PHOTOGRAPHING THE MEXICAN REVOLUTION

THE WILLIAM & BETTYE NOWLIN SERIES
in Art, History, and Culture of the Western Hemisphere

PHOTOGRAPHING THE MEXICAN REVOLUTION

COMMITMENTS, TESTIMONIES, ICONS

JOHN MRAZ

UNIVERSITY OF TEXAS PRESS AUSTIN

Printed in China
First edition, 2012

Requests for permission to reproduce material from this work should be sent to:
Permissions
University of Texas Press
P.O. Box 7819
Austin, TX 78713-7819
www.utexas.edu/utpress/about/bpermission.html

The paper used in this book meets the minimum requirements of ANSI/NISO Z39.48-1992 (R1997) (Permanence of Paper). ∞

Designed by Lindsay Starr

LIBRARY OF CONGRESS CATALOGING-IN-PUBLICATION DATA

Mraz, John.
Photographing the Mexican Revolution : commitments, testimonies, icons / John Mraz. — 1st ed.
p. cm. — (The William and Bettye Nowlin series in art, history, and culture of the Western hemisphere)
Includes bibliographical references and index.
ISBN 978-0-292-73580-4 (cloth : alk. paper)
ISBN 978-0-292-73794-5 (e-book)
1. Mexico—History—Revolution, 1910–1920—Photography. 2. Mexico—History—Revolution, 1910–1920—Pictorial works. 3. Photography—Mexico—History. 4. Historiography and photography—Mexico. I. Title.
F1234.M93317 2012
972'.030222—dc23 2011033193

To revolutionaries . . .
before and behind the cameras

Contents

Acknowledgments ix

INTRODUCTION 1

CHAPTER 1
The Porfiriato: From the Studio to the Street 17

CHAPTER 2
Representing the Revolution 39

CHAPTER 3
The Myth of the Casasolas 45

CHAPTER 4
Learning to Photograph War 53

CHAPTER 5
The Zapatista Movement and Southern Cameras 93

CHAPTER 6
Photographing the Reaction 123

CHAPTER 7
The Caudillo of the Cameras? 167

CHAPTER 8
The Advantages of Photographing the Constitutionalist Movement 193

EPILOGUE
The Icons of the Mexican Revolution 233

Notes 259
Bibliography 295
Index 309

Acknowledgments

This book was made possible by the generosity of many Mexicans and their institutions. It is, first of all, a product of the Instituto Nacional de Antropología e Historia (INAH), and was written at the invitation of director Alfonso de Maria y Campos as part of the celebration of the centenary of the Mexican Revolution. Luis Ignacio Sainz, administrative secretary of the INAH, was instrumental in carrying out this project, which was closely linked to my work as curator of the photographic exhibit *Testimonios de una guerra: Fotografías de la Revolución Mexicana*. I also thank Miguel Ángel Echegaray, Abraham Guerrero, and Benito Taibo of the INAH for their contributions to this work.

Both the book and the exhibit are based to a great extent on the holdings of the Fototeca Nacional of the INAH, and I am grateful to director Juan Carlos Valdéz for his assistance and that of his staff, among them Mayra Mendoza and Heladio Vera. The Fototeca researcher who has contributed most to this effort is Daniel Escorza, who has looked for images in relation to themes I have proposed, has generously offered information from his own investigations in illustrated magazines, has answered innumerable questions, and has provided his articles as references. Moreover, I thank Escorza and researcher Patricia Massé Zendejas for having allowed me to see a selection they had prepared for a photographic exposition on the revolution. I would also like to recognize the contribution of the director of the INAH organization in Morelos state, Eduardo López Calzada, and of Paloma Corona, director of the INAH-Morelos Fototeca, for having organized three congresses on the imagery of the revolution, from which I learned much.

Research in other archives was important, and I am grateful to the following for their participation: Archivo General de la Nación; Archivo Roque González Garza of the Universidad Panamericana; Fondo Andrés Angulo, INAH-Tlaxcala; Instituto de Investigaciones sobre la Universidad y la Educación, UNAM; Harry Ransom Humanities Research Center, University of Texas; Departamento de Información y Documentación de la Cultura Audiovisual, Benemérita Universidad Autónoma de Puebla; Colección Gráfica y de Sonido del Instituto Nacional de Estudios Históricos de las

Revoluciones Mexicanas; Fototeca del Centro de las Artes, Monterrey, Nuevo León; and Fondo Cachú, Dirección de Artes Visuales de la Fundación Televisa. I also thank photographers Elsa Medina and José Hernández-Claire for modern images of revolutionary icons.

In the course of this project I have consulted with many people who have responded generously. Samuel Villela is the researcher whom I have tormented most with my questions, and he has treated me with the altruism for which he is well known. Among other researchers who have helped me are Ricardo Pérez Montfort, Ariel Arnal, Fernando del Moral, Arturo Guevara Escobar, Miguel Ángel Berumen, José Antonio Rodríguez, Max Parra, Jack Womack, Miguel Ángel Morales, Jesús Vargas, Ángel Miquel, Jorge Carretero, Paul Vanderwood, Fernando Osorio, Acacia Maldonado Valera, Bernardo García Díaz, Tom Benjamin, Christine Rousset, Javier Pérez Siller, Adriana Zavala, Samuel Brunk, Rebeca Monroy, Julio Broca, and Enrique Villaseñor; I thank them all for their unselfish collaboration. I consulted with New Zealand photo historian John Turner thanks to a Hood Fellowship at the University of Auckland, a result of the invitation of Kathy Lehman and Walescka Pino-Ojeda, who offered a stimulating space in which to discuss issues of revolutionary photography. I am also grateful to Jaime Vélez Storey and the two anonymous readers of this manuscript. Their suggestions helped to make this a different book than the Spanish version, as did the feedback I received from public lectures at Princeton University, Harvard University, the University of Utah, the Universities of California at Berkeley and Santa Cruz (and the Casa de la Universidad de California in Mexico City), and the Museo Regional de la Laguna–INAH. Obviously, the knowledge I acquired from both printed and oral sources in the year after I turned in the Spanish-language manuscript has made this a better work, as has Theresa May's enthusiasm, which "infected" the UTP editorial staff, and me as well. (All translations are my own.)

It has been possible to write this book thanks to various constants in my life. Agustín Grajales, director of the Instituto de Ciencias Sociales y Humanidades "Alfonso Vélez Pliego" at the Benemérita Universidad Autónoma de Puebla, demonstrated his usual leadership and comprehension in allowing me to dedicate myself to this project between 2008 and 2010. Gustavo Cubero was vital as an assistant in yet another book, and for the exposition; Mayra Uribe Eguiluz proved invaluable in finishing this version. Finally, Eli Bartra listened to my ideas, corrected the text, offered suggestions, and put up with my frustrations as I dealt with one of the most extraordinary— if at times inordinately stressful—opportunities that I have been offered since I decided to live in Mexico.

PHOTOGRAPHING THE MEXICAN REVOLUTION

Introduction

The armed struggle in Mexico from 1910 to 1920 offers an exceptional case of revolutionary photography. But before examining the singularity of the Mexican experience, we should ask, "What are we talking about when we talk about 'revolutionary photography'?" A primary instance—and one relevant to the task I carry out in this book—is the imagery produced during armed movements that have the objective of radically transforming the existing socioeconomic and political structure, and which defeat the old regimen to implant a new order. Now, not all the photography produced during this period was made by "revolutionary photographers," because that concept would be limited to those committed to forces of genuine popular mobilizations. There have been few revolutions, and even fewer that have been covered extensively by photography; it could well be that we would find no more than the Mexican, the Soviet, the Chinese, the Vietnamese, the Cuban, and the Nicaraguan revolutions. Moreover, the photography of these conflicts has been little studied in terms of authors and their allegiances, while discussions of the images' contents are often uninformative and/or erroneous.[1]

The concept of "revolutionary photography" is usually applied to photos made after the conflict has ended. In a strict sense, this would be "postrevolutionary photography," because the imagemakers did not have to risk their lives in deciding to which side they belonged. This photography could be considered "revolutionary" because the societies are in the process of constructing systems that are profoundly different from those that existed before combat began. These photographers participate in the cultural effervescences, identifying social problems, suggesting ways to resolve them, and celebrating—in a few cases, constructively criticizing—the advances of the new societies. In Mexico, the individual about which most has been written in relation to this type of imagery is Tina Modotti; in the Soviet Union, the photographer who has received the most attention is Alexander Rodchenko; and in Cuba, the imagemakers who most stand out are Korda (Alejandro Díaz Gutiérrez), Raúl Corrales, Osvaldo Salas, and Mayito (Mario García Joya).[2]

This term has also been employed in an intrinsic sense in relation to those photographers who have metamorphosed the medium itself. Sometimes they have been linked to transformative situations—for example, Modotti and Rodchenko; in other occasions they have been influenced by these visual climates of opinion, as were Edward Weston and Paul Strand in Mexico of the 1920s and 1930s. Manuel Álvarez Bravo is the Mexican who best represents this third instance because his modernist stance in opposition to picturesque and pictorial photography transfigurates the folkloric.[3] His is the most progressive way of incorporating Indianist elements, which are at the center of *lo mexicano* in the postrevolutionary period.

It is not my intention in this book to examine either postrevolutionary photography or that which innovates the medium. This work centers on the photography made during the period 1910 to 1920—above all by Mexicans—in an attempt to discover who made these images, why, to what ends, with what intentions, and for whom they were taken. It seems clear—once we leave behind the myth that Agustín Víctor Casasola was *the* photographer of the revolution—that many others covered the long civil war. Some of them were linked to certain groups, and in the course of this project I have discovered a pattern of commitment that has been little commented upon in previous studies (and completely unexplored in the photography of other revolutions). I believe that specific photographers can be linked to the contending forces in broad strokes—and with strong possibilities of erring—in the following way: Manuel Ramos was the preeminent photojournalist of the Porfiriato; the agency of Heliodoro J. Gutiérrez was linked to the Maderista movement both on the northern frontier and in Mexico City, making it the first photographic protagonist on the side of the revolutionaries; Gerónimo Hernández was a Maderista imagemaker during the truncated presidency; the photographer most engaged with the Orozquista rebellion seems to have been "El Gran Lente" (the Great Lens), Ignacio Medrano Chávez; Amando Salmerón was the photographer of Emiliano Zapata, although there were other photographers connected to that movement, among them Cruz Sánchez and Sara Castrejón (one of the few women to participate with a camera); an individual named Hernández appears to have been the imagemaker for Domingo Arenas, an agrarian revolutionary from the Puebla region; Eduardo Melhado may have photographed reconstructions of La Decena Trágica (the Tragic Ten Days) and thus could be considered as having been a Huertista; the Cachú brothers, Antonio and Juan, were the photographers closest to Pancho Villa; and although the Constitutionalists had many imagemakers, Jesús H. Abitia has been considered *the* Constitutionalist photographer.

How did they express their commitments visually? What aesthetic strategies did they employ to take sides and offer their bit to the struggle? What identities and identifications were generated with their images? What sorts of fears must have been associated with appearing in photos, taking them, signing them, and circulating them? How did the "visual economy" function in terms of production, distribution, consumption, and conservation, both immediately and in the long run?[4]

That which is really novel about Mexican photography during the armed struggle is the fact that photographers were committed to revolutionary groups that were at war with each other. Hence, the term "revolutionary photography" is problematized, because the images of the Gutiérrez agency or Gerónimo Hernández are as "revolutionary" as those of Medrano Chávez, just as Abitia's are as "revolutionary" as Salmerón's or the Cachú brothers', despite the war that their armies waged against each other. At the same time, many photojournalists worked for illustrated magazines whose owners and editors were generally conservative, even Porfirian; however, the periodicals were chameleon-like, changing their lines to adapt themselves to a turbulent situation. Perhaps the foreigners were the only ones able to be impartial (and not always); among them, Hugo Brehme stands out.

In this study I highlight the commitments that I have been able to uncover. The revolutionary situation required, on occasions, that photographers identify with one or another group. At the same time it offered them the opportunity to use their artistic and technical capacities to express themselves—and to have their material and equipment paid for. There is a fundamental difference between those who write and those who photograph: it costs money to create technical images; photographers must face expenses for film, chemicals, cameras, tripods, assistants, and equipment.[5] We must always ask of predigital imagery, "Why was this photo made?"

We could also rephrase Jean-Paul Sartre's famous question about writing to ask, "For whom does one photograph?"[6] The most direct way to demonstrate commitment and have it paid for was to be subsidized by a caudillo; obviously, those that had more money for arms, munitions, and uniforms also had more for photography.[7] Nonetheless, there were other ways to earn a living with imagery and, perhaps, express a point of view: work for the illustrated magazines or in a news photo agency; have a studio or a film business; be employed by an institution with an interest in documenting the war, such as the Cruz Blanca Nacional (National White Cross); and, moreover, sell postcards to publications, or in a store, or to the very people pictured therein as souvenirs.

It would appear that art historian Laura González is correct in asserting that "The revolution was covered by more or less professional photographers."[8] The photojournalists from Mexico City were important in picturing the revolution; for example, metropolitan photographers made about half of the photos in this book. They did not, however, leave the city often, and it is a common misconception that their media sent them to cover the war. In the main, the illustrated magazines got the images of scenes outside of Mexico City from photographers they called their "correspondents," but who were probably the owners of local studios. I believe it could be argued that regional photographers, most likely with studios (but who also sold their imagery to local and national publications when possible), were the ones who really documented the revolution, particularly as they attached themselves to one group or another.

Photographers with a political consciousness must have found that the revolution represented a unique opportunity, for taking photographs is a passionate occupation. Although the evidence of commitment is, at times, circumstantial, we can imagine that many thought in ways similar to the filmmaker Salvador Toscano, who wrote to Venustiano Carranza insisting on the importance of counteracting the effects of films produced for or about other leaders (such as Pancho Villa, who had signed a famous contract with the Mutual Film Corporation): "The masses are easily impressed by movie scenes, which are a faithful copy of life. Their effect can be greater than that achieved with propaganda in a hundred newspapers."[9] Hence, one can imagine a scenario in which commitments were made in greater and lesser degrees, and grew stronger or weaker, according to the relation with the caudillo, the luck of his movement, and the market for images.

It is important to note that the task of establishing commitments is particularly complex because it is difficult to identify the authors of the images. The research of Ignacio Gutiérrez Ruvalcaba on the Casasola Archive in the Fototeca Nacional, a fundamental source of revolutionary photographs, has demonstrated that "Agustín Víctor Casasola erased photographers' names from the emulsion of many thousands of negatives"; moreover, the archive itself "is made up of the work of at least 483 photographers."[10] The problem of determining authorship is not limited to the Casasola photographs, as can be seen in the example of one of the more impactful photos from the Veracruz invasion. The image of a U.S. sailor with his rifle pointing down at some dead Mexicans—as if he were on tropical safari in the arches of the Hotel Diligencias—has appeared repeatedly in the picture histories produced by Gustavo Casasola (Figure I-1). Although the usual Casasola practice of not giving credit to other photographers implied that Agustín Víctor had shot the scene, the grain of the copy published in the histories indicates that it was copied from a magazine of that period. At any rate, Casasola did not sign this photo, but other photographers did. For example, the left side of another version (Figure I-2) bears the following legend: "No. 33, Muertos in Diligencias (Dead in Diligencias) Abril 21-1914, P. Flores Perez, Fot.," indicating that it was taken by Ponciano Flores Pérez, a resident of the port city who was active during the occupation. According to historian Bernardo García Díaz, the area around the Hotel Diligencias was "one of the strongest centers of resistance to the invaders," a comment he placed in the cutline for this photo.[11] But Walter P. Hadsell evidently made the image that the historian published (Figure I-3); handwritten on the left side is the label "Hadsell, V Cruz, 3371, Killed in Front of Hotel Diligencias."

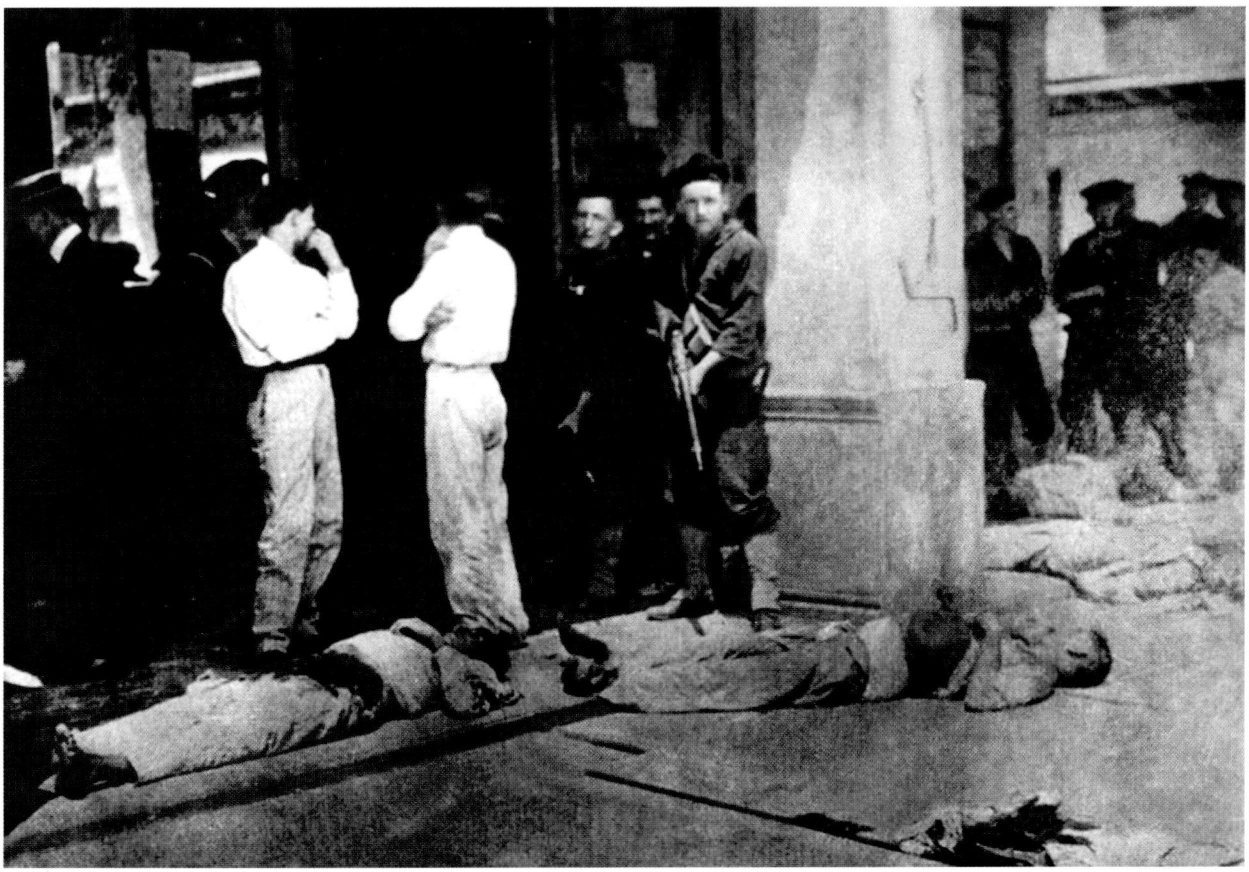

I-1. U.S. sailors with dead Mexicans, Hotel Diligencias, Veracruz, April 1914. © Inv. #627284, Fondo Casasola, SINAFO-Fototeca Nacional del INAH.

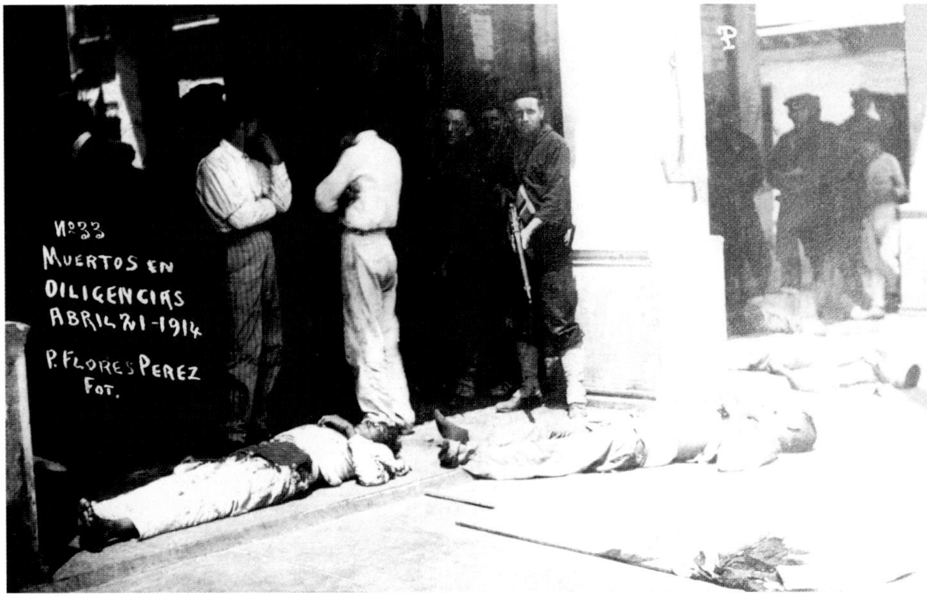

I-2. U.S. sailors with dead Mexicans, Hotel Diligencias, Veracruz, April, 1914; Ponciano Flores Pérez? © Archivo General de la Nación, Fondo Propiedad Artístico y Literaria, Flores Pérez, "Intervención norteamericana," 24.

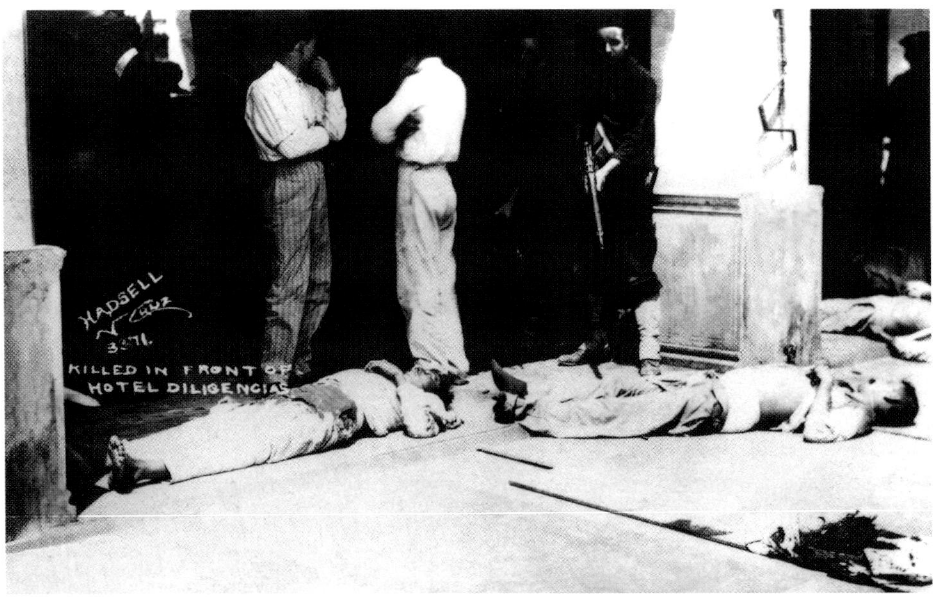

I-3. U.S. sailors with dead Mexicans, Hotel Diligencias, Veracruz, April, 1914; Walter P. Hadsell? Archive of Bernardo García Díaz.

Plagiarism of images—by erasing the name they bear and signing them—was constant during the Mexican Revolution (and in the wider world of international photography).[12] Nevertheless, the confusion generated around the authorship of the image made in front of the Hotel Diligencias does not end with the legends scratched into the emulsions. According to Daniel Escorza, the first time this photo appeared was in the weekly *La Ilustración Semanal* in May 1914; although this magazine sometimes credited its "correspondents," such as Samuel Tinoco, in this case there is no indication of who made the photo.[13] Even if credit for the image had been given, that would not prove who really made it, because one finds photos in the illustrated magazines of the period that seem to have been credited to photographers who didn't make them. That observation notwithstanding, publication of a photo with credit (in a national magazine) offers a surer lead about authorship than a signature on the negative itself; misidentifying an image would expose the periodical and the photojournalist to a complaint, something that could not occur with postcards. There are a number of articles in magazines accusing one another of publishing copyrighted photos, answered by assertions from the accused as to their rights to the images.[14]

The photo of the dead lying before the Hotel Diligencias arches entered quickly into international circles: the French magazine *L'Illustration* published it in May 1914 without giving credit to any photographer.[15] Years later it was included in the now-classic volume that Anita Brenner brought out in 1943, *The Wind That Swept Mexico*, in which credit was given to the "Brown Bros." agency; however, the contrast and retouching make it apparent that the image is a copy.[16] Moreover, it is cropped on the left side, where the signature of Flores Pérez or Hadsell might have appeared. Finally, it could have been taken by one of the invaders, because it was a "popular card bought and sent by participants on both sides of the battle lines."[17] These examples of its circulation, both in the period of its making as well as years afterward, reveal how problematic it is to trust what we see on the surfaces of images or what we read beneath them in publications. The semantic debility of photographs in general is also demonstrated—in this case by the fact that we cannot identify which side the photographer was on: it would be just as easy to imagine that a Mexican took it as a denunciation—*La Ilustración Semanal* published it "in case anybody doubted it"—as it would be to think that one of the invading forces made the image to show a hunter with his trophies.

I have attempted to overcome problems of accurate identification with a methodology that cross-references archival photographs, images printed in illustrated magazines and picture histories, interviews of the photographers, and articles written during the revolution, as well as investigations carried out afterward of both photography and the revolution. I have privileged certain images and constructed a narrative that has been consistently propelled by the visual, given that it is based on a photographic exhibit that I curated, *Testimonios de una guerra: Fotografía de la Revolución Mexicana*. In this sense it has not been an investigation of the twenty or thirty years that the photography of the revolution deserves, but a study that synthesizes prior research and my own. As curator of the national exhibit for the centennial of the Mexican Revolution, I have written this work in a situation that had its advantages and disadvantages: I was able to enter into unexplored archives, but I have had to write within a time frame uncomfortable for a historian.

On rereading the text, I notice that the words "it appears" or "it seems to have been" crop up repeatedly. Such phrases will perhaps lead readers to infer that my observations are based on scanty evidence, but in some cases that is all that currently exists. Although it is important to open new photo archives and conserve and circulate the images they contain—in order to have the "previously unpublished photos" about which such an ado was made during the centennial, I believe that it may not be as important as producing previously unpublished research on the archives that we know. We are working in a field with great difficulties, and the only way to advance is to formulate hypotheses and attempt to identify the photographers as well as what they photographed. We must be open to taking risks and committing errors, from which we surely can learn more than from our successes. Although I have indicated the mistakes of my friends and colleagues, I hope that I have pointed out more of my own made in previous works. I do not consider this book to be a definitive history of the revolution's photographs and photographers, but a map indicating possible roads on which to advance in its study.

In developing my analysis, I have been guided by the idea that photographs offer historians a "double testimony": they tell us about the authors who made them, and they show us frozen fragments of past scenes.[18] The categories I use as a heuristic device to distinguish between these two distinct "testimonies" are "history of photography" and "photohistory," which necessarily employ two distinct research methodologies.

Insofar as this work is a history of photography, I have attempted to examine the commitments of the imagemakers in relation to their personal backgrounds, their aesthetics, their equipment, and their experiences during the armed struggle. I have also attempted to unearth the stories behind the making of the photos—why they were made, and why they were made the way they were—even when their authors are unidentified. Writing a history of photography also implies studying the circulation of images. In general, I have focused on the illustrated magazines because they also had their commitments, and reviewing the published images can open important windows onto the photographers and the events depicted. Further, I have carried the issue of image dissemination beyond the period of combat to study the history of five icons of the revolution. I cannot say that my understanding of how to do histories of photography has been much influenced by traditional art history, above all the aspect of that discipline that emphasizes "influences," for I find the concept of "climates of opinion," developed by historian Carl Becker, to be more useful.[19] I believe that the photographers of the revolution existed within a climate of technovisual opinions and possibilities that we are only beginning to understand.

At the same time that I have written a history *of* the photographs, and *of* the photographers and their imagery (and its circulation), I have been involved in an effort to historicize *with* photographs, using them as documents that testify about social relations and details of daily and material life. That is, I have produced a species of photohistory in which I attempt to discover what technical images can tell us about some of the social aspects of this period as a function of their unique capacity for "mechanical reproduction," their indexicality, their "transparency," their capacity to embalm "That-which-was."[20] Photographs testify to the presence of groups often absent from written histories, such as women and children. They also record differences in the armies' armaments, the destruction of the bombings, and life in the camps and on top of the train cars, among other things. In this enterprise I have had to base my identifications largely on those provided by Gustavo Casasola in his picture histories; he lived during the revolution and knew how his father, Agustín Víctor, had identified the images. Although I recognize that his works contain significant errors, they have served as a point of departure that I have corrected from other sources.

I have also attempted to draw out meanings in photographs by adding another level of testimonies, those of participants in the revolution. These texts are situated in an oblique relation to the images; that is, they do not derive from the pictures, but are included in an attempt to suggest ways of seeing them that go beyond simple description.

We confront a unique problem in both history of photography and photohistory: photographs are polysemic, and they can be used to illustrate anything. Whether they are too "thin" or too "thick" is a crucial theoretical question.[21] In other words, are the connotations and denotations of photographs so fickle because these images are semantically weak, and hence can be assigned any meaning by accompanying text, or because they are so full of information, so replete with so many possibilities, that they offer themselves to seemingly infinite readings? Whether resulting from one or the other instance, the only solution is to historicize photographs by embedding them in the contexts from which they came, as well as those which have given them subsequent meanings.

One of the great temptations of historians who use photographs in their analyses is that of psychologism, or making psychological judgments from "apparent" expressions of sentiment—for example, deducing depression from a non-smiling face. The classic example of this is Michael Lesy's *Wisconsin Death Trip*, in which the historian juxtaposed photographs of deadly serious people in Wisconsin around 1900 with state reports, news items, and stories of epidemics, suicides, homicides, insanities, bankruptcies, arson, early deaths, and ghosts. He concludes, "If a man didn't kill himself or if a woman didn't murder her own children, the countryside [offered] two varieties of psychic identity. . . . The character type of genteel success now described as obsessive-compulsive, and the character type of failure now called paranoid."[22] Historian Robert Levine also fell into this temptation in describing the reaction of the Brazilian underclass to being photographed: "Some lower-class men and women stared at the camera listlessly; others appear to be carefree. Whites, who were usually European immigrants, and blacks, likely slaves or ex-slaves, showed similar degrees of weariness, but whites usually wore shoes and were better dressed."[23]

Although histories of photography and photohistories are related to the study of the mentalities of the imagemakers and the photographed, it is crucial to insist that using photographs to document mentalities is completely different from arguing for psychological readings of them. Mentalities are long-term, deeply ingrained sociocultural patterns, whereas psychology, at least as it appears in photographs, is an immediate emotional state: sadness, joy, disappointment, chagrin. The problem with this approach becomes obvious if we consider exposure times. When films and lenses were slow, people did not look happy because they could not hold a smile for the length of time required; it became a blur.[24] Thus, they necessarily had to maintain a straight face (something perhaps a result as well of posing's ordeals). Today, however, exposure times are usually in the range of from $1/250$ to $1/60$ of a second. Obviously, no one could seriously propose to make a psychological analysis based on such a tiny fraction of time, although the photographs of Zapatistas in Sanborn's restaurant (see Figures 7-21 and 7-22) lure us to do so.

The Mexican Revolution occurred just as photography was being defined as a medium. In the same way that we find horses next to airplanes, and ancient cannons on the same battlefield as modern artillery, one sees a great variety of photographic equipment: old and heavy cameras together with the new, lighter, more portable ones that became available as the revolution advanced. Wars stimulate technological development, and U.S. preparations to enter World War I, and that cataclysm itself, produced dramatic advances in photographic equipment. Many photojournalists used reflex (single-lens reflex) cameras, which could be carried and operated in a handheld fashion, enabling photojournalists to go to the news rather than wait for it to come to them and their stationary apparatus; the even more portable Graflex camera was employed at times.[25] The reflex cameras offered more mobility and the capacity to capture action; the visor on top allowed photographers to focus on subjects without covering their heads with a dark cloth. The other camera employed by professionals during the revolution was the view, which required the use of a tripod.[26] Some photojournalists—above all the older ones, such as Manuel Ramos—used view cameras; however, these were generally favored by studio and postcard photographers, probably because they were, in the words of photo historian Naomi Rosenblum, "an instrument of great sensitivity and precision, provided the subject was immobile."[27] Finally, Kodak Brownies must have been popular among the wealthy and the middle class, but it appears that they did not document the war; moreover, there is no evidence that the common soldiers of the revolution made the small-format photos taken during World War I by soldiers from more-prosperous nations. The differences between the cameras determined, to some extent, whether one captured combat scenes or was limited to posed groups, and the degree to which photos were spontaneous or directed.[28] If, however, the variations between the cameras produced different kinds of photographs with their particular aesthetics, in the distribution of photos there was much filtration between the genres, with photojournalistic images circulating as postcards and vice versa.

The attitudes of photographers, and the public, were as important as the technology. For those with pretensions—and informed about international movements—Pictorialism represented the way to elevate photography to an art in order to legitimate it, particularly that which was made in the studios. For example, photojournalist Ezequiel Álvarez Tostado, editor of the news magazine *La Ilustración Semanal*, published covers with soldiers posing in the midst of cactus and the national flag which have no credibility for our eyes (see Figure 6-29).[29] Photo historian Marion Gautreau has explained this phenomenon, noting that "It was habitual for the photographers to pose soldiers (or individuals disguised as such), so as to offer images more acceptable to what the editors and readers expected to see of the armed struggle, images that were almost impossible to capture on the battlefield."[30] Nonetheless, at the same time photojournalists were creating their own space thanks to the increasingly sophisticated equipment, the innovative formats of the illustrated publications, and modern culture's appetite for the realist effect. This confrontation between art and documentary resulted in codes of realism that varied greatly, much the way that premodern and modern elements rub up against one another in photos of the conflict.

Readers may be surprised at the "primitive" aesthetics of many photographs.[31] It is important to remember that most of these pictures were made by provincial studio photographers and photojournalists who were largely inexperienced in covering live news. It appears that photographing combat was "very nearly impossible" at this time, and that many photos that purport to be of troops going "over the top" were in fact training exercises.[32] Photo historian Susan Moeller evidently expected to find more interesting imagery than she discovered while investigating the photographs of a war that was taking place at the same time:

> What seems so disappointing about the World War I photographs is the near-total absence of either a sense of the horror or the thrill of the danger. The photographs are remarkably static—more so than the camera technology insisted. They portray neither a sense of emotion nor one of movement. No photographs were published during the war of individual faces showing the glazed eyes of the shell-shocked or the naive look of the recruits.[33]

According to historian of photography Jane Carmichael, "Very little has been written on the photographers of the First World War."[34] Despite that deficiency, it would appear that they belonged to essentially three groups: official imagemakers attached to the armed forces, photojournalists, and amateurs. Press photographers were severely restricted by the commanders and largely excluded from the most important battle area, the Western Front.[35] "Most journalists were not allowed anywhere near the front . . . [and] photographers labored under the same—if not worse—constraints."[36] Sometimes they were incorporated, along with other professional photographers, into the services and given commissioned status, but they were subject to very strict military and civilian censorship. Working under the shadow of the censor and ever conscious of what would and would not pass, imagemakers took few controversial photographs; those that were deemed acceptable were "mundane and uninspired."[37] The role of the "embedded" photographers was that of providing images for home-front publications and propaganda material, but there appears to have been little consciousness among the military hierarchy of the importance of photography in the struggle, particularly in the beginning. Carmichael notes that "Despite the shift from hostility to welcome in 1916, it remained fundamental to most military thinking that any form of reporting should be limited and occupy a lowly place in the overall scale of priorities."[38] This resistance to modern media is a crucial difference with the Mexican Revolution, in which all the caudillos understood the importance of projecting themselves and their movements visually.

Another important distinction between the images of these cataclysms is the role of amateur photographers. This group may well have provided the most interesting pictures of World War I, thanks to small, readily available cameras. At times soldiers were encouraged by the press to provide photos for publication; for example, the French magazine *Le Miroir* offered ten prizes for outstanding photos of the war, with the best awarded 30,000 francs.[39] The freedom enjoyed by amateurs varied according to their commanders, the war zones in which they found themselves, and the time period. They appear to have been most important in the beginning of the conflict: "The first year and a half of the war on the Western Front and at Gallipoli was recorded chiefly by amateur photographers."[40] The most striking of these images were those of the 1914 Christmas truce, which show German and British soldiers fraternizing, but there are many candid pictures of troops eating in the trenches and shielding themselves from the cold, wet mud. Further, while private cameras were increasingly restricted on the Western Front, they abounded in other theaters of war. In contrast, there appears to be very little amateur imagery of the Mexican Revolution, although that may be a function of the lack of research on this aspect. Nonetheless, one can conclude for the moment that while professional photographers were largely excluded or embedded by the armies of World War I, they provided the vast majority of imagery of the Mexican Revolution.

Comparing photographs is a methodological key to analyzing them, and another obligatory parallel is with the photography of the Soviet Revolution, which began in 1917. Unfortunately, this imagery appears to have been little studied, and I have no choice but to make impressionistic remarks based on one photohistory that uses images to illustrate a text and in which no photographers are identified.[41] Despite these limitations, it appears that these pictures were taken by professional photographers who carried relatively sophisticated cameras. This is clear, above all, in the capture of movement within the frame, an aesthetic characteristic of modern (1930s on) photojournalism. In pictures probably taken by military photographers, soldiers attempt to flee the German advance, their legs blurring against the ground behind them.[42] One of the most famous of this revolution's images, shot from on high on 17 July 1917 in Saint Petersburg, shows demonstrators running away from machine-gun fire.[43]

Other photographs of the Soviet Revolution that spark interest are those of prerevolutionary squalor, such as people sleeping in crowded cellars and eating in filthy dining halls; these images are reminiscent of Jacob Riis's work in the United States, and of those made by John Kenneth Turner in Mexico.[44] It is difficult to imagine the public for whom these photos were intended. There are many images that document destruction, executions, mounds of cadavers, and the hunger faced by the populace, who evidently were reduced to cannibalism at times.[45] The participation of children and women (sometimes as combatants) is also depicted, at times as refugees in flight. Some photos that purport to be of combat are in fact training exercises; others may be of actual fighting, but taken from the air.[46] There appears to be little amateur photography, and the identification as to commitments will have to await studies of the different factions' media.

Perhaps the most accomplished photographer of the Mexican Revolution was a German who came to live in Mexico, Hugo Brehme, for whom I acquired a new respect in the course of this project.[47] He had studied photography in Erfurt, Germany, at the beginning of the century and afterward joined a geographic expedition to German colonies in Africa, but he caught malaria and had to return to his native country.[48] His liking for hot lands led him to travel to Veracruz in 1906; he went on to Mexico City and remained there. A particularly gifted technician, with an eye for exotic beauty, he would in the coming years turn out to be one of the most important photographers in Mexico.[49] Although much research is still to be undertaken, the surviving photos indicate that he must have covered the revolution extensively. He took photos of the centennial, and of the demonstrations when Porfirio Díaz fell on 25 May 1911; of Maderismo in power, the Tragic Ten Days, the U.S. invasion of Veracruz, and the entrance of the Constitutionalists, as well as the Conventionists, into Mexico City in 1914; he also photographed different groups around the city, notably the Zapatistas.[50] In the 1920s and '30s he constructed what some scholars of Mexican photography consider to be "a graphic system of *lo mexicano*," creating a "visual vocabulary" of *mexicanidad* that constitutes "the base of today's national identity."[51] His romantic and bucolic vision was expressed in a nineteenth-century style that would be directly confronted by the modern photography of Edward Weston, Tina Modotti, and Manuel Álvarez Bravo.

The Mexican Revolution received extraordinary coverage by photographers and cineastes—commercial and amateur, national and international—from its very beginning. The battle for Ciudad Juárez in May of 1911 attracted some 1,500 "Kodak fiends" from El Paso, who daily went down to the Rio Grande or stood in relative safety on rooftops to shoot the action.[52] As the struggle developed, photographers and filmmakers poured into Mexico to document the world's first great social conflagration, taking advantage of the relatively free access to the action, especially compared to the strict censorship exercised during World War I. Film historian Jay Leyda reflected on the exceptional documentation of this war in modern media, stating that he had once fantasized about making a movie that would "attempt to bring together the newsreel footage of this world-shaking event, filmed by cameramen sent there from every film-producing country of the world. I even dreamed of a fascinating world tour, digging in London and New York newsreel archives, finding Mexican footage in Copenhagen and Stockholm . . . in Berlin and Vienna."[53]

George Leighton selected the images for Anita Brenner's book, and he affirmed that "No revolution has ever been so thoroughly photographed."[54] Art historian Olivier Debroise agrees with Leighton, writing, "Few wars have excited the imagination like the Mexican Revolution. Few have been so extensively represented, so intensely observed."[55] The Mexican Revolution was probably the most photographed of such events for nearly a half century, largely because of its duration; also, its proximity to the United States allowed materials and equipment, and photographers, to enter easily due to the extensive and essentially unguarded border. The Mexican revolt was much longer than the Soviet uprising (which lasted about a year, from February 1917 to March 1918, although fighting continued until 1921), the Cuban struggle of some two years (from December 1956 to 1 January 1959), and the Chinese conflagration, which lasted about three years (from 1946 to 1 October 1949). The Sandinista rebellion in Nicaragua (1962–1979) was of long duration, but there is no evidence of extensive photo archives. I believe that the Vietnamese struggle against France and the United States (1848-1975) must have replaced the Mexican struggle as the most photographed revolution, because of the development of both technology and media consciousness.[56]

What can be argued is that the Mexican Revolution is one which has generated great interest in conserving its images. This interest in conservation has resulted, in part, from public interest in picture histories, but it is also a product of "the perfect dictatorship," the felicitous turn of phrase with which Nobel Prize–winning novelist Mario Vargas Llosa described the rule of the Partido Revolucionario Institucional (PRI). The party dictatorship subsidized the construction of a history in images that present it as the legitimate heir of the painful events that produced modern Mexico. Obviously, the winners write history, so it is not surprising that many more photos exist of the Constitutionalist movement than of the other armies. For the same reason, there are few images in the Fototeca Nacional of manifestations supporting Porfirio Díaz, despite the fact that Agustín Víctor Casasola must have made many while working for the pro-government newspaper *El Imparcial*.[57] The official historiography of the postrevolutionary period gave priority to Constitutionalism among the revolutionary forces and sent the Porfiriato to the cellar of the Black Legend. The visual economy of the armed struggle assured that more images were made of Constitutionalism; photo historian Miguel Ángel Berumen states that they took many more photographs of Pablo González, Venustiano Carranza, and Álvaro Obregón than of Pancho Villa, and, moreover, that the photos of Emiliano Zapata are 5 percent of those made of Villa.[58]

The challenges of this investigation have been several. Our vision of the revolution's photography is necessarily mediated by the fact that we are limited to analyzing the images we can find in archives and those published during and after the armed struggle. The photos we know best are those that a metropolitan photojournalist (Agustín Víctor Casasola) accumulated with a vision to posterior uses—or which a victorious army conserved. Where are those that were hidden out of fear that they would provide evidence of a commitment to a lost cause?[59] The competition between photographers to establish credit for the images complicates the situation, as do prior identifications of authorship, including names they themselves have written over the emulsion. Above all, the extraordinary number of photos of the armed struggle made by so many photographers imposes its own challenges. To a certain point, the visual variety of the mechanical eyes offers a parallel to the cacophony of the revolutionary voices.

CHAPTER 1

The Porfiriato: From the Studio to the Street

LIKE THE MEXICAN REVOLUTION ITSELF, the photography of the armed struggle had its roots in the Porfiriato, since the great majority of the professional photographers who covered it were formed in the illustrated press and the photographic studios of that period. Moreover, although the subjects that appear in the images were radically "other," it seems that the ways of photographing them were established prior to the rebellion. An image that evokes the progress of Porfirian rule offers an example: treasury minister José Limantour viewing the public works that channel water from Xochimilco to Mexico City from atop a construction, his head shielded from the tropical sun by the umbrella held by an assistant (Figure 1-1). Bringing drinking water into the metropolis and draining the Valley of Mexico to prevent flooding were among the great engineering accomplishments of the late Porfiriato. It was considered of such importance that Miguel Casasola was contracted by the Mexico City government to register this process, from 1906 to 1912, and he may well have taken this photograph.[1] The image is photojournalistically modern in that it captures the people spontaneously, without asking them to pose. Along with other images found in the Casasola Archive, it contradicts a much-repeated commonplace that Olivier Debroise articulated thusly: "To make photographs at the beginning of the twentieth century, it was still necessary to ask history to stop long enough to make the picture. For this reason, photography in the final years of the Porfiriato still largely conformed to the formal, static models established by the studios."[2]

In the photo, Limantour and the other men—dressed inappropriately for the spring heat in dark suits, stiff-collared shirts, waistcoats, and ties—stand above and apart from the laborers, who, in work clothes and sombreros, gaze up at them. An embodiment of the extreme class differences heightened by vertiginous modernization, this image is an early (candid) version of what Tina Modotti would compose during the postrevolutionary effervescence to portray "Those on top and those on the bottom."[3] Soon, however, those who are here in the foreground, but blurred and facing away from the camera, will be the focal point for revolutionary photographers.

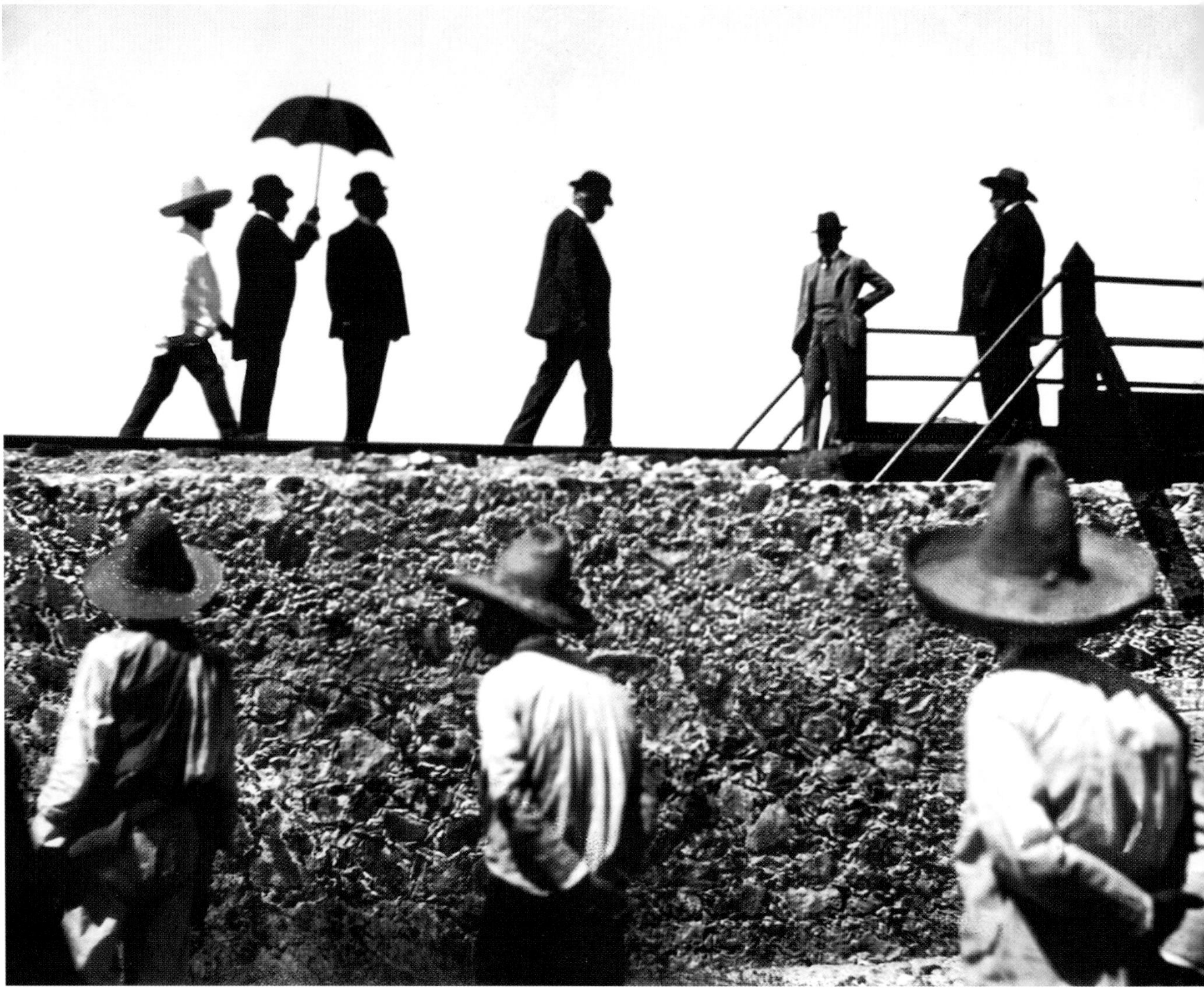

1-1. Government minister José Ives Limantour (shaded by umbrella) in Mexico City for the opening of the works to bring drinking water from Xochimilco, 18 March 1910; Miguel Casasola? © Inv. #35001, Fondo Casasola, SINAFO-Fototeca Nacional del INAH.

Perhaps the critique was evident to *El Imparcial*'s editor, because Rafael Reyes Espíndola, the founder of the first mass media company in Mexico, did not publish the photo at the time. Reyes Espíndola was closely allied with Díaz and founded, among other publications, the magazine *El Mundo Ilustrado* and the newspaper *El Imparcial.* In order to privilege imagery, the editor imported from Europe the best high-volume rotogravure presses and Linotype machines, cutting-edge technology that he acquired thanks to a government subsidy of 1,000 pesos a week, which gave him an insurmountable advantage over his rivals.[4] The fact that impartiality was not a priority for Reyes Espíndola can be appreciated in another spontaneous photo, that of his brother, Luis Reyes Espíndola, heading up a bunch of paperboys from *El Imparcial* who were recruited to support the sixth (and last) reelection of Díaz (Figure 1-2). The editor's publications fundamentally transformed Mexican journalism, employing the illusory objectivity of photography to make it appear that they were engaged in an ostensible search for the apparent truth. Projecting the image of objectivity was in line with the positivist precepts of the official ideologues, the Científicos, who backed *El Imparcial*;

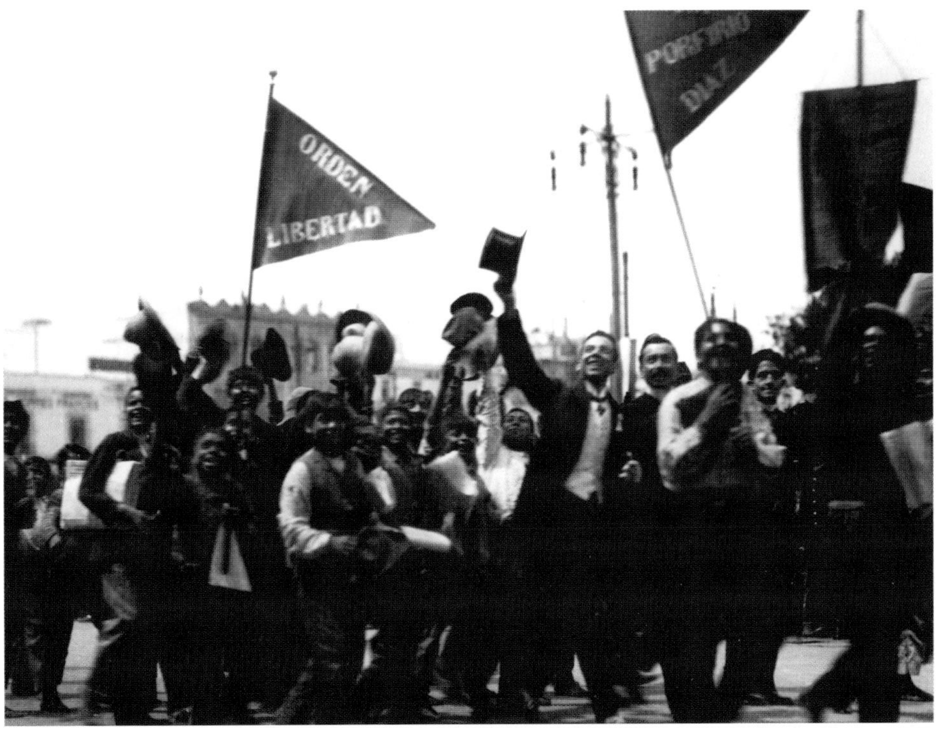

1-2. March of newsboys calling for the reelection of Porfirio Díaz, led by journalist Luis Reyes Espíndola (with top hat), Mexico City, 2 April 1909. © Inv. #663555, Fondo Casasola, SINAFO-Fototeca Nacional del INAH.

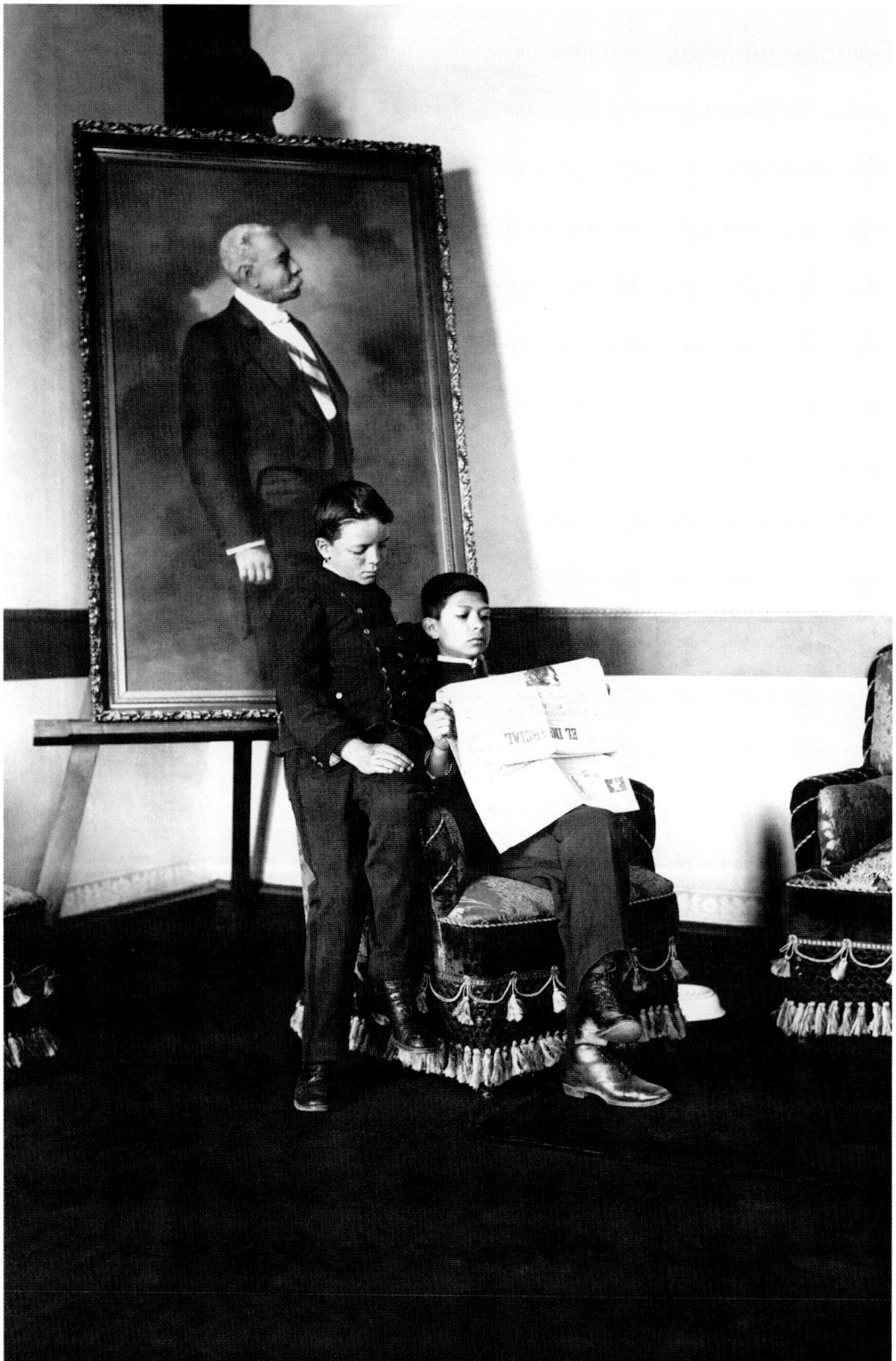

1-3. Boys reading the newspaper *El Imparcial* under a portrait of Porfirio Díaz, ca. 1910. © Inv. #5067, Fondo Casasola, SINAFO-Fototeca Nacional del INAH.

this position was also in accordance with the "end of ideology" established by Díaz's blurring of liberal and conservative battle lines.[5]

Designed to prioritize the ocular, *El Imparcial* was originally subtitled "Illustrated Morning Daily."[6] Although the newspaper covered official acts of the president, the governors, ministers, and diplomats—as well as the cultural activities of the upper class—police reports (*nota roja*) comprised its center. Its pages were filled with news of disasters, train crashes, streetcar accidents, fires, thefts, murders, suicides, and assaults, which planted fear and "demonstrated" that the country needed the firm hand of a dictator. One macabre example was the coverage of an execution of three campesinos in Chalco for having killed a policeman (Figure 1-4). The photograph combines the spectacular fact of a triple execution with elements usually associated

1-4. Execution of Marcelino Martínez, Arcadio Jiménez, and Hilario Silva for murder, Chalco, Mexico state, 28 April 1909; Agustín Víctor Casasola? © Inv. #196863, Fondo Casasola, SINAFO-Fototeca Nacional del INAH.

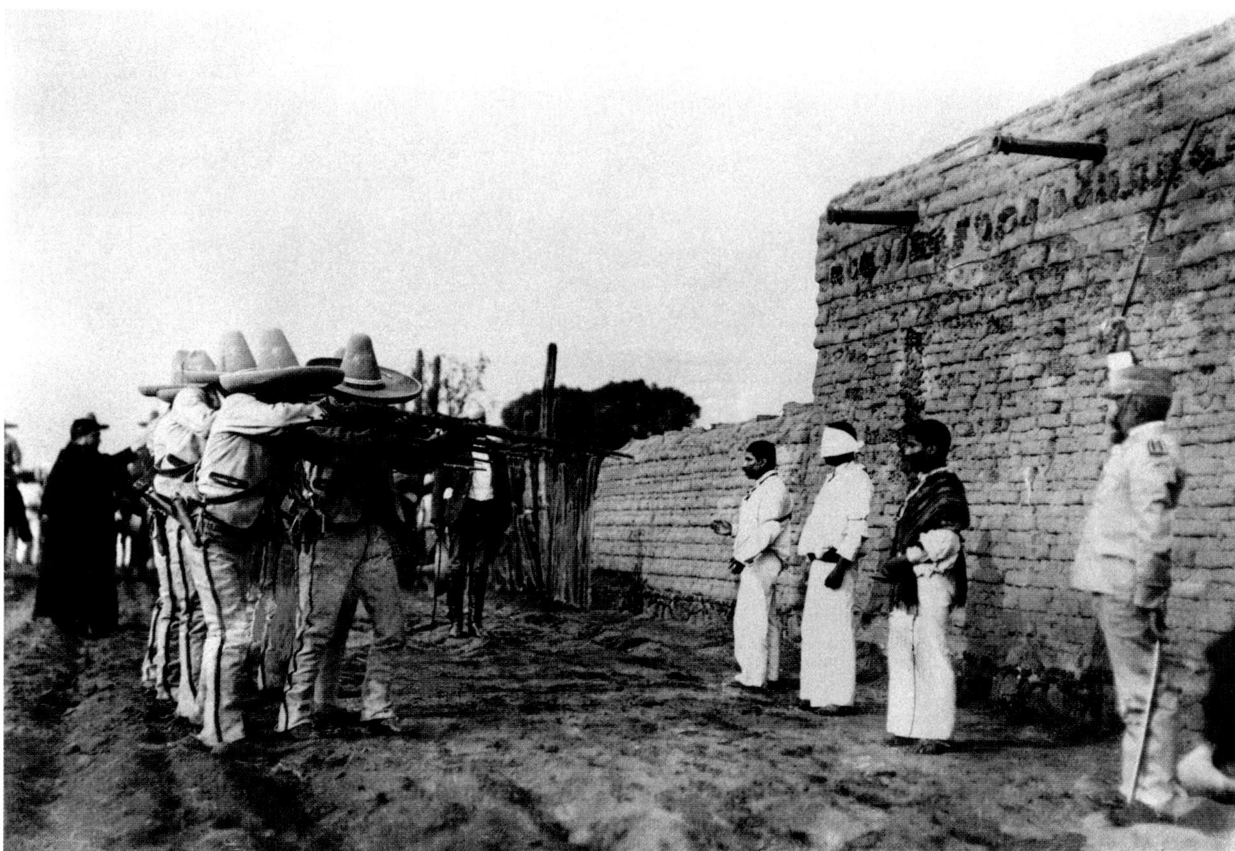

with the exotic of the Mexican countryside, such as the broad-brimmed sombreros of the Rurales and the typical white clothing of the peasants. It may have been intended as an object lesson for Mexicans who might disturb the Pax Porfiriana—"an example so that the law, interests, and people would be respected"—as well as an advertisement to foreigners who required order for their investments.[7] *El Imparcial* put the story on the front page for three days and provided ample graphic reportage with six photos and texts that demonstrated the newspaper's thirst for blood:

> The bodies fell simultaneously, slowly backward, and a hoarse whisper flowed from either the enormous holes made by the bullets or their tightly pressed lips. The clothing smoked from the gunpowder, and their contractions denoted an extraordinarily cruel suffering. A death rattle, like that of a sheep with its throat cut, escaped from the three bodies. Their families sobbed, and their cries filled the countryside. Those of us who were present will never forget it.[8]

While the sensationalism of *El Imparcial* was designed to play to the lowest instincts, the magazine *El Mundo Ilustrado* was directed toward the refinements of the well-to-do: "Our weekly has always been for the elegant people of Mexico, and should therefore be an echo of the gatherings and entertainments to which they concur."[9] The magazine published photos of society congregations: banquets, balls, and fiestas, as well as the sports that developed in the Porfiriato, from basketball to horse races, all of which took place in a stable and progressive culture, relaxed and harmonic in deserved well-being. The constant charity fairs were also featured: a seemingly infinite number of kermesses, carnivals, and *jamaicas* were fashioned to show concern for the "other half," though they really served as little more than band-aids for the era's extreme social injustice. The poor were excluded from the pages of *El Mundo Ilustrado*: in fact, the only Indian who ever appeared in the magazine was a dead one.[10]

Although it may appear paradoxical, the presence of the less fortunate at charity events could produce an uncomfortable reaction, as may have been registered in Figure 1-5. Four well-dressed women at a kermess walk arm-in-arm toward the photographer, their white dresses reflecting a light that leaves the rest of the scene in grey shadows. Two women return the camera's gaze, but the other two look instead at a tiny indigent woman and her daughter; dressed in rags and barefooted, they were probably attempting to sell their meager goods (see the basket). We might find expressions of disgust on the faces of the wealthy women, but more important than any psychological reading are the manifest indicators of class in the contrast between the elegant clothing of the women and the tatters in which the poor are dressed. Moreover, the women in white are almost a head taller than the poor mother, a difference in size that indicates a substantial dissimilarity in diet and genetics. The appearance of the impoverished in the middle of an event organized for the wealthy may have been a bit vexing, for the woman closest to the destitute mother and child appears to pull the skirt of her dress aside to avoid contact with such miserable and filthy creatures. There were laws governing the interaction between the classes in public spaces: "When a '*pelado*,' that is to say, a person dressed in the white campesino clothing (*calzón de manta*) and a reed sombrero, would be confronted on the sidewalk by a 'gentleman' in a suit and elegant hat, and he did not step down, the gentleman would then tell him, 'Step down, *pelado*.' If he did not do so, he would be taken to the policeman on the corner and accused of insult."[11]

1-5. Wealthy women passing by a poor woman and child at a charity bazaar in Tacubaya, Mexico City, ca. 1904. © Inv. #276381, Fondo Casasola, SINAFO-Fototeca Nacional del INAH.

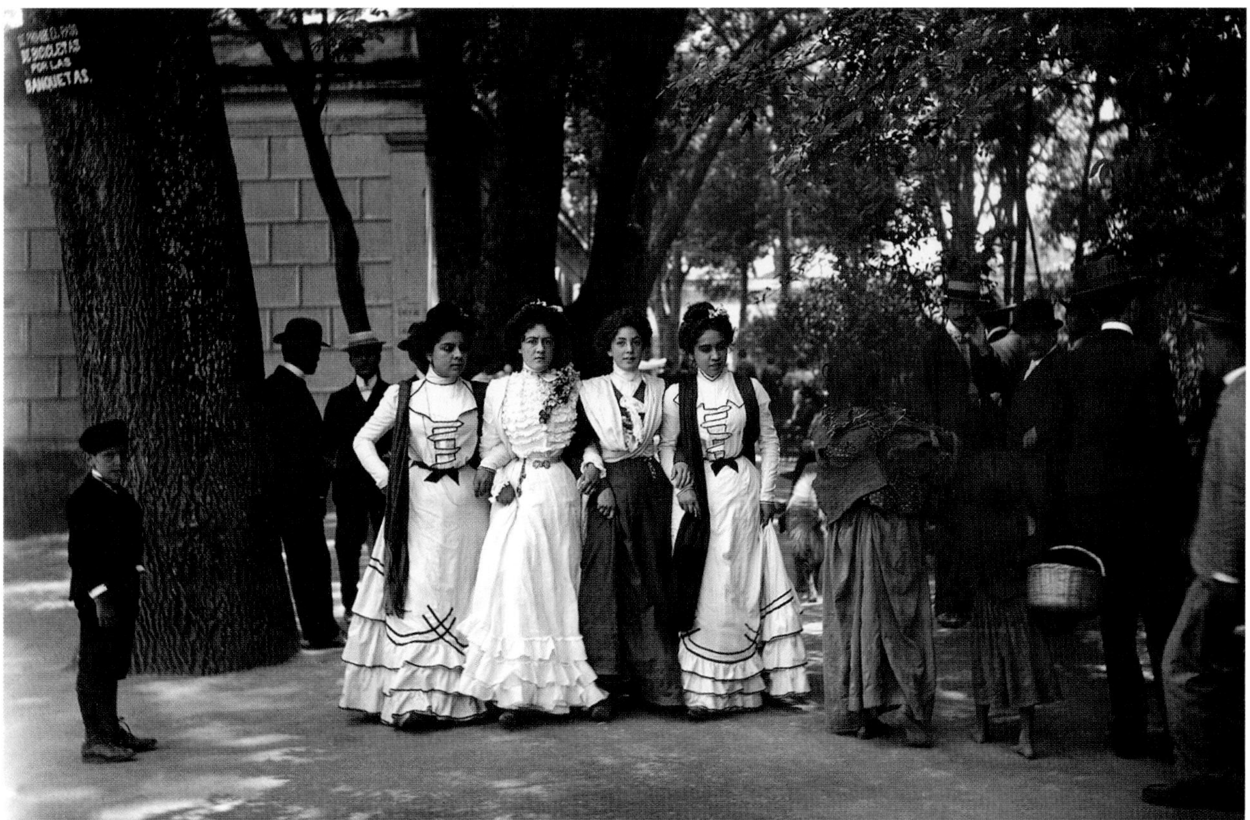

Porfirian legislation attempted to divide the use of Mexico City by marginalizing the less fortunate, but the needs of the poor to have access to the central areas of the capital in order to sell their goods or labor, as well as buy their necessities, blurred "the artificial borders between a modern city, where public and private functions were clearly separated, and another city, where elite models of behavior seemed less important."[12] As historian Pablo Piccato has argued, "Peddlers . . . fought a constant battle against authorities to occupy those areas of the city where customers and money were accessible."[13] Although vendors had circulated throughout Mexican history, for Porfirian authorities they were an "unnatural" element of the city's ambience, "an agent of social conflict, struggling for space against established merchants and respectable neighbors."[14]

Attempts to create an ideal city in which the poor masses were segregated from the wealthy, modernizing elements of society were doomed to failure for several reasons. The underclass had a more "horizontal" conception of the city than the Porfirian elite and, like water, flowed through the points of least resistance. Further, the constant arrival of migrants from the countryside made it difficult to indoctrinate the populace, while new means of transportation, such as streetcars, facilitated access to the supposedly off-limits center. Finally, the very needs of the economy itself dictated against such a policy. As historian John Lear has asserted, "The Porfirian project of ridding the center of the poor and of controlling their behavior proved contradictory and ultimately unsuccessful . . . [for] the presence of these poor and working people was fundamental to the needs of the urban economy."[15]

The "Great Men" who had created Porfirian Mexico were at the magazine's core, and the presence of Díaz was ubiquitous: he is featured opening new markets, medical schools, electric plants, theaters, and jails; unveiling statues of great leaders; receiving homage from foreign governments; heading up charity festivals; making trips throughout the republic; opening sessions of Congress; giving awards to the best military students; celebrating his silver wedding anniversary; appearing at military parades; and celebrating his reelections at balls and banquets.[16] The Porfiriato was a regime of image, and at its nucleus was Porfirio Díaz.

The era's photojournalism took place in a context dominated by the publications of Rafael Reyes Espíndola. The editor was a shrewd judge of talent and had formed an impressive group of visual collaborators, including Manuel Ramos, Ezequiel Álvarez Tostado, Abraham Lupercio, and Gerónimo Hernández, as well as correspondents from different parts of the country, such as José María Lupercio in Guadalajara. Among the photographers who documented Porfirian progress for *El Mundo Ilustrado* was the German Guillermo Kahlo, who provided images of modernity such as the train stopped for a portrait on the Metlac bridge (Figure 1-6).[17]

In 1905, Agustín Víctor Casasola was invited to join *El Imparcial*'s staff.[18] He had similar commercial instincts to those of Reyes Espíndola, combined with a love of photography; once he chose the camera as his medium, he seems rarely to have put it down.[19] He had worked as a reporter as well as photographer for various publications, but he devoted himself full time to his new profession as a photojournalist upon joining *El Imparcial*. His extraordinary dedication began to gain him a reputation in 1910, when he earned a 25 peso bonus for "excessive achievement of duties," jumping into

1-6. Train on the Metlac bridge, 1903; Guillermo Kahlo. © Inv. #843539, Fondo Casasola, SINAFO-Fototeca Nacional del INAH.

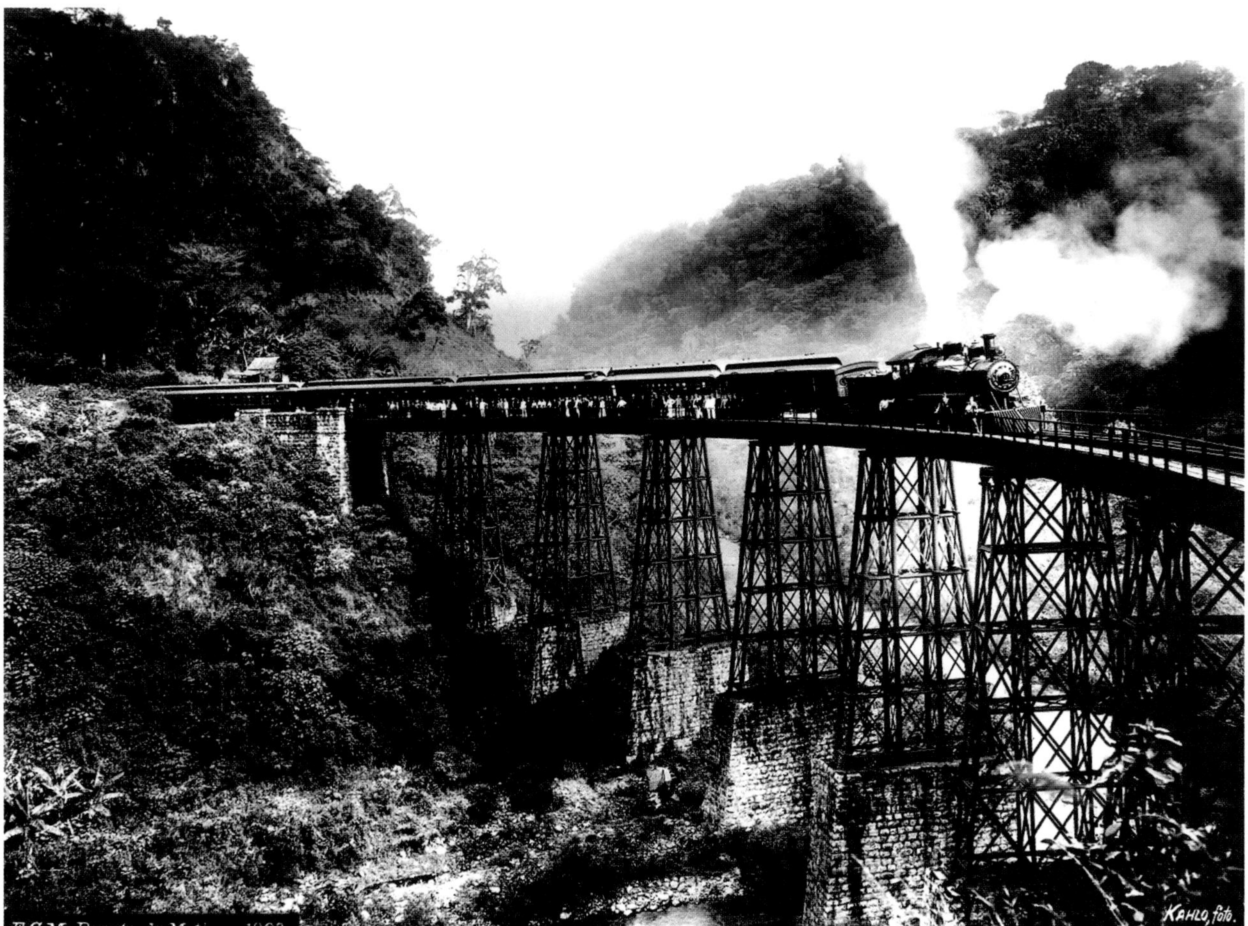

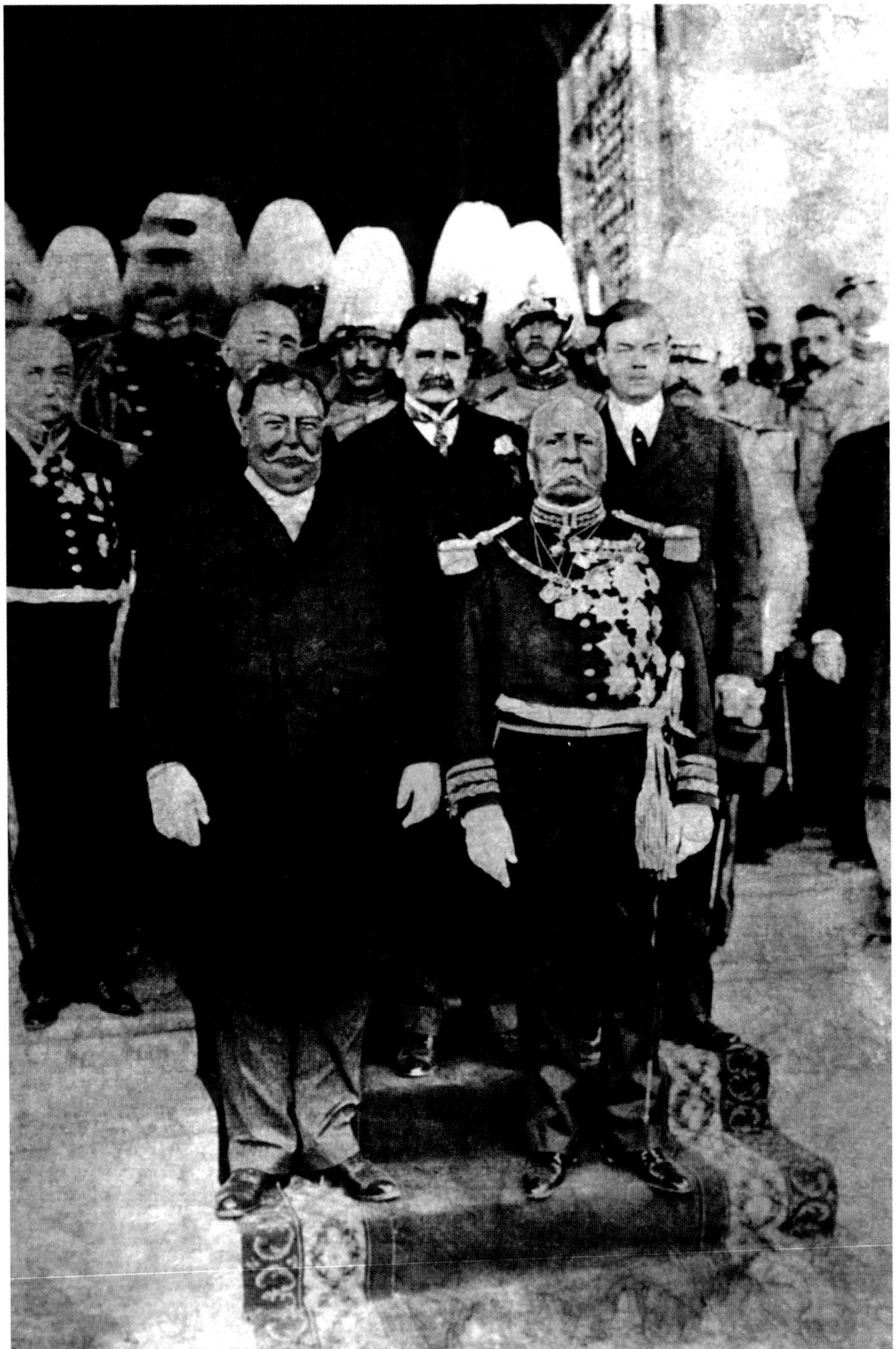

1-7. Porfirio Díaz in uniform next to U.S. president William Howard Taft, El Paso, Texas, 11 October 1909; Manuel Ramos. © Inv. #33925, Fondo Casasola, SINAFO-Fototeca Nacional del INAH.

a bullring to capture the action up close.[20] It was surely the connection of Agustín Víctor with the periodicals of Reyes Espíndola that led Debroise to assert that Casasola was "the official photographer of Porfirio Díaz," because the only evidence he offers is the fact that the photojournalist accompanied the dictator to Veracruz when he sailed into exile.[21] Nevertheless, almost all the metropolitan press photographers shared his attachment to the regime. It has been habitual to consider Agustín Víctor an obligatory reference of Porfirian photography, but my research indicates that other photojournalists were more important.[22] Moreover, to judge by a 1906 article in *El Tiempo Ilustrado*, Casasola did not figure among "the Mexican photographers that have elevated to a true art what was formerly considered a mere hobby or a way to earn a living."[23] Obviously, Casasola and other photojournalists would be excluded from "Mexican Artist Photographers," an article that paints a line between the "artistes" of the camera and those who have to live from their profession; this position also points to an aesthetic tension that would continue throughout the revolution.

If the Porfiriato had an "official" photojournalist, it was Manuel Ramos, about whom his daughter, Teresa Ramos Sánchez, commented, "He must have been the photographer of Don Porfirio . . . whenever he talked about him he took off his hat."[24] Ramos was the head of photography for both *El Imparcial* and *El Mundo Ilustrado*.[25] He later photographed the revolution, but "he didn't like Madero, nor the Villistas nor the Zapatistas."[26] Hence, his work opens windows onto the imagery that dominated the Porfiriato, and, moreover, it permits us to contemplate an experience that must have been relatively typical of the capital's photojournalism. The dictator's official acts were at the center of Ramos's photos, including one taken when he traveled to the northern border to cover the 1909 meeting of Díaz and U.S. president William Howard Taft (Figure 1-7).

On that occasion Ramos was sent by the magazine *Arte y Letras*, which affirmed that the first U.S. president to visit Mexico came "lavishing praise for our progress, our peace, our liberal conquests."[27] In a climate full of contradictions and opposition to a dictatorship that seemed interminable—and given the polysemia of photographs—the image of the bemedalled general surrounded by a multitudinous military escort contrasts strongly with that of the progressive, democratically elected president, dressed in civilian clothes and accompanied by only two aides. According to the revolutionary Salvador Alvarado, "On the one hand, all the simplicity of a true democracy, on the other, the pomp and vainglory of an oriental sultanate. One president, simply dressed; the other president covered with crosses, medals, ribbons, and jewels. In sum, all the ostentation and splendor of an ORIENTAL MONARCH."[28]

Like the rest of the metropolitan photojournalists, Ramos depicted the progress incarnated in the public works and new buildings inaugurated by Díaz. The images offered visual and ostensibly objective testimonies of clean and well-paved avenues, always taken in the wealthy zones, creating the illusion that Mexico City looked like a European city, even though, in that period, it was actually a "sewer" according to historian Manuel González Navarro.[29] Ramos also extensively covered social activities, such as elitist sports like riding and polo, as well as charities: kermesses, *romerías* (pilgrimages), *zarzuelas*, fiestas, theater performances, and beneficial works.[30] One of the Porfiriato's most recognized graphic reporters, he won prizes in photographic contests for his picturesque images of romantic landscapes and "Mexican types." Picturing the real situation of the underprivileged was vetoed from the illustrated magazines, so Ramos disguised members of his family as if they were poor, well behaved, and clean; his daughter remembered that the photojournalist often had his wife dress herself up as a little Indian maid.[31]

The fact that Ramos would deck out his family to look like ordinary people indicates the degree to which the media marginalized the great majority of the population. In this way the Mexican masses were excluded from the nation of order and progress constructed by the illustrated press, which reduced the panorama of social and ethnic variety in Mexican society to the successful and the criminal. There appears to have been no critical photography produced in Mexico (and perhaps nowhere in Latin America) of the sort that was being made in the United States during this period by Jacob Riis and Lewis Hine. This could be attributed to the economic difficulties of independent publications in obtaining the equipment to make photogravure, which left those photographers that might have had an interest in criticizing the Porfirian regime without any place to publish their work.

Among negatives from the Casasola Archive that might have a critical intention, one possibility shows a family of vegetable sellers outside a market (Figure 1-8). Ignacio Gutiérrez has argued that while it is generally true that Casasola did not take denunciatory images, he believes that this photo "offered little possibility of being considered part of the official photography associated with the Porfiriato."[32] Nonetheless, this picture does not appear to have been motivated by a social consciousness of class oppression because the subjects smile at the camera, involved in a task that is evidently profitable and gratifying. Critical imagery of the Porfiriato is probably limited to that made by foreigners such as C. B. Waite and Winfield Scott, who took pictures to promote businesses such as rubber and coffee plantations, mines, real estate, and tourism, all of which were often constructed and controlled by foreign investors.[33]

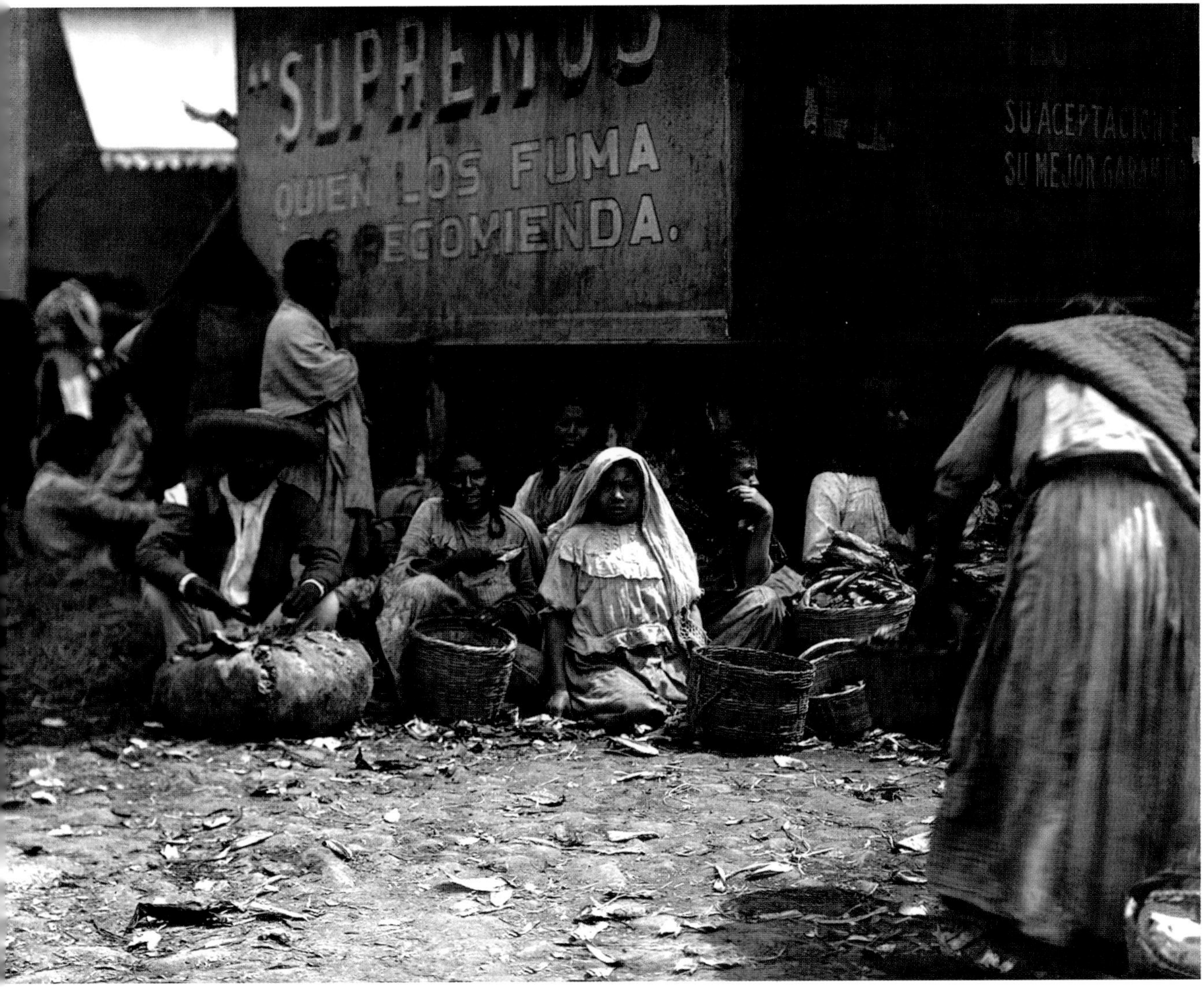

1-8. A family of vegetable sellers, ca. 1905. © Inv. #6030, Fondo Casasola, SINAFO-Fototeca Nacional del INAH.

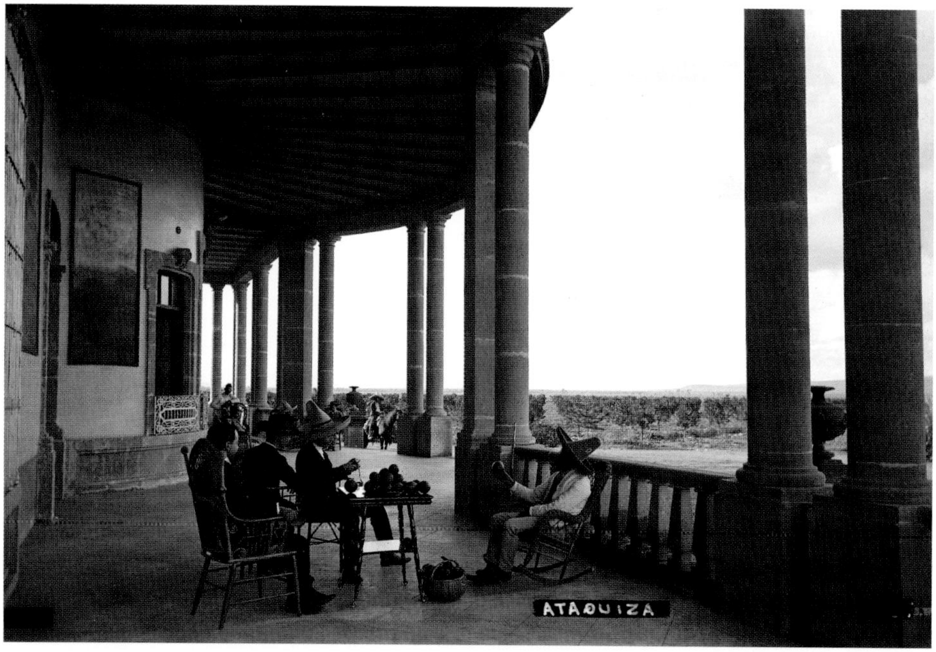

1-9. Hacienda of Ataquiza, Jalisco, ca. 1905; Winfield Scott. © Inv. #120452, Fondo Casasola, SINAFO-Fototeca Nacional del INAH.

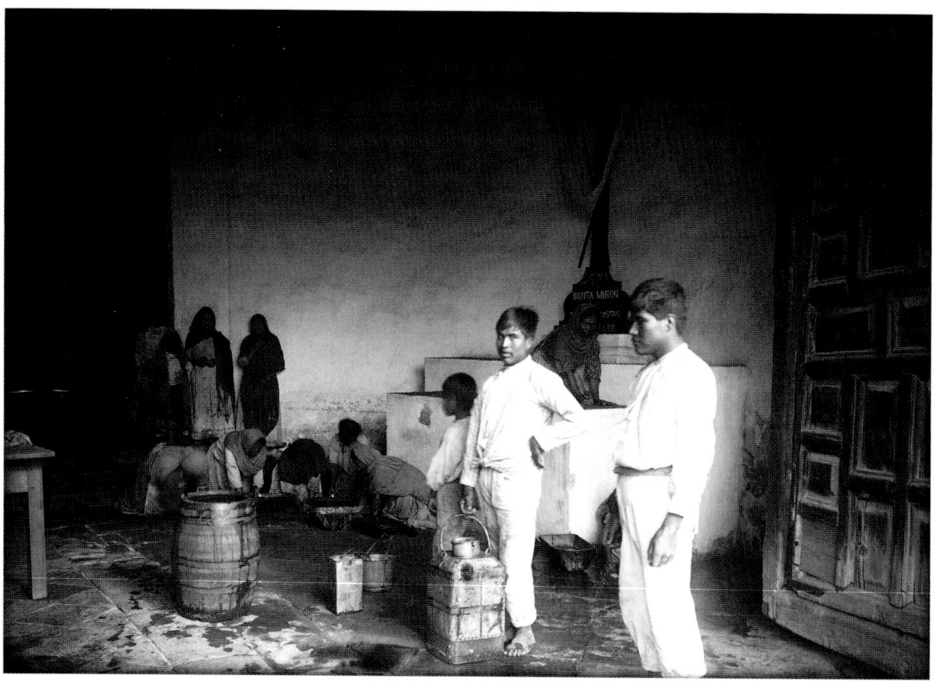

1-10. Campesinos in the patio of a hacienda, 1911; C. B. Waite? © Inv. #120001, Fondo Casasola, SINAFO-Fototeca Nacional del INAH.

Although their motives were those of celebrating the creation of a new and dynamic Mexico, as well as bringing tourists to exotic (but safe) locales, Waite and Scott made some images that were at the same time indexes of the crushing poverty and underdevelopment in which so many Mexicans lived. There was no lack of photos celebrating the luxury enjoyed by the *hacendados*, such as the owner of the Ataquiza hacienda (Figure 1-9), but images of barefooted campesinos standing in the midst of such opulence, the women cleaning floors on their knees (Figure 1-10), or seated in front of their simple huts (Figure 1-11), documented the abysmal class differences during the Porfiriato.

1-11. Campesinos, central Mexico, ca. 1907; Winfield Scott. © Inv. #458159, Fondo Casasola, SINAFO-Fototeca Nacional del INAH.

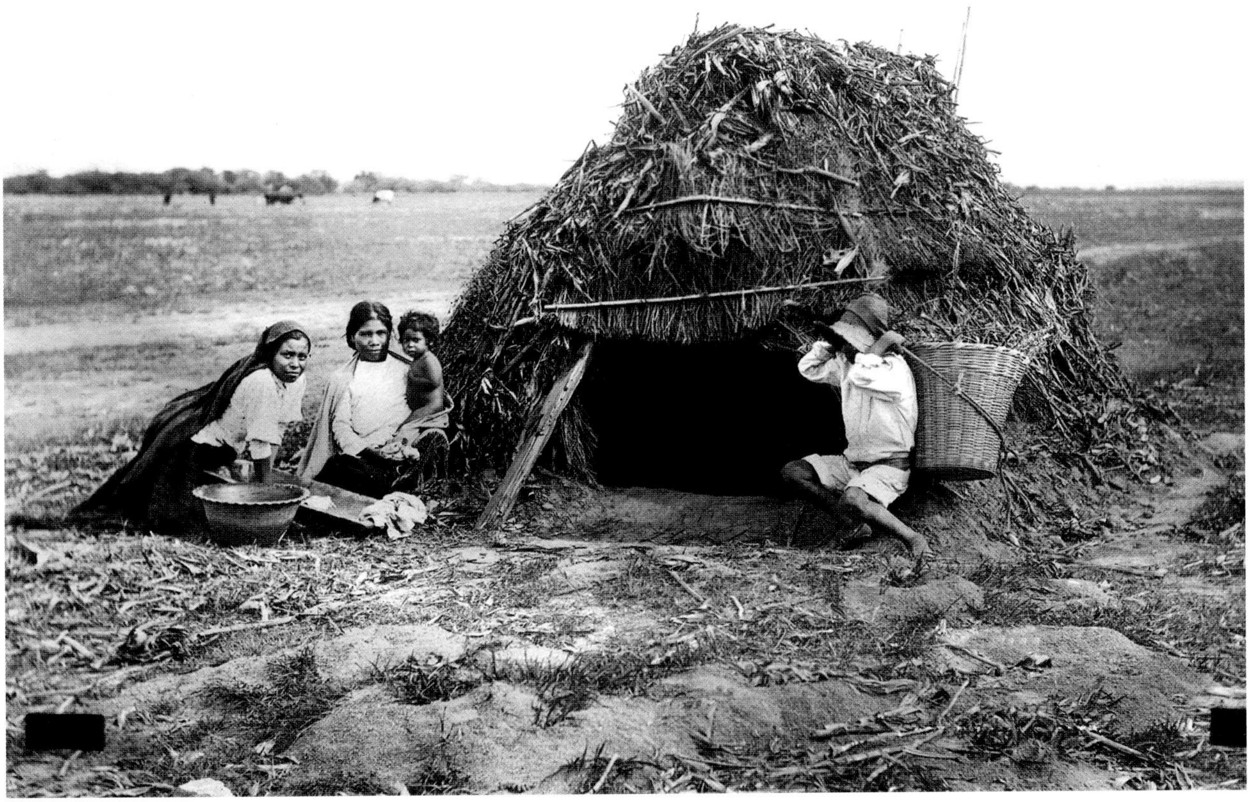

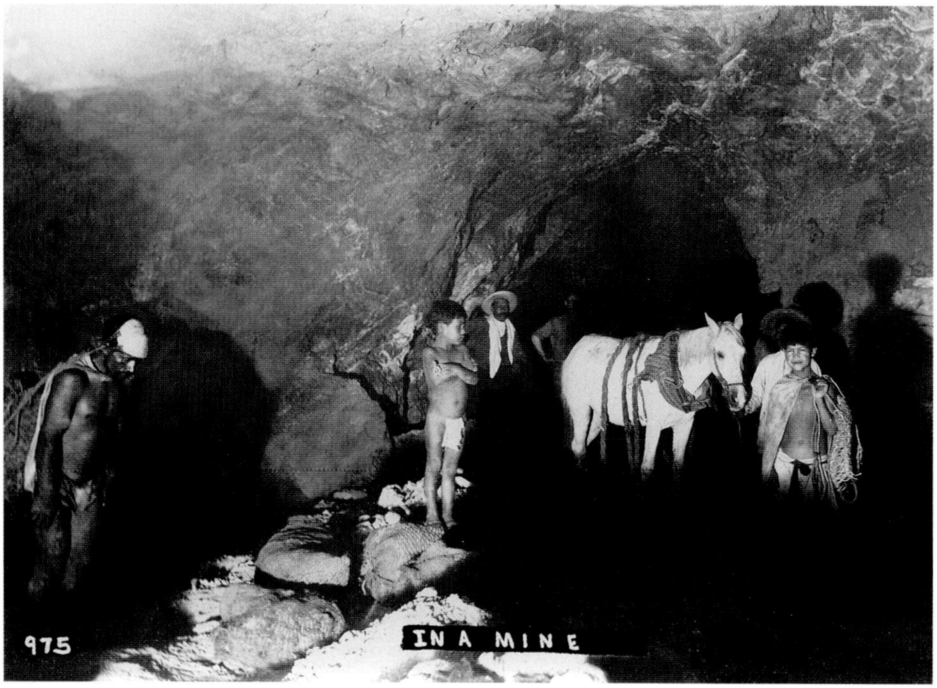

1-12. Miners, ca. 1905; Winfield Scott. © Archivo General de la Nación, Fondo Propiedad Artístico y Literaria, C. B. Waite, "Trabajo y tecnología," 1.

Foreign photographers were especially attracted to the fate of children: girls and boys in rags huddling together in the countryside and the cities, entire families participating in communal delousing.[34] One photo shows laborers in the depths of a mine, including two nearly naked young boys (Figure 1-12). A witness of life under Díaz offered the following testimony, which corroborates, and helps us understand, the lack of clothing worn by miners: "I remember having seen the seminude miners descend into the hot entrails of the earth and come up to the surface in the midst of icy winds, covered only with something placed in their crotches and tied to their belts."[35] Several images of children point to a complex intertwining of poverty and pornography still to be investigated: a boy covered only with a jacket begs, with hand extended, "Give me a penny"; two children stand in the middle of misery, the genitals of the boy exposed by the lack of clothing; young girls bathing in a stream shyly cover their genitals and yet-to-develop breasts (Figure 1-13).[36] This latter is a complex image, for the barbed wire behind the girls that keeps them from escaping the camera could also be a reference to the barriers—or could in fact be one of the fences—that were enclosing communal lands. Of course, one would not wish to ascribe a critical

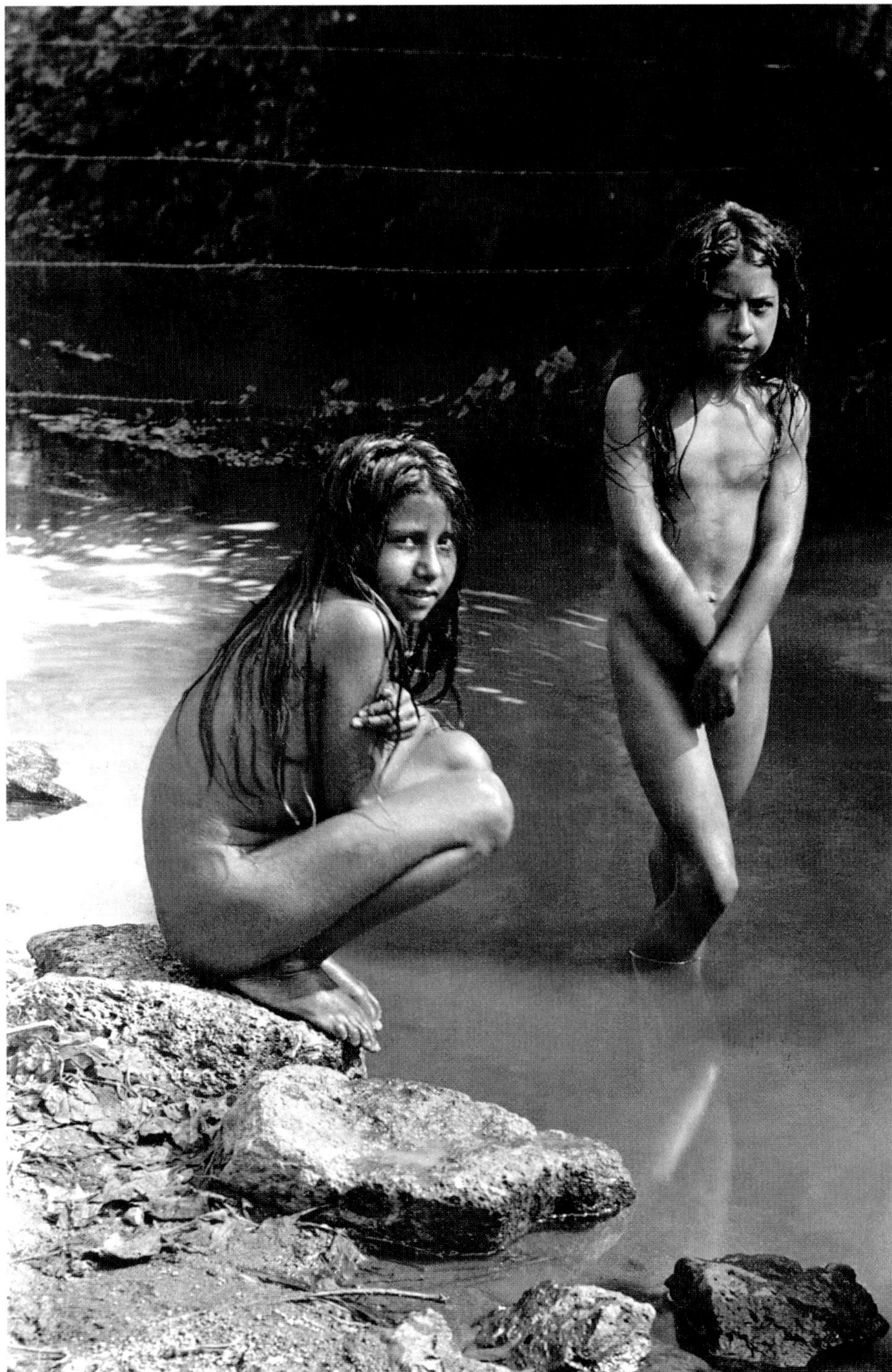

1-13. Girls bathing, ca. 1905; C. B. Waite or Winfield Scott.

eye to either Waite or Scott; rather, they simply recorded what was before them: in this case, the imagemaker has captured "innocent" (nonthreatening) female sexuality, embarrassed at being caught naked but unable to flee exposure.

We do not know if these images entered into a well-developed market in Europe, where erotic postcards of young girls numbered five times those printed of adult pinups.[37] It is worth noting, however, that both Scott and Waite were suspected of making child pornography. Scott ran afoul of the law in the United States, where he was accused in 1894 of using his position as the director in charge of creating a photographic register of Chinese immigrants to convince young girls to pose nude for him.[38] Waite was arrested in 1901 for trying to send through the Mexican mail photographs of "completely naked children presenting their deformed and hairless bodies," and he spent three days in jail for violating postal codes against "indecent" images.[39] *El Imparcial*'s reporter raged against "travelers who look for the most ridiculous, the most degenerate, and the most miserable in Mexico, exhibiting us in a state of barbarity"; he was incensed by what he described as typical tourist pictures made by "J. G. Wheite" [*sic*] of "miserable huts, the indispensable woman grinding corn, the market carrier, the water seller, and the drunk . . . dirty and uncombed women with their clothes torn, and men made into degenerates by all the vices."[40] Nevertheless, a functionary who was alert to the services that Waite provided to the government must have called the police and *El Imparcial* on his behalf, for three days later the paper stated that all was due to a mistake (while providing a model of the images preferred by the regime): "El señor Waite has spent much time traveling around the country to take pictures of the most beautiful and notable monuments, the most picturesque landscapes, and the best buildings of Mexico."[41]

The centennial of independence, celebrated in September 1910, was "the last waltz" of the Porfiriato. The regimen spent a fortune to show invited foreigners a Mexico City that was developed, modern, and cosmopolitan. The participation of many photojournalists who would soon be photographing the revolution was key. Among them were Manuel Ramos, Agustín Víctor and Miguel Casasola, Gerónimo Hernández, Samuel Tinoco, Ezequiel Álvarez Tostado, Eduardo Melhado, and Heliodoro J. Gutiérrez, who published their images in newspapers, illustrated magazines, postcards, and the many sumptuous volumes that were dedicated to the celebration.[42] The illumination of certain parts of the city was an important protagonist and a visual metaphor for the centenary because the new "ideal" city had been extensively electrified, and many federal buildings were profusely illuminated by "torrents of electricity"; as the centennial's chronicler, Genaro García, described it: "The city was wrapped in a true mantle of light, whose immense tongues of fire ascended to the heavens, as if the city had been consumed in a vast fire or consecrated on a colossal pyre in memory of its heroes."[43]

Photographing the luminous city must have offered a double certification of the up-to-date: the images not only testified to Mexico's electrical capacity, but also demonstrated the technological capabilities of the photographers. One such was made by Hugo Brehme (Figure 1-14). He also may have begun during the centennial to explore his later folkloric vein: one photo taken in the middle of the historical parade shows an Indian dressed as "Un gran señor méxica" (a great Aztec sire) (Figure 1-15).[44] One of the few ways in which an Indian could get a good seat for the centennial's activities was to disguise him- or herself as an aristocrat from an ancient (and idealized) civilization; the less privileged of Porfirian society were otherwise largely kept away from the festivities.[45] One person who lived through the revolution as a child remembered how that segregation was described: "My father told us how the army had formed a barrier at 8 or 10 blocks all around the Zócalo in order to make sure that Indians—those that were dressed in the cotton pajamas and straw sombreros—couldn't get within that area."[46]

1-14. LEFT Electric company illuminated for the centennial of independence, Mexico City, September 1910; Hugo Brehme. © INAH: Hoffman-Brehme, 004.

1-15. RIGHT "Un gran señor mexica" (A great Aztec sire), historical parade celebrating the centennial of independence, Mexico City, 15 September 1910; Hugo Brehme. © INAH: Hoffman-Brehme, 017.

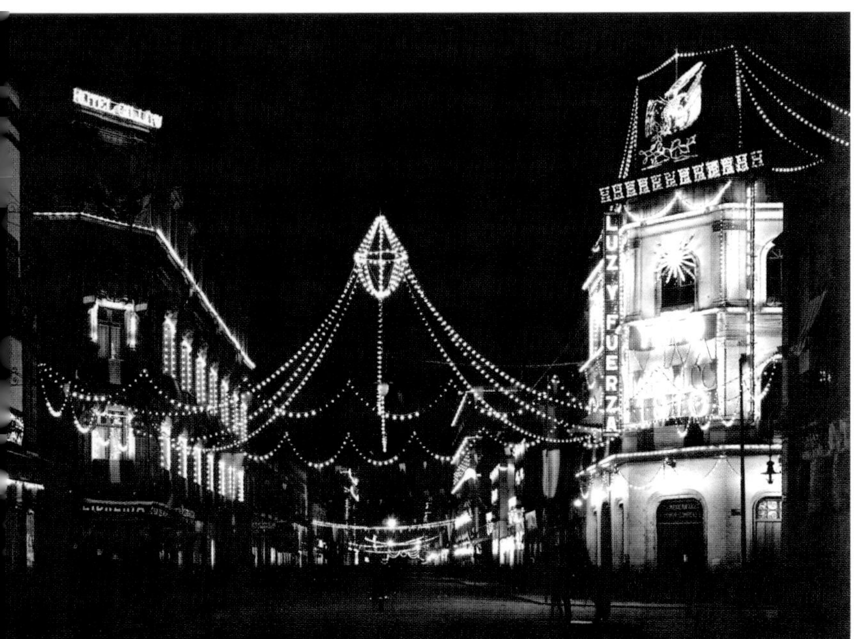

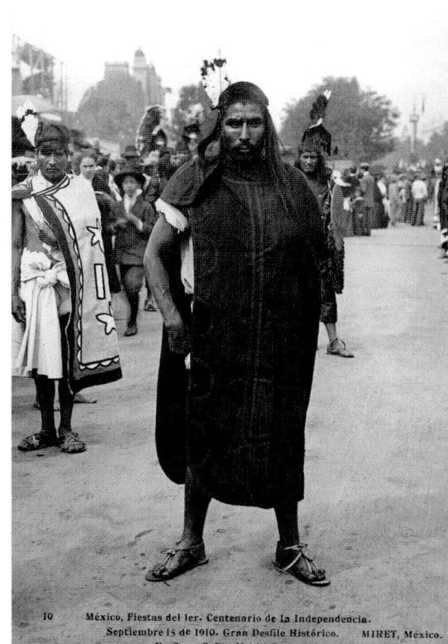

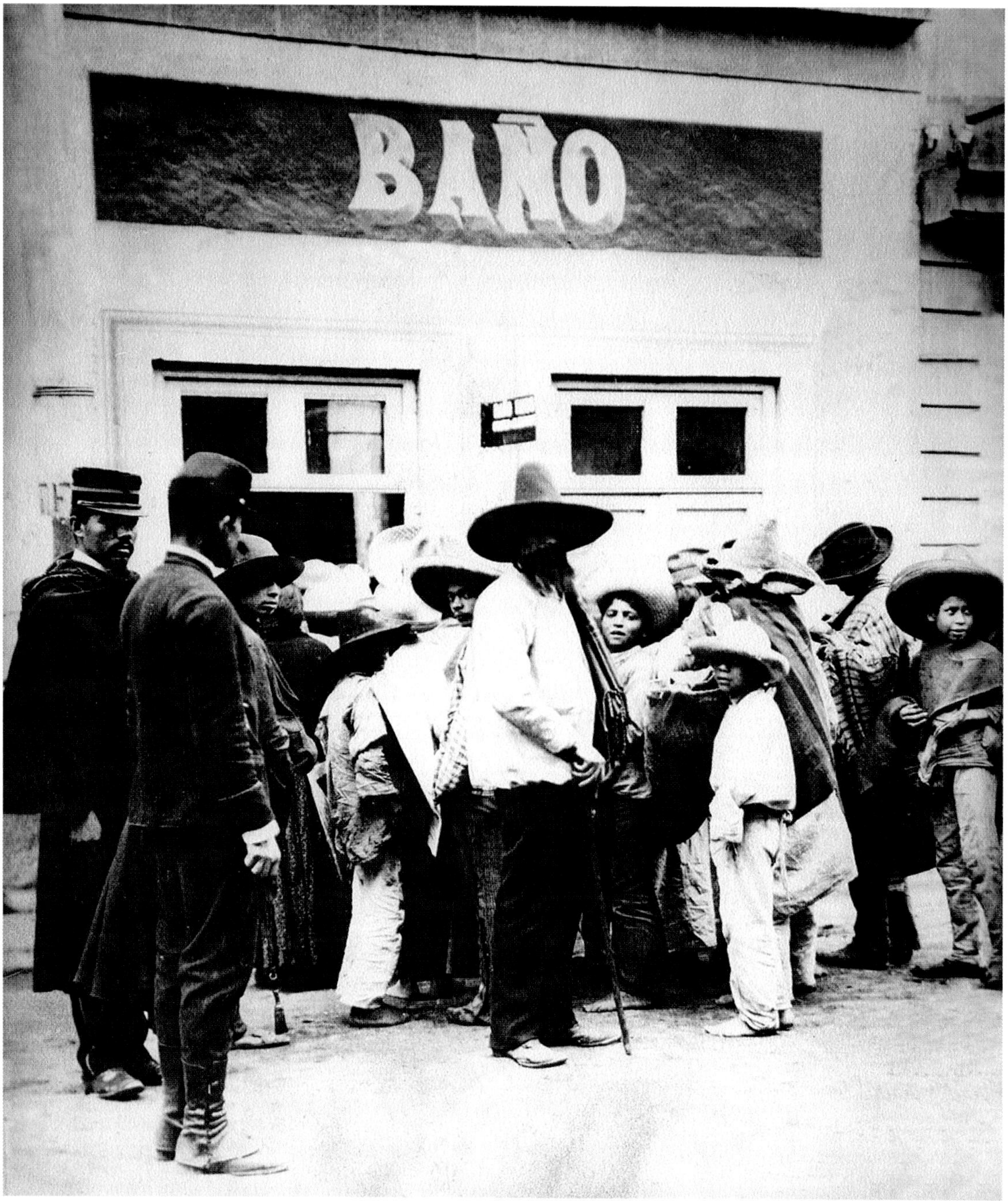

1-16. Police and poor people in front of a public bath, Mexico City, ca. 1910. © Inv. #673264, Fondo Casasola, SINAFO-Fototeca Nacional del INAH.

1-17. Colonel William Green (center, with raised hand), owner of the Cananea Copper Company, and Rafael Izábal (in bowler hat), governor of Sonora, attempt to convince workers to return to the mines. Behind them, a group of armed Rangers and volunteers from the United States stand in front of the company store, Comisaría de El Ronquillo, Cananea, Sonora, 2 June 1906. Archive of John Mraz.

Being excluded was not a new experience for those from the underside; they had been banished from the imagistic world constructed by the press long before. Given their absence, we might well ask what motivated a photographer to take an enigmatic picture of some poor people under the watchful eye of police outside a public bath (Figure 1-16). Was it meant to praise the forces of order, which maintained the poor at bay? Or was it a denunciation of how the less fortunate were corralled and harassed by the police? There was little space for the masses in Porfirian media, but a well of rebellion prepared the stage for their appearance.

One image of the incipient uprising shows Colonel William Green, owner of the Cananea Copper Company, and Rafael Izábal, governor of Sonora, attempting to convince workers to return to the mines (Figure 1-17). The photographer is unknown, but it could well have been someone who accompanied the armed Rangers and vigilantes

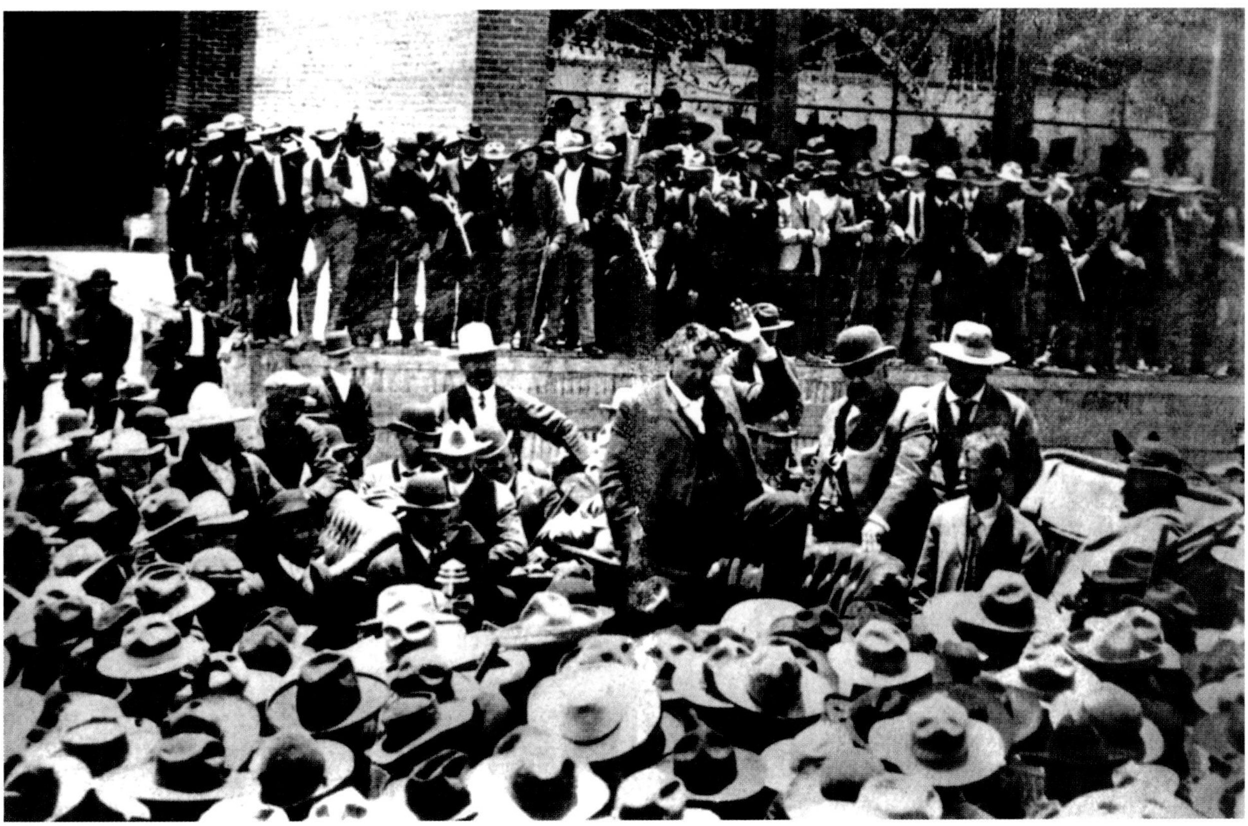

from the United States shown standing guard in front of the company store, a testimony to neocolonialist imposition. The picture was made as part of a series of twenty postcards that circulated widely, and the author was without doubt a colleague and an antecedent of Walter Horne, who would soon be producing 5,000 postcards a day about the revolution and the U.S. troops on the frontier.[47] The postcards of the workers in Cananea also could have been souvenirs for the trespassers from Arizona, but to the editor of the newspaper *El Correo de Chihuahua*, they had a different meaning: Silvestre Terrazas published an image of the U.S. contingent to criticize the official version of the strike; it was the first time his periodical printed a photo.[48] Hence, this image from Cananea foreshadows several things: the mass rebellion that would soon explode; the semantic debility of photographs, which would be used according to the contexts in which they appeared; and the infiltration of U.S. photographers who came to cover the first great social revolution of the modern world.

2-1. FACING Pascual Orozco and his general staff, Chihuahua, April 1911. © Inv. #34289, Fondo Casasola, SINAFO-Fototeca Nacional del INAH.

CHAPTER 2

Representing the Revolution

THE MEXICAN REVOLUTION changed the face of the country. Suddenly, ordinary people were appearing in photographs, newspapers, illustrated magazines, and documentary films; the underdogs projected a force that overflowed the constrictions of the "popular type" model within which they had been shoehorned (Figure 2-1). The conventions of the photographic studio continued in place for those acquainted with them, as can be appreciated in the classic three-quarter pose that Roque González Garza (who stands on Pascual Orozco's left) assumed on putting his head at the haughty angle preferred by "Great Men," as if he were indifferent to the photographer or the public, and deserving of his nickname "the Divine Countenance."[1] As Susan Sontag

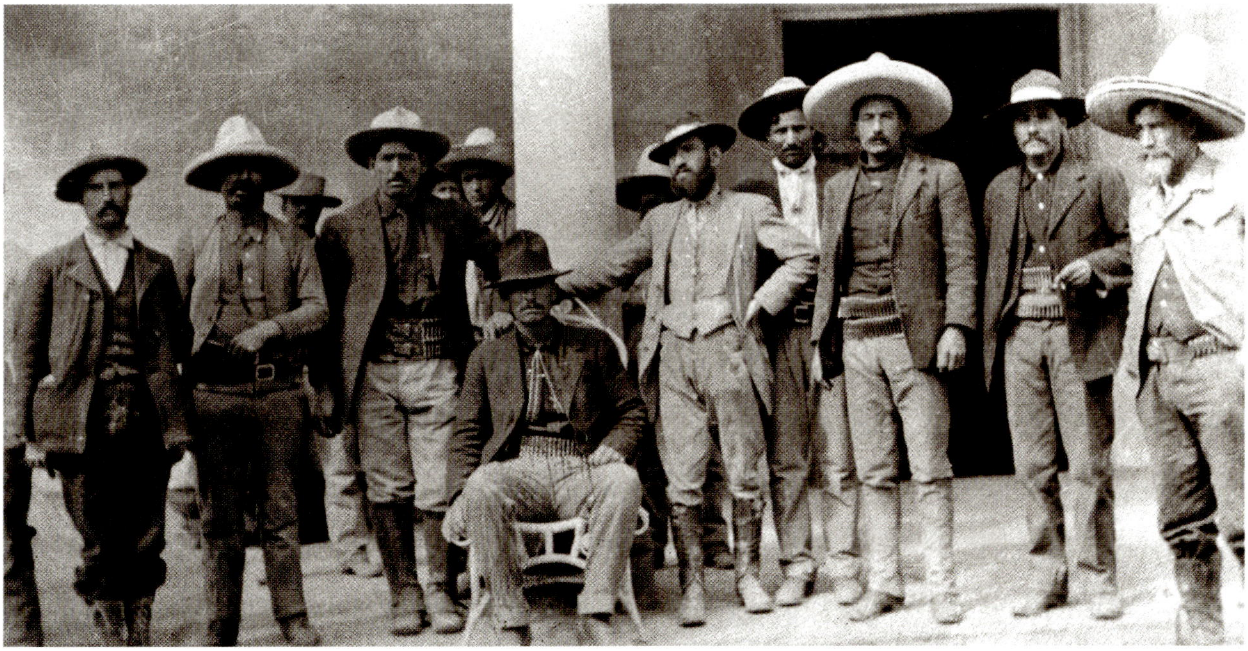

observed, "for politicians the three-quarter gaze . . . soars rather than confronts, suggesting instead of the relation to the viewer, to the present, the more ennobling abstract relation to the future."[2]

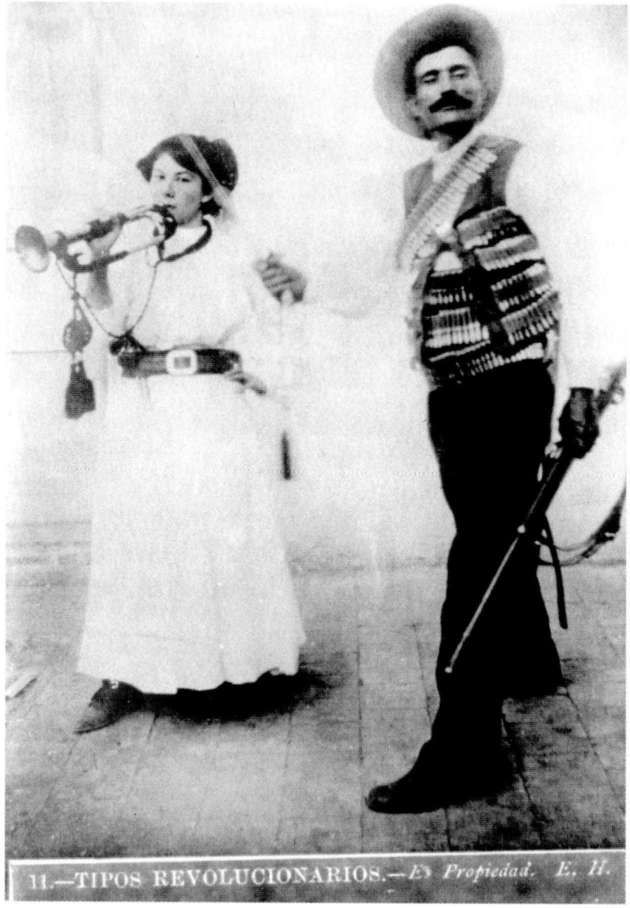

2-2. *Tipos revolucionarios* (Revolutionary types), Ciudad Juárez, Chihuahua, May 1911; E. Herrerías. © Inv. #373891, Fondo Casasola, SINAFO-Fototeca Nacional del INAH.

The other men, new protagonists ignorant of the required poses, return the camera's gaze. Moreover, the established forms weighed so heavily that some photographers, such as E. Herrerías, believed there was a market for "revolutionary types" (Figure 2-2).[3] Those from the underside began to enter the periodicals alongside the suits and Victorian dresses that had so dominated Porfirian representation, although the magazines continued to refer to the Maderistas as bandits and rebels until the resignation of Porfirio Díaz in May of 1911. Combatants with crossed cartridge belts—a pose that became a trope of Maderismo—were only the most spectacular of the apparitions (Figure 2-3). As nonconformity and unrest spread, images of striking seamstresses and villagers protesting against their town's caciques joined the illustrated magazines' familiar fare of upper-crust social activities.[4]

The great majority of photojournalists—above all in the capital—shared the conservative, though always opportunist, positions of the periodicals that paid their salaries and also provided materials and a place to publish their images. Other photographers linked themselves to revolutionary movements and leaders who rapidly recognized the importance of circulating their visages as propaganda for themselves and their causes; caudillos employed photographers and cineastes, usually Mexicans, and/or included them in the ranks. Foreigners with cameras poured into Mexico to cover a war that was news all over the world, and in which the relative lack of control allowed them access to all fronts. The photographs were published in newspapers and illustrated magazines, and also appeared as postcards, for which there was an enormous demand within and outside of the country. Newsreels and documentary compilations became very popular, and some photographers—among them Jesús Abitia, Eutasio Montoya, and Ignacio Medrano Chávez—worked in cinema as well.

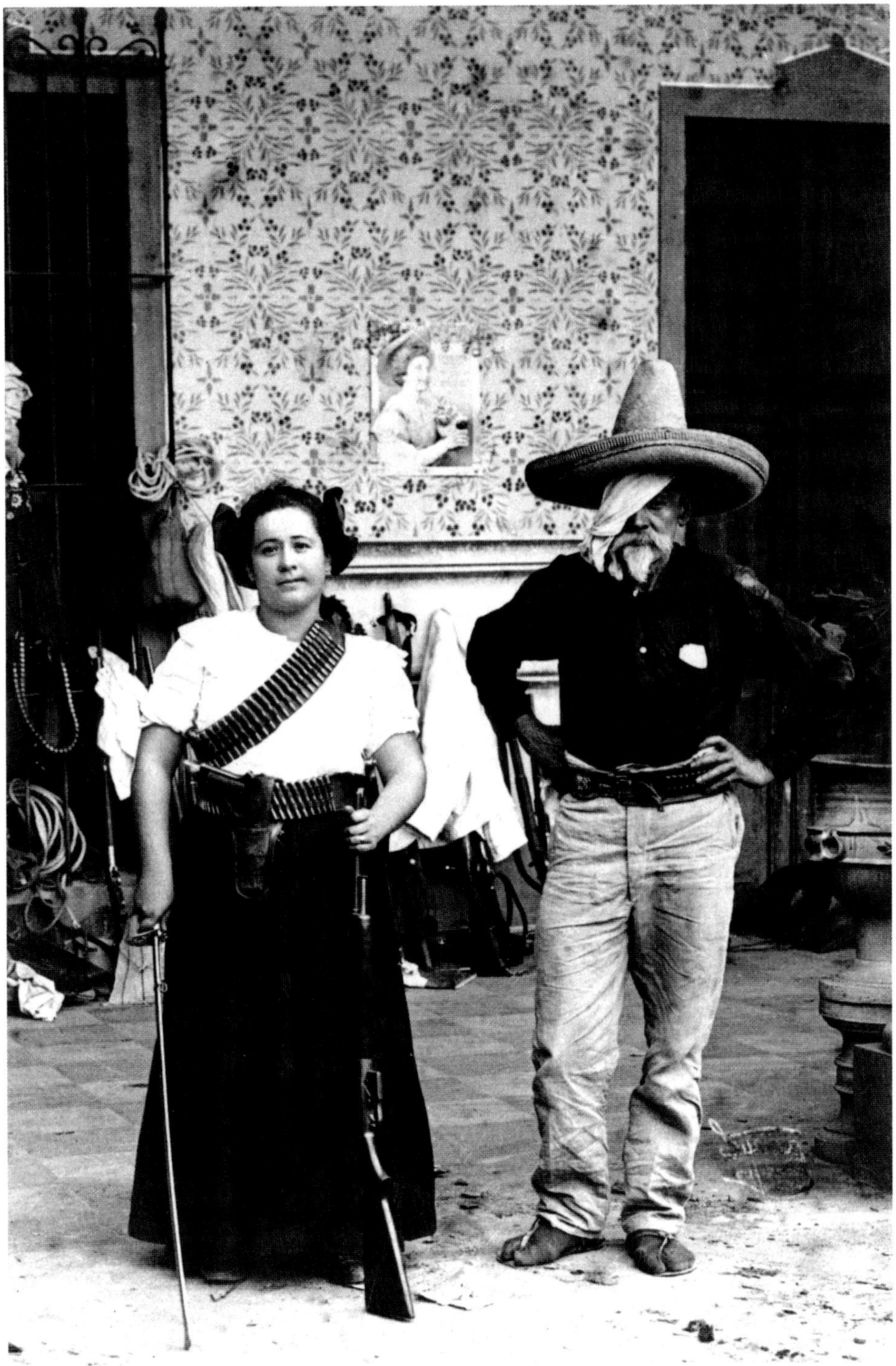

2-3. Herculano de la Rodia and his daughter, Clara Rodia de Peña, rich miners from Durango who joined the Maderista revolt, 1911. © Inv. #186519, Fondo Casasola, SINAFO-Fototeca Nacional del INAH.

THE CAUDILLOS AND PHOTOGRAPHY

Leaders seem not only to have understood the power of modern media, but also to have had a fascination with their portraiture; moreover, they had the funds to make it happen. Typical of the sort of images that were produced are those of Leonides Corral in the north, and of Jesús Figueroa, member of a family of caciques in Guerrero (Figures 2-4 and 2-5). Although much of the evidence of such obsession is circumstantial—for example, the many photos made by José Mora of Pablo González dressed as an aviator to demonstrate his modernity, or atop pyramids to link himself to the deepest roots of *mexicanidad*—there are a few testimonies about such a proclivity.[5] Martín Luís Guzmán, an intellectual close to many revolutionary leaders, was a particularly sharp observer and articulately narrated the insistence with which Venustiano Carranza had himself photographed:

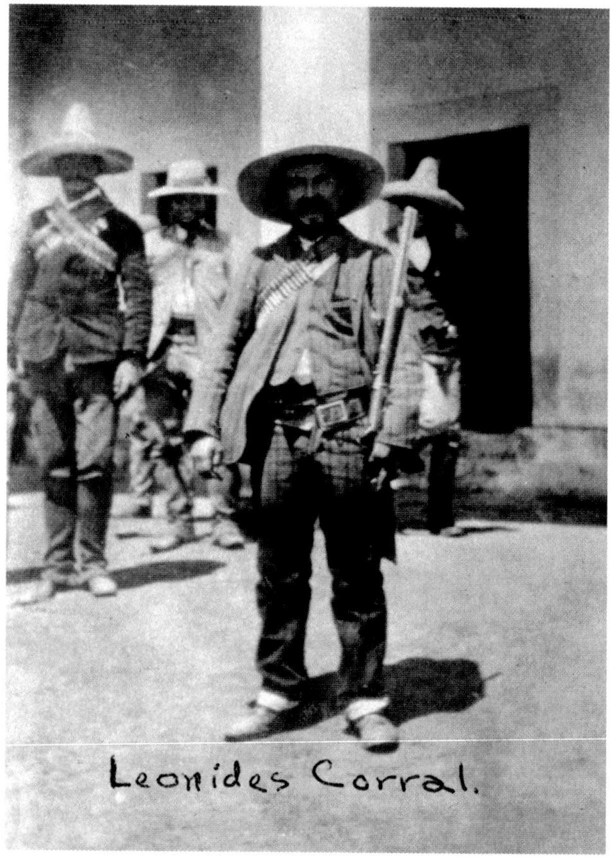

2-4. Leonides Corral, Villista leader, Bustillos, Chihuahua, May 1911; E. Herrerías. © Inv. #373897, Fondo Casasola, SINAFO-Fototeca Nacional del INAH.

> History has not yet determined what was at the bottom of Don Venustiano's love of having his portrait made: if it was a primary urge or a political recourse of a hidden and transcendent nature. Was Carranza pleased by his own image, knowledgeable perhaps of the attraction revealed in his features by the oratory of "the flowery beard"? Tender narcissism of sixty years! Or could it be rather that the Commander-in-Chief, annoyed at running into Madero's portraits all the time, aspired to substitute them with his own?[6]

The attraction that the camera held for Carranza is apparent in the many photos where he assumes the classic pose of looking away from the camera, as does González Garza in Figure 2-1. Perhaps the affinity of Salvador Alvarado has been less known, but it is Guzmán who, again, offers us an apt description:

> It was clear at first sight that Alvarado was a megalomaniac, but an honorable one, that is, those who don't hide their megalomania or disguise it. On his

desk he had a complete arsenal of his photographs, in a multitude of sizes, poses, and forms; there were those in the "imperial" format and those in the "*tarjeta de visita*" format, with a cardboard back and without it, in uniform and in civilian clothes, of his head and of his entire body, with kepis and without kepis. . . . When we were leaving he decided, spontaneously, to give us photographs of himself. He looked at the group of three and then, slowly observing us, one by one, he said easily, "Let's see: what shall I give to whom?" On one of the biggest he wrote an enormous signature and gave it to Miguel Alessio Robles. Another, not quite as big, he signed with moderation and gave it to [Eduardo] Hay; finally, he gave me one of the smallest and least scenic, after signing it with a small, careful signature. In his judgment, he had measured us, with his eyes, as if on a scale.[7]

2-5. Jesús Figuero and his soldiers, Guerrero, 1911. © Inv. #36793, Fondo Casasola, SINAFO-Fototeca Nacional del INAH.

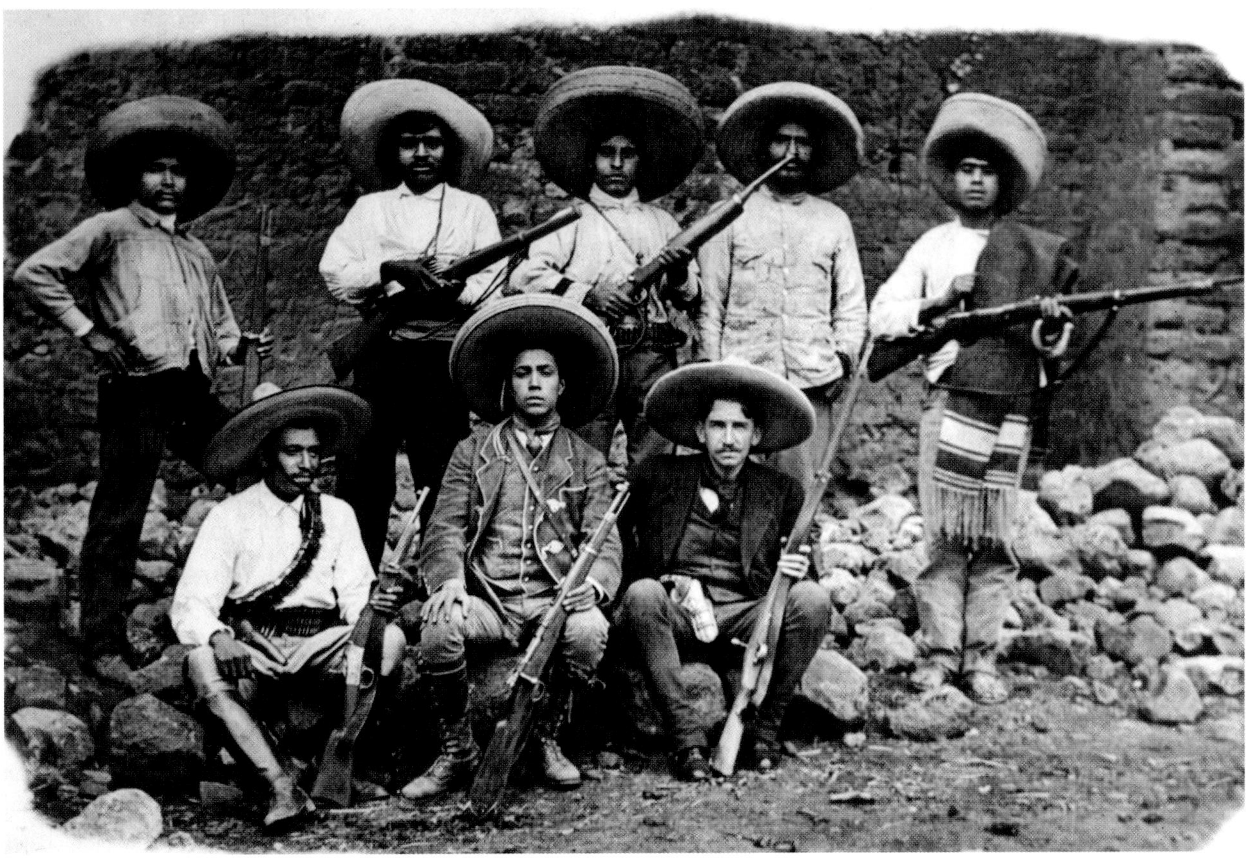

For John Reed, a few months in the north of Mexico were enough to discover the disposition of the caudillos to have themselves pictured. Recalling his experiences with Tomás Urbina, he wrote:

> In the patio the General was talking with his mistress, a beautiful, aristocrat-looking woman, with a voice like a handsaw. When he noticed me he came up and shook hands, saying that he'd like to have me take some pictures of him. I said that that was my purpose in life. . . . For the next hour I took photographs of General Urbina: General Urbina on foot, with and without sword; General Urbina on three different horses; General Urbina with and without his family; General Urbina's three children, on horseback and off; General Urbina's mother and his mistress; the entire family, armed with swords and revolvers, including the phonograph, produced for the purpose, one of the children holding a placard upon which was marked: "General Tomás Urbina R."[8]

The photography of the revolution was produced for a variety of complex and dialectical reasons. On the one hand, the caudillos comprehended the need to employ modern media to promote their causes, and, at the same time, their vanity and self-worship impelled them to have photographers at hand to document their historical feats. On the other hand, the photographers with a political consciousness saw the possibility of putting their art at the service of principles in which they believed. As the revolution grew longer and crueler, the polarization of forces required that they declare which cause and caudillo they served. In some cases, the commitments of the photographers are transparent; in others they appear veiled by the ostensible "neutrality" of the press. Nonetheless, in a revolutionary situation, few have the luxury of remaining on the margins; the insistent question is: Which side are you on?

CHAPTER 3

The Myth of the Casasolas

HISTORY IS CONSTRUCTED, and deconstructed, and reconstructed interminably. Hence, an examination of the complex role played by photographers in the Mexican Revolution must begin with a critical reflection on an accepted truth that Ignacio Gutiérrez paraphrased in a few words: "To date, it is generically claimed that 'the Casasolas are the photographers of the Mexican Revolution.'"[1] It could be said that there are parallels between the Casasolas' "kidnap" of revolutionary photography and the PRI's monopolization of that watershed event. The official history concocted by PRI ideology invented "the Revolutionary Family" to obscure the fact that the armed struggle was defined by a war to the death between groups that were in fact irreconcilable.[2] In a similar way, the "objectivity" attributed to Casasola imagery blurs the commitment of imagemakers aligned with particular causes, and obviates the question of whether photographs made during the revolution were neutral or created with the intention of serving a cause.

The Casasola myth began to establish itself during the 1920s, but it had its genesis in Agustín Víctor Casasola's practices during the armed struggle of the prior decade. The photojournalist seems to have been less concerned with making a commitment to any particular group than in developing strategies to compete with the myriad of foreign photographers covering the war, and ensuring that the photographs would be available for future uses, commercial and historical. In 1912 he founded a news photo agency, the Agencia Mexicana de Información Gráfica. There he accumulated images from many sources, beginning with the photo archive of *El Imparcial*, which closed in 1914.

Casasola was both a photojournalist and an entrepreneur, contracting men to work for him, as well as purchasing and copying images. He invites comparison to Mathew Brady, who referred to himself as an "impresario" while organizing a corps of twenty men to cover the U.S. Civil War.[3] Historian Alan Trachtenberg observed that "More than any other American, Brady shaped the role of the photographer as a national historian," and the same could be said of Casasola.[4] However, his was also a typically

Mexican business, formed around the family: he founded the agency with his cousin Gonzalo Herrerías and incorporated family members, including his brother Miguel, his sons Gustavo, Ismael, Agustín, and Mario, and his daughters Dolores and Piedad. Among the photographers who appear to have worked for him or sold him their images are Eduardo Melhado, Abraham Lupercio, Samuel Tinoco, Gerónimo Hernández, Víctor León, Luis Santamaría, Manuel Ramos, Antonio Garduño, José María Lupercio, and Hugo Brehme.[5] A review of the images in the Casasola Archive makes it clear that Agustín Víctor systematically copied photos from the illustrated magazines—a not uncommon practice of established photojournalists with agencies—such as the image of the terrified Zapatista children taken by Samuel Tinoco and originally published in *Novedades* (Figure 3-1).[6]

Because Agustín Víctor was not very forthcoming in identifying the authors of images in his archive, for many years he was described as "*the* photographer, by antonomasia, of the Revolution."[7] He had presented himself in that role as early as 1921—at least implicitly—by excluding the names of the photographers whose images he incorporated in his *Albúm histórico gráfico*, a practice that Gustavo continued in all the publications that came out of the Casasola Archive.[8] It appears, however, that only in a 1926 interview did Agustín Víctor begin to present himself as the photographer that had documented the revolution in its entirety, claiming to have participated in "all the phases of the revolutionary epoch, and very particularly with the Constitutionalists and Don Venustiano Carranza, in Querétaro, where [I] spent a long period."[9] With Agustín Víctor's death in 1938, the writer of his obituary made a further contribution to the myth: "Since the Revolution began, Casasola, carrying his camera on his back like a 'Cyrenian' and with his children and his brother Miguel, became the official photographer for different Revolutionary divisions and brigades."[10]

In 1988 the PRI made him a key element of identity, eulogizing him in a publication that was part of a series on "Cultural Nationalism: Forgers of Mexico," where they consecrated the Casasola myth, dubbing him "the graphic chronicler of the Mexican Revolution" and asserting that "Casasola took the camera into all of history's corners . . . [and] was present in every civic and military activity of the armed movement."[11] Antonio Rodríguez, a Portuguese Marxist art critic exiled in Mexico, intuited that Agustín Víctor must have acquired images from other photographers, and he credited him with the historical foresight to construct an archive with which to recount the epic struggle: "Casasola was everywhere, with Pascual Orozco and with Felipe Ángeles, now in front of Huerta, and later together with Carranza; but when his gift of ubiquity failed him, he looked for his better colleagues and, with no sense of inferiority, acquired their photos, thinking of the documentary collection that he would donate to the future so that such a vivid page from Mexico's history would not remain empty."[12]

Another strategy to explain the difficulties that such travels would have entailed has been to include the entire family. Gustavo Casasola may have inaugurated this tactic in 1960, when he asserted, "The Casasolas were in the north, in the west, in the south and in Veracruz during the U.S. intervention."[13] A text in the magazine *Siempre!* followed Gustavo's lead, alleging that "Various family members covered the Revolution. Some in the north, another in the south, another in the northeast, and the rest covered Mexico City. Agustín was the photographer for the 24th Brigade, that was with the Constitutionalist army."[14] The PRI hack who composed the Casasola panegyric also tried to extend the enterprise to the family: "The Casasola family members

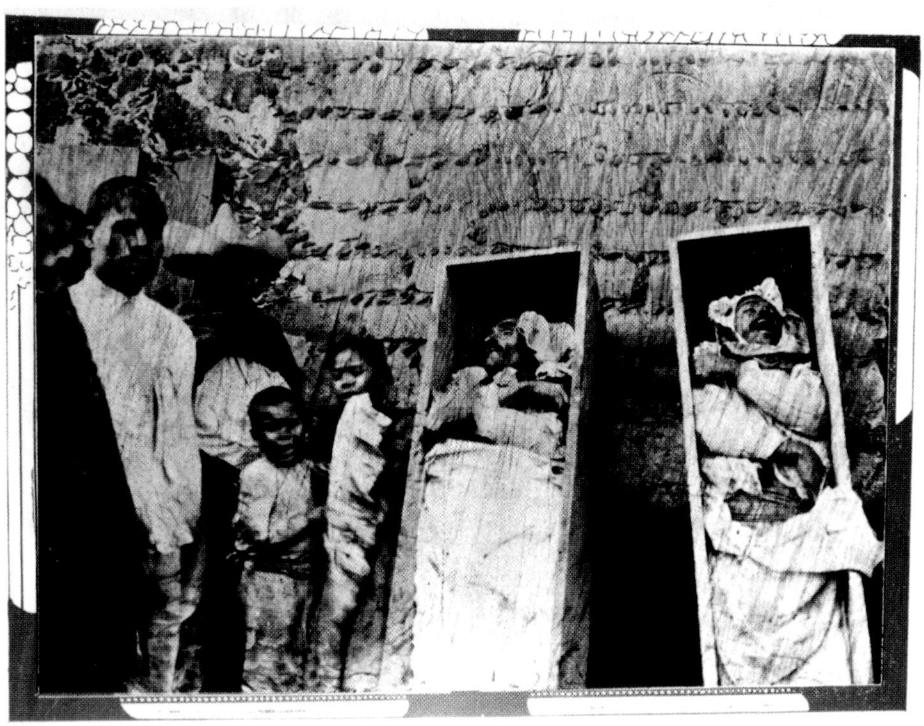
LA BESTIA HUMANA EN AYOTZINGO.—Cuadros son que ponen terror en el ánimo, los que se desarrollaron en ese desdichado pueblo, al sufrir un [illegible] bandidos zapatistas que, como la mala hierba, crecen y se desarrollan, sin que sea posible destruirlos. [illegible] Municipal después del furioso asalto, lo muestra elocuente- [illegible] en ese mismo pueblo en que tantas fechorías come-

3-1. Children sob next to executed Zapatistas, Ayotzingo, Morelos, January 1913; Samuel Tinoco, *Novedades*, 22 January 1913. © Inv. #63752, Fondo Casasola, SINAFO-Fototeca Nacional del INAH.

took direct part in the work. Some went to the north of the country, to the south, to the northwest, and others in the capital widely covered the armed movement."[15] Nonetheless, this strategy is problematic, because only Miguel and Gustavo (born in 1900) would have been old enough to participate in the civil war.

Recent scholarship seems to indicate that the Casasolas' coverage of the revolution was largely limited to Mexico City. Agustín Víctor did accompany Porfirio Díaz to Veracruz when the dictator left Mexico in 1911, and according to Ignacio Gutiérrez, he and Miguel also made images in Morelos of federal troops fighting the Zapatistas.[16] He eventually ended up in Querétaro, where he was connected to the Constitutionalists, an army to which many professional photographers attached themselves.[17] Miguel Casasola apparently preferred dynamiting trains for Obregón's army to being a photographer, abandoning his camera in 1914 and returning to it only in the 1920s.[18] Gustavo was sent, at age fourteen, to cover the Convention of Aguascalientes, but the other Casasola children were too young to do anything but help in the laboratory. My own experiences with the Casasola Archive have left me with the distinct impression that Agustín Víctor´s photography during the revolution was an extension of the political and social imagery he had made of the ruling class for *El Imparcial*: the caudillos in turn—Díaz, Madero, Huerta, Villa, Zapata, Carranza, Obregón—and their general staffs, as well as pictures of their womenfolk visiting the underprivileged. Studies analyzing the negatives and comparing the credits given to published photos with images from the Casasola Archive have confirmed my suspicion.[19] Even more important, my recent investigations in the illustrated magazines of the revolutionary period indicate that photojournalists Samuel Tinoco, Abraham Lupercio, and Antonio Garduño received many more credits for pictures than did Agustín Víctor, while Ezequiel Álvarez Tostado was much more important than him in the world of modern media.

Agustín Víctor did photograph warfare on at least one occasion, when he, Miguel, and other photojournalists documented La Decena Trágica, taking what would have to be included among early instances of real combat photography in the world. Nonetheless, coverage of that conflict, which resulted in Madero's overthrow, had been preceded by Jimmy Hare's photography of the U.S. intervention in the Cuban movement for independence in 1898, and the Japanese-Russian war of 1905; Hare (and other foreigners) had also taken war photos during Madero's uprising on the northern frontier in 1911.[20] Whatever his participation in La Decena Trágica, rather than a "revolutionary" photographer, Agustín Víctor was a committed entrepreneur, a lover of photography, a visionary of the picture histories that would become so central in constructing national identity, and an excellent photojournalist who was probably most at home in conservative publications. What made him exceptional were his organizational capacities, his extraordinary work habits, and his ability to get along with everyone, particularly those in power.

In the past Agustín Víctor Casasola was considered "*the* photographer of the revolution"; today he is a question mark because it has become increasingly difficult to determine which pictures he took. Nonetheless, he founded an archive that contains a half million images and is considered vital to national identity: "[The images] are in our life and our history because they have become indissolubly integrated into our Mexican patrimony."[21] The use that Agustín Víctor made of his collected archive in the *Albúm histórico gráfico* began the process of his mythification, but it was consolidated by the multivolume series with thousands of photographs that Gustavo published and republished for more than fifty years: *Historia gráfica de la Revolución*, *Historia gráfica de la Revolución Mexicana*, and *Seis siglos de historia gráfica de México*.[22]

In his original picture history, Agustín Víctor had pretended to objectivity, "free from all partisanship and naked of all political passion."[23] Gustavo followed his lead by creating an eminently positivistic discourse with almanac-like prose and a profusion of photographs, expressing the son's belief in his own capacity for "objective observation."[24] Gustavo stated that he initially attempted to solicit the aid of historians, perhaps following in the footsteps of his father, who had invited prestigious historiographers to participate (if minimally) in the *Albúm histórico gráfico*. However, Gustavo decided that they were "too partial and tendentious," and he determined to write all the texts himself, guided "by a documentary rather than a political idea," and "without accepting advice or ideas from anybody."[25] In a book on his father that Gustavo published, the articles he commissioned refer time and again to the "objectivity" of the Casasola project.[26] The original intention of Agustín Víctor in collecting such a vast archive is said to have been that of producing "an objective history of the country," and it is argued that the very nature of photographs offers an "equilibrium" that is beyond the "destructive" historiographic battles over the meaning of the revolution because they cannot be manipulated like words![27] Obviously, Gustavo's comprehension of photography—a polysemic medium that can be made to signify anything the accompanying text dictates—was as naive and reactionary as his understanding of the historical endeavor.

Technical advances (and perhaps greater financing) allowed Gustavo to heighten photography's power. He abandoned the crude retouching of Agustín Víctor's *Albúm histórico gráfico*, leaving behind a nineteenth-century model of illustrationism to adopt a modern format in which photographs appear as windows onto the past, a transparency that purports to speak for itself, although—as always—the context created by the image choice and texts determines the pictures' meanings. Whatever Agustín Víctor's commitment during the revolution, the photos in his archive have been packaged in the picture histories in such a way as to create both the myth of his authorship as well as the lie of their objectivity.

Before he (and Gustavo) began to use that archive to produce the *historias gráficas* that would so mark their nation's culture, Agustín Víctor focused on achieving recognition for photojournalists, who had evidently received little respect during the Porfiriato. In 1911 he created the first Association of Press Photographers in Mexico and set the stage for the continued adulation of patriarchy while meeting with interim president Francisco León de la Barra. Casasola expressed his gratitude for "having inaugurated a stage of photojournalistic freedom almost unknown here," and hastened to assure de la Barra that the purpose of their association was to provide fraternal aid in the spirit of the old mutualist organizations rather than the new labor unions that were appearing: "Ours is not an industrial mass that opposes our productive force against the businesses that require our services; it is a cordial grouping of good and honorable men."[28]

The principal activity of the association appears to have been the organization of the inaugural exhibit of photojournalism in Mexico, *Primera Exposición de Arte Fotográfico* (First exposition of photographic art). Agustín Víctor personally guided the recently elected Francisco I. Madero through the exposition and may have photographed him with Ezequiel Álvarez Tostado (Figure 3-2). In an effort to stay close to the presidential figure, and to disassociate himself from the anti-Madero sentiments of *El Imparcial*, Casasola sat next to Madero in the group photo.[29] The exhibit itself demonstrated the aesthetic tensions between an incipient photojournalism and the Pictorialist picturesqueness that was supposed to legitimate photography as an art. Photo historian Rebeca Monroy described its contents: "In spite of the armed conflict, few images in the exposition were testimonies to it. On the contrary, all seemed interested in replicating the *costumbrista* genre of traditional customs and dress, landscapes, and bucolic portraits; few showed signs of a documentary modernism."[30]

When photojournalists were threatened, Agustín Víctor was in the front line of their defense. He attempted to interview Emiliano Zapata in 1912, but—according to the photojournalist—the leader refused to receive him and warned him to leave immediately, which he did.[31] However, a train that was somehow related to this affair in El Jilguero was attacked, and journalists were killed, including Ignacio Herrerías, the Casasolas' cousin and an important member of the Mexico City press corps.[32] Agustín

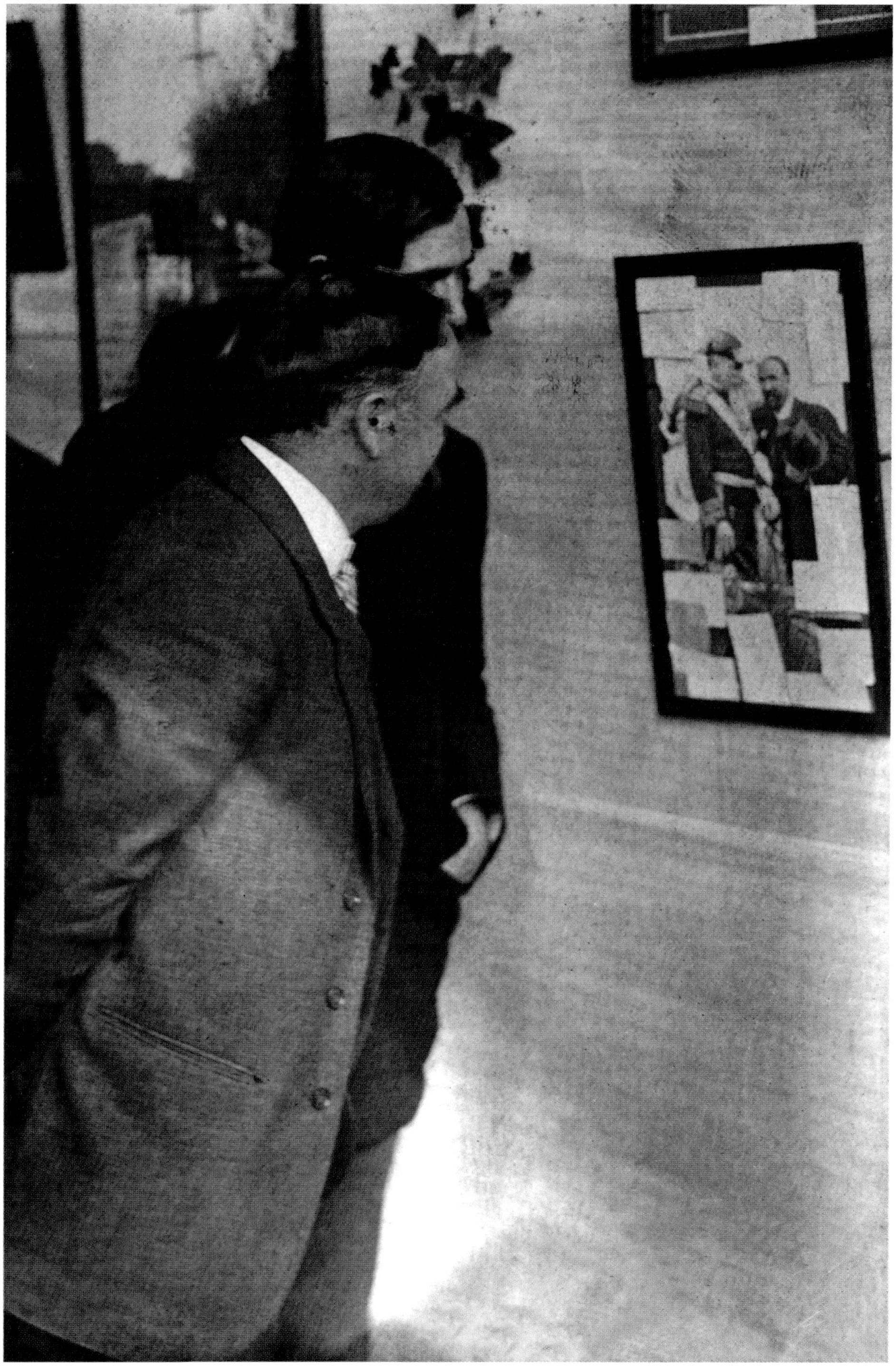

3-2. President Francisco I. Madero at the first exhibit of photojournalists, with Ezequiel Álvarez Tostado, Mexico City, 15 December 1911. © Inv. #36629, Fondo Casasola, SINAFO-Fototeca Nacional del INAH.

Víctor led the protest against their assassination.[33] Notwithstanding the importance of his activities in organizing the photojournalist guild, Casasola's fame rests largely on the picture histories produced from his archive and the classic revolutionary icons that appear therein, forming a fundamental element of the nation's visual identity. All have been attributed to Agustín Víctor Casasola at one time or another, a process brought about by their "kidnapping" in the *historias gráficas* since the 1920s.

CHAPTER 4

Learning to Photograph War

MADERISMO WAS ONE OF THE MOST photographed revolutionary movements. This is due principally to the proximity of the United States, although the transformation of Francisco I. Madero's consciousness as to the importance of modern media was also crucial. In the beginning Madero was a man of words: the book *La sucesión presidencial en 1910*; the proclamation "El plan de San Luis Potosí"; his numerous discourses. "The Apostle of Democracy" had won his nickname for his extended political speaking tour throughout the country, and though the correspondent of *La Semana Ilustrada* found him at first to be "a declared enemy of photography and, above all, of posing," one can imagine that Madero's contact with the masses convinced him that the new visual media were going to be significant in his bid to unseat Porfirio Díaz.[1] As he went about the country during 1909 and 1910, he founded anti-reelection clubs everywhere, and the act of making photographs to celebrate the new associations served to cement the ties among participants, who thus identified themselves publicly with Maderismo (Figure 4-1). Appearing in such a photograph was taking a stance against the regime, and a risk because images were employed, at times, to identify insurgents.[2] One can imagine that sometimes it must have presented a problem for the photographers as well.

Later, in open rebellion, Madero showed the respect he had for photographic imagery by carefully staging the meeting of the revolutionary junta at the Casa de Adobe in Ciudad Juárez on 30 April 1911, at which some fourteen photographers arrived. As photo historian Miguel Ángel Berumen remarked, "Madero knew that images of him and his followers would be published, and that the face they put on for the photographers would play a decisive role."[3]

At times, Madero's contact with photographers was of a completely different order than issues of representation. In January 1910, Madero's campaign arrived in Hermosillo, where imagemaker Jesús H. Abitia had gotten together those followers who dared to go to the train station to receive the candidate, "despite the open hostility displayed by the garbage collectors for the city and the henchmen and the

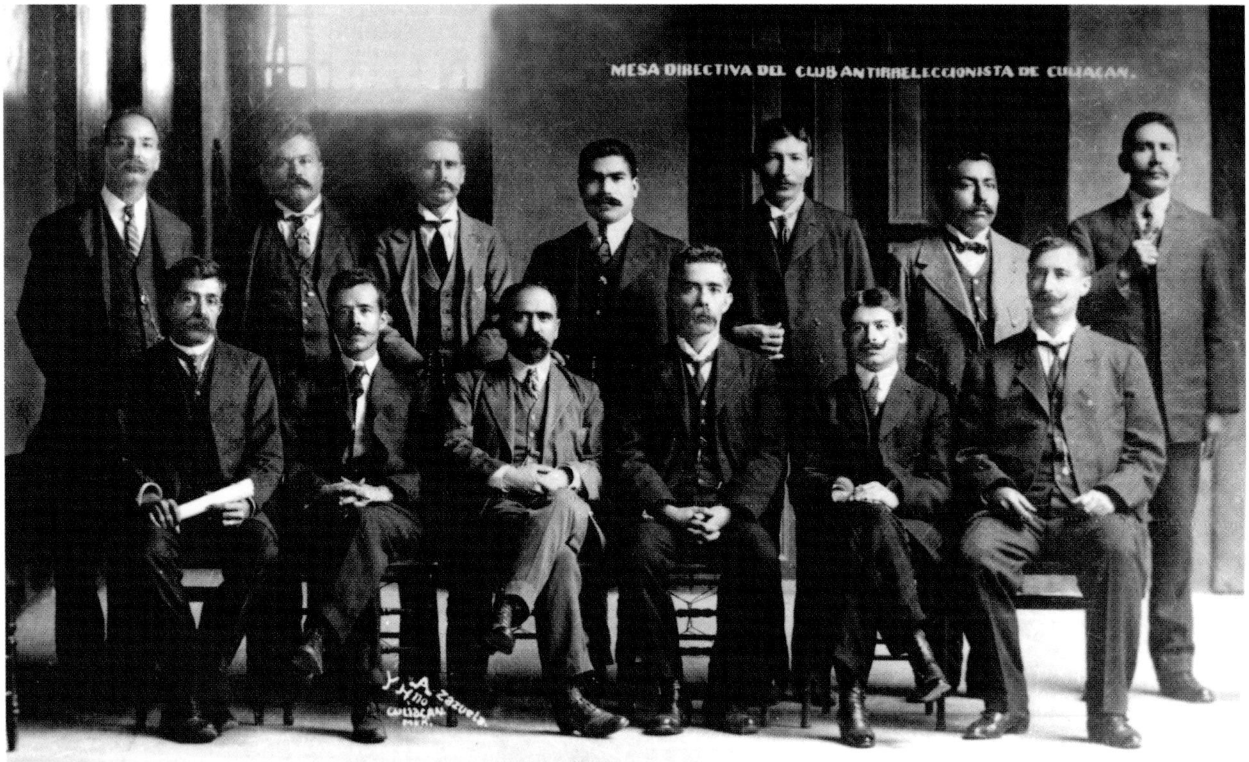

4-1. Francisco I. Madero with leaders of the anti-reelectionist club of Culiacán, Sinaloa, 1909; A. Zazueta. © Inv. #641904, Fondo Casasola, SINAFO-Fototeca Nacional del INAH.

disguised policemen that the prefect and other caciques sent."[4] Madero and his wife were refused lodging by the hoteliers, with the exception of the Sonora Hotel, "a whorehouse." Abitia was the only photographer in Hermosillo, and his wide net of contacts informed him of plans to assassinate Madero. He arranged for the candidate and his wife to leave the hotel under the cover of darkness and brought them to his house, where "they slept peacefully, while I and my brothers guarded them all night, armed with a .30-30 carbine."

The next day the Maderistas tried to hold a meeting, but "a group sent by the government stopped the reunion by insulting Madero with obscene language and yelling at him: 'Death to Madero!, Shut up crazy!' Outraged, the candidate confronted the henchmen and rebuked them saying, 'I knew this would happen, but I came because I want you to see that I don't fear you.' . . . Seeing that it was impossible to hold the meeting, we went to the station, followed by the henchmen and a hostile group that never stopped insulting Madero and me and my brothers." Abitia and his family were persecuted, and he escaped to Arizona, later rejoining Madero in Ciudad Juárez. After Díaz's resignation, Madero invited Abitia to accompany him to Mexico City, but he preferred to return to Hermosillo. There he remained until Victoriano Huerta's coup of 1913; fleeing the repression, he joined up with his childhood friend Álvaro Obregón and became a Constitutionalist photographer.

Once he had risen in revolution, Madero was conscious that his movement's success depended, in part, on the image generated in the United States. As Berumen has written, "Madero didn't waste any opportunity to win terrain in the camp of public opinion, because he knew how important a good image of the revolution could be, above all to attain recognition as a legitimate force by the United States."[5] In fact, the proximity of the United States and the interest of U.S. publications in the Mexican events resulted in the great majority of photographs on Maderismo being made by U.S. photographers, particularly those from the border.[6] To cover the coming battle for Ciudad Juárez, *Collier's* magazine assigned the famous photojournalist Jimmy Hare, who arrived on 15 April 1911, a day before the Maderista contingent. In contrast, *La Semana Ilustrada* sent Samuel Tinoco more than a month later, 18 May, eight days after combat had ended.[7]

Some Mexican newspapers showed more interest than the magazines. *El Tiempo*, a Catholic periodical that carried out a moderate critique of the government from the right, named Ignacio Herrerías their war correspondent, and on 13 April he left for the north, where he interviewed Madero. Herrerías published the interviews in his famous daily column, "In the Revolutionary Camp," and his commitment to Maderismo is clear (within his objectivist stance as a journalist). He also took photos of the revolutionary leaders, although with a nonprofessional camera, the little Kodak 3 "A" folding model (see Figure 4-7).[8] The editors of the Mexican magazines feared censorship, and they had little sympathy for Maderismo, but the attraction of revolutionary activities for U.S. publications can be measured by the fact that by June 1911, one magazine alone, *Collier's*, had published more than a hundred photos on these events. With a market like that, and open access, professional photographers such as Otis Aultman, Homer Scott, Walter Horne, Jim Alexander, Harvey Kiefer, Fred Feldman, and Hare produced a significant quantity of pictures.

Ciudad Juárez was flooded by imagemakers from the United States who wanted to participate in the media phenomenon that the Maderista rebellion represented. Berumen aptly noted that "great quantities of photographers and photographs were generated in the same instant, so that we can see photographers photographing

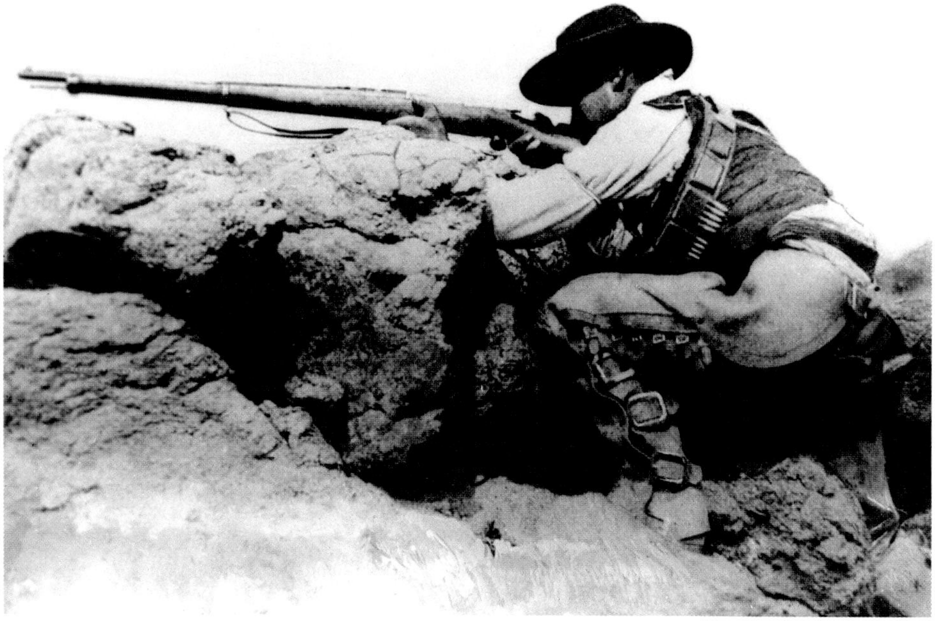

4-2. Rebel sharpshooter, Chihuahua, May 1911; *La Semana Ilustrada*, 31 March 1911. © Inv. #643393, Fondo Casasola, SINAFO-Fototeca Nacional del INAH.

photographers who are taking photographs of photographers."[9] Among those who carried cameras were two women, Esther Eva Strauss and Clara Goodman. Strauss was a professional who worked in Fred Feldman's studio; she made images that provided a feminine perspective of the struggle, whether of women posed in what would become a classic scene—toting rifles and draped in cartridge belts—or spontaneously expressing grief as they come to pick up the bodies of their dead.[10] Goodman was an amateur who was visiting El Paso and decided to cross the border to take photos of the Maderista camp and the center of Ciudad Juárez; her case was evidently not unusual, because many of the images found in family albums were made by women.[11] Another amateur, "excited, like many residents of El Paso, to document the revolutionary army," was Melville Jean Herskovits, who later became a famous anthropologist.[12]

It is probable that Figure 4-2, an image of a rebel rifleman, was made by one of the U.S. photojournalists. The photo was published in *La Semana Ilustrada* on 31 March 1911, before Tinoco arrived at the border, and it is not signed by H. J. Gutiérrez, Carlos Harris, Ignacio Herrerías, or E. Herrerías, the Mexican photographers who might have been present. Further, it reproduces the U.S. myth of the indomitable and lonely sharpshooter, which had been born with the long rifles used to win independence from England, and fortified by those of the pioneers in conquering the West. It is a very modern representation, photojournalistically speaking—well posed, framed, and focused—with a close-up on an individual in action, something seen rarely in photographs of the revolution, because most are of groups. It seems to me that it was made by a photojournalist with some experience in war because (although it is directed and not spontaneous) he knew how to re-create a pose that makes you think the image was made in the midst of combat.[13]

Some images of the battle for Ciudad Juárez could be identified as having been made by U.S. photographers. Jimmy Hare arrived with the experience of having covered previous conflicts, among them the Cuban-Spanish-American War in 1898, and that of Russia and Japan in 1904–1905. The *El Paso Daily Herald* celebrated his presence by announcing that "No war is official until it has been covered by Jimmy Hare's camera."[14] Hence, it is not surprising that he made the best combat images, demonstrating his well-known valor by crossing the line of fire to take different angles of a revolutionary group advancing on the federal headquarters, to which Hare arrived before the rebels themselves (Figure 4-3).[15] Worried for his safety, the *Collier's* editor wrote to Hare, "Do not take any more foolish chances. You were sent to take photographs, not to indulge in mock heroics. You will be of no use to either your family or *Collier's* if dead or wounded." Hare answered: "Have evidently misunderstood my assignment. Will send you El Paso sky line and some pretty pictures of flowers in the park."[16] Otis Aultman and Homer Scott also made photos during the battle for Ciudad Juárez, and there are various in which the danger they faced is obvious. Berumen commented that "Homer Scott's fascination for the line of fire was well-known."[17] Their courage notwithstanding, the fact that they were studio photographers from El Paso, more accustomed to taking portraits than to covering events, made their images less successful than Hare's. In any case, the combat photos of Hare, Scott, and Aultman show spontaneous scenes that our modern eyes find preferable to those of revolutionary caciques posed with their followers.

Aside from the combat imagery, few photos of the Maderista movement appear to be spontaneous; one is of a rebel prisoner in the hands of federal forces (Figure 4-4). The majority of Maderista images follow the aesthetic established by studio photography (or that of postcards), showing leaders such as Rafael Cepeda in San Luís Potosí (or Pancho Villa in Chihuahua, Ignacio Bonilla in Culiacán, Jesús Figueroa in Oaxaca) posed with their followers (Figure 4-5). Certain of these pictures permit us

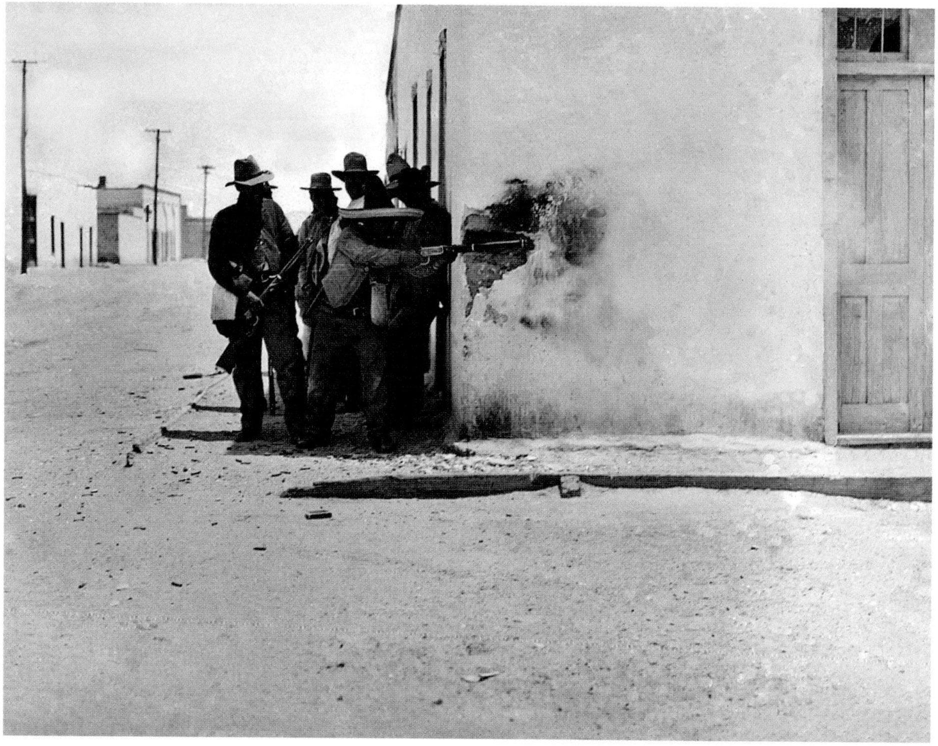

4-3. Maderista combatants, Ciudad Juárez, May 1911; Jimmy Hare. Harry Ransom Humanities Research Center, University of Texas, Hare 1307.

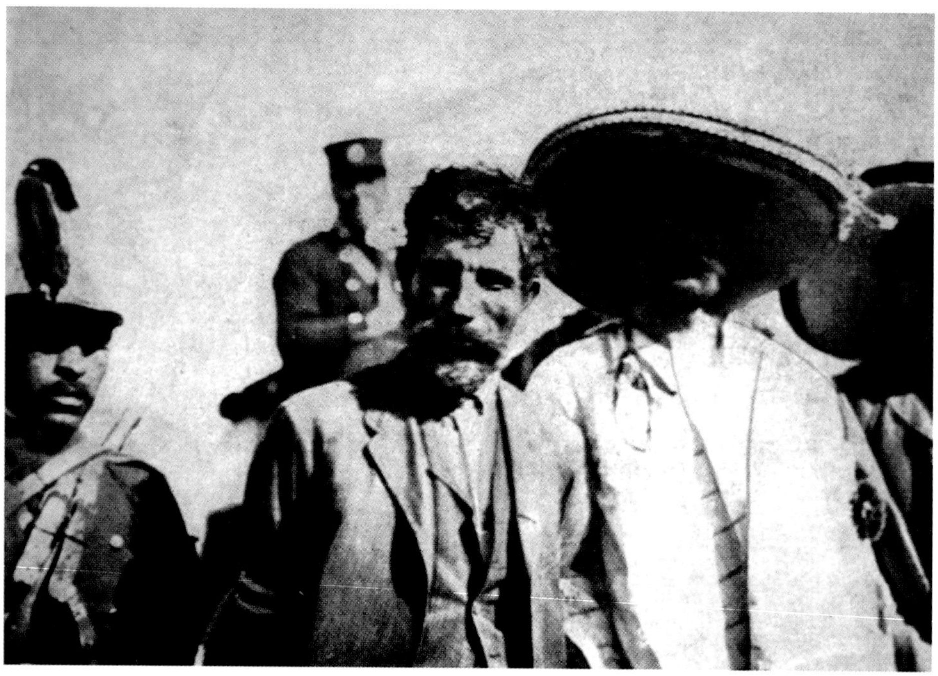

4-4. Maderista prisoners being conducted by federal soldiers; Chihuahua, May 1911. © Inv. #34327, Fondo Casasola, SINAFO-Fototeca Nacional del INAH.

to perceive the development of leaders' consciousness of the mass media. Berumen asserts that "Villa [began] to understand the worth and the importance of photographs in Ciudad Juárez."[18] The researcher recounts that the watershed event occurred on 26 April 1911, when Villa received the grade of colonel from Madero, "in front of the attentive and meticulous gaze of dozens of reporters and photographers, as well as almost two thousand 'spectators' from both sides of the border." From that date forward, he changed his clothing to project a new image that differentiated him from the rest of his army. In Figure 4-6, we see Pancho Villa dressed in the same clothing as his followers, which informs us that the photo was made before 26 April, the day on which Villa changed "his dark *ranchero* suit for that of a townsman, and his black *charro* hat for a beige *americano* style," as he appears in a photo taken by Ignacio Herrerías (Figure 4-7). Villa would eventually be wearing the uniform designed by the Mutual Film Corporation, but his mediatic projection as a revolutionary leader began in Ciudad Juárez.[19]

4-5. Rafael Cepeda and other revolutionaries, San Luis Potosí, 1911; García. © Inv. #37901, Fondo Casasola, SINAFO-Fototeca Nacional del INAH.

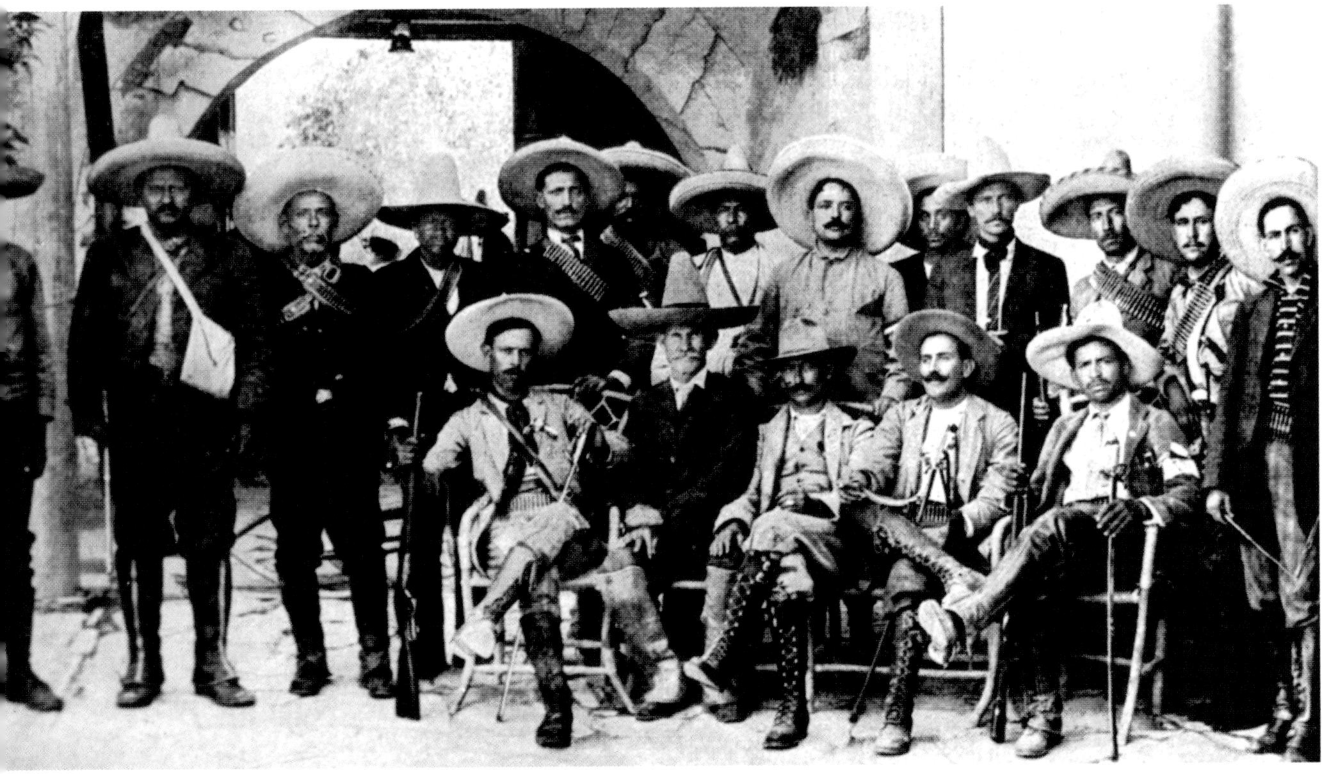

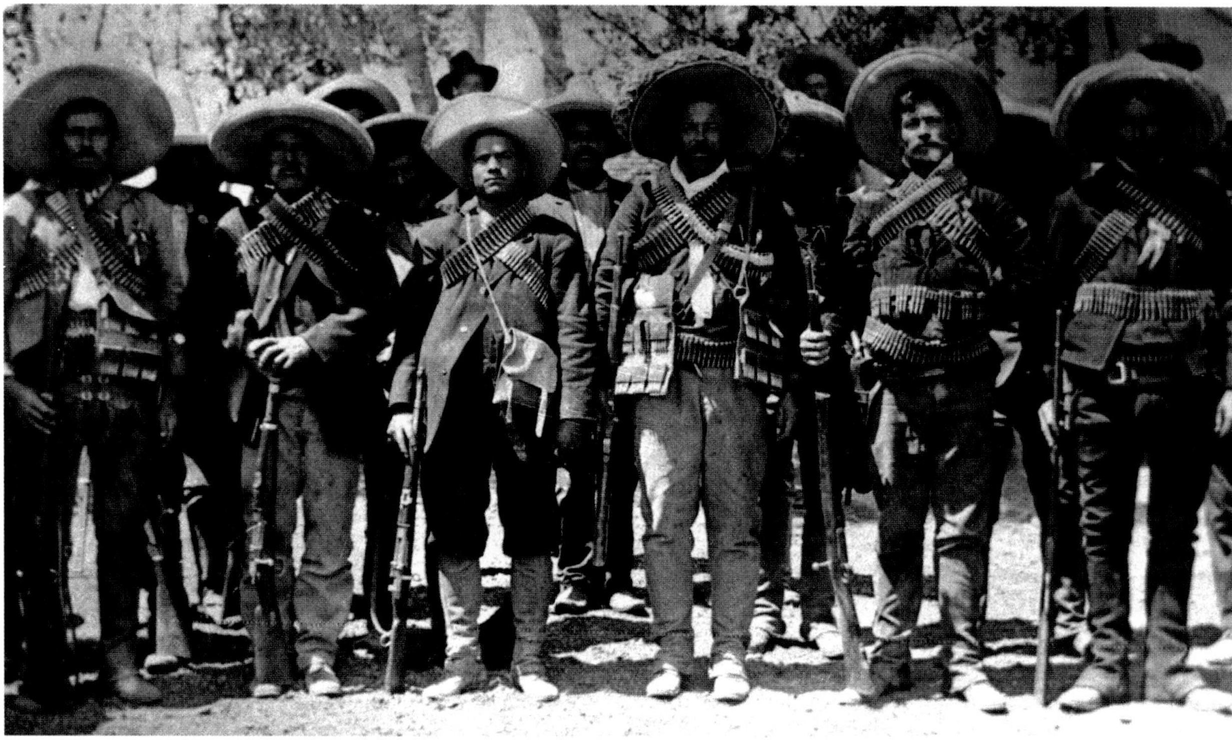

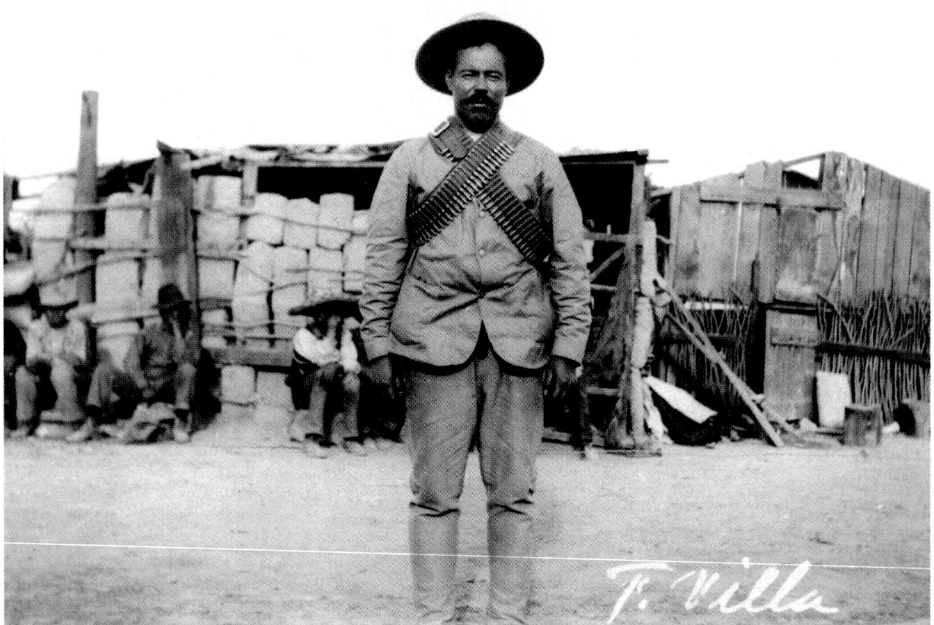

4-6. ABOVE Pancho Villa with members of his forces in a Maderista camp, Ciudad Juárez, Chihuahua, April 1911. © Inv. #6194, Fondo Casasola, SINAFO-Fototeca Nacional del INAH.

4-7. LEFT Pancho Villa, Ciudad Juárez, May 1911; Ignacio Herrerías. © Archivo General de la Nación, Fondo Propiedad Artístico y Literaria, I. Herrerías, "Revolución," 19.

The regional studio photographers who were suddenly called upon to cover a rebellion did so with the only aesthetic they knew, and many images of Maderismo show soldiers that appear in scenes that (to us) have little credibility. One such picture shows Yucatecos, under the orders of José Cantón, pretending to protect a train station (Figure 4-8). The image from Yucatán at least has the advantage of having been taken in the open air; one of Tomás Garza Flores and his soldiers was clearly staged in a studio—and a few months after the triumph of Maderismo (Figure 4-9). The codes of realism changed, albeit slowly, on moving from the studio to the street.

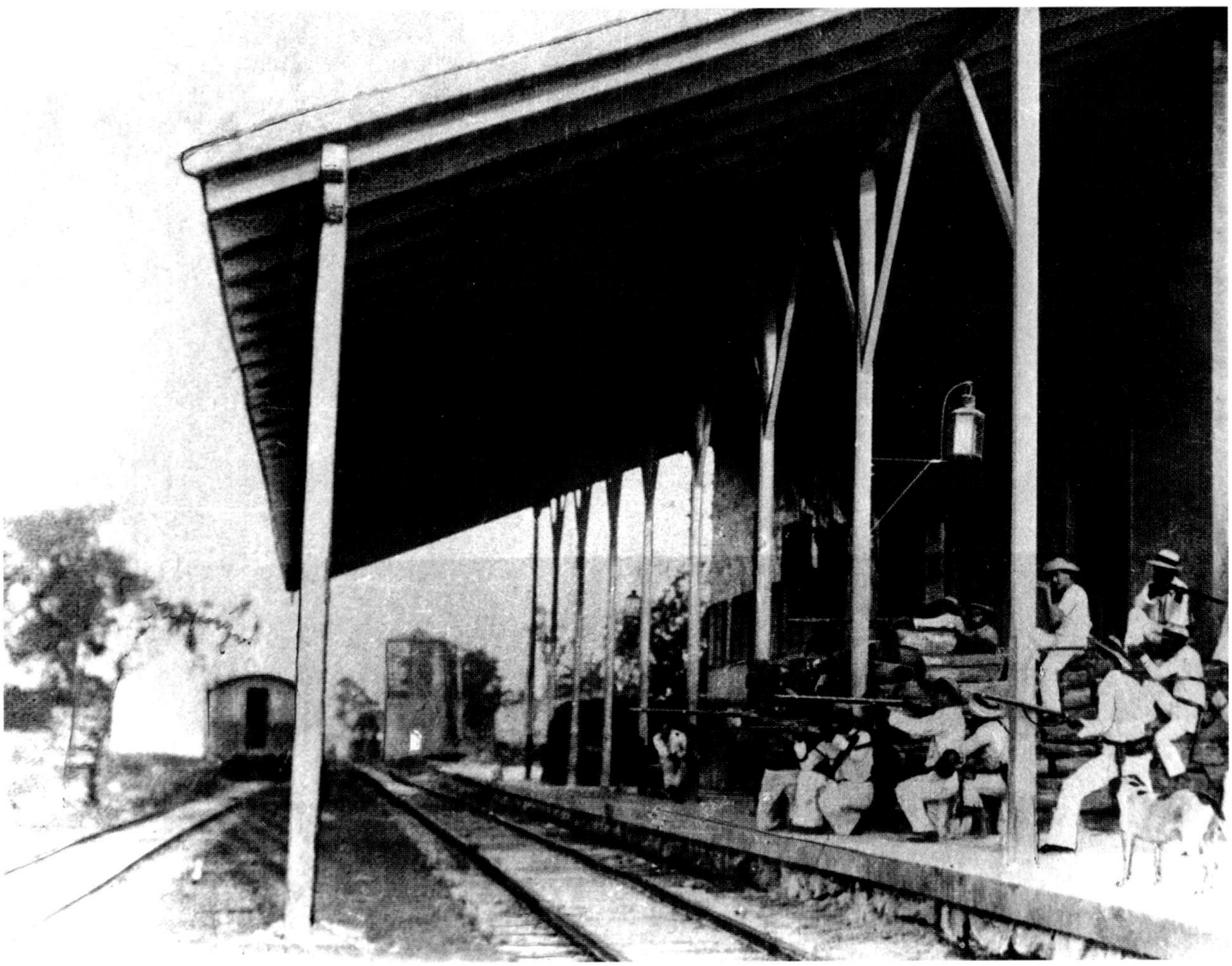

4-8. Maderista troops under the command of José Cantón, Temax?, Yucatán, 1911. © Inv. #641407, Fondo Casasola, SINAFO-Fototeca Nacional del INAH.

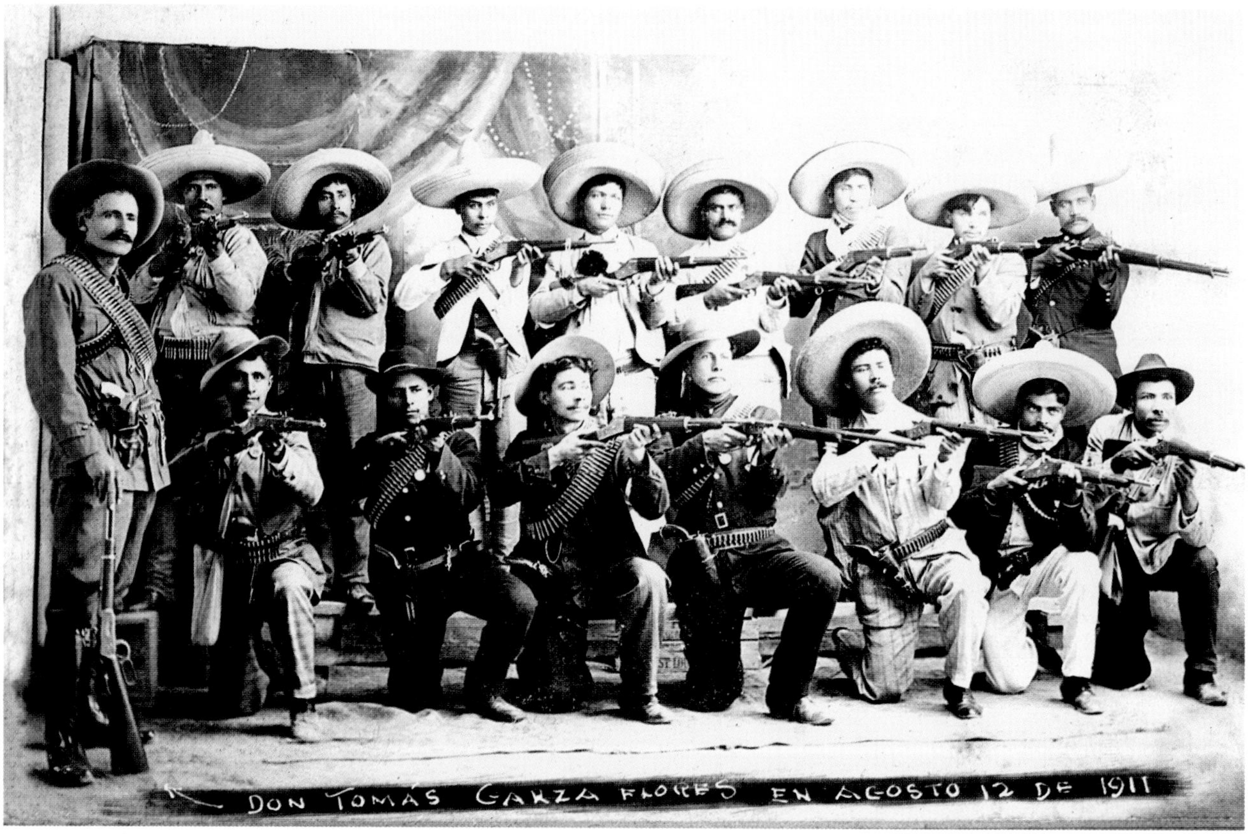

4-9. Tomás Garza Flores and his soldiers, Monterrey, Nuevo León, 12 August 1911. © D. R. 10069, Fototeca del Centro de las Artes, Flores Varela.

Whether posed or spontaneous, some of the photos made during the Maderista rebellion provide information about certain aspects of social and material facets of the war. They clearly demonstrate the differences between the federal army and the revolutionary movements in terms of equipment, and such discrepancies are immediately visible on comparing their camps: the well-provided Porfirian forces, with all the facilities to live in the open; the Maderistas in improvised camps with their families (Figures 4-10 and 4-11). The contrast between the arms used by the opposing sides is also apparent in the photos. The variety of rifles that the Figueroistas carry in Figure 2-5 is an indication of the problems that the revolutionaries faced, because it made it difficult to interchange munitions on the battlefield, compared to the federal army in which all carried the same weapons. The photo of the old cannon from the era of French intervention is another reminder of the rebels' deficiencies, although

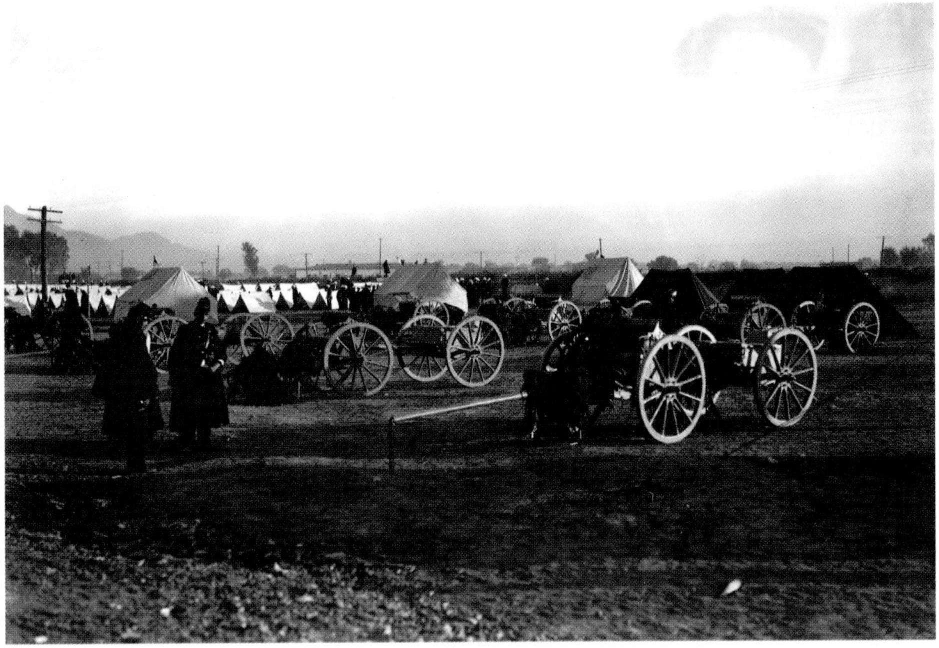

4-10. RIGHT Camp of the federal army, Ciudad Juárez, May 1911. © Inv. #34255, Fondo Casasola, SINAFO-Fototeca Nacional del INAH.

4-11. BELOW Maderista camp, Chihuahua, May 1911. © Inv. #5893, Fondo Casasola, SINAFO-Fototeca Nacional del INAH.

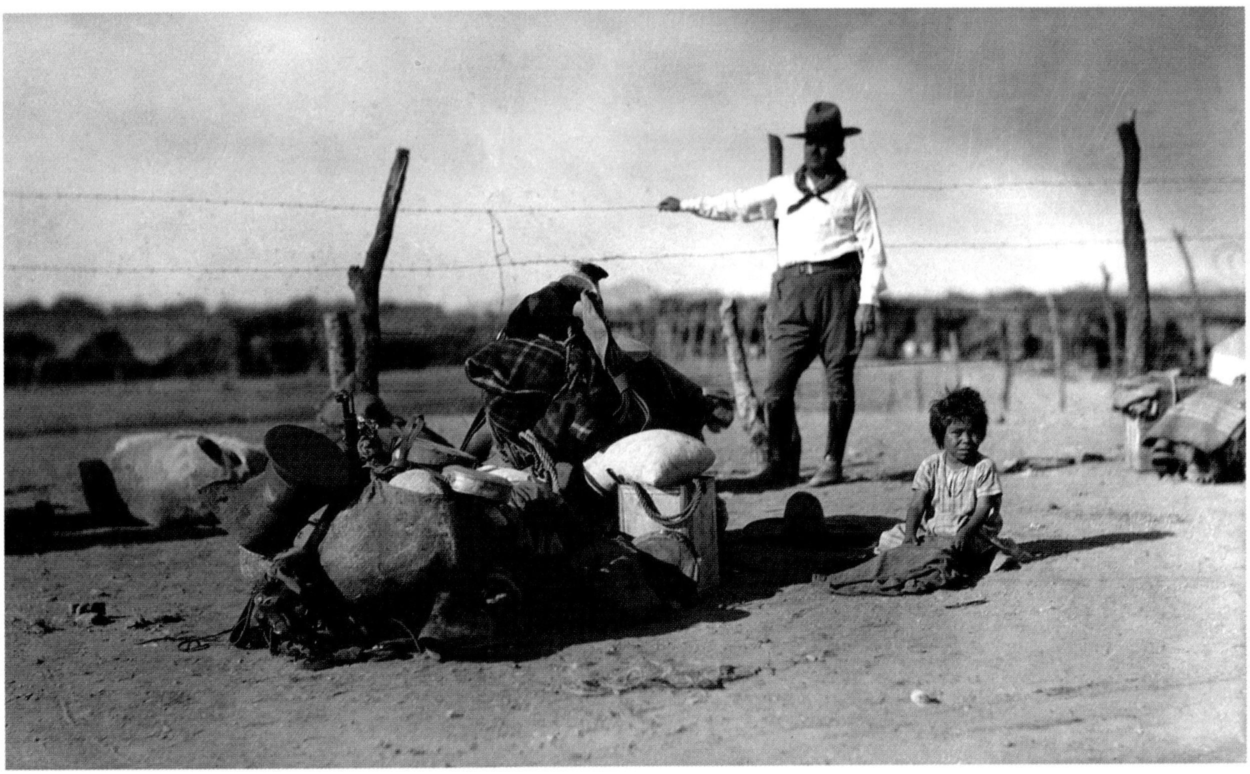

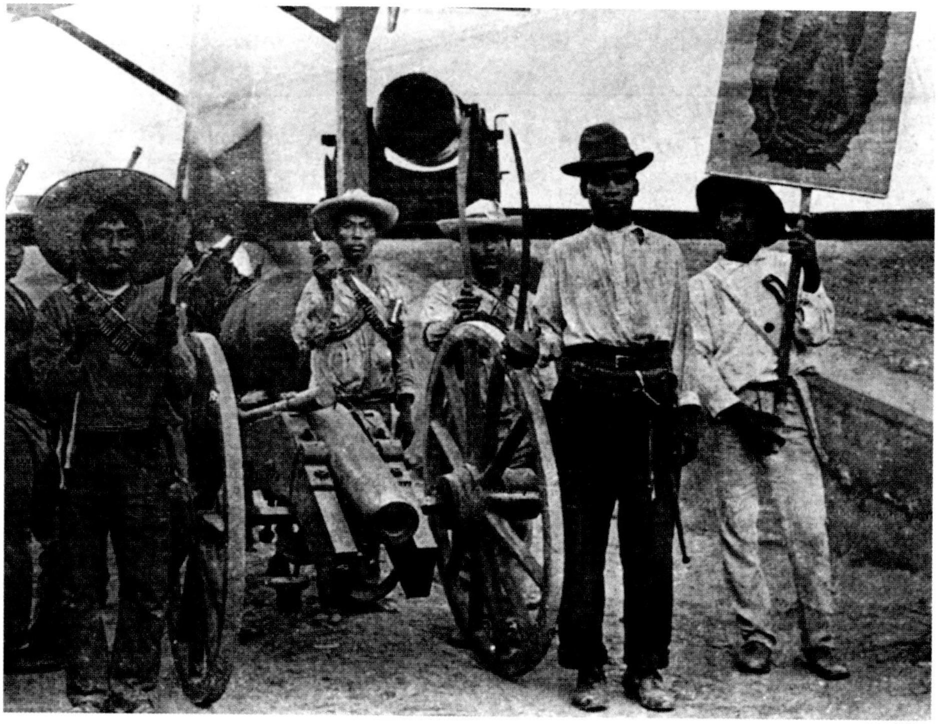

4-12. Cannon from the mid-nineteenth century and a banner with the image of the Virgin of Guadalupe, coast of Sinaloa or Nayarit, 1911. © Inv. #37995, Fondo Casasola, SINAFO-Fototeca Nacional del INAH.

this image also serves to demonstrate that reverence for the Virgin of Guadalupe was not limited to the Zapatistas (see Figure 4-12). Photos of the destruction rained on Ciudad Juárez by artillery show the devastation that would be a constant over the following years, as do images of refugees, many of whom fled to the United States.[20]

The outstanding Mexican photographer of the Maderista movement signed his images "H. J. Gutiérrez." It was previously believed that Heliodoro Juan Gutiérrez Escobar had united with Maderismo on the northern border. Berumen, the leading historian of the northern revolution's photography, asserted that "Gutiérrez left his work as a photographer for *El País* to travel north and join the revolutionary army."[21] Recent research by photo historian Arturo Guevara Escobar seems to have changed the story: he argues that the photos signed "H. J. Gutiérrez" were made by an agency, Fotografía H. J. Gutiérrez, the Chicago Photo Studio. This business was dedicated generally to the production of postcards, but it carried out a wide range of activities that included advertising photography, social events, historical registers, and duplication of documents, as well as sales of frames and drawings.[22] Heliodoro J. Gutiérrez had founded the studio during the century's first decade, and he employed members of his family, the three Escobar brothers, as photographers. It appears that Aurelio Escobar Castellanos went to the north, perhaps in a similar situation to that of Antonio Ocañas, the cineaste who worked for filmmaker Salvador Toscano. Ocañas—"an anti-reelectionist to the death" (as Toscano wrote)—was a follower of Madero and, according to Toscano, "pestered so much to go to Ciudad Juárez" that he gave him permission and, moreover, money, film, and a camera to make movies.[23] Ocañas wanted to make propaganda for the Maderista cause; Toscano was more interested in the economic possibilities of distributing films on exciting events.

The decision to send Aurelio Escobar to the north could have corresponded to two interests: that of Escobar to link himself to the Maderista movement and that of Gutiérrez to obtain new material for postcards.[24] Escobar's commitment to Maderismo would seem to have proved itself later: he fled the country shortly after Huerta's coup but returned with his fall and was at the Estudio H. J. Gutiérrez when Zapata went to have his portrait made there.[25] Mexico City's photojournalists arrived late to cover the rebellion, since their media didn't have much interest in publicizing challenges to the regime. It was different for the postcard studios, who were motivated by profit rather than the governmental subsidies that financed the press. Postcards were one of the passing fads of modern visual culture; they enjoyed an enormous popularity between 1890 and 1920 because they brought the world and its events to the coffee table, where every family had its precious albums. We have no information about postcard circulation in Mexico, but the numbers in the United States give us an idea of their attraction: in 1906, 770,500,000 postcards were mailed; in 1913, the number had reached 968,000,000.[26]

It is at least ironic that postcards advertised the Maderista challenge to the Porfiriato, because "the first Mexican postcards devoted a disproportionate attention to Porfirio Díaz's administration, glorifying it and praising the country's progress under his rule."[27] Its prior function notwithstanding, the medium would now serve other masters: Escobar arrived in the north at the beginning of April, and the first photo that registered the presence of the H. J. Gutiérrez agency in the revolution was taken in the middle of that month in Casas Grandes, Chihuahua, documenting a group of Maderistas in front of what must have been a Wells Fargo office of messenger service and transportation (Figure 4-13).[28]

Another photo signed "H. J. Gutiérrez" is more enigmatic. We see three young, well-dressed men, two of them with ties, in a scenario that mixes modern and classic armament: a machine gun and a sword held high (Figure 4-14). Many Mexicans were

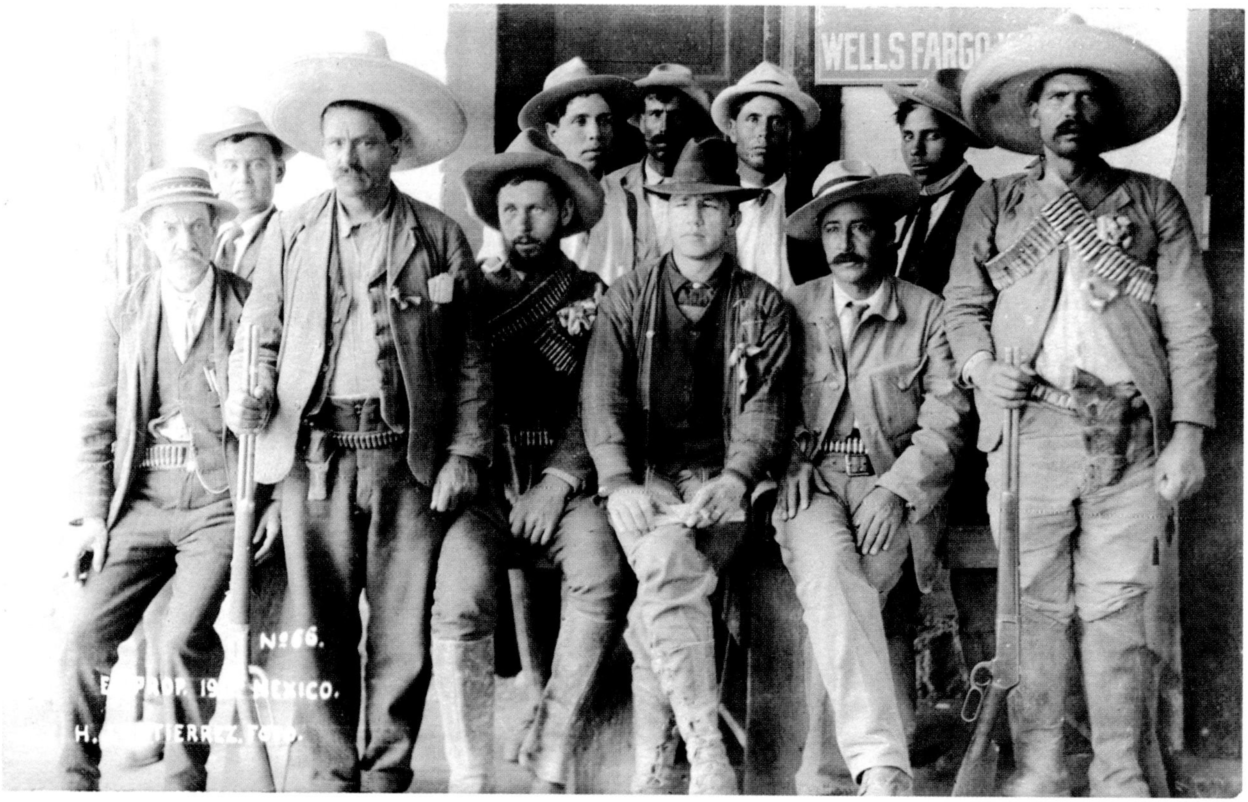

4-13. Maderista revolutionaries, Chihuahua, April 1911; Aurelio Escobar Castellanos, for the agency of H. J. Gutiérrez. © Inv. #373835, Fondo Casasola, SINAFO-Fototeca Nacional del INAH.

photographed who wished to demonstrate their revolutionary fervor as a souvenir, probably often after the triumph of Maderismo. At times they came from the other side of the border, since, as historian Willivaldo Delgadillo described it, "The revolutionary camp became a sort of amusement park for the children and young men of the border. For weeks, many people lived with the revolutionaries, and in some cases the rapport was such that they let them take photographs with cartridge belts and rifles."[29]

This picture, however, is part of a series of (at least) four images that show these men in what appears to be a weapons workshop.[30] It is unusual to see combatants dressed in this way in other photos from Ciudad Juárez, but these men represent the attraction that Maderismo had for the younger generation of privileged Mexicans. The man in the foreground is Ismael Reyes Retana, son of a Porfirian senator who had sent him to study engineering in Boston.[31] When the rebellion began, Reyes Retana returned to Mexico, abandoned his father's house, and joined up before the victory of

Ciudad Juárez. When he presented himself to Pascual Orozco dressed in his customary elegance—with jacket and tie, pants sharply pressed and shoes well shined—he was asked what such a fop could possibly do for the cause. His response was that—thanks to his education—he could keep the machine guns functioning. Reyes Retana was named lieutenant engineer and may have commissioned the photographs from Escobar; it is also possible that the photographer himself may have seen this imagery as a way to represent the Maderistas as decent people rather than the bandits portrayed by the Porfirian press. Further, the Retanas were a prominent family and belonged to the Maderista wing that Escobar appears to have favored in images of José de la Luz Blanco, Samuel Vázquez, Castulo Herrera, and the Ponce brothers. Arturo Guevara believes that Aurelio Escobar focused on these prominent Maderista families as a way of "catapulting" them mediatically, while the photographer only pictured Orozco in the midst of crowds.[32]

4-14. Lieutenant Engineer Ismael Reyes Retana and other Maderistas with a machine gun, Ciudad Juárez, Chihuahua, May 1911; Aurelio Escobar Castellanos, for the agency of H. J. Gutiérrez. © Inv. #373853, Fondo Casasola, SINAFO-Fototeca Nacional del INAH.

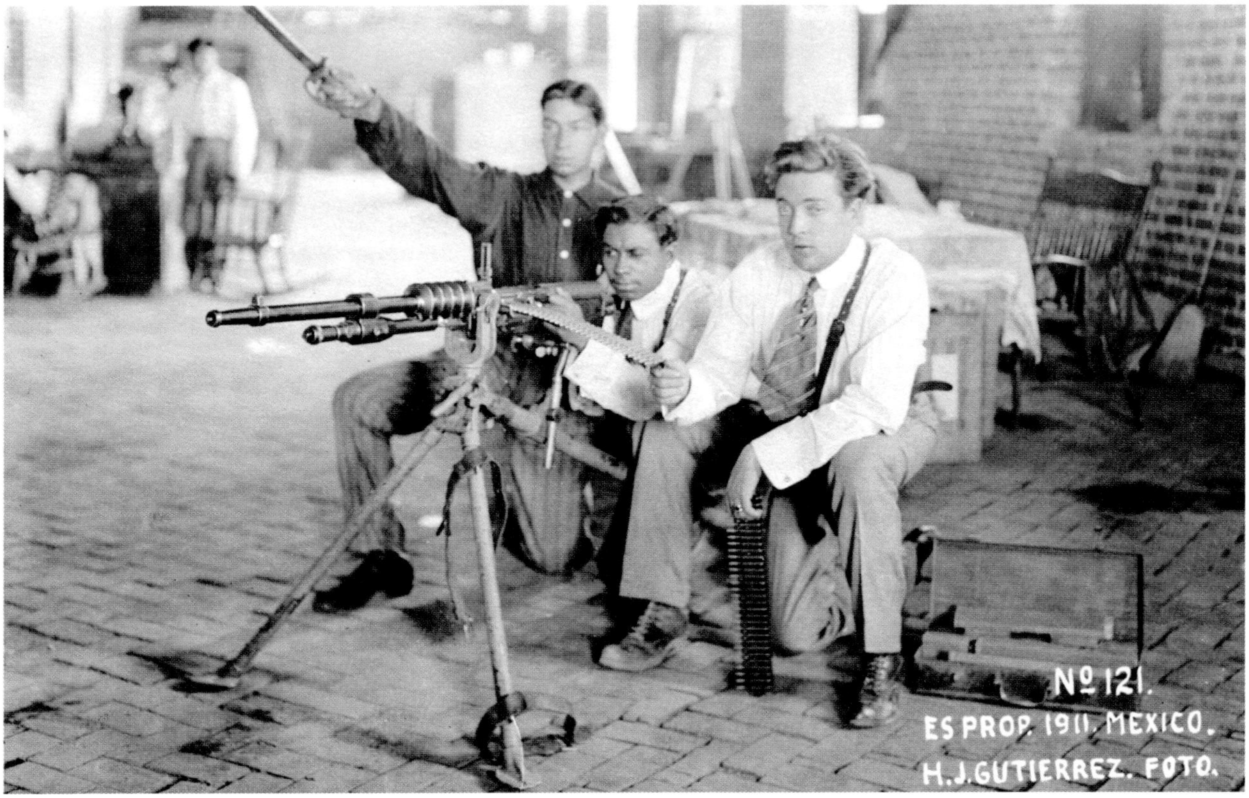

The aesthetic of many Escobar images is that of postcards and not photojournalism; the participants are clearly posing, as if in a studio, although the photographic acts take place beyond a set. Perhaps they are an expression of Escobar's experience and training, as well as the Gutiérrez agency's market. The equipment Escobar used also played its role, because the Gutiérrez photographers employed view cameras, which required tripods, while photojournalists preferred reflexes, which they could carry about.[33] The portraits of Herlinda Perry made by the Gutiérrez agency not only evidence the postcard style but also provide enticing leads about a fascinating case still to be investigated. This woman was photographed in Ciudad Juárez with a .30-30 carbine and loaded down with cartridge belts over her shoulders and around her waist, but we know nothing more about her (Figure 4-15).[34]

Another revolutionary Herlinda, this one named González, also offers a story in search of a teller. She appears with armed Maderista women and girls in a picture accompanied by the following typewritten phrase: "Orozco and Villa equipped these *señoritas*, knowing that they would help the anti-reelectionist party in the Revolution. They hid arms and distributed the Plan de San Luis Potosí. Herlinda, the oldest, directed her sisters; Rebeca, the youngest, was seven years old. María, my sister, had a master's degree and directed the San Diego School, Chihuahua, June of 1911" (Figure 4-16).[35] This photo is in the Roque González Garza Archive, and one scholar has ventured the notion that Gutiérrez was "the favorite photographer" of that revolutionary leader.[36] Nonetheless, the possibility also exists that Eustasio Montoya made it, as the writing on this photo is similar to that found on other images that are his.[37]

Both photos of the Herlindas belong to what we might call the performance trope of "women with crossed cartridge belts" that historian Gabriela Cano has identified with the Maderista movement.[38] The most famous woman to adopt that pose was Elena Arizmendi, who founded the Mexican White Cross to care for wounded revolutionaries, and was close to Madero and José Vasconcelos. She became a celebrity figure thanks to the attention she received from the media as an attractive, intelligent, and powerful woman. As Cano recounts, "The physical attractiveness of Elena and her delight in showing her beauty led to the massive circulation of her portraits in the press and as postcards in the aftermath of the battle for Ciudad Juárez. Her image was also captured by Salvador Toscano's camera during Madero's visit to a White Cross hospital."[39] Her notoriety as a femme fatal (she was Vasconcelos's extramarital lover) added a dash of moralism to the envy that men felt on having to follow her orders. She made a photo with crossed cartridge belts as part of a Vasconcelos joke, and when it was published in the press, underlings, in a ploy to remove her, accused

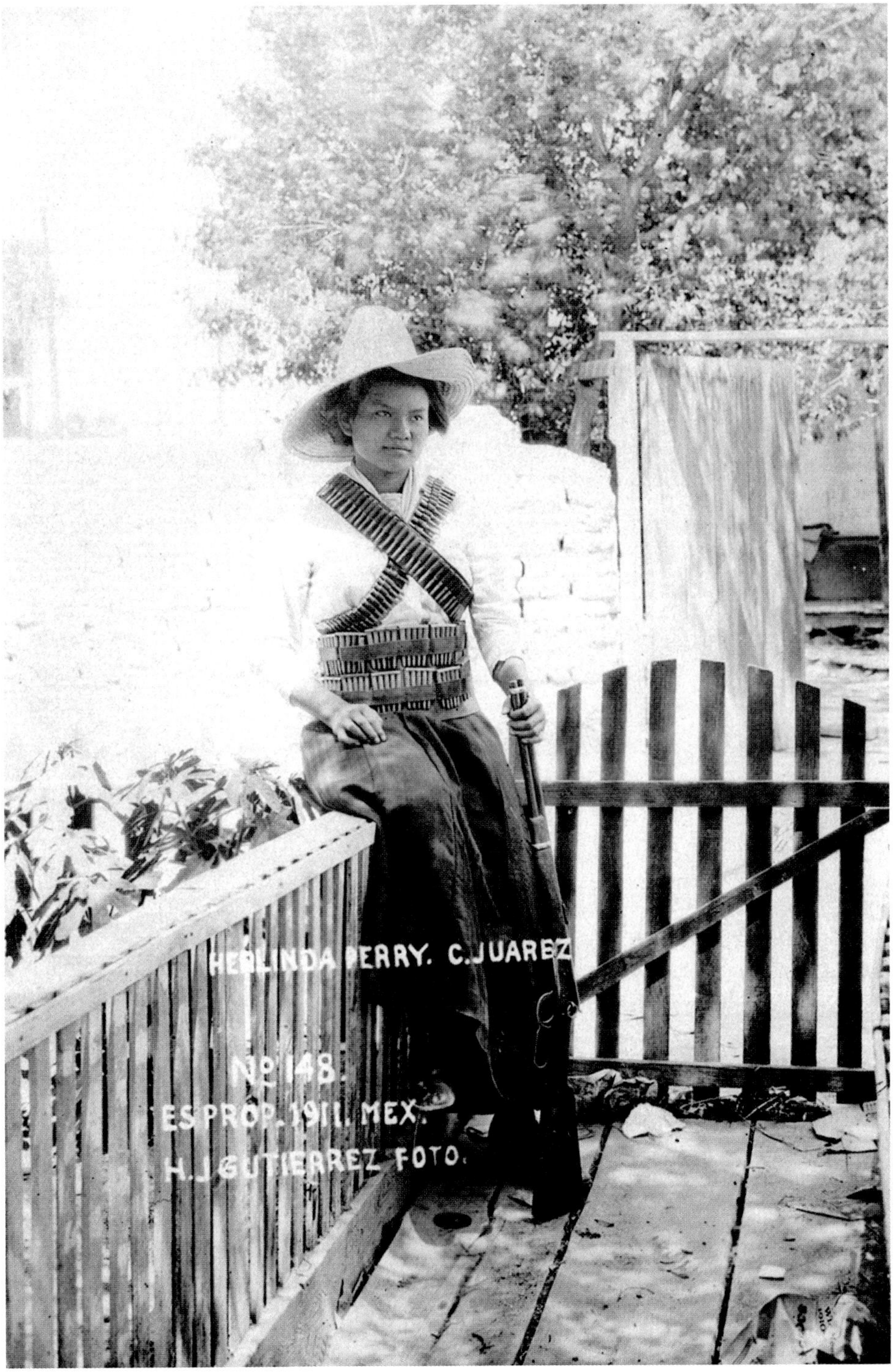

4-15. Portrait of Herlinda Perry, Ciudad Juárez, Chihuahua, May 1911; Aurelio Escobar Castellanos, for the agency of H. J. Gutiérrez. © Inv. #373880, Fondo Casasola, SINAFO-Fototeca Nacional del INAH.

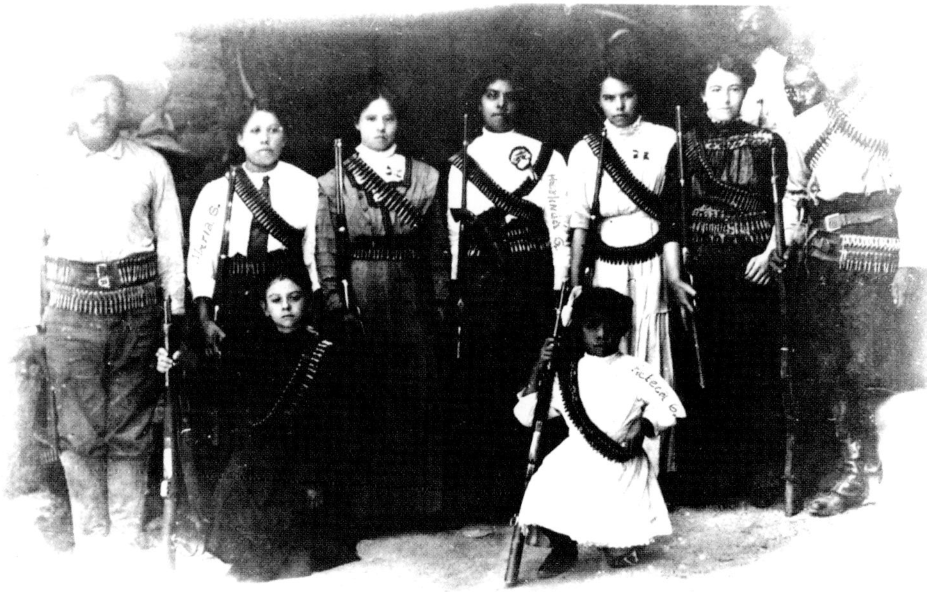

4-16. Herlinda González and other Maderistas, Chihuahua, June 1911; Eustasio Montoya? © Archivo González Garza, Universidad Panamericana, 03.046, Registro 156.

her of violating the neutrality of the health organization. It appears, however, that the leaders of the revolution liked the photo, and José Guadalupe Posada reproduced it in a lithograph titled *La maderista*, which became the cover for a collection of songs about the revolution.[40]

The great majority of the northern photos made by the Gutiérrez agency are not in what I consider a postcard style. Nonetheless, the complexity of this issue can be seen in one image that is splendidly photojournalistic—that of Pascual Orozco receiving congratulations after taking Ciudad Juárez on 10 May 1911—yet clearly a postcard (Figure 4-17). Hence all types of images were reproduced as postcards, and we should always keep in mind that there was much filtration between postcards, photojournalism, and studio photography.[41] There are many panoramic images with a very wide field of vision, taken from on high, of Maderista troops in formation, reunited in front of strategic places, marching in line, or celebrating the triumph of the battle for Ciudad Juárez—all good examples of Berumen's assertion that Gutiérrez was "a lover of shots from on high."[42] Other photos show public buildings in Ciudad Juárez, usually with revolutionaries standing outside, but taken at such distances that the individuals are unidentifiable. For us, with so many information media, it is difficult to imagine these images as postcards, but they provided pictures of events in an era without television or the Internet. Photos showing the destruction of Ciudad Juárez must have encountered a public avid to see the effects of the war, because several are labeled "Ruins in C. Juárez."

After the victory of the Maderista movement, it appears that Escobar accompanied Madero on the train to Mexico City.[43] He (or other Gutiérrez photographers) documented the triumphal reception in the train station and the multitudes that gathered outside Madero's residence in photos that are much more congested than those of the north, whether because of the context of the photographic act or as a result of the photographer's decision.

The slight evidence offered by the images themselves indicates that other photographers of the Gutiérrez agency in Mexico City may have shared Escobar's interest in anti-reelectionism. The agency covered the anti-reelectionist convention, took pictures of Madero and Emilio Vázquez Gómez, and made various shots of the Partido Nacionalista Democrático, one of the groups that arose with Maderismo.[44] The

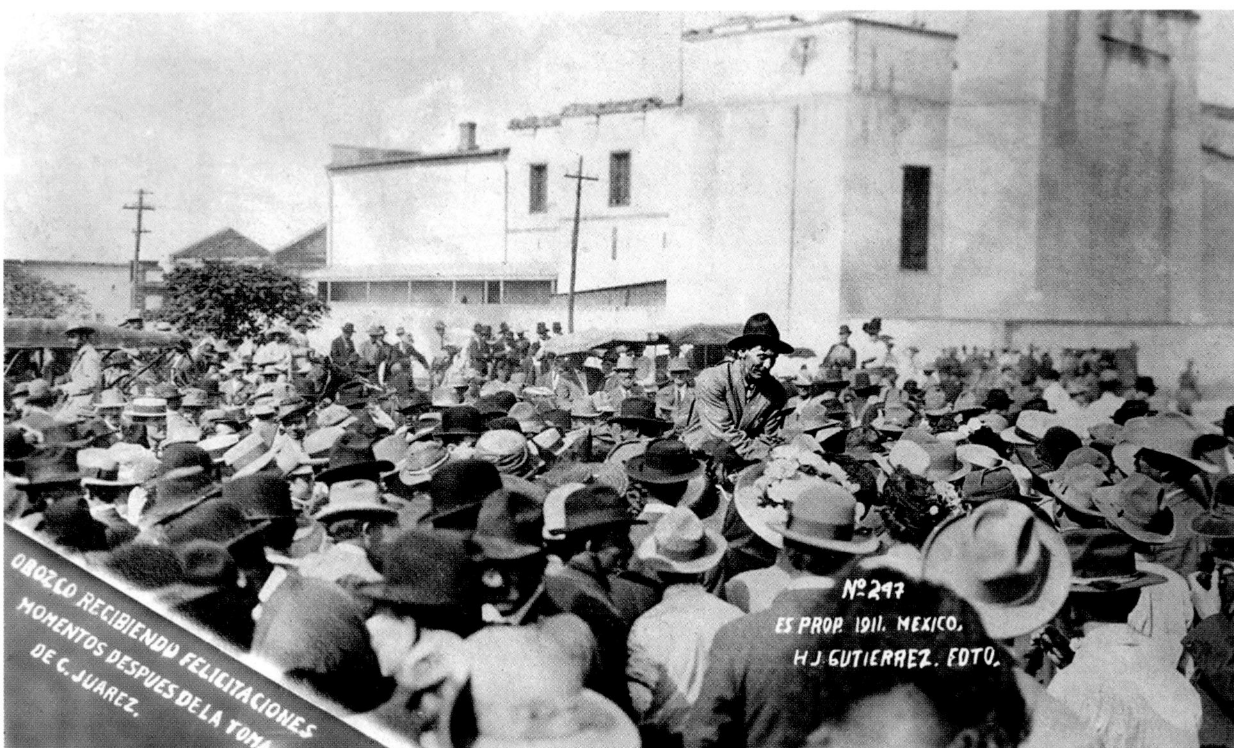

4-17. Pascual Orozco receiving an ovation after taking Ciudad Juárez, May 1911; Aurelio Escobar Castellanos, for the agency of H. J. Gutiérrez. © Archivo González Garza, Universidad Panamericana, 03.036, Registro 222.

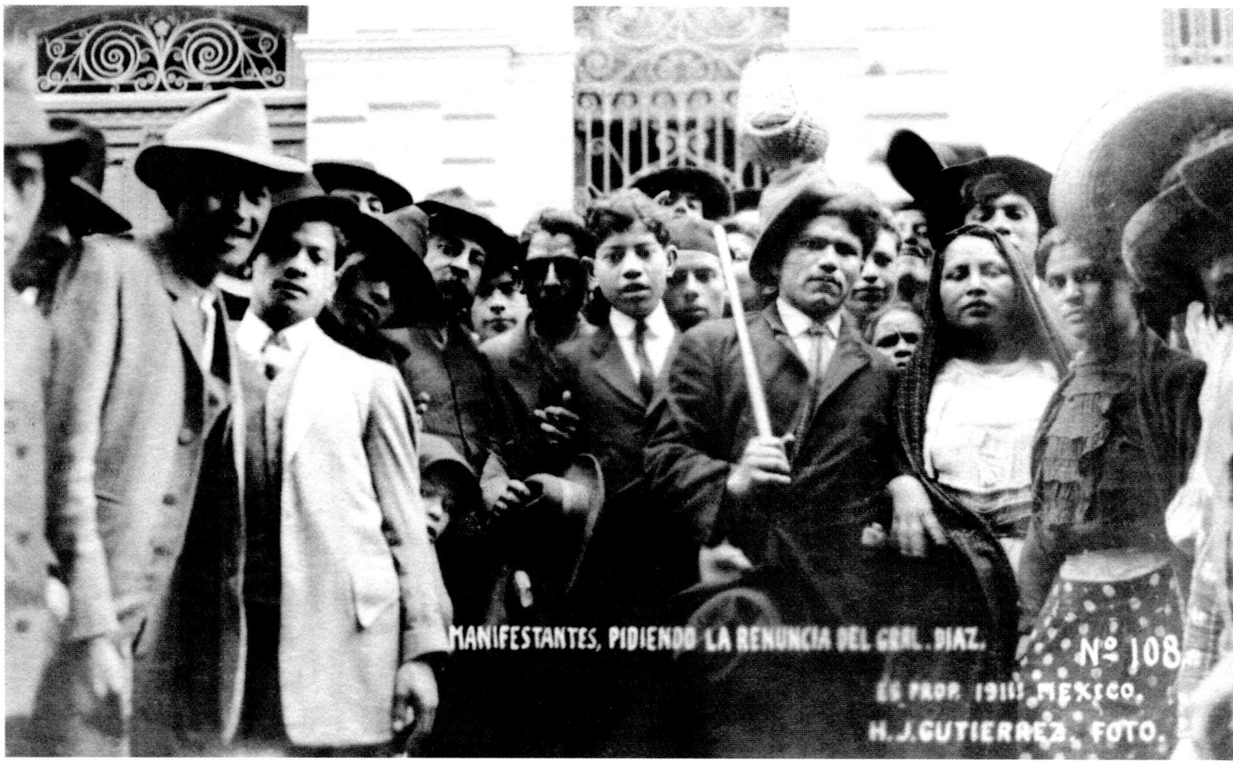

4-18. Protestors demanding the resignation of Porfirio Díaz, Mexico City, 22–25 May 1911; Agency of H. J. Gutiérrez. © Inv. #373882, Fondo Casasola, SINAFO-Fototeca Nacional del INAH.

Gutiérrez studio obviously had an interest in covering the popular protests against Porfirio Díaz in the last days of his reign. Some photos are in the postcard style, with people posing, empowered by a slight low angle (Figure 4-18).[45] Others show scenes from on high, documenting demonstrations in the street and in front of the Chamber of Deputies, as well as soldiers guarding Díaz's residence. Even more indicative of the stance taken by the Gutiérrez agency in favor of Maderismo are the inscriptions found on several photos; in one from the north the individuals pictured are referred to as "Officers of the Liberating Army."[46]

Other Gutiérrez agency photos have writings on them that describe scenes in Mexico City as part of a "Demonstration for the popular candidate Francisco I. Madero" and narrate a situation in Morelos thusly: "The people of Cuernavaca cheering Sr. Madero."[47] Finally, photos of General Gabriel M. Hernández, after having taken the city of Pachuca, as well as of revolutionaries in Jalisco, offer more reasons to think that the Gutiérrez studio supported Maderismo.[48] In sum, the existing images upon which are written "H. J. Gutiérrez" support two hypotheses: one, that several different photographers worked at the same time for what we now know was an agency; two, that the Gutiérrez studio was the first photographic protagonist on the side of the revolution because of its committed participation in the Maderista movement in different parts of the country.

Anti-reelectionism awoke a series of rebellions throughout Mexico, and one can imagine that local leaders sought ways to publicize themselves at the same time that photographers sought to link themselves to movements—or simply tried to earn a living with their craft. Although the names (and images) of the great majority of them are still to be discovered, one about whom we know a little was Mauricio Yáñez of Sinaloa.[49] Of the surviving photos made (or, at least, signed) by Yáñez there are several of the caudillos in that region: Conrado M. Antuna on horseback in Sinaloa; Melquiades Meléndez (or Justo Tirado) in front of his revolutionary troops in the streets of Culiacán; and Manuel Bonilla, accompanied by Juan Banderas ("el Agachado") and other revolutionaries, in Culiacán in 1911 (Figure 4-19).[50]

The most interesting of Yáñez's photos is that of General Ramón F. Iturbe in Mineral de Topia, "accompanied by his Feminine General Staff," according to *La Semana Ilustrada* (Figure 4-20).[51] Years later Iturbe recounted the history of this image.

> Here is a cute story. The town's prettiest girls had taken refuge in the U.S. Consulate because the Federales had given me a bad reputation of carrying women off, and they were frightened. That was not true; I never carried a woman off, but for them Iturbe was a bandit. The consul presented me to them, and they noticed that I wasn't like people said. We became friends, and four of them wanted to have a picture taken with me, holding arms. From that photo another legend was born: that Iturbe, rebel leader, had a feminine General Staff. The photo became famous in the capital, being published in magazines and newspapers.[52]

It is difficult to say whether Yáñez was committed to Maderismo or more-local movements. Among his photos are those of a rebellion in Culiacán in April 1912, probably an expression of the centrifugal tendency that was produced during Madero's presidency; they include pictures of the uprising in the city, a participant (Roberto Almada), and cadavers in Huanacatle, Sinaloa.[53] Among his known photos are those of Huertistas in 1914: some officers on the warship *Guerrero* and leaders on horseback accompanied by their prisoners, "rebels apprehended in the combat for Conchis, Mazatlán."[54]

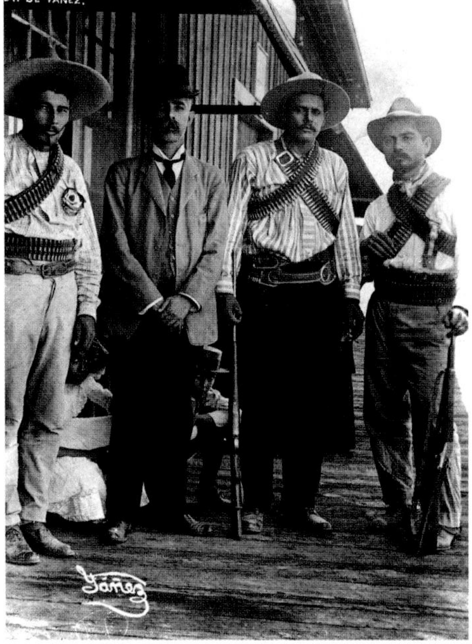

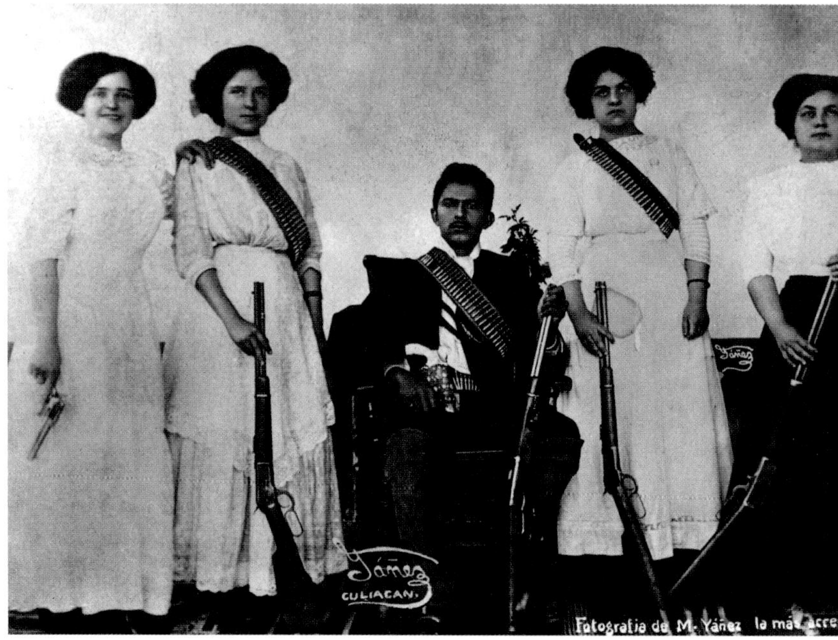

4-19. LEFT Manuel Bonilla, accompanied by Juan Banderas (El Agachado) and other revolutionaries, Culiacán, Sinaloa, 1911; Mauricio Yáñez. © Inv. #34262, Fondo Casasola, SINAFO-Fototeca Nacional del INAH.

4-20. RIGHT General Ramón Iturbe, accompanied by what was said to be his "Feminine General Staff," Topia, Durango, March 1911; Mauricio Yáñez, *La Semana Ilustrada*, 28 April 1911. © Inv. #186666, Fondo Casasola, SINAFO-Fototeca Nacional del INAH.

If our knowledge of Yáñez is extremely limited, we know even less about other regional photographers involved with Maderismo. One was Carlos Harris, who signed several photos. Berumen described him succinctly: "He was living in Chihuahua city when the revolution broke out, and was one of the pioneers in documenting it. Beginning in November of 1910, he took photos of the armed struggle, and continued to do so when Madero headed it up in March of 1911. The next year he founded the agency 'La Rochester,' with which he documented much of the Orozquista rebellion, above all the federal forces."[55] Another name that appears is that of José P. Arriaga, a studio photographer in Mexico City and a collaborator of *El Universal Ilustrado*.[56] Although it is not clear when he arrived, he was in Ciudad Juárez during the Maderista rebellion and made photos of Madero's camp near Ciudad Juárez.[57] Manuel L. Andrade took several photos of Maderistas, including one in which they are riding to Cerro Grande, Chihuahua.[58] J. Z. García signed one photo of revolutionaries in El Saub, Durango.[59] Another García took a photo of Rafael Cepeda in San Luis Potosí during 1911 (see Figure 4-5 above). It also appears that a photographer who stamped "F. K. MEXICO" on his images was in Ciudad Juárez during the uprising and made several photos of Maderista leaders.[60] Finally, after the triumph of Madero in the 1911 elections, a

V. Carmona, correspondent of *La Semana Ilustrada*, and a Villalobos made photos of his reception in Saltillo and Guadalajara, respectively.[61]

Few Mexican photographers can be established as having been committed to Maderismo, but it is even more difficult to find imagemakers for the other side. One might be Luís Ramírez Pimental, who took pictures of federal forces after their triumph in the Aldama ambush; they pose proudly, the officers with their hands on their swords, and the soldiers holding their rifles.[62] According to Berumen, "Established in the city of Chihuahua, he was one of the pioneer photographers of the armed struggle in the area, with images that date from 1910. The photographs he made in 1911 and 1912 were massively commercialized."[63] It is not easy to know what Ramírez Pimentel's commitment might have been—if he had one—because the little evidence that exists is contradictory. There is a photo of "Revolutionary leaders," but it is not known whether this was the photo that was used to identify the Portillo brothers, Maderistas for whom a trap was set to kill them.[64] Another of his images is that of the "Revolutionary train in Bachimba canyon, 3 July 1912," which must have been one of the military expeditions of General José González Salas, on its way to fight against the Orozquistas.[65] Among other possible candidates is one N. González, who made a photo of what appear to be Maderista arms and flags captured by the Rurales, who pose next to them.[66]

Some magazines, such as *La Semana Ilustrada*, published a good deal of photography on the northern revolution, beginning in March of 1911. It is not clear who made these photos—whether they were Mexicans from the region and/or U.S. photojournalists—but the illustrated weeklies' editors must have felt themselves trapped between various factors: the growing demand to know what was happening in the north, their own class interests, and the possibility of being censored. They expressed their position thusly: "Attempting to provide our readers with news in all its forms, *and only for that reason*, we continue in our labor of presenting in *La Semana Ilustrada* graphic information about the revolution in the north. . . . Our burning desire is to please the public."[67] Maderistas were usually identified as "rioters" and labeled "seditious," while the leaders were invariably designated *cabecillas*—a term of opprobrium in that period—at the head of "hordes." It does not appear that the magazines sent photojournalists until later, but they nonetheless insisted on their determination to provide "the latest word of graphic information on the revolution."[68] When the correspondents finally arrived—"the atmosphere still reeked of powder and the last shots were heard"—the magazines crowed about it by publishing photos of Samuel Tinoco and Ignacio Herrerías.[69]

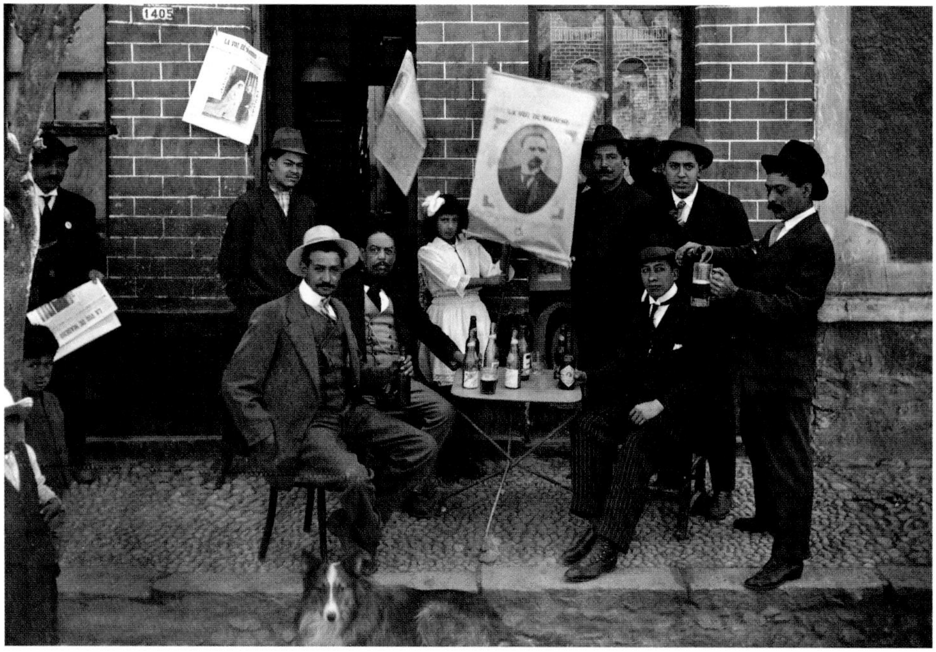

4-21. Maderistas, Mexico City, 1911. © Inv. #186139, Fondo Casasola, SINAFO-Fototeca Nacional del INAH.

In general, the Porfirian magazines used photos to furnish evidence against the Maderista movement. They were testimonies of the destruction loosed by the rebellion: "For those who believe that the news about the attack on Ciudad Juárez was exaggerated, the photographs will show, with all their horrible sincerity, the degree of extermination. The artillery totally destroyed many buildings, mowing down hundreds of human lives."[70] They also served to discredit Maderismo, recurring to nationalism by documenting the participation of U.S. citizens in that movement: "A group of these men was surprised by the photographic camera of our correspondent right before the attack on Ciudad Juárez. These foreigners in the Maderista ranks have caused, despite sympathy for the movement, a bad effect."[71]

After Madero's victory, the democratic fervor and his own capacity to promote himself visually placed his image everywhere; Martín Luís Guzmán noted that "you run into a portrait of Madero at every step (Figure 4-21)."[72] Always opportunistic, the illustrated press changed its tune. *La Semana Ilustrada* prided itself that "the man of the day" had posed "for our magazine."[73] *El Mundo Ilustrado* published photos of Madero with engineering students; the encounter was "an agreeable surprise" for the youths, who "sang songs about politics, commending Madero's democratic works."[74]

The same magazine showed images of the multitudes that received Madero in Puebla, where "he was the object of all sorts of attention and demonstrations of affection," and Xochimilco, a place where "he was received with enthusiasm and a limitless affection by the friendly Indians."[75]

Among the metropolitan photojournalists, Gerónimo Hernández was a "decided Maderista from the epoch of Porfirio Díaz," and he may have taken the dynamic photo of the leader in the moment he cast his ballot in the elections of October 1911 (Figure 4-22).[76] The graphic reporters attempted to get close to the winner: they invited him to their photographic exposition, and he arrived to be pictured with them and tour the exhibit, standing for a moment in front of a photo of himself talking with General Bernardo Reyes (see Figure 3-2 above).[77]

4-22. Francisco I. Madero voting, Mexico City, 1 October 1911. © Inv. #68491, Fondo Casasola, SINAFO-Fototeca Nacional del INAH.

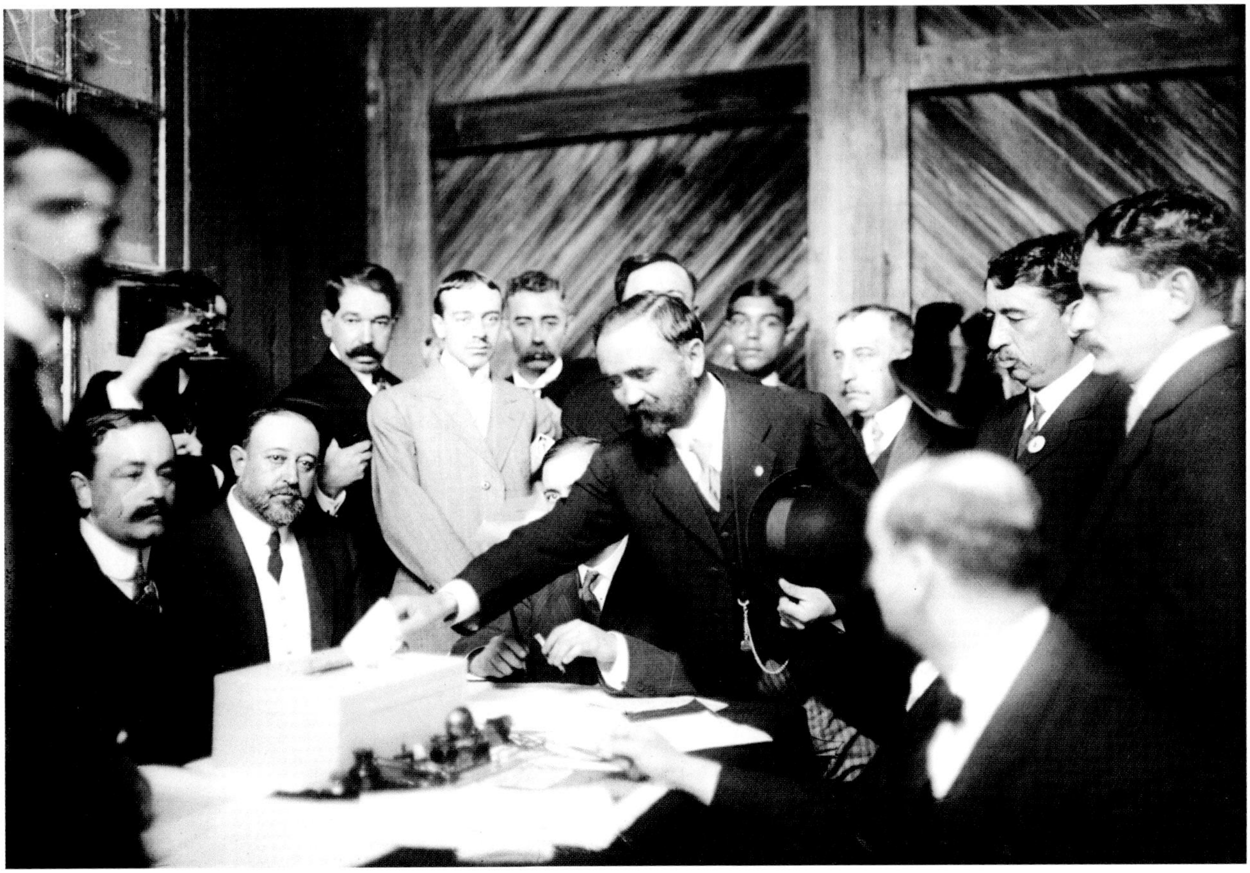

Once again, Maderista photographers saved the Apostle's life. The Rousset brothers—Antonio, Guillermo, and Benito—had a photo studio in the city of Puebla. According to agrarian leader Gildardo Magaña, "They were affiliated with the revolution, and *compañeros* of Aquiles Serdán, in the difficult days."[78] Founders of the anti-reelectionist club in Puebla, the Roussets had hidden Aquiles in 1909 when he fled the Porfirian police; a revolutionary *corrido* recounts how they organized a meeting in the plaza of San José together with the Serdán brothers.[79] Although they came from an accommodated family, and represented the moderate wing of Maderismo in Puebla, they were nonetheless instrumental in obtaining weapons for the planned uprising of 20 November 1910.[80] They went to Mexico City and bought 130 arms that they took to Puebla and concealed in their studio.[81] The police arrived to confiscate the guns three days before the insurrection, and in the course of their search devastated the house/studio interior, breaking the furniture and ripping up the mattresses and bedding.[82] Thanks to a tip from within the police, no arms were found; they had been removed, hidden under the bulky clothing of women connected to the movement.[83] The Roussets were arrested and set to be executed, but they managed to escape and find their way to the railway hub, Apizaco, dressed as sellers of *rebozos*.[84] As a consequence, their studio "was destroyed by the Porfirian henchmen, and since they could not work or find any way to earn a living, the Rousset brothers fled to the north, crossed the border on 13 April 1911, and presented themselves to the Junta Revolucionaria Maderista that was in San Antonio, Texas."[85]

In San Antonio they took photos of Maderista leaders such as Emilio Vázquez Gómez and Gildardo Magaña, linking themselves to the Junta's activities in organizing Madero's return to Mexico.[86] After Díaz left the country, the Rousset brothers went back to Puebla, where in July 1911 they found themselves occupying the room next to some Puebla politicians who were planning to assassinate Madero.[87] They warned the Maderistas, who arrested the reactionaries. Nonetheless, the interim government of Francisco León de la Barra had little desire to antagonize powerful interests in Puebla. The role played by the media, "which never liked the revolutionary leaders," was decisive.[88] "The Porfirian press screamed to high heaven against Madero," and the prisoners were liberated.[89]

The Roussets were photographed with different revolutionary caudillos, as in a photo in which they appear with Emiliano Zapata.[90] They may well have been combatants as well as propagandists and photographers, and were certainly in the forefront of the revolutionary struggle: they were arrested in Puebla in 1914 along with "forty-two of the principal doctors, lawyers, engineers and professional men . . . and sent to the front in chains to fight with the military forces against the Americans"; on the list of those "prominent men of Puebla," the Rousset brothers are first.[91] Imprisoned in San Francisco de las Peñas, they were sentenced to be shot by Victoriano Huerta, but the officer designated for that task, General Rubio Navarrete, refused to carry it out. They continued their opposition and were eventually named "Veterans of the Revolution, in the First and Second periods, and with the decoration of Revolutionary Merit."[92]

As Madero's presidency advanced, the press became more and more problematic for him. In part, it was understandable: after thirty years of the suffocating Porfirian peace, the many demonstrations of a people who finally saw the possibilities of being their own rulers must have appeared chaotic to the accommodated owners of the publications. In Mexico City, the new liberty produced a frenzy of union activities; among them, the most important and contestatory organization was the Casa del Obrero, whose members dared to ask for luxuries such as having Sunday off (Figure 4-23). Outside of Mexico City, the centrifugal effect of the revolution appeared to

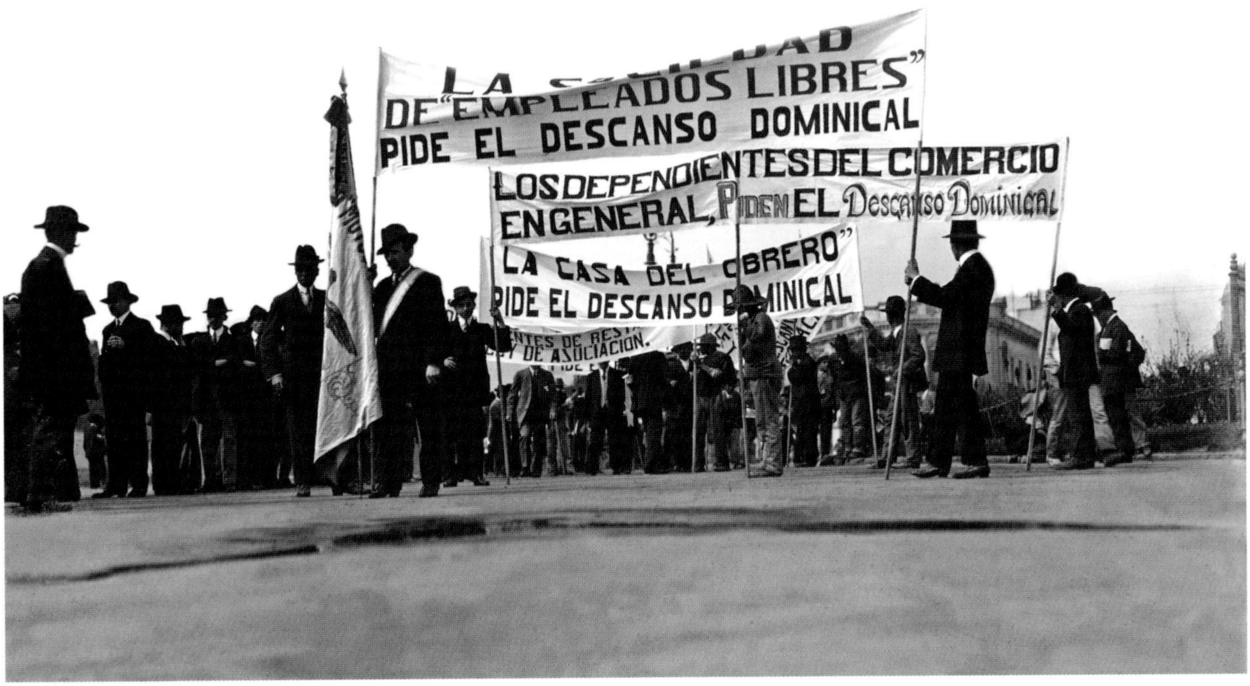

4-23. Protest by members of the Casa del Obrero (Home of the Worker) to demand Sundays off, Mexico City, summer 1912. © Inv. #36373, Fondo Casasola, SINAFO-Fototeca Nacional del INAH.

offer the regions the opportunity to free themselves from both federal control and that of the state governments. The new leaders kicked out the caciques imposed by Porfirio Díaz, who had been agents of centralism, and attempted to replace them. One example was the Chegomista movement in Juchitán, Oaxaca, organized by José Gómez toward the goal of achieving a degree of autonomy; "By the end of 1911 it constituted the biggest armed movement in the country" (Figure 4-24).[93]

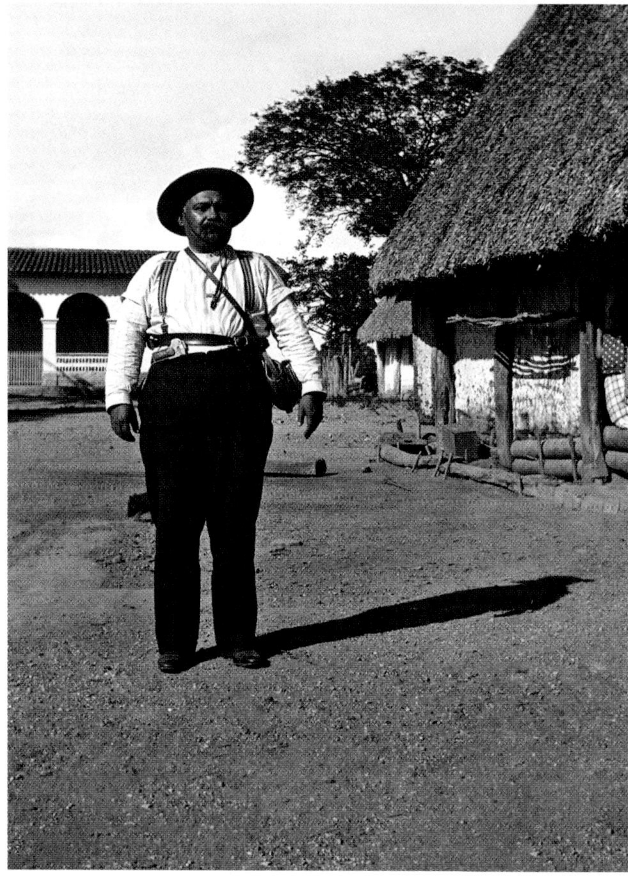

4-24. José (Che) Gómez in Juchitán, November 1911. © Inv. #16945, Fondo Casasola, SINAFO-Fototeca Nacional del INAH.

Another uprising inspired by the Maderista rebellion was the "interrupted revolution" in Chiapas.[94] There had been no armed revolt against the Díaz regime, so the state continued under the control of the local Porfirian elite based in Tuxtla Gutiérrez. The seed had been planted, however, and with León de la Barra in the interim presidency, liberals from San Cristóbal de las Casas rose up against the establishment. Chamula Indians participated on the liberal side; this raised the ever-present threat of caste war, a consideration that may have facilitated Policarpo Rueda's candidacy to the governorship, as he represented an attempt to conciliate the struggle between the two power bases and the interests they represented. Rueda may well have had good relations with the Chamulas, for their leader, Jacinto Pérez ("Pajarito"), appeared with a great following when the new governor entered San Cristóbal on 15 July 1911.[95] It is estimated that some 10,000 Chamulas paraded in his honor, headed up by a giant who carried the banner of the troops, and two dwarfs who trotted alongside the colossus. Among other activities, Rueda was photographed with both the giant and the dwarfs (Figure 4-25).[96] Historian Prudencio Moscoso Pastrana recounted that the camera made the behemoth nervous, and he jumped back when it clicked, while the dwarfs remained tranquil in front of the apparatus.

What are we to think of this photograph (and that of the giant)? What purpose was served, what message was intended, with these folkloric images of Indian freaks that seem to have stepped out of a circus, standing next to an eminently modern man in front of an improvised tarp? To which public were these photos directed? Why does Rueda appear with these individuals, and what is behind these spectacles? It is important to recognize that Rueda seems to have had a genuine concern for the Chamulas. He may well be the unidentified man who participates in a photograph of the profilmic reconstruction of an incident in which the ears of Chamula prisoners were cut off for having supported the liberal cause; the Ladinos from Tuxtla showed the race hatred (and fear) they had for the Indians, who were the only prisoners to whom this punishment was meted out.[97] Further, the dwarfs and the giant had been the headliners of the parade, and thus the individuals who would naturally be featured in photographs. Rueda may have participated in these (and other) images as a way of showing his solidarity with the Chamulas and demonstrating their support for him and his policy of conciliation. Other photographs could well have been made in which Rueda and Jacinto Pérez appeared together, but these images of the dwarfs and giant may be the only survivors of that encounter.[98]

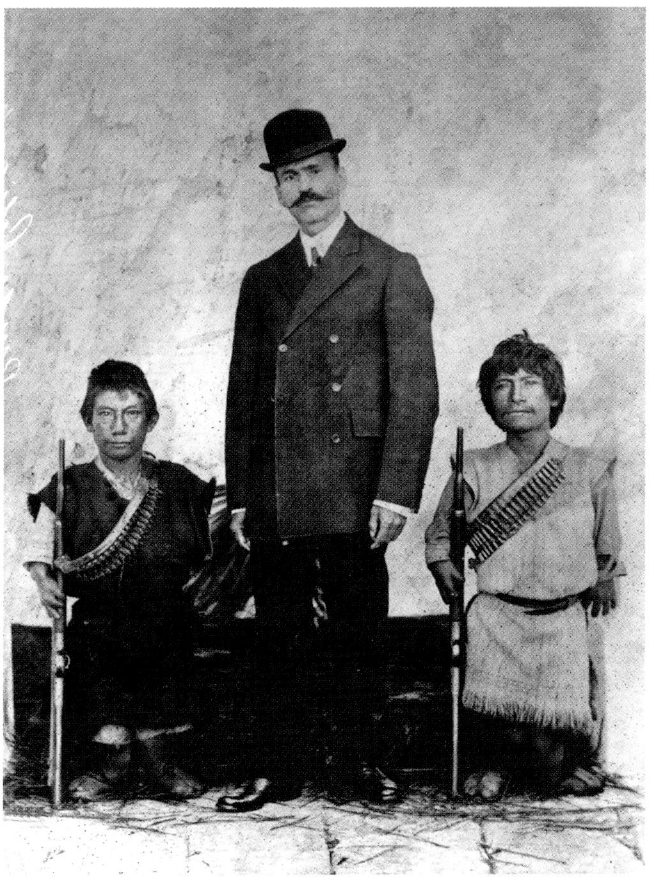

4-25. Governor Policarpo Rueda with two Chamula Indian dwarfs who were revolutionaries, San Cristóbal de las Casas, Chiapas, 15 July 1911. © Inv. #34261, Fondo Casasola, SINAFO-Fototeca Nacional del INAH.

Regardless of whether they are a result of the fact that these men led the parade, or that these photos were the ones chosen to survive, they are spectacles—and hence raise questions about colonialist representation and, specifically, Indianist photography.[99] The Chamulas are shown as being irredeemably "other," both by virtue of belonging to another culture and by having dramatically abnormal body types. If, as anthropologist Catherine Lutz and sociologist Jane Collins have argued, "Exotic dress alone often stands for an entire alien life-style, locale, or mind-set," the effect is doubled with physical aberrations.[100] The traditional *chuj* (woolen shift), the primitive footwear and bare feet, the wild uncombed hair, the darker (perhaps dirty) skins, and the strange smashed and elongated bodies set the Chamula dwarfs and giant off from the well-furbished "normality" of Rueda, who wears a double-breasted coat, a derby hat, and highly polished shoes. Such disjuncture must have had different meanings for Rueda's friends and enemies. To his liberal Ladino allies, Rueda's appearance in the scene was likely reassuring: these creatures might look grotesque and ferocious, but they are made nonthreatening by his presence and validation of them as they are. To his conservative opponents, the images may have carried the threat of a caste war, with the Indians demonstrably on the side of the liberals. The representation of their abnormalities also demonstrates photography's polysemia. They could be examples of what Homi Bhabha called the "degenerate types [that] justify conquest."[101] Showing them with weapons, however, might be interpreted as a "rescue" of the physically challenged: though they suffer nature's whim, they are capable of joining a revolutionary movement and carrying their load.

The fact that the Chamulas are armed sets the images well outside the usual humanist conventions of portraying indigenous peoples as victims—the dead, dying, and misfunctional—or in a sentimental fashion, as vanishing races or lost cultures. It is also a bit of a contradiction with Rueda's professed concern to disarm both sides.[102] Nevertheless, the armament also integrates them into the modern world, as does the tarp backdrop that partitions them off from their own culture and geography while enveloping them in the atmosphere of an itinerant studio: a tabula rasa of the new revolutionary space in which a social leveling would take place, transforming human relations—among them that of the races.[103]

The most direct challenge to Madero's presidency came from one of his old allies, Pascual Orozco. The Orozquista movement was, at least in the beginning, an extension of Maderismo, and for that reason I here consider its imagery. The photographer most committed to Orozquismo could have been the man who called himself "El Gran Lente" (the Great Lens), Ignacio Medrano Chávez. According to historian Jesús Vargas, "He was as Orozquista as all of Chihuahua in 1912, [although] his position was not as defined as those of other artists."[104] Medrano Chávez was a cineaste as well as photographer, and he had filmed the 1911 entrance of Maderistas into Chihuahua city.[105] Vargas claims that "He was the most important photographer in Chihuahua during the first half of the twentieth century. Many of the photos that became known during the revolution bear the signature of his studio."[106] It would appear that he had a close relationship with the rebels, as he made some photos in Chihuahua on 6 March 1912 of Orozquista followers waiting for their leader, and General José Inés Salazar signing Orozco's protest against Madero (Figure 4-26).[107] In April of 1912, Medrano Chávez had access to Benjamín Aranda's workshop, where the munitions were made for Orozco's army; the handwriting makes me think that he made this photo, although he may not have signed for aesthetic reasons or to hide his identity even beyond that provided by his nickname (Figure 4-27). In May, El Gran Lente photographed the taking of San Diego.[108] Among other images made by Orozquistas, we find one of an armed group in their car in a hacienda patio, which has a sense of being a postcard made as a souvenir (Figure 4-28).

On the other side of the Madero-Orozco conflict, the photography appears to have been made largely by professional photojournalists. It would appear that they came from the north, armed with the most modern of cameras, Graflexes that weighed about as much as a Mauser carbine, around ten pounds.[109] Because these cameras used celluloid film instead of glass plates, their portability permitted surprisingly modern images, such as that of a radio operator and federal officials (Figure 4-29). A close-up that spontaneously captures soldiers in what appears to be the midst of combat,

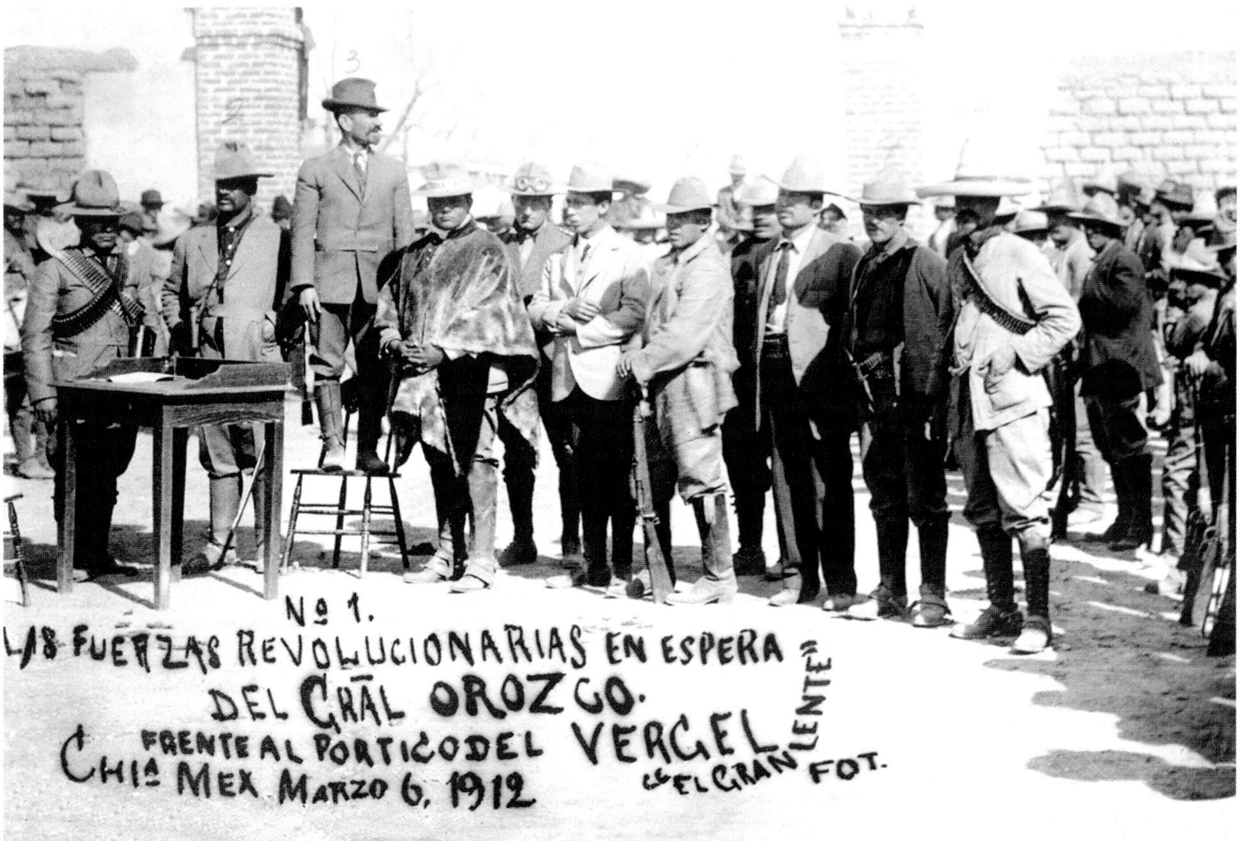

4-26. Orozquista forces waiting for Pablo Orozco, with General David de la Fuente standing on a chair, Chihuahua, 6 March 1912; El Gran Lente (Ignacio Medrano Chávez). © Inv. #36809, Fondo Casasola, SINAFO-Fototeca Nacional del INAH.

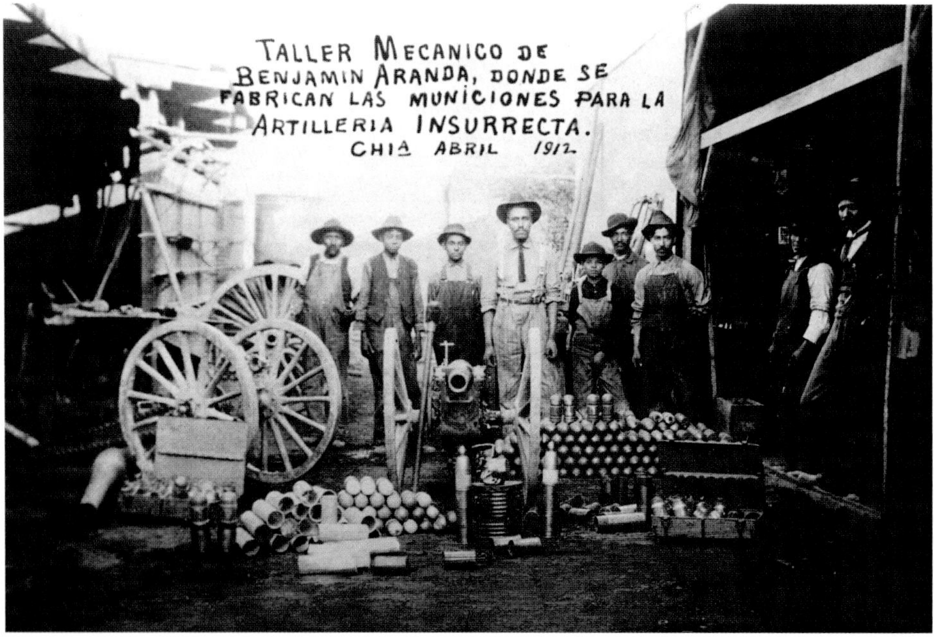

4-27. "Mechanical workshop of Benjamín Aranda, where the munitions for the rebel artillery were made," Chihuahua, April 1912; El Gran Lente (Ignacio Medrano Chávez). © Inv. #36818, Fondo Casasola, SINAFO-Fototeca Nacional del INAH.

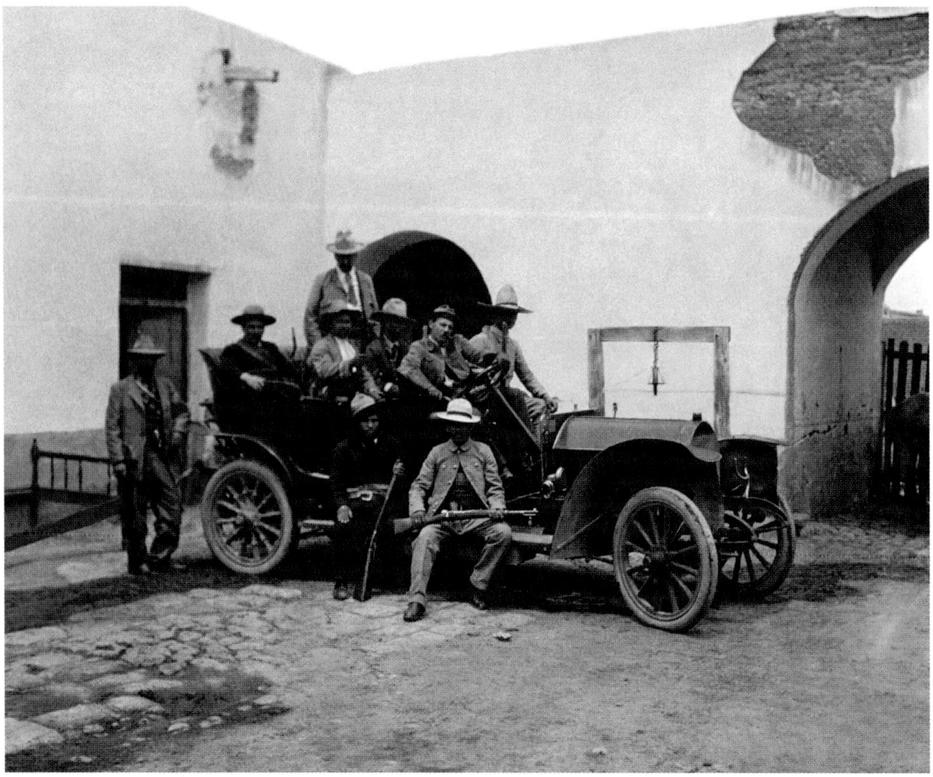

4-28. Orozquistas, Chihuahua, 1912. © Inv. #36773, Fondo Casasola, SINAFO-Fototeca Nacional del INAH.

the photo represents the advantages enjoyed by the federal forces, both in the documented technology and the way of photographing it. The composition is before its time, for this style of picturing would not really be seen widely until the small-format 35 mm cameras made possible the innovative coverage of the Spanish Civil War by imagemakers such as Robert Capa and Gerda Taro, who created a new photojournalist aesthetic embodied in Capa's famous saying: "If your photos aren't good enough, you're not close enough."[110]

4-29. Radio operator and federal officers in combat against the Orozquistas, Chihuahua, 1912. © Inv. #36700, Fondo Casasola, SINAFO-Fototeca Nacional del INAH.

Another photo that was probably taken by a photojournalist shows a doctor holding an amputated leg (Figure 4-30). The image almost seems to be a macabre variation of the pictures in the well-known series of types and occupations produced by the German photographer August Sander. Those images were published under the title of *The Face of Our Time* in 1929, but Sander "incorporated portraits that he had

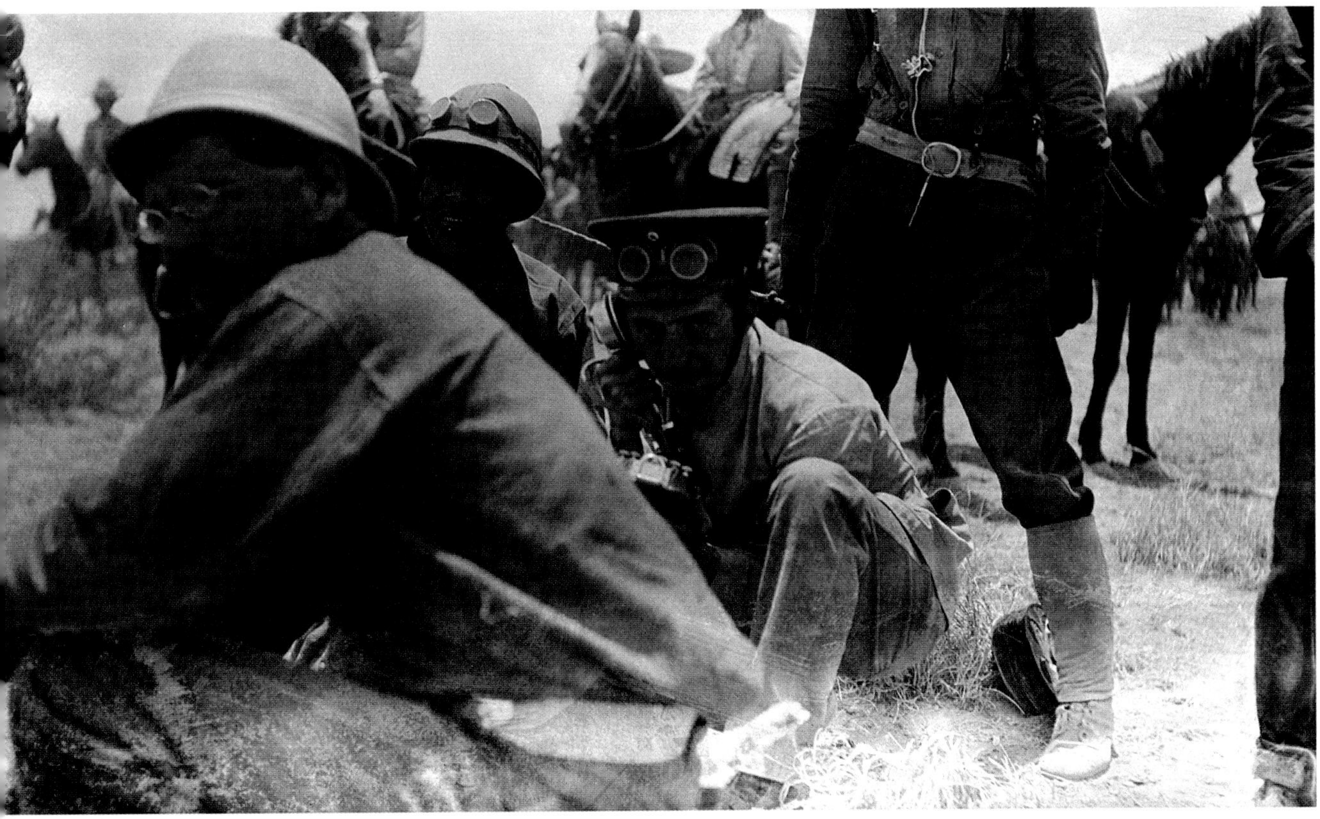

created over the previous decades."[111] Of course, the Mexican who photographed the doctor probably had never seen any Sander images; the image was more likely produced for the *nota roja*. Gruesome police reports had a long trajectory in Mexico, thanks to *El Imparcial*, and one can speculate that this photo was made with that public in mind. That newspaper made a visual critique of the rebels, publishing on its first page a lithograph created with a photo of some Orozquistas with a bottle and a guitar in Chihuahua in June 1912 (Figure 4-31).[112] Charles Harris formed his company La Rochester and extensively covered the response to Orozquismo in the north; in one photo he documented some Coahuila volunteers (perhaps dynamiters) who had joined up to fight against the insurrection (Figure 4-32).[113] The photo that Manuel Ramos took of the embrace between Pascual Orozco and Victoriano Huerta (Figure 4-33) must have given some satisfaction to the dean (and most Porfirian) of the photojournalists, as it signaled the possible end of war in the union of revolution and reaction.

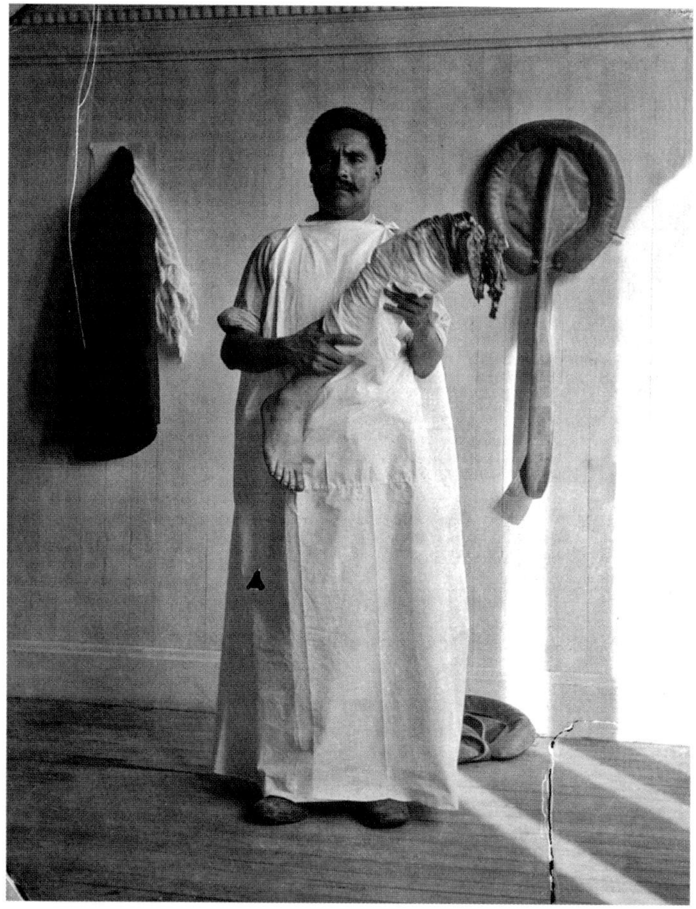

4-30. Doctor with the amputated leg of a federal soldier, Chihuahua, 1912. © Inv. #36758, Fondo Casasola, SINAFO-Fototeca Nacional del INAH.

I sense a development in Mexican photojournalism between the Maderista and the Orozquista movements. Those advances notwithstanding, one of the most intriguing images of that conflict was taken by an amateur, the doctor for Villa's División del Norte, Alemán Pérez. It could well be that the attraction of this slice of time and space, in which we see Villa at the point of being executed (Figure 4-34), resides in the unique capacity of photography to embalm "that-which-has-been."[114] The circumstances of this photo are the following: Victoriano Huerta and Pancho Villa were in a power struggle, exacerbated by the differences between a professional officer and a revolutionary; once Orozco had been defeated, Villa was no longer necessary, and Huerta found a convenient excuse to have him shot in Jiménez, Chihuahua, at the beginning of June 1912. The testimonies that serve to elucidate this incident were collected by historian Friedrich Katz. Huerta had ordered General

4-31. FACING Orozquistas with a bottle, Chihuahua, June 1912; A. Ruíz Sandoval. © Inv. #643310, Fondo Casasola, SINAFO-Fototeca Nacional del INAH.

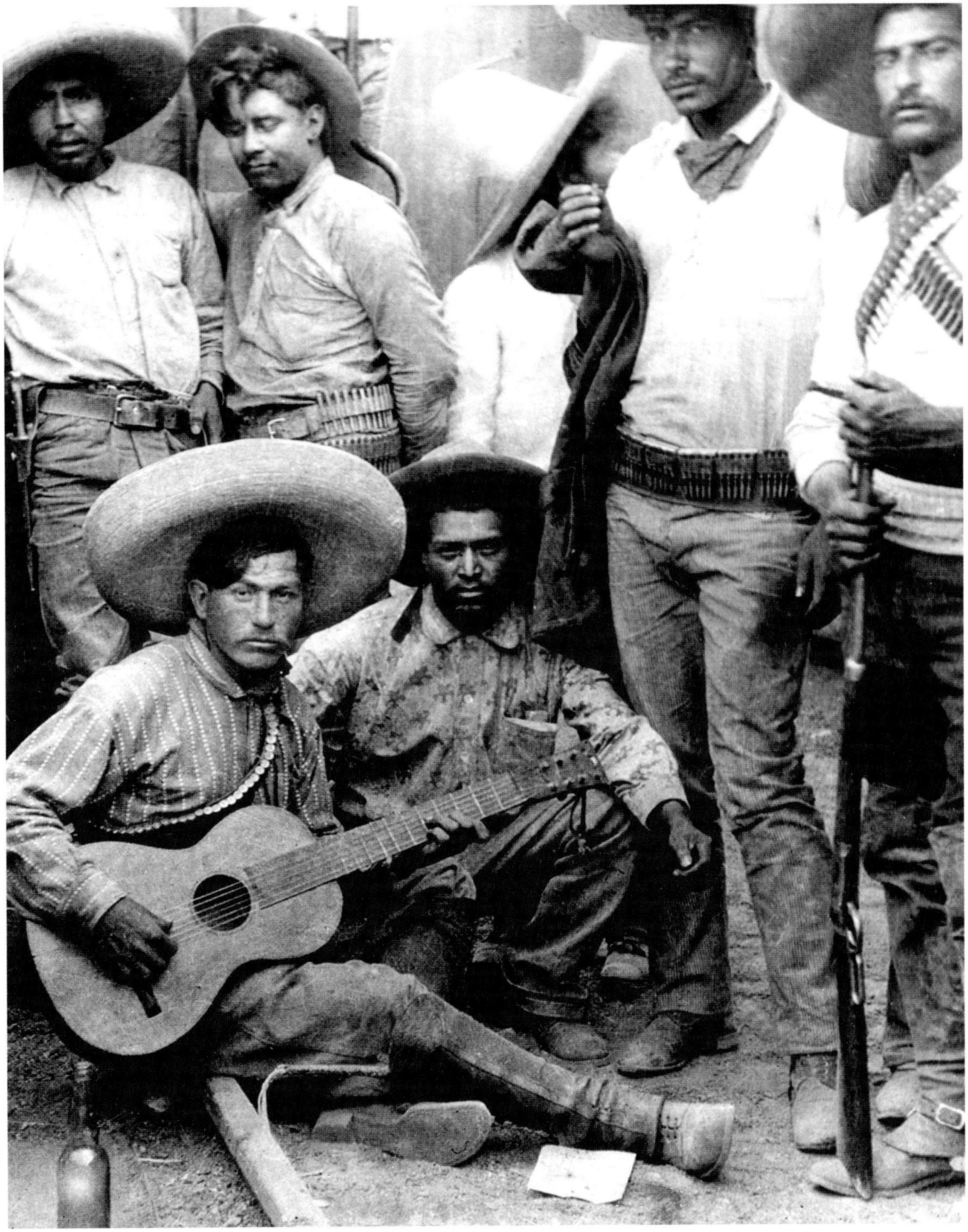

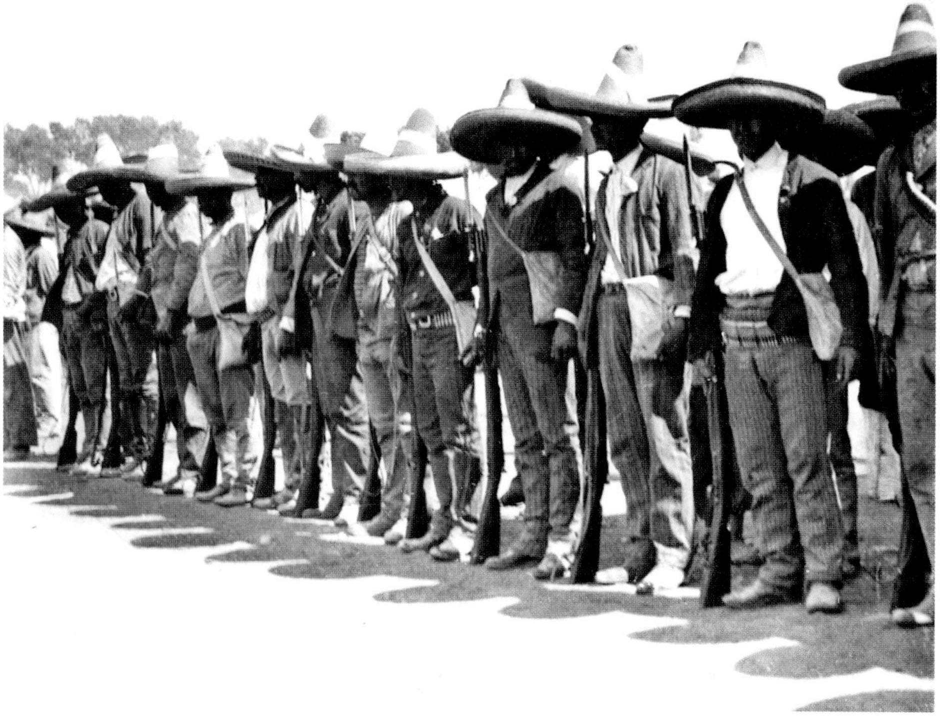

4-32. Volunteers (dynamiters?) from the state of Coahuila during the campaign against the Orozquista movement, 1912; La Rochester. © Inv. #643412, Fondo Casasola, SINAFO-Fototeca Nacional del INAH.

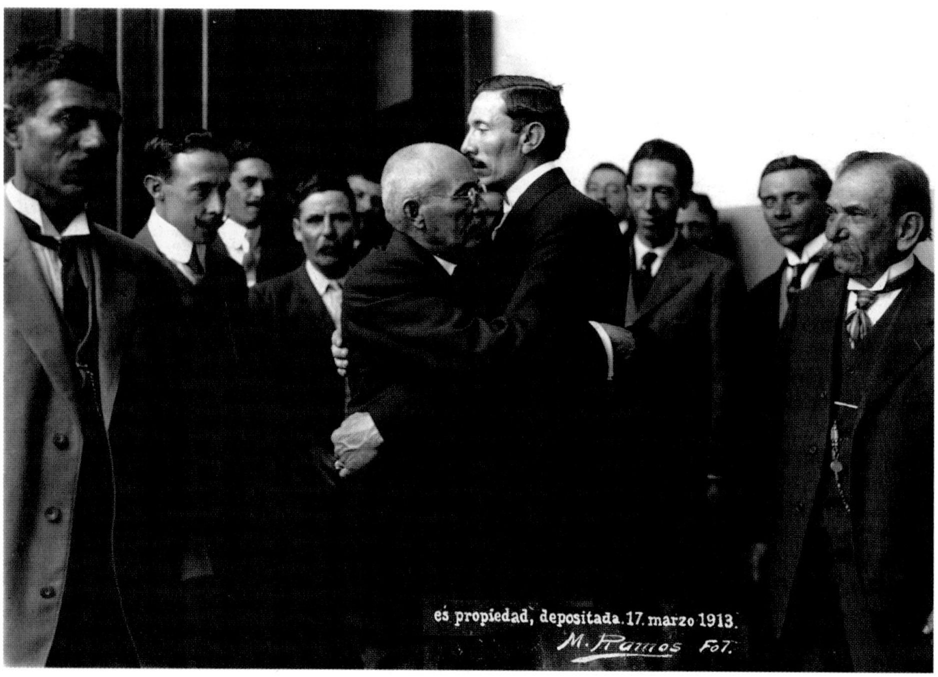

4-33. Pascual Orozco and Victoriano Huerta, Mexico City, 14 March 1913; Manuel Ramos. © Inv. #455163, Fondo Casasola, SINAFO-Fototeca Nacional del INAH.

Guillermo Rubio Navarrete to execute Villa, an order he effectively avoided carrying out; the career officer remembered, "I saw Villa kneeling and weeping, loudly begging not to be shot and to be allowed to see General Huerta. He was kneeling, holding one foot of Colonel O'Horan, and behind the group, consisting of him and Colonel Castro, was the execution squad with their arms at rest."[115] This scene must have become the object of commentaries, because Villa later made reference to it: "At the time I hardly knew whether I was weeping from mortification or from fear, as my enemies said. I leave it to the world to assess whether my tears in these supreme moments were due to cowardice or to despair at seeing that I was to be killed without knowing why."[116]

4-34. Villa at the point of being executed on the orders of Victoriano Huerta, Jiménez, Chihuahua, June 1912; Doctor Alemán Pérez (of the División del Norte). © Inv. #68170, Fondo Casasola, SINAFO-Fototeca Nacional del INAH.

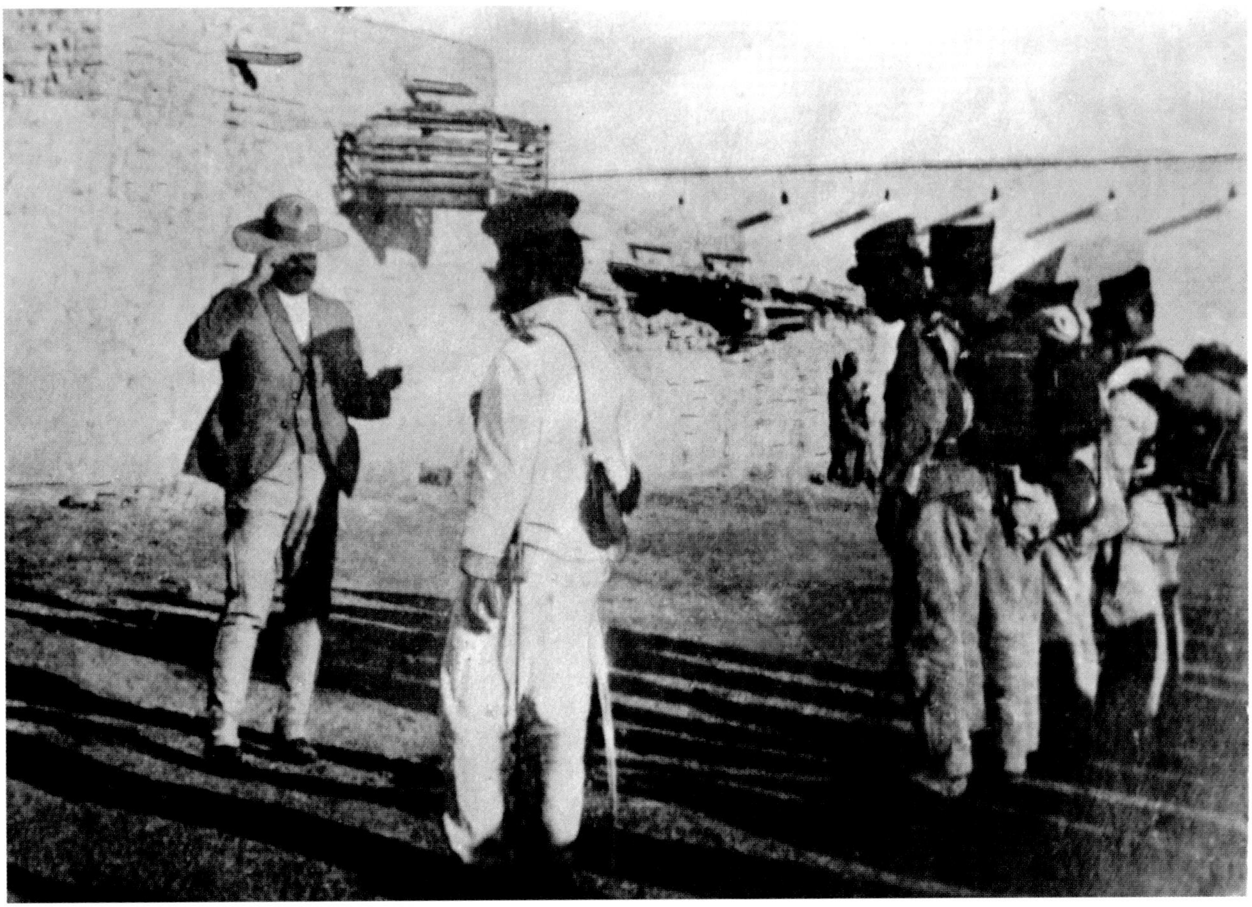

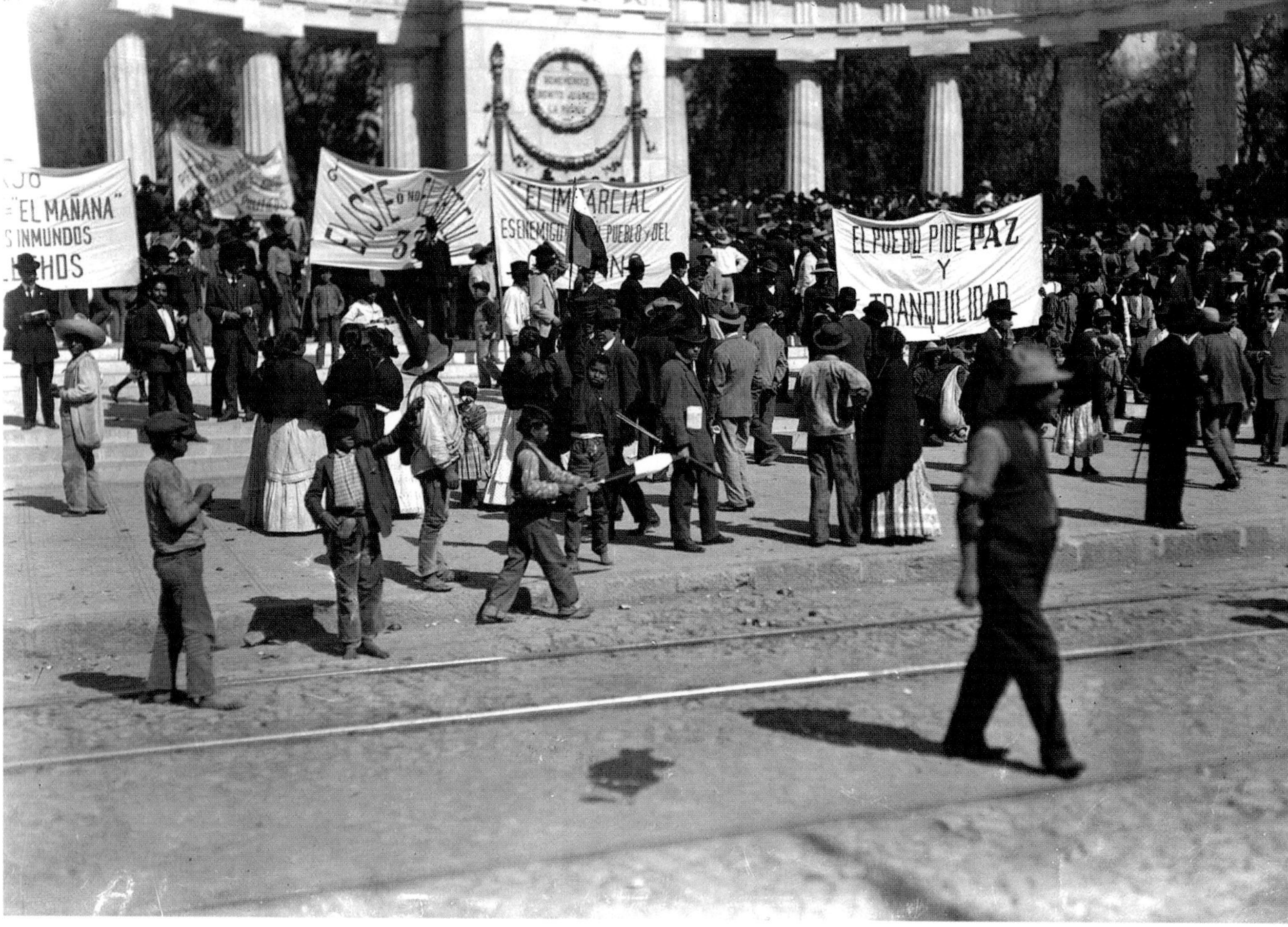

4-35. Protests against the Mexico City press for irresponsible criticism of President Francisco I. Madero, 1 January 1912. © Inv. #36982, Fondo Casasola, SINAFO-Fototeca Nacional del INAH.

Despite his triumph over Orozco, Madero seemed too weak to the (still) Porfirian press to control the new forces that threatened their privileges. Once they understood that Madero really believed in freedom of expression, they attacked him "in bitter, scurrilous and obscene terms; for the first time in Mexican history, the literate public enjoyed the spectacle not only of a free press, but also of a press mercilessly lampooning the head of state."[117] Although he was staunchly conservative, the poet Juan José Tablada advised Vice President José María Pino Suárez of the danger he and Madero faced, in the strongest of terms:

> Finally, growing more and more excited, Pino Suárez asked me if in my judgment the situation was dangerous. Without vacillating, animated by the good faith of that man and the trust he demonstrated in me, I told him that, yes, the situation was not only dangerous, but that it became more so every day, since the government seemed to tolerate the excesses of a certain press that systematically encourages the military leaders, exciting them almost to rebellion. I had hardly said this when Pino Suárez, getting up out of his seat and raising his arms to the heavens, declared, "It's clear! It's evident! I am tired of telling the president that this negligence will cost us our lives; we are going to pay for this with our heads!"[118]

The Maderistas organized to defend themselves, and the group (*porra*) led by Gustavo Madero protested against the irresponsibility of newspapers such as *El Imparcial* in a demonstration on 1 January 1912 (Figure 4-35). Nonetheless, the press would play a role in poisoning public opinion against Madero and creating the climate for a revolution that was the last thing they desired.

The Zapatista Movement and Southern Cameras

HISTORICIZING THE PHOTOGRAPHY of the Zapatista revolution required me to rectify a mistaken opinion that was left by an impression I received from a cinematic experience. Some years ago I saw the film *Memorias de un mexicano*, which contains a sequence of Emiliano Zapata and Pancho Villa seated on either side of Eulalio Gutiérrez at a long table in the National Palace's dining room during the brief period that the Conventionists occupied Mexico City.[1] It seemed obvious to me at the time: on one side, the northerner, grinning and relaxed, accustomed to the camera's gaze; on the other, the campesino who came from deep Mexico—timid, nervous, and withdrawn in front of modern media. I thought that Villa was the great publicist, and that Zapata had been ignorant of, and resistant to, the necessity of projecting his image. In one of the revolutionary icons, it is Villa who sits in the presidential chair, Zapata at his side; according to historian Ricardo Pérez Montfort, "Villa blustering and smiling, Zapata mistrustful and inhibited."[2] (See Figures E-15 and E-17.)

Over the last twenty years or so, I have been preaching about the dangers in photohistory of surrendering to the temptation of attempting psychological readings from photographs, without noticing that I myself had a prejudice caused by a camera.[3] My idea that Zapata had a limited consciousness in relation to modern media continued until the watershed study by anthropologists Blanca Jiménez and Samuel Villela demonstrated that Amando Salmerón was invited by the caudillo to become "the photographer of the revolution in the south."[4] What is even more surprising is the fact that Salmerón was not the only imagemaker to make that commitment: photographers such as Cruz Sánchez, Sara Castrejón, and a certain Hernández have appeared as other protagonists of the southern camera. Moreover, the only film made on a cause that eventually lost was *La revolución zapatista*, which celebrated that movement.[5]

It was important that the southern revolutionaries had their own visual media because they were vilified without respite in those of Mexico City. Pérez Montfort described the portrait offered of those forces: "The image of both Zapata and the Zapatistas, was full of lucubrations, aggressive speeches, epithets, and disqualifications."[6]

In the illustrated press, Zapatismo was always portrayed as the greatest enemy, and its supporters were referred to time and again as bandits, bad weeds (*malas hierbas*), and criminal hordes. According to Marion Gautreau, "Both the Zapatistas and their leader were objects of a systematic stigmatizing: the publications invariably underlined the ferocity and barbarity of the southerners, without ever mentioning their agrarian ideals or vindicating the nature of their struggle."[7] Photo historian Ariel Arnal carried out a significant study on the photographic representation generated around Zapata, concluding that "The image of the southern leader published in the press attempts to locate Emiliano Zapata within the traditional iconographical type of the bandit."[8]

The owners of the publications acted in terms of their class interests and took advantage of the metropolitan repulsion for campesinos to ensure that no favorable images of Zapatismo were published. At times, however, the government itself intervened. During the Huertista dictatorship, Gerónimo Hernández tried to register three photos of Emiliano Zapata with the governmental agency charged with author's rights in order to establish his authorship, but his petition was rejected. For that office, the problem was not plagiarism but politics: "Being that it is public and notorious that the referred Zapata is caught up in rebellion, and that the circulation of these photographs would produce an agitation to commit that very crime, which is punishable, such circulation has no licit object."[9]

One might imagine that the vision constructed by the magazines and newspapers was an expression of their tendency to be on the side of those in power, and that when the Zapatistas arrived there, things would change. As the southern army closed in on Mexico City in August of 1914, such appears to have been the case, if we were to judge by the fear expressed in the magazine *Novedades* that the press had abandoned its usual line:

> Times change: up until recently the Zapatistas, who were considered to be bandits and an emblem throughout the world of barbarity and savagery, begin to be called by adjectives that praise them. It is now written in capital letters that Emiliano Zapata is the Generalissimo of the Liberating Army of the Republic, and that his ends are *high and noble*; very soon we will have to consider these *worthy citizens to be most honorable and generous*. This is what we are made to think by a reading of the periodicals in these sad and bitter days. Those that a month ago were bloody *cabecillas*, bandits, and assassins begin to be called misters and generals.[10]

According to Pérez Montfort, a significant transition occurred in the middle of the revolution: "After 1914 the Zapatista movement was increasingly recognized until it acquired the rank of 'revolutionary.' Emiliano Zapata would stop being 'Attila' to become the 'Caudillo of the South.'"[11] Historian Samuel Brunk is in agreement with Pérez Montfort; he argues that "Between mid-1914 and mid-1915 Zapatismo was at full crest, and so was Zapata's national reputation. Poems were written for and about him, and there were so many requests for his photograph that he ran out of prints to distribute. Even the minister from Japan was said to have two such pictures on his desk."[12] Nonetheless, I believe that the racist and classist ideology of the owners of the illustrated publications expressed itself in anti-Indian and anti-campesino representations that essentially did not change until Zapata's death in 1919 permitted his entrance into the pantheon of revolutionary heroes. Arnal, for example, does not encounter any modifications in the course of the armed struggle: "Even during the period that the Conventionists were in power, the press defined the struggle against Zapatismo as the confrontation between the savage from outside and civilization as symbolized by Mexico City."[13] Gautreau, as well, asserts that the anti-Zapatista discourse only "changes radically in the 1920s"; ironically, the transformation is effected "with the aid of the same photographs" that had been employed to attack that movement, indicating, once again, photography's polysemia and the ways in which images' meanings are determined by the contexts in which they appear.[14]

There are certain fissures in the official visual ideology that give pause. Arnal has focused on some images of captured Zapatistas, noting that "Photographs of tied-up prisoners forced to pose next to their captors abounded in the illustrated press" (Figure 5-1).[15] Such a profusion makes me hypothesize that the image of the "Zapatista prisoner" could be considered a trope of the *nota roja*. Arnal compares two photos that appear to belong to this group of pictures.[16] In a photo taken, and probably directed, by Abraham Lupercio for *La Ilustración Semanal*, we see what could be a *lépero*, an urban indigent, posing as if he were a captive surrounded by his "captors" (Figure 5-2). The federalist soldiers incarnate the different corps of the armed forces—two officers from distinct army troops, a marine, and an armed civilian volunteer of the militia—in a representation of national unity, an indispensable requisite to confront the otherness of Zapatismo. Arnal compares this image of staged submission to another photo that appears to be spontaneous (Figure 5-3). The researcher never found this picture published, and he speculates that it may be because it does not provide the image required by the illustrated magazines: "In spite of his condition, the prisoner's attitude and stature imposes itself, placing him above his captors. Neither their laugh,

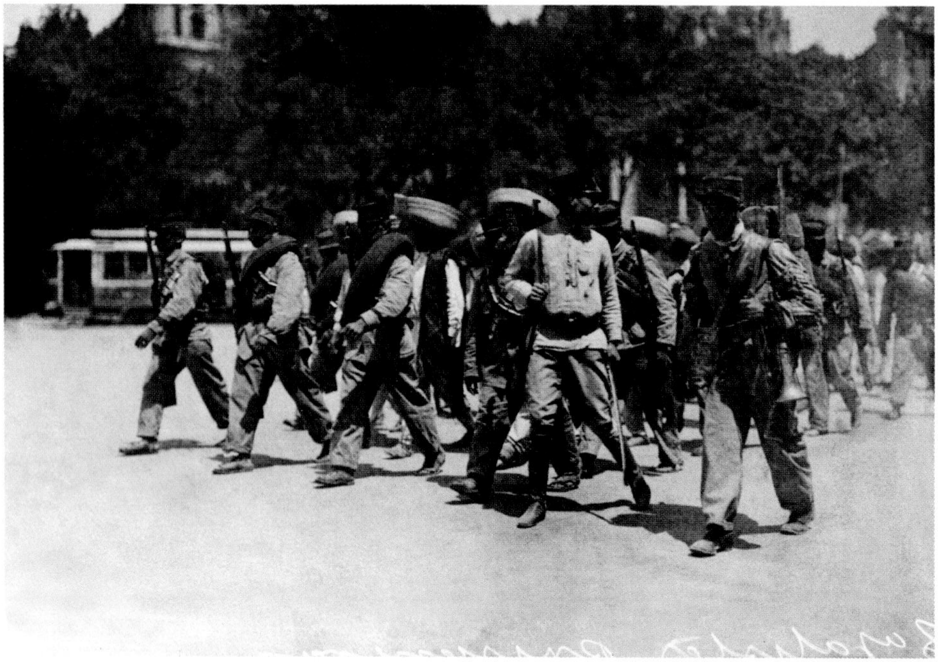

5-1. Zapatista prisoners being escorted in Mexico City, 1911. © Inv. #36324, Fondo Casasola, SINAFO-Fototeca Nacional del INAH.

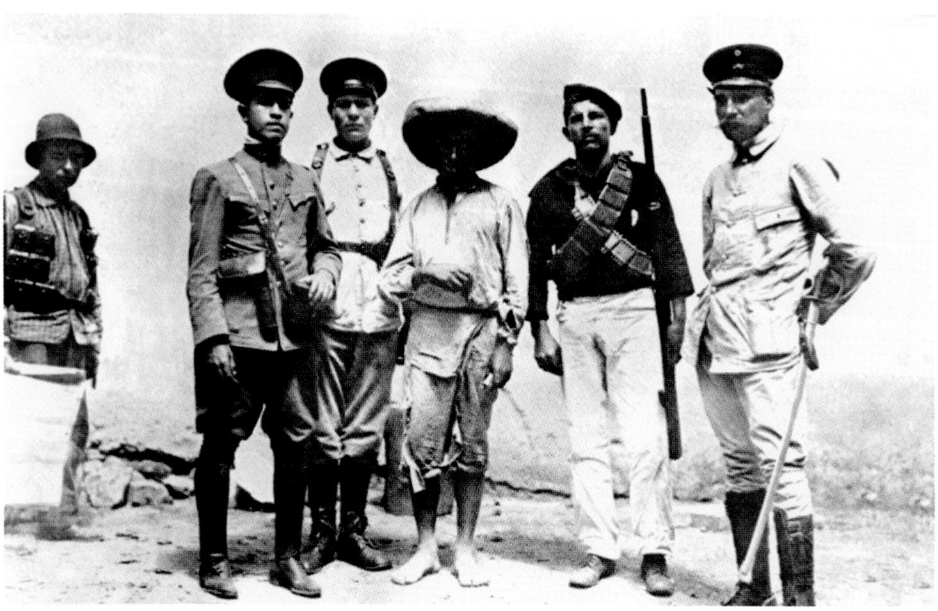

5-2. Group with a "Zapatista prisoner," Mexico City, July 1914; Abraham Lupercio, *La Ilustración Semanal*, 27 July 1914.

nor the rope that ties him, nor the clothing that is much poorer than that of those who show him as a trophy, can intimidate the gaze he launches at the camera."[17]

Another image that offers the possibility of being a message outside of the official line is one of terrified children (Figure 5-4). The magazine *Novedades* attempted to determine the reading of this photo by accompanying it with a reference to "the Zapatista bandits executed in the same town in which so many misdeeds were committed."[18] According to Gautreau, the illustrated press recurrently exhibited Zapatista cadavers "without much reserve on the part of the editors."[19] Nonetheless, there is a

5-3. Zapatista prisoner, Mexico City, ca. 1911. © Inv. #6031, Fondo Casasola, SINAFO-Fototeca Nacional del INAH.

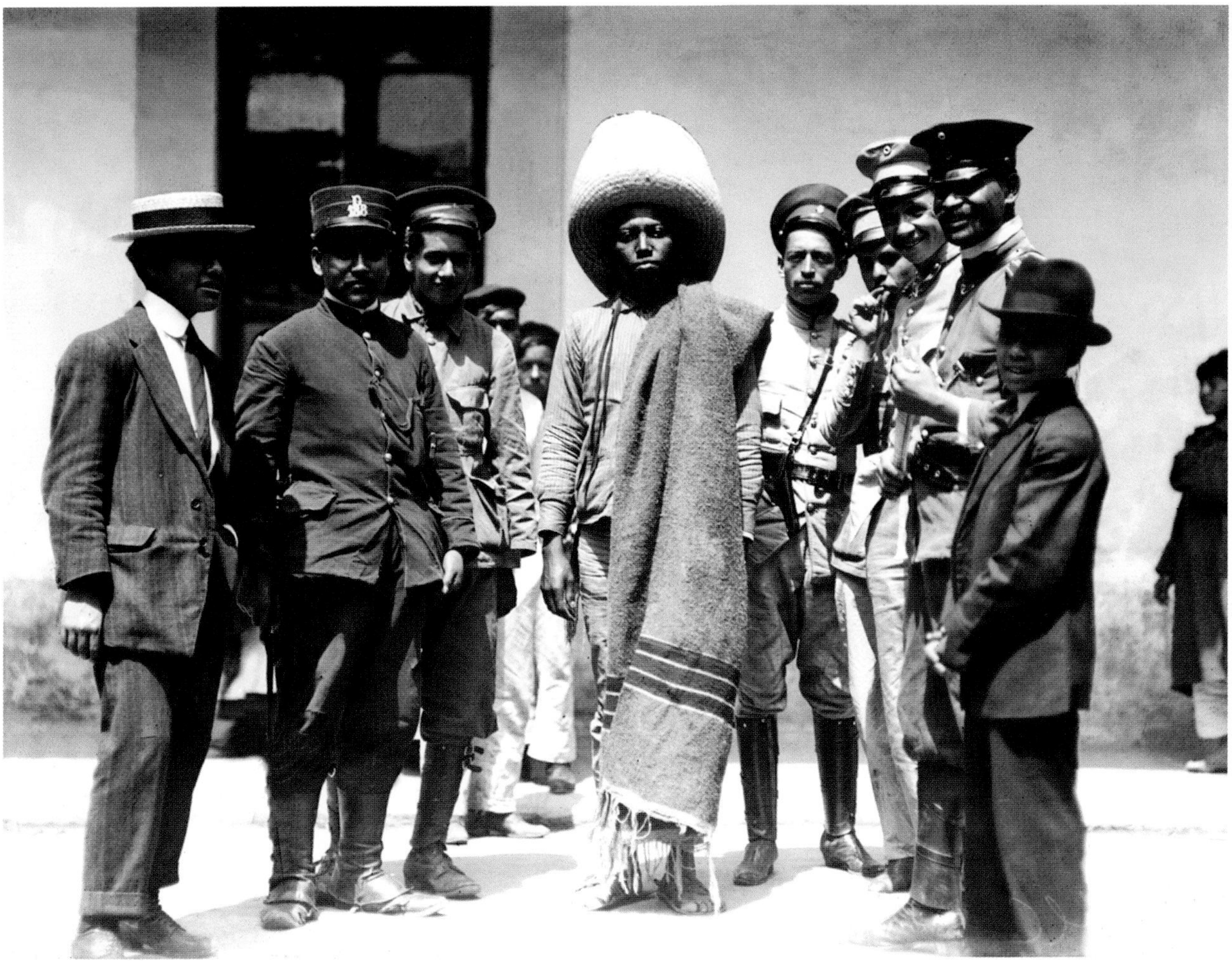

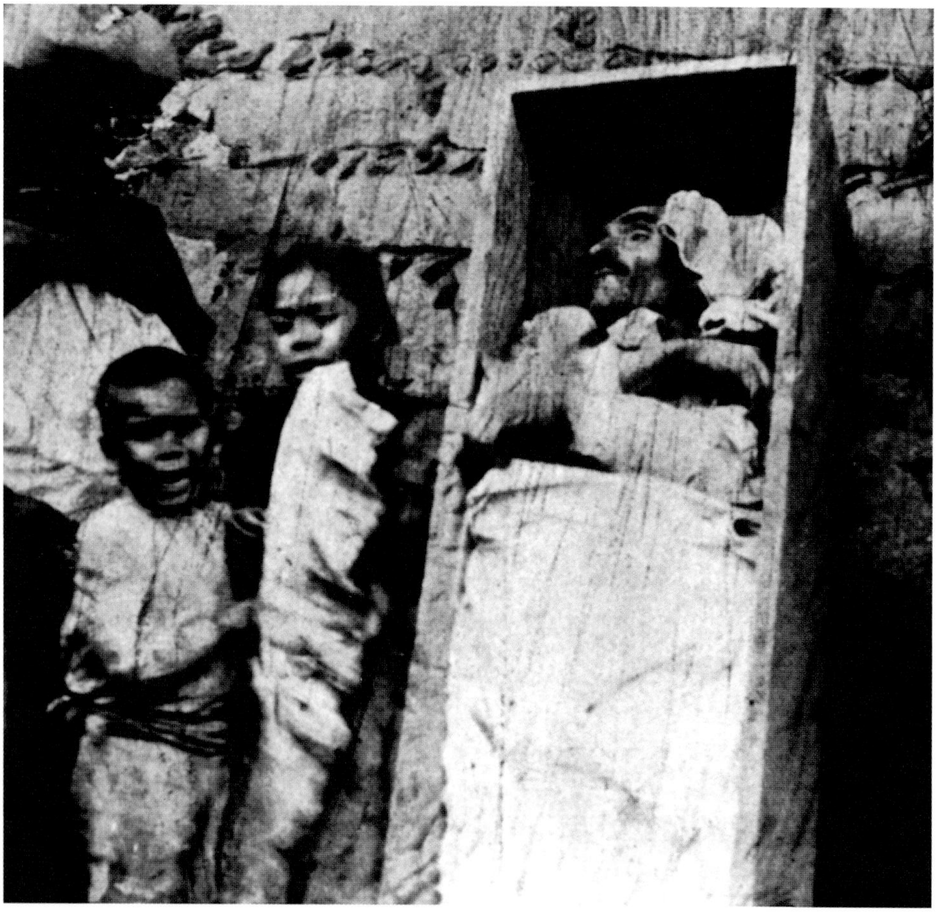

5-4. Children sobbing next to executed Zapatistas, Ayotzingo, Morelos, January 1913; Samuel Tinoco, *Novedades*, 22 January 1913. © Inv. #63752 (detail), Fondo Casasola, SINAFO-Fototeca Nacional del INAH.

disjuncture between the magazine's cutline and Samuel Tinoco's rendering, which catches the children in a scene that we are today very accustomed to seeing in photos from Vietnam, Yugoslavia, Iraq, or any other unfortunate part of the world, but which is unique, in my experience, within the photography of the Mexican Revolution. It is almost impossible to imagine that Tinoco could have remained immune before the scene of the children sobbing, their faces full of terror, next to their father's body; the boy's gaze beseeches compassion. It is better to conceive of this photo as an attempt to humanize the perception of Zapatistas among the metropolitan public than think that the anti-Zapatista prejudice of the city's photojournalists was it so enrooted that it would not permit them to see with their hearts.[20]

According to the illustrated press, journalists should have had little reason to feel sympathy for the Zapatistas since they were apparently the only revolutionary group that attacked reporters. There had been a brief honeymoon between the capital's media and the Zapatistas, captured in a photo of a bunch of photojournalists and rebels during Madero's tour of Morelos and Guerrero in June 1911 (Figure 5-5). By August of 1912, however, the differences of class and culture had been reestablished, and from the struggle between the new Maderista government and Zapatismo arose the case of the El Jilguero interview. Agustín Víctor Casasola described it fourteen years afterward: "Journalistic fever had made reporters search for new sensations, and led them to attempt to interview Emiliano Zapata in his den."[21] Among the journalists

5-5. Southern revolutionaries in a group portrait with photojournalists and cameras, Morelos, 1911. © Inv. #5710, Fondo Casasola, SINAFO-Fototeca Nacional del INAH.

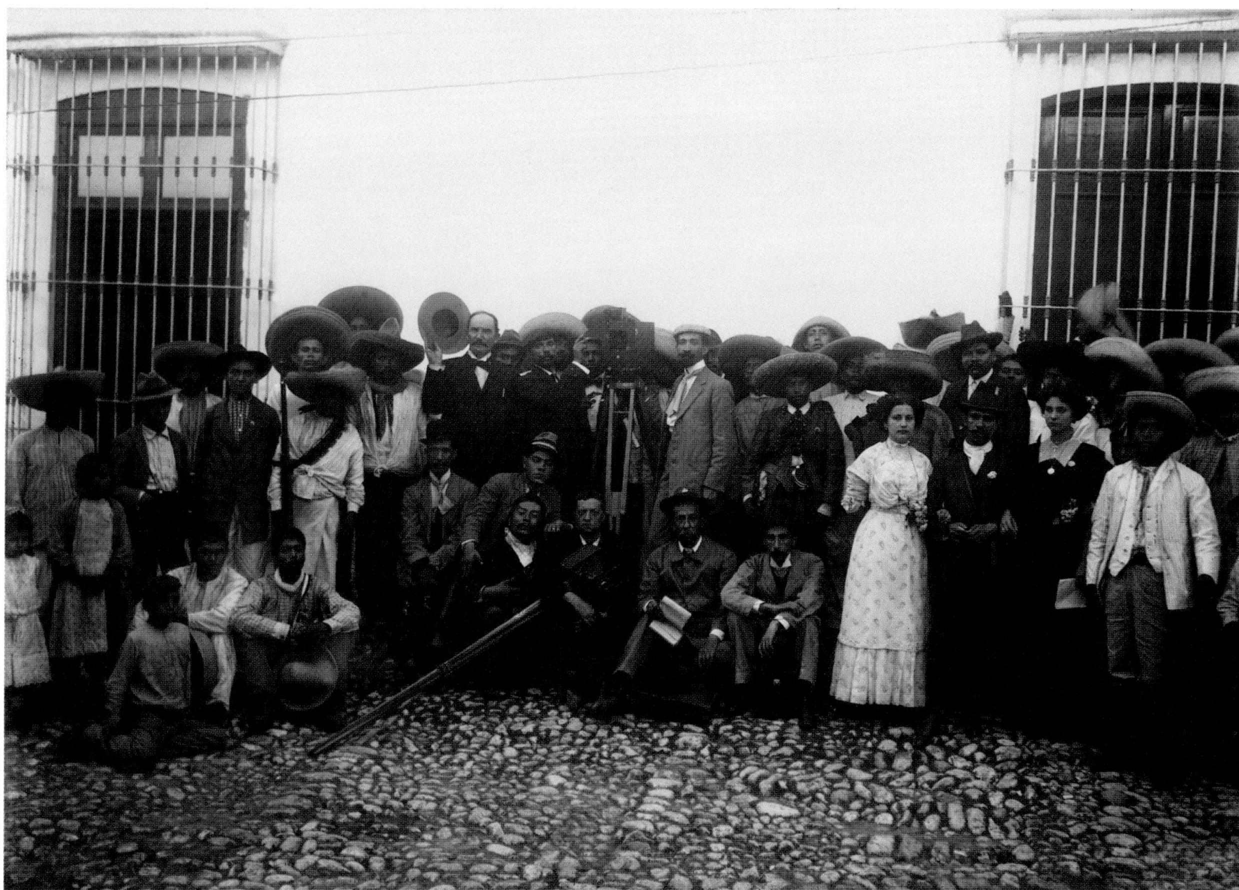

who went to Morelos with this intention were photographers Agustín Víctor Casasola, José Soriano, and Gerónimo Hernández.

They arrived in El Jilguero, and, by the quantity of photos of this encounter that have survived, it is clear that they felt the liberty to document it in images that show the Zapatistas and the journalists interacting, even relaxing at an informal rodeo.[22] At least one photo was taken in which they appear with Zapata: him seated with his escort, and them standing behind.[23] The visual evidence notwithstanding, Agustín Víctor painted a very different picture, saying that the caudillo, "Indignant, answered that he did not want to even see the journalists, much less receive them; that they should retire from the camp immediately if they didn't want a scare. The threat was made in such a form that they decided to get out of that dangerous place as fast as they could."[24] As they were leaving Zapatista territory, they ran into other members of the press that were on their way to interview Zapata, among them Ignacio Herrerías, Casasola's cousin, who had interviewed Madero in April 1911; "Despite our indications that they should not go on, and full of enthusiasm and pride, the journalists continued on the train."[25]

That train was attacked by Zapatistas, and three journalists died: Herrerías, Rivera (a photographer), and Humberto León Strauss. Portraits of the "press martyrs" appeared in the magazine *Artes y Letras*, and the text reveals the way in which Zapatistas were not even accorded recognition as human beings: "The barbarous death, the vile assassination, ended our colleagues' lives in an insolent cruelty like that of Zulus and cannibals. Civilization has cried in all its voices: the enemy is not political, nor social, it is not even human; it belongs in a zoo."[26] It is telling that Agustín Víctor took the train attack personally: "Zapata prepared that for us. The attack was against us, not those boys."[27] For Zapatista Gildardo Magaña, it was simply an "unfortunate incident of war."

> The train was attacked with fire directed toward the car of the escorts, who answered back with their own bullets. Who could have known, in those moments of tremendous excitement, when the rifles' roar mixed with curses, that three of the individuals who were among the soldiers were three journalists that attacked the revolution, but from the columns of their metropolitan dailies? How many times did those same newspapers, for which they worked, cruelly attack the revolution and disfigure the facts and mitigate the crimes committed by the federal soldiers. . . . And, we never called them savages![28]

In 1913, *La Semana Ilustrada* published a whole page about the "Assault of a train with journalists by Zapata's hordes," in which it described how that "criminal horde treated the journalists in a brutal and infamous way."[29] Nonetheless, a year later another case of relations between journalists and Zapatistas came up that was as complex as the El Jilguero interview attempt. *La Ilustración Semanal* recounted the drama of "Those who stared down the Mauser's barrel" in 1914.[30] One of the leading photojournalists in this period, Abraham Lupercio, was captured with other members of the press: "These four brave colleagues ventured into the Zapatista camp, where they were apprehended and taken to San Nicolás Totolapa to be shot; they escaped through diplomacy." The full-page photo shows the seven Zapatistas who captured the journalists, whose portraits appear in four ovals above (Figure 5-6). We are, once again, in front

5-6. Journalists and Zapatistas, San Nicolás Totolapa, August 1914; Abraham Lupercio, *La Ilustración Semanal*, 3 August 1914.

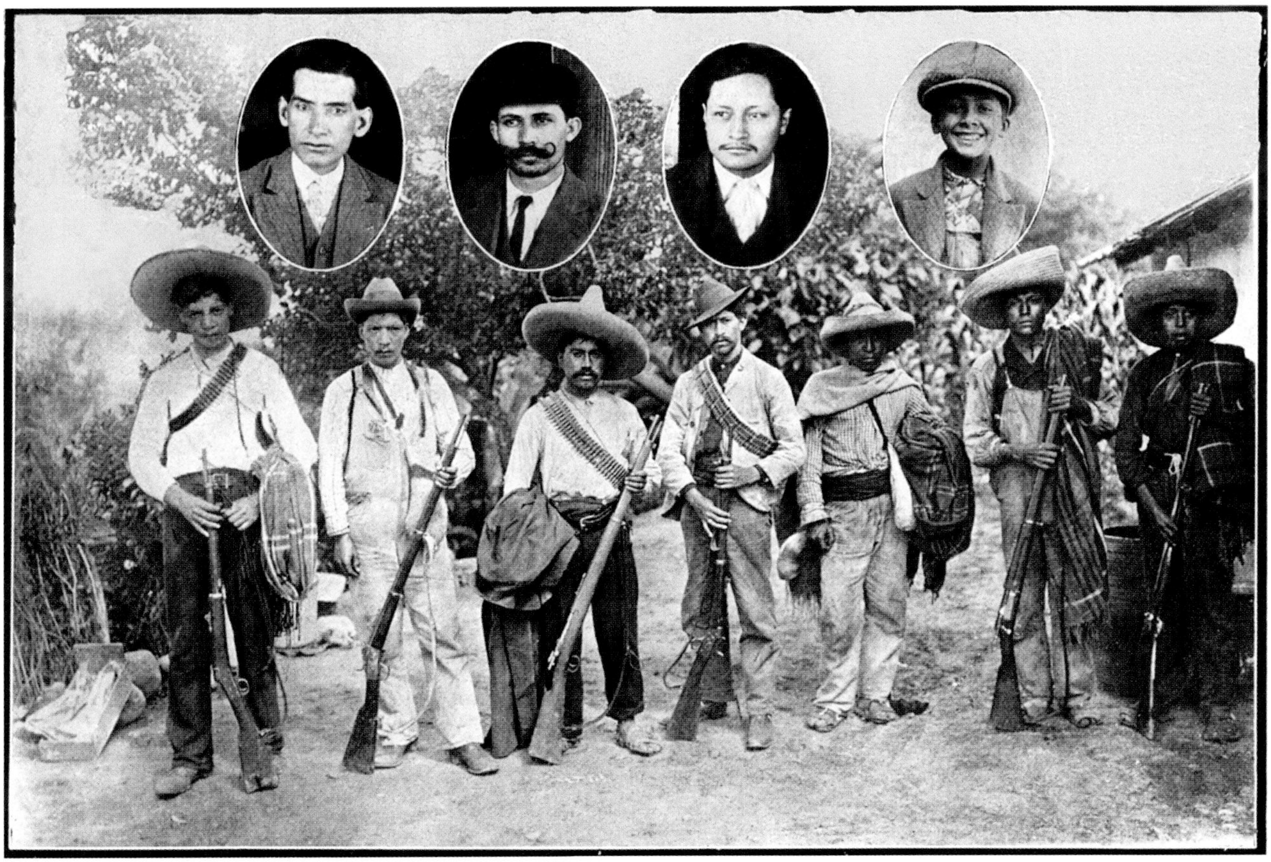

of photography's polysemia and its insistent documentalism. Although the mediatic table is set to make this another story of the Zapatistas' barbarity, the fact that they pose tranquilly for Lupercio personalizes them; rather than seeing them as *types* of savages, the camera reveals their individuality and, most important, their humanity.

Arnal comments that "The Mexico City press rarely published images of Zapatistas in their territory."[31] According to him, this is due to two reasons: on one hand, "not just any photographer was capable of entering the Zapatista camp to make a reportage"; on the other, there was always the possibility of censorship if "the enemy was shown as he really was or, better said, as he—the enemy—would like to have appeared."[32] If Lupercio's purpose was that of representing the Zapatistas in such a way as to change the predisposition of the metropolitan mind that perceived them as savages—as "that 'other,' the indomitable, vicious, and armed campesino-Indian"[33]—is still unknown. One might suspect that Lupercio was left with a good impression of the Zapatistas since they freed the journalists in the moment they identified themselves. This detail is not mentioned in the magazines, but a recent book narrates that "When Lupercio explained the true reason behind his presence, the revolutionaries desisted from the execution, posing afterwards for photographs."[34] Both this photo and Tinoco's of the sobbing children offer intriguing possibilities for alternative readings.

Among the official photos of Zapatismo, we find some taken literally from the federal side; one or another might be of combat. That which has been published frequently, always attributed to Casasola, is one about which we have limited information, but which is of the contradictory type that opens up interesting questions (Figure 5-7). The picture has been used to illustrate different periods, but it was evidently made in Jonacatepec, Morelos, 18 August 1912, and published two days later in *El Imparcial*.[35] It thus served to illustrate the offensive of the Maderista government against the Zapatistas in the precise moment that the press was ferociously attacking that movement for the deaths of Herrerías, Rivera, and Strauss. To our eyes, the image is clearly directed: it could have resulted from a collaboration between the press and the army to stage a media event, or it could have been a training exercise between uniformed soldiers and others dressed in campesino clothing (or campesinos recruited for the narrative tableau vivant). The fact is that nobody would expose themselves in combat as the participants are doing for the photo, above all guerrillas whose survival depends on their capacity to hide.

What moves me to interrogate this photo is the text that accompanies it, which the newspaper evidently thought necessary to include so that the public would believe it was real. The photo's cutline stresses its veracity—"A valuable photograph, taken at the precise moment of combat between Zapatistas and federals"—and provides a lengthy narrative that looks like a dispatch sent from the front: it describes the battle (and victory) of greatly outnumbered federal troops over Zapatistas and, above all, narrates the situation of the photographer, engineer León Salinas, whose purpose "was to obtain an instant photo for *El Imparcial*."

> Jonacatepec, 18 August 1912, 20 federals against 200 Zapatistas. Francisco Mendoza and Felipe Neri against the 37th under the command of Captain Emilio Guillemín. Photo by Engineer León Salinas. The Zapatistas draw near: toward the southeast and among the brambles you can see some silhouettes of a compact group of armed individuals, with their cartridge belts, their enormous sombreros, and their rifles ready for combat. Señor Salinas placed his camera over the ground [i.e., on a tripod] when the first shot was fired. . . . Instantaneous: two instant photos were obtained, one of them good, in a relatively short period of time, because he had just set up the camera when a bullet hit a rock near it. That made him leave off the enterprise, and after two hours of fire the battle ceased with victory cries of the triumphant federal soldiers.[36]

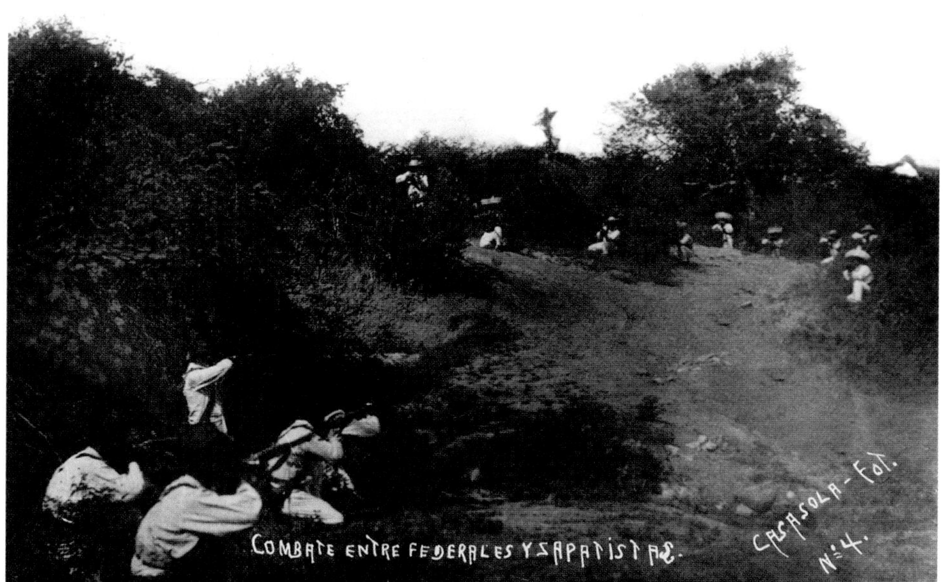

5-7. Military exercise (or a staged media event) involving federal soldiers and Zapatistas (or federal soldiers dressed as Zapatistas), Morelos, 1912; León Salinas. © Inv. #643135, Fondo Casasola, SINAFO-Fototeca Nacional del INAH.

The text (above all, in its entirety) could well be the longest narrative about a photographic act during the revolution that was published in a periodical of the period. What is its purpose? Like movies that begin with "Based on a true story," a photo that requires a long text to legitimate it is particularly suspicious. Perhaps, as Arnal suggests, it was an idea of Capitan Guillemín, who collaborated with the photographer and/or reporter to make an essay that would promote him.[37] Nonetheless, the press's interest was surely other. I believe that the journalists wanted to revenge themselves mediatically for the deaths of their colleagues, and that periodicals wanted to augment sales by putting a good combat photo—of which there were few—accompanied with a front-page report of a victory direct from the battlefield. Saying that the "instants" were made by an amateur such as Salinas adds to their realism, when in fact they seem to have been made by an experienced photojournalist.[38]

So much effort to make credible the image leads me to ask: Was *El Imparcial*'s public of such visual sophistication as to require it? If this is so, how can we explain that other publications such as *El Mundo Ilustrado* and *La Ilustración Semanal* dedicated covers to photos of soldiers clumsily posed, shooting at the enemy in the midst of scenes containing magueys and the national flag (see Figure 6-29). Salinas's photo and the text also represent a challenge to the notion that there is a lineal development of visual literacy, a growing sophistication that produces changes in codes of realism. In 1912, this photo evidently required a long explanation; today, scholars with experience in utilizing visual sources continue to publish it as if it had been taken in the eye of the hurricane of combat.[39]

One of the few photos made during the Mexican Revolution that could be of combat is of federal troops who appear to be charging against the Zapatistas (Figure 5-8); if so, it is an exceptional image for its time because it appears that few combat photos were taken in World War I.[40] Now, there is no evidence that this is not an training exercise, but the poor composition, the elements that enter from beyond the frame, and the fact of being so close to the troops in action give the impression that the photo was taken under difficult conditions. Only years later would it occur to photojournalists to imitate the crudeness of spontaneous photos by shooting "slightly out of focus" in order to make them look like they were taken in combat.[41] The picture is an anomaly in the photography of the Mexican Revolution because the photos to which we are accustomed—of exercises—have been taken at greater distances and with much better compositions. The fact that it is identified in the *Historia gráfica de la Revolución Mexicana* as being from one particular place, Amecameca, indicates that it was published initially in relation to fighting in that region.[42] Its appearance in the *Historia gráfica* attributes it implicitly to Agustín Víctor Casasola, but the negative in the Fototeca Nacional—showing the original picture pinned to the wall with tacks to photograph it—makes it obvious that he reproduced the photo from a periodical, and from thence took the identification. Knowing who made the photo could provide a clue about photojournalism in this period and coverage of the revolution. Ignacio Gutiérrez has asserted that Agustín Víctor and/or Miguel took photos in Morelos during 1912 of battles between federal troops and Zapatistas, but this was not one of them.[43]

Even when we don't know who took them, photos still provide details of material and social aspects of the war between the Zapatistas and the federal forces. The difference in armament is evident on comparing an image of the federal artillery (Figure 5-9) with one of a poor Zapatista cannon (Figure 5-10). It is difficult to know the

5-8. Federal soldiers attacking the Zapatistas, Amecameca, 1911. © Inv. #64398, Fondo Casasola, SINAFO-Fototeca Nacional del INAH.

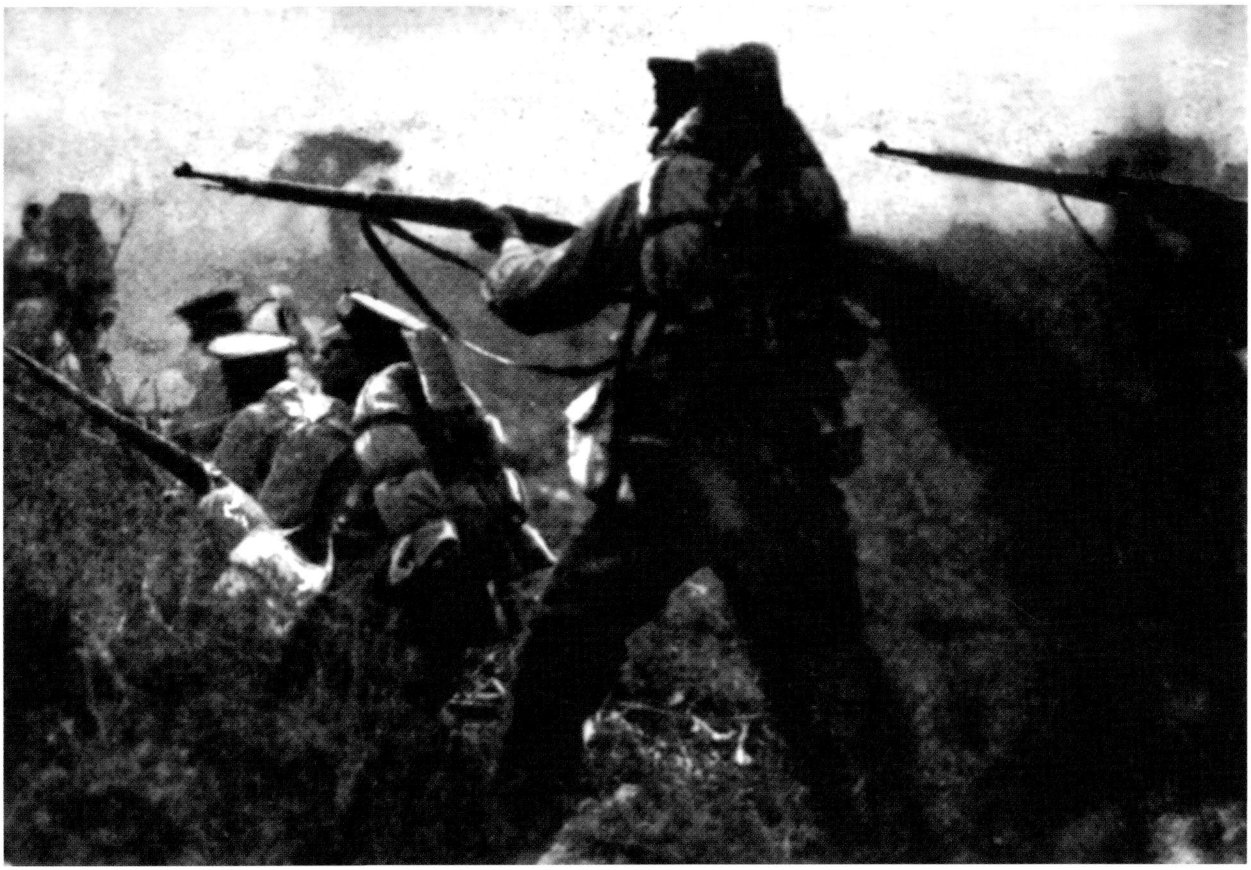

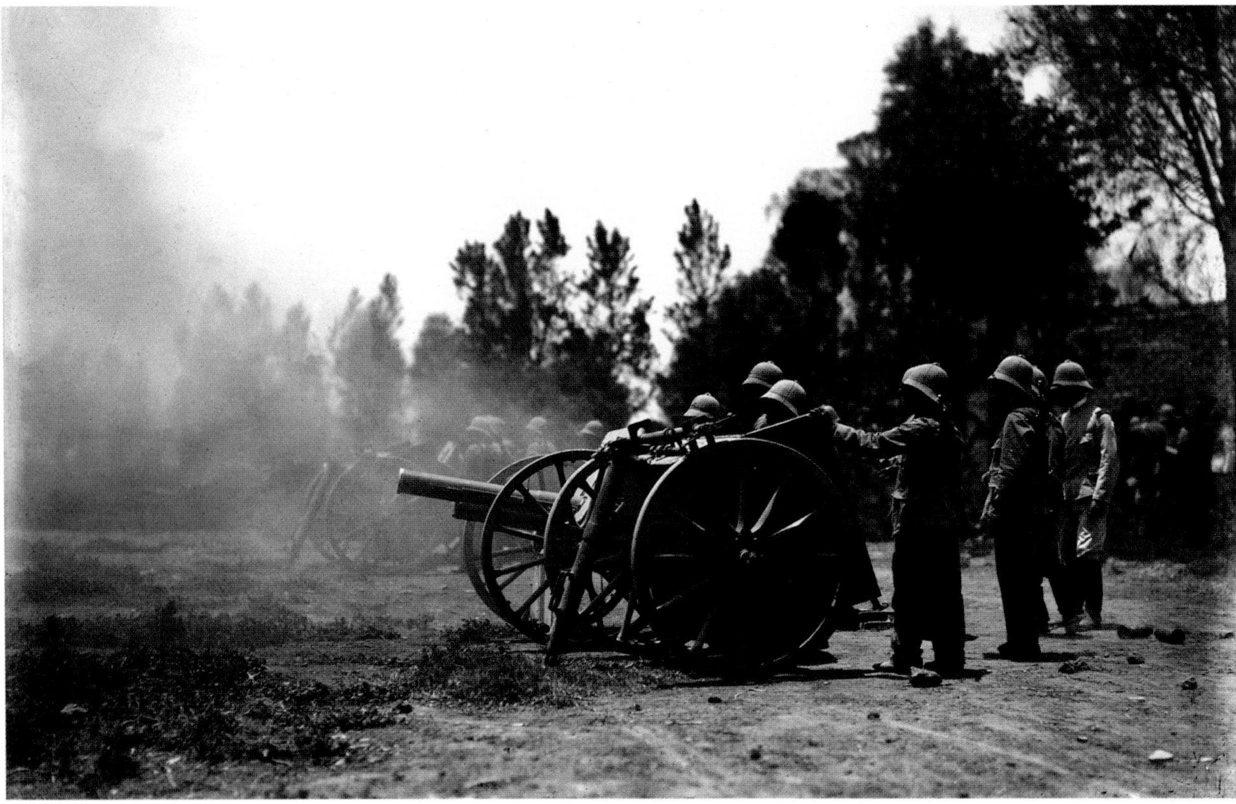

5-9. Federal artillery against the Zapatistas, Morelos, 1912. © Inv. #36839, Fondo Casasola, SINAFO-Fototeca Nacional del INAH.

reason why federal officers, dressed in civilian clothes, and a Zapatista general, Jesús Gil, found themselves in the train station of San Lázaro in January 1912.[44] The most probable explanation is that the image belongs to the trope of "Zapatista prisoner" that was plentiful in the capital's press. The cannon had presumably been captured in the war against the Zapatistas that began in November 1911 and was being taken to Mexico City. Perhaps it is shown as part of a media event to document the successes of the federal army, but there is no public present, and it is not clear why the officers are dressed as civilians if the idea was to visually celebrate the army. The presence of the Zapatista general is equally enigmatic since he ought to be accompanied by captors identifiable as such by their arms and uniforms (and their arrogance). The photo's semantic debility permits us to see it as a demonstration of federal victory or as a document of the enormous inequality of the resources available to the Zapatistas and the federal army.

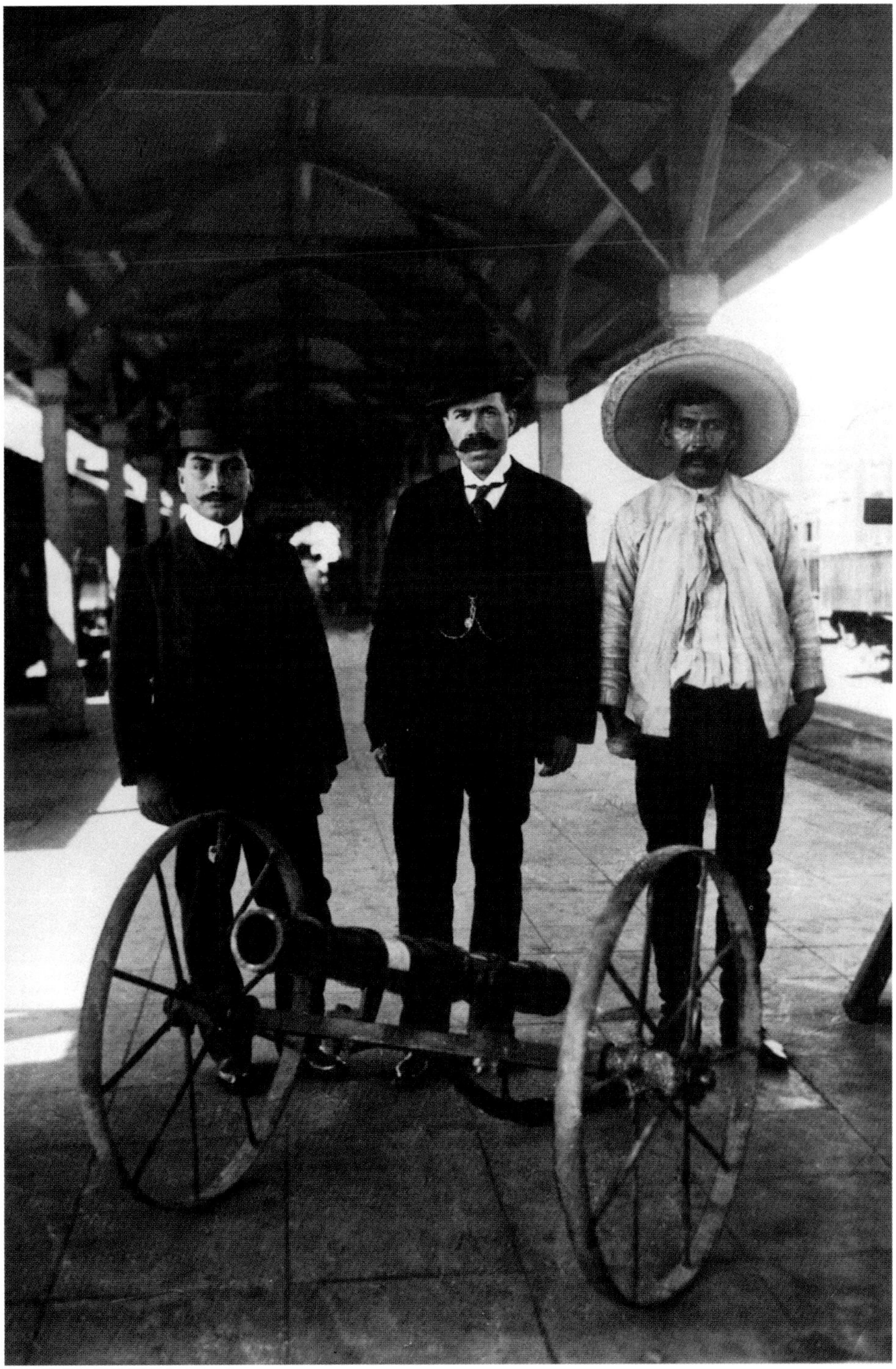

5-10. Zapatista cannon and (*left to right*) Major Edmundo Bazán, Colonel Eduardo Reyes, and Zapatista general Jesús Gil on the patio of the San Lázaro train station, Mexico City, January 1912. © Inv. #186448, Fondo Casasola, SINAFO-Fototeca Nacional del INAH.

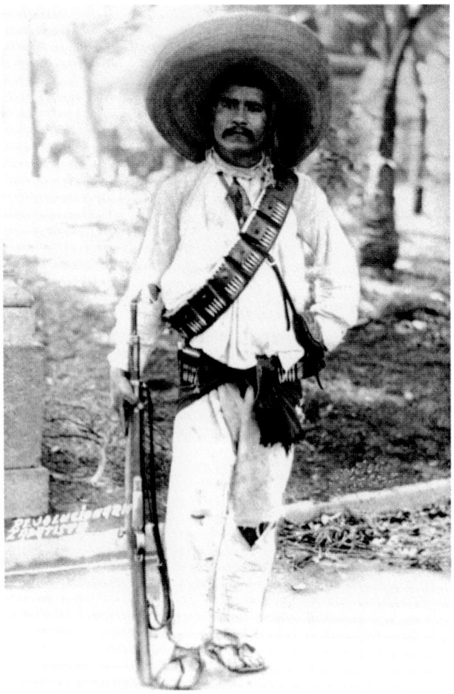

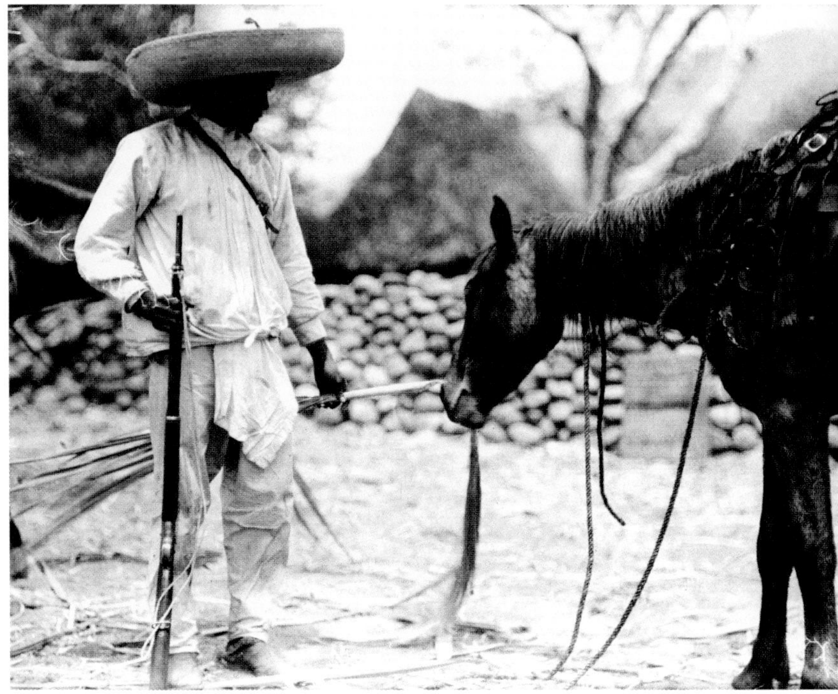

5-11. LEFT Zapatista, ca. 1915. © Inv. #4930, Fondo Casasola, SINAFO-Fototeca Nacional del INAH.

5-12. RIGHT Zapatista feeding his horse, Morelos, ca. 1914. © Inv. #5929, Fondo Casasola, SINAFO-Fototeca Nacional del INAH.

Even when we find a Zapatista with a modern weapon, as in the image of a guerrilla armed with a bolt-action, clip-loading rifle that appears to be the Steyr-Mannlicher carbine that certain Constitutionalist soldiers carried (see Figure 8-24 below), the worn-out clothing and sandals document the asymmetry of the forces (Figure 5-11). The picture of a Zapatista feeding his horse presents us with one of the most mundane and indispensable details of war, incarnated in Napoleon's saying, "An army marches on its stomach" (Figure 5-12). Aside from being a social document, it represents the Zapatista as a human being in the midst of a generous act; for that reason, it may have been taken by a photographer for that side.

The Zapatista imagemaker about whom we have the most information is Amando Salmerón, member of a photographic dynasty founded by his father, Protasio Salmerón, in Chilapa, Guerrero.[45] Beginning as a young man in the paternal studio, Amando slowly replaced Protasio; by 1910 the business was his. He made officialist photos of Porfirio Diaz's visit to Chilpancingo, and of the festivities for the centennial of independence with Governor Damián Flores. However, it was a moment to explore the possibilities of resistance, and Salmerón entered as a correspondent of *El*

Tiempo, a moderate critic of the Díaz regime. He began to express his true sympathies in the studio photograph he made of Eucaria Apreza, "The hero of the revolution in Guerrero and a symbol of feminine participation in the explosion of the southern revolution."[46] He photographed Apreza with a newspaper in hand to represent her as a person who stayed informed about national events. According to Villela, she belonged to "an anti-reelectionist club, had personal contact with Madero and the Serdáns in Puebla, and aided the first uprising in Chilapa."[47] Salmerón soon found himself photographing campesinos in open rebellion, such as the celebration of the taking of Chilapa by the Ramírez brothers in April 1911. With the triumph of Maderismo, the photographer dedicated himself to making portraits of the new rulers, such as the representatives in the Twenty-second Constitutional Congress and "Don Eladio Miranda, first Maderista municipal president in Chilapa, with the new leaders, officers, and countrymen celebrating the triumph of the Maderista revolution."[48]

Following Huerta's overthrow of Madero, Salmerón lost no time in aligning himself with the Carrancista and Zapatista opposition. He photographed Julián Blanco and others who followed the Constitutionalist cause, but his heart was Zapatista. He made many images of the leaders and ordinary soldiers posing both in his studio and on "real" stages, among them a Zapatista wedding celebrated in the patio of a house and the court-martial of a Huertista.[49] Salmerón's proclivity for the pose—and the collaboration of the Zapatistas with his photographic project—can be appreciated in the images of troops formed for his camera, sometimes with bows and arrows.[50] Some spontaneous photos by Salmerón exist, among them one of a prisoner on his way to be executed and another of some affluent citizens led by Bishop Campos y Ángeles fleeing the theater of operations (Salmerón described them as "capitalists" in the title he put on the photo).[51] However, his artificial images of "combat" indicate that his conception of documentary realism (or his experience on the battlefield) was not very developed; he placed the soldiers on top of one another in positions that would never occur in reality.[52] Nonetheless, Zapata recognized his commitment and his utility to the cause; their friendship is demonstrated in the dedications inscribed on the photographs' backs by the leader, as well as the .30-30 carbine he gave to Salmerón.

The photographer made portraits of the caudillo on several occasions, among them one on horseback (Figure 5-13); although there are many photos of Zapata mounted, very few are portraits. It was not unusual for Zapata to have his portrait made, and several photographers did so, including Abraham Lupercio, Heliodoro J. Gutiérrez, and Antonio Garduño, something that, in itself, demonstrates his consciousness of the medium's worth. In all of his portraits he is dressed as a *charro* (a Mexican horseman),

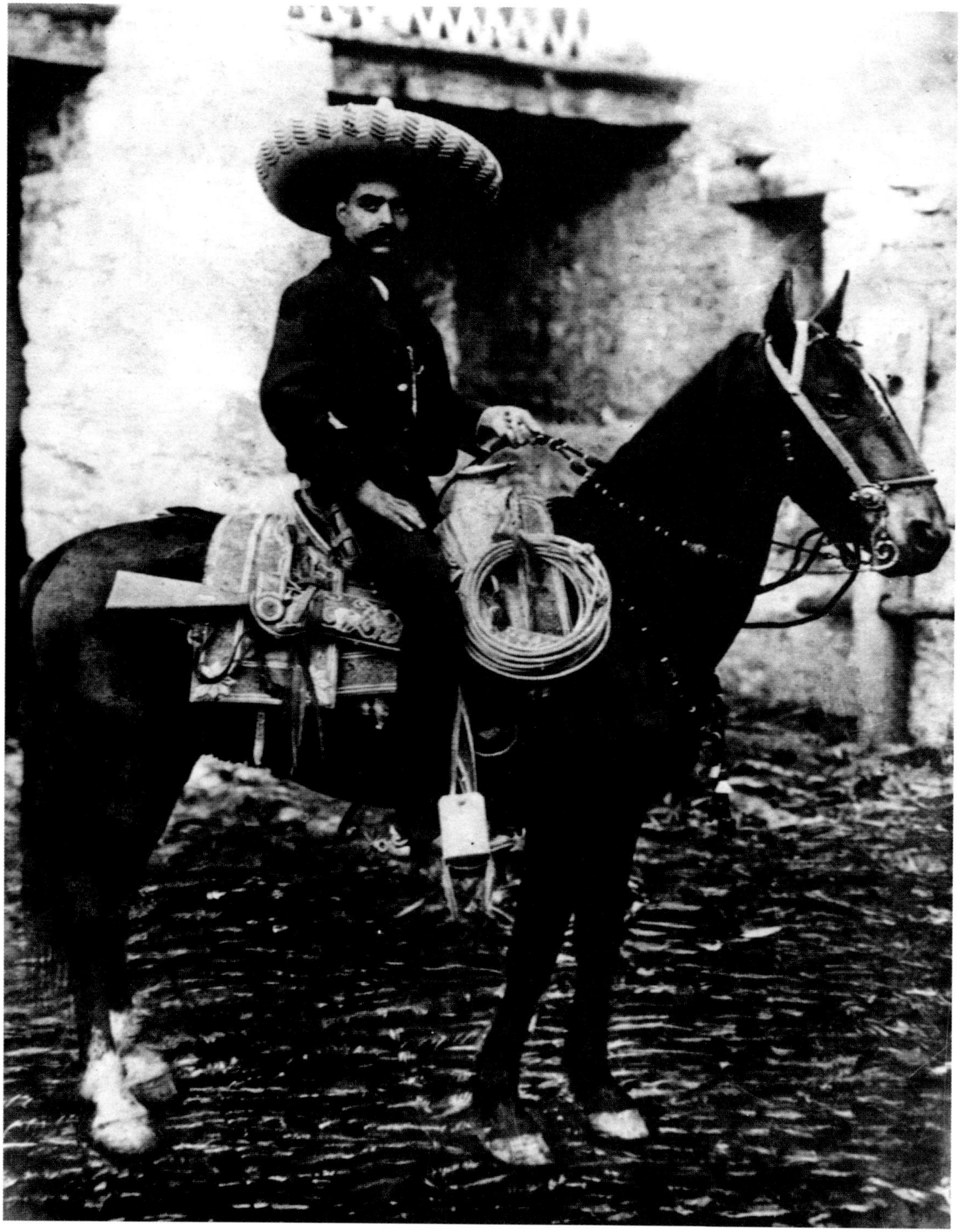

in tight pants, white shirt, silk scarf, a short jacket that was sometimes embroidered, riding boots, and a wide felt sombrero. This attire distinguished him from his troops, who wore the loose white clothing typical of campesinos; it does not appear that the decision to differentiate himself was a result of contact with modern media, as was Villa's case, because Zapata had always dressed in this way.[53]

On comparing this photo with one of General Ignacio Maya (mounted on the same horse) taken at the same time in the patio of the stables of the Hotel Álvarez in Chilapa, Arnal argues that Salmerón photographically distinguished the leader from his follower:

> The composition of both photos, as well as the angles from which they were taken, inevitably favors the caudillo above his subordinate. While the image of Maya is taken from the same angle as the saddle, the photograph of Zapata has been focused from a slightly low angle, which in conventional photographic language increases the sensation of the subject's visual power. Moreover, Maya is slightly bent over his horse, an effect that is sharpened even more by the rifle he holds in his hands. Zapata, though, is seated completely straight on his horse, maintaining a visual rigidity but with a smooth strength marked by his forearm, which rests easily upon his thigh. The *charro* Emiliano Zapata has demonstrated aesthetically that he deserves the place he occupies in the southern movement.[54]

One could say that it is the collaboration between Zapata and Salmerón that legitimates the commander photographically. Their closeness (and the shrewdness of the leader in terms of media's importance) produced one of the few documents in which a revolutionary caudillo expressly manifested the desire that a photographer serve the cause. Rescued by Jiménez and Villela, Zapata sent a letter to Salmerón after the taking of Chilpancingo containing explicit instructions.

> General Headquarters in Chilpancingo
> March 26, 1914
> Señor Amando Salmerón Chilapa
>
> Very dear sir and friend:
>
> As a result of the taking of the state capital by insurgent troops, and the complete defeat of our enemies, I recommend that you come immediately to this city, in the moment you receive this letter, bringing with you your camera and other

5-13. FACING Emiliano Zapata, Chilapa, March 1914; Amando Salmerón. © Inv. #63434, Fondo Casasola, SINAFO-Fototeca Nacional del INAH.

equipment necessary to take images of Chilpancingo, the major points of combat, and the leaders, officers, and soldiers of the bad government, who have fallen prisoner.

I salute you and await your arrival tomorrow.

With nothing more for the moment and expecting your punctuality, I repeat my sincere attentions, your friend and servant.

El General Emiliano Zapata

Note.—I await you tomorrow in Tixtla, expecting your punctuality. Bring the photographic plates of the group you took in Tixtla, and take another couple dozen.[55]

An overdue investigation remains to be carried out on Cruz Sánchez, a professional photographer who was also municipal president of Yautepec, Morelos.[56] Almost nothing is known about him, and little about his photography, although Zapatista colonel Octavio Magaña wrote the following on the back of a portrait of the imagemaker: "This is photographer Cruz Sánchez, Municipal President of Yautepec, who valiantly defended the interests of his town and to whom is owed a great deal of the graphic material on the Southern Revolution."[57] In view of this vacuum, it is worth reproducing a text that appeared about Sánchez in 1932, when the memory of his revolutionary activities was still fresh.

> Artist photographer Cruz Sánchez fought against the big landowners and defended the rights of the peoples stripped of their communal lands. Elected municipal president of Yautepec, he held that post for various years with probity and honor, earning his countrymen's gratitude. Señor Sánchez is a man of character: he made himself; desiring to exercise an honorable profession, he dedicated himself to photography, which he came to dominate. In 1917 he was at the point of being executed by Carrancista leaders, subordinates of Pablo González.[58]

Sánchez was a Zapatista photographer, and among early evidence of his activities in favor of agrarian justice is a portrait of Jovito Serrano; he was taken prisoner in 1905 for demanding campesino rights and died in prison, "one of the first victims of the Morelos caciques."[59] Miguel Ángel Berumen asserts that Sánchez was "perhaps the author who most photographed the Zapatistas; in many cases, his images constitute the only testimonies of some officers."[60] There is no doubt of the value of portraits of individuals who probably left few written traces of their existence—for example, that of

Refugio Sánchez, the Zapatista leader in Tepotzlán, and his followers (Figure 5-14).

Cruz Sánchez may also have had a conception of photography that went beyond the studio. It is surprising, but it seems that he may have used his camera to document the expansion of the haciendas that were taking over the common lands; at any rate, a photo of the "Atihuyán hacienda, property of Pablo Escandón, which absorbed the lands of Yautepec," makes that speculation possible.[61] The southern revolution was directly linked to expansion of the haciendas, which acquired the land and, ipso facto, the labor of campesinos who had no other way to feed themselves. Did Sánchez have a consciousness that photographs could serve as witnesses capable of recording over time those extensions of the haciendas, with the purpose of offering them

5-14. Refugio Sánchez, Zapatista leader in Tepotzlán, Morelos, ca. 1914; Cruz Sánchez. © Fondo Magaña-Cerda, 10550, Instituto de Investigaciones sobre la Universidad y la Educación—UNAM.

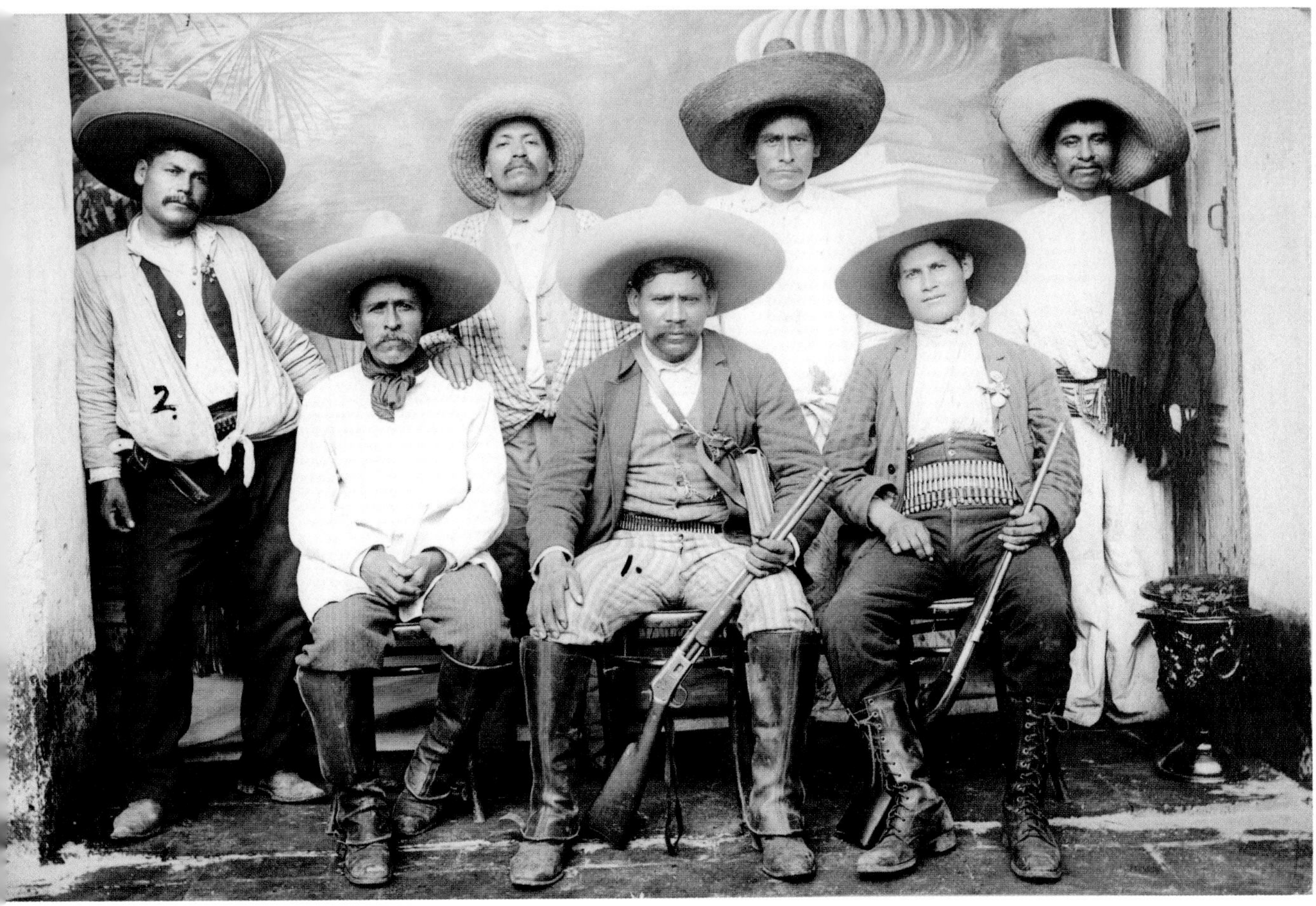

as testimony in the innumerable court cases that the campesinos filed against big landowners before the revolution exploded? We do not yet know, but during the armed struggle he used his camera to document the atrocities against communities committed by federal troops as part of the campaign to force the campesinos to enter concentration camps in order to minimize the aid they gave to the Zapatistas. He photographed "Peaceful neighbors hanged in Yautepec, by Juvencio Robles' soldiers," as well as burned houses and the damage caused by shootouts.[62]

There are two, perhaps three, other imagemakers who may have been linked to the southern movement: Sara Castrejón of Guerrero, someone named Hernández from Puebla city, and an individual named Herrera of Texmelucan, Puebla. We know of Hernández only through his photographs in the Fondo Dr. Andrés Angulo of INAH in the state of Tlaxcala.[63] Based on the limited evidence of some twenty surviving images, it is possible that Hernández was the photographer of Domingo Arenas, the important agrarian leader in the area of Puebla and Tlaxcala. Hernández made several photos of the Arenas brothers and their troops: Domingo and Cirilio are elegantly dressed for their portraits in suits, vests, and ties; the soldiers wear the familiar campesino clothing. The photographer followed Arenas into different situations, both when the leader was a Zapatista, and when he later became a Constitutionalist. He even documented "The last supper of General Arenas," shortly before he was "betrayed and assassinated by Zapatista fanatics," as Angulo wrote over a portrait of Domingo and Cirilio. The most radical project of Domingo Arenas was establishing agricultural colonies, the only revolutionary leader to develop this ordered strategy for redistributing the hacienda lands and organizing the new towns with their authorities, streets, houses, and schools.[64] Hernández carefully pictured the leader placing the first stone of the Colonia Hidalgo in Texmelucan, Puebla, capturing the ceremony in several shots (Figure 5-15). From Herrera we have a couple of photos that celebrate the taking of Tlaxcala city in May 1911 by agrarian revolutionaries Benigno Zenteno and Victorio Meneses and their troops.[65]

According to Samuel Villela, Sara Castrejón was certainly the first woman to photograph the revolution, and she may have been the only Mexican woman to do so; in fact, she may have been the first woman in the world to photograph war.[66] Castrejón was born in 1888 in Teloloapan, an enclave of such cultural abundance that it was known as the "Athens of Guerrero." Her family must have been relatively comfortable because her father was a lawyer and her brother became a jeweler.[67] At the age of eighteen she went to study photography in Mexico City, where she remained a year; it is not clear whether she matriculated in the Escuela de Artes y Oficios de Mujeres

(School of Arts and Professions for Women) or if she simply worked with established photographers to acquire the necessary skills. It was, of course, unusual for a woman to enter into this occupation, and even more uncommon to go off to the metropolis to study at such a tender age. She returned to Teloloapan and in 1908 opened her studio, a typically Mexican business in which she was assisted by her sister, Dorotea, and her brother, Joaquín. She may have gone back to Mexico City at times in order to buy materials, and perhaps participated in the magazine *La Ilustración Semanal.*[68]

5-15. General Domingo Arenas placing the cornerstone for the Colonia Hidalgo, Texmelucan, Puebla, 1916; Hernández. © Fondo Andrés Angulo, INAH-Tlaxcala.

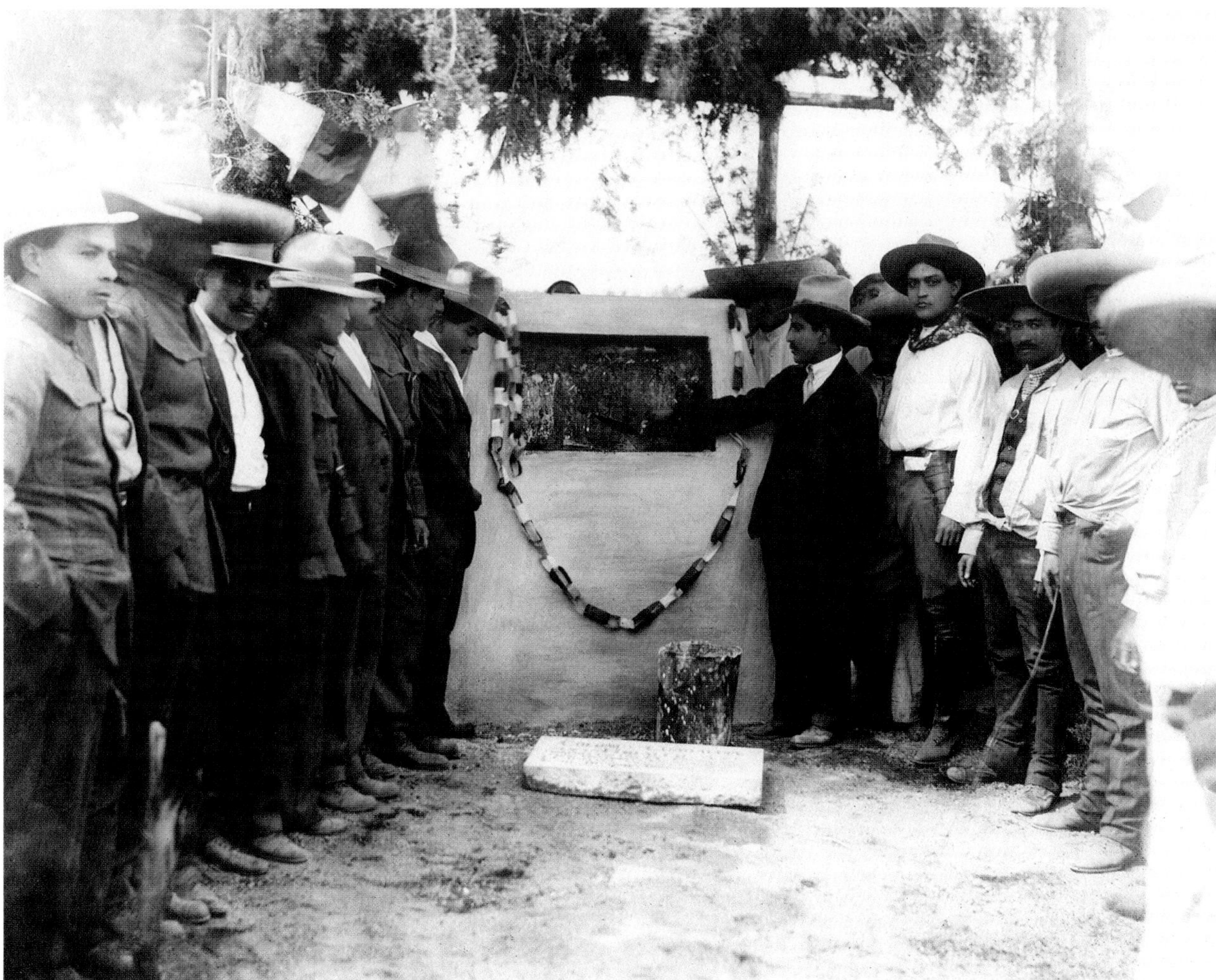

Castrejón never married, and this may have been a determining factor; as photo historian Eli Bartra has asserted about Natalia Baquedano, another woman photographer in this period, "The fact that she was without children or husband was no doubt important in allowing her to dedicate herself to her art."[69] As a studio photographer, Castrejón's portraits were her staple, though it appears that she staged many outside to emphasize the rural environment. She produced postcards, one of which is the only to be found from Guerrero that celebrated the centennial of independence.[70] Among her surviving pictures of the Porfiriato is a striking image of a poor campesino taken in what would appear to be the patio of a hacienda.[71]

As Villela makes clear, Castrejón was a studio photographer, not a photojournalist. Nonetheless, she made a documentary image of Maderista troops entering Teloloapan on 26 April 1911, the first photograph of the southern rebellion to be taken.[72] Shot from a rooftop, perhaps that of her house, the photo captures the column of horsemen stretching off into the distance. She also used her experience of photographing in the countryside to record a Maderista camp on the outskirts of Teloloapan, an image that captures a scale of operations seen in few photos during this period.[73] She made several images of the principal leaders posed in front of an improvised backdrop—a studio photo made outside—including Jesús H. Salgado, a wealthy *ranchero* from the same town who joined the Maderista movement and was later one of the most important Zapatistas in Guerrero. The photographer also collaborated with Salgado to stage a scene in her studio that represented Dr. Severo Herrera García in the act of donating money to the revolutionary cause. Perhaps it was Castrejón's gender consciousness, and a certain commitment to Salgadismo-Maderismo in its first stages, that led her in 1911 to photograph the combatant Colonel Amparo Salgado dressed in cartridge belts and holding a rifle that was not just a prop, as is often the case in studio portraits from the revolution (Figure 5-16). This image is beyond doubt the first made of a female revolutionary in Mexico.

Although much of her archive was lost, it is clear that Castrejón continued photographing throughout the revolution, capturing *pronunciados* (rebels) as well as those from the other sides, often posed in front of the same backdrop.[74] When the Salgadistas rose up against Madero in 1911 for his failure to carry out the expected agrarian reform, Castrejón pictured those forces and the federal troops sent to put them down. She continued her policy of photographing all who required her services after Victoriano Huerta overthrew Madero in 1913, for she made photos of the Huertistas that arrived in Teloloapan. As resistance to the dictator developed, more Zapatista and anti-Huertista soldiers came to have their pictures made, including the female

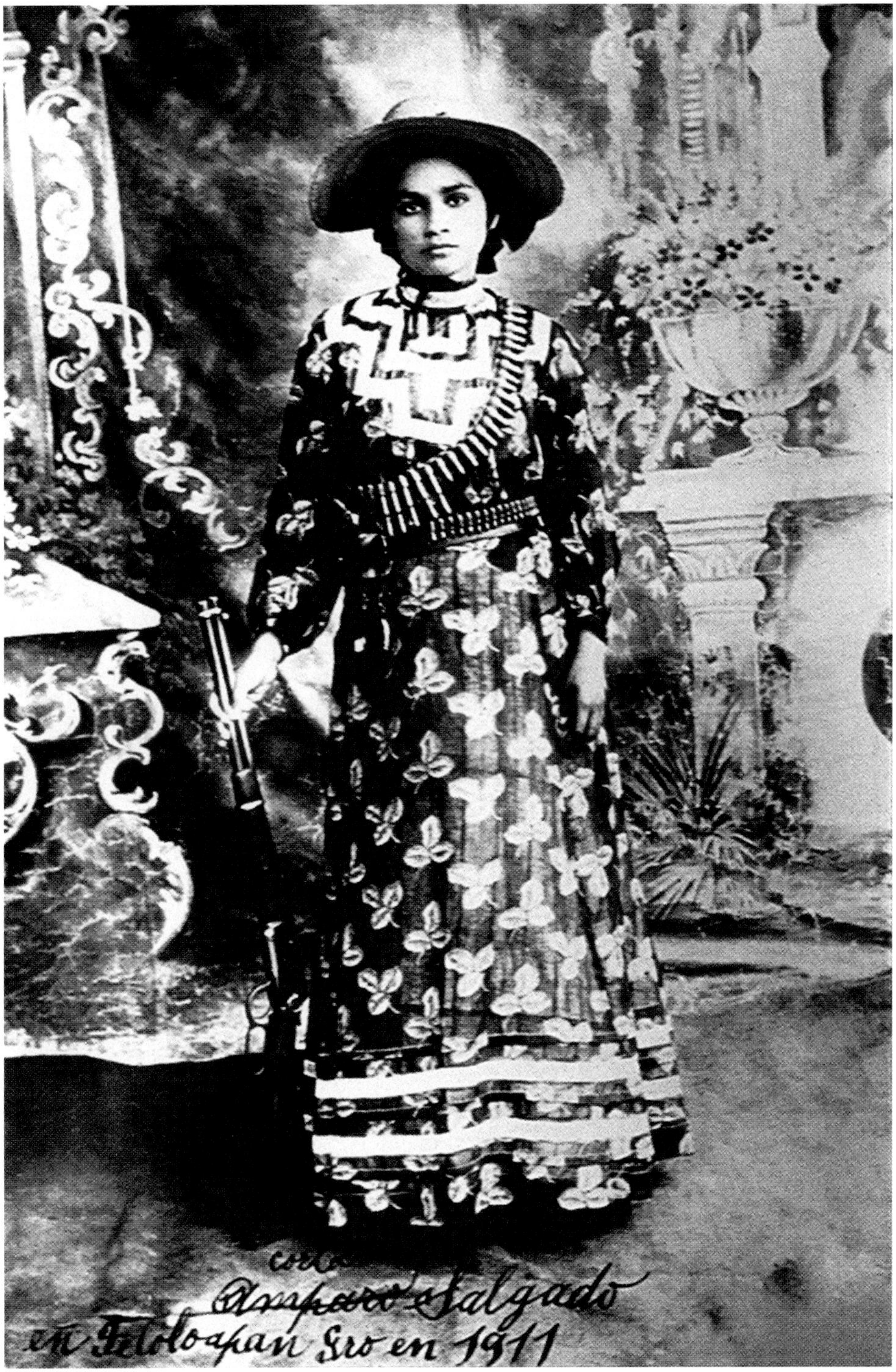

5-16. Zapatista colonel Amparo Salgado, Teloloapan, Guerrero, 1911; Sara Castrejón. Archive of Enrique del Rayo Castrejón.

agrarian revolutionary Colonel Carmen Robles.[75] When the Constitutionalists gained ground, they replaced the Salgadistas and Zapatistas in Castrejón's studio. Among her tasks was that of photographing executions; sometimes she made portraits beforehand of those to be shot because, according to Villela, "Families of the condemned asked that photos be made as souvenirs of their loved one."[76] It was a situation similar to that of the Cachú brothers, who photographed hanged revolutionaries at the behest of their relatives (see the following chapter). At other times, federal officers asked her to photograph the executions to provide evidence that they had carried out their orders. When the different factions would arrive in the night to ask her to photograph those who were to be shot, the five women in the house hid in the places that they had prepared until Joaquín could determine that there was no threat of rape. Her brother always accompanied her, carrying the camera and tripod. Castrejón said that she was not greatly affected by photographing executions and saw it as part of her job. Berumen had signaled the contributions of U.S. photographers Esther Eva Strauss and Clara Goodman on the border during the Maderista movement, but until the publication of Villela's work, those of Mexican women behind the camera were yet to be uncovered.

The participation of women in the Mexican Revolution is a theme that has sadly been ignored.[77] As that history is written, I would imagine that photographs will provide valuable information and leads that can be followed. For example, photos insistently document the presence of women as officers and combatants in the Zapatista forces, as does the image of Carmen Robles in Guerrero after the battle of Iguala in May 1911 (Figure 5-17).[78] The relation between Carmen and another Zapatista colonel named Robles—Amelia, who would become Amelio—is not clear.[79] At any rate, photography has been important in rescuing both Robles from being forgotten, as well as demonstrating that "Various women had commanding positions within the Zapatista army."[80]

At times it seems that the force of the female Zapatistas resulted in unexpected images. Arnal disentangles the representation of the nuclear family—enclosed within the elbows akimbo of the women—in a photo made by Hugo Brehme of the Zapata brothers and their wives (Figure 5-18). He points out that it is vital to analyze this photo against the backdrop of the "*soldadera* and her Juan," which the capital's press constantly invoked to describe women during the revolution.

> The attitude of the three women that appear in the photograph represent distinct ways of dialoguing with the camera. She on the left-hand side of Eufemio Zapata is in a relaxed position, which she reaffirms with the position of her arms, the

look, and the slight smile. This pose assumes a serene dialogue with the photographer, full of dignity and confidence. On the other side, the challenging flirtatiousness of Emiliano's woman, Josefa Espejo, imposes itself on Brehme's control, which permits her to "visually control" the event. Finally, the frank smile (almost a laugh) of the woman seated at the left of the frame—the only person who has definitely liberated herself from the photographer's control—emphasizes the sensation of insecurity in the photographic pose of the two principal personages: the Zapata brothers. For that reason, I believe that this photo is, paradoxically, an image of feminine vindication rather than a photograph of masculine politics. To the degree possible, the women impose order and dignity through their body language. They challenge, in their own way, the presence of the photographer and his machine that hunts personalities.[81]

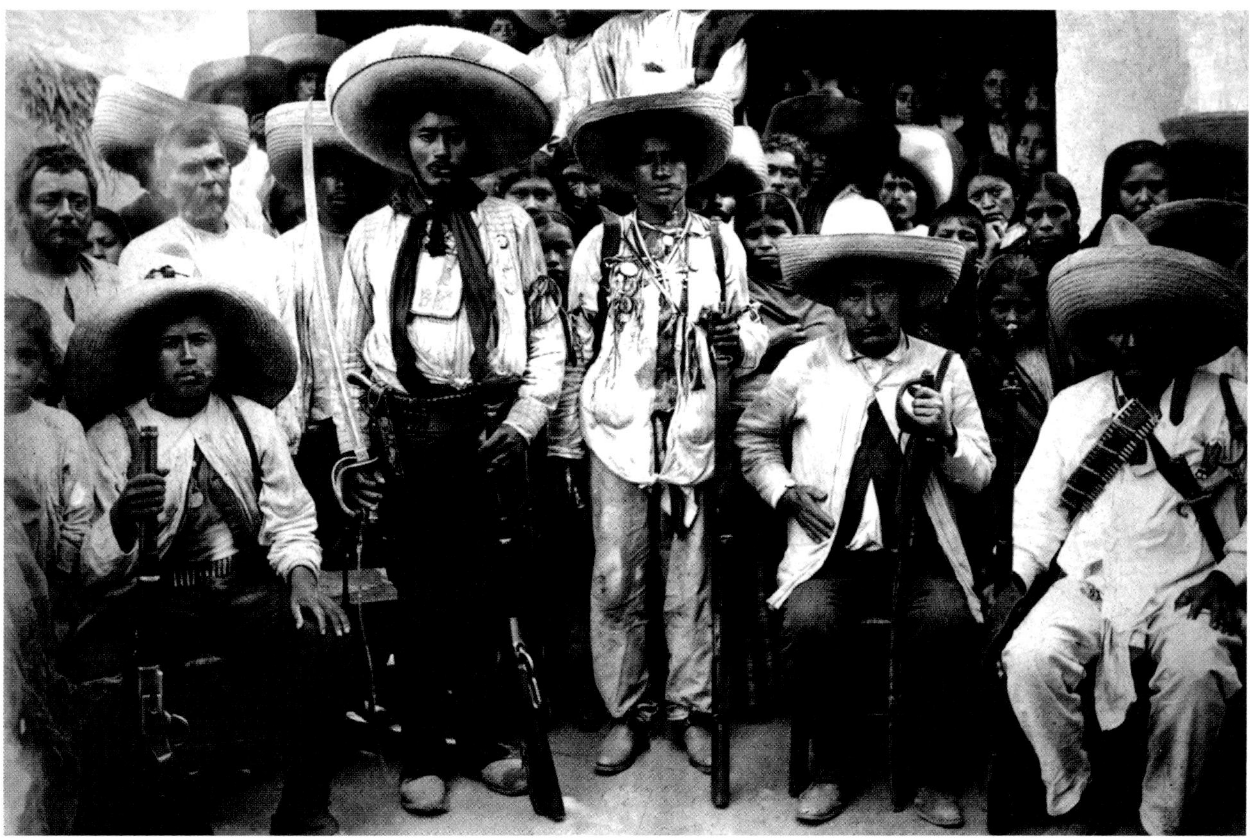

5-17. Zapatista colonel Carmen Robles, Guerrero, ca. 1913. © Inv. #33833, Fondo Casasola, SINAFO-Fototeca Nacional del INAH.

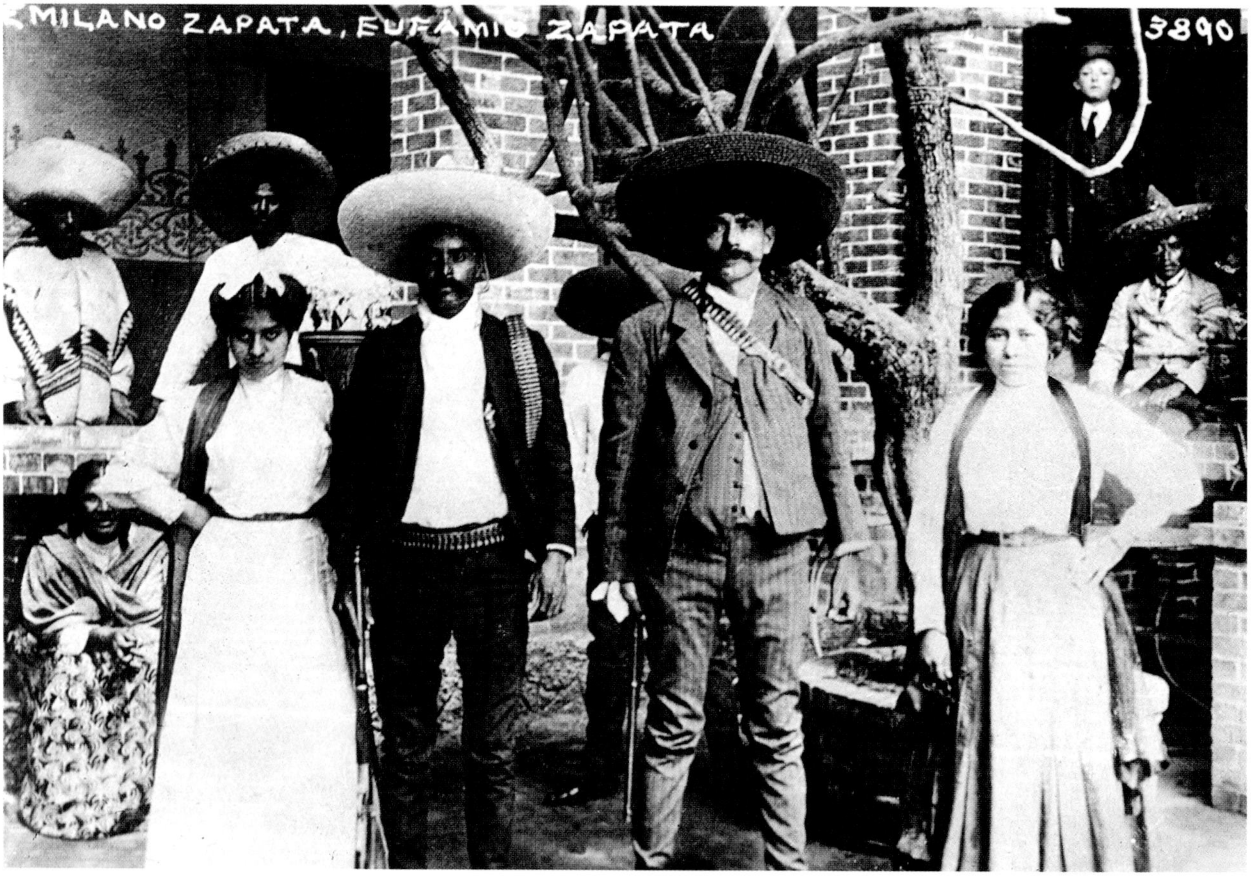

5-18. Emiliano and Eufemio Zapata with their wives (Josefa Espejo and ?), Cuernavaca, June 1911; Hugo Brehme. © Inv. #5672, Fondo Casasola, SINAFO-Fototeca Nacional del INAH.

Hugo Brehme (and the fact that the Zapatistas controlled Cuernavaca at this moment) permitted these women to project their power; in contrast, a Mexico City photojournalist, Luis Santamaría, captured the opposite side in his contribution to the trope of the "Zapatista prisoner": women in a very different situation—Emiliano Zapata's family apprehended by Huertista soldiers.[82] One can imagine that Brehme's attraction to the exotic (and saleable) is what led him to travel to Morelos to picture the Zapatistas in 1911. It is difficult to know what the relation was between Brehme and the southern rebels, but it would seem that he was able to get close to them, to judge by the photos in which they pose for him.[83] It could well be that Zapata facilitated Brehme's access because he felt that a foreigner would be more neutral than the metropolitan photojournalists, and that the image would travel outside Mexico.

Whether or not he made the famous icon of the guerrilla that we have credited him with (see Figure E-1), there is no doubt that Brehme was present in Cuernavaca during 1911, and that he took several images, such as the entrance of Zapatistas in that city.[84] I suspect that Brehme went to Morelos to photograph the Zapatistas in the moment of Madero's victory, when the two groups were still allied. It is difficult to imagine that "a person so apolitical as Hugo" had any commitments to any revolutionary group; rather, he needed to earn his living by selling images as postcards and to illustrated magazines.[85] Also, Brehme considered himself an artist; his commitment was aesthetic. Among the most striking examples of this are the shots from on high of Zapatistas, a strategy that would later be seen in his photos of La Decena Trágica and the U.S. invasion of Veracruz; in an often-reproduced photo, we see Zapatista cavalry extend themselves over the plains until they are lost in the distance (as with Castrejón, this is an aesthetic strategy little seen in Mexico or during World War I).[86] The period between Díaz's resignation and the election of Madero as president was a magic moment in which the whole country seemed united against the old regime. A daring photographer such as Brehme could feel relatively secure with the feared Zapatistas, despite encountering a culture that must have seemed shockingly different. After suffering a serious fright during La Decena Trágica, Brehme decided to leave with his family for the United States.

CHAPTER 6

Photographing the Reaction

THE EVENTS OF THE REVOLUTION most photographed by Mexicans occurred during La Decena Trágica, 9–18 February 1913.[1] The coup d'etat that overthrew Francisco I. Madero's government began in the plot of Félix Díaz, Manuel Mondragón, and Bernardo Reyes; the latter died in the first battle, to take the National Palace. It was, in a certain sense, another instance of the Latin American military destroying a newborn democracy with the connivance of the United States. There is an aura of uncertainty created by the mask that Victoriano Huerta wore as the commander of Madero's defense: he engaged in a "phony" war designed to reduce the troops loyal to the president and gain advantage with the plotters; at the same time he mercilessly bombarded the civilian population to ensure their eventual acceptance of Madero's overthrow.[2] The disorder generated by a cannonade that seemed to make no sense was accompanied by the confusion caused by seeing soldiers fighting on different sides but wearing the same uniform; chaos and peril reigned.

La Decena Trágica was documented extensively by photographers, from the more experienced photojournalists and postcard producers to amateurs. Among the graphic reporters were Samuel Tinoco, Eduardo Melhado, Ezequiel Álvarez Tostado, Manuel Ramos, Abraham Lupercio, Agustín Víctor Casasola, Miguel Casasola, Gerónimo Hernández, Ezequiel Carrasco, and Antonio Garduño. It was also an attraction for photographers who functioned more freely, selling their images as postcards or to the illustrated magazines, both national and international; those who were present included Sabino Osuna, Hugo Brehme, Félix Miret, C. B. Waite, and the photographers of the Heliodoro J. Gutiérrez studio.[3]

The constant filtration between media continued: Tinoco and Melhado joined up to commercialize postcards of events they had covered for their magazines, and they signed these images with a "TM."[4] With so many photographers, it is not surprising that there were moments of "crossed fire": carrying his reflex camera, Gerónimo Hernández runs to look for another shot while, behind him, Madero arrives at the National Palace on the first day of La Decena Trágica (Figure 6-1).

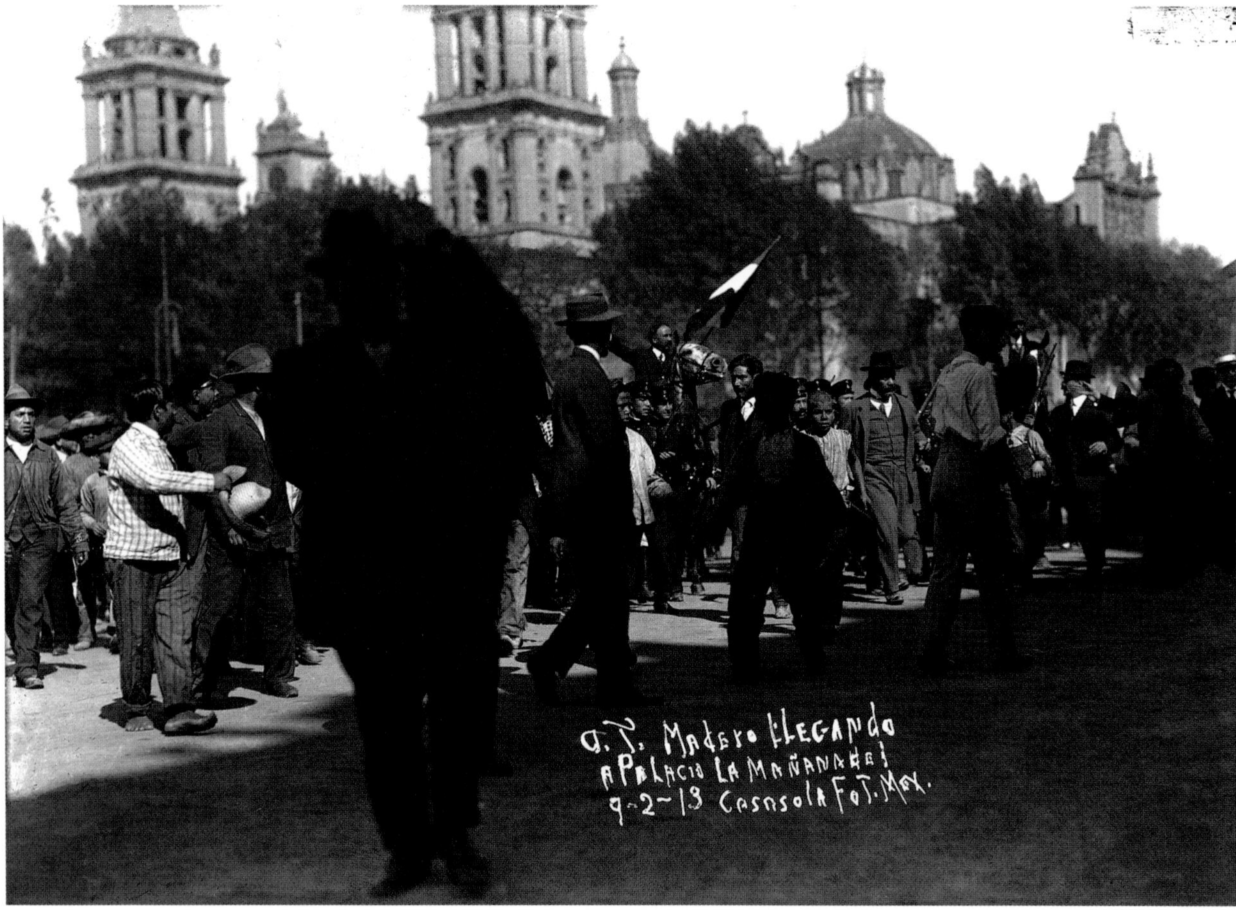

6-1. Gerónimo Hernández running with his reflex camera while behind him President Francisco I. Madero arrives at the National Palace on the first day of La Decena Trágica (the Tragic Ten Days), Mexico City, 9 February 1913. © Inv. #37276, Fondo Casasola, SINAFO-Fototeca Nacional del INAH.

The muddle that characterized these ten days was reproduced, to a certain point, in the photographic representations. It is difficult to determine if some of the photographers had commitments with one group or another during the fighting, although they could have chosen sides afterwards, as did the illustrated magazines (always in function of the editors' class interests and according to who was in power). Contradictions present themselves on attempting to untangle the identities of the image-makers. For example, both Osuna and Miret signed Figure 6-2, an image of some women "Giving drink to the thirsty," as Osuna wrote on his copy.[5] A picture of a federal artillery post was also signed by Osuna and Miret, and there is also a copy without a signature.[6] Among the other photos that Osuna and Miret both signed are two that merit special attention for their sharp focus, the careful composition that individualizes the soldiers, and poses that give the sensation of spontaneity: one of federal combatants with a machine gun and another of students in the military college.[7] This *mano a mano* between Miret and Osuna reaches its extreme with an image of a group of soldiers shooting around a corner: for Osuna, these are "Federal soldiers firing," but Miret wrote over his copy that they are an "Advance party of Felicistas," a name that was used for the rebels because Félix Díaz was the leader most identified with the uprising as it was occurring.[8]

I tend to think that Osuna made the images in dispute. Rebeca Monroy asserts that this postcard producer "was one of the photographers who most amply covered the events, making some 300 plates. . . . In all his images, Osuna's experience is evident, and particularly so in the portraits of the rebel soldiers and leaders, for the

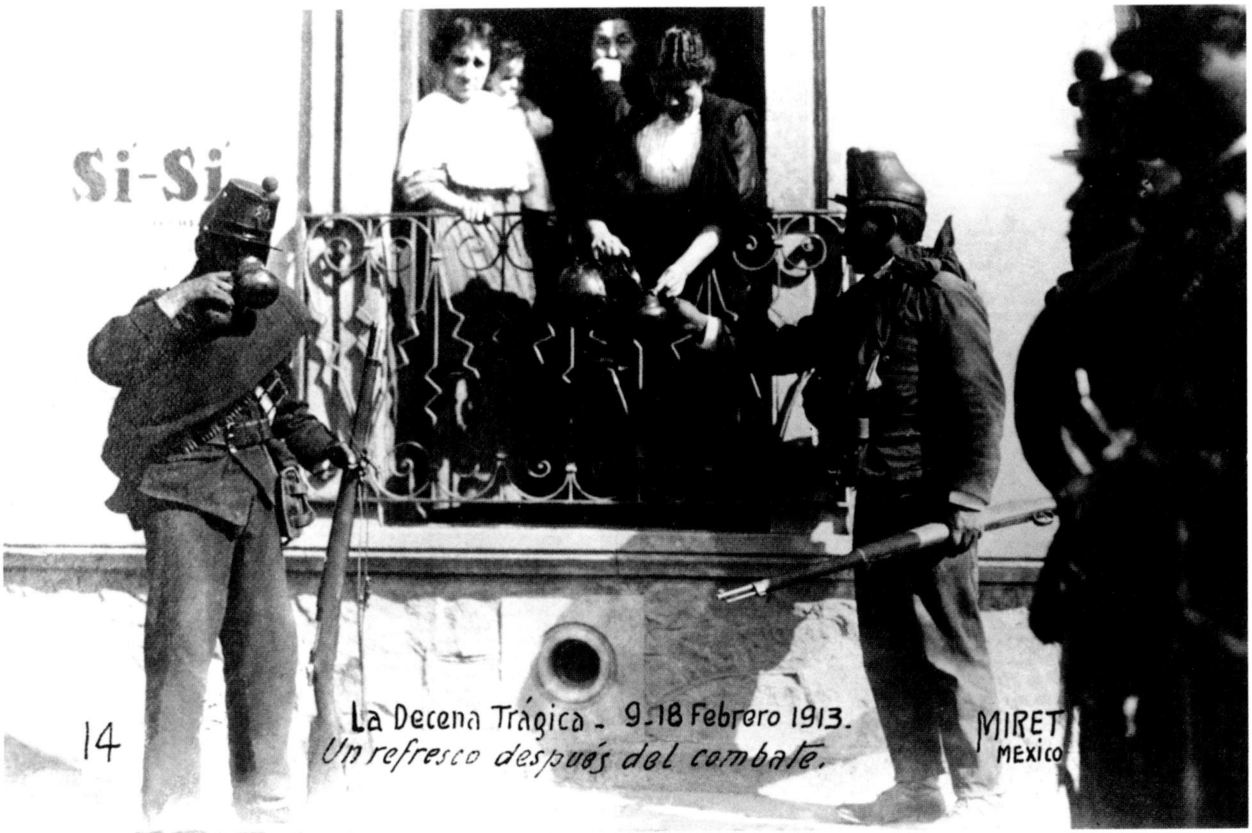

6-2. Women offering water to soldiers, Mexico City, February 1913; Félix Miret. © Inv. #455220, Fondo Casasola, SINAFO-Fototeca Nacional del INAH.

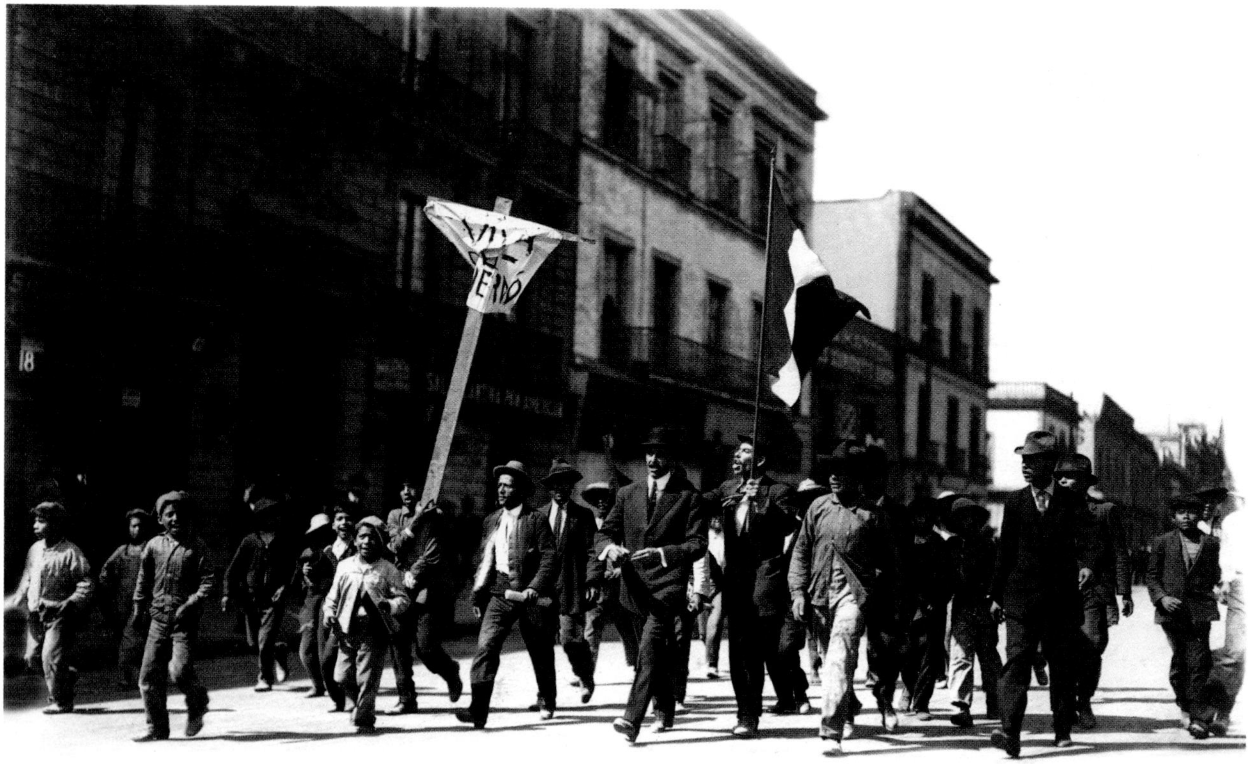

6-3. The last demonstration in support of President Francisco I. Madero, Mexico City, 17 February 1913. © Inv. #451478, Fondo Casasola, SINAFO-Fototeca Nacional del INAH.

posed attitudes—the influence of studio photography—that these people present to the camera."[9] Miguel Ángel Berumen praises Osuna's "extraordinary technical quality," stating that "he left perhaps some of the best graphic testimonies of the revolution."[10] Osuna contemplated making an album about the events and began documenting La Decena Trágica from the president's march to retake the National Palace on the morning of 9 February until "The last Maderista demonstration," as he wrote on his copy of Figure 6-3.[11] He photographed the insurgents from within the Ciudadela as well as the loyal soldiers outside, shooting with their rifles as well as at rest; he took pictures on streets full of dead humans and animals, and inside destroyed buildings. Finally, he made a portrait of the coup leaders after their victory.

Other postcard makers also brought their experience to documenting La Decena Trágica. Collaborators of the H. J. Gutiérrez agency were in the streets photographing buildings in ruins, the rubble, the federalist artillery, and some Felicistas who posed in the Ciudadela (Figure 6-4). This photo was made on 18 February, after the detention of Madero; staging a scene with representatives of different factions of the disloyal—soldiers, students of the Military School for Applicants, and civilians—would seem to be designed to demonstrate the amplitude of discontent with Madero.[12] Arturo Guevara Escobar asserts that Aurelio Escobar Castellanos was the photographer for the Gutiérrez agency during this event, together with his assistant, Enrique Escobar Castellanos.[13] If that is so, we would have to ask ourselves why someone so committed to Maderismo—Aurelio Escobar was one of the first to cover the rebellion in the north in 1911 and would exile himself from Mexico a few days after Madero's fall—would have wanted to make a photo so clearly staged to communicate a political message that he must have found repugnant.

C. B. Waite, the well-known postcard photographer who had represented the progressive and the picturesque of the Porfiriato, found himself in Mexico City, although his family had fled to the United States almost a year before. In 1912 his brother, manager of the Esmeraldas Mining Company, had been decapitated by Indians in Magdalena Etla, Oaxaca; they also set fire to his ranch. It was surely one of the many

6-4. Armed Felicista supporters (soldiers, students of the military school, and civilians) pose in Mexico City, 18 February 1913; H. J. Gutiérrez Agency. © Inv. #641936, Fondo Casasola, SINAFO-Fototeca Nacional del INAH.

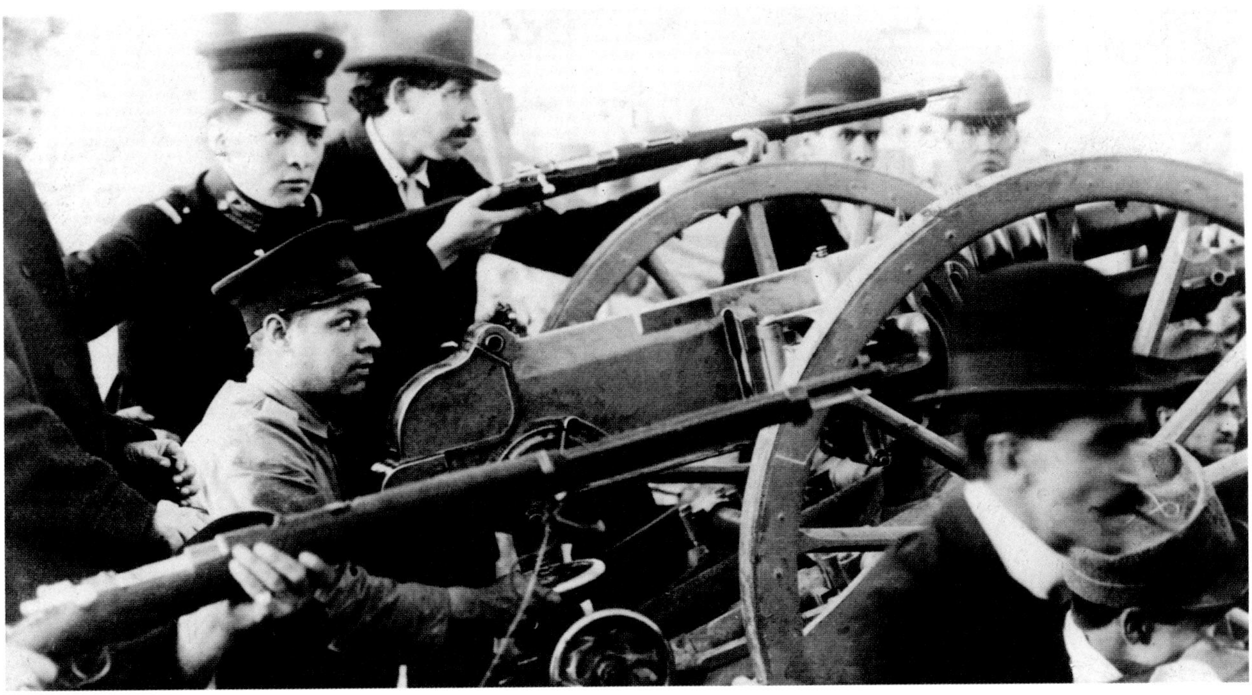

agrarian disputes turned violent by the expectations created by the Maderista rebellion, because the newspaper reported that "The cause of the Magdalena Indians' attack resides in their battle with the ranch's owner, who acquired the area's water for ten years."[14] Despite his brother's tragedy, his family's departure, and the fact that he was no longer active as a photographer, C. B. Waite was probably living in Mexico City to safeguard his properties. It would appear that he kept a low profile during La Decena Trágica, but once the coup had been consummated, he registered the damage suffered in different locations. He paid special attention to the YMCA building, perhaps anticipating that U.S. illustrated magazines would be interested. Within the damaged edifice, he reconstructed a scene with three men—a civilian machine gunner, and two Felicista soldiers, one of whom was "playing dead"—in which he expressed his reactionary vision of the revolution.[15] A representative of the popular backing for the coup, the civilian points a machine gun at an imaginary enemy through a closed window.[16] According to Waite's representation, the antidemocratic forces are those on which foreigners ought to count; they are the ones willing to fight for their interests, and they are disposed to pay the price, to judge by the "dead" Felicista soldier on the YMCA floor.

Hugo Brehme was surprised by the onset of La Decena Trágica while returning from work. According to his grandson,

> One morning in February of 1913, Hugo left his studio in the center to take the streetcar home. Suddenly, the streets became deserted: businesses rolled down their metal curtains, and houses shut their doors and windows. For the first time, Hugo understood that his life was in danger, and he began to knock desperately on doors, but they remained closed. He started running, only to stop and knock again on more doors, and this went on until finally a Good Samaritan opened one.[17]

I don't know if the story is true or one of those family fables that become sacred. A photo exists that bears the date of 9 February and identifies the place as the Ciudadela; it shows a row of dead loyal soldiers.[18] It would seem that the photographer recovered quickly from his scare. Nonetheless, since the federal assault on the Ciudadela did not begin until the morning of 11 February due to Huerta's dilatory tactics, it could be that the writing on the photograph is mistaken (or that the dead resulted from the taking of the Ciudadela by the Felicistas at midday on 9 February). At any rate, Brehme pictured death and destruction in the streets; his may have been a more intimate photography—for example, in documenting a bedroom destroyed by the bomb fragments rather than wider shots of buildings in ruins. It would appear that he took more photos of the loyal troops than of the insurgents, capturing the anxiety and bewilderment on the faces of families in the Rinconada de San Diego, one of the government forces' main positions (Figure 6-5). In another photo he portrayed a typical war scene, capturing the calm between battles and the necessity to pass the time playing cards or watching (Figure 6-6). The fright that the photographer experienced during La Decena Trágica, as well as a worsening situation, made the Brehme family decide to move to the United States in 1914; however, on what was supposed to be their last night, they went to the theater, and upon their return found that thieves had stolen "a good part of their belongings."[19] They were thus forced to remain in Mexico, and Brehme became famous by photographing it.

6-5. Maderistas, Rinconada de San Diego, Mexico City, February 1913; Hugo Brehme. © INAH-Hoffman-Brehme, 090.

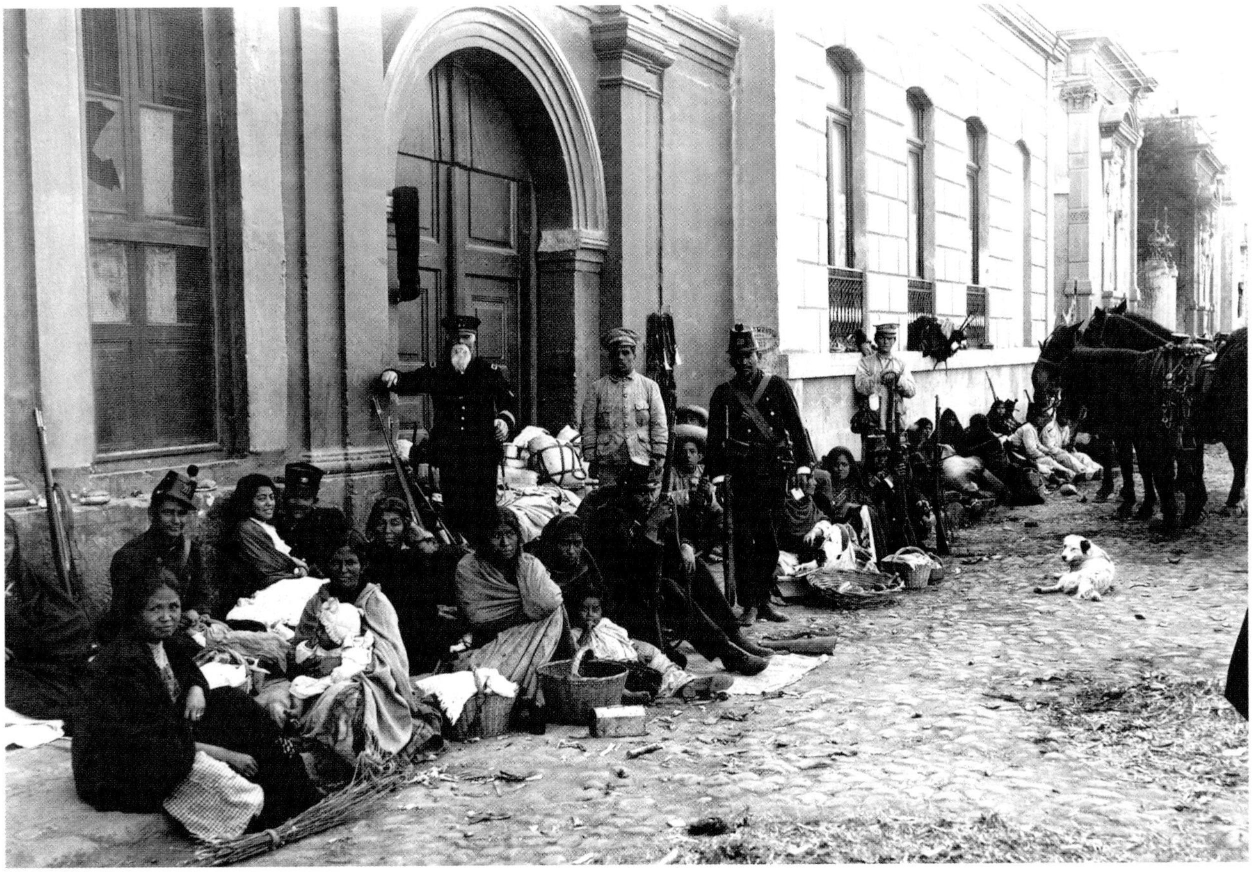

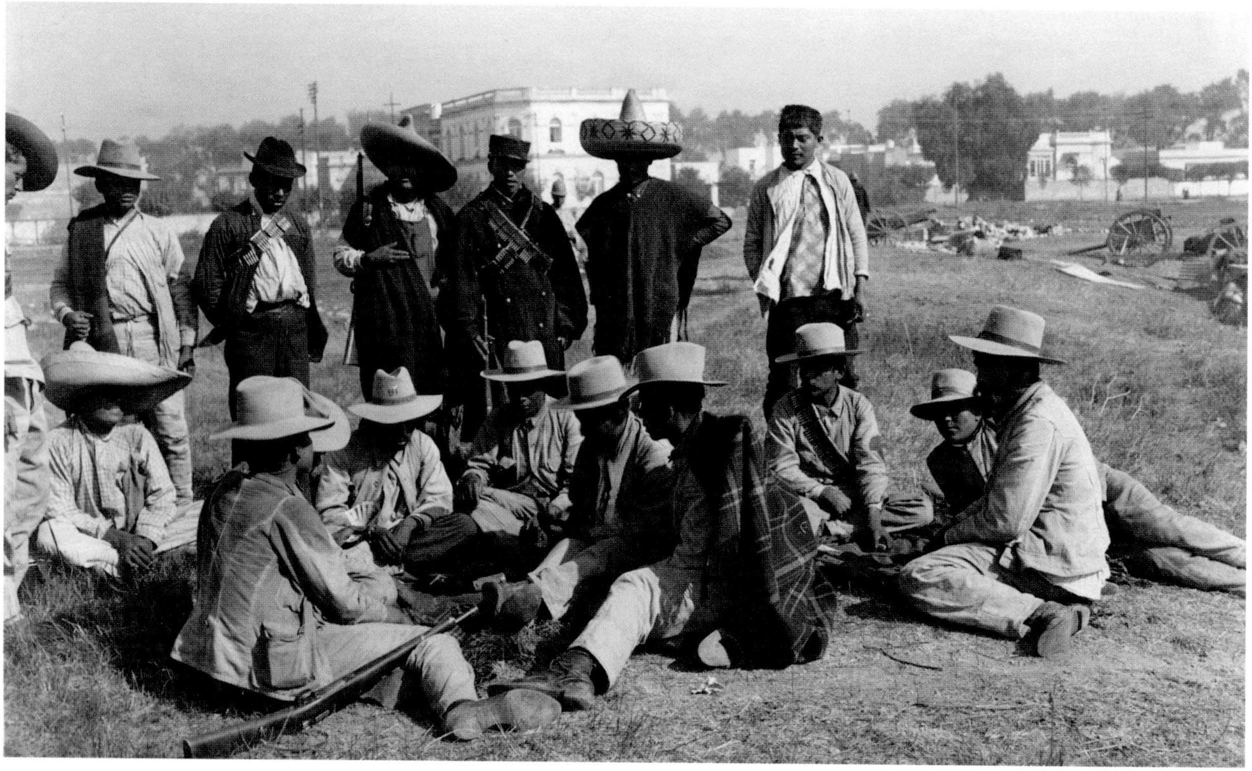

6-6. Maderistas playing cards, Mexico City, February 1913; Hugo Brehme. © INAH-Hoffman-Brehme, 092.

It is probable that photographers were in more immediate danger during La Decena Trágica than at any other moment of the revolution. José Ángel Aguilar provided a description of what the experience must have been for many: "Dozens of photographers risked their lives to capture scenes and images, printing their plates in distinct parts of the city. . . . On occasion, they had to leap among cadavers; others had to take refuge behind walls, their bodies curved and in a continual uncertainty."[20] It was said of the Casasolas that Agustín Víctor "became so familiar with bullets that he didn't get a scratch, but his brother Miguel took a couple of stray rounds through his legs."[21] Although it has been asserted that "Casasola covered events from the beginning," we do not know which photos were made by the brothers.[22] But the danger they all faced is evident in images such as one showing a large group of men, women, and children—relatively well off to judge by their clothing and skin color—hiding in a refuge to wait out the bombardment (Figure 6-7). José Juan Tablada wrote a moving narrative in his diary.

> The cannonade has continued all day, exasperating, savage, infernal, sowing death in the city and ruining properties. Five days of diabolic cannonade within a city is something shameless and an unheard of barbarity. Hundreds of widows and orphans are crying in this instant; the women and children suffer, the hunger begins to be felt in the homes of the poor people who don't eat because they can't work. And tomorrow the plague will come! The prospect could not be more distressing.[23]

6-7. People hiding from the bombardment, Mexico City, February 1913. © Inv. #451474, Fondo Casasola, SINAFO-Fototeca Nacional del INAH.

The magazine *Novedades* emphasized the courage of its photojournalist: "We want to make very special mention of our well-informed photographer, Samuel Tinoco, for the magnificent service of information that he has provided by constantly exposing his life. We give a public testimony of our praise."[24] Although his medium extended

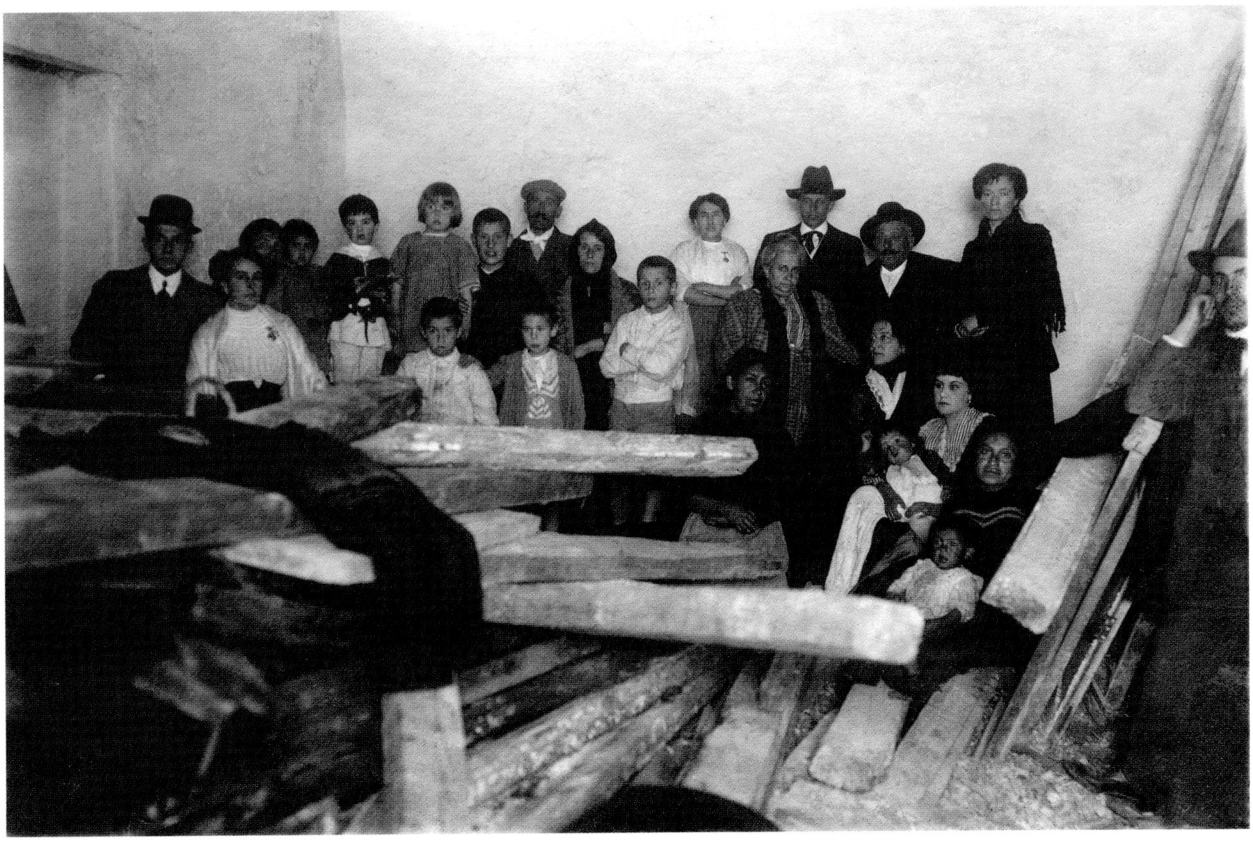

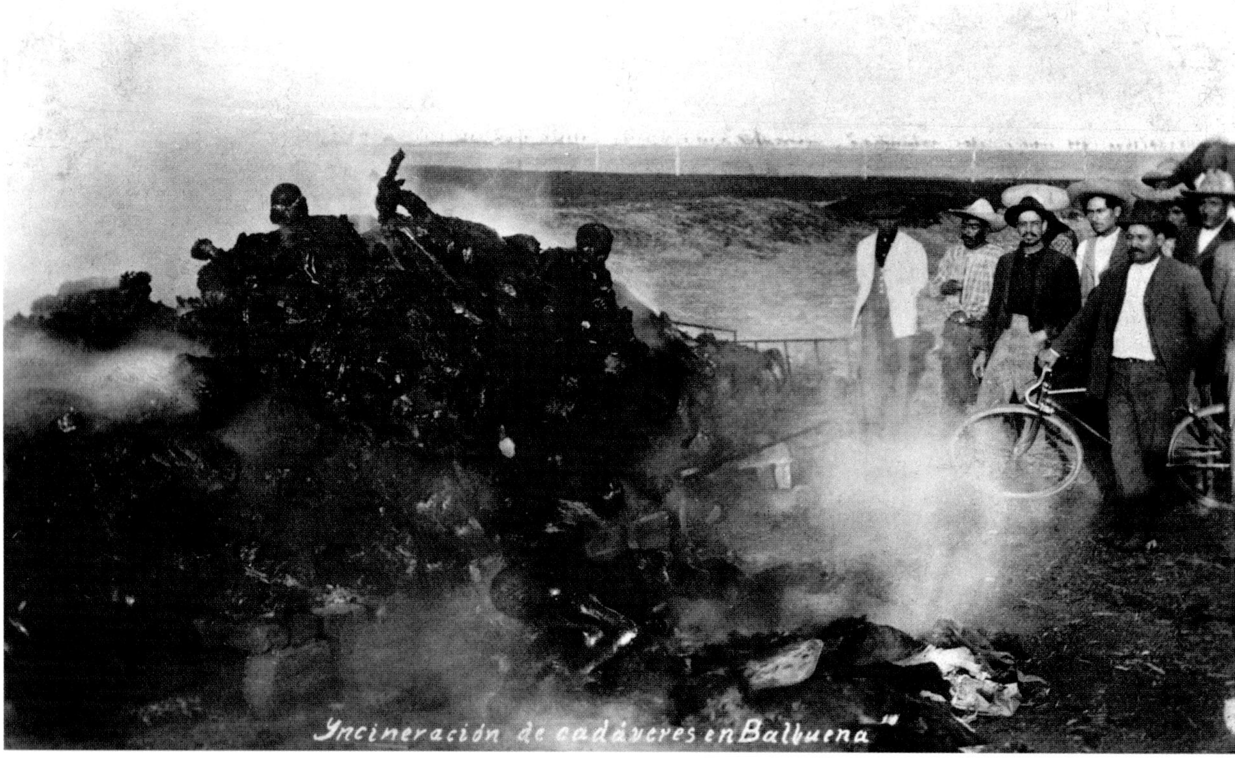

6-8. Cadavers being burned in Balbuena, Mexico City, February 1913; Samuel Tinoco, *Novedades*, 5 March 1913. © Inv. #37306, Fondo Casasola, SINAFO-Fototeca Nacional del INAH.

him recognition, historians have still not taken account of his contributions. In part this is due to the fact that other photographers have received credit for images that Tinoco took: for example, Osuna signed two photos that are credited to Tinoco in *Novedades*.[25] Another instance is provided by a splendid Tinoco photo of people running to save their lives, which was included in the book *Jefes, héroes y caudillos* as if it had been made by Agustín Víctor or Miguel Casasola, Manuel Ramos, or another of the photographers whose names appear therein.[26] Further, Miret signed an image that Tinoco made of Felicista artillery in the street.[27]

The photographs published in *Novedades* make it clear that Tinoco was all over during La Decena Trágica, photographing the bombardments, the wounded, soldiers on both sides, the burning of the newspaper offices, destroyed buildings, troops in front of the magazine's building, and cadavers piled up to be burned in order to avoid an epidemic (Figure 6-8).[28] When the crisis passed, *Novedades* documented "the overflowing happiness of Tuesday 18"—as the magazine described the demonstrations of support for the insurgents—using Tinoco's images to illustrate: "With immense enthusiasm, the people went into the streets and throughout much of the city, singing and acclaiming the generals Díaz, Mondragón, and Blanquet."[29] As seen from above, however, the crowd looks pretty sparse.

The participation of other photojournalists is still to be researched. One of the most established and conservative, Manuel Ramos, must have thought he had everything to lose, because "his photographs were not taken at the moment of the events, but when the action had ended, capturing only the desolate panorama of what was left after combat. This would lead us to believe that the graphic reporter was often not present during the military action, but that he arrived afterwards."[30] In relation to the question of political commitment, there are different possibilities to explore. On the side of the loyalists, the production of Gerónimo Hernández must be examined because he was a Maderista and worked for the newspaper that most supported the revolutionary government, *Nueva Era*; identifying his images in the Fondo Casasola of the Fototeca Nacional could provide evidence of his position.[31] It will be important to discover what photojournalists Abraham Lupercio, Ezequiel Álvarez Tostado, and Antonio Garduño did during these days. I have been able to identify few photos by them, though they were among the most important graphic reporters in that moment.[32]

Eduardo Melhado could be the photojournalist who most identified with the insurgents. He evidently had very direct access to them, photographing Félix Díaz and Manuel Mondragón drawing on a blackboard inside the Ciudadela "to calculate the artillery fire"; he also made photos of a media event with "the winning generals," as he wrote over one image.[33] Melhado had been a portraitist around 1900, with a studio on Bolívar Street.[34] He began in 1911 as a photojournalist for the newspaper *Amigo del Hogar* and later went on to the magazines *El Mundo Ilustrado*, *Revista de Revistas*, and *La Ilustración Semanal*. He also continued to work in his studio, to judge by his advertisements in *Revista de Revistas* during 1916 offering to make portraits with "a card that reproduces with total fidelity the face's movement."[35] He probably photographed the U.S. invasion of Veracruz in 1914 and then returned to Mexico City, where he pictured Venustiano Carranza on different occasions.

I have not been able to identify many Melhado photos of La Decena Trágica, but one of Felicista soldiers demonstrates his political position, his extensive experience, and his modern vision (Figure 6-9). The image has a force that is unusual in the revolution's photography: with great technique, he focused on Felicista soldiers who are circumscribed within a brick wall, creating a play between their visages and the structure. Aesthetically successful and eminently pictorial, the photo reminds me of images that great photographers such as Paul Strand and Walker Evans would make in later decades by framing people against houses of weathered wood. As a metaphor, the relation between the "hard wall" and the "hard men" asserts that these Felicistas are going to be man enough to put down social uprisings such as that of the Zapatistas and restore the Porfirian peace. Conservatives accused a "weak" Madero of lacking the toughness that these soldiers incarnate. Alarmed by an extended period of chaos, those who had something to lose looked for a new Díaz, and La Decena Trágica seemed to provide new leadership. Photographic historian Rosa Casanova has hypothesized that there were "posterior stagings mounted for the triumphant group"; both Figure 6-9 and Figure 6-4 could belong to this media operative.[36]

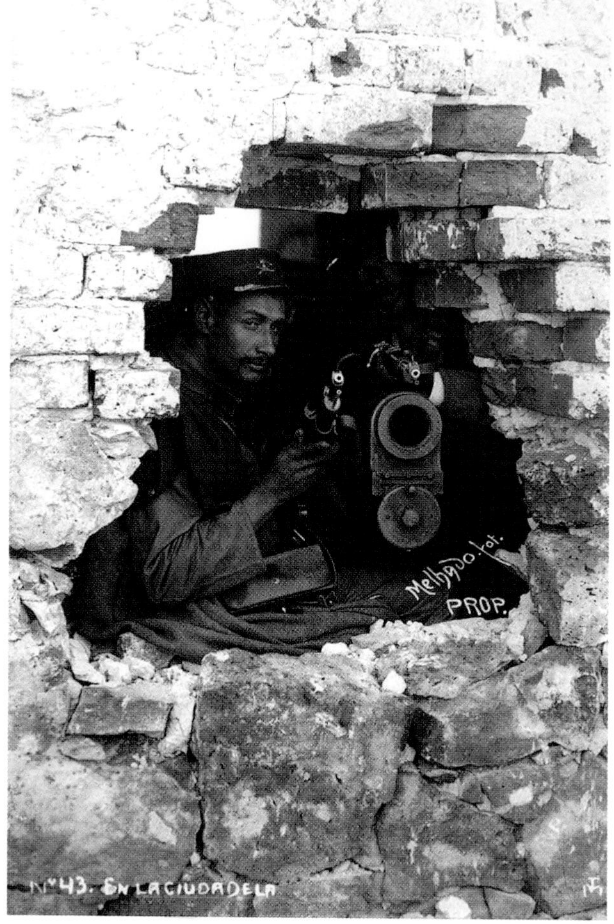

6-9. Soldiers with a cannon, Mexico City, February 1913; Eduardo Melhado. © Archivo General de la Nación, Fondo Propiedad Artístico y Literaria, Melhado, Decena Trágica, 7.

As was to be expected, the illustrated magazines favored the coup. Most of them waited until the insurgent triumph to express that, but *El Mundo Ilustrado* felt safe enough to pontificate in the middle of it: "Public opinion is still pending but, to tell the truth, the majority is anti-Maderista."[37] For *La Semana Ilustrada*, everything was a result of the "popular fury" that could not be contained until it had destroyed Madero's house and made a so-called spontaneous assault on the car in which Madero and Pino Suárez had been placed, resulting finally in their deaths.[38] *Novedades* also emphasized the role played by the "*pueblo*, crazy with enthusiasm and joy" at the defeat of Madero: according to this magazine, the Maderista newspaper *Nueva Era* "was burned by the *pueblo*," but the right-wing newspapers *El País* and *La Tribuna* had been destroyed by the "Porra," a group of followers supposedly contracted by Gustavo Madero to intimidate the opposition press.[39] For *Novedades*, the Maderistas were at fault for having "bloodied the streets of our city," and it praised the Felicistas' "great valor and firm decision": "Many of them are young and from the country, but it is not strange that they showed such valor, encouraged by the example of their illustrious leaders."[40]

Photographs of La Decena Trágica and Huertismo provide information about various facets of social life in the middle of war. In the first place are images of destruction: hundreds of photos document the damage suffered in Mexico City, from buildings photographed from a distance to rooms within homes. The violence produced refugees, who took advantage of the 16 February truce to flee to safer places (Figure 6-10). Photographs are also testimonies to the participation of women and children. In Figure 6-11 we see a woman helping a wounded person in the street; her uniform would seem to indicate that she belonged to an organization such as the

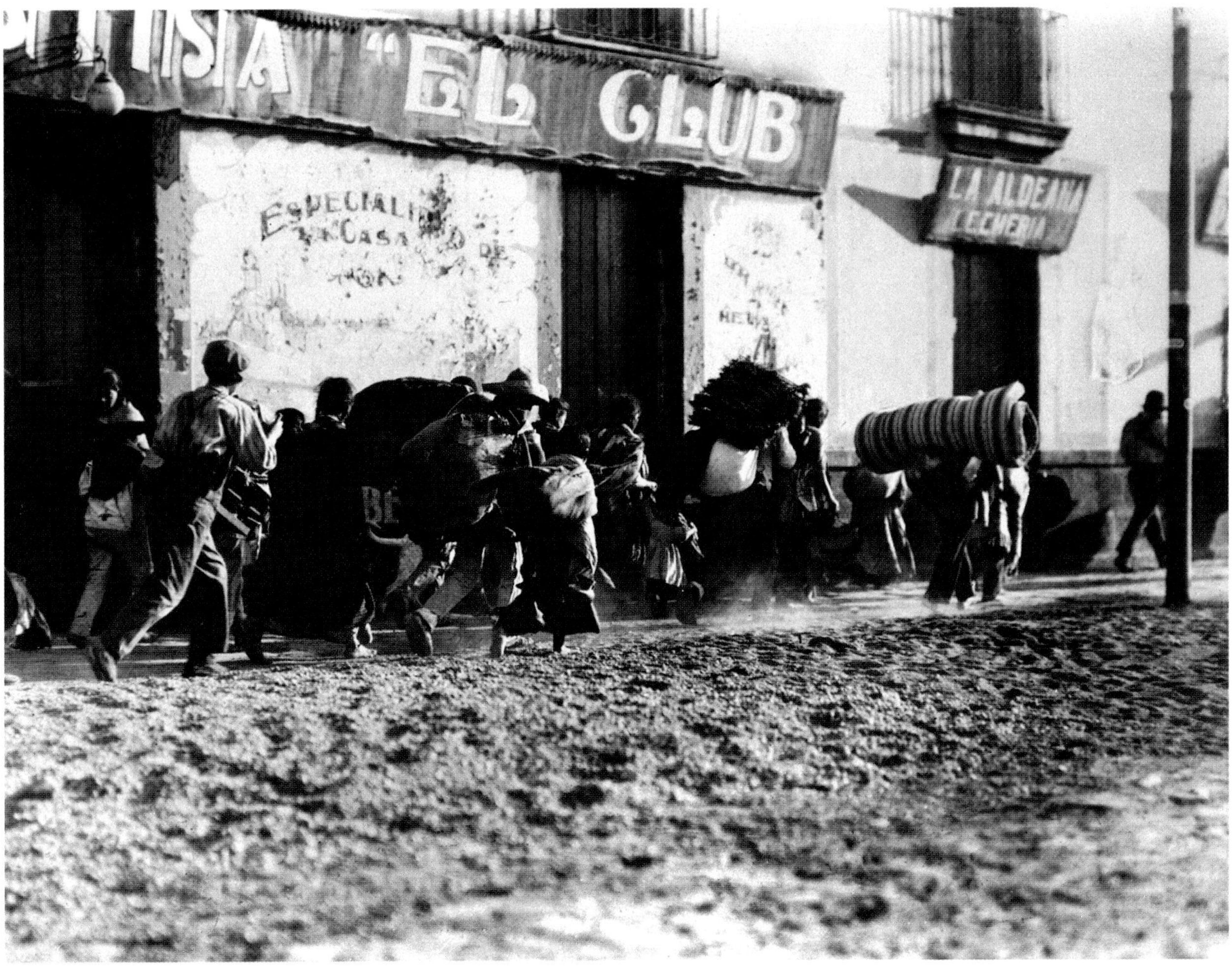

6-10. People fleeing from the combat zone during the day of truce, Mexico City, 16 February 1913. © Inv. #37311, Fondo Casasola, SINAFO-Fototeca Nacional del INAH.

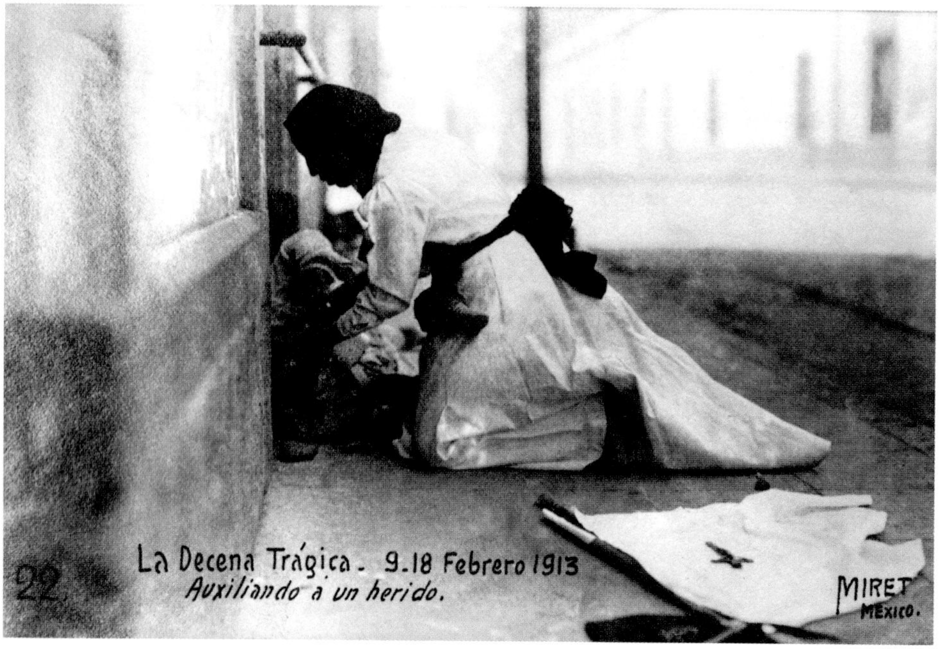

6-11. A woman helping a wounded person, Mexico City, February 1913; Félix Miret. © Inv. #451501, Fondo Casasola, SINAFO-Fototeca Nacional del INAH.

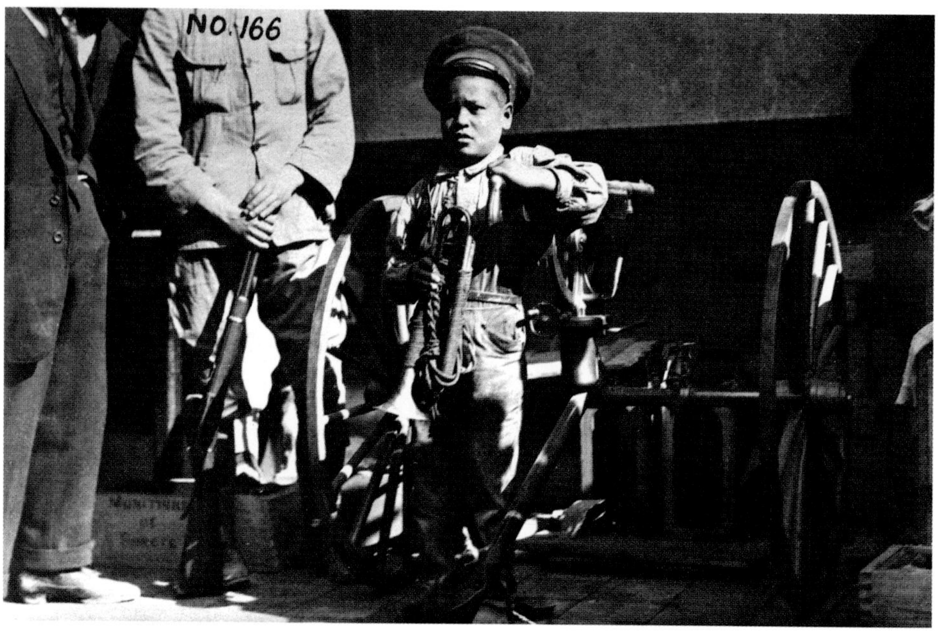

6-12. Nine-year-old trumpet player, Mexico City, February 1913; Antonio Garduño. © Inv. #37466, Fondo Casasola, SINAFO-Fototeca Nacional del INAH.

White Cross.[41] Historian Enrique Krauze affirms that one boy trumpeter who was among the insurgents was nine years old when Antonio Garduño photographed him (Figure 6-12).[42] With Victoriano Huerta's ascent to power, children would be massively incorporated into the revolution.

Gang pressing (the *leva*) was the most notorious method of forced conscription to fill the ranks of the federal army. Madero had considered it "immoral" and attempted to institutionalize an obligatory military service.[43] Huerta, however, had no such scruples and depended on the *leva* to provide the necessary cannon fodder. Historian Michael Meyer affirms that it had never been employed "as extensively as during the summer and fall of 1913," when previously respected age considerations were ignored.[44] Although I have seen no images of the *leva* published in illustrated magazines, memorable scenes were documented, including one of urban inhabitants rounded up by what appear to be Rurales (Figure 6-13). In the photo's center are young boys, two of whom may wear uniforms from an orphanage. Denied the opportunity to return

6-13. Young boys gang pressed by Rurales, Mexico City, ca. 1913. © Inv. #5301, Fondo Casasola, SINAFO-Fototeca Nacional del INAH.

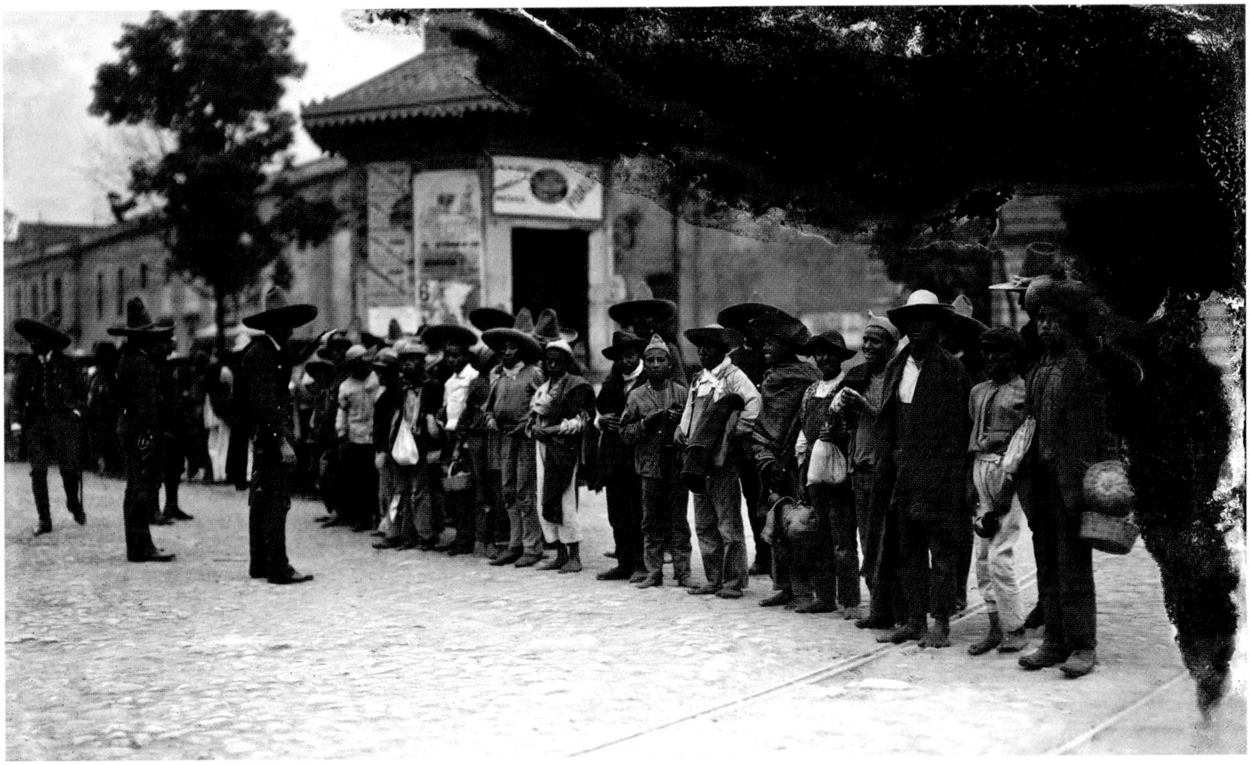

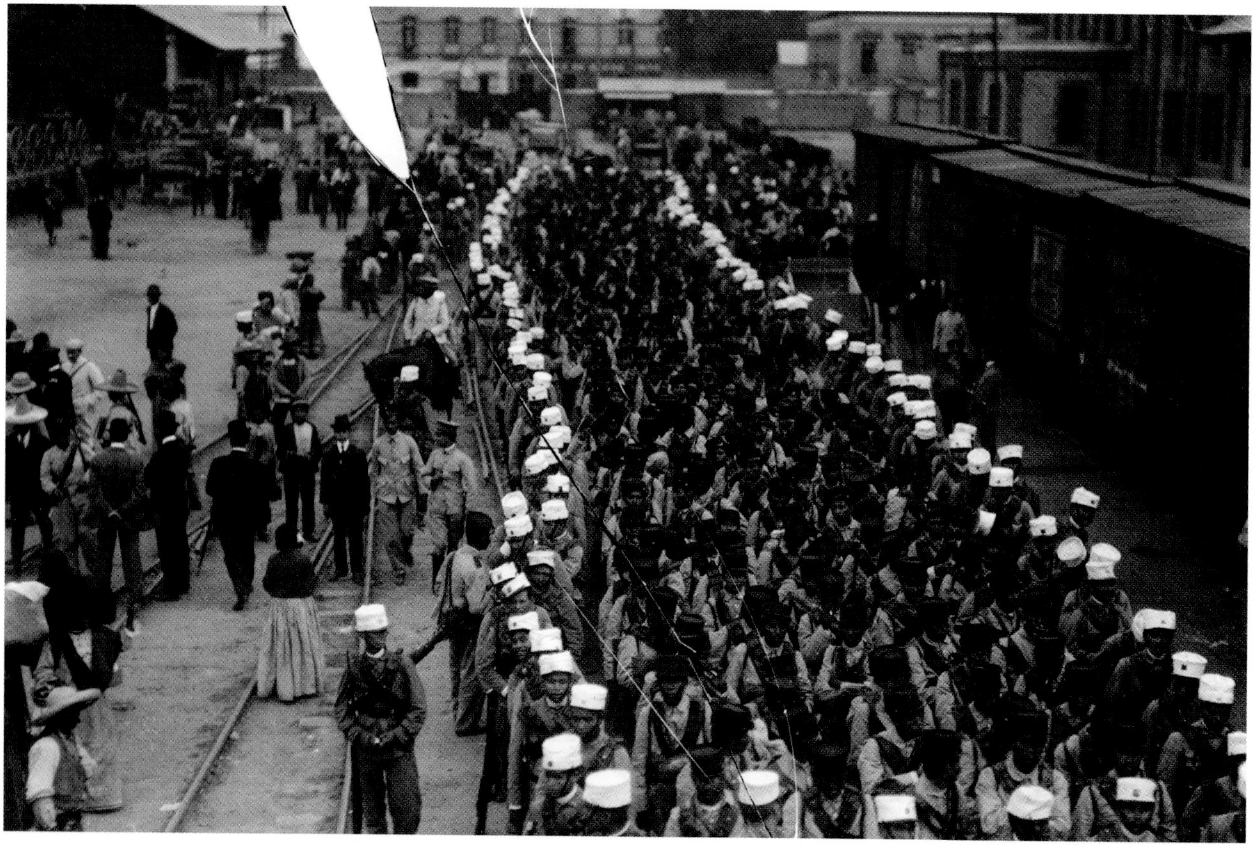

6-14. Soldiers who have been pressed into service being taken to the railroad station surrounded by military police wearing white hats to distinguish them, Colonia Station, Mexico City, ca. 1914. © Inv. #818041, Fondo Casasola, SINAFO-Fototeca Nacional del INAH.

to their homes to gather their belongings or say goodbye, the conscripts were bathed, shaved, uniformed, and shoed; then, controlled between rows of military police who were distinguished by their white caps, they were sent to the train station (Figure 6-14). Each state was assigned a quota according to population, and the *leva* was applied throughout the country. Sometimes the conscripts passed through Mexico City, as did some soldiers from Juchitán who were probably photographed in April 1913, perhaps as part of a media event to demonstrate national support for Huerta's government (Figure 6-15).[45]

Francisco Ramírez Plancarte was living in Mexico City and made the following observations about the effect that the unbridled *leva* had on those who had not yet taken a position in the revolution.

On observing that the *leva* began to everywhere take its victims, a sentiment of justice and a profound protest of indignation came over us, the neutrals, those of us that had maintained ourselves apart from the struggle. We desired with all our forces that the revolution triumph, because that would signify the tranquility of the families sunk in the saddest helplessness, and exposed to mendacity or prostitution, as a result of the misery caused by the missing fathers, husbands, sons, and others who sustained them.[46]

6-15. Soldiers from Juchitán, Mexico City, October 1913. © Inv. #641417, Fondo Casasola, SINAFO-Fototeca Nacional del INAH.

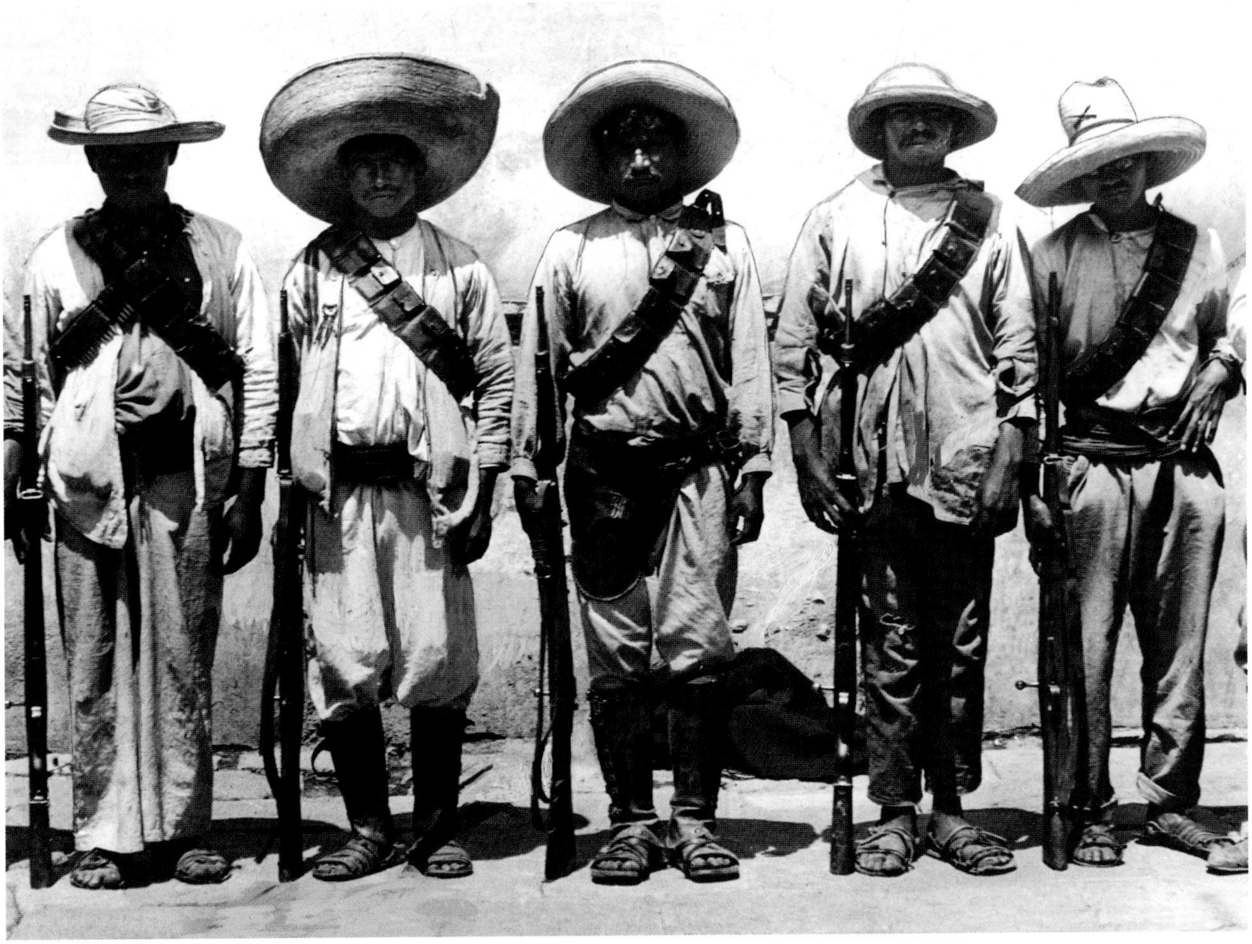

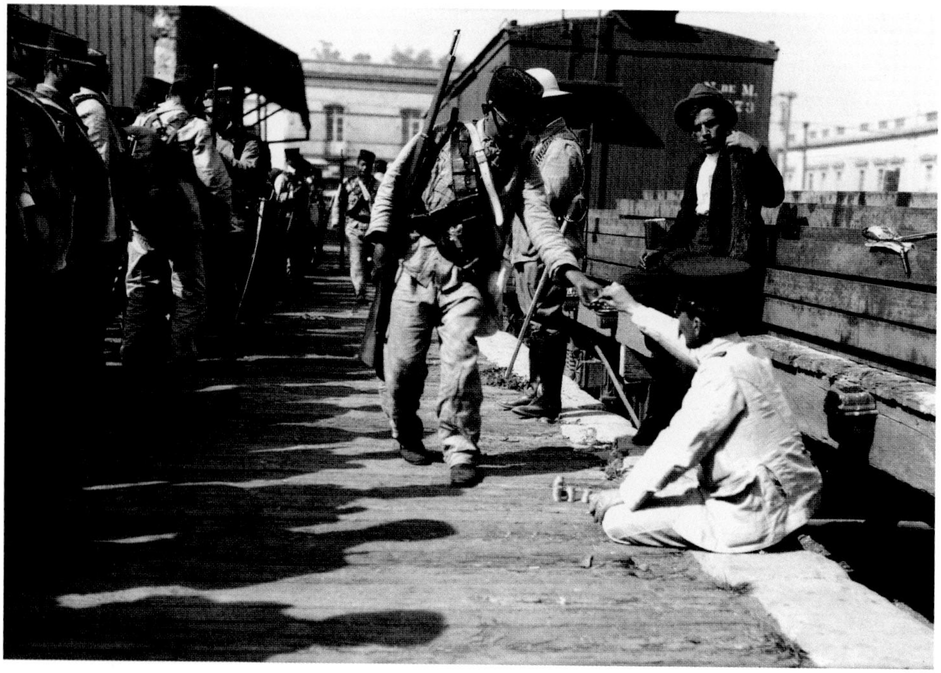

6-16. LEFT Payday for federal soldiers, Mexico City, ca. 1913. © Inv. #6085, Fondo Casasola, SINAFO-Fototeca Nacional del INAH.

6-17. BELOW LEFT Federal soldiers, Mexico City, ca. 1913. © Inv. #642773, Fondo Casasola, SINAFO-Fototeca Nacional del INAH.

6-18. BELOW RIGHT Federal camp, ca. 1914. © Inv. #38101, Fondo Casasola, SINAFO-Fototeca Nacional del INAH.

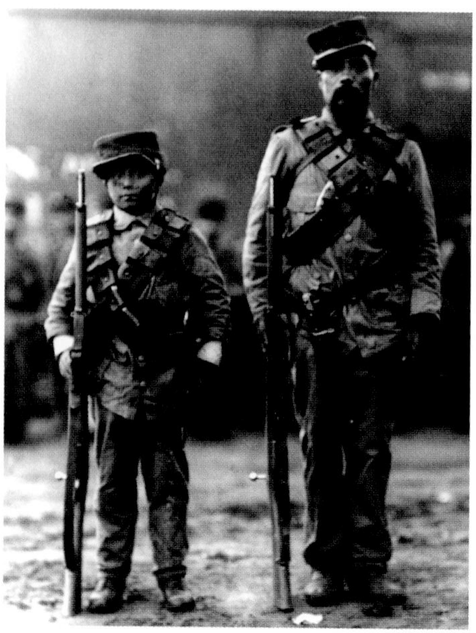

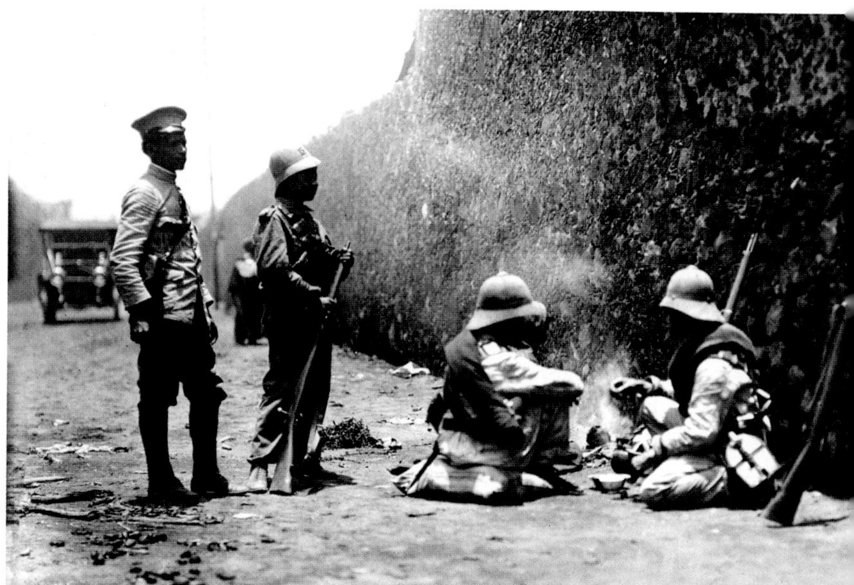

As in the Porfiriato, the rules of Huertismo were "the carrot or the stick" of the social jungle. In an economy that was constantly deteriorating, the army offered employment; in Figure 6-16, a soldier picks up his pay (*soldada*). Many children were surely attracted to join up by the possibility of being paid for adult labor (which they did anyway), and some probably followed their fathers in enlisting (or were grabbed by the *leva* at the same time [Figure 6-17]). Soon they found themselves in federal camps, despite their tender years (Figure 6-18). And, perhaps, they would presently be standing to honor a fallen comrade, such as Captain Librado Cervantes, in Tacámbaro, Michoacán, in 1913 (Figure 6-19).

6-19. Federal forces with the body of Captain Librado Cervantes, Tacámbaro, Michoacán, 1913. © Inv. #38105, Fondo Casasola, SINAFO-Fototeca Nacional del INAH.

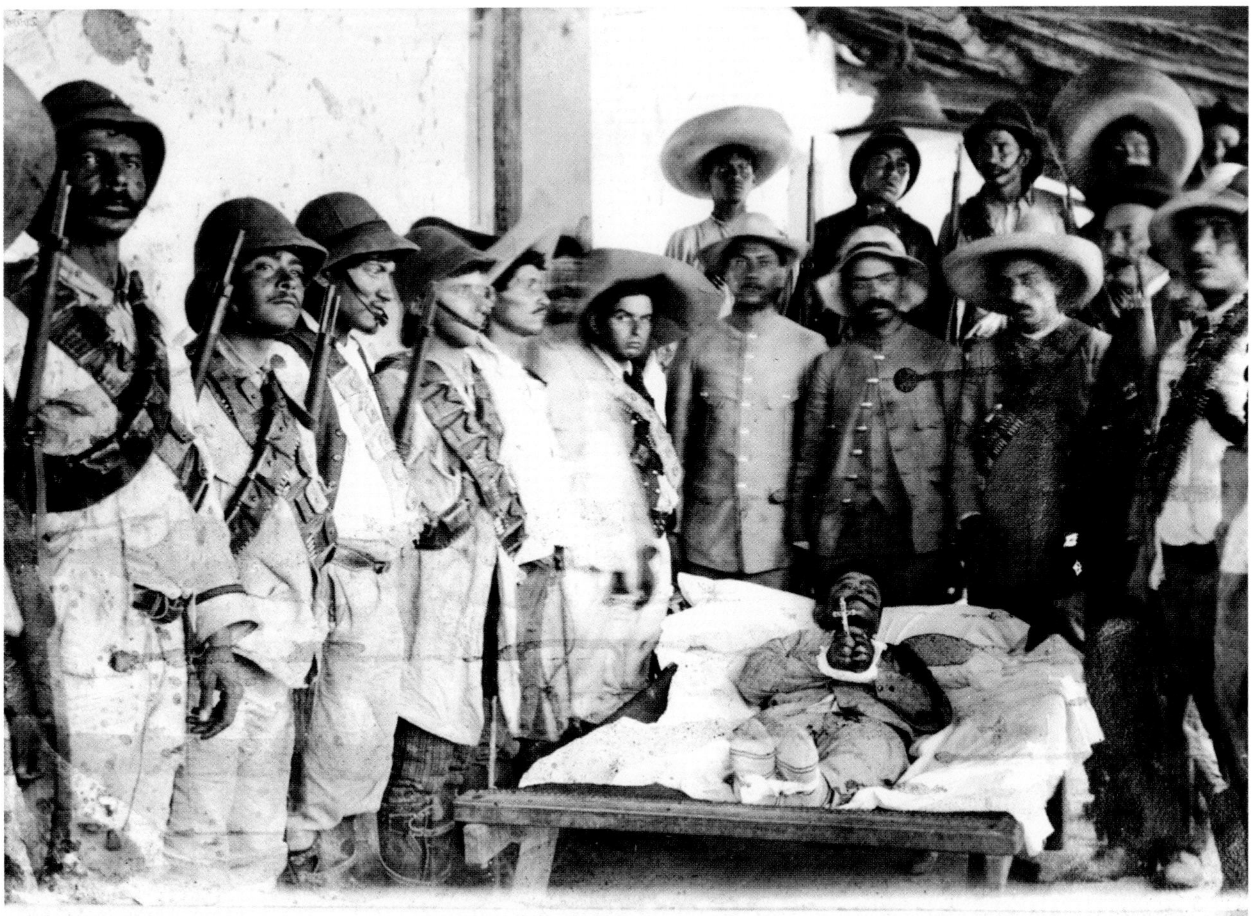

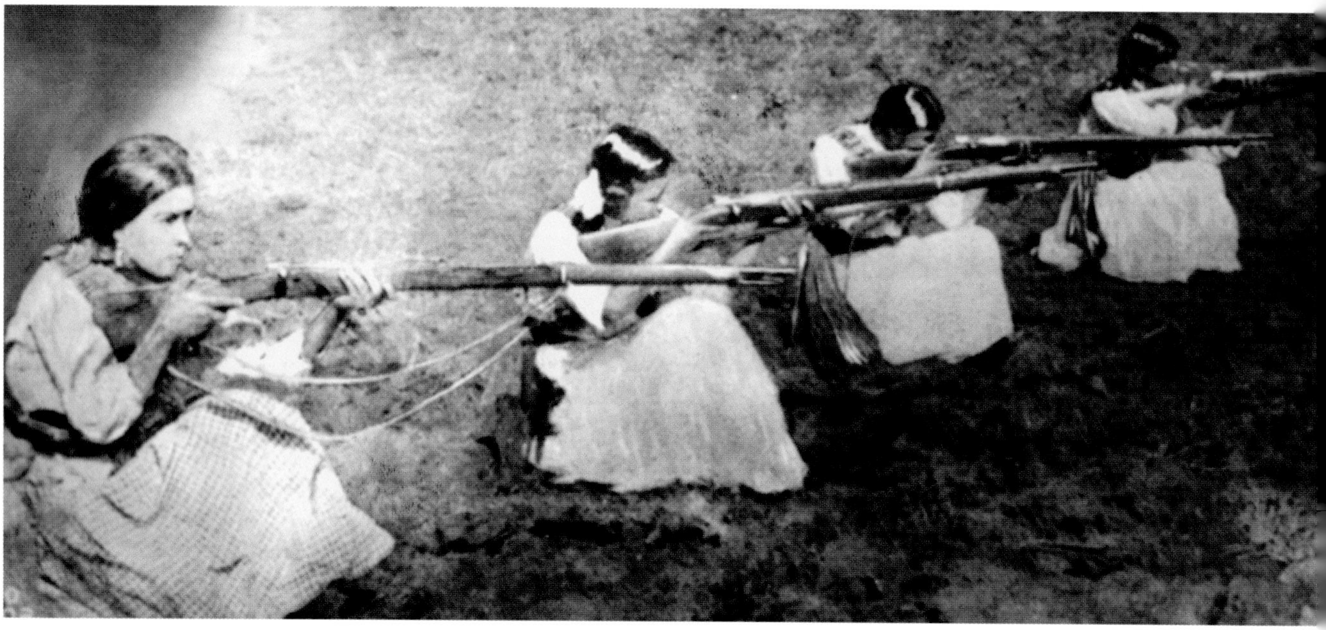

6-20. Women learning how to shoot to defend themselves, Ario, Michoacán, February 1914; J. Guerrero, *La Ilustración Semanal*, 3 March 1914. © Inv. #63945, Fondo Casasola, SINAFO-Fototeca Nacional del INAH.

Rather than advertising war's disasters, the periodicals preferred to emphasize the militarization of society to defend Huertismo. *La Ilustración Semanal* printed several photos from their correspondent in Michoacán, a J. Guerrero, of women's participation in the counter-revolutionary movement, under the title "The Services of the Amazons in the Lines."[47] In accordance with the exaggerated warmongering of Huerta's regime, they made them appear as if they were incorporated in the regular army, identifying them in one image as a "Group of sharpshooters from the 48th battalion in Ario" (Figure 6-20).[48] There are few photos of women shooting, and this one has a history beyond the magazine and Huertismo. When Gustavo Casasola published it, he inserted it within the context of the 1916–1918 struggle of the Constitutionalists against the bandits who "fell like hungry vultures over Michoacán towns"; the cutline of the image affirmed that "The Michoacán women, so punished by the bands of José Inés Chávez García, prepare themselves to defend their towns."[49] Historian Luis González described Chávez García as "the country's most celebrated bandit, who made his entrance under Villa's flag. His tactics were 'strike and run,' and his triple purpose was to loot, to rape the girls, and to set fire to the ranches. . . . His men looted and killed, deflowered virgins, raped women in the presence of their husbands, and committed other excesses. The leader loved seeing his soldiers have a good time."[50]

The photo could have served in the *Historia gráfica de la Revolución Mexicana* as a veiled reference to the rapes that were constant during the revolution, as tends to be the case in chaotic situations; obviously, as for so many other calamities of war, there are no photographs.

Rape was, nevertheless, as constant during the revolution as it is invisible in its histories. Hence, it is important to include one of the few verbal testimonies to the danger Mexican women faced, which was so widespread that it could come from any quarter. Ignacio Méndez Alonso lived through the revolution as a child, and he remembers what happened when the forces that his family was attached to took a town and occupied a house in which they found three girls.

> We all threw ourselves on the food. The girls watched us, trembling with fear, and it was then that someone said, "I was hungry, but on seeing these cuties, I know what I'm going to eat instead." "No," said a woman who was with us, "Poor girls, don't do anything to them!" "Shut up, old woman. It'd be better if you didn't get into this because we may just finish up with you." As he said that, he grabbed one of the girls, who cried for help. Others followed his lead and dragged the other girls to a room from which we soon heard their yelling and crying.
>
> Then something terrible happened. Some sixteen or eighteen men were with us, and their lowest instincts had been awakened. As there were only three girls in the house, they turned on the four young women that were with us, among them my sister Dominga. The women didn't want to, but the men said, "We don't want to beat you up, but you'll do it one way or the other." Although they were crying, they obeyed and were taken to the room with the other girls. I didn't comprehend then what had happened. I was a child and only heard the women crying and cursing the men. Later, when I was an adult I understood that they had been raped by our own people.[51]

For those who felt themselves attracted to the new possibilities of democracy, the ferocity of the Huertista reaction was such that they had to take a position: either join up with the revolutionaries or suffer the consequences. In Michoacán, 1913 was known as "the year of the hanged," and one way that the brothers Juan and Antonio Cachú earned their living was picturing hanged Maderistas (the following year, they would leave their native state to join up with agrarian revolutionaries, eventually becoming Villistas) (Figure 6-21). According to Miguel Ángel Berumen,

> It was prohibited to cut them down, and the families were uncertain of what would happen to their dead, so they went to the Cachús to have them make a posthumous portrait of their loved one, which they conserved as a souvenir. . . . It was important that the entire body of the deceased be seen very sharply, so the photographers would ask some person to hold the swinging body to make it still. Once the cadaver's movement was controlled, with impressive sangfroid the Cachús photographed it as if it were any studio portrait.[52]

As central a protagonist of the war as death was the train, and it was much more present in photographs. "The revolution was made on rails," said the railroad leader from Puebla, Guillermo Treviño, and trains and stations appear constantly as the context of photographed activities.[53] Within this genre, one of the tropes that developed was that of the train station farewells between federal soldiers and their "loved ones." I suspect that most of these images were taken during Huertismo, and that they were media events for the magazines.[54] In general, the photos of the goodbyes focus on couples: the soldier—well dressed and equipped with weapon, pack, and full cartridge belts—and his girlfriend, wife, or mother.

An intriguing variant of the train station photographs can be seen in Figure 6-22. The image offers the opportunity to examine how an art historian analyzes the photography of the revolution, for Leonard Folgarait focused exclusively on this picture in discussing the work of Agustín Víctor Casasola.[55] Having assigned authorship of the photo, Folgarait went on to assert that the date of the picture is between 1912 and 1917, though "most certainly" 1915. Exact dating is apparently unimportant in art history, for he explains, "The possible five-year span of time does not concern me terribly here, as the historical events of the Revolution during this entire period were paradoxically consistent in terms of the overall chaos . . . of rural peoples fighting on behalf of different causes, all of which called themselves revolutionary." The geographical location is as nebulous as the chronological: "Here is neither city nor open country." Folgarait believes that what we are seeing is an assemblage of people who were organized into "photographable fashion": "The photographer here has decided that a candid shot would somehow not have caught the version of reality he and his photojournalistic context sought. Now we need to examine why this *organized* version of reality was preferred over the given but now invisible one."

In looking for an explanation behind the photo's creation, Folgarait stated that his analysis was driven by his consciousness of the heterogeneity of the revolutionary forces. He argues that the image was constructed to demonstrate a national unity within a mixed population.

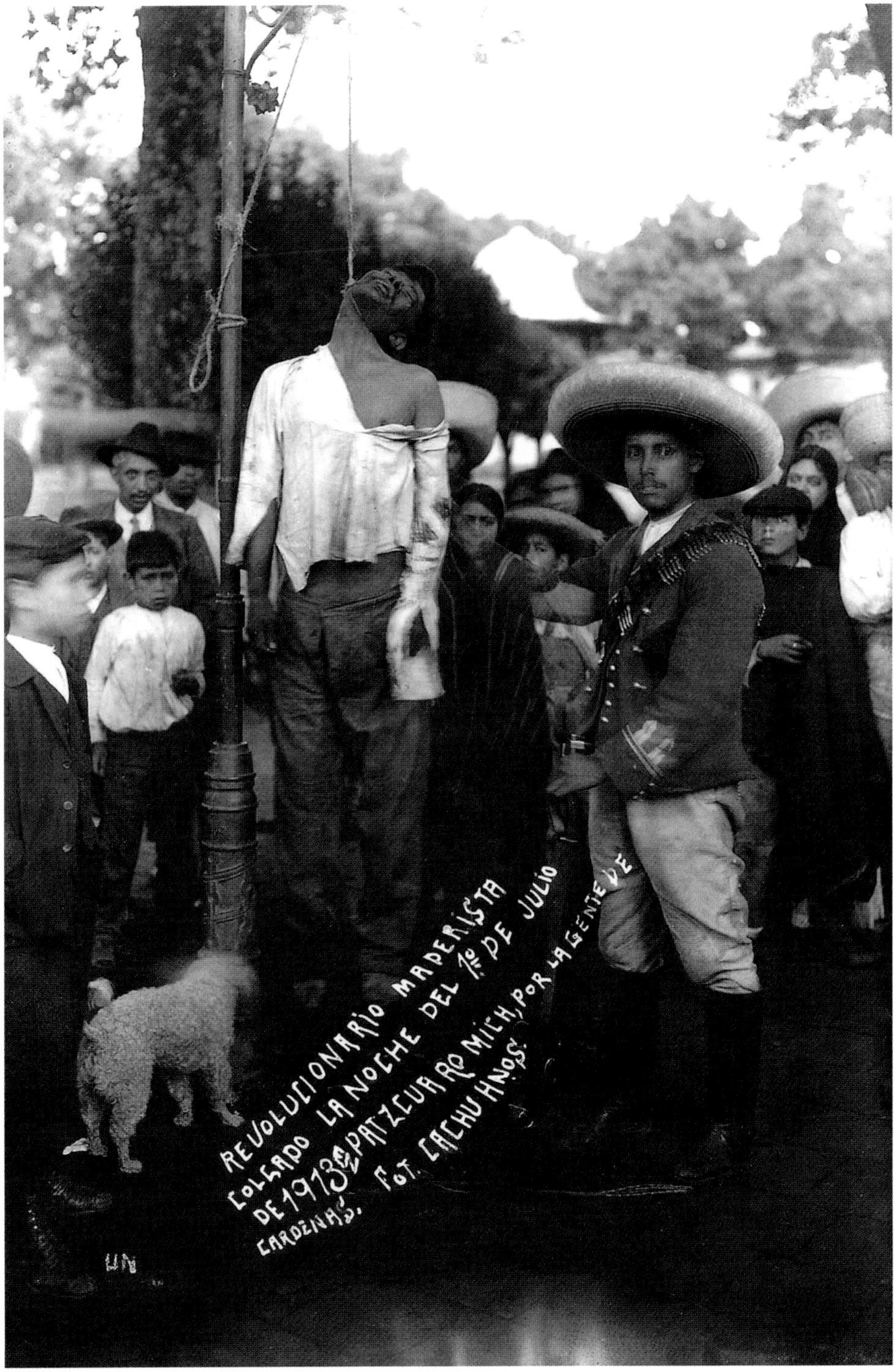

6-21. "Maderista revolutionary hanged on the night of 1 June 1913 in Patzcuaro, Michoacán, by the people of Cárdenas"; Cachú brothers. © Fondo "Cachú-Ramírez Juan," Departamento de Información y Documentación de la Cultura Audiovisual, Benemérita Universidad Autónoma de Puebla.

This is not a cohesive group in terms of personal appearance. . . . This is clearly a cross section of generic types of Mexicans, removed from their home communities and randomly brought together. . . . This is an inventory of populations in an imaginary grouping that might connote a "nation." . . . Urban and rural underclasses are mixed in throughout. This is Mexico displaced, then cobbled together, ready to be transported and recombined again, a coming together of the wished-for nation, an amalgamation being truly forged, guaranteeing that the widest possible cross section is always maintained. . . . This cross section of the peoples of Mexico is exactly the union that each of the major groups contesting for power wished to lay claim to.[56]

6-22. Train station scene, Mexico City (?), ca. 1913. © Inv. #6360, Fondo Casasola, SINAFO-Fototeca Nacional del INAH.

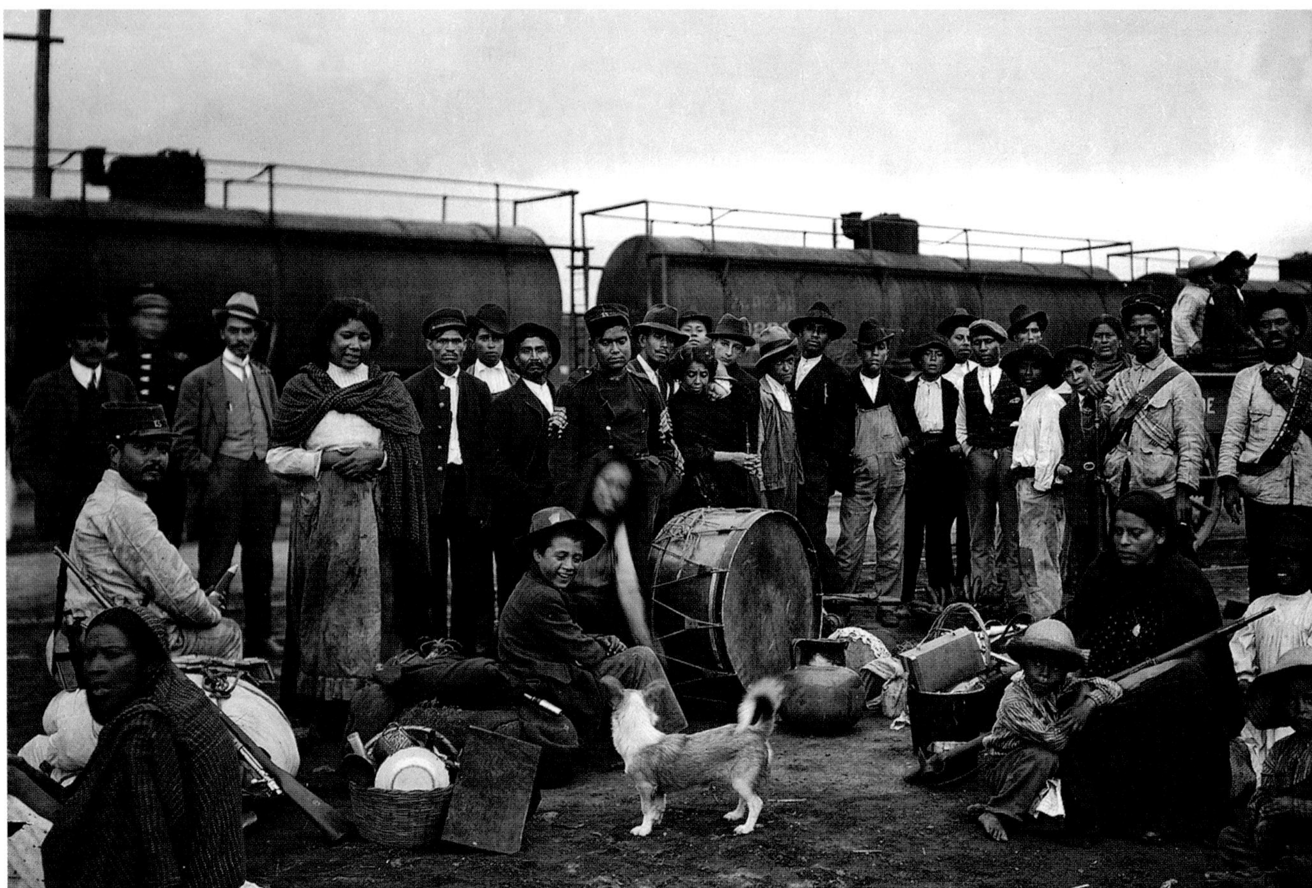

The first steps in critiquing Folgarait's analysis are to ask whether in fact that picture shows what he contends it does, and whether the photographer would have been involved in such a construction of nationhood. The people are clearly of urban extraction, and the soldiers are clothed in federal uniforms, indicating that they are likely members of Huerta's forces. The men in the back dressed in modern clothing are a composite of the sorts of individuals who are found around important railway centers, such as inspectors, telegraphers, private security, and crossing guards.[57] Several of the men are connected to the railroad, most of them workers, in their customary overalls and unique hats, and one is a disheveled official (conductor?) of some sort. A trio of younger males are probably food sellers (see the bananas at their feet). A couple of better-dressed men—with ties, jackets, and more elegant headwear than the others—stand to the side, their hands in their pockets. Six women are in the image, one of whom has been recruited to pose as a *soldadera*-combatant with a rifle that has evidently been given her to that end; the pose seems so strange to her son that he smiles at the photographer in complicity. If this photo represents an *intention* to create a cross section of Mexico or an inventory of its populations, we would have to ask whose vision it is.

One is struck by the absence of campesinos. At this point in time, Mexico was predominantly agricultural, and country people formed the vast majority of the revolutionary armies. Folgarait alludes to the figures on the wagon as "representatives" of the campesinos, but they are almost certainly workers for the national railroads, for they are sitting high on a modern work vehicle of that company. He also attempts to find peasantry in "the seated women wearing shawls," but only the one on the far left could possibly be identified as a campesina. The question arises: Whose concept of national unity would exclude campesinos? Obviously, country people would be present in any Zapatista or Villista construction of national being because peasants were the very base of those forces; and they would also appear in a Constitutionalist depiction because of the ideological incorporation of campesinos in that movement. The eminently urban and militarized vision here embodied is that of Huertismo: if this is Mexico, it is a Mexico of the reaction, and not the revolution, because these are not revolutionary forces. In imagining that this image somehow encapsulates a broad search for Mexican identity, the art historian has engaged in an anachronistic endeavor, projecting upon an image made in the midst of the armed struggle a message of national unity that would be elaborated in the years after 1920.

We could ascribe this image to Agustín Víctor Casasola (or some other metropolitan photojournalist) and see this configuration of individuals as *his* construction of national unity, made in the service of reactionary propaganda. A couple of possible scenarios come to mind. One narrative could be the following: the photographer went to make some typical *soldadera* images in the patio, finding or taking the woman who is sitting with the rifle to participate with the soldiers. When he started shooting, unoccupied railway workers and sellers wandered over and gathered around; some of them leaned forward to make sure they got into the picture. Another possible explanation is that the young men standing in the background were recruited—or gang pressed or volunteered—to serve in Huerta's army. They do not appear to have been gathered en masse (as were the men in Figure 6-14), though they are enclosed in the photo by armed soldiers. The fact that they seem to have (more or less) willingly entered into the military might link them to some key event that galvanized the country; perhaps they had volunteered to go off and fight against the U.S. invasion of Veracruz in April of 1914, and the soldiers were to accompany them to make sure they got there. Maybe the *soldadera* was being utilized as a mediatic recruiting tool: she may have marched with the soldiers and military band (see the member in front of his drum) on a sweep through Mexico City that ended up in one of the railroad stations where the photojournalist posed the image as propaganda for Huerta's war effort. At this point, the federal army was suffering great shortages, a fact indicated by uniforms that are dirty, worn, and mixed. The photograph is not without its metaphors, but they are visual allusions to the militarization of society, the forced recruitment, and—whatever the intentions of the photojournalist—the decadence of the Huertista cause.

Life itself occurred on top of the trains for many people: they slept, they ate, they loved, they gave birth—and they died, because many *soldaderas* fell off of them.[58] Photographic researcher Miguel Ángel Morales found my affirmation that the *soldaderas* traveled on top of the trains to be "reckless and erroneous": "Anybody that has ever traveled in a train, even one for children, will know how difficult it is to stand up and how dangerous it would be to travel on top of or underneath a car in movement."[59] Morales's assertion notwithstanding, there is no doubt that people traveled on top of the trains, despite the danger, as can be appreciated in researched histories—for example, that by Elizabeth Salas—and in documentary films made during the revolution. In the absence of a quartermaster corps dedicated to feeding the troops, it was necessary for families to accompany the soldiers; in Figure 6-23 we see women cooking on top of a car. The trains not only carried combatants (and their families) and armament, they were weapons themselves at times (Figure 6-24). For obvious reasons, they were the object of attacks, either by means of destroying the tracks (Figure 6-25) or by blowing up the trains (Figure 6-26).

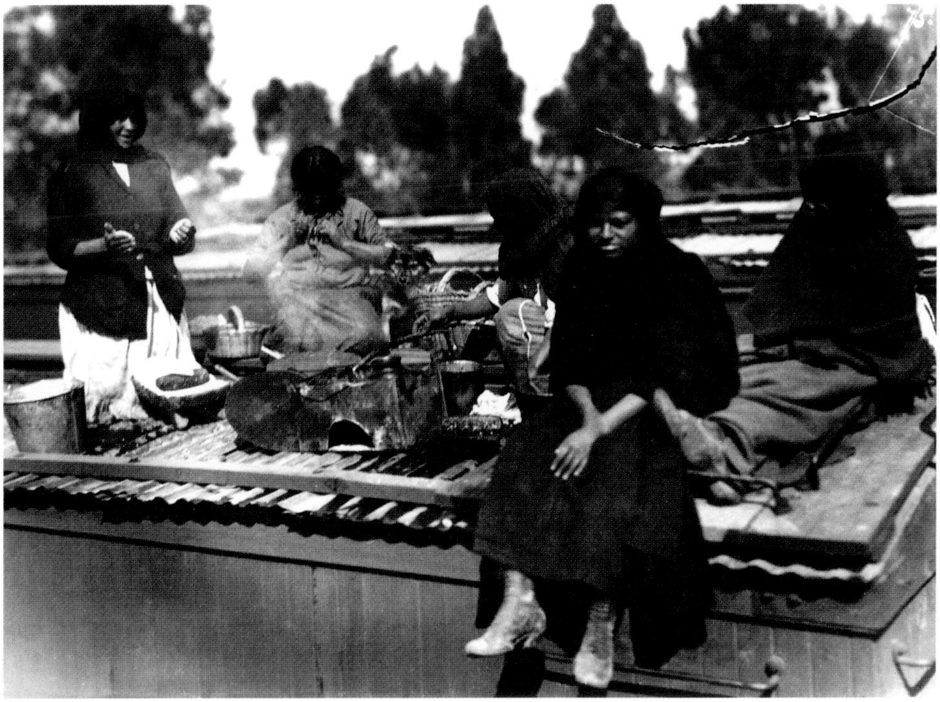

6-23. Women cooking on top of a train, ca. 1914. © Inv. #643154, Fondo Casasola, SINAFO-Fototeca Nacional del INAH.

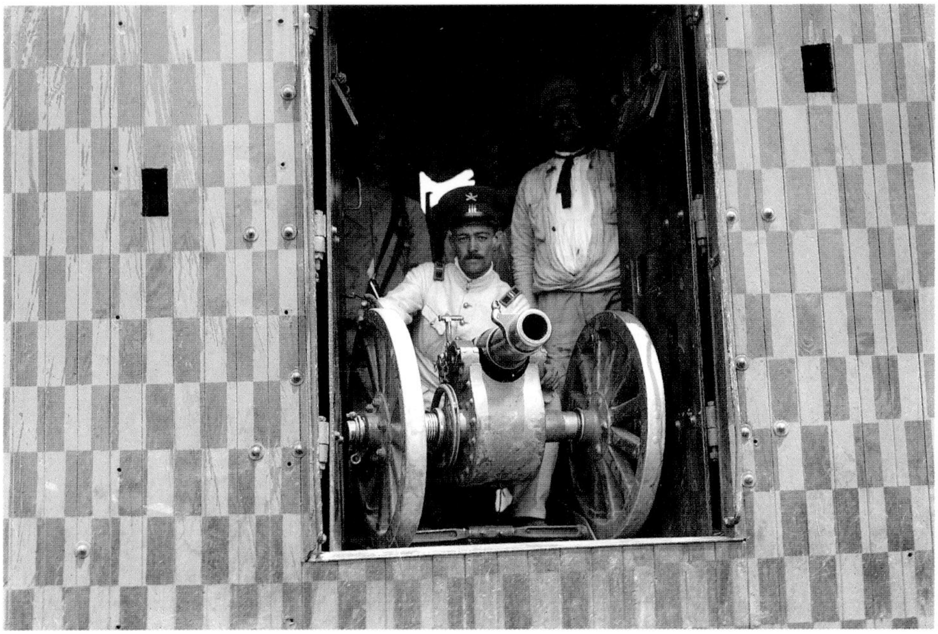

6-24. Armored train, Mexico City, ca. 1913. © Inv. #65930, Fondo Casasola, SINAFO-Fototeca Nacional del INAH.

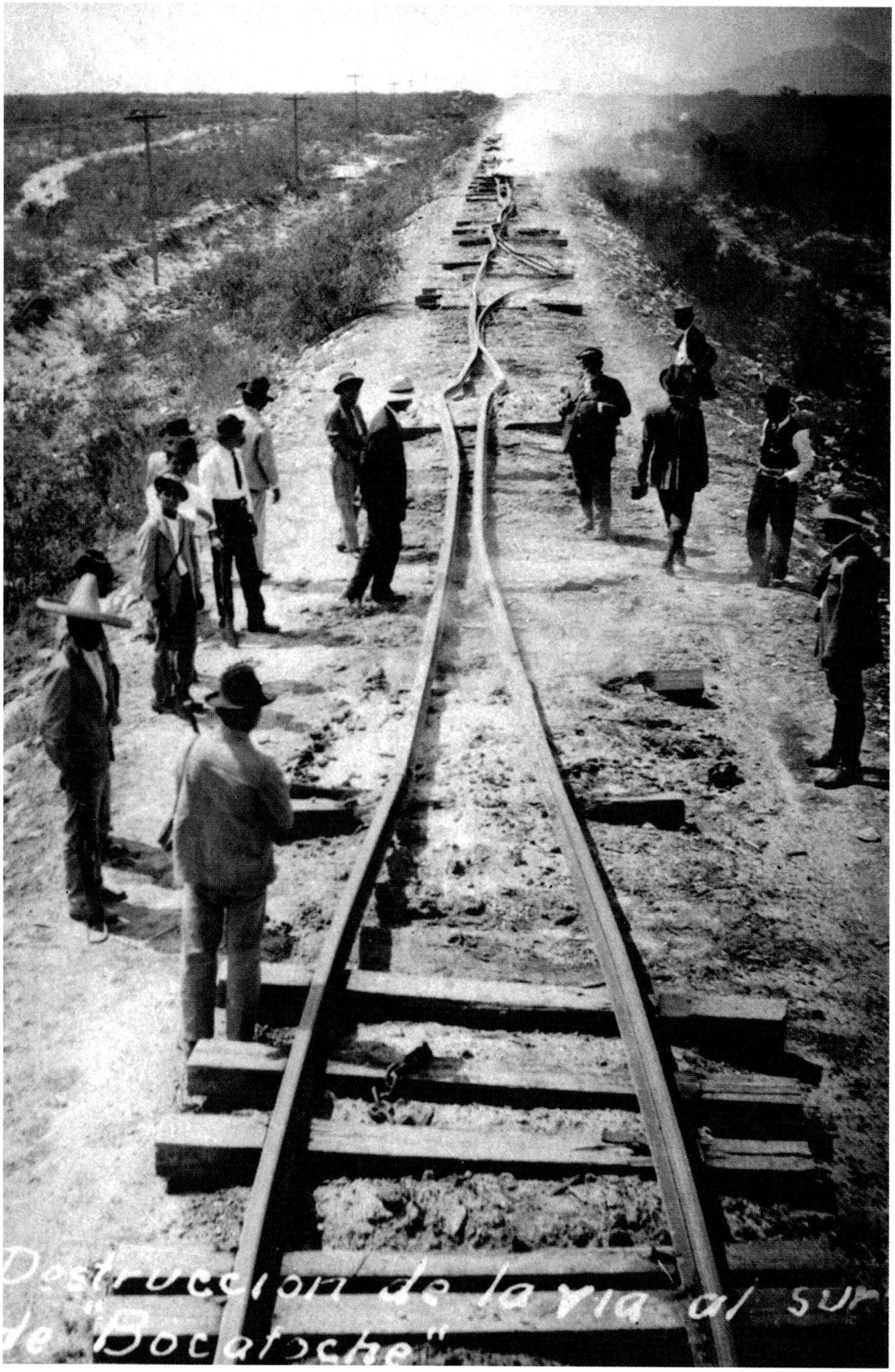

6-25. Destroyed rails, Bocatoche, Coahuila, ca. 1913. © Inv. #32942, Fondo Casasola, SINAFO-Fototeca Nacional del INAH.

The interruption of the regular train service greatly affected the economy, which suffered an enormous lack of liquidity: the treasury was empty, the *leva* depleted the workforce, and European bankers hesitated to loan money because of the United States' refusal to recognize Huerta's regime. Even in Mexico City, "conservative and Porfirian to the core," the discontent with the problems grew together with opposition to Huertismo.[60] In spite of the Thermadorian dictatorship, the moral ground had fundamentally shifted in the two and a half years since the overthrow of Díaz. The extraordinary development of popular consciousness—and the grade of desperation which people must have reached—can be seen in a photo taken by Abraham Lupercio of "a commission of workers that present themselves to the President of the Republic in search of work" (Figure 6-27).[61]

The protests took on less respectful forms, and the refusal to accept the betrayal of the Maderista revolution was expressed in schemes designed to overthrow the dictatorship. Some students planned to rise up in arms against Huerta, but they were

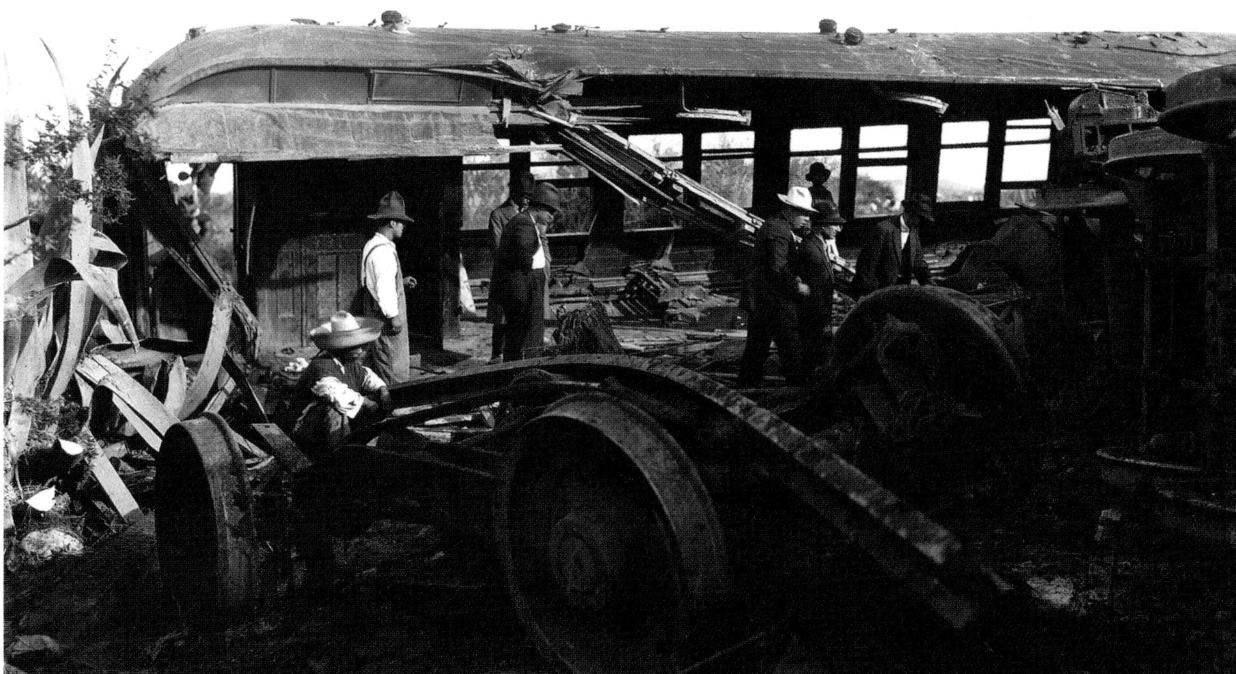

6-26. A train that was blown up, ca. 1914. © Inv. #5950, Fondo Casasola, SINAFO-Fototeca Nacional del INAH.

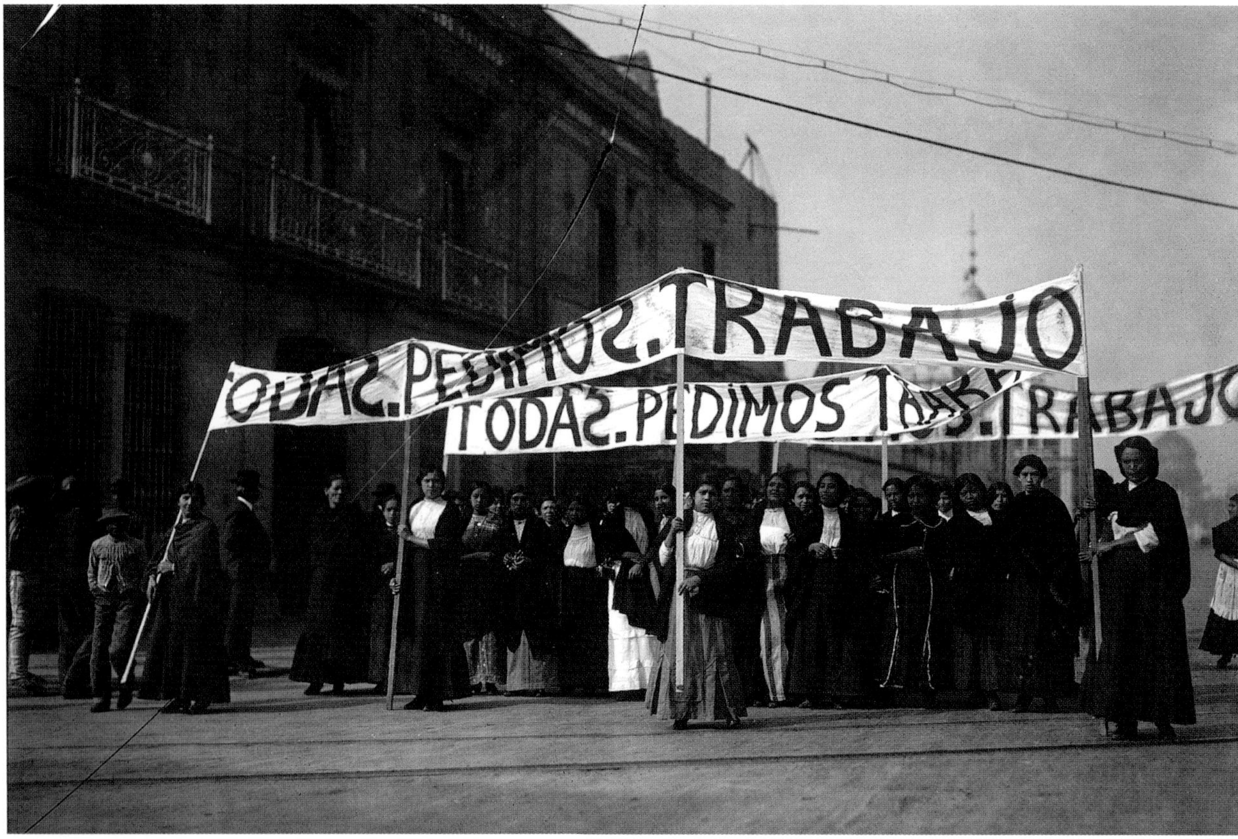

6-27. Women demanding work, Mexico City, December 1913; Abraham Lupercio. © Inv. #5336, Fondo Casasola, SINAFO-Fototeca Nacional del INAH.

arrested in San Lucas Xochimanca, 24 April 1913, before they could act.[62] It was hard to get a plot off the ground because Huerta's secret police were everywhere; witnesses affirmed that "The situation was very difficult; vigilance was extraordinary and one had to be very careful about what they said. One couldn't talk about the revolution because there were 'rats' (*soplones*) and many police reserves all over the place. Because of that everything was veiled and clandestine."[63] Congressman Néstor Monroy conspired with some workers to assassinate Huerta, Félix Díaz, and Aureliano Blanquet; they were captured in Mexico City, 13 July 1913 (Figure 6-28).[64] Most of the prisoners return the camera's gaze, knowing that they will soon be killed. Among the classic repertory of revolutionary photos are those in which men stare back at their executioners while waiting for the rifles' discharge (see Figures 8-29 and 8-30); here we see how others look into the face of death.

6-28. Federal deputy Néstor Monroy and a group of workers who were captured by police for plotting against Victoriano Huerta and who will shortly be killed, Mexico City, 13 July 1913. © Inv. #37723, Fondo Casasola, SINAFO-Fototeca Nacional del INAH.

The wide and contradictory range of visual culture in this moment can be illustrated by comparing three photos: one staged for the cover of *La Ilustración Semanal* (Figure 6-29), another of the Felicista soldiers in the Ciudadela (Figure 6-9, above), and the third published in a French magazine (Figure 6-30). We do not know who took the photo of the soldier posing for the Mexican magazine, but if Ezequiel Álvarez Tostado did not take it personally, he had it made as director (Figure 6-29).[65] The style is antiquated, as if it were staged in a studio; although it occurs outside, its realism does not reach the level of the postcards made by Aurelio Escobar during the Maderista movement. Typical of studio imagery, this picture is full of obvious and imposed symbols: the patriotic icons of the maguey and the national flag and, moreover, a transparently capitalist allegory: a fence of barbed wire indicates that the soldier is there to protect private property.

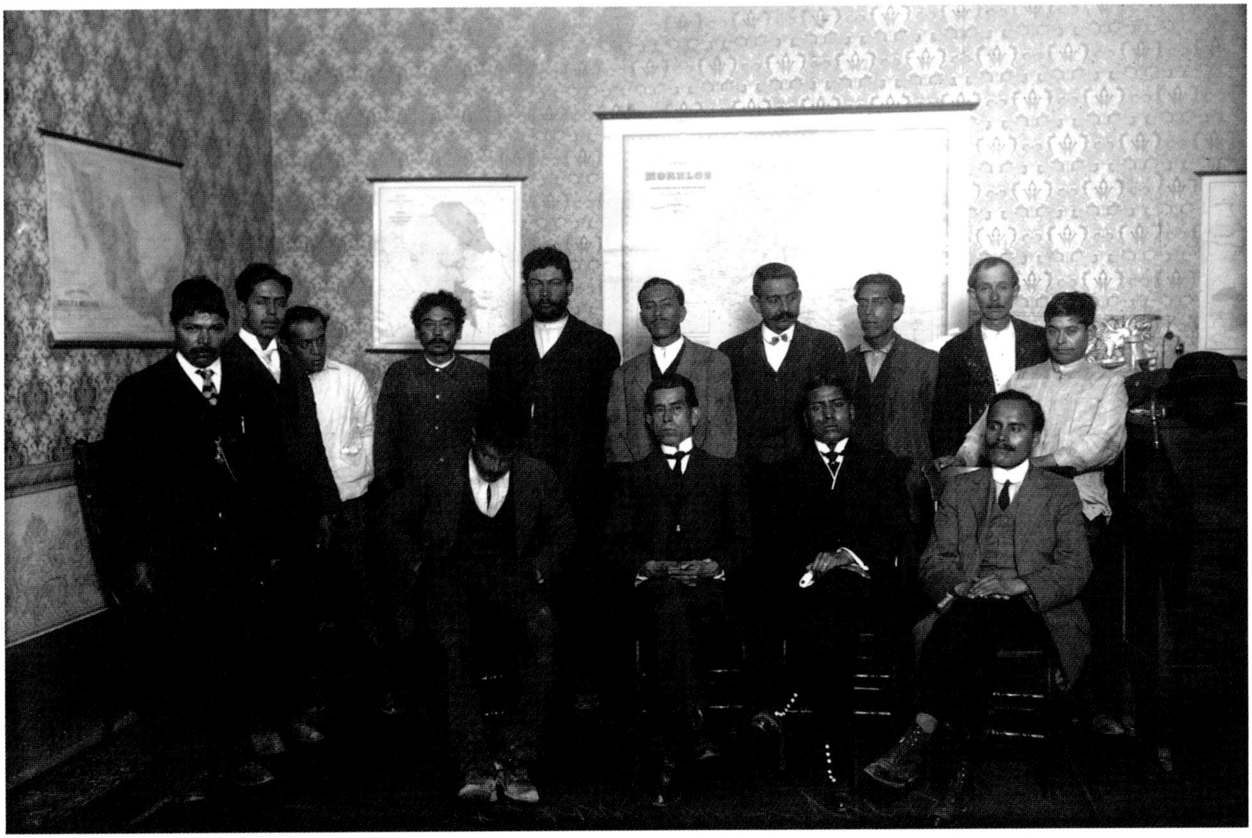

The symbolism of the magazine cover photograph belongs to nineteenth-century aesthetic practices. Modern photography would employ more subtle metaphors such as the brick wall in the photo from La Decena Trágica taken by Eduardo Melhado (Figure 6-9 above). Melhado's photo incarnates the metaphysic that art historian Gretchen Gardner describes as that of a "spontaneous witness": "a type of photography that emphasized chance, alert presence in the real world and quick response."[66] Thanks to the invention of small-format cameras and fast film on plastic rolls, "The heyday of spontaneous witness was the period of high modernism between the two world wars and into the 1950s."[67] Melhado was a modern photojournalist: as Henri Cartier-Bresson would in the following decades, he used his camera to hunt for and to discover the world, possibilities created precisely by photographic technology. His is an advanced aesthetic of photography in which the significance of a scene appears to derive from a reality that Melhado found, rather than one he imposed upon the photograph.[68] Melhado recognized photography as a new and distinct medium; Tostado wanted to imitate art. The difference between these imagemakers foreshadows that which would occur in Mexico during the 1920s between modernists such as Edward Weston, Tina Modotti, and Manuel Álvarez Bravo, and traditionalists such as Hugo Brehme and Luís Márquez.

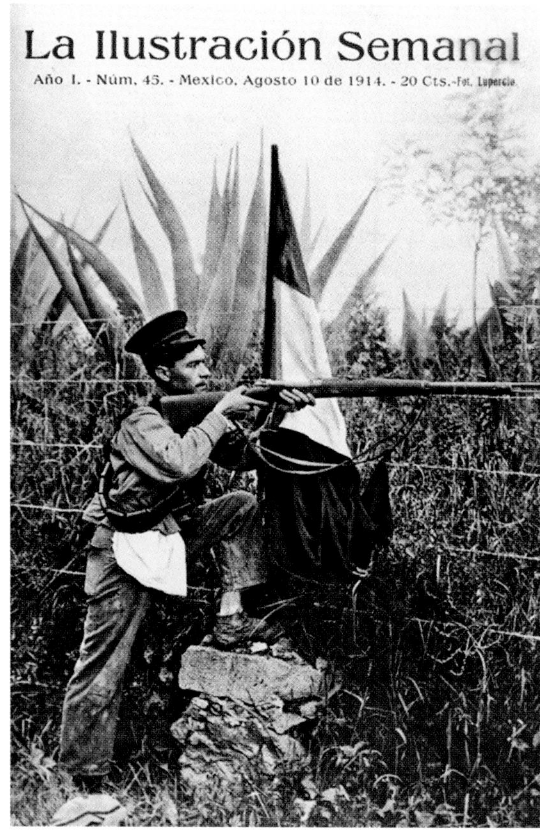

6-29. Cover of *La Ilustración Semanal*, 10 August 1914; Ezequiel Álvarez Tostado.

Although Tostado's photo does not correspond to our codes of realism and credibility, he was following premodern, nineteenth-century models that still found expression in the Pictorialist movement. His interest was to produce art, not document reality. When he was interviewed in the midst of the Huertista regime, he spoke with a certain disdain of photojournalism and, implicitly, of documentary imagery. In fact, it seems that this photographer-impresario-lithographer did not recognize the historical moment through which his country was passing.

> My tendencies and habits have led me to artistic photography and principally to that of landscapes. There is no doubt that, from the journalistic point of view and above all of daily newspapers, the information of the moment, the fact surprised in the public world, the fire, the murder, the *nota roja*, are worthy of taking into

> account, and their reproduction forms an archive of national life, the history lived and laid out before the readers' eyes. But, if it is true that within this meritorious labor one can produce great works, artistic works, it is no less true that it does not lend itself to express the temperament and personal inclination of the individual as does free photography.[69]

Given his position, it is ironic that Tostado directed a news magazine, *La Ilustración Semanal*, whose first issue appeared in October 1913.[70] The only illustrated magazine of general news directed by a photojournalist in the history of Mexico, this publication could represent an effort to "recapture" the photographic space that amateurs were winning with their capacity to document spontaneously the scenes offered by the revolution. For Tostado, it was important to take into account the levels of development: "We who have spent years behind unpolished glass and under a focusing cloth must differentiate ourselves from those who go out with their Kodak under their arm one fine morning in search of the science to make photographs."[71] The fact that he could produce a magazine of high quality on good paper—which began to become scarce in the middle of the war—and pay photographers and correspondents to cover different fronts indicates that he had contacts in the high spheres of Huertismo. Olivier Debroise asserted that Tostado was a "committed follower of Madero," but my suspicion of his links to the Huertista regime deepens upon knowing that Tostado left for Cuba with the arrival of the Villistas and Zapatistas in December 1914 (he would later join the Constitutionalists).[72]

A photo published on a two-page spread in the French magazine *L'Illustration* on 20 June 1914 is diametrically opposed to the cover of *La Ilustración Semanal* (Figure 6-30). The image of Huerta and his accomplices drinking alcohol (probably brandy, as that was Huerta's favorite libation) must be situated within a genre that would only develop in the following decade in a technologically advanced Germany, and today has reached its maximum expression in paparrazi imagery. With the invention of the small-format cameras that used rolls of 35 mm plastic film, photographers such as Erich Salomon and Tim Gidal became famous in the 1920s and '30s for their "candid" photos that caught politicians in indiscrete situations.[73] Evidently, this photo was taken by the French magazine's correspondent M. Louis Botte, and indicates a familiarity with the technology that permitted such a shot (without Huerta's bodyguards noticing), as well as a consciousness of the uses to which it could be put. Published a month before Huerta resigned (and shortly before the First World War would wipe news of Mexico off the pages of European magazines for four years), the

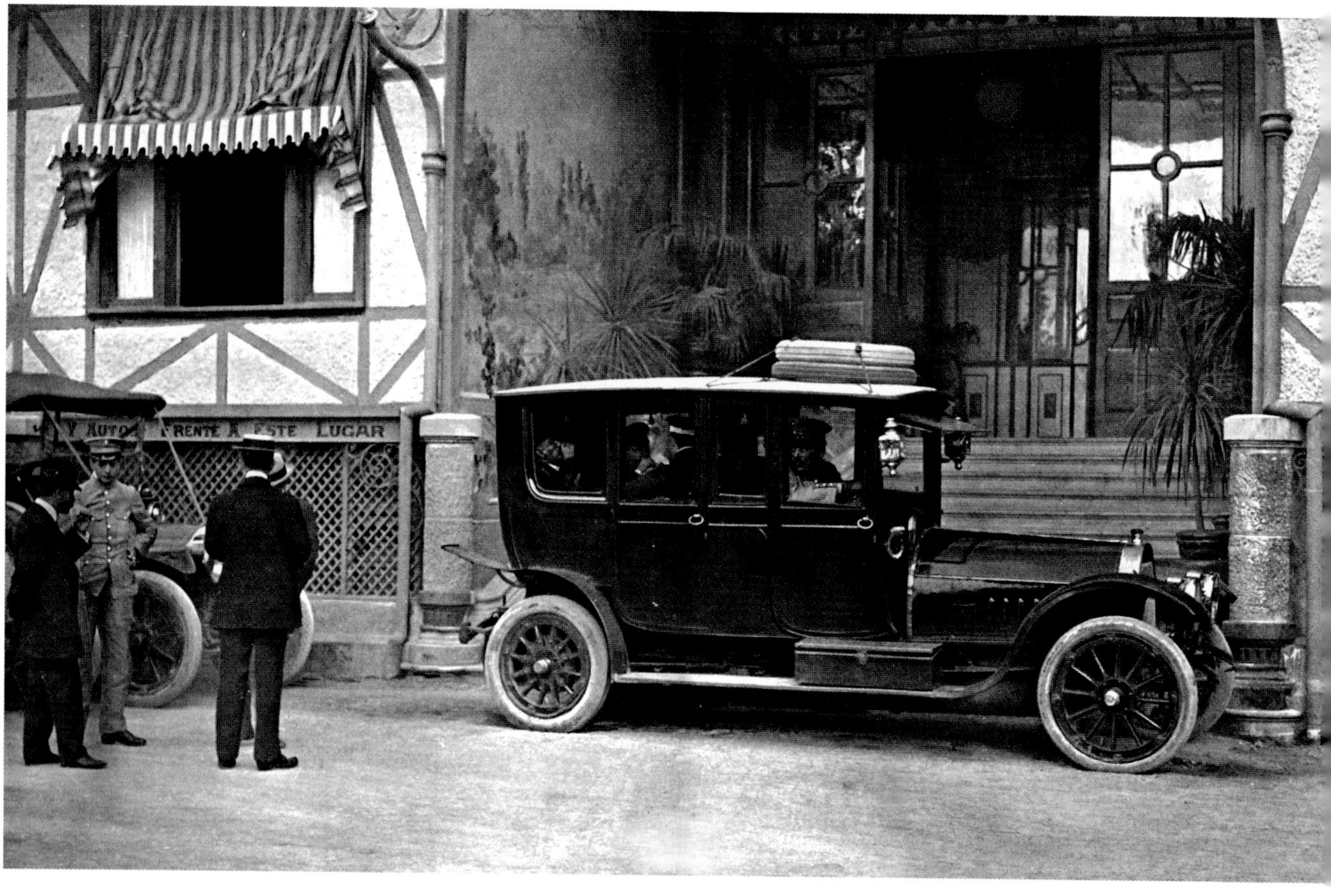

6-30. President Victoriano Huerta and friends drinking in his car, Mexico City, June 1914; M. Louis Botte, *L'Illustration*, 20 June 1914.

photo documents Huerta's alcoholism, "which has been so criticized by the U.S. press and President Wilson."[74] Two months after the United States had invaded Veracruz, the picture represented a way of putting pressure on Huerta and, at the same time, ridiculing the puritanical morality of a nation that had decided to oust the dictator for essentially two reasons: to keep the revolution from radicalizing, and to ensure that Mexico would be retained within the imperial sphere.

When U.S. troops entered the port of Veracruz on 21 April 1914, they came accompanied by navy photographers in ships equipped with darkrooms. Historian Paul Vanderwood has described how Veracruz and the northern border served as a laboratory for U.S. armed forces that would soon enter the First World War: it permitted them to try out new equipment, logistical procedures, ground operations, and information gathering.[75] Veracruz was the first place where U.S. forces began to incorporate photographs as a fundamental element of reconnaissance. They took photos of the Mexican installations and lines of defense, sometimes from airplanes, which were being used for the first time in U.S. history against an enemy. I imagine that pictures were part of the propagandistic machinery designed to ensure that opposition to the intervention would not develop within the United States, whether from isolationists or leftists.[76] Although this aspect of the invading army has not been researched, photographs in the Library of Congress—including one of a Mexican band marching in front of a contingent of U.S. sailors in their white dress uniforms—indicate that it must have been important.[77] Because the navy did not permit nonmilitary professional photographers to accompany the fleet, those assigned to the ships "earned extra money photographing the crews in personalized pictures which became postcards."[78] It is also probable that many of the marines and sailors carried Kodak Brownies to document their bellicose tropical tourism. The military photographers and the amateurs produced a significant quantity of images taken from the side of the invaders. Also, the invasion attracted "a large number of special correspondents," including recognized writers such as Richard Harding Davis and Jack London.[79] Among the foreign photojournalists who arrived in Veracruz was the ever-present Jimmy Hare, sent by *Collier's*.[80]

The imperial media machine was as powerful as the military, and that was surely the reason that *La Ilustración Semanal* became involved in a journalistic resistance against the U.S. press. The magazine reproduced "A clipping from the *World* of New York, which shows how the U.S. government has tried to glorify those that attack our sovereignty"; the photos are of dead and wounded invaders, as well as a boat with cadavers.[81] The Mexican periodical also published images of the invading army taken by foreign photographers (and probably rephotographed from U.S. magazines), but they recontextualized them with commentaries such as the following: "We publish this information because we esteem it to be of great interest to us as documents for the history of the Yankee infamy; we suppress the commentaries of the U.S. press because of their hateful nature"; and "Photographs of the Yankee disembarkation in Veracruz, published in the U.S. with denigrating notes about our country."[82] It also pointed to the presence of military cineastes charged with producing propaganda by reproducing a photo of "Prisoners in San Juan de Ulúa forced to cheer the Americans for a movie," an act in violation of today's Geneva Convention.[83]

It is not easy to establish authorship of the photographs taken from the Mexican side, but Samuel Tinoco was present, along with others we know only as Torresilla

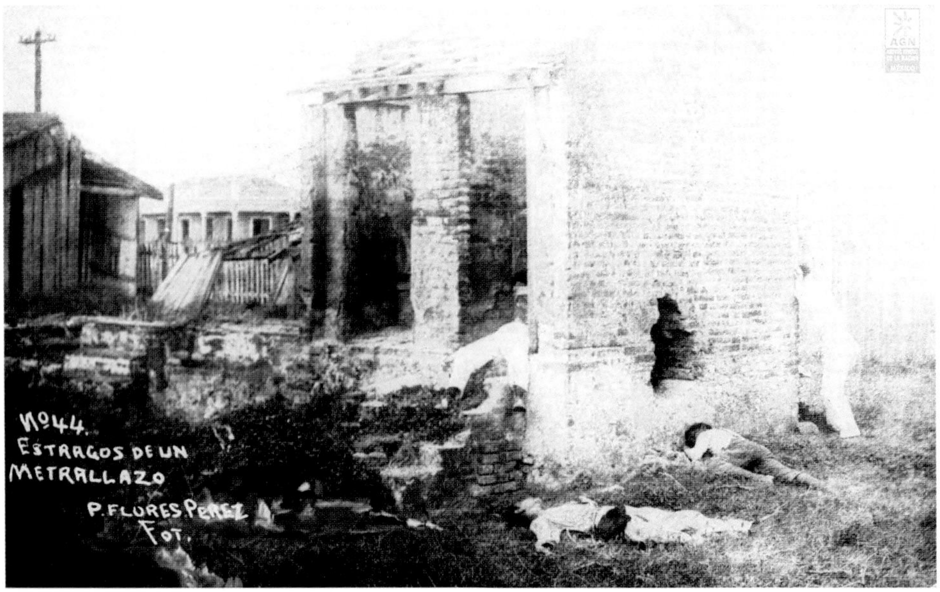

6-31. "Destruction caused by a machine-gunning," port of Veracruz, April 1914; Samuel Tinoco. © Archivo General de la Nación, Fondo Propiedad Artístico y Literaria, Flores Pérez, "Intervención norte-americana," 16.

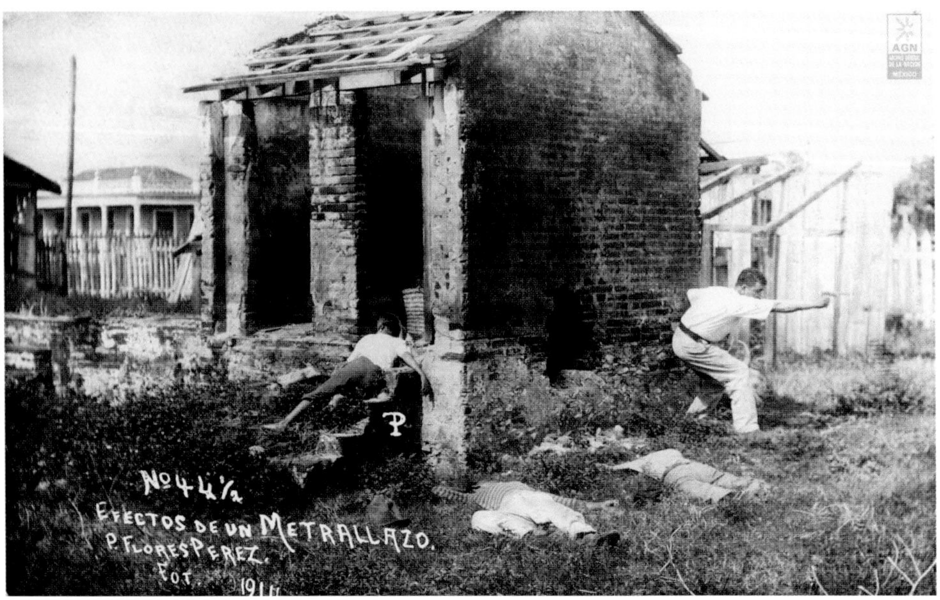

6-32. "Effects of a machine-gunning," port of Veracruz, April 1914; Samuel Tinoco. © Archivo General de la Nación, Fondo Propiedad Artístico y Literaria, Flores Pérez, "Intervención norteamericana," 17.

and Guerrero; Eduardo Melhado may also have been in the port.[84] Their images (and surely some taken by U.S. photographers) were used by the illustrated magazines to testify to the calamities caused by the invaders. In the first place are photos of the destruction and civilian casualties provoked by the occupation. It appears that the Mexican photojournalists arrived too late to cover the combat (which lasted about a week), so they staged scenarios to represent the cadavers (the destruction caused by days of bombardment was such that it would be a real backdrop for a long time). Tinoco, for example, evidently directed some Veracruzanos to "play dead" (and pose as members of the resistance) in front of a destroyed house (Figures 6-31 and 6-32).[85] Other photos document those wounded during the invasion (Figure 6-33) and Mexican prisoners guarded by sailors in uniforms stained with coffee grounds and dirty boiler water to camouflage them (Figure 6-34); both of these pictures were made in the first days, although it is not clear who took them.[86]

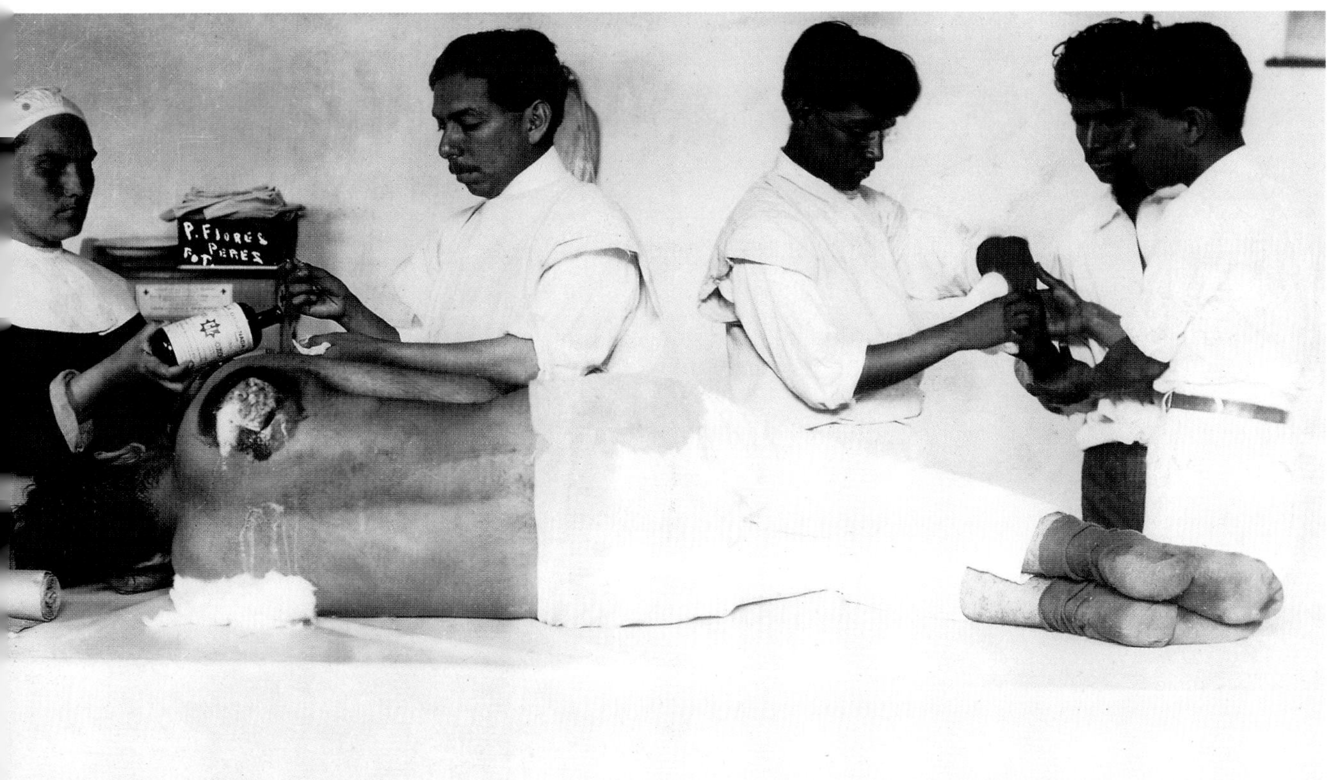

6-33. Nurses with wounded, port of Veracruz, April 1914. © Inv. #373917, Fondo Casasola, SINAFO-Fototeca Nacional del INAH.

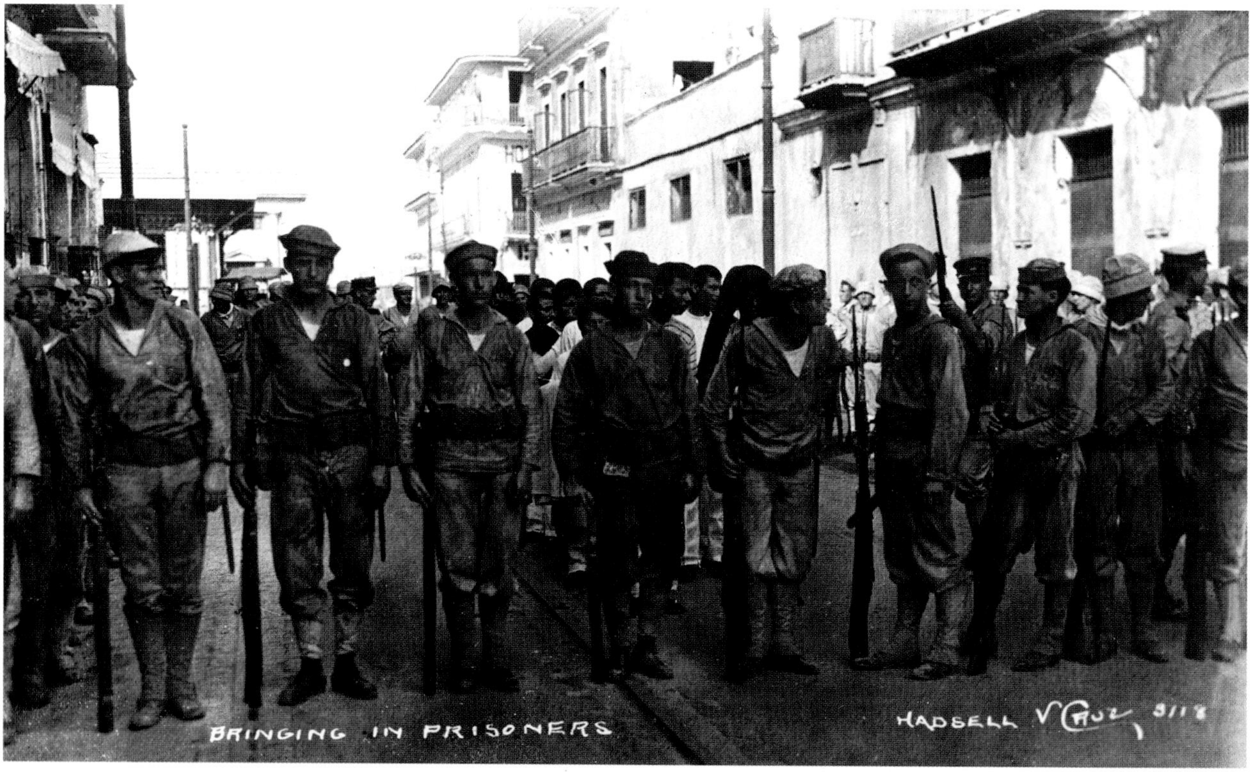

6-34. U.S. sailors in uniforms dyed with coffee grounds and dirty boiler water to camouflage them, with Mexican prisoners, port of Veracruz, April 1914. © Inv. #627278, Fondo Casasola, SINAFO-Fototeca Nacional del INAH.

The Mexican periodicals criticized the invading forces' lack of respect for the law. *Novedades* demonstrated U.S. racism with a photo of a urinal reserved for the invaders: "Despite their much-lauded equality before the law, they prohibit negroes to get near whites. In Veracruz, they have created a place Mexicans can't go. They treat us like they treat negroes!"[87] A photograph taken by Félix Miret and published in *La Semana Ilustrada* pictured a sailor standing in front of a store, ostensibly proving that he was permitting it to be sacked: "With the motive of the raising of prices for goods of prime necessity in Veracruz, the Americans had no problem in letting the people serve themselves, as can be seen in the photograph."[88]

Photographs were used to prove the existence of, and to incite, resistance in a call for national unity. Some images from Veracruz showed volunteers in training; one group of well-dressed shooters (Figure 6-35) were probably students from Mexico City whom Huerta had strong-armed to go to the port. Protests throughout the country were documented by the illustrated magazines: Abraham Lupercio covered those in Mexico City extensively, an individual named Rojas photographed demonstrations in Aguascalientes, Pichardo covered protests in Toluca, *Novedades*'s correspondent in Puebla provided images of "enthusiastic people who prepare themselves to receive military training for the war against the Yankees," and *La Semana Ilustrada* dedicated a page to "Patriotism in the states."[89] The publications called upon images to convince their countrymen of the need to resist: "Heaven hopes that viewing these photographs raises the spirit of Mexicans and contributes so that all, each in their sphere, inflamed by holy love for the Fatherland, offer themselves to save it from the painful trance in which it finds itself."[90]

National symbols were also incorporated into the resistance. One cover of *La Semana Ilustrada* showed a soldier "Haranguing the *pueblo*": he carries a banner in which an image of the Virgin of Guadalupe had been inserted in the darkroom.[91] Photos of

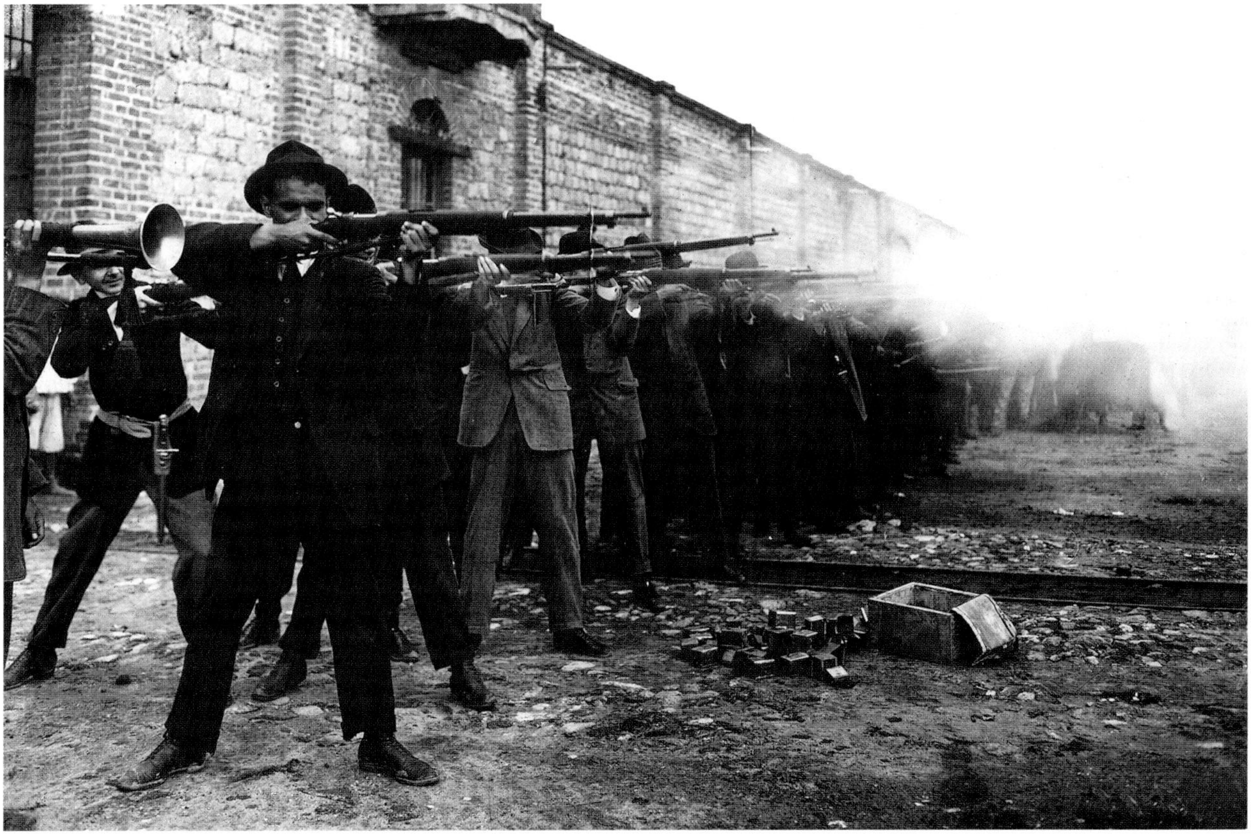

6-35. Students preparing to resist the invasion, port of Veracruz, April 1914. © Inv. #627277, Fondo Casasola, SINAFO-Fototeca Nacional del INAH.

dead heroes such as José Azueta and Virgilio Uribe appeared often. While Huerta remained in power, the media promoted him: the front page of *El Imparcial* carried a large portrait of the dictator holding a banner of the Virgin of Guadalupe, with an eagle and cactus behind.[92] Nonetheless, neither the pleas of the publications for national unity, nor their lies—such as the one that alleged that the Zapata brothers "will join the government"—served; Huerta became more and more unpopular.[93] *Novedades* hoped that images would wake up the nation: "We publish these photographs just so that the *pueblo* of Mexico, so indifferent to this situation, does not forget the offense and has the spirit to revenge it."[94] When the United States finally decided to leave Veracruz, the image that incarnated that news was a photo by Abraham Lupercio of "The Commander-in-Chief of the Revolution, Don Venustiano Carranza," reading a telegram from President Woodrow Wilson, 15 September 1914.[95]

As always, there was much filtration between the mediums of photojournalism and postcards. For example, Félix Miret is most known as a postcard producer, but he went to Veracruz as a correspondent for *La Semana Ilustrada* and photographed the occupation, apparently arriving at the end of May.[96] According to Ricardo Pérez Montfort, Veracruzano Ponciano Flores Pérez "reunited an extraordinary album of more than 70 photographs of the invasion that circulated around the world."[97] Nonetheless, it is difficult to know which of those images he took and to determine his participation in this event. I would say the same of Walter P. Hadsell, a U.S. citizen who had lived in the port some ten years and had a store of photographic materials, La Kodak, where he sold postcards, cameras, and film, which he developed and printed. Miguel Ángel Berumen believes that Hadsell's images are particularly outstanding.

> The scenarios and angles were well known to him. . . . His situation as a U.S. citizen converted Hadsell into the perfect interlocutor for the Marines, who opened the door easily to certain strategic places that were vetoed for other photographers. . . . Nonetheless, Hadsell did not conform himself with privileged military placements and, faithful to his custom, roamed all about the port to document the fighting.[98]

It could be that Hadsell's presence in the port allowed him to cover the first day of combat, as the text on Figure 6-36 alleges, but this image is problematic for two reasons. First, it is credited to Tinoco in *La Ilustración Semanal*, and, moreover, another copy was signed by Flores Pérez.[99] Second, I do not believe that it is of combat because the entire image reveals three men (on the left-hand side) talking calmly in the line of fire.[100] I suspect that Tinoco staged the scene and asked the federal soldiers to act as if it were combat. Further, it is useful to point out that the image of the sailors in the dyed uniforms (Figure 6-34)—which would indicate that it was taken in the first days—was published in *La Ilustración Semanal*, but credited to *La Semana Ilustrada*.[101] The roles played by Hadsell and Flores Pérez during the invasion are still to be defined, as is that of Melhado. It also remains to be determined whether any photos were made during combat since even the great Jimmy Hare does not seem to have arrived in time.

Another photographer who already knew Veracruz and documented the invasion was Hugo Brehme. It is not clear what the market was for Brehme's imagery, as I have never seen his photos of the invasion published in the illustrated magazines nor reproduced as postcards. What can be appreciated about his work is its visual force, as well as the search for angles and themes that other photographers seem not to

6-36. Federal soldiers, port of Veracruz, April 1914; Samuel Tinoco. © Inv. #451566, Fondo Casasola, SINAFO-Fototeca Nacional del INAH.

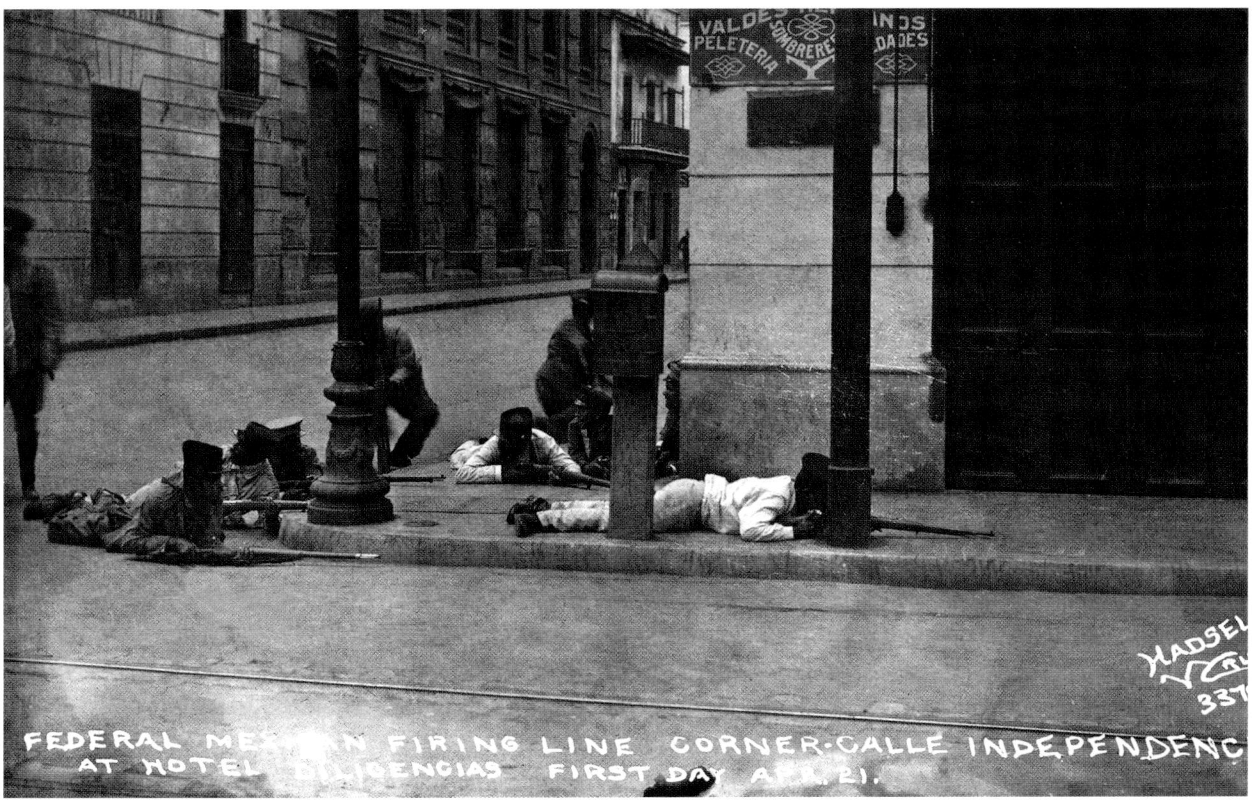

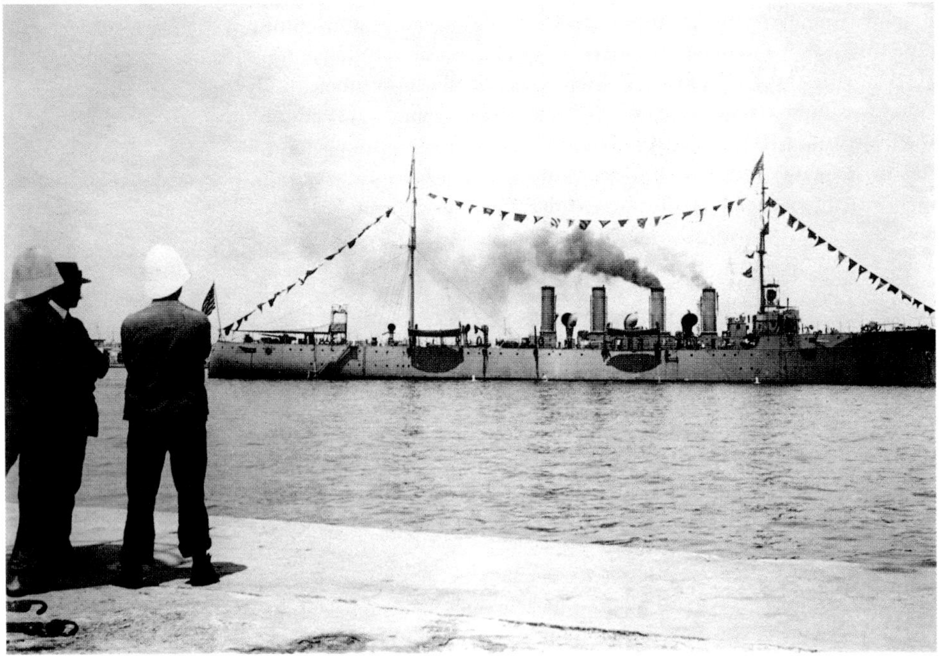

6-37. U.S. battleship, port of Veracruz, April 1914; Hugo Brehme. © INAH-Hoffman-Brehme, 135.

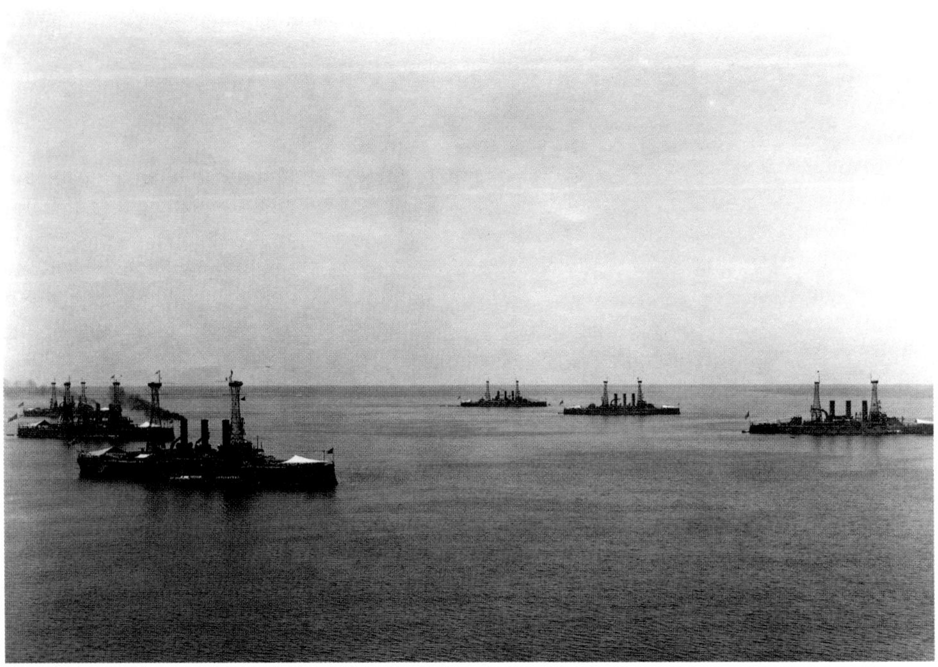

6-38. U.S. warships, port of Veracruz, April 1914; Hugo Brehme. © INAH-Hoffman-Brehme, 176.

have explored. The image of Mexicans gazing at a U.S. warship (Figure 6-37)—one can barely see the flag over the shoulder of the man on the right—transmits a sensation of how the defenders must have felt overwhelmed by U.S. power. A shot from on high of the U.S. warships (Figure 6-38) permits us to appreciate the enormous display of force that the fleet represented, and it is the only one I know of that was made by someone not in one of the U.S. navy planes. Brehme was able to convince the captains of both U.S. and German ships to let him photograph the crews formed on the decks, but it is difficult to know how he could get access to the prison, San Juan de Ulúa, and make a photo of such intimacy as Figure 6-39.[102] One might think that, of all the photographers in Veracruz, it was Hadsell who had the best opportunities

6-39. Mexican prisoner (*left*) and U.S. guard, port of Veracruz, April 1914; Hugo Brehme. © INAH-Hoffman-Brehme, 184.

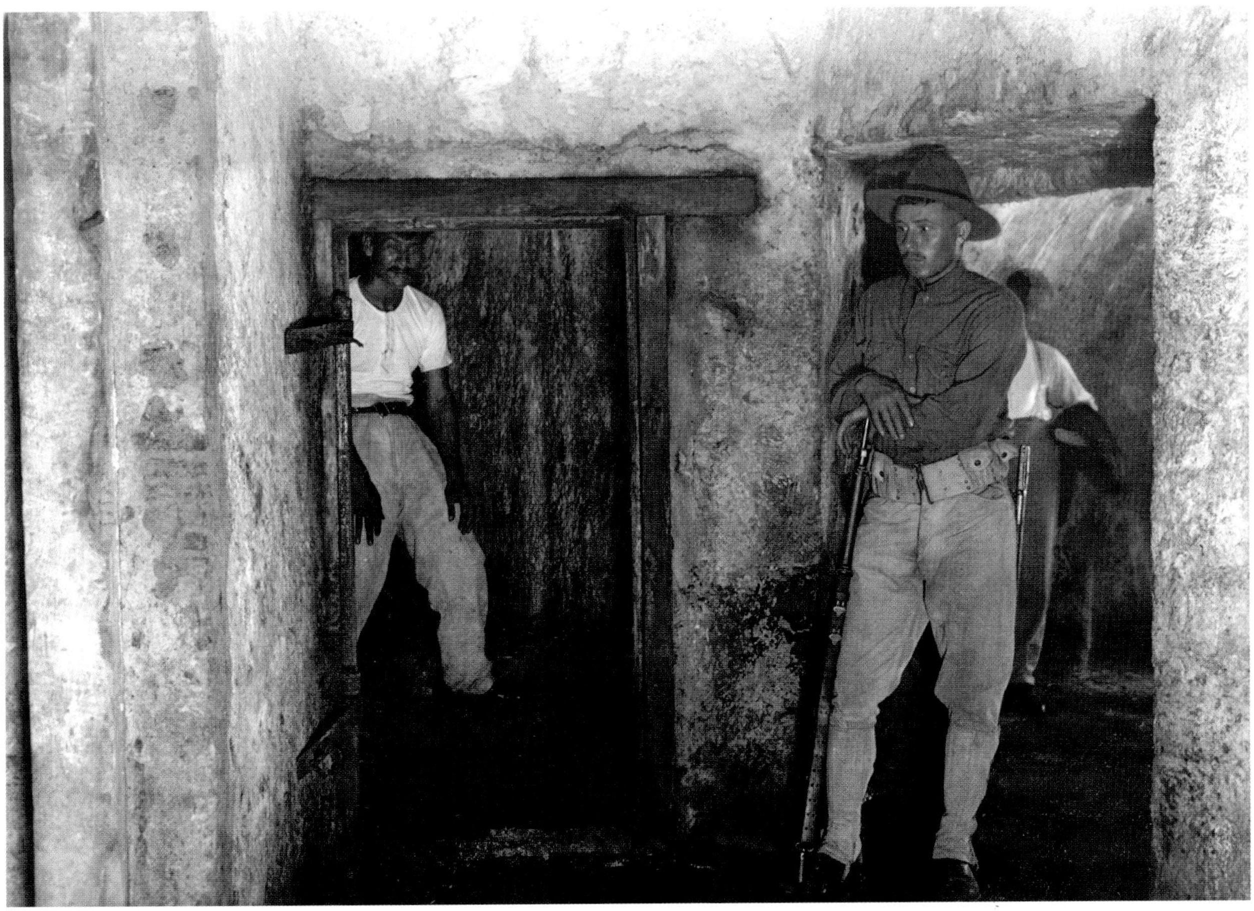

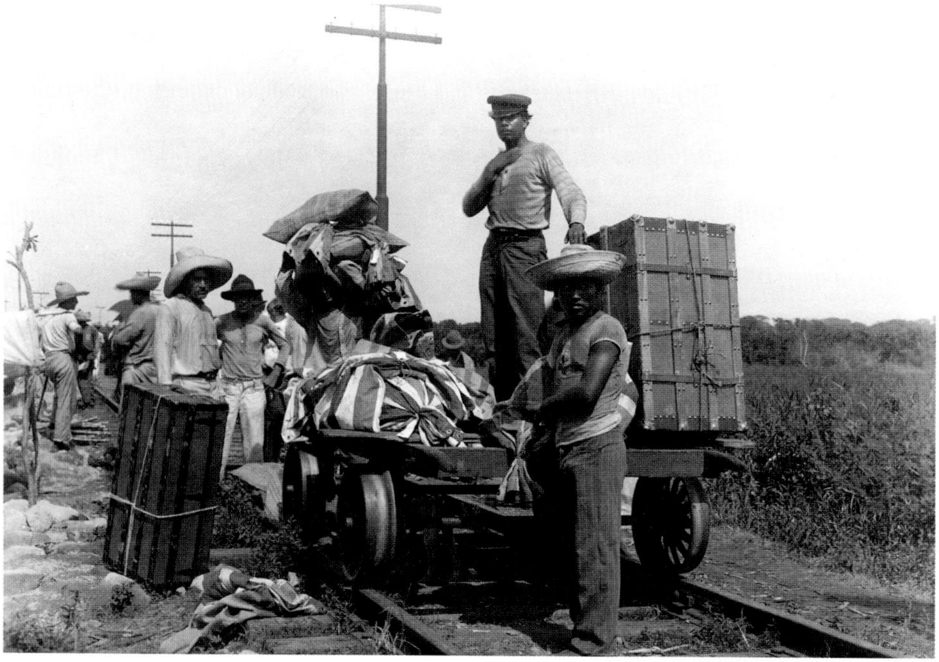

6-40. Refugees fleeing from the port of Veracruz, April 1914; Hugo Brehme. © INAH-Hoffman-Brehme, 188.

to get close to the invaders and document the relations between them and the Mexicans. Evidently, it did not occur to Hadsell to get into the prison, much less to make a picture of such intensity: hunched over, the Mexican gazes from his cell while the Negro guard stands tall but appears to have doubts that are not found on the faces of the triumphant white soldiers.[103]

Brehme also took pictures of refugees (Figure 6-40). Vanderwood reproduced postcards of U.S. residents in Veracruz who had to flee the Mexican ire provoked by the invasion, but I know of no published photos or postcards that show Mexicans who had to leave their city.[104] With the resignation of Huerta in July of 1914, the fragile alliance between the Constitutionalists and the Villistas-Zapatistas ended, and the revolution entered its most radical phase. Increasing numbers of refugees had to choose among their belongings for those that would best help them survive outside of their homes, their towns, and their habitual lives; they would be ubiquitous figures in the revolutionary scenario, although not necessarily in photographs. Brehme, however, found the refugees of such importance that he recorded them in several images taken in Veracruz.

CHAPTER 7

The Caudillo of the Cameras?

THE PHOTOGRAPHY MADE DURING the apogee of the Villista movement (1913–1915) represents a watershed in the revolution's imagery. Perhaps, then, it is no coincidence that Villa is the only caudillo who appears in a picture with a camera in his hands; what's more, his son Agustín was photographed when he was four years old standing behind a film camera of the "Hearst International News Pictorial."[1] During three long years of combat, Mexican photographers acquired experience in traversing the difficult terrain of picturing war, and there is a notable development in both their capacities and their equipment. With the economy in shreds, a camera must have offered different ways of earning a living, whether linking oneself to a caudillo, selling sensationalist photos to illustrated magazines, and/or working for one of the organizations that acquire particular importance during war, such as the Cruz Blanca Nacional.

To the degree possible, photographers adopted medium-format cameras (5 × 7)—or smaller ones (4 × 5)—which permitted them to move easily and capture spontaneous scenes while still obtaining publishable images.[2] Laura González comments that "The visual repertory of war photography was enriched by new visual forms derived from the extended use of light and instant apparatus."[3] Probably first seen in the hands of foreigners—for example, John Reed—the new cameras, as well as photographic equipment and materials, must have entered the country as easily and constantly as did arms, uniforms, and supplies. The most portable camera (other than the Brownie) was the Graflex, whose negatives of celluloid were 3½ × 5¾ inches; they were seen in the north as early as the Orozco rebellion of 1912. Although relatively mobile, they seem not to have as sharp a focus as the reflex or the view, in part because they required a learning process, particularly if the operators were not going to employ tripods.[4] The panorama of photographic technology must have been extensive, however, and the daily omnipresence of imagemaking equipment—sometimes as ubiquitous as arms—created a consciousness that led some of the photographed to disregard them, and some of the photographers to construct unique narratives.

Friedrich Katz found Villa's modernity worthy of comment: "It is remarkable how profoundly a semiliterate man like Villa understood the importance of public relations and of influencing the media on behalf of his movement."[5] His explosion onto the world stage as a modern figure came after taking Ciudad Juárez in November 1913. Villa already had a strong presence in the popular imagination—thanks to his audacious victories and the myth that began to be constructed with songs, stories, and images—and he brought a consciousness of photography's importance acquired in his experiences during the Maderista rebellion. Nonetheless, the feat of getting a train full of his soldiers into the center of Ciudad Juárez without firing a shot—a Trojan horse on rails that took the federals by complete surprise—"propelled him to world fame in a matter of days. . . . With the capture of Juárez, Villa's fame grew by leaps and bounds both in Mexico and north of the border."[6] Villa carried out this feat aided by his command of modern communications, in this case the telegraphs that kept the tracks open by assuring Huertista headquarters in Ciudad Juárez that the train was commanded by federal officers.[7]

In January 1914, Villa signed a contract with the Mutual Film Corporation to document his activities. As cinema historian Aurelio de los Reyes has written, "Villa demonstrated an unusual intuition for publicity by utilizing cinema for his propaganda. His intelligence is apparent in accepting U.S. cameramen in his ranks, because they were the most capable of exhibiting his pictures outside of Mexico."[8] The contract itself became part of Villa's myth: it has been asserted that it contained clauses such as "It was agreed that Villa would carry out his battles in daylight," and "If the cameramen don't get good battle scenes, Villa promises to re-stage them."[9] According to Katz, "The actual contract in fact contained no such clauses. There was absolutely no mention of reenactment of battle scenes or of Villa providing good lighting."[10] Thanks to the agreement, John Davidson Wheelan was present to make a production still of Villa while cinematographers were filming him prior to the battle of Ojinaga. This image immediately circulated around the world and has become an icon of the revolution (see Figure E-10).

Aurelio de los Reyes has asserted that "Thanks to Villa's ability for publicity, his military campaign was meticulously inventoried by U.S. photographers and cameramen, from the taking of Ojinaga to the fall of Torreón."[11] The Mutual Film Corporation was so pleased with Villa's cooperation that while the documentaries were being shot, they signed another contract to make a fiction film (which included some documentary footage), *The Life of General Villa*, with the soon-to-be-famous actor Raoul Walsh in the role of Villa as a youth (the mature Villa was played by the caudillo himself). For Katz, modern communications were the key to the leader's rapid ascent to power: "The favorable treatment that Villa received in films and other media in 1914 was of great importance to his standing both in Mexico and in the United States. By treating him as a national leader long before there was a basis for this, the media facilitated his rise to national and international prominence."[12]

Among the foreigners who were attracted to both Villa and modern media was John Reed, who carried cameras during the four months he was with the Villistas at the beginning of 1914. Literary critic Jorge Rufinelli affirmed that the journalist had a very particular interest in the relation between image and text: "He insisted in indicating which photos, of those that he sent or of the mountain of rolls dispatched to Paul Thompson, should accompany his articles; he was conscious of the power of visually representing the revolution, and the necessity of transmitting it in more than words."[13] It appears that Reed was photographed with Villa according to a letter of 17 February 1914 to Carl Hovey, editor of the *Metropolitan Magazine* in New York, who had contracted him to write about the revolution: "Villa trusts me now, and tomorrow I'll take a picture with him in uniform. Don't say that I am an officer of that army, or just say it as a joke. Be careful, do what you want but make it obvious that it is a joke. Mexicans don't understand these things very well, and they could expel me from the country. And, aside from all that, I do not want to pose as a war hero when in truth I'm not fighting."[14]

It does not appear that the international fame which Villa enjoyed was reflected in Mexican media, where he was generally ignored. While participating in the Maderista movement, he was photographed on horseback; next to the image (which circulated widely later) the text referred to him as a *cabecilla*.[15] When he took Torreón in September 1913, *La Ilustración Semanal* showed the streets full of cadavers as a result of "the entrance of Villa's bandits."[16] The iconographic image made by Wheelan offers an interesting example of the difference between his treatment by the national and the international media: taken in January 1914, the photo was published in the United States, Great Britain, Germany, France, and Spain before it finally appeared in a Mexican publication (after Huerta's fall).[17]

Even after they had transformed Villa from a "bandit" to a "revolutionary leader," the Mexican illustrated magazines tried to domesticate him. *La Semana Ilustrada* published "an interesting photograph of the Constitutionalist leader Francisco Villa, in which he appears wearing a military uniform."[18] In fact, the uniform was designed by the Mutual Film Corporation, and it appears that he was not allowed to use it except when they were filming.[19] Dressing the guerrilla fighter in civilized clothing represented an attempt on the part of the U.S. company to civilize him, a pretension that found a favorable response in the Mexican media. Miguel Ángel Berumen confirms my impression of the treatment Villa received in the Mexican press, sustaining that the influence of the country's mass media in the construction of Villa's myth "was very little": "It was not until April of 1914 that there was a daily guaranteed propaganda in favor of the Villista cause, with the founding of the newspaper *Vida Nueva* in Chihuahua."[20]

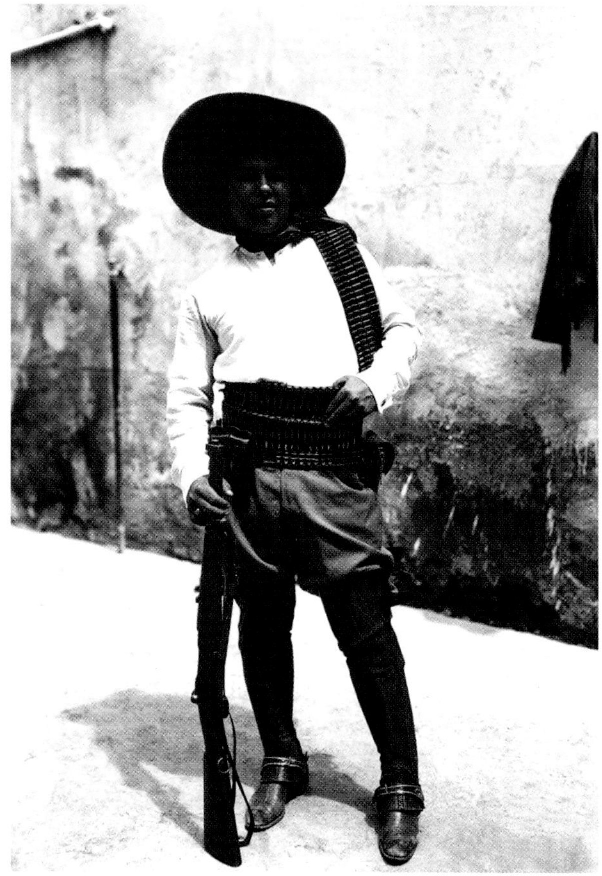

7-1. Villista commander, ca. 1914. © Inv. #6043, Fondo Casasola, SINAFO-Fototeca Nacional del INAH.

7-2. FACING Villistas in front of a train, ca. 1915. © Inv. #32579, Fondo Casasola, SINAFO-Fototeca Nacional del INAH.

Despite the Mexican magazines' lack of interest in the Villista movement, surviving photos indicate a fundamental change in the revolution's imagery. Of course, the posed portraits so characteristic of the early years do not disappear. One of these portraits is said to be of a Dorado, the elite corps whose members Villa chose personally; I do not know if he was a Dorado, but he was probably a Villista commander (Figure 7-1).[21] Nonetheless, in other images, while some subjects pose, others turn their backs on the camera, occupied with their tasks (Figure 7-2). Other photos are clearly spontaneous: one shows a Villista crossing the street, his face covered by the rifles he carries (Figure 7-3), and in another, a group butchers a cow to feed their regiment, with only one of the nine men looking at the photographer (Figure 7-4). The scenes captured by some photographers are of a modernity so radical that it would not be seen again until the Spanish Civil War. For example, Figure 7-5 (perhaps taken by a Hugelman) could be one of the few combat images taken during the revolution: it shows Villistas charging toward federal positions in Zacatecas in June 1914, the battle that signaled Huerta's definitive defeat.[22] The men run, weighed down by their arms and boxes (munitions?); one has fallen, though we do not know whether he was hit by fire or simply tripped; another man huddles over. A photo of the federal artillery wagon also has a strong action sense thanks to the animals that are blurred by movement and the cloud of dust that envelopes the scene (Figure 7-6). Finally, the picture of a stretcher crew in Zacatecas, photographed with surprising proximity, has a spontaneity difficult to find in imagery two years before (Figure 7-7).

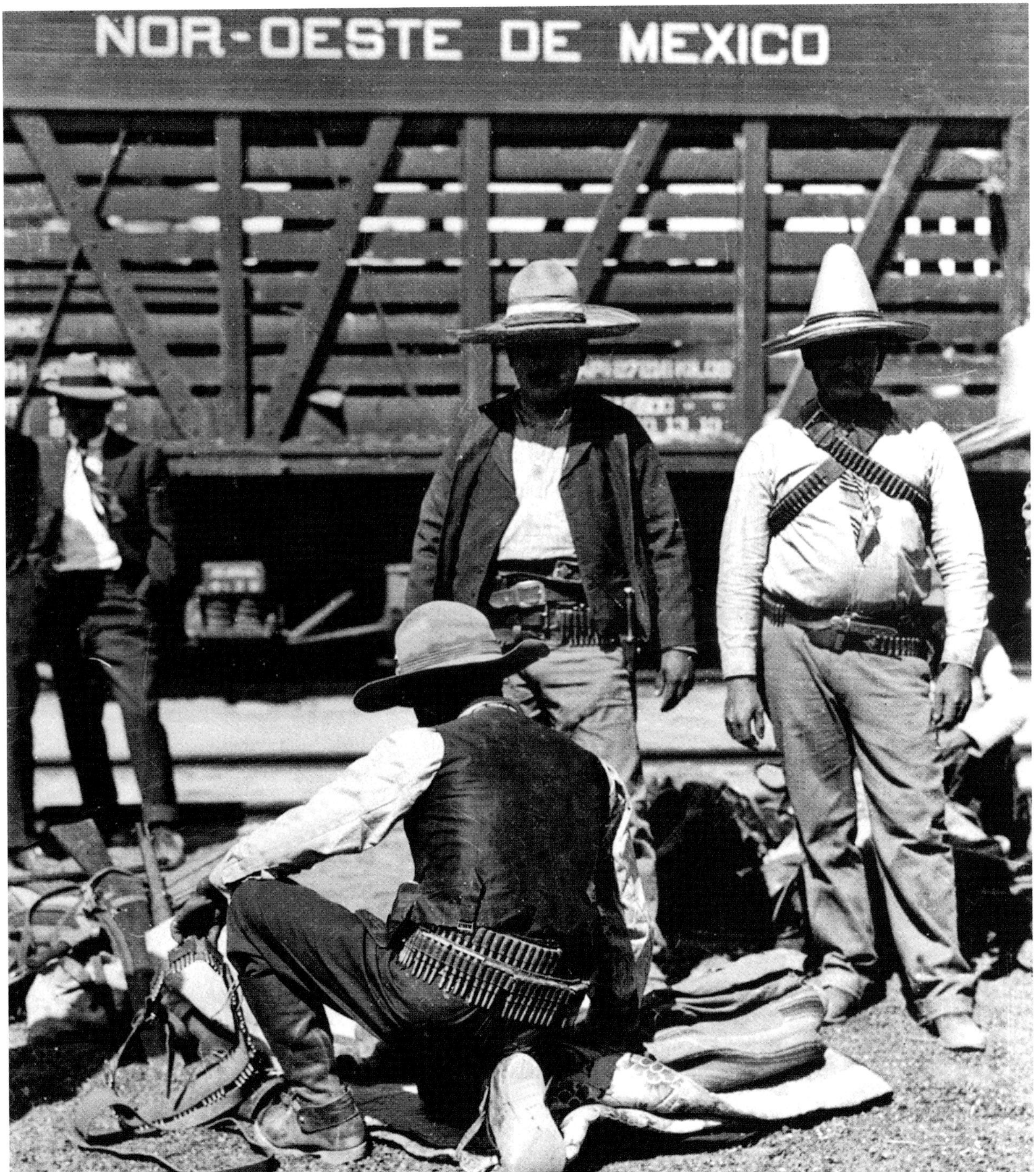
NOR-OESTE DE MEXICO

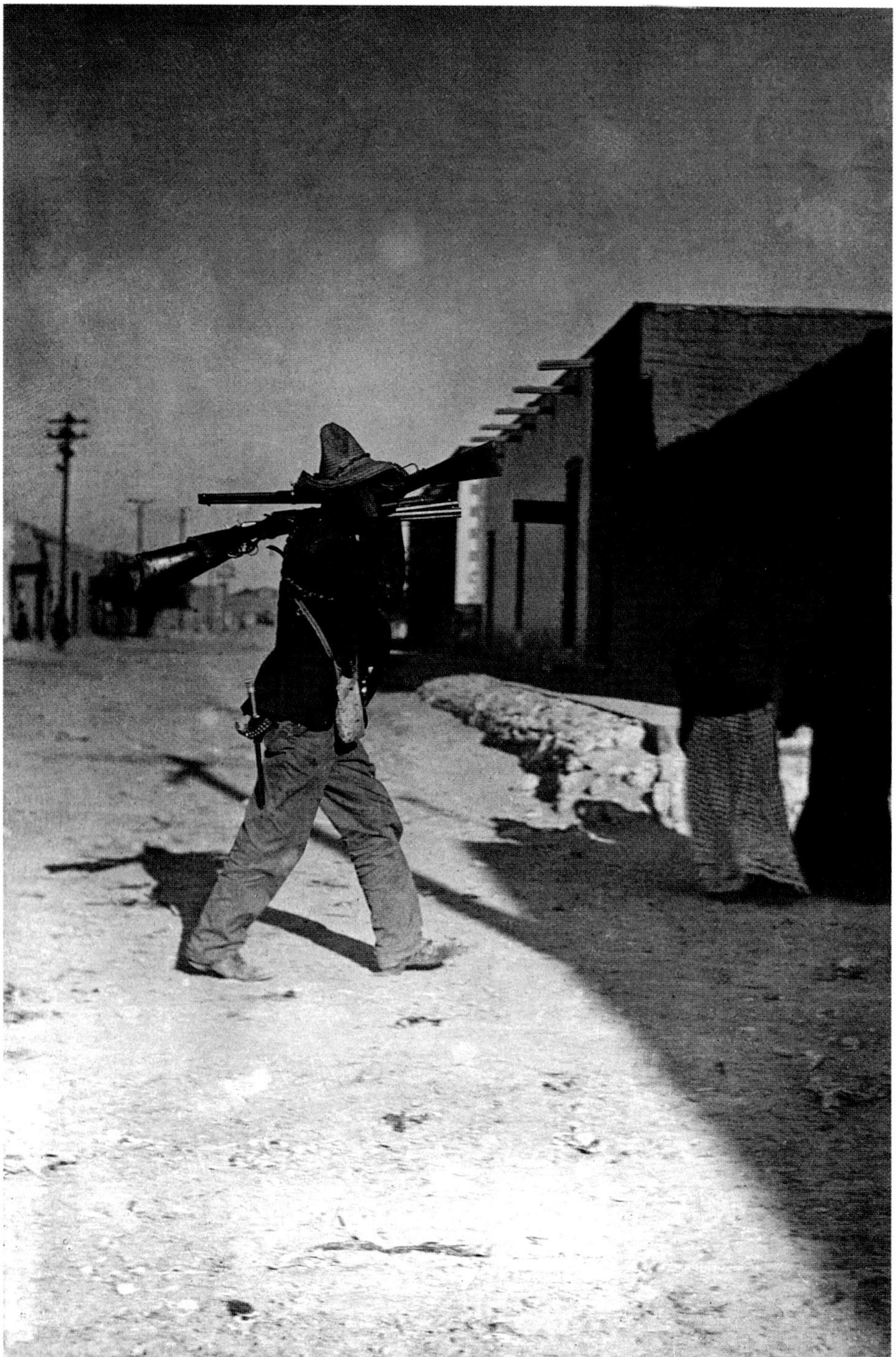

7-3. Villista with rifles, Ciudad Juárez, November 1913. © Inv. #5904, Fondo Casasola, SINAFO-Fototeca Nacional del INAH.

A fascinating figure of the revolution's visual world is Eustasio Montoya, a dual Mexican-U.S. citizen born in San Antonio, Texas.[23] Montoya was one of the "hybrids" who combined the filming of documentaries with photography, like Jesús Abitia and Ignacio Medrano Chávez. He appears to have been a prolific maker of pictures, and filmed more than 40,000 feet of material.[24] According to cinema historian Fernando del Moral, "As a freelance documentary maker of his time, he thought it was important to record in images the events that, according to his criteria and possibilities, he had the opportunity to capture and exhibit, such as civilian, military, and diplomatic episodes."[25] Montoya may have begun to photograph the revolution as early as June

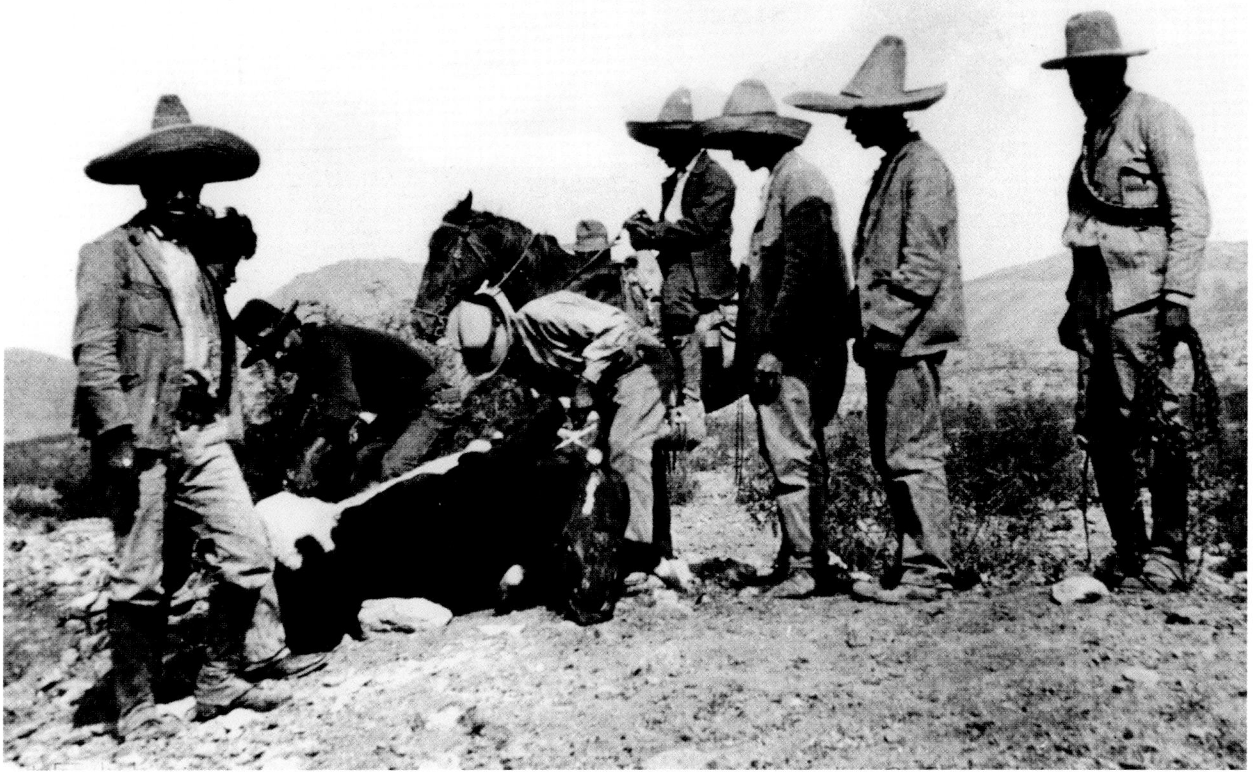

7-4. Revolutionaries butchering a cow to supply their regiment, ca. 1914. © Inv. #643244, Fondo Casasola, SINAFO-Fototeca Nacional del INAH.

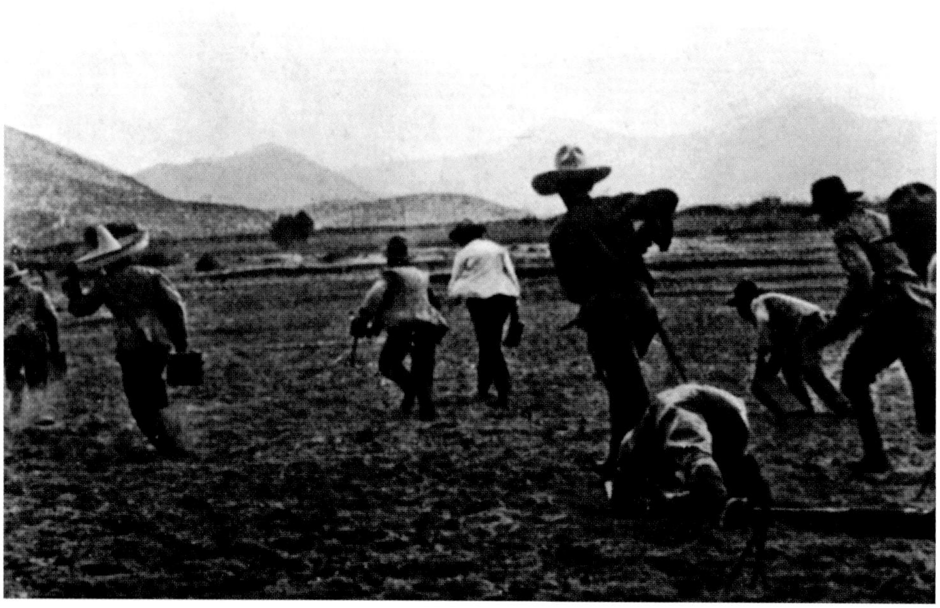

7-5. Villistas advancing on Zacatecas, June 1914; Hugelman? © Inv. #37837, Fondo Casasola, SINAFO-Fototeca Nacional del INAH.

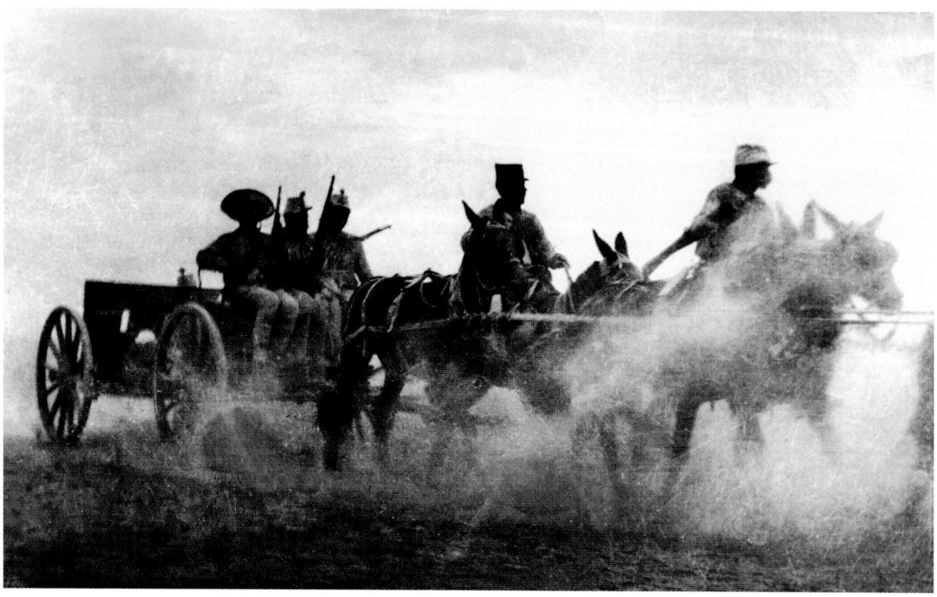

7-6. Federal artillery wagon in Torreón, ca. 1913. © Inv. #624171, Fondo Casasola, SINAFO-Fototeca Nacional del INAH.

1911, with the photo of the armed anti-reelectionist women (see Figure 4-16). He was captured by Villistas under General Roque González Garza in 1913 and appears to have served as a photographer with them during that year.

In 1914 Montoya became the official photographer of the health organization La Cruz Blanca (the White Cross), an institutional affiliation that linked him with Constitutionalism, as Pablo González was the honorary president.[26] Leonor Villegas de Magnón, the Maderista-Constitutionalist revolutionary who founded La Cruz Blanca, said that Montoya "eventually became the semi-official photographer of Carranza."[27] He filmed a documentary of the battle of Villaldama, Nuevo León, in 1915 for the Carrancistas when they defeated the Villistas, and photographed Constitutionalist leaders.[28] Years later Montoya described his wanderings during the revolution: "I was

7-7. Wounded person being carried, Zacatecas, 1914. © Archivo González Garza, Universidad Panamericana, 03062, Registro 152.

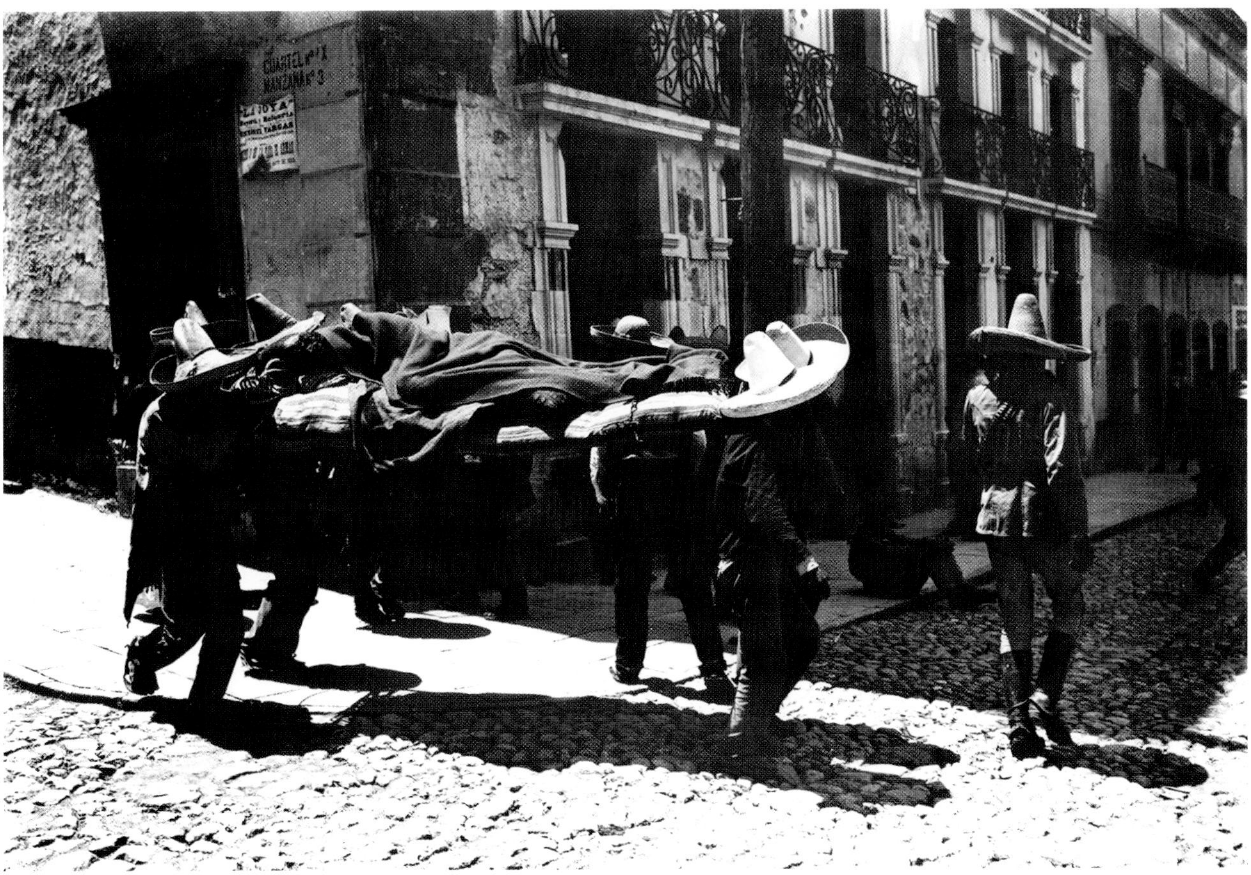

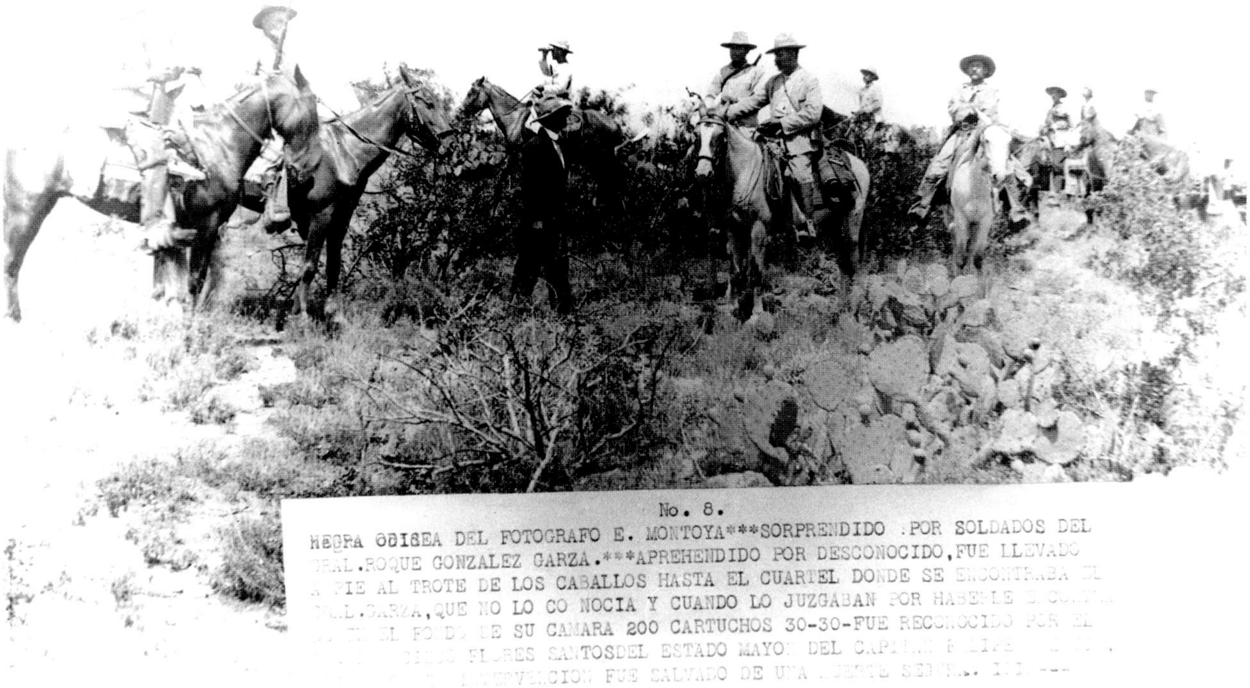

7-8. "Black odyssey of photographer E. Montoya," a directed photograph reconstructing Montoya's capture by Villista troops, Coahuila, 1913; Eustasio Montoya. © Archivo González Garza, Universidad Panamericana, 04016, Registro 104.

in different parts of the country, suffering many wants and great dangers, twice escaping execution. Throughout the revolution, and at the risk of my life, I took pictures of everything important that I could."[29]

We owe Montoya for two dazzling narratives. The first is a photo he directed to reconstruct his capture in 1913 by Villistas in Coahuila (Figure 7-8). This must have been one of the times that he escaped the firing squad, because he wrote on the photo:

> Black odyssey of photographer E. Montoya surprised by the soldiers of General Roque González Garza. Apprehended when he was not recognized, he was taken at a horse's trot to headquarters where he was shown to General Garza, who did not know him. When he had been tried for having been found with 200 cartridges of .30-30 caliber in the bottom of his camera bag, he was recognized by Francisco Flores Santos of Capitan Felipe Muzquiz's general staff, whose intervention saved him from a certain death.

A number of interesting questions arise from this photo. How was Montoya able to convince the Villistas to participate in the staging? How quickly did he establish a relationship with them so as to allow this? What motivated Montoya to re-create this scene? For whom was it intended, by Montoya and by the participating Villistas? Reconstructing history through photographs has a long trajectory in Mexico, beginning with a picture that the surgeon general of the Mexican army, Pedro Vander Linden, staged to represent the amputation of a soldier's leg during the U.S. invasion of 1847.[30] However, I know of no other photo from the revolution that was so carefully re-created, and with such a descriptive text; it could offer a path to a fascinating story.

Another Montoya photo is a narrative without words. A group of unarmed civilians, apparently photographers, look at the body of someone who appears to belong to their group (Figure 7-9). It would seem to be a daily experience for them, to judge by their sad but resigned features. The photographer (the fourth camera present) documented more than their grief: there are two cameras (and a box to carry another) of the view type that are light and mobile, although they all require tripods. The one on the right is a Kodak Poco, a medium-format (5 × 7) camera, but the one on the left appears to be a more advanced and smaller model, and could be a 4 × 5.[31] Beyond the evidence of technological advance (and media presence), I wonder about the history behind the image. Was it made in homage to a photographer who died in the battle of Colombia, Nuevo León, in 1913? If so, was the scenario constructed to recognize him or to protest his death?

Montoya was, finally, a Constitutionalist photographer who made photos for the Villistas only until he could escape from them. In contrast, the brothers Juan and Antonio Cachú were died-in-the-wool Villistas according to Berumen.[32] In 1900 Antonio began to work with a German photographer, Juan Kurt (J. C. Curd), in Patzcuaro; his brother Juan joined him three years later. They did theater as well as photography, founding a family entertainment company with another brother, Luís, and traveling around various states in the country's center. From their surviving photographs, we know that they were in Patzcuaro in 1913, making portraits of families on country outings and of federal officers posing in uniform, documenting the Huertista forces defending Patzcuaro, and taking pictures of hanged revolutionaries (see Figure 6-21). They must have had a studio, even if it was only a mobile backdrop, because they made several portraits of "revolutionary couples" wearing cartridge belts and armed with modern rifles, the men sitting and the women standing behind.[33] I believe that these portraits come from the first phase of the Cachús' work; its style belongs to the previous century and is very similar to that of the known studio photographer in Guanajuato, Romualdo García.[34]

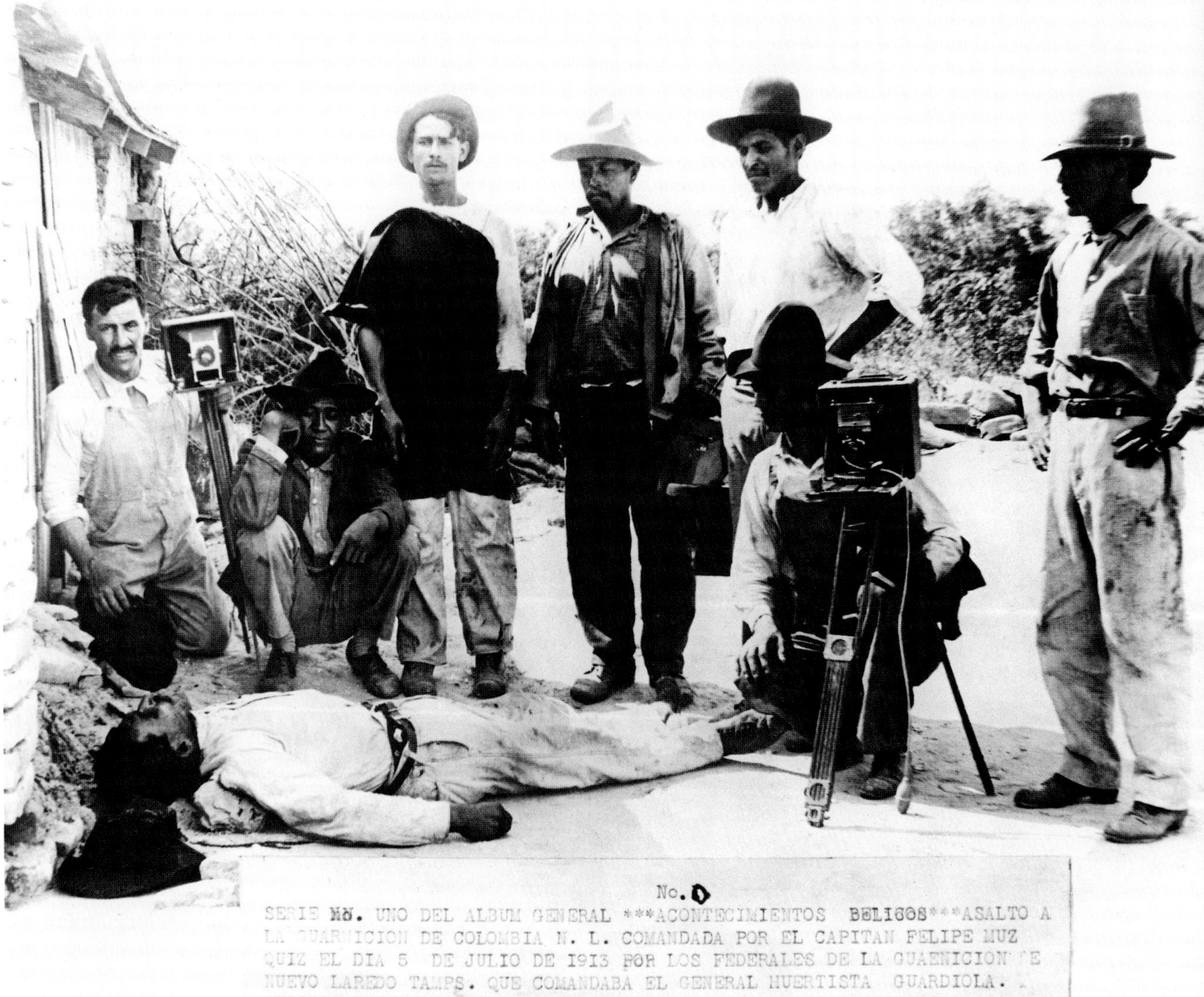

7-9. Photographers and a dead man in Nuevo León after being attacked by Huertistas, 5 July 1913; Eustasio Montoya. © Archivo González Garza, Universidad Panamericana, 04.011, Registro 23.

At the same time the Cachús began to move outside and toward more spontaneous scenes of the revolution; for example, the photo of a Maderista captured by Huertistas who will promptly execute him. I suspect that it was as much the push of the repression as the pull of their ideals that led them to leave Michoacán and link themselves to the forces of agrarian revolutionary General Alberto Carrera Torres in 1914. At any rate, they seem to be related to that movement, because they made (at least) two photos of the executed General José Pérez Castro (Figure 7-10).[35] Pérez Castro was a reactionary guerrilla who may have been simply one of the many bandits who took advantage of the chaotic situation to loot, rape, and kill. Allied with Huerta and Pascual Orozco, he joined the latter in sacking the city of León, Guanajuato, on 1 August 1914. When the city was retaken by Carrera Torres, one of the first to promulgate an agrarian reform, Pérez Castro was captured and executed. Photographs of the dead commander were probably taken to celebrate the victory over the reactionary forces and to demonstrate the control of banditry by the revolutionaries. What might be called the "punctum" in this photo—that which elevates it beyond banal voyeurism of the morbid and horrific—is the finger that points to the destroyed visage.[36] Those who were going to be executed had an obsession about not being shot in the face (see the stories below about Figures 8-29 and 8-30). Hence, the Cachús could either have arranged the arm to make the finger point at the head, or they could have taken advantage of a serendipitous occurrence, but it would appear that their photograph is meant to indicate how bandits and counter-revolutionaries would be treated.

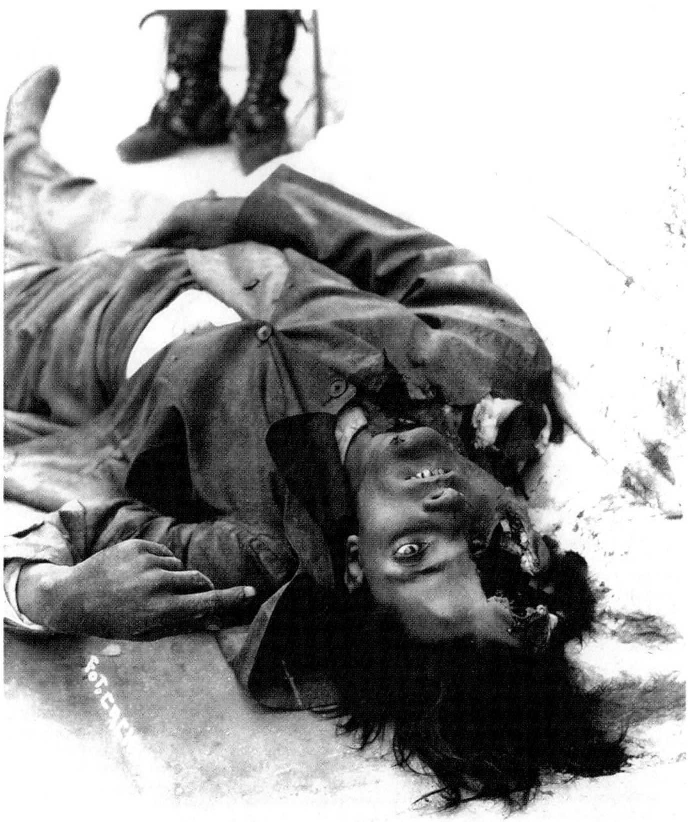

7-10. General José Pérez Castro, executed in León, Guanajuato, 3 August 1914, by General Alberto Carrera Torres; Cachú brothers. © Fondo "Cachú-Ramírez Juan," Departamento de Información y Documentación de la Cultura Audiovisual, Benemérita Universidad Autónoma de Puebla.

Reconstructing the story of the Cachús and their commitments demonstrates the complexity of historicizing the revolution's photography from "survivors." For example, their link to Villismo is clear in the University of Puebla archive, where there are numerous images of Villa's personal train car, both without and within, as documented in photos of his personal bathroom, his

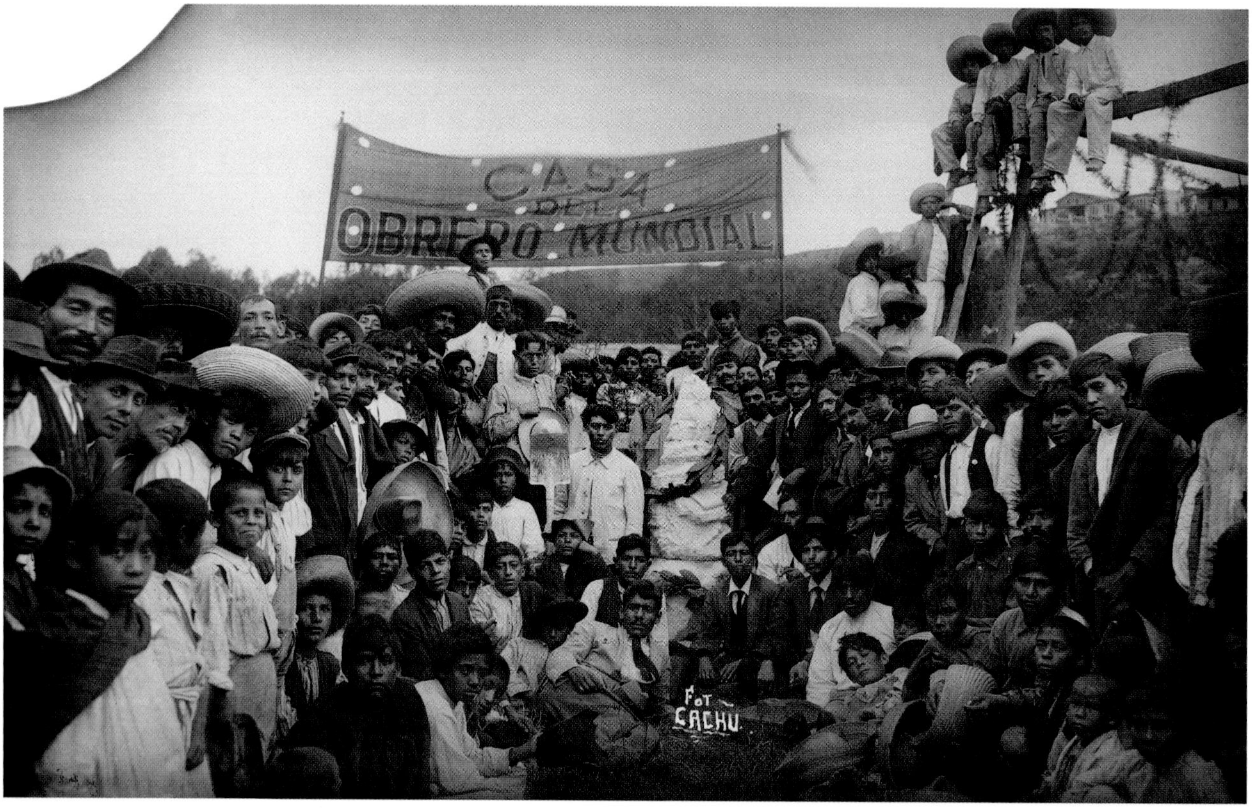

7-11. Regional meeting of the Casa del Obrero Mundial, Michoacán?, ca. 1915; Cachú brothers. © FJC_2008_02_001_125, Fondo Cachú, Dirección de Artes Visuales, Fundación Televisa.

furniture with "PV" engraved upon it, and his photos on the wall.[37] They probably joined the División del Norte at the end of 1914. Having studied medicine, Antonio entered into a medical brigade. Juan also had a medical background, but it appears that he gained Villa's confidence and was entrusted with confidential commissions.[38] Their photography always retained something of a studio style, but it became more documentary; for example, it seems they photographed various scenes during the battle of León, Guanajuato, including at least one spontaneous shot of the Red Cross "fulfilling its duty" by collecting bodies.[39] Berumen says, "The Cachús' sympathy for Villismo was famous, and they became objects of political persecution as the movement lost ground in the country's south and center. Juan was apprehended in Pátzcuaro at the end of 1916."[40] Antonio had died in 1916, and Juan may have decided to join the Constitutionalists after being captured; certainly, the photos from the Televisa archive would seem to point in that direction.[41] One is of a regional gathering of the Casa del

Obrero Mundial, the workers' organization closely linked to Obregón (Figure 7-11). In another image, though it is difficult to determine the troops pictured, the officers look like Constitutionalists (Figure 7-12). In 1918 Juan moved to Mexico City, where he opened a studio and was named a "Photographer of Health Inspection" for the Council of Health by an order signed personally by President Venustiano Carranza.[42]

Few Mexican photographers of the Villista movement are known. One may have been a Robles who lived in Zacatecas city; the only existent images by him are related to the taking of that city by Villistas in June 1913. He had some relation with the magazine *Novedades*, which published five of his photos in the 2 July issue, three that emphasized the deaths and destruction caused by combat, as well as the lines of people waiting for water.[43] One Robles picture is of the advance party entering Zacatecas, which could indicate that he had information about their arrival and, perhaps, did not

7-12. Review of revolutionary troops, Michoacán?, ca. 1915; Cachú brothers. © FJC_2008_02_001_771, Fondo Cachú, Dirección de Artes Visuales, Fundación Televisa.

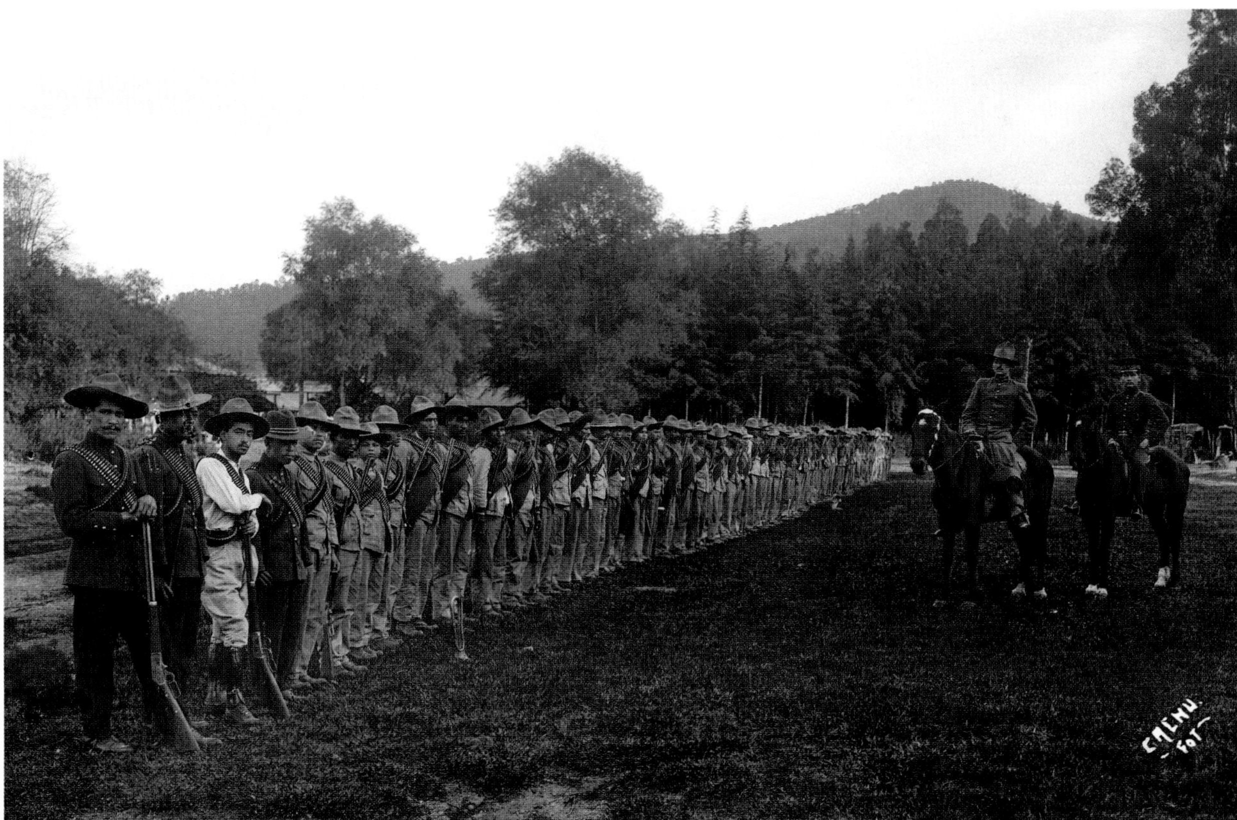

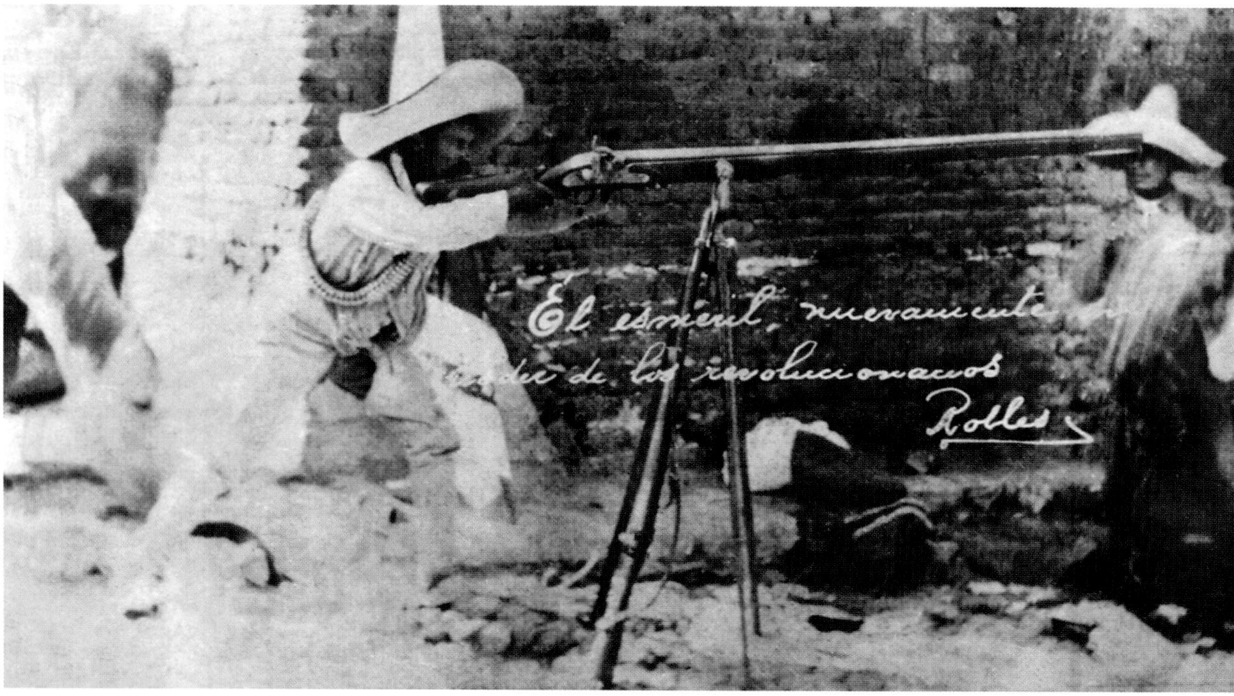

7-13. Revolutionary soldier shooting with the weapon called "El Esmeril," Zacatecas, July 1913; Robles. © Inv. #38021, Fondo Casasola, SINAFO-Fototeca Nacional del INAH.

fear them. The other photo is of Villista general Pánfilo Natera offering guarantees to the populace, a pro-Villista position that is unique in the illustrated magazines in this moment and very difficult to encounter in a photo before Huerta's fall. In the following issue of the magazine, another Robles image was published: a Villista shoots a weapon that looks picturesque, but which was "of great importance" according to *Novedades* (Figure 7-13).[44] Josaphat Martínez also may have had a certain relation to Villismo, according to Fernando del Moral, who states that he studied photography in the United States during the revolution but returned to Mexico to cover the Convention of Aguascalientes in 1914.[45] There he made a photo of Villa on horseback that (according to what Martínez told his family) the caudillo "liked" and asked him "if he was satisfied with his remuneration."[46] It probably was taken during the convention, as Gustavo Casasola also situates it in that context; however, the photo that appears in the *Historia gráfica de la Revolución Mexicana* is not signed.[47]

The Convention of Aguascalientes and the Convencionistas' subsequent entrance into Mexico City were, according to historian Adolfo Gilly, "The acme of the revolution in the world, when they became owners of Mexico City, assuming the representation of the masses throughout the country. . . . The occupation of Mexico City by the campesino armies is one of the most beautiful and moving episodes of the entire Mexican Revolution."[48] That, however, was not the opinion of the city's dwellers beforehand, who feared the appearance of Zapata's forces both because of metropolitan prejudices and the fact that the Carrancistas—who had just left the city—had pillaged the capital, leaving behind "a deep print of discontent because of their continual abuses and scandals, their flaunting of impunity, their despotic and rude attitude, and, above all, the irritating disrespect with which they perceived civilians."[49] The first Zapatistas arrived at 11 p.m. on 24 November; this contingent is passing by the Portal de Mercaderes (Figure 7-14).

7-14. Florentino Antonio, Felipe Antonio, Chico Antonio (*left to right*), and other Zapatistas entering Mexico City, Portal de Mercaderes, at 11 p.m. on the night of 24 November 1914. © Inv. #33846, Fondo Casasola, SINAFO-Fototeca Nacional del INAH.

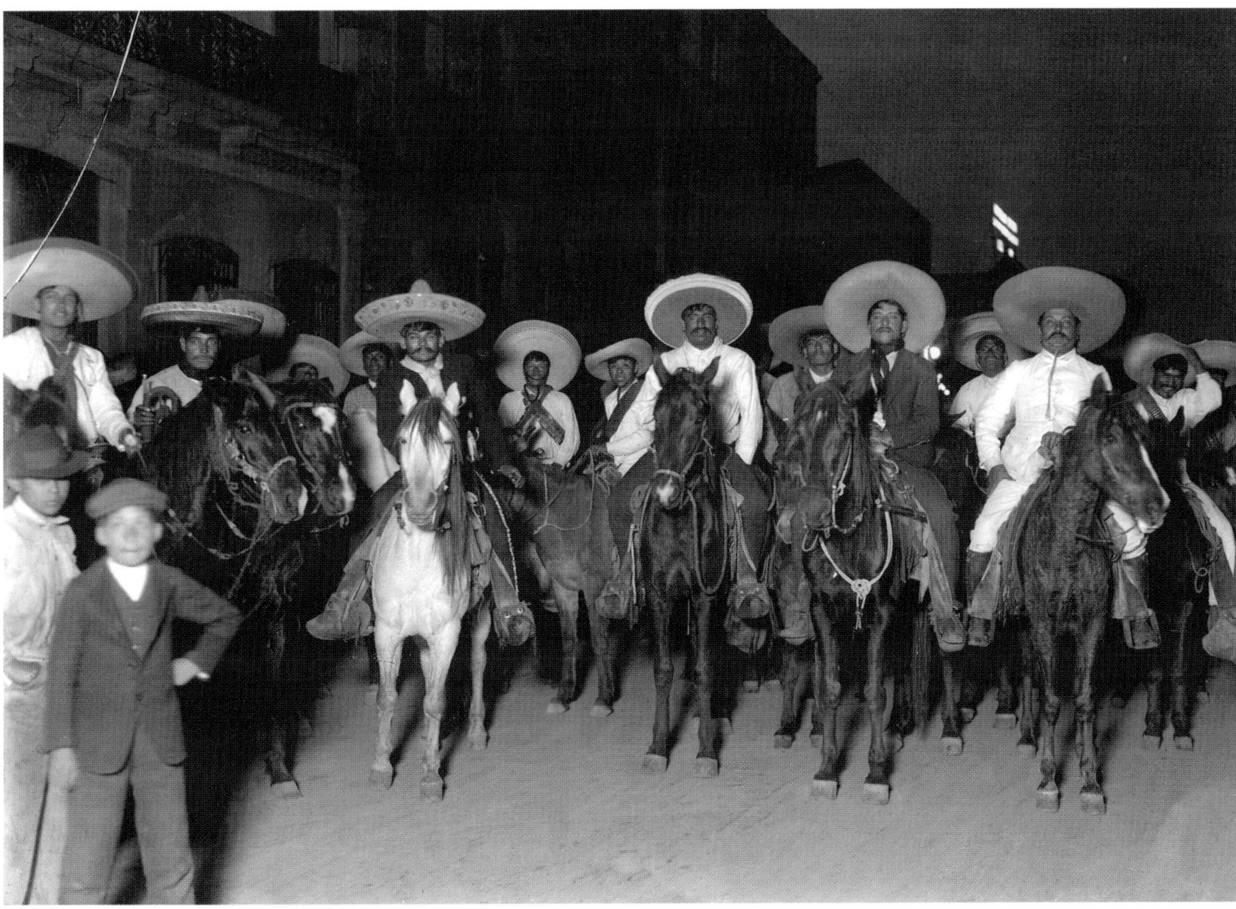

Francisco Ramírez Plancarte witnessed their arrival and noted how the media had conditioned the city's inhabitants to perceive the Zapatistas:

> Many were the stories of ferocious savagery that the government press had published about how the Zapatistas carried out their traitorous and bloody assaults, as well as their perverse instincts, and the reprehensible methods they employed to torture their prisoners. The popular voice recounted numerous of their acts, all very repugnant and carried out with such refinement of cruelty that just hearing them made us feel an intense nervous tension.[50]

Despite the constant brainwashing carried out by the media, the capital's residents were pleasantly surprised by the Zapatistas. Ricardo Pérez Montfort describes the difference between what the urban dwellers expected and what they encountered: "The capital's press had divulged an image of Emiliano Zapata and the Zapatistas that did not correspond to what passed in front of the citizens' eyes."[51] John Womack narrates the Zapatistas' entrance: "The first southern contingents filtered quietly, almost embarrassedly, into the capital. Uncertain of their role there, they did not sack or plunder but like lost children wandered through the streets knocking on doors and asking for food."[52] An eyewitness was astounded: "In the center we saw something amazing and incredible: the Zapatistas, slandered by the potentates as 'bandits,' were sleeping on the benches and eating beans with chile and hard tortillas out of humble clay pots, on the ground, when inside the houses there was money to throw succulent banquets."[53] Ramírez Plancarte says, "The general opinion about the Zapatistas was highly favorable, and it was also dangerous to opine differently."[54]

Whether it was due to the unanticipated discovery that campesinos were human, or because they now had some input into the media, both the publications and the photographers seem to have treated them pretty well. Most of the illustrated magazines had succumbed during 1914 to the "formidable" paper crisis (and other revolutionary infirmities) "that has made even the most opulent dailies reduce their circulation and their size."[55] The editor of *La Ilustración Semanal*, Ezequiel Álvarez Tostado, had fled to Cuba when the Conventionists arrived, and the magazine limited itself to publishing photos of Zapatistas on horses in the center with neutral titles such as "The Zapatistas in Mexico City."[56] This attitude seems to have found an echo among the photographers; for example, the photojournalist who must have most resented the presence of radicals in the capital was the Porfirista Manuel Ramos. This photographer "did not identify with the revolution in the least," but he made a pair of images with a little-expected perspective.[57] In one photo Zapatista riders carrying banners file past the National Palace; the low angle and backlighting make the horsemen and raised flags seem to rise out of a dust devil that envelopes them in clouds.[58] The other Ramos photo that would seem to be discordant with his ideology—or a commentary about the ambiguity of photography—is one of the revolution's great icons, Villa, in the presidential chair, with Zapata next to him (see Figure E-18).

For Heliodoro J. Gutiérrez and Aurelio Escobar, Zapata's brief stay in the city offered them different opportunities: Gutiérrez made a portrait of the leader, while Escobar reestablished contact with him; the result was one of the classic portraits of the caudillo.[59] Gutiérrez's young goddaughter, Consuelo, was in the Chicago Photo Studio and told the story of how Zapata arrived on 6 December between the parade that revolutionary troops made through the Zócalo and the meal celebrated with Villa and Eulalio Gutiérrez in the National Palace. The children lived above the studio and had come back from the parade to eat, when a little brother interrupted to announce that "Aurelito just came in with a bad man." According to Consuelo,

> The man who arrived with Aurelio Escobar was Zapata. He entered the house very well dressed, with a precious *charro* suit, a little beige suede jacket, and on its back an eagle embroidered in gold. Black pants with shining silver buttons down the sides, and a wide sombrero. They were going to take some photos. My little brother repeated that he was a bad man, perhaps because he had made a face at him. Zapata had a box full of coins, all *caballitos*, there was a thousand, to pay my godfather for his work. At least that day money arrived, because we were tired of not being paid. A crowd waited expectantly outside, while inside Zapata chatted cordially with Aurelio Escobar. They knew each other, because Aurelio had been a guest of the "Attila of the South" in 1912, and he now corresponded with a good cognac.[60]

Photographs taken during the few months that the Conventionists occupied the city provide details about daily life. Food was scarce, as "fruits, vegetables, and cereals didn't arrive in the city; even if there were any in the near states, they couldn't be transported because the railroads were destined exclusively to military ends."[61] Hence, it was not unusual to find people with baskets forming lines to wait for something edible to arrive (Figure 7-15). One person who lived through the war described what the experience was like: "Families had to stand in line entire days and nights to obtain food; the women took small stools in order to move along in the line, and seat themselves for minutes. Some had to stay in line during two or three days and nights

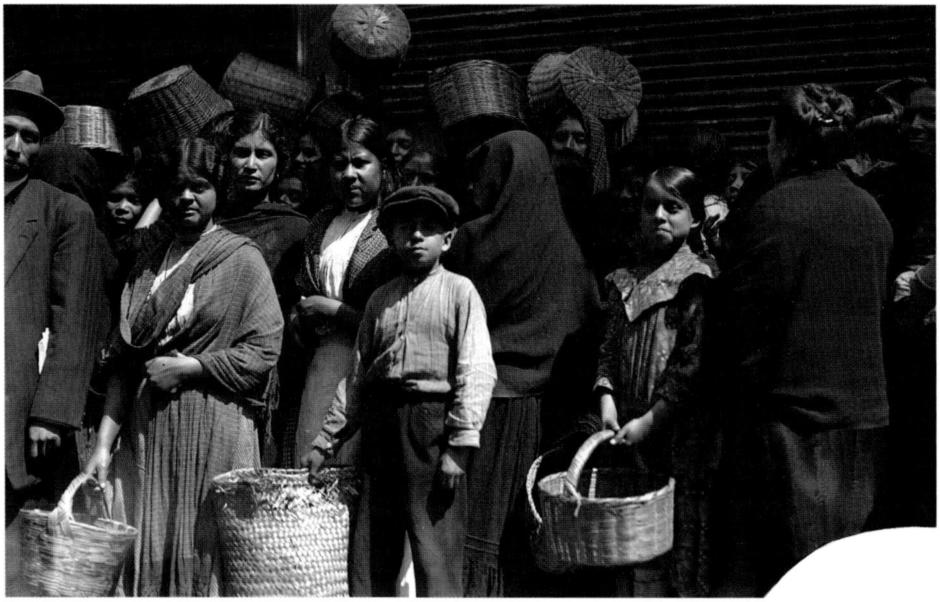

7-15. People waiting for food, Mexico City, ca. 1915. © Inv. #5999, Fondo Casasola, SINAFO-Fototeca Nacional del INAH.

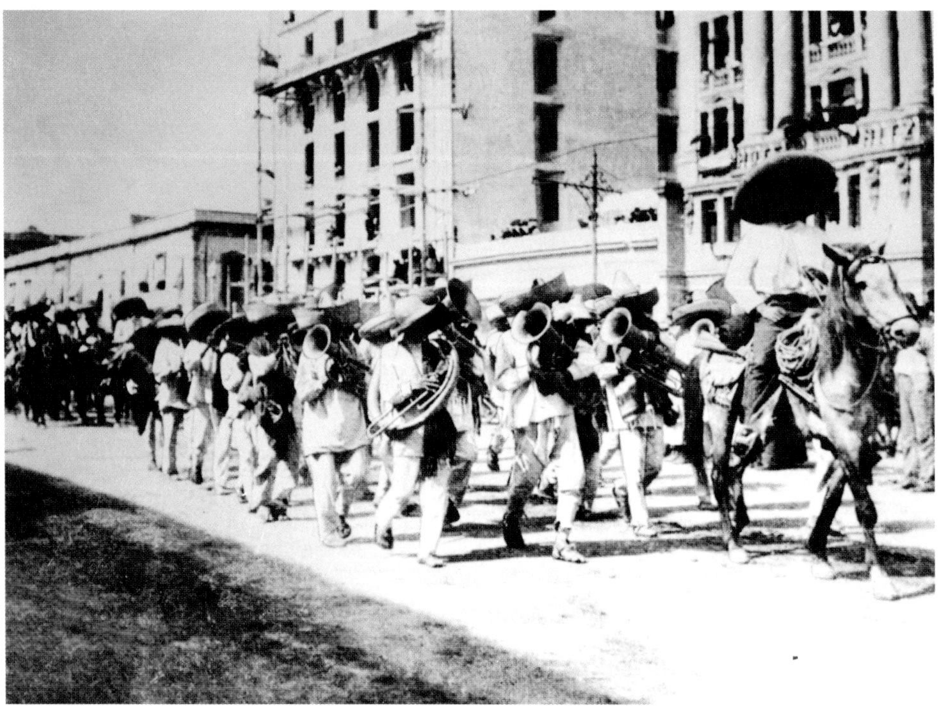

7-16. Zapatista band, Avenida Juárez, Mexico City, 6 December 1914. © Inv. #6117, Fondo Casasola, SINAFO-Fototeca Nacional del INAH.

because when they arrived at the store everything was gone, and they had to wait until more bread and milk were brought."[62] Historian Berta Ulloa commented that "The most palpable contrast to these problems was the music played in public places."[63] One moment of much music was the triumphal entrance of the Conventionist army, 6 January 1914, in which a Zapatista band appeared (Figure 7-16). Gustavo Casasola witnessed the march of 50,000 soldiers and said, "The bands of music in the parade played so much and so long that any recess was imperceptible."[64]

Photographs can be testimonies to elements that are often marginalized in written histories, as well as witnesses of mentalities. The image of the Zapatista delegates in the Convention of Aguascalientes shows the *charro* clothing that the leaders wore (note the contrast between the modern hats and felt sombreros) and signals the presence of underdogs in their moment of power (Figure 7-17). Another image that

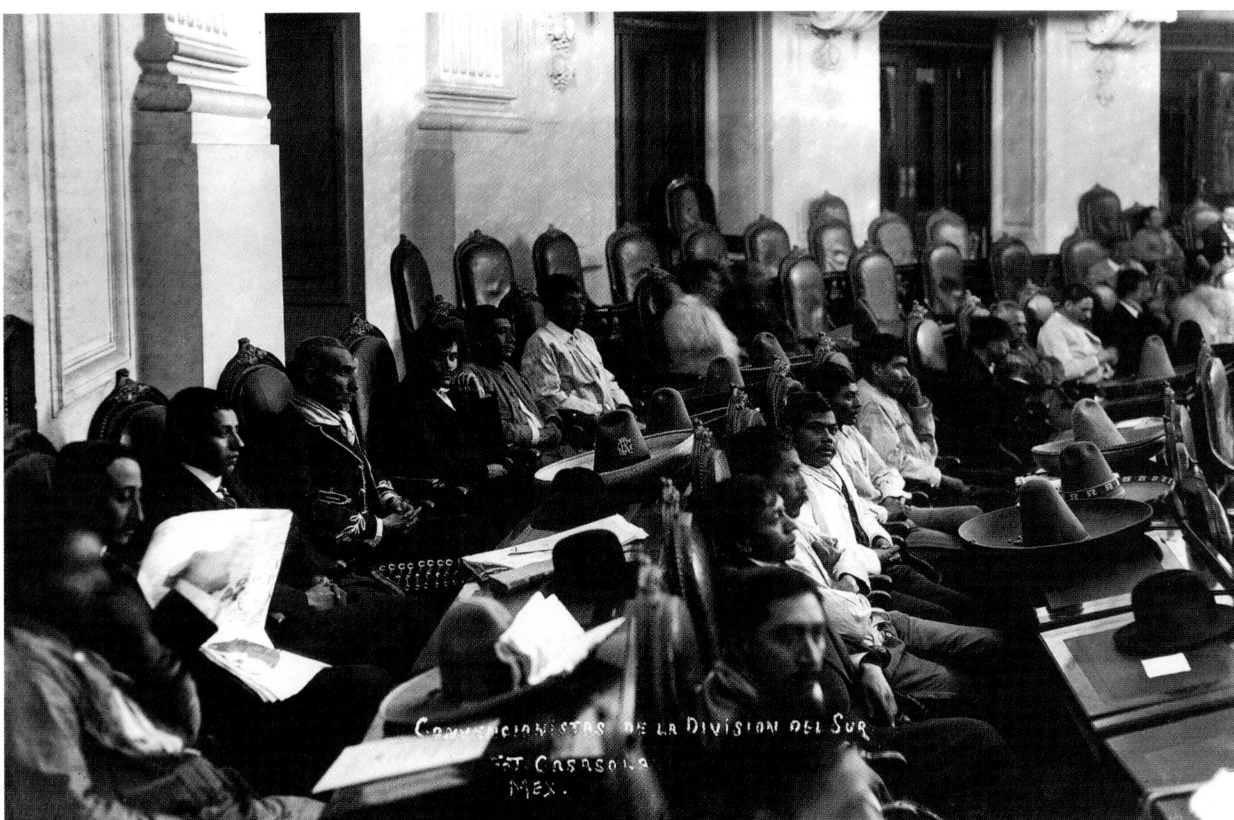

7-17. Zapatista delegates at the Convention of Aguascalientes, Mexico City, January 1915. © Inv. #638585, Fondo Casasola, SINAFO-Fototeca Nacional del INAH.

documents the determination of subalterns to play a protagonist's role—and, moreover, their consciousness of the necessity to organize to promote their interests—is that of "the First Regiment of the Socialist Brigade of Mexico, Feminine Sex" (Figure 7-18). In March 1915 these women demonstrated their decision "to defend Mexico City if it were attacked again by Constitutionalist troops"; it is a little-known episode and revolutionary group, but their existence—and the participation of women beyond that of the typical *soldadera*—was documented photographically.[65] The images also provide evidence of the Virgin of Guadalupe's importance to the Zapatistas, the only army to systematically incorporate a religious figure in their representations. One photo shows a cavalry contingent under her banner, accompanied by followers in the street (Figure 7-19). In another, of Zapatistas visiting the Basilica of Guadalupe, we can spot tiny cards with an image of the Virgin in their sombreros (Figure 7-20).[66]

7-18. "First Regiment of the Socialist Brigade of Mexico, Feminine Sex," Mexico City, March 1915. © Inv. #818038, Fondo Casasola, SINAFO-Fototeca Nacional del INAH.

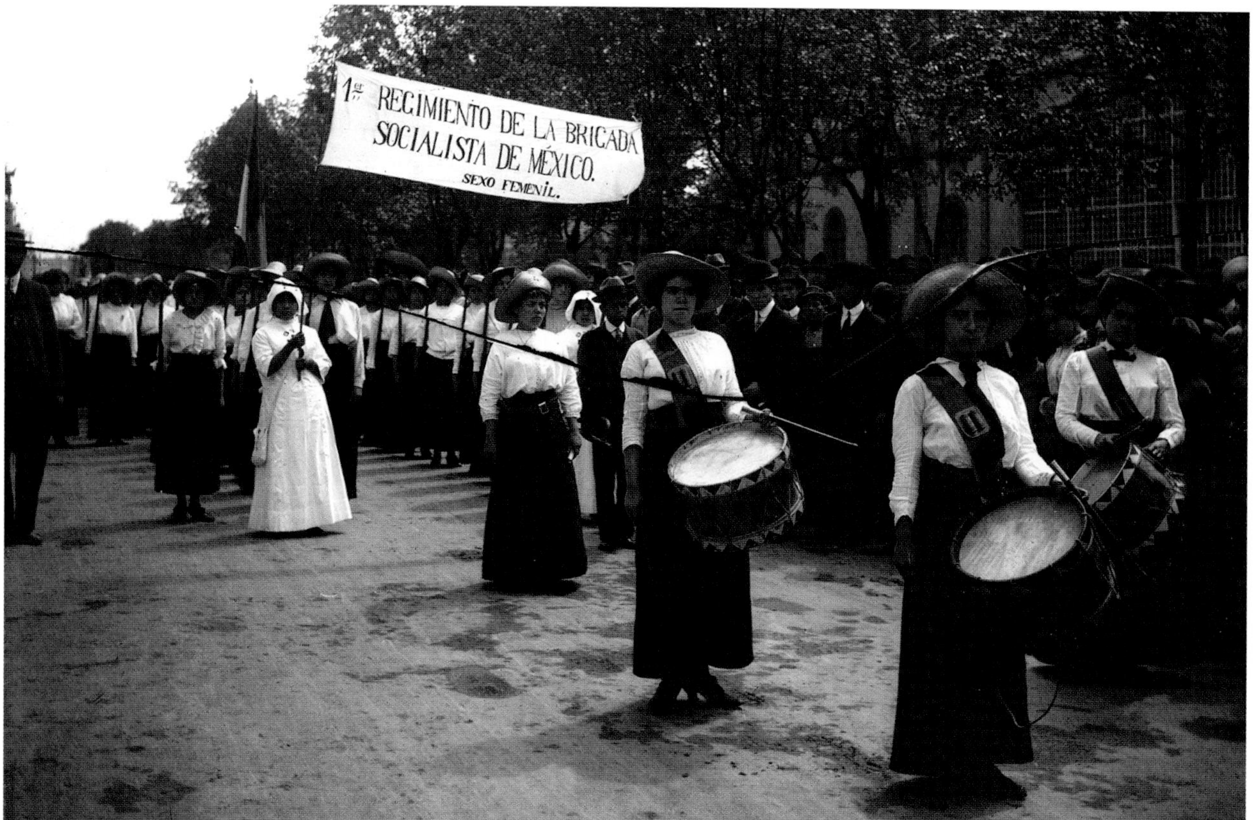

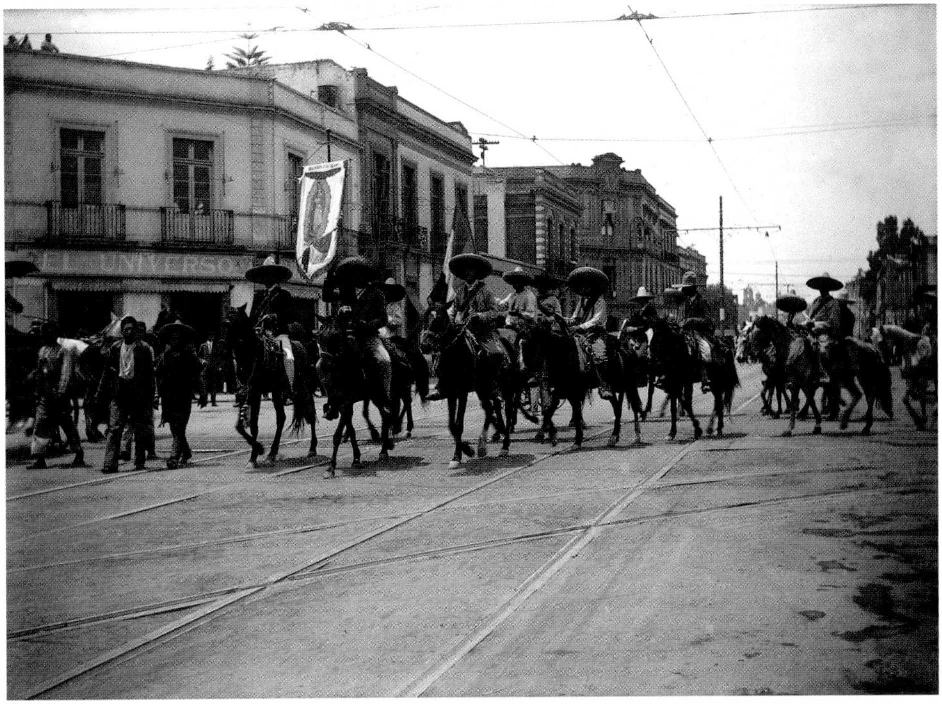

7-19. Zapatistas under a banner with the image of the Virgin of Guadalupe, Mexico City, December 1914. © Inv. #65296, Fondo Casasola, SINAFO-Fototeca Nacional del INAH.

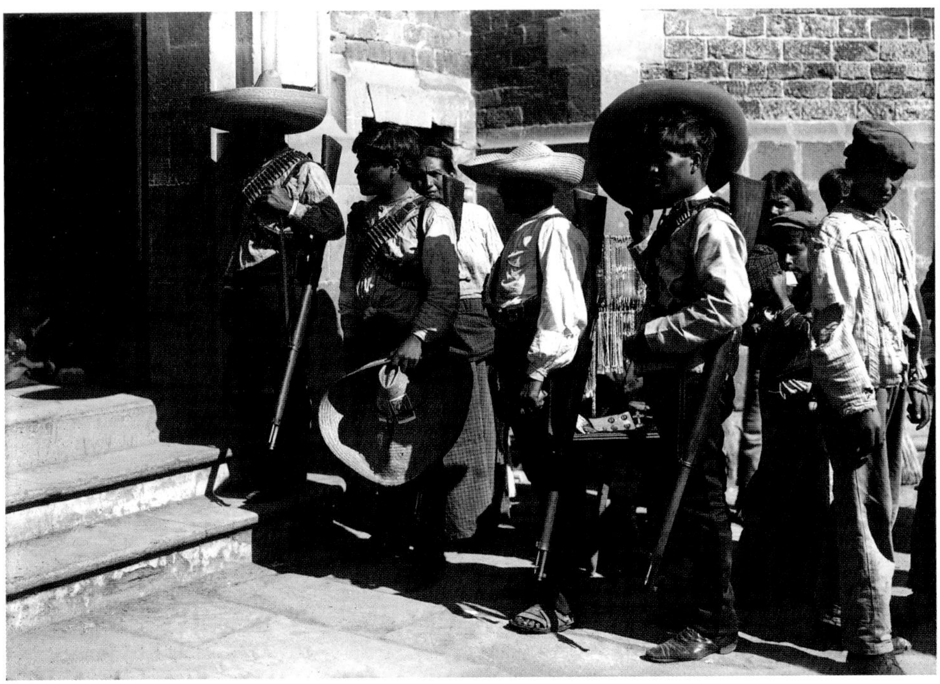

7-20. Zapatistas in the Basílica of Guadalupe with tiny cards bearing the image of the Virgin of Guadalupe in their sombreros, Mexico City, December 1914. © Inv. #6267, Fondo Casasola, SINAFO-Fototeca Nacional del INAH.

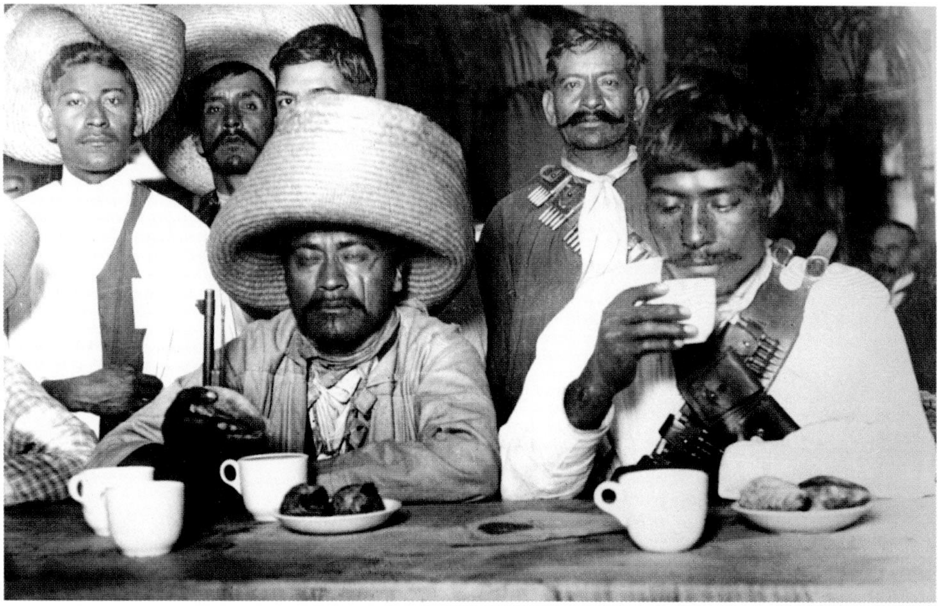

7-21. Zapatistas in Sanborn's restaurant, Mexico City, December 1914. © Inv. #33532, Fondo Casasola, SINAFO-Fototeca Nacional del INAH.

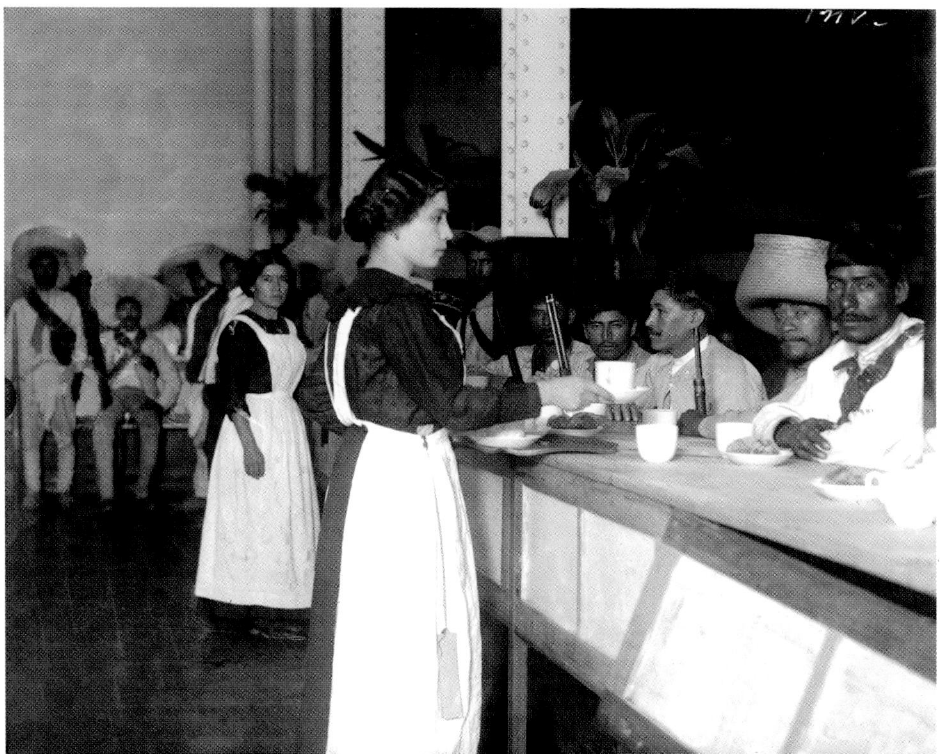

7-22. Zapatistas in Sanborn's restaurant, Mexico City, December 1914. © Inv. #6219, Fondo Casasola, SINAFO-Fototeca Nacional del INAH.

The temptations and complexities of attempting to realize psychological readings from historical photographs, discussed in the introduction, can be appreciated in comparing two pictures of Zapatistas in Sanborn's restaurant during the Constitutionalist occupation of Mexico City. In one photo they are almost incarnations of the image which many urban residents had of them: scarred, violent men who appear ready to cut your throat for the pleasure of it (Figure 7-21). In the other, they look like harmless campesinos, a bit disoriented at finding themselves in an unfamiliar situation (Figure 7-22). Obviously, neither of these readings offers us the "truth" about the Zapatistas. What they do instead is more important: they evidence the fact that these men—like all the Conventionists in Mexico City—were occupying a space that had formerly been denied them.

CHAPTER 8

The Advantages of Photographing the Constitutionalist Movement

THE IMAGE THAT PANCHO VILLA PROJECTED—and the images of him that were projected—have left the mistaken impression that the Villistas were the group that most promoted itself with modern media. My research in photographic archives, illustrated magazines, and picture histories indicates that Constitutionalism was the most photographed movement and, moreover, was depicted by more photographers than all the other forces combined. Marion Gautreau's investigations confirm this hypothesis, asserting that the Constitutionalist leaders were the most published in the illustrated magazines.[1] Miguel Ángel Berumen believes that the "overvaluation" of Villa has skewed the big picture: "There are a lot of photographs of Villa but he is not the most photographed man in the revolution, as many think. We found fewer photos of Villa in archives and published than of Carranza, Obregón, and Pablo González; Pablo González is in first place, if you discount the photos of Carranza and Obregón as presidents."[2] Although the dominance of Constitutionalist photography appears clear, it is still necessary to question whether that perception is not an expression of a well-known pattern in historiography: the documents of the winners are collected and preserved, while those of the losers are dispersed and many times lost.

Notwithstanding the importance of bearing in mind the above methodological observation, I believe that there were more Constitutionalist photographers, and that they took more pictures for the same reason the movement won the war: they had more money. The number of photographers and images is a testimony to the leaders' vision of modern media usage. Martín Luis Guzmán described Carranza's obsession with having himself pictured, and the funds he dedicated to that purpose.

> The figure of Venustiano and the photography of the revolution interpenetrate. Carranza arrived in Sonora not only fleeing, but dirty and shabby; when all expected him to call for a bath, they heard with surprise that the First Leader of the Constitutionalist Army only wanted to have a portrait made. This was a bountiful

> event for revolutionary photography: from that point dates its consciousness of its destiny as an activity called to great things; from that point the thrust, soon growing, later booming, of its economic development. From then on Venustiano cultivated such a tenacious and overwhelming inclination to do everything possible to appear in effigy, that his kindly smile and the glint of his glasses promptly became the photographers' fat times, a true lark of light: a golden and twinkling light. His portraits brought thousands of pesos to Hermosillo; due to shortages in Sonora, even more money went to U.S. laboratories in California, where the really big jobs were done: print runs of a hundred or two hundred thousand, impressions on expensive paper. And all this, already important, was only the beginning of the photographic era; later, not content with static images of the Commander-in-Chief, the supreme directors of the revolution recurred to cinema.[3]

Abitia made both cinema and photography for the Constitutionalists. Because revolutions offer such fertile loam in which to cultivate the chimeras of "Great Men," Abitia, like Casasola, has also become a myth that overshadows other imagemakers. In his case, the legend is that he was *the* Constitutionalist photographer: according to the *Diccionario histórico y biográfico de la Revolución Mexicana*, "In 1919 Venustiano Carranza, the president of Mexico, designated him 'The Constitutionalist Photographer.'"[4] Abitia himself, however, always recognized the participation of others; for example, he titled his autobiography "Memories of a Constitutionalist Photographer."[5] There he told the story of the recognition he received in 1913 from Carranza, a demonstration of the caudillo's astuteness in promoting his movement: "He was delighted to find out about the propaganda I was making for the revolution in films and photographs, and on dedicating a portrait of him that I myself had taken, he called me a 'Constitutionalist photographer.'"

Born in Chihuahua in 1881, Abitia's father was a liberal agronomist who "talked about the injustices of the Porfirian government."[6] Jesús was a childhood friend of Álvaro Obregón, and they organized circus functions in which the kids played instruments—guitars, drums, and a cardboard violin—made by Abitia.[7] Later, the two friends were named schoolteachers, although Obregón was only thirteen years old and Abitia was twelve. His interest in photography began in 1895, when he saw the Lumiére outfit that a family member had brought from Paris: "He began to show the inhabitants of Uruachic that extraordinary invention, teaching me how it functioned. The movies, some 30 to 40 meters long, left my neighbors with their mouths hanging open; but what positively fascinated me was the apparatus itself. My irresistible addiction to cinematographic technology, and photography, was born at that point, and they have been the passion of my entire life."[8]

As soon as he could, Abitia asked a store in his town to order photographic equipment for him. He acquired a little wooden camera (of 2½ × 2½ inches) and the materials to develop and print film. "With that outfit," he recalled, "I began to take photos and make money."[9] He later went to Chihuahua city to buy a medium-format camera (5 × 7), with which he traveled about the mountain towns as a professional photographer. In 1903 he moved temporarily to Mexico City "in search of wider horizons."[10] He wanted to buy a movie camera but didn't have the money, so he decided "to continue studying photographic art, under the tutelage of the Valleto brothers, then the capital's best photographers."[11] The Valletos certainly knew their profession, but it was a curious choice for someone who would enter into rebellion against the favorite subjects of that studio. According to photo historian Claudia Negrete, "The Valleto brothers photographed the great society of Mexico, to which they came to belong"; what is more, "It was the photographic company chosen to register the most important moments of the life of President Díaz and his wife."[12]

After three or four months in the capital, Abitia returned to Chihuahua, dedicating himself to artistic tours and practicing his new photographic knowledge. In 1908 he moved to Hermosillo, Sonora, and opened a photo shop; according to him, "It became the city's most favored studio in a short time, with the result that, without it being my intention, the established photographers closed their doors and left me an open field."[13] Abitia prospered, but the strike in Pinos Altos, Chihuahua—"the first in the country"—and the labor uprisings in Río Blanco and Cananea made him "think that a change of government was necessary."[14] He organized a Society of Workers and Artisans "to better the economic, social, and cultural conditions of the working classes," and he received the Magonista newspaper, *Regeneración*.[15] He linked himself early to the rebellion, saving Madero and his wife during a visit to Hermosillo in January 1910, an act for which Abitia and his family were persecuted by the government. Two of his brothers fled south to make Maderista propaganda, eventually reaching Oaxaca and Chiapas.

Abitia stayed in Hermosillo, "carefully watched by the police and harassed by the caciques."[16] He had some work pending that was "very important" to the governor and the army, but he found out that once he had turned it in, they were going to arrest him and "send him to the Islas Marías to cure him of his rebelliousness." Abitia finished the job immediately and left it with a brother, with instructions not to let the Federales know about it until he had arrived safe and sound in Arizona. He escaped disguised as a campesino—changing his straw sombrero for a cap and a raincoat to cross the border—and when the police arrived to arrest him the next day, they were "very upset." Abitia lived in El Paso and there acquired his first movie camera; he returned to Mexico a few days before Diaz's resignation. He had left his photo store in the hands of a friend, Jesús Azueta Franco, and it had prospered. Abitia discovered on his return that he had accumulated important capital and fourteen employees.

Invited to form part of the new government, Abitia was elected to an important post in Hermosillo, "taking advantage of that position to benefit the working classes by distributing lots of vacant lands so they could build homes." The reactionaries in city hall didn't like his attitude and got rid of him by commissioning Abitia to go to Mexico City to meet with Madero. Although he found out en route about the coup, he continued on and stayed in the capital for ten days photographing the damage caused by the fighting during La Decena Trágica. Attempting to return to Hermosillo, he was identified as a Maderista in Colima and had to escape, keeping one step ahead of the authorities until he finally arrived at the border and was able reunite with Obregón in Nogales.

Obregón invited his old friend to collaborate with him, and "Abitia was designated, first by Obregón and then by Carranza, the 'official' photographer of Constitutionalism."[17] He was incorporated into the general staff but wished to maintain his civilian status; he told Obregón that in doing so, "I can carry out the civilian or military commissions to which you name me and, moreover, have a certain liberty of action to make movies and a picture history of the revolution."[18] Abitia followed the Constitutionalist forces—"Sometimes at the side of Venustiano Carranza, other times at that of General Hill or General Diéguez, but principally together with General Obregón"—documenting the battles, the triumphs, the camp life, and, above all, Carranza and Obregón.[19] He filmed an enormous quantity of material; by August 1916 he had shot "nearly 60,000 feet of film."[20] This was edited into feature-length documentaries such as *La campaña constitucionalista* and was much later made into two compilation films, both titled *Epopeyas de la Revolución*.[21]

The most pampered of the revolutionary photographers, Abitia was assigned a caboose to carry his equipment, which he would buy on trips to Havana. He certainly did not lack money, above all because he was entrusted to design the new bills for the army, a revolutionary mission he carried out with his photos: a portrait of Madero on the front and on the reverse an image of the cannon "Zaragoza," which sunk the Huertista warship *Morelos* in Mazatlán in 1914 (Figures 8-1 and 8-2). The privileges that he enjoyed did not save him from the dangers of war. Once, while filming an

8-1. FACING TOP Constitutionalist bill designed by Jesús H. Abitia, 1914. Archive of Ángel Miquel.

8-2. FACING BELOW Group of artillerymen with the cannon called "Zaragoza," which sunk the federal warship *Morelos* off Isla de la Piedra, Mazatlán, 1914; Jesús H. Abitia. © Fondo Barragán, 2581, Instituto de Investigaciones sobre la Universidad y la Educación—UNAM.

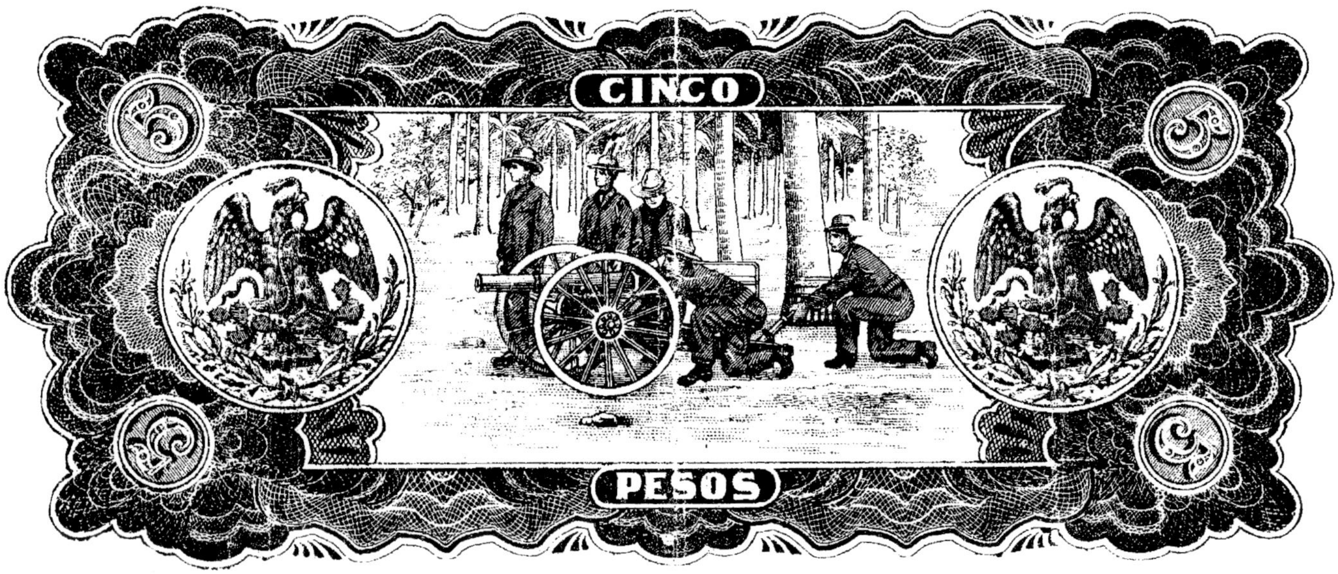
CINCO
PESOS

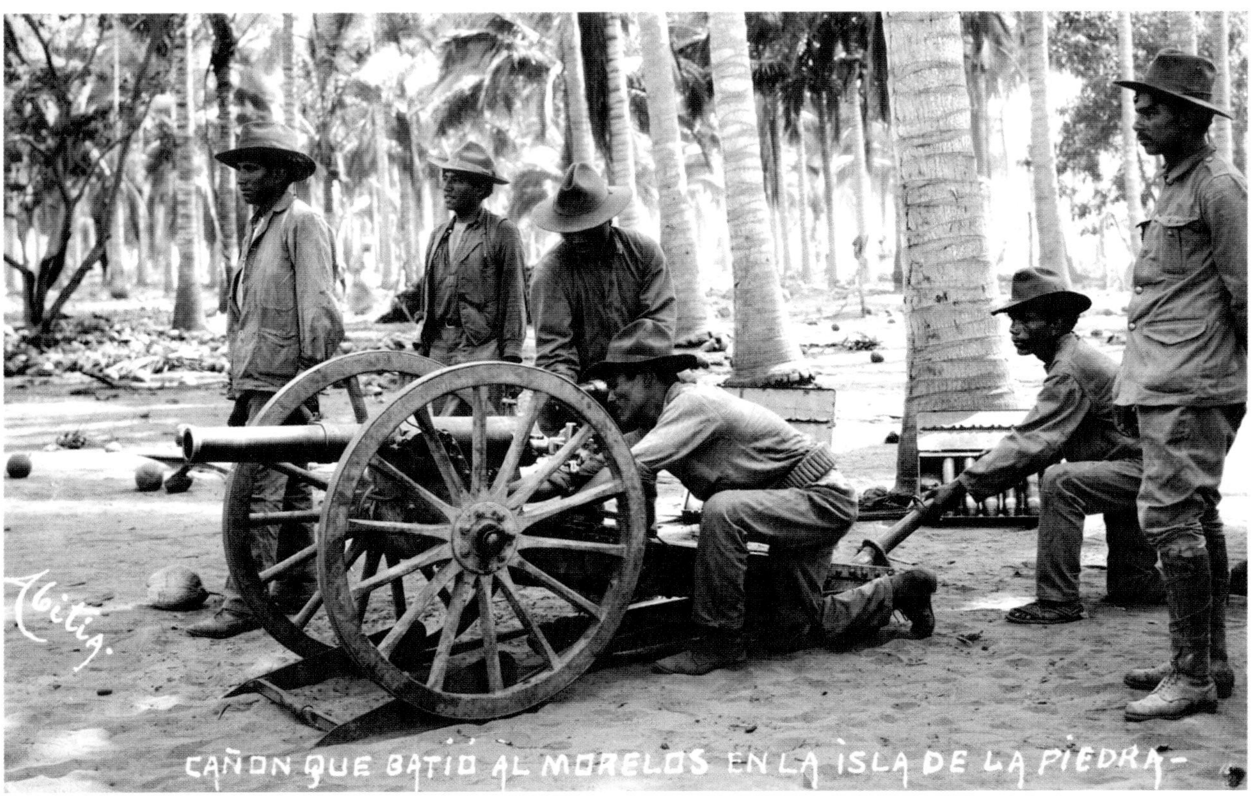
CAÑON QUE BATIÓ AL MORELOS EN LA ISLA DE LA PIEDRA-

artillery duel with the famed Villista general Felipe Ángeles, his equipment saved his life: "A grenade exploded at my feet and a piece of shrapnel hit the camera, knocking me down; when I got up I saw that the camera and tripod had been rendered useless, but I was uninjured."[22]

The photographs that Abitia took throughout the Constitutionalist campaign must have served a variety of purposes, but they were always focused on making "great propaganda for the cause."[23] One of his images that is most openly propagandistic is that of the "Heroic General Obregón" seated on his horse; taken against backlighting that frames his silhouette against the landscape, the image shows the revolutionary leader contemplating the future country he will create (Figure 8-3). Film historian Ángel Miquel is the researcher who has most studied Abitia, and he found several series of postcards that the photographer produced for the leaders, although they were probably also sold to soldiers. Miquel identifies the first series as a register of the northern campaign against the Huertista army in 1913 and asserts that "As opposed to those who portrayed cadavers, destroyed houses, and fires, Abitia's is a less-crude description of the war," focused on "the leaders and soldiers preparing themselves for the battles, fighting, resting, and even enjoying a bullfight."[24]

Abitia understood that his role was to show the leaders—and successes—of an integrated army. Miquel commented on one postcard of Mayo Indians with bows and arrows "that is particularly significant because it extends equality to this group traditionally discriminated against, making them one more member of the army."[25] There are also postcards of the booty obtained, such as captured artillery pieces and war materials. Miquel comments that these postcards "were not composed with an aesthetic sense, but they complied with the task of clearly showing what they wanted to portray."[26] The researcher compares the first postcard series with those Abitia made two years later, concluding that "They represent a step further in his development as a photographer. He achieved some images, such as the train car covered with branches where the wounded caudillo convalesced, or that of riders in the open after the decisive battle, taken with a twilight illumination in which the emotion of the represented gains in intensity on being united with forms of great beauty."[27]

Abitia was just one piece in the Constitutionalist propaganda machine, which included the contracting of many photographers and the founding of an English-language magazine to promote their interests in the United States, *The Mexican Review*.[28] Created by George F. Weeks, a U.S. citizen who became one of Carranza's closest advisors, the periodical was published monthly from October 1916 to December 1921, and in its very first number defined itself as "A Journal Devoted to the Enlightenment of the American People in Respect to the Hopes, Ambitions, Beneficent Intentions and Accomplishments of the Constitutionalist Government."[29] The magazine was directed toward U.S. politicians, intellectuals, journalists, bankers, businessmen, unions, and the Mexican emigrants who found themselves in that country. Rather than a critique of Carranza's enemies, such as Villa and Zapata, it strove to create a positive image of the Constitutionalists as the Mexican authority capable of establishing normalcy for U.S. investors. This message was conveyed in images that legitimized Carranza by visually equating him with U.S. president Woodrow Wilson; for example, their portraits appeared on the cover of the first issue.[30] Although the use of pictures does not appear to be very experimental and is limited largely to leaders' visages, photo historian Jaime Vélez Storey argues that "The propagandistic rhetoric was accompanied by images that exalted the political and cultural symbols of Mexico as a visual referent and a historical shield of national integrity."[31]

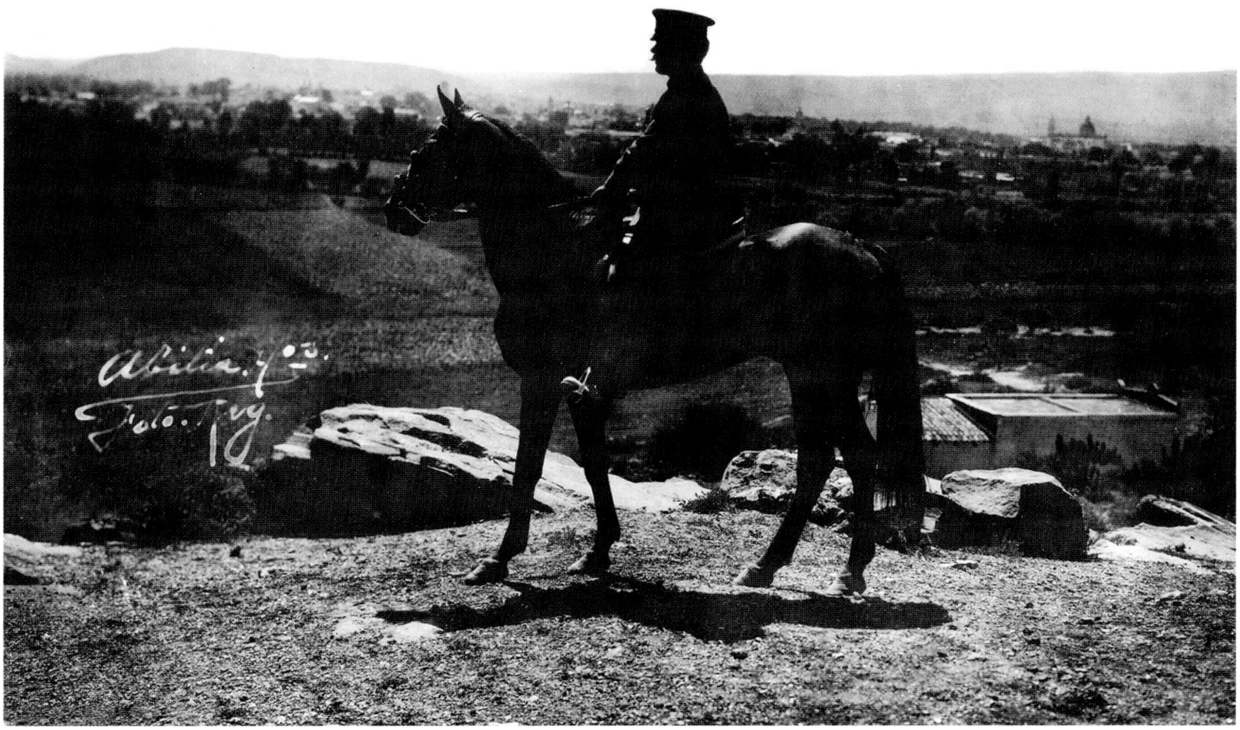

8-3. General Álvaro Obregón, ca. 1914; Jesús H. Abitia. © Inv. #374012, Fondo Casasola, SINAFO-Fototeca Nacional del INAH.

It was necessary to arm a media offensive to defend Constitutionalism from the attacks of the metropolitan press, which continued with its established pattern of being on the side of whoever was in power, and thus was anti-Constitutionalist until Huerta's resignation in July 1914. For example, in April 1913, *Novedades* published several photos by Samuel Tinoco of troops embarking in trains, while critiquing "the anti-patriotic and devastating revolution. The rebels, in their desire to cause more harm to the nation, as if enough blood had not been spilled, are completely destroying the vast and rich region of the north."[32] After Huerta's defeat, the same magazine dedicated itself to rescuing Francisco I. Madero from the oblivion to which he had been condemned by the media so that his ideals "would come back in style."[33] In subsequent issues, *Novedades* covered the exhumations of Huerta's victims, among them Belisario Domínguez, with photos by Antonio Garduño, reviling against the "cruelties and horrors of General Huerta" and "the frightful crimes committed by his followers to impose his government."[34] When revolutionary troops arrived in the capital in August 1914, photos by Garduño and Almagro documented the multitudes that filled the Zócalo, while the cutlines signaled how Obregón had "conquered sympathies."[35] For *Novedades*, the Constitutionalists, including Pancho Villa, had changed from being *cabecillas* into "revolutionary leaders" with the abdication of Huerta.

Other illustrated magazines also demonstrated their chameleon-like character. During August 1913, Lucio Blanco carried out one of the first repartitions of land as a result of the revolution. *La Semana Ilustrada* placed over the photograph of that act the title "Despoil to share"; below, the cutline complained, "Lucio Blanco celebrated the distribution of the lands he stole from their legitimate owners. The *cabecilla*, aided by Manuel Urquida, shares among his retinue the fruit of the booty" (Figure 8-4).[36] After Huerta's fall, this magazine celebrated leaders Pablo González and Pancho Villa, while it published photos of Madero, "whose assassination cries for vengeance," and the exhumed cadaver of General Rafael Tapia, "valiant Constitutionalist leader, vilely assassinated."[37]

La Ilustración Semanal used photos from its correspondents in the states to document the material advantages of the Huertista army: Ignacio Ocampo y Amezcua showed the fortifications defended with large-caliber artillery in Mazatlán; a López in Guaymas portrayed machine guns and troops that appear to be Yaqui Indians who "have battled heroically against the rebels"; and a photographer named Guerrero visually flaunted the public services brought by military occupation: "Federal soldiers repair the sidewalks in one of El Oro's streets to make the city beautiful."[38] Regional imagemakers also provided testimonies of the destruction wrought by the revolutionaries, and the punishment they received. Pictures by "P. Reygaud Jr." illustrated "the damage caused by Jesús Carranza's hordes on his way to Montemorelos," and R. Rojas photographed an execution in Aguascalientes.[39] On finding himself without the Huertista backing he had received, the editor, Ezequiel Álvarez Tostado, indicated his preference by dedicating a cover of *La Ilustración Semanal* to Carranza, an honor usually reserved for beautiful women.[40] In the same issue a photo by Antonio Garduño portrayed a young Constitutionalist artilleryman with a certain sympathy (Figure 8-5).

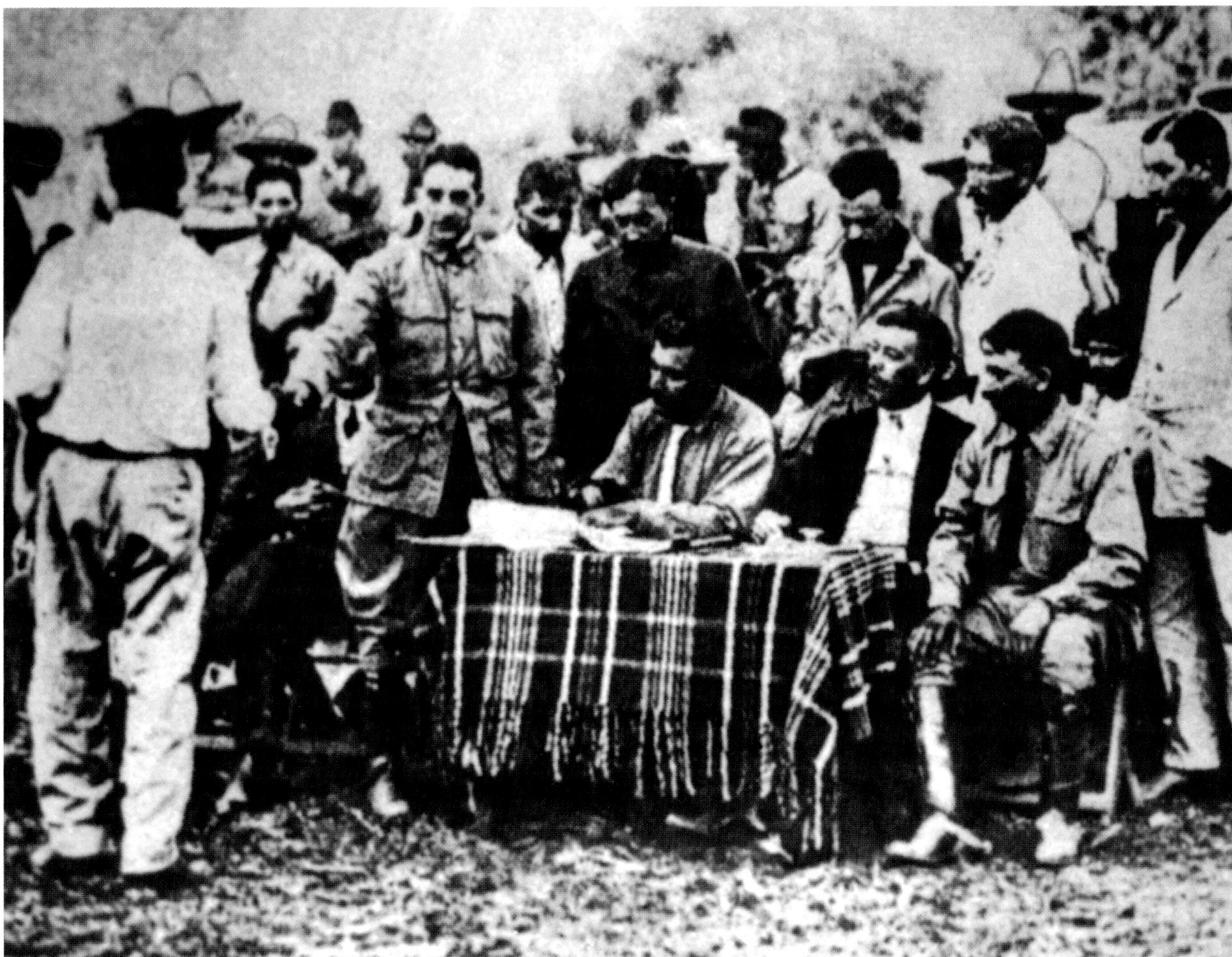

8-4. First distribution of land as a result of the revolution, carried out by Lucio Blanco in Matamoros, Tamaulipas, August 1913; *La Semana Ilustrada*, 30 September 1913. © Inv. #40720, Fondo Casasola, SINAFO-Fototeca Nacional del INAH.

The metropolitan photojournalists must have generally sided with the Constitutionalists, above all when they had to choose between them and the Conventionists. Some, such as Gerónimo Hernández and Luis Santamaría, enlisted directly in the Carrancista army; there is no evidence that they were military photographers.[41] Agustín Víctor Casasola asserted that he had participated "very particularly" in the Constitutional Congress, during which he "spent a long time" in Querétaro.[42] It appears that Eduardo Melhado remained in Mexico City after returning from Veracruz, dedicating himself to making typical photographs of social events and the *nota roja*. Nonetheless, his commitment to Carrancismo was expressed in photos of the commander of the Constitutionalist army; later, *Revista de Revistas* sent their "special photographer" to portray an "Intimate Carranza" in his home, as president.[43]

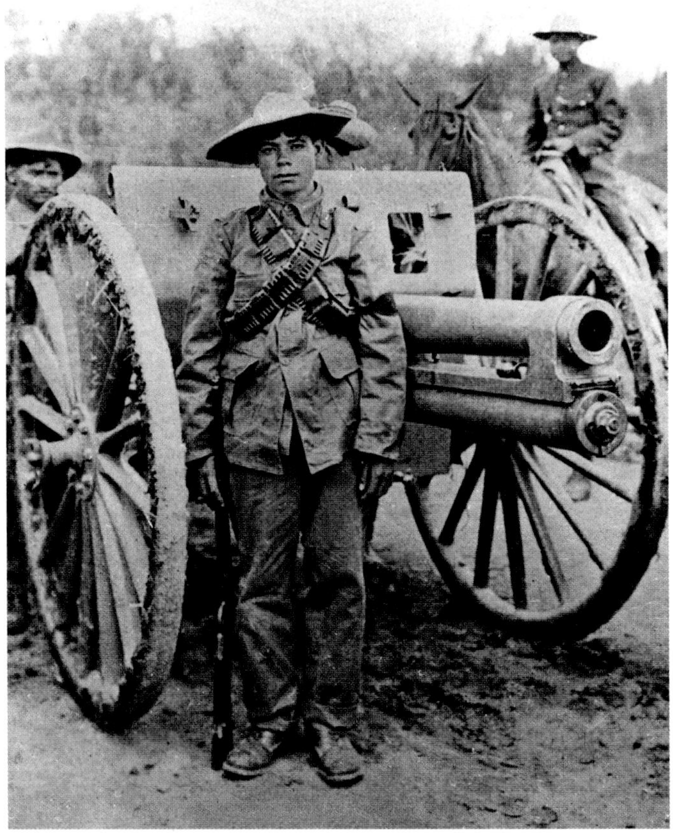

8-5. Young Constitutionalist artilleryman; Antonio Garduño. © Inv. #638387, Fondo Casasola, SINAFO-Fototeca Nacional del INAH.

José Mora had a very direct relation with Constitutionalism. Berumen affirms that he "was the official photographer of Pablo González," and photos signed by Mora showing González in Cuernavaca, Querétaro, Oaxaca, Puebla, el Desierto de los Leones, and Mexico City seem to confirm that hypothesis.[44] González is portrayed in various roles: as a victorious general on horseback—photographed from a low angle that visually empowers him—entering Cuernavaca in 1916; as a revolutionary administrator who visits girls in an orphanage; as the supermodern man, dressed as a pilot and standing next to his airplane; as a Mexican who cares about the ancient past, climbing a pyramid in Teotihuacán or visiting ruins in Mitla.[45]

Like González, Mora was ferociously anti-Zapatista. He documented the mutilated bodies and destroyed machines of different trains derailed by the Zapatistas, writing ironically on one image, "The progressive southerners in their dark attacks"; another photo—which is clearly of a training exercise—bears the text "Beating back the Zapatistas."[46] It seems that what Mora most desired for the Zapatistas was death:

he took a photo of González in front of a tomb that Mora described sarcastically as "a monument to those who signed the Plan de Ayala."[47] It is not surprising that Mora is most known as the photographer of Zapata's corpse after he was assassinated in 1919. He made images in two different locations: one where the body was placed for public exhibition, where people crowded and pushed to get into the frame and have their faces recorded next to the caudillo's mutilated visage; the other at the funeral, showing women sitting stoically next to the remains of the rebel leader.[48]

The experience of the sisters Adriana and Dolores Ehlers demonstrates both the participation of Mexican women in representing the revolution and Carranza's interest in promoting his movement through modern media. The Ehlers are better known in the cinema world, but they began their professional lives by opening a small photography studio in the patio of their house in the port of Veracruz. There they taught themselves photography and had a level of success, above all with women: "With a camera that a friend loaned us, we began a business that was well accepted by the public, above all the feminine, because we could make portraits that showed a certain cleavage, and with women draped in gauzes, things that couldn't be done in studios run by men."[49] Their family was staunchly anti-Porfirista, and their house was a place for dissidents to meet; "the sisters joined the Maderista movement, and were part of the committee that received Francisco I. Madero in the port."[50] In 1915 Veracruz was the provisional capital for a time. When Carranza went to visit an orphanage, the director contracted the sisters to take photos: "Carranza could only smile on seeing two girls taking photographs, and above all so young to be dedicated to such a strange profession. He asked that we show him what we had done when we finished; of course, he knew of our revolutionary activities."[51]

Days later the sisters went to Carranza's house to give him copies of the portraits. He showed much interest in them, asking what their greatest ambition was, and the sisters replied: "To perfect our work in photography by going to study in the United States."[52] Carranza sent them there as part of "many cultural commissions" that were dispatched to the north, and they were given scholarships to study photography in Boston for a year.[53] After they became interested in cinematography, they were granted another year of study in Washington. They later entered a school that was linked to a factory of cinema equipment, of which they became representatives in Mexico City when they returned in 1919 and mounted a cinema laboratory (which Obregón, as president, would give to Jesús Abitia).

The brothers José and Pedro Mendoza lived in Mexico City and were closely linked to the Carrancista movement through the intellectual Isidro Fabela.[54] In their archive is an album commissioned by Fabela of Carranza's triumphant tour throughout the country, in which images can be found of receptions in important centers such as Monterrey, Guanajuato, Celaya, Monclova, and Irapuato, as well as in small towns: Huichapan (Hidalgo), Cuatrociénagas (Coahuila), Hércules (Querétaro), and La Barca (Jalisco).[55] Photo historian Alberto del Castillo noted their "well-realized professional framings that construct a certain documentary aesthetic of the revolution with interesting close-ups on the multitudes; on occasion they also projected images designed to glorify the 'First Chief.'"[56] Some of their compositions seem to be made from a cinematographic perspective. In one image Constitutionalist cavalry ride through the northern desert; shot from a distance, they are buried in the scarce vegetation in a way that would appear to be camera setups for a documentary filmmaker.[57] Whether the Mendozas made films—as did other photographers such as Abitia, Eustasio Montoya, and Ignacio Medrano Chávez—is yet to be investigated.

Among other photographers linked to the Constitutionalist movement are Fernando Sosa, José Cruz Salazar Cázares, L. O. She, Refugio Z. García, and a Rodríguez. Sosa collaborated in publications such as *La Ilustración Semanal*, *El Pueblo*, *El Heraldo de México*, and *El Liberal*; his work as a photojournalist notwithstanding, he seems to have personally followed Carranza about, photographing him in a variety of places, including Puebla, Córdoba, and the port of Veracruz.[58] He remained with the leader up to the very last moment: he took a photo of him at midday on 20 May 1920, some twelve hours before Carranza was assassinated in Tlaxcalantongo, Puebla.[59] José Salazar enlisted in the Constitutionalist army in Piedras Negras, Coahuila, in 1913, and was described in his military file as "a photographer in different acts of service"; he photographed Constitutionalists in Saltillo, Monterrey, and Tampico, documenting in one photo the reception given the leader: "The *pueblo* salutes Commander General V. Carranza."[60] L. O. She was established in Monterrey and followed the Constitutionalists from Coahuila in 1913 to Puebla in 1914, and onto Tlalnepantla in 1917.[61] The relation of García and Rodríguez with Constitutionalism is less defined. Refugio Z. García had a studio in Monterrey called Light and Shadow; later he became a photojournalist for the magazine *Zig-Zag* and the newspaper *El Porvenir*.[62] He photographed Carranza on various occasions during his stays in Monterrey, but García also documented the federal artillery defending the city from the Cerro del Obispo.[63] Rodríguez made one or two photos of Carranza, but it is not clear to what purpose.[64]

Hugo Brehme continued to photograph in Mexico City and its surrounding towns after his return from Veracruz. He was in the city in August 1914, as evidenced by images of the Constitutionalist forces entering the capital (Figures 8-6 and 8-7). They

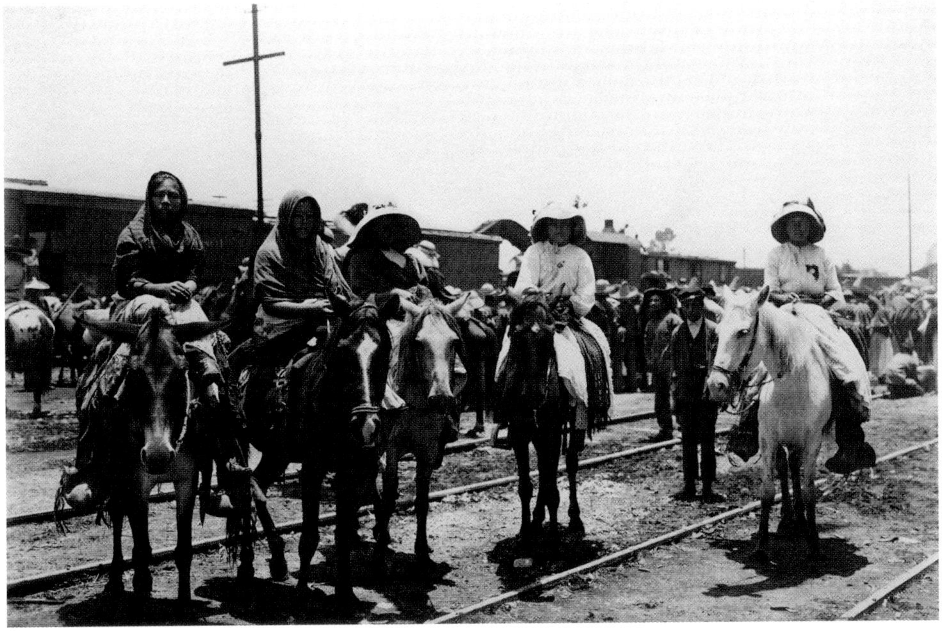

8-6. Women who accompanied the Constitutionalist army as it entered Mexico City, 1914; Hugo Brehme. © INAH-Hoffman-Brehme, 131.

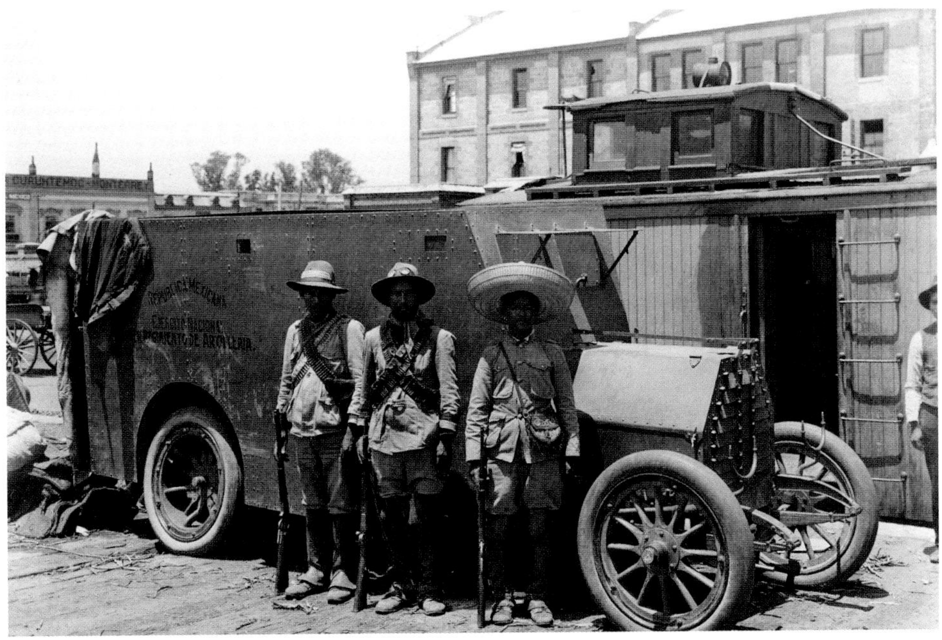

8-7. Armored car, entrance of the Constitutionalist army into Mexico City, 1914; Hugo Brehme. © INAH-Hoffman-Brehme, 127.

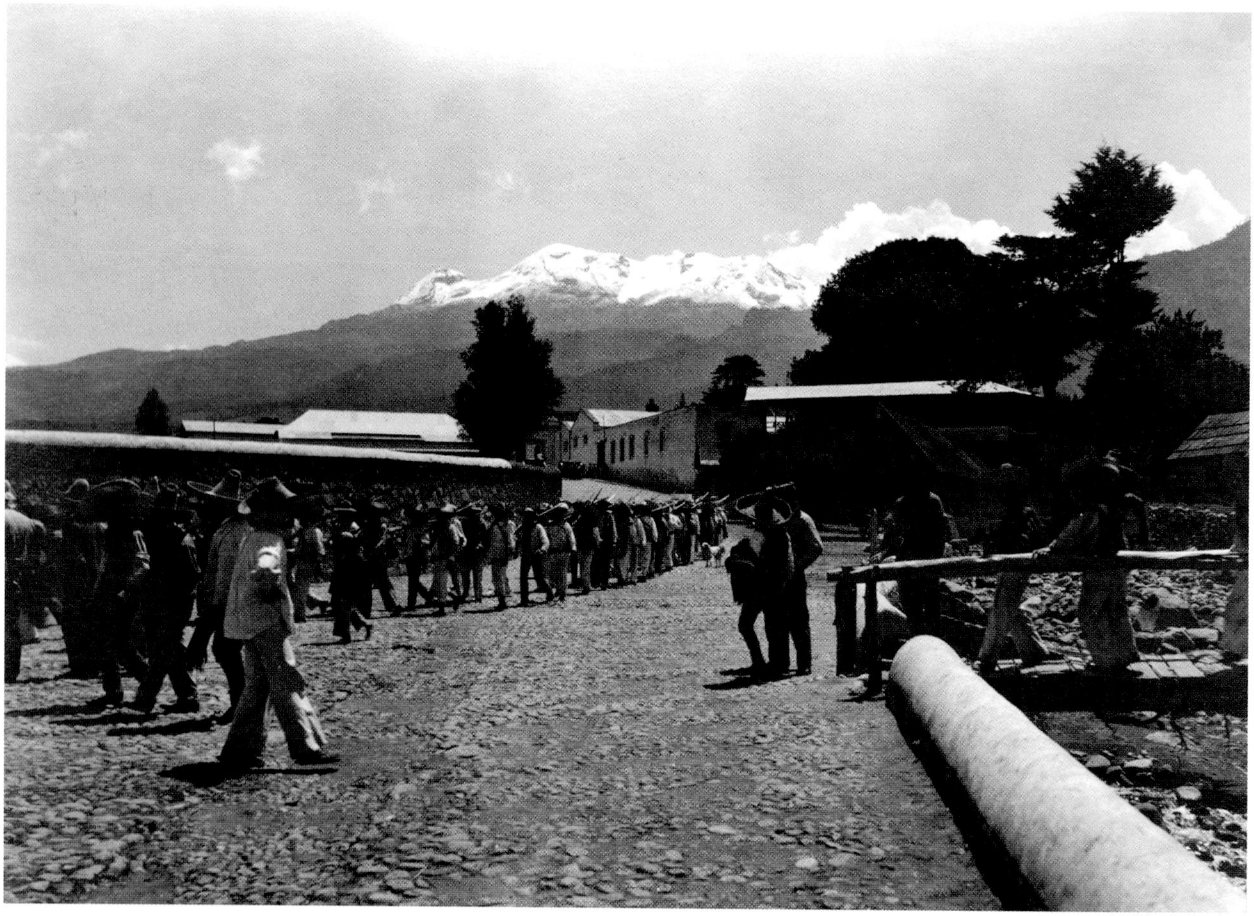

8-8. Troops marching through Tomacoco, near the volcano Iztaccihuatl, ca. 1915; Hugo Brehme. © INAH-Hoffman-Brehme, 30.

show the enormous variety of technological development during the revolution: women sit on horses that have surely just been taken off the trains, and men pose in front of an armored car, an example of the material advantages enjoyed by the Constitutionalists. Brehme took several photos in the neighboring towns, indicating that he must have circulated freely in those areas. One photo that prefigures his picturesque and panoramic renditions of the 1920s is of a troop marching through the town of Tomacoco, with the extinct volcano Iztaccihuatl providing the backdrop (Figure 8-8). In another photo a group poses with arms and drums (Figure 8-9). The clothing worn by the townspeople is a mix of campesino and urban dress: some wear the typical white *calzón* and have wide sombreros made of *petate*, but others are clad in modern apparel, and the man in the center wears worker's overalls. The fact that all the rifles are of different calibers indicates that they are irregular forces. They may have been the sort of self-defense groups that developed during the revolution to repel bandits, and they probably also served as barriers against the entrance of the Zapatistas into the city. Although Brehme took photos of the Villistas during the Conventionist occupation, I have found no pictures of the revolution by him after January 1915.[65]

Photographs of the Constitutionalist movement reveal a wide spectrum of social details. For example, an image of a woman combatant demonstrates feminine participation beyond that of the classic camp follower. Figure 8-10 is, in fact, a detail cropped from a larger image, a spontaneous photo taken by Abraham Lupercio of some federal soldiers carrying the body of a sailor killed by Zapatistas in July 1914

8-9. Townspeople near Mexico City, ca. 1915; Hugo Brehme. © INAH-Hoffman-Brehme, 29.

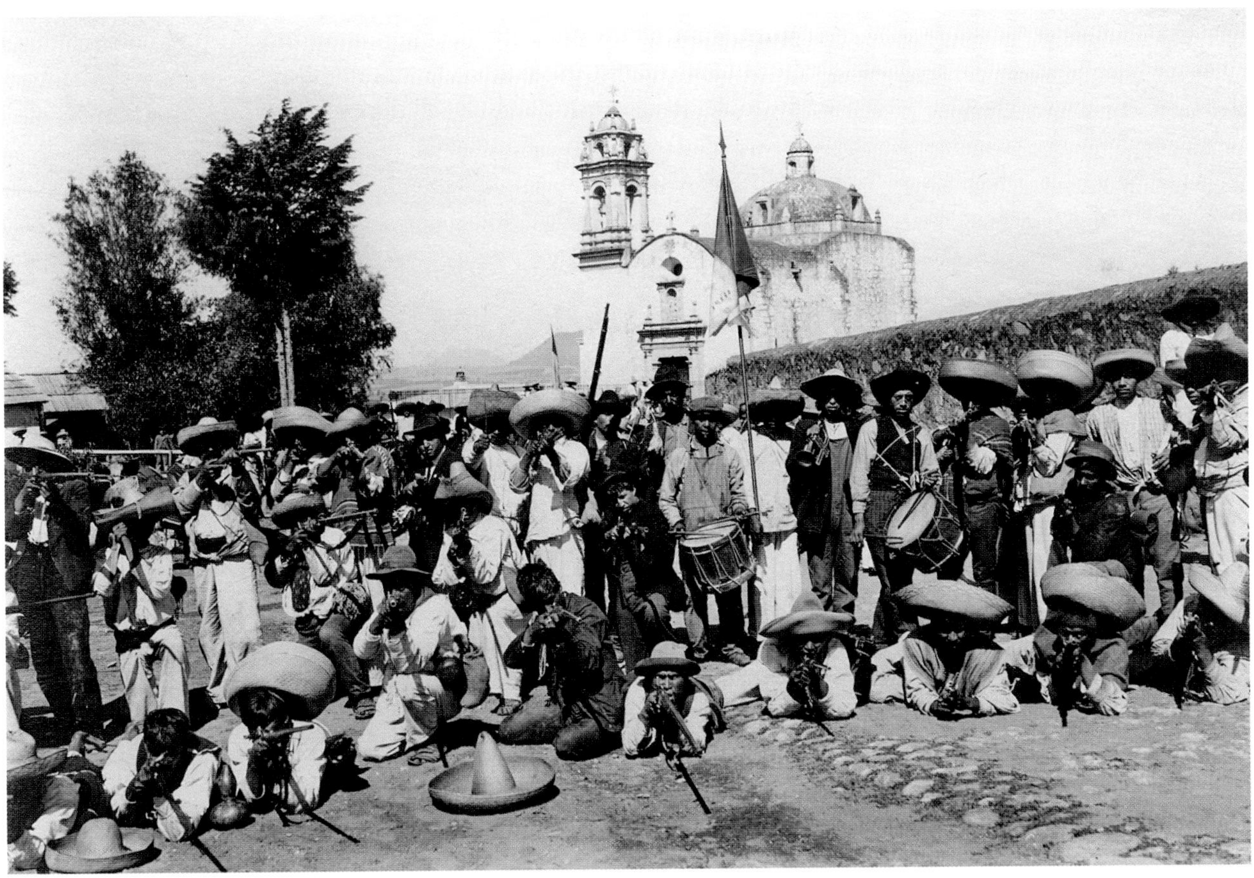

(Figure 8-11).[66] The mix of soldiers and civilians, of men and women, shows the mobilization of the town of Xochimilco in response to the Zapatista threat, in the precise moment that Huerta's resignation had left the army and the inhabitants of Mexico City exposed to the revolutionary forces.

Testimonies to the scarcities suffered by the populace of Mexico City, and the conflicts they produced, can be found in images which were probably made primarily by metropolitan photojournalists. In Figure 8-12 we see a Constitutionalist soldier using his rifle butt to push back men and boys who appear to be waiting for something, probably work. Hunger spread as the revolution prolonged, and the years 1915–1918 were especially difficult. Political decisions also played their part: according to Alan Knight, "As the new Constitutionalist elite consolidated itself in power, matters grew worse rather than better."[67] The authorities took advantage of shortages to traffic in foodstuffs and profit personally, while at the same time food was often exported to secure arms and foreign exchange. As a result, several photos document women with empty baskets in search of food or in the midst of a protest (Figure 8-13). Francisco Ramírez Plancarte described the extreme situation that he had lived through.

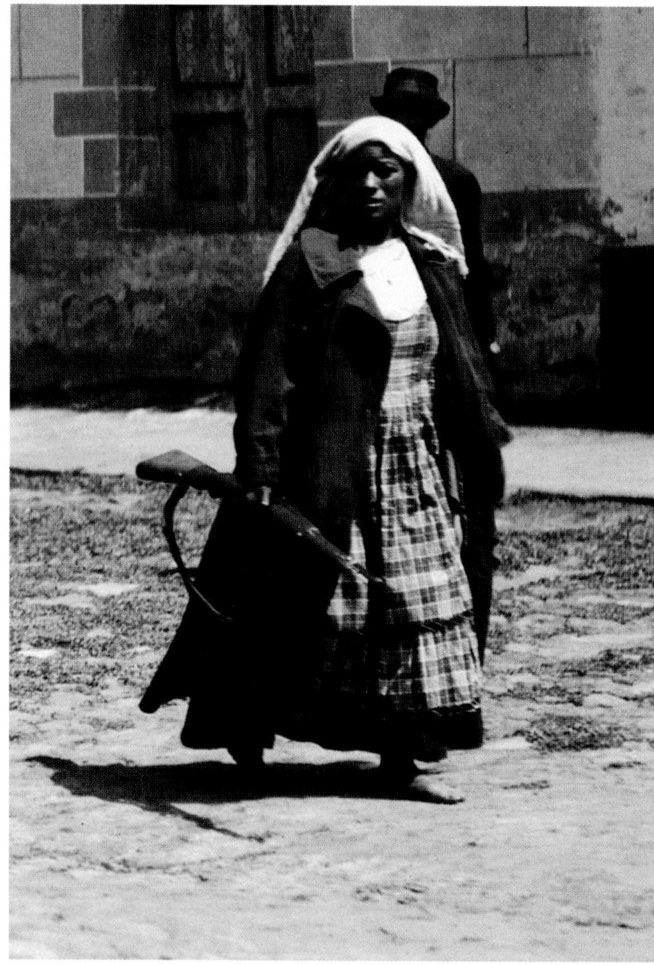

8-10. Constitutionalist combatant, Xochimilco, July 1914; Abraham Lupercio. © Inv. #5317 (detail), Fondo Casasola, SINAFO-Fototeca Nacional del INAH.

> People's hunger became so great that not a few fainted. A multitude of indigent individuals picked up fruit peels from the ground, and notwithstanding the fact that they were impregnated with dirt, they put them anxiously and voraciously in their mouths. Others poked with poles among the great mountains of garbage around the markets, in the hope of finding some leavings of poultry, fruit, vegetables, or entrails, even if they were rotten, their sole desire being that of somehow placating the hunger that devoured them.[68]

8-11. Federal soldiers and civilians carrying the body of a sailor killed by Zapatistas, Xochimilco, July 1914; Abraham Lupercio, *La Ilustración Semanal*, 27 July 1914. © Inv. #5317, Fondo Casasola, SINAFO-Fototeca Nacional del INAH.

Protests broke out against scarcities and the hoarding of food by the shopkeepers, but the trigger was usually related to problems caused by the different monies that were circulating. According to John Lear, "Protests almost inevitably occurred when the new occupiers of the city canceled the previous faction's currency."[69] Figure 8-14 is of a demonstration that included the demand for money with real value: "The people are dying of hunger. They don't have anything but bad papers and worse bills." What is curious about this photo is the presence of men in the foreground,

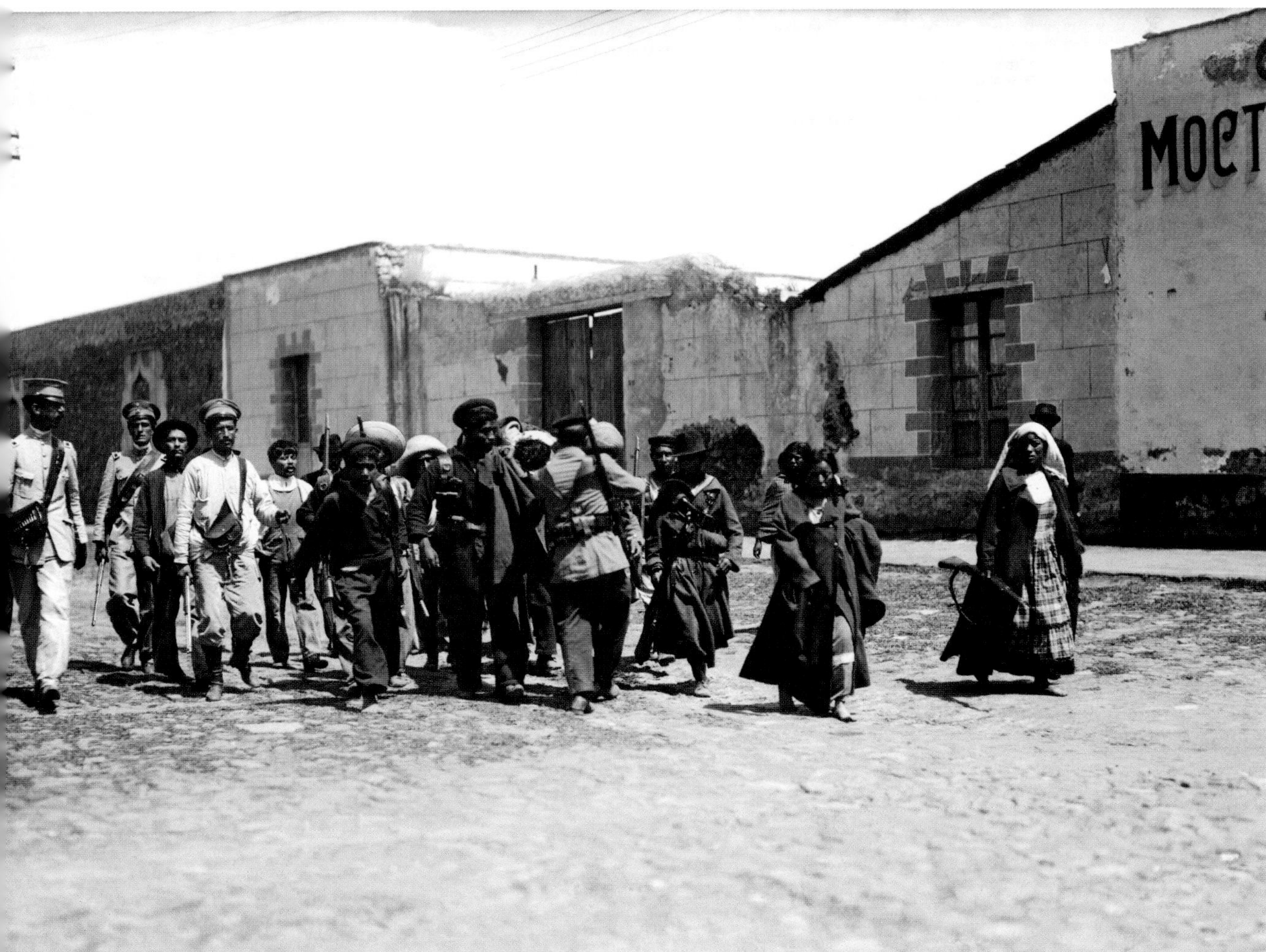

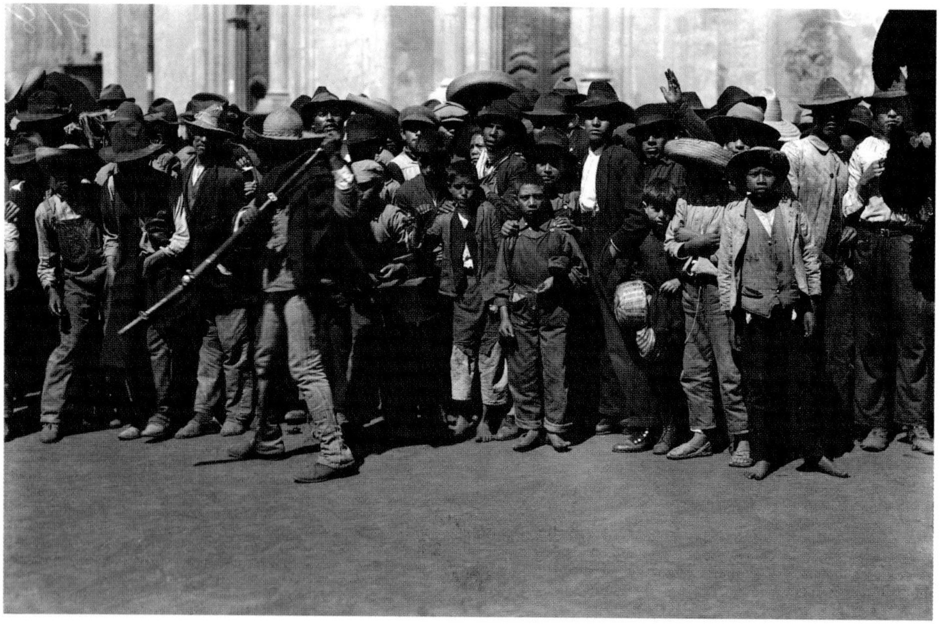

8-12. Constitutionalist soldier using his rifle butt to push back a group of men who were probably looking for work, Mexico City, 1915. © Inv. #41461, Fondo Casasola, SINAFO-Fototeca Nacional del INAH.

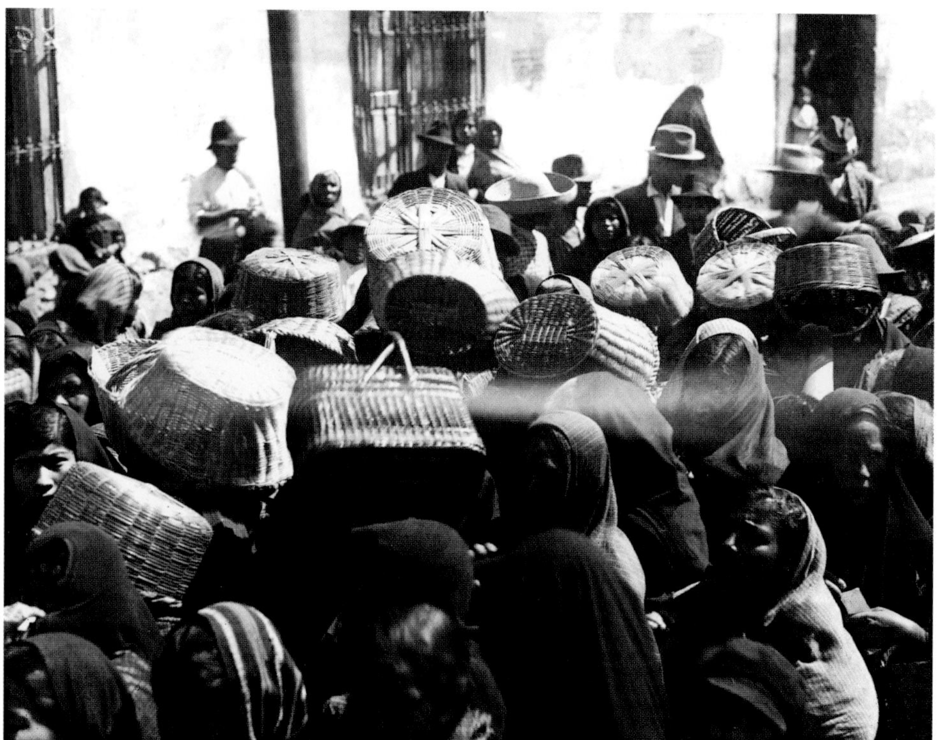

8-13. People looking for food, Mexico City, ca. 1915. © Inv. #6348, Fondo Casasola, SINAFO-Fototeca Nacional del INAH.

because it was women who generally searched for food, and according to Lear, it was they who organized protests related to its scarcity. For that reason, the photographer who took Figure 8-15, showing distribution of corn, focused on the women with children; we do not know if it is a scene constructed by the photographer or staged as a media event, but the absence of multitudes makes me suspect that it is more a case of visualizing public relations than of providing comestibles. The same observation could be made in relation to Figure 8-16, showing children in front of their plates in an orphanage: we are reminded of scarcities, and of the myriad of orphans left by the revolution, but it could well have been a photo made for publicity ends.

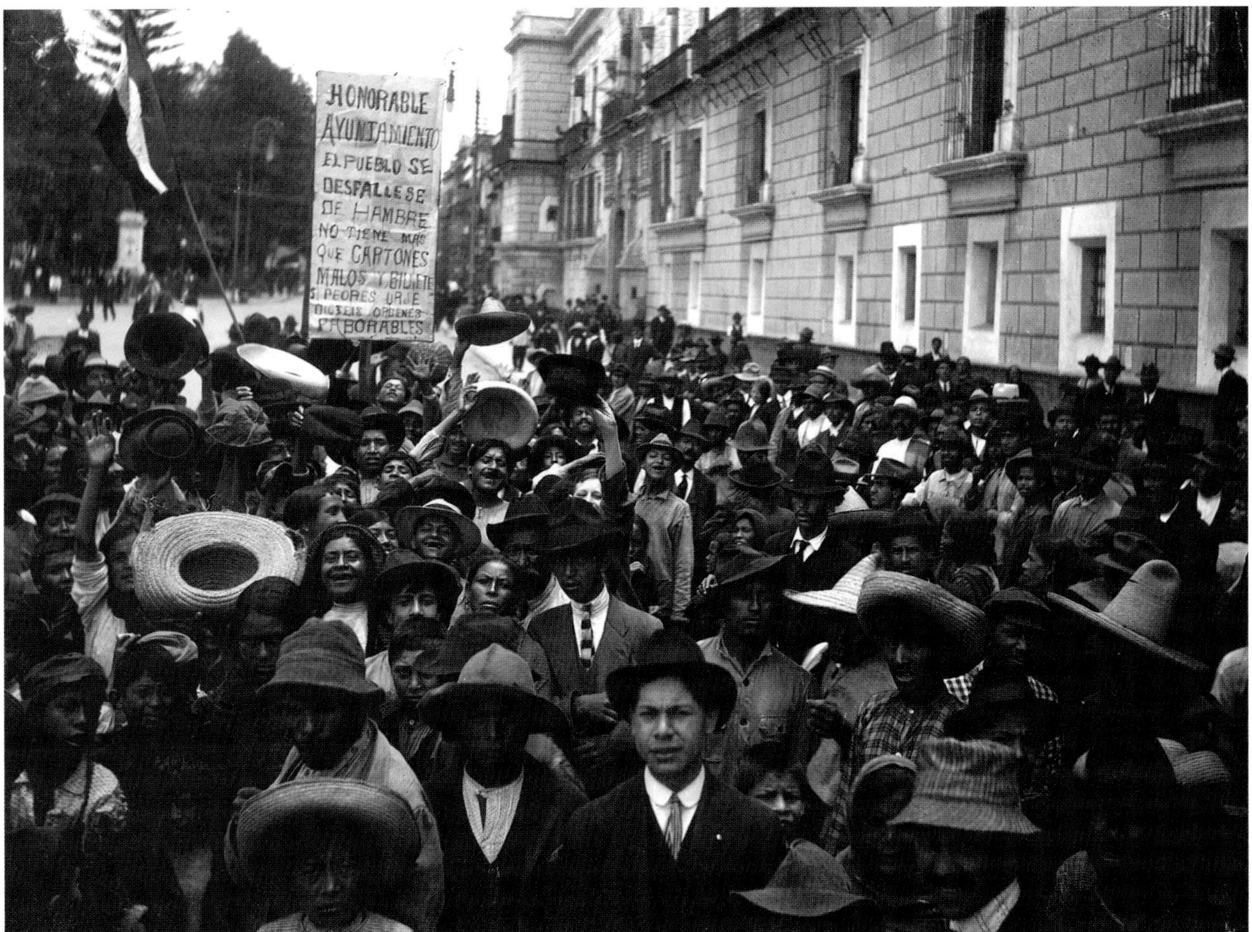

8-14. Protest against hunger and devalued paper currency, Mexico City, ca. 1915. © Inv. #5074, Fondo Casasola, SINAFO-Fototeca Nacional del INAH.

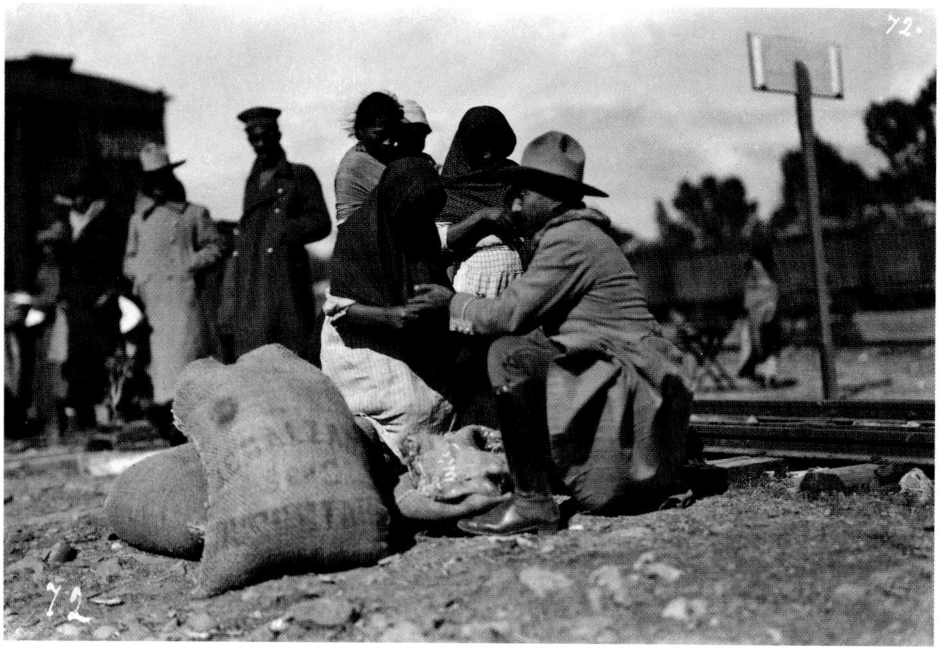

8-15. Distribution of corn, ca. 1915. © Inv. #6398, Fondo Casasola, SINAFO-Fototeca Nacional del INAH.

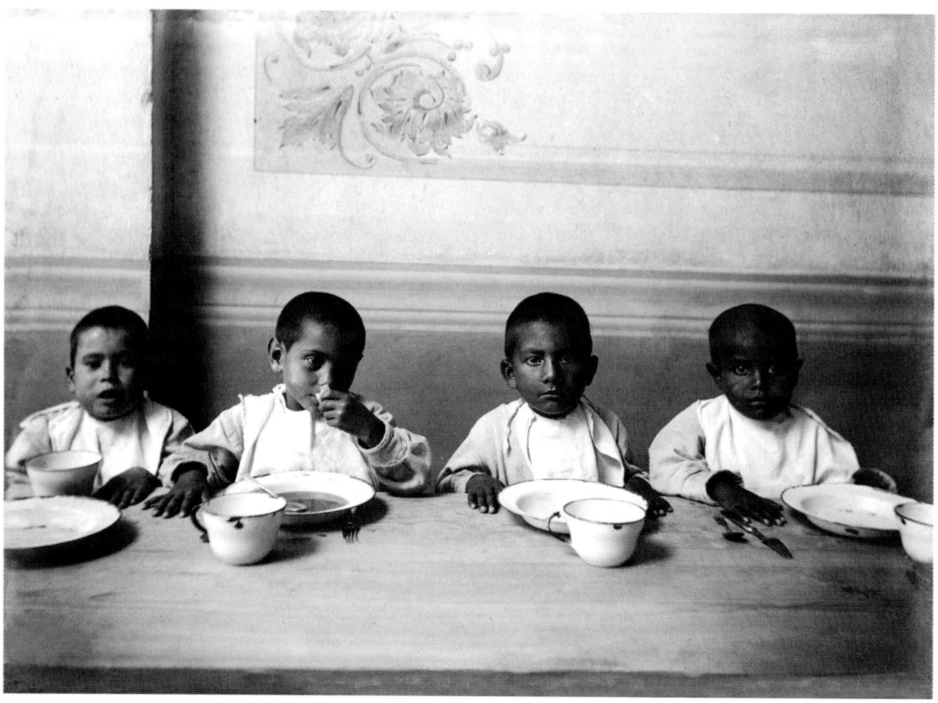

8-16. Children in an orphanage, Mexico City, ca. 1915. © Inv. #6230, Fondo Casasola, SINAFO-Fototeca Nacional del INAH.

It appears that the Constitutionalists tended to employ symbolic acts rather than direct themselves to the problems of scarcity and different monies. For example, they blamed the shopkeepers, who were mainly foreigners and hence an easy target because of the always latent xenophobia. When they refused to pay a special tax, Obregón had them arrested, and who continued to resist were forced to sweep the streets under the guard of armed Yaqui soldiers (Figure 8-17). Ramírez Plancarte recounted their dilemma with little sympathy.

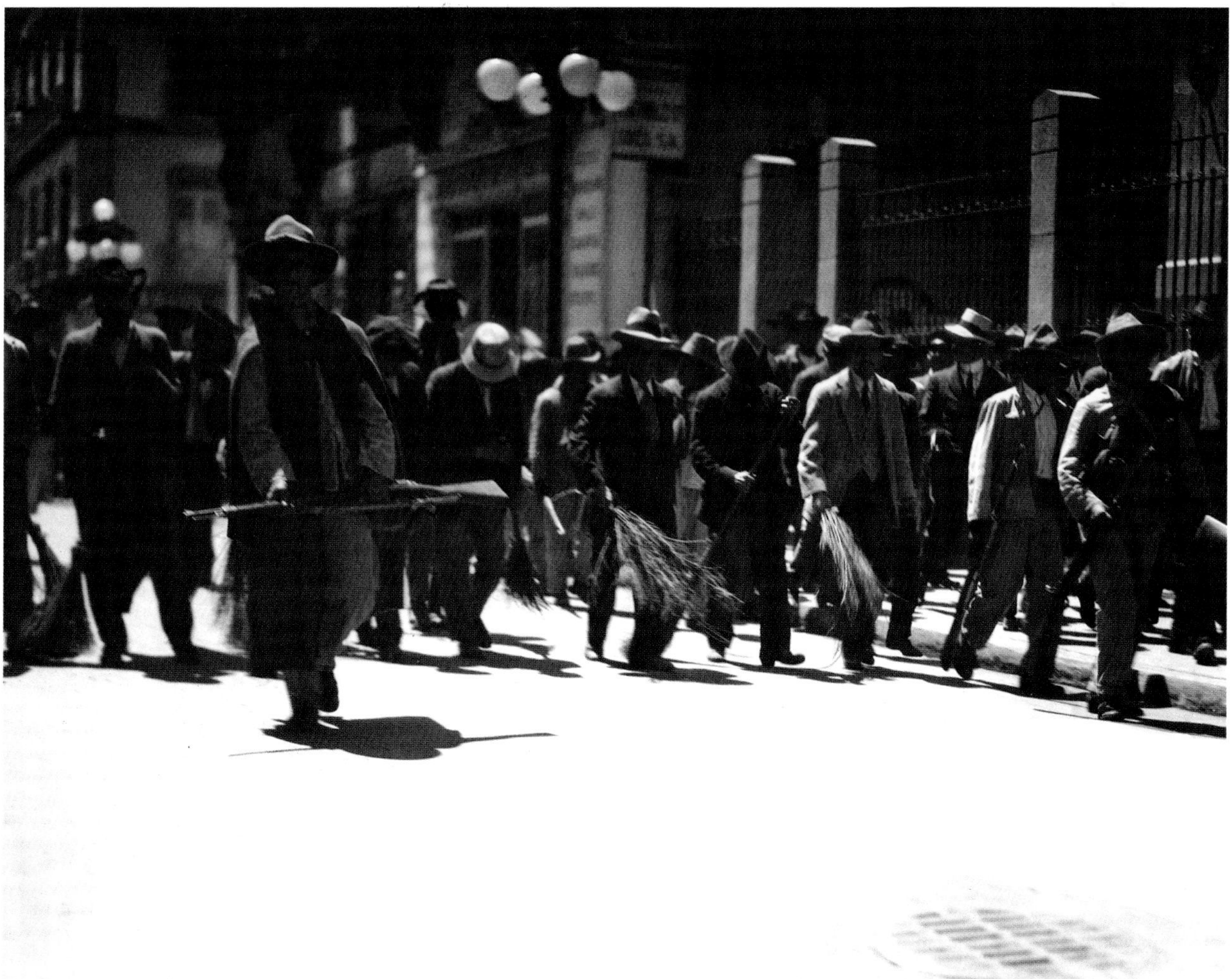

8-17. Shopkeepers, mostly foreign, forced to clean the streets by Álvaro Obregón, Mexico City, February 1915. © Inv. #41469, Fondo Casasola, SINAFO-Fototeca Nacional del INAH.

> All the air of petulance, the insolent pride and haughty stare that was so much of their being behind their counters, where they were the lords of life and death, disappeared as if by magic. With their faces livid, their lips trembling, and their bodies flaccid, they arrived dragging their feet before a triple line of Yaquis who looked contemptuously at them. They were followed by the mocking smiles of the curious who crowded to see them, some of which said sarcastically, with a nasal tone, as they passed by: "*Olé* boys, have a good time!," dragging out the syllables in a malignantly ironic way that imitated their accent and way of speaking.[70]

Other problems, as grave as hunger, were also documented in photographs. The lack of water was constant, both because of the demands made by the occupying armies and the lack of maintenance. Families waited long hours to fill their buckets with the precious liquid (Figure 8-18). Yet even when water was available, it was often not without its problems. Eduardo Vargas Sánchez again offers a nightmarish testimony.

> Men were killed on both sides during the shootouts, and their bodies fell into the water, where they rotted. It occurred to me to send for some of the long ropes and poles that were used in the poorer neighborhoods to hang clothes out to dry, and we employed them and a sort of apron to pull out some of the lighter corpses. However, when the giant Yaqui Indian soldiers fell to the bottom of the springs it was impossible to get them out. They were especially heavy because they usually wore cartridge belts crossed from their left shoulder to their right hip and from their right shoulder to their left hip, as well as two more around their waists. That was the water that was consumed in the city, and was the source of all kinds of diseases.[71]

Charcoal was another hard-felt scarcity, for food could not be cooked without it. Within houses, the inner doors and frames were disjoined and the flooring itself was pulled up to make cooking fires.[72] Outside, the trees in Chapultepec Park were cut down to burn (Figure 8-19).

In their weakened condition, people easily became ill. The "Spanish" flu of 1918-1919 was a respiratory pandemic that swept the world, killing between 20 and 50 million people, and causing serious problems in the enfeebled population of Mexico.[73] Compared to other epidemics in the country, such as typhus, it was short-lived, with the worst stage lasting about three months, September–November 1918. Venustiano Carranza had been installed as president of Mexico, and the revolution had

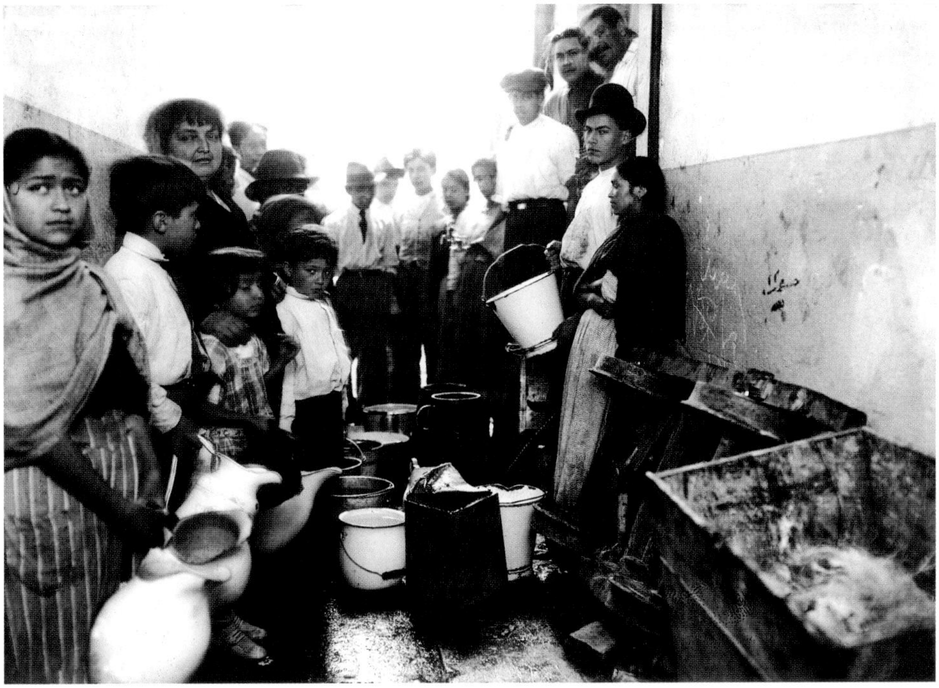

8-18. Families waiting for water, Mexico City, 1915. © Inv. #41444, Fondo Casasola, SINAFO-Fototeca Nacional del INAH.

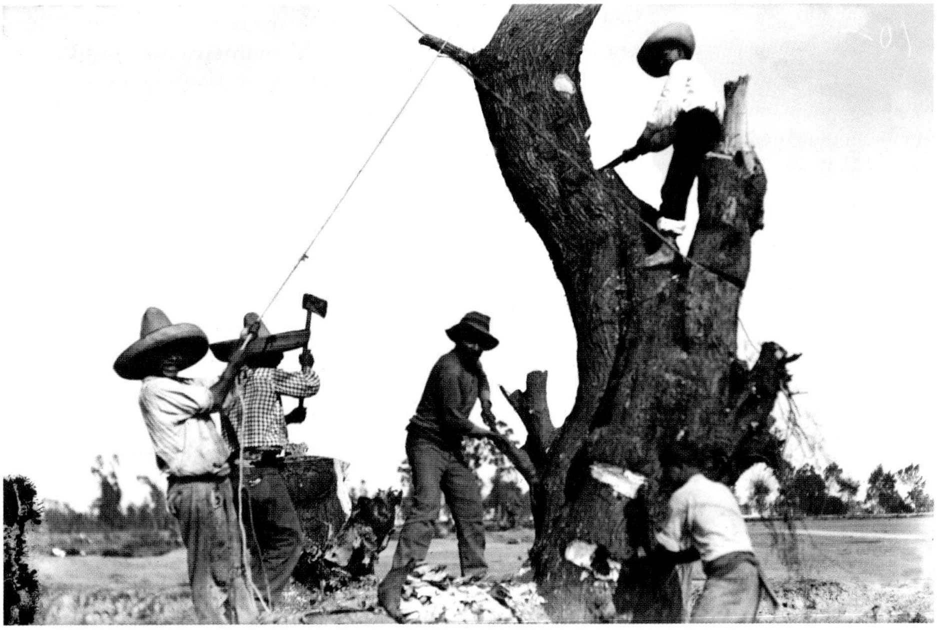

8-19. Cutting trees in Chapultepec Park for lack of charcoal, Mexico City, 1915. © Inv. #41455, Fondo Casasola, SINAFO-Fototeca Nacional del INAH.

essentially been decided in favor of the Constitutionalist forces. Although the nation enjoyed some measure of peace, the widespread destruction and lack of maintenance of sanitary facilities, the malnutrition of a disease-weakened population, and insufficient numbers of doctors, medicines, and hospital beds all contributed to make the Mexican mortality rate from the flu the third highest in the world (some 300,000 deaths, or 20 per 1,000 people).[74] The government's sanitary policies during the outbreak took on several forms: transportation between infected communities was interrupted; gathering places such as theaters, clubs, schools, and bars were closed; and people were advised to keep away from reunions, to cover their mouths and noses when coughing and sneezing, to avoid kissing or shaking hands when greeting, and to breathe through the nose rather than the mouth.[75] The ill were required to report to hospitals, but those were quickly filled to capacity.

Because the Constitutionalists were such masters of public relations, Figure 8-20 may have been a setup designed to convince Mexico City residents of an active campaign to combat the flu. Although historians have yet to substantiate the allegation, one survivor's recollection suggests that the government may have resorted to extreme measures to control the disease's spread. Arcadio Rico de la Cruz remembered the following episode.

> One day, around three in the afternoon, word spread in the house: "Here comes the brigade of nurses." I had my head wrapped up and was under a blanket, but I very quickly took off the wrapping and threw the blanket aside, rolled up my sleeves and stood up; I had to hold on to the wall at all times but I wanted to try to whistle. I did all that so that I wouldn't be given the death pills (the pills the nurses handed out so that people would die). Fortunately, they didn't come in the house, and I got over my scare.[76]

The social chaos led to great urban tumults; the police had been decimated by the *leva* (forced military service) and desertion, above all because they had to confront undisciplined and armed soldiers.[77] Although there are few photos of criminality and violence, a photojournalist documented one street battle that evidently occurred when some thieves were surprised while assaulting the temple of Santa Brígida (Figure 8-21).[78] Finally, the militarization of society appears to have produced a lack of respect for laws and civilized comportment; the spread of a bellicose mentality can be seen in the photo of President Carranza with little boys holding wooden rifles (Figure 8-22).

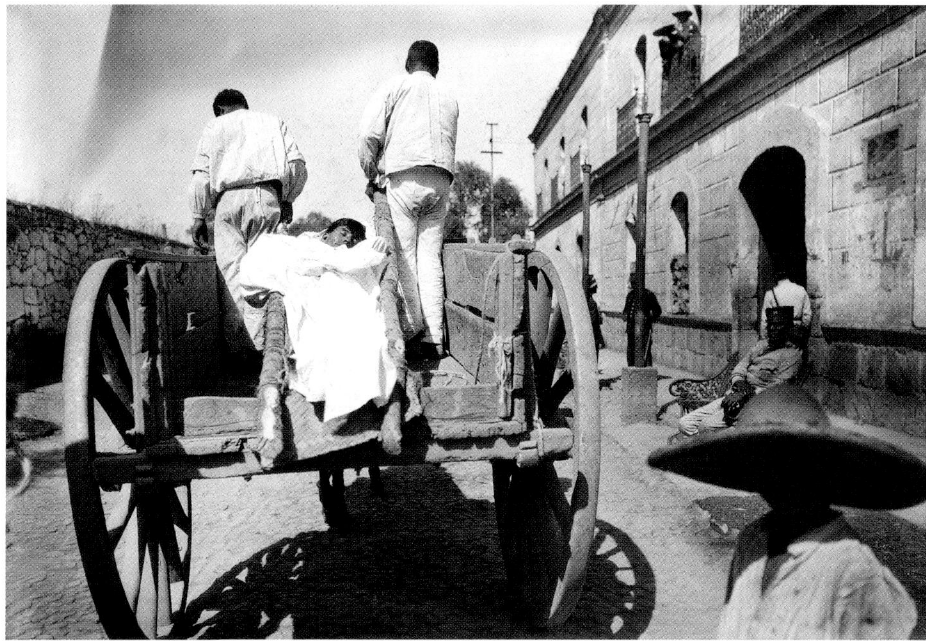

8-20. Soldier sick with the "Spanish" flu, Mexico City, 1918. © Inv. #75735, Fondo Casasola, SINAFO-Fototeca Nacional del INAH.

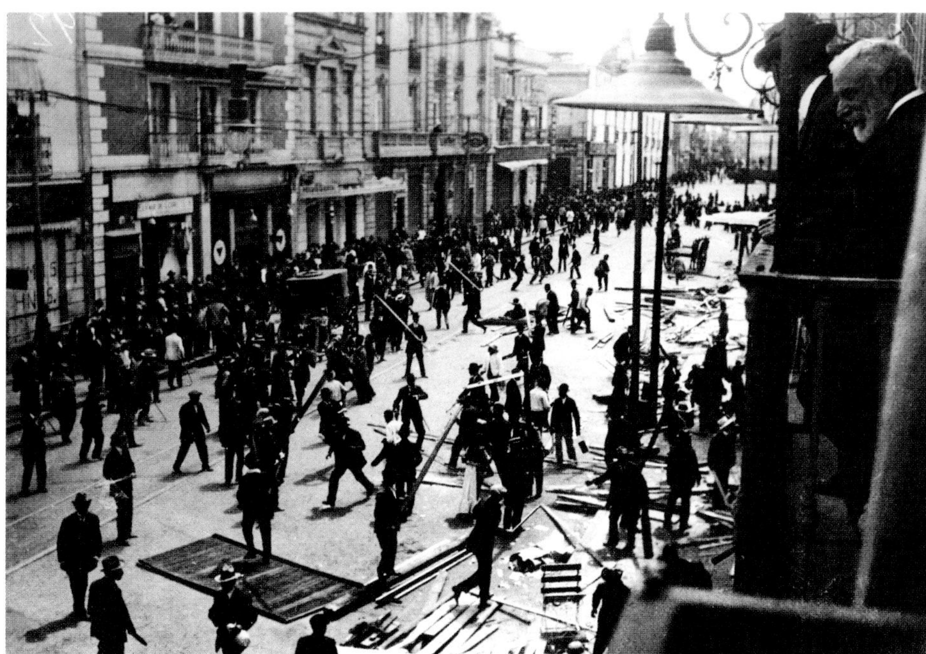

8-21. Riot in the city as a result of the assault on the temple of Santa Brígida, Mexico City, 1915. © Inv. #41481, Fondo Casasola, SINAFO-Fototeca Nacional del INAH.

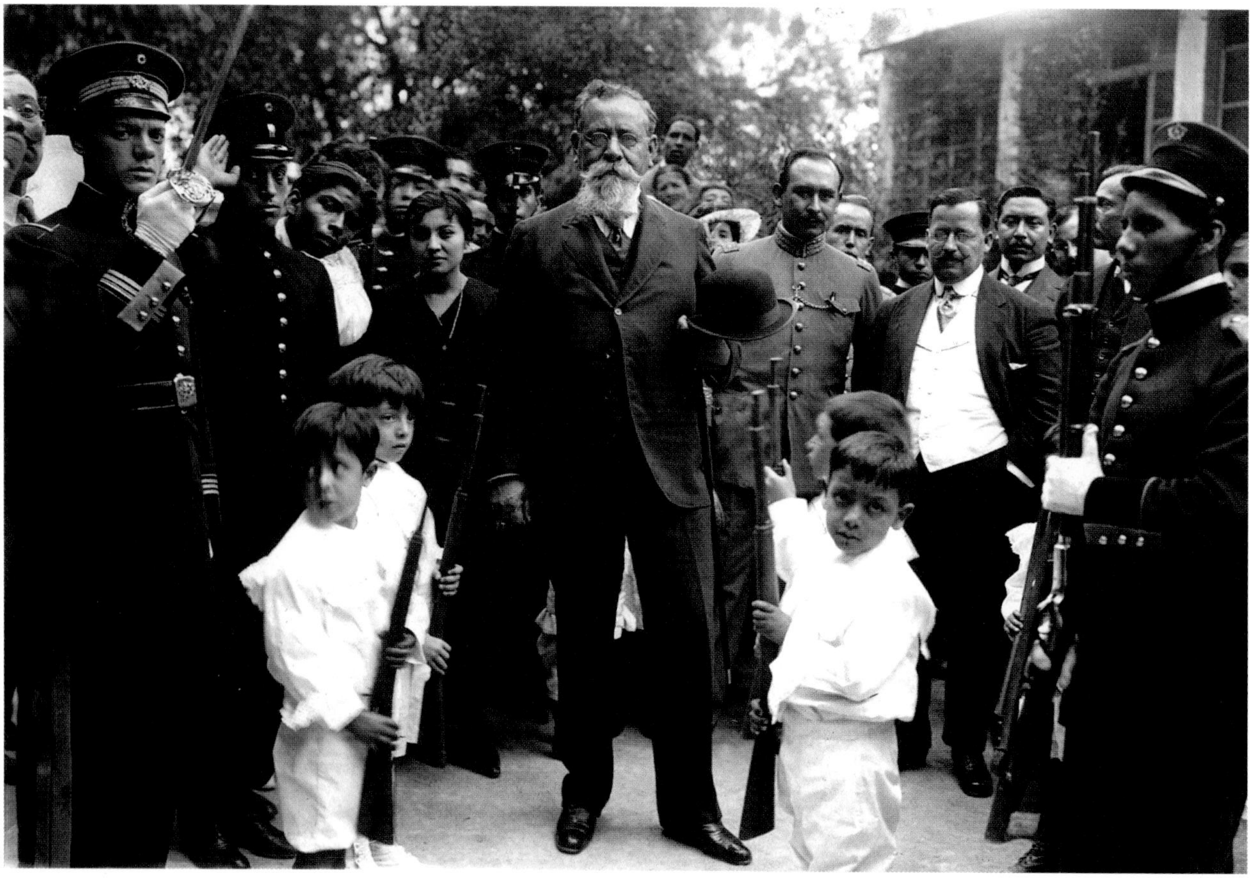

8-22. President Carranza with boys carrying wooden rifles, Mexico City, 1918. © Carpeta Venustiano Carranza, F.C. 209, Colección Gráfica y de Sonido del Instituto Nacional de Estudios Históricos de las Revoluciones Mexicanas.

The extensive documentation of the Constitutionalist movement opens windows on various facets of the revolution. For example, an image of a hospital showing soldiers in their beds and attended by doctors is another instance of the advantages which those forces enjoyed (and may have been the reason behind making the photograph) (Figure 8-23). But as Martín Luis Guzmán reminds us, war is hell, even for those with the upper hand.

> I looked at the double row of beds, the cots spread around in the rooms full of wounded, and it was strange to discover in every bed (or every pallet or every chair) the master work of a diabolic entertainment. Separately, each wound revealed the existence of a particular category of bullet, of the acting personality in

each projectile at the moment to deliver the blow. There were bullets that denosed and dechinned; those that multiplied idly the purifying escapes of the organism; those that perforated the abdomen to produce peritonitis; those that left in the brain an eternal din of cataracts or an irresistible shining, more intense than if the sun were within the eyes; those that created for the rest of one's life, foci of cold, of breakdown, of pain, of embarrassing inertias in the organs of the most necessary and constant functions. That soldier who can never sit! That other, who has to complete his vocal cavity with the palm of his hand in order to be able to eat! That one who can't bend his left knee nor straighten his right! That one within whom the slightest variations of temperature accumulate, with the sensation of hot coals or of an ice floe all along his spine![79]

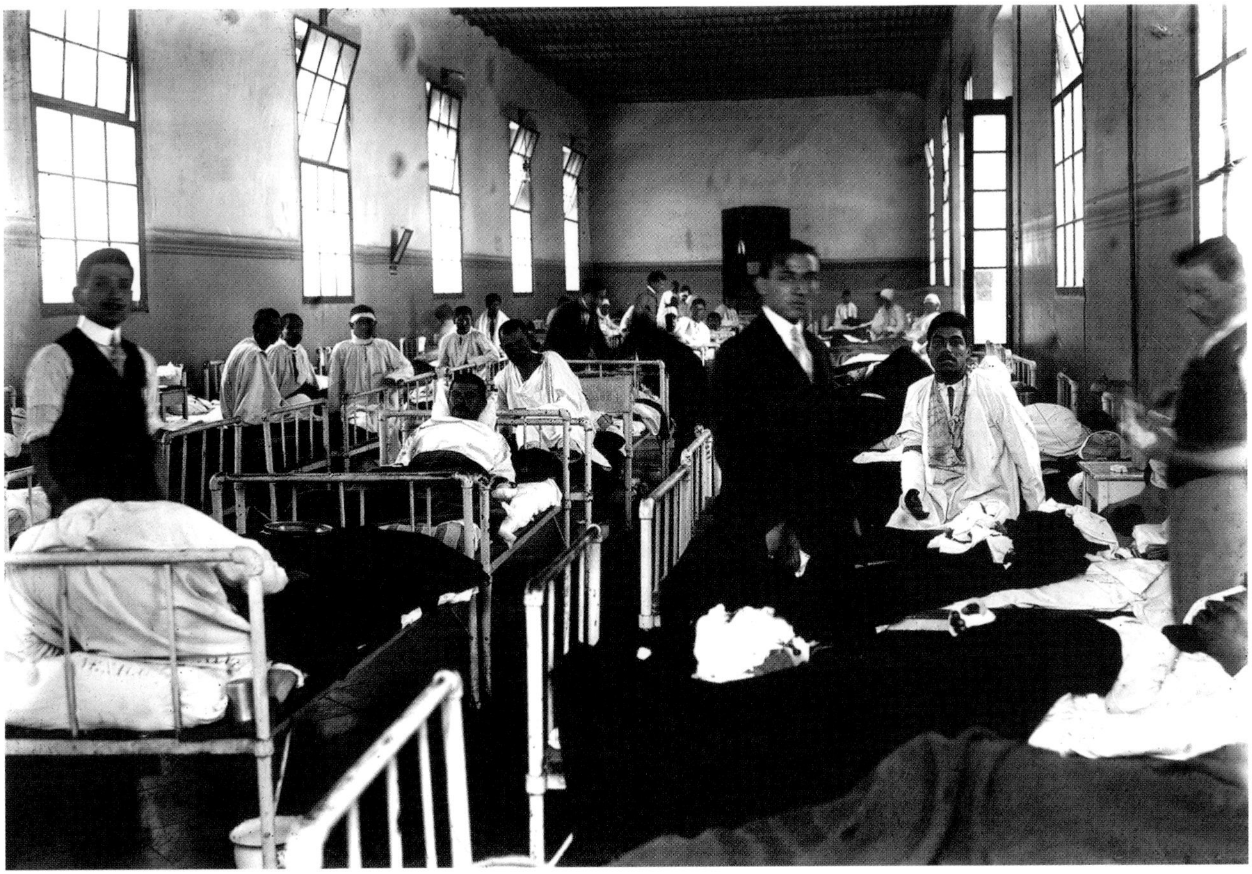

8-23. Military hospital, Torreón, Coahuila, ca. 1915. © Inv. #64597, Fondo Casasola, SINAFO-Fototeca Nacional del INAH.

Photographs permit us to appreciate the modernity of some of the armament that caused such damage, at least in the group equipped with Steyr-Mannlicher carbines, the standard weapon for the Austro-Hungarian army (Figure 8-24). The fact that all these Constitutionalist soldiers had the same rifle permitted them to interchange ammunition if one ran out, and if their weapon jammed, they could use that of a wounded or dead *compañero.* A strong contrast is offered by an image of the Yaqui (or Mayo) Indians (Figure 8-25). I would imagine that this photo was made prior to 1914, as there are images of Mayos in Sonora in 1912 and 1913, armed with bows and arrows, who are identified as "Obregón's first contingents," as well as of Zapatistas in Guerrero in 1911 also armed with these primitive weapons.[80] In Figure 8-26, new Constitutionalist recruits have been given .30-30 carbines and cartridge belts, but they still lack uniforms and, above all, shoes. Nonetheless, it does not appear that it was unusual to begin training them to shoot before providing them with uniforms: in Figure 8-27, an officer gives orders through a trumpeter. Trumpets were a constant

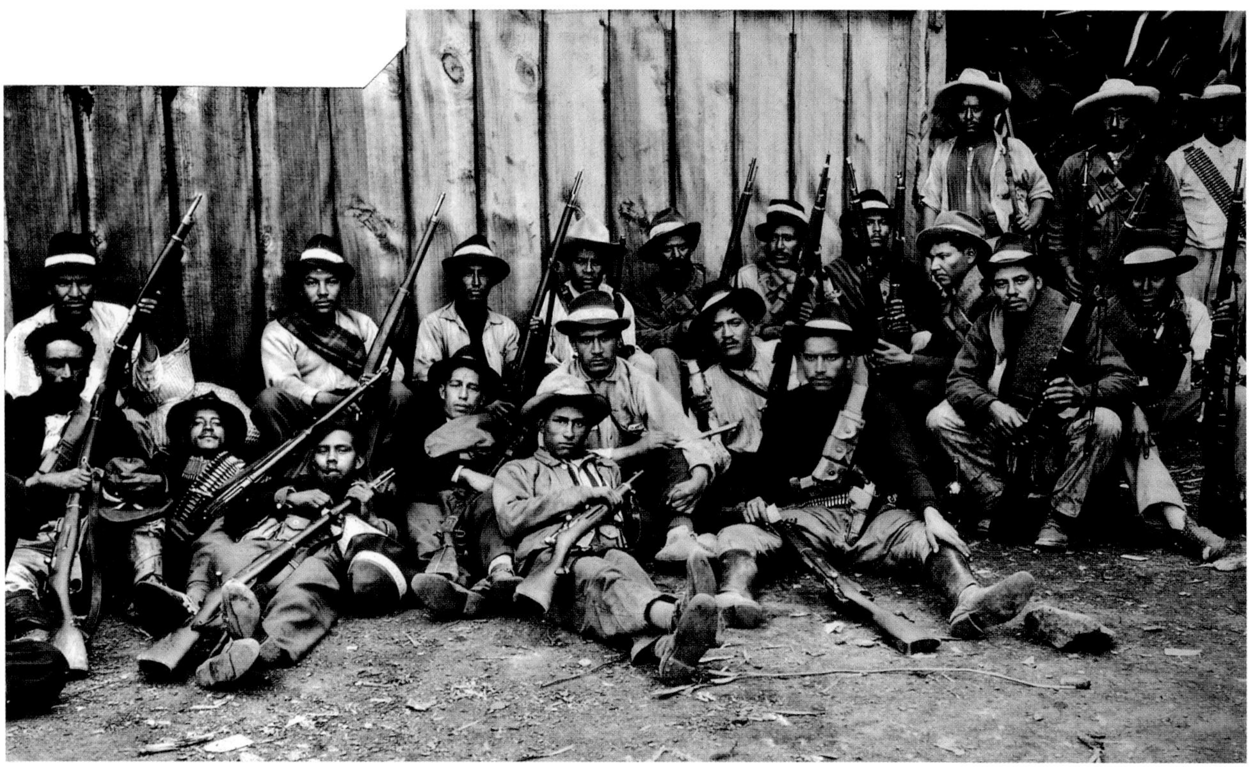

8-24. Constitutionalist revolutionaries with Steyr-Mannlicher carbines, ca. 1914. © Inv. #37838, Fondo Casasola, SINAFO-Fototeca Nacional del INAH.

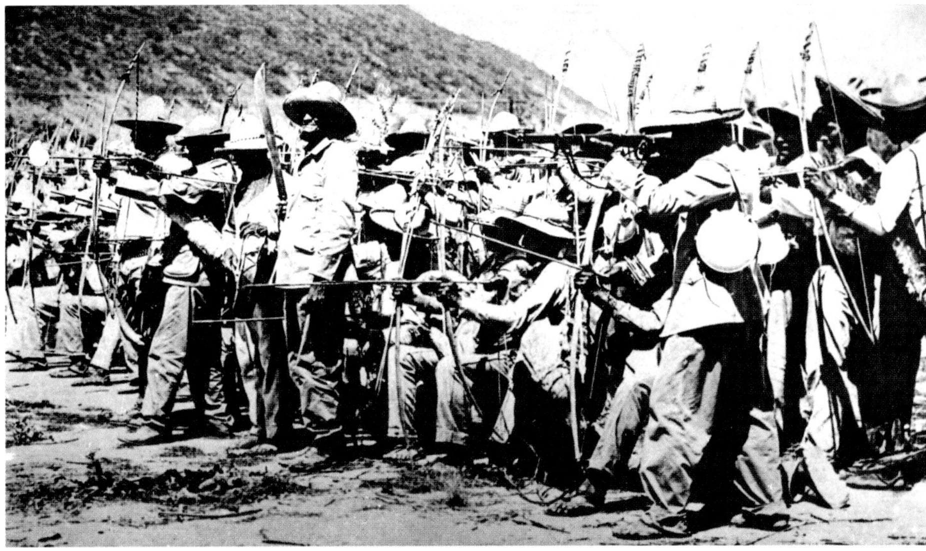

8-25. Constitutionalist battalion of Yaqui (or Mayo) Indians with bows and arrows, Sonora, ca. 1912. © Inv. #670059, Fondo Casasola, SINAFO-Fototeca Nacional del INAH.

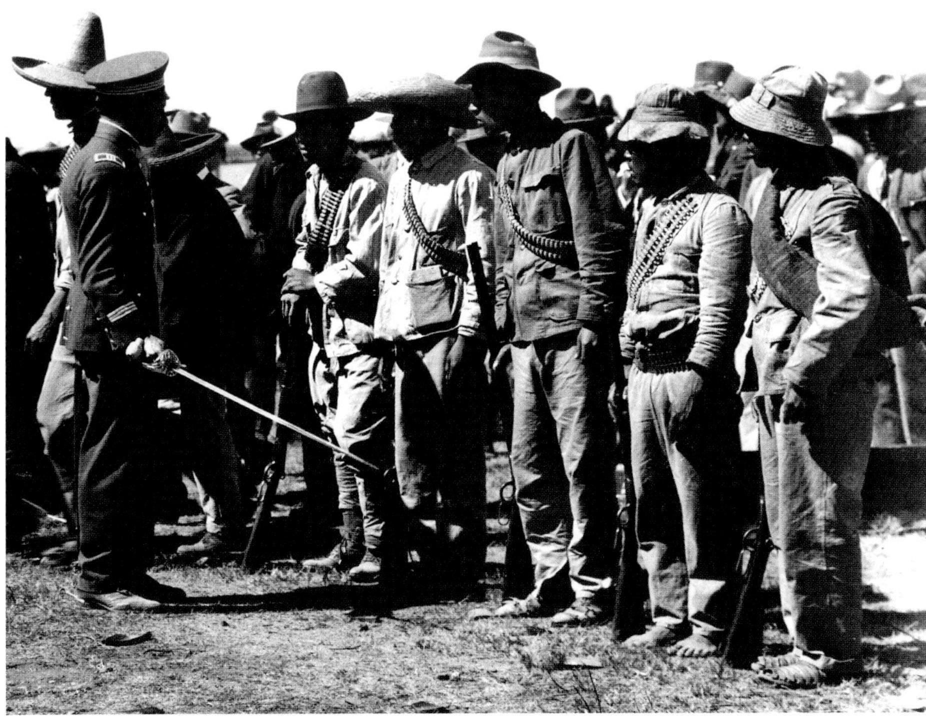

8-26. Constitutionalist recruits, ca. 1915. © Inv. #624157, Fondo Casasola, SINAFO-Fototeca Nacional del INAH.

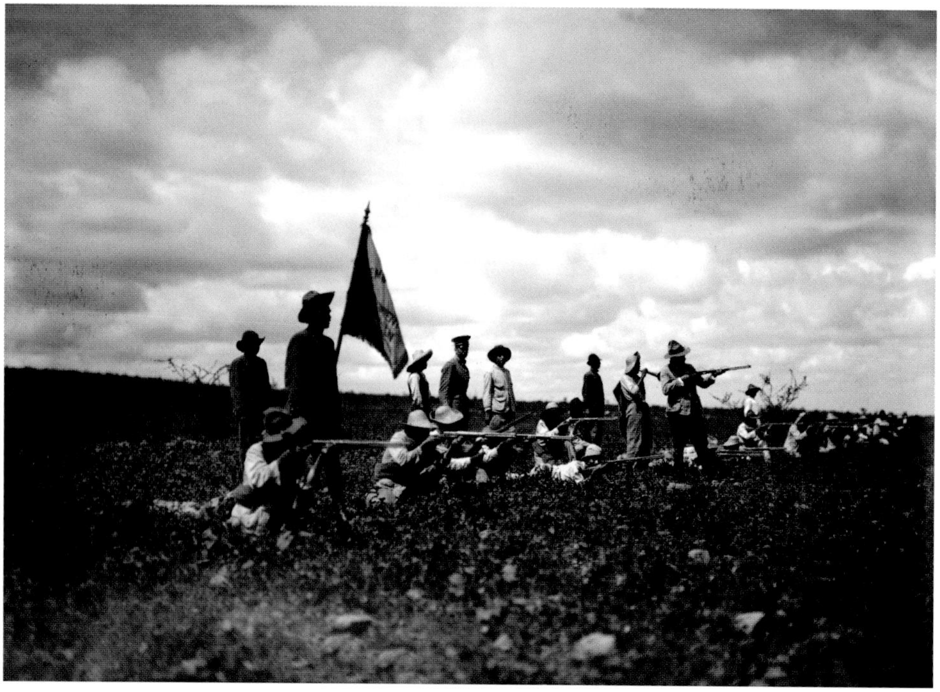

8-27. Training Constitutionalist recruits to shoot, ca. 1915. © Inv. #39253, Fondo Casasola, SINAFO-Fototeca Nacional del INAH.

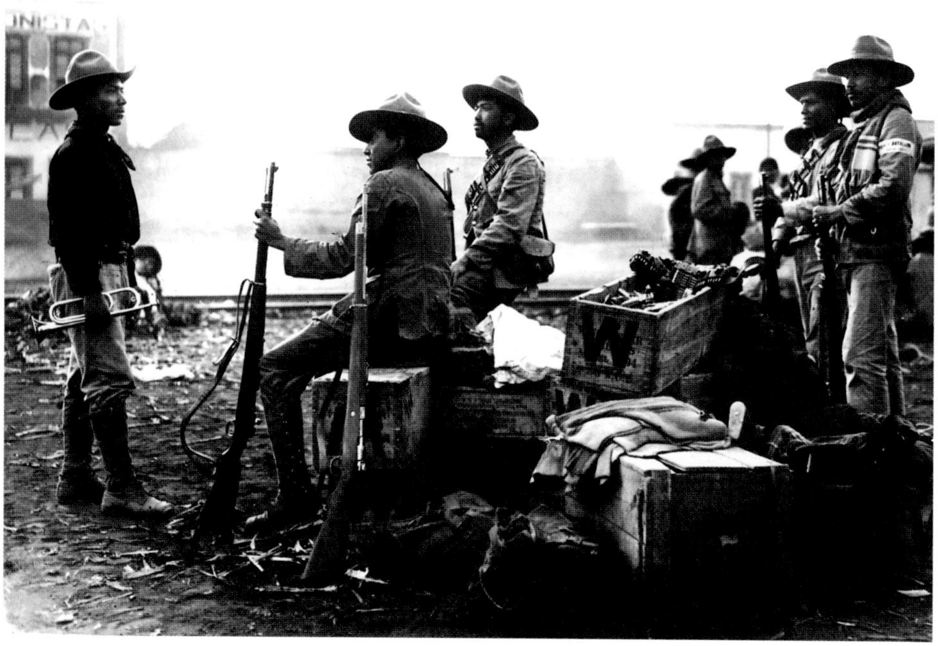

8-28. Trumpeter with troops guarding boxes of ammunition, ca. 1915. © Inv. #662658, Fondo Casasola, SINAFO-Fototeca Nacional del INAH.

presence in all the armies, but to Guzmán, its use in Carranza's forces "always sounded indefectibly Porfirian."[81]

The revolution produced its fair share of execution imagery. Some of the photos are classics in which men demonstrate inconceivable valor in extreme circumstances, such as that of Fortino Sámano (Figure 8-29). According to Gustavo Casasola, Captain Sámano was convicted of theft and violence; on the road to the place of execution, "He was as serene as if he was going to a ceremony. . . . Smiling and chewing on a cigar, he stood in front of the wall and asked them to shoot at his chest. With extraordinary sangfroid he awaited the volley."[82]

8-29. Execution of Fortino Sámano, Mexico City, ca. 1915. © Inv. #6013, Fondo Casasola, SINAFO-Fototeca Nacional del INAH.

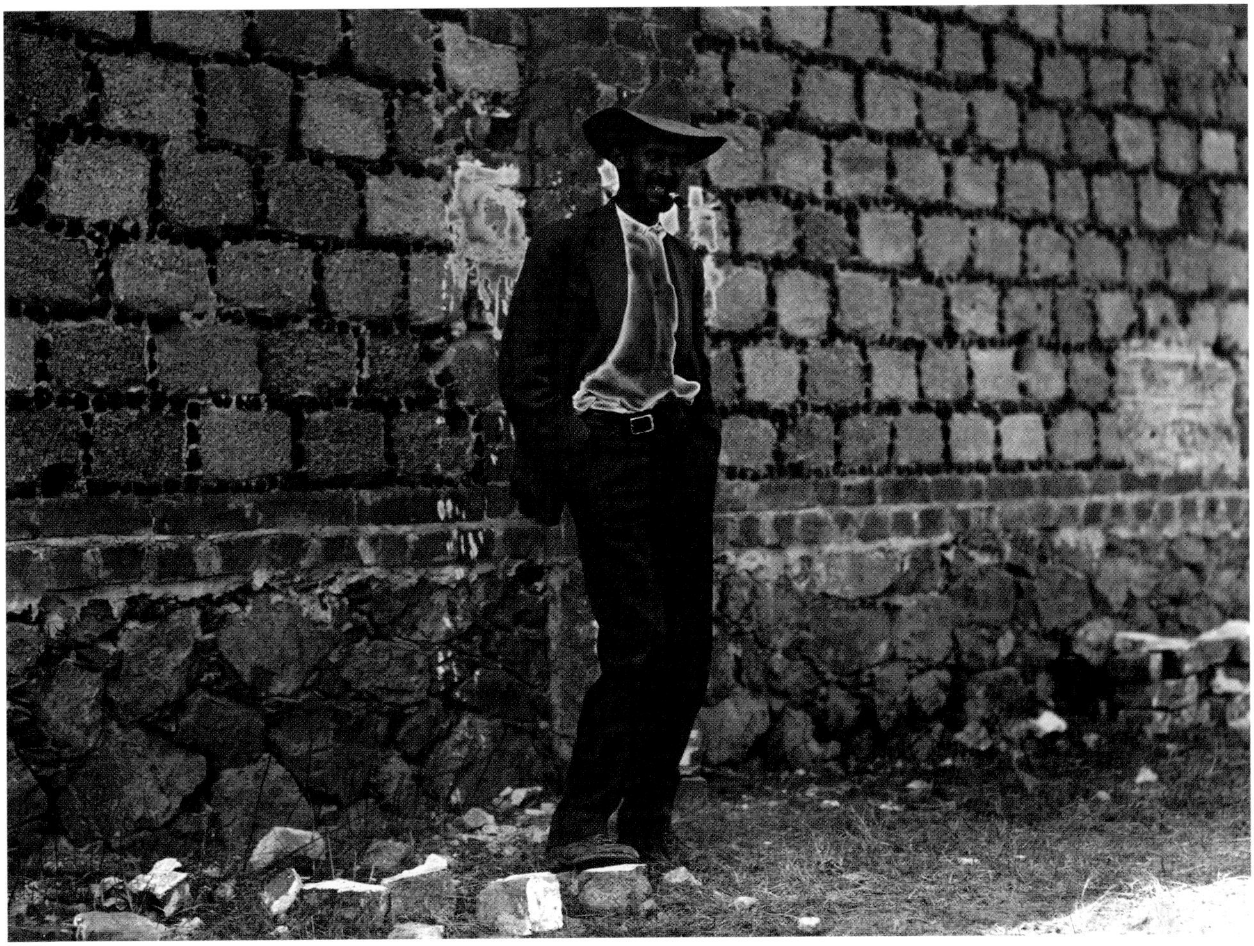

Major Maximiliano Lobo Guerrero seems to have demonstrated a similar serenity when he was executed, although more details permit us to appreciate the stress he suffered (Figure 8-30). A Constitutionalist combatant, he said in his last letter that "They are the only army that can save my beloved Mexico."[83] Despite his articulated loyalty, he was tried for crimes that included insubordination, theft, counterfeiting, and desertion; he was convicted of all except desertion and sentenced to be shot. A reporter from *El Pueblo* emphasized Lobo Guerrero's fortitude, which surprised him: he answered his questions just a few hours before the execution "very naturally," laughing after saying, "Hope dies last." The journalist described Lobo Guerrero as "tranquil and serene," and reported that he spoke directly to the firing squad, "*Compañeros* in arms! I say goodbye to you, shoot at my body."[84]

According to the memory of Constitutionalist general Francisco Urquizo, Lobo Guerrero must have been preoccupied about being shot in the face. "He asked for a good meal, a bottle of cognac, cigarettes; he barely slept during his last night. He found the stamp of the Commander of the guard, and for long hours was repeatedly stamping it on his naked chest over his heart."[85] In the photo he appears to be showing the squad the stamped portion of his body as a way of indicating that they should shoot there in order not to disfigure his face. Urquizo described the scene a bit differently than did *El Pueblo*'s reporter.

> His eyes, before tranquil, opened widely in fear. He recovered a bit, and threw away the cigar on which he had been chewing nervously; he tore open his shirt violently with both hands, showing his nude chest stained with the purple ink on the side of his heart. He pulled himself up with arrogance and said quickly, as someone who feared not having sufficient time to do so, as someone who desires anxiously to end a process that has been incubating a long time, "Let the bullets come!"[86]

Being able to look death in the face as Sámano and Lobo Guerrero did must be an uncommon attribute. I would imagine that the great majority of people would react as did Alfonso Aguilar, a deserter from the Constitutionalist army. As he was about to be shot, he covered his face and appeared to cry while the soldiers stared (Figure 8-31).

Among the complex legacy that the Constitutionalist revolution left Mexico during the last century are anti-clericalism, nationalism, and social reform. There had always been isolated acts against priests who abused the faithful entrusted to them, but they were relatively few and did not form part of any group's official position. Knight comments that the situation changed when the Constitutionalists took control of the

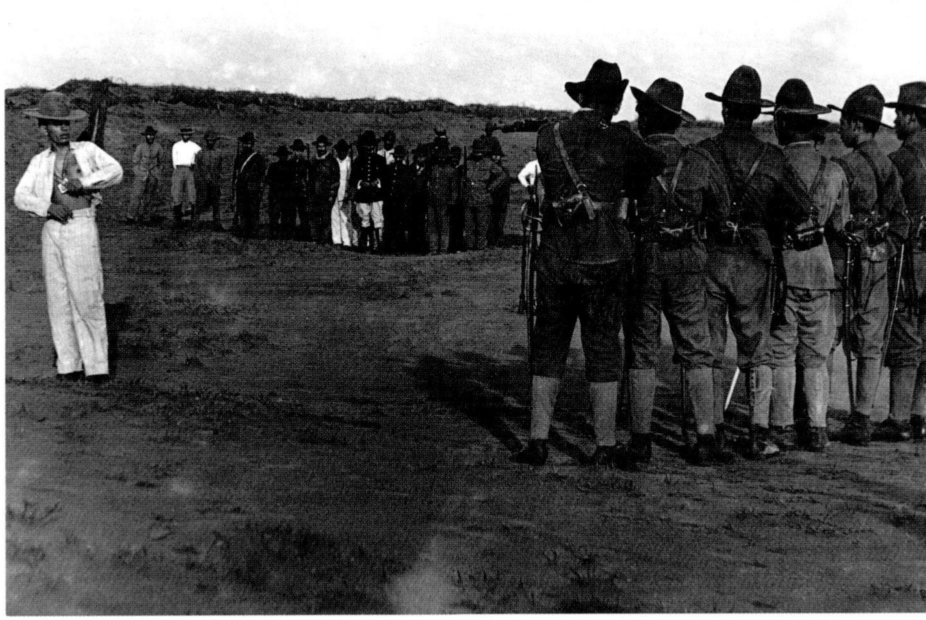

8-30. Execution of Máximo Lobo Guerrero, Veracruz, June 1915. © Inv. #643137, Fondo Casasola, SINAFO-Fototeca Nacional del INAH.

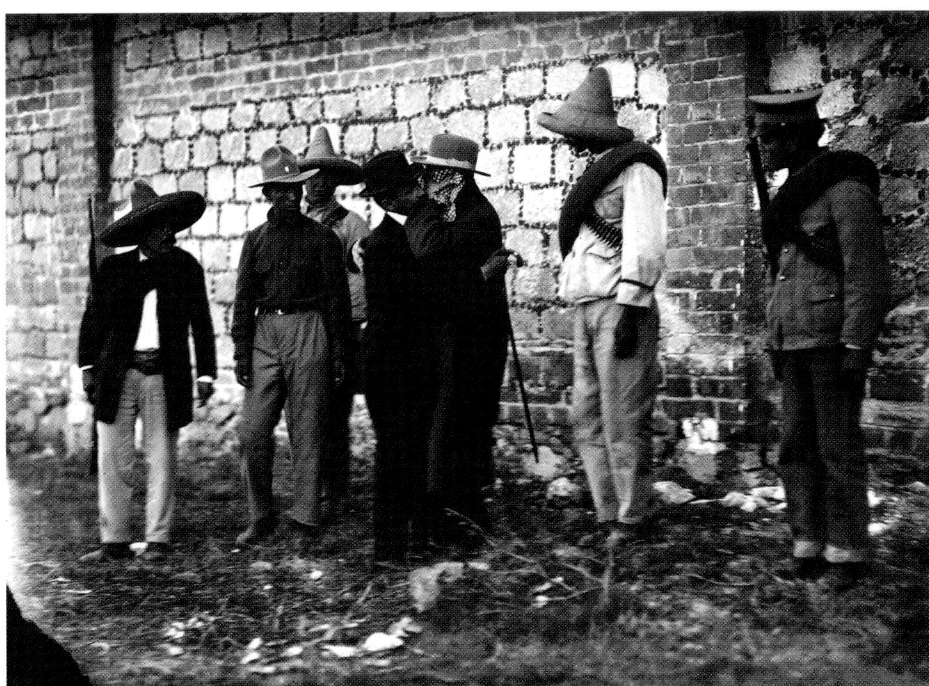

8-31. Execution of Alfonso Aguilar, Mexico City, ca. 1916. © Inv. #6331, Fondo Casasola, SINAFO-Fototeca Nacional del INAH.

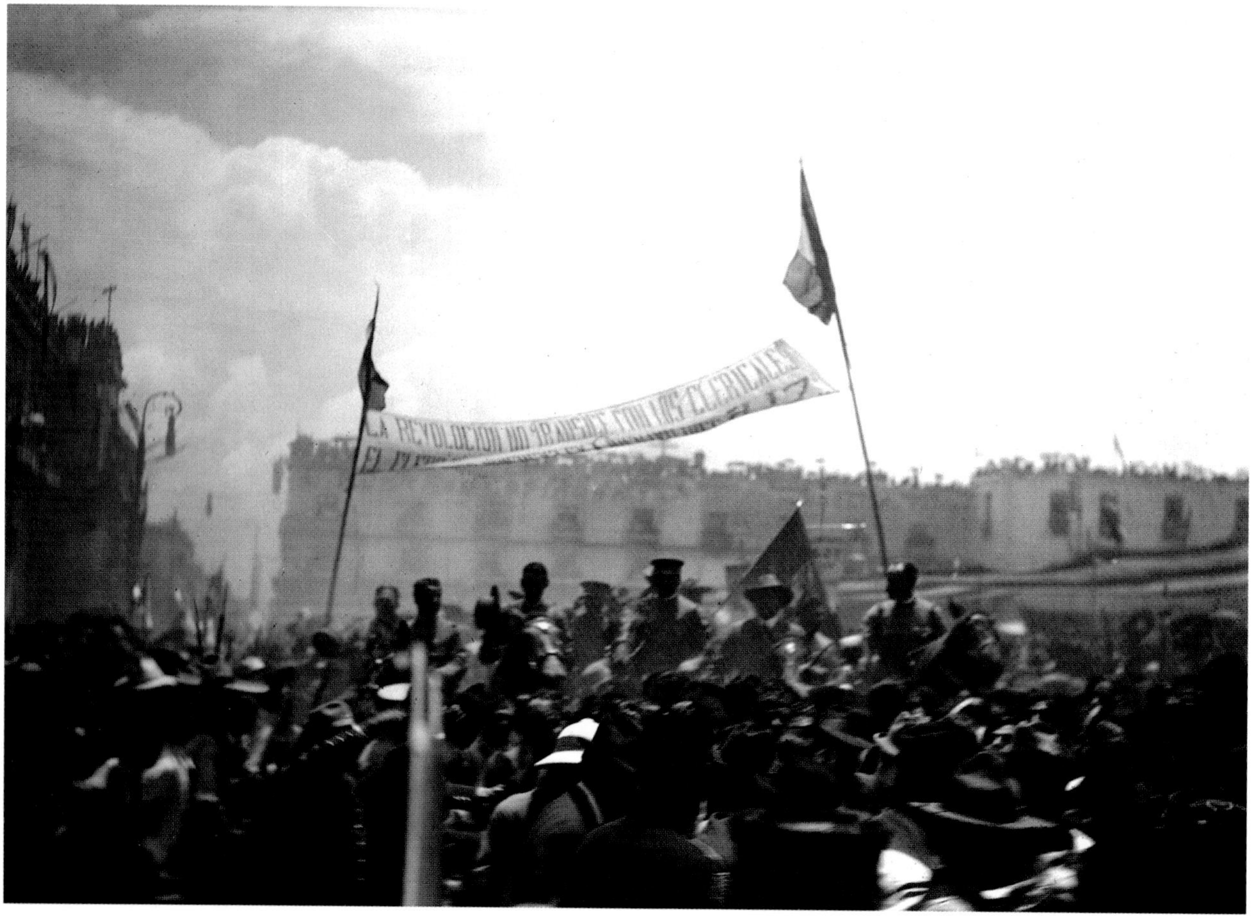

8-32. Anticlerical banner over Constitutionalist troops, Mexico City, ca. 1916. © Inv. #38925, Fondo Casasola, SINAFO-Fototeca Nacional del INAH.

revolution, because their triumph "marked the entrance of anti-clericalism—hitherto a minor, shadowy figure—to the centre of the official revolutionary stage."[87] Figure 8-32 shows Constitutionalist officers participating in a demonstration under a banner affirming that the revolution should not compromise with the clergy. Constitutionalism is also the movement most identified with nationalism: Carranza's vision of the nation was more developed than that of Villa or Zapata, and he refused to negotiate Mexico's sovereignty. When Villa attacked the town of Columbus, New Mexico, the United States sent troops under the command of General John Pershing. The Constitutionalists fought against the invasion, and some U.S. soldiers—black cavalrymen—were captured in person and in photographs (Figure 8-33).

The social reforms carried out by the Constitutionalists are encapsulated in Articles 27 and 123 of the 1917 Constitution. According to historian Charles Cumberland, "Article 123 constituted the most enlightened statement of labor protective principles in the world to that date."[88] One of the ways in which the government intervened was by means of inspectors for the secretary of industry, commerce, and labor who visited factories and businesses. One of those inspectors was Juan de Beraza, whose visits had taken him from toy factories to the "French lingerie" establishment. In December 1919 de Beraza took his revolutionary task seriously enough to investigate the situation of women workers in eleven mills and outlets of *nixtamal* (ground corn meal), and he decided that photography offered an additional tool to document his research. De Beraza may have been the photographer—the photos are small-format and could have been made with a Kodak Brownie—or he could have taken a photographer along; in any case, he is the intellectual author of Figure 8-34.

8-33. U.S. soldiers taken prisoner in Carrizal, Sonora, June 1916. © Inv. #63512, Fondo Casasola, SINAFO-Fototeca Nacional del INAH.

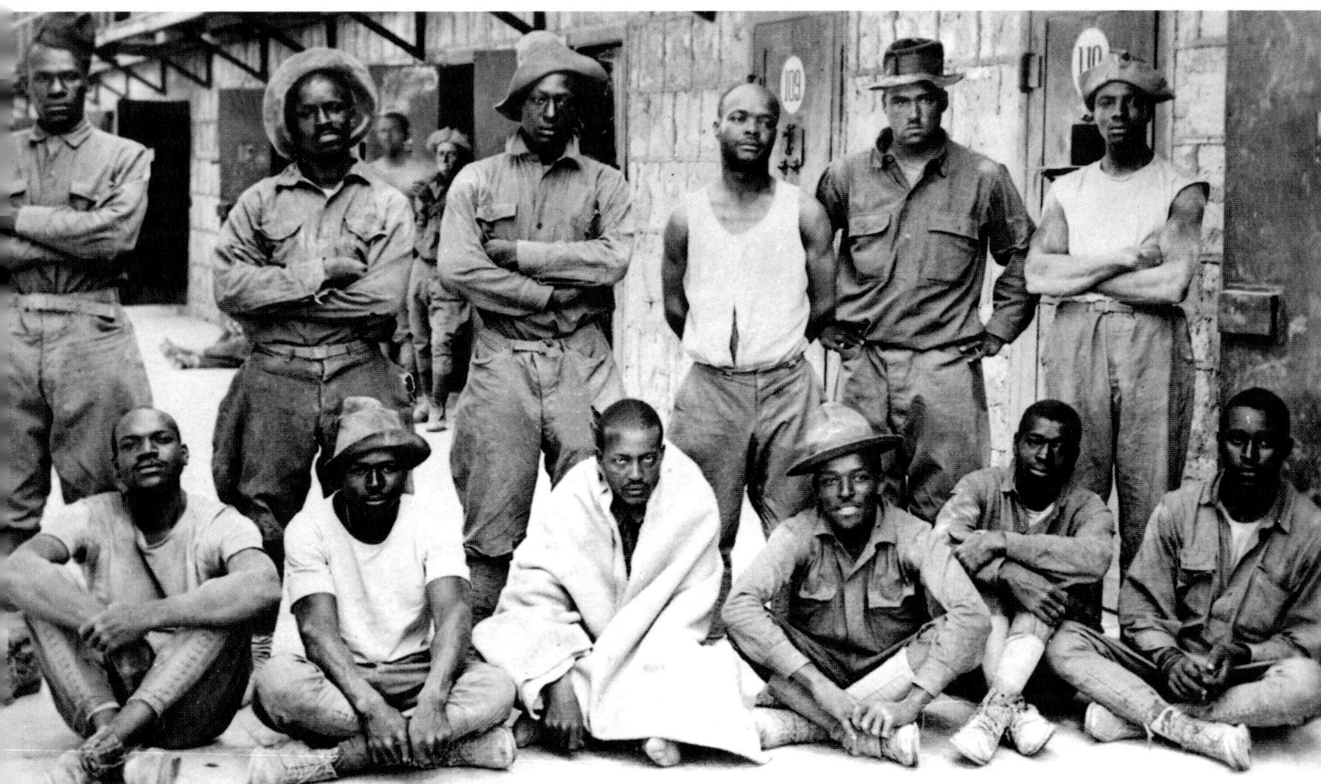

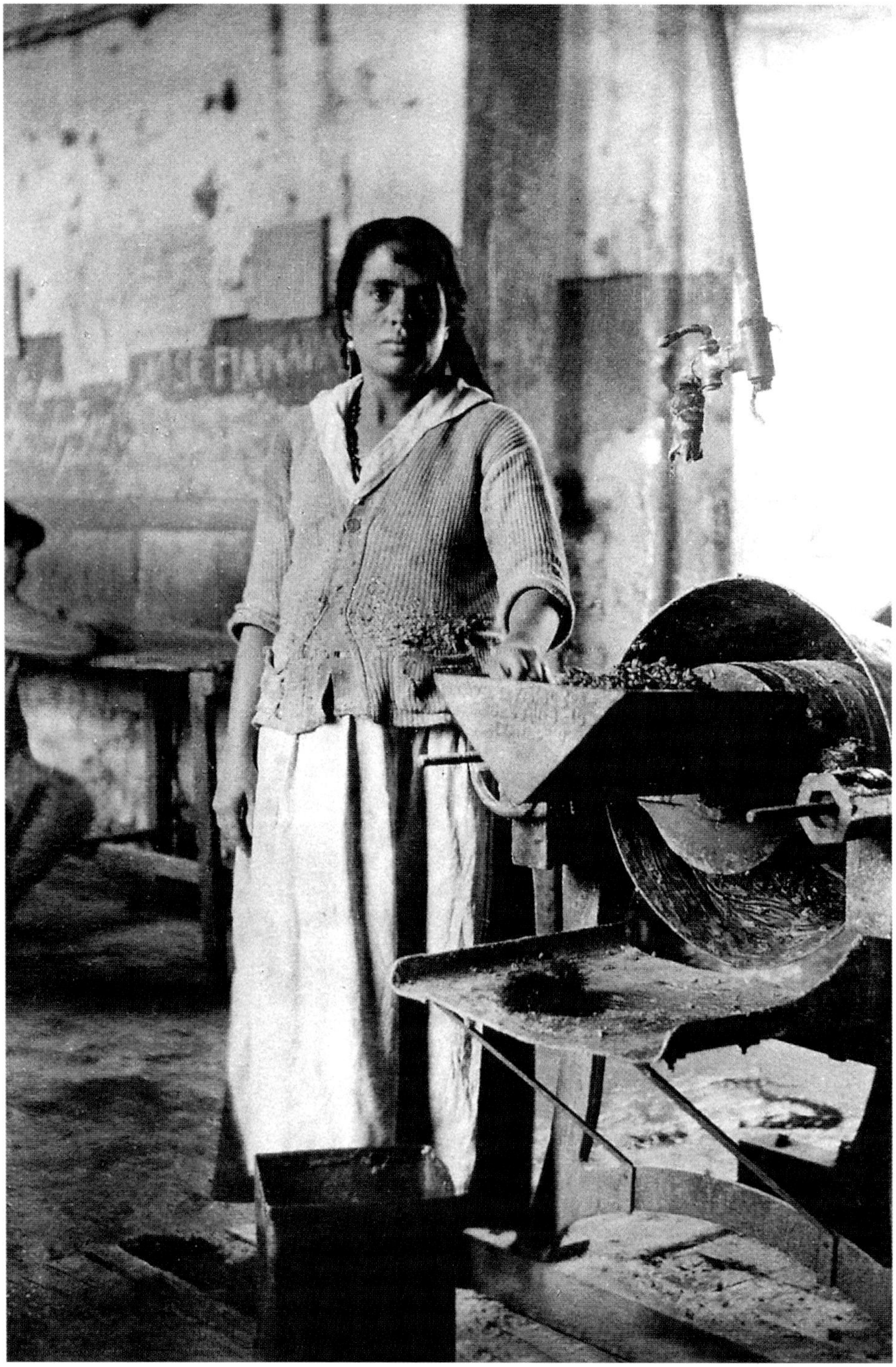

8-34. Luz Duani Vda. de Guzmán (widow of Guzman), worker in a *nixtamal* mill called "Casa Blanca," Distrito Federal, February 1919; photo made by, or under the orders of, Juan de Beraza, inspector for the secretary of industry, commerce, and work. © Archivo General de la Nación, "Ramo del trabajo," 172-12.

De Beraza found a strong contradiction between law and reality. Article 123 contained far-reaching reforms related to women and childbirth: for example, women were to be given a month of rest with full pay (and other benefits) after giving birth, including two extra rest periods a day to nurse. When interviewed by de Beraza, the woman in this photo, Luz Duani (a widow with six children), asserted that the company "didn't give them anything."[89] The article legislated an eight-hour workday and forbade women to work overtime. Those de Beraza talked to normally labored from 4 a.m. until 5 p.m., "without considering the time they spend liquidating accounts, which usually lasts until seven or eight at night." For a workday of thirteen to sixteen hours a day, the women received the "miserable salary" of $.62 to $1.50, when the cost of living in Mexico City was around $2.50 a day, and even though Article 123 required that the minimum salary "satisfy the normal necessities of the worker's life, education, and honest pleasures."[90] Although the article obliged owners to pay a legal salary, de Beraza noted that "They pay them nothing for the sale of the company's corn meal, which averages daily 1,000 kilograms. The salaries must come out of the *maquila* [the corn brought in by clients to be ground], and if there's no *maquila* they pay them nothing." Article 123 stipulated that indemnification be provided for accidents or work-related illness, but the women told de Beraza that not only did they receive no aid or compensation, but they lost their jobs and were immediately replaced. The women were virtual prisoners in the *nixtamal* mills: they practically never left because their bosses insisted that they sleep there to guard the machinery, with neither toilet facilities nor ventilation, and only a thin, flea-ridden mat between them and the cold, damp cement floor (not exactly the sort of housing Article 123 contemplated in its clause that "all businesses must provide comfortable and hygienic habitations for their workers"). Without exception, the women despised their "coarse and despotic" boss, who treated them "worse than animals," and some complained of sexual harassment, stating that he subjected them to "lewd and suggestive language when they turned in their accounts." De Beraza summed up the women's situation: they were treated "like slaves."

The Mexican Revolution was, above all, a popular agrarian rebellion, and the Constitutionalists were constantly pushed by the other forces to incorporate campesino demands in their program, and in the Constitution as in Article 27. This reform granted the communities constitutional rights to the restitution or distribution of lands, which could be expropriated in the national interest. Perhaps Figure 8-35 represents a moment in the process of measuring lands for redistribution. Agrarian reform was negligible under Carranza, but it had been institutionalized as a national

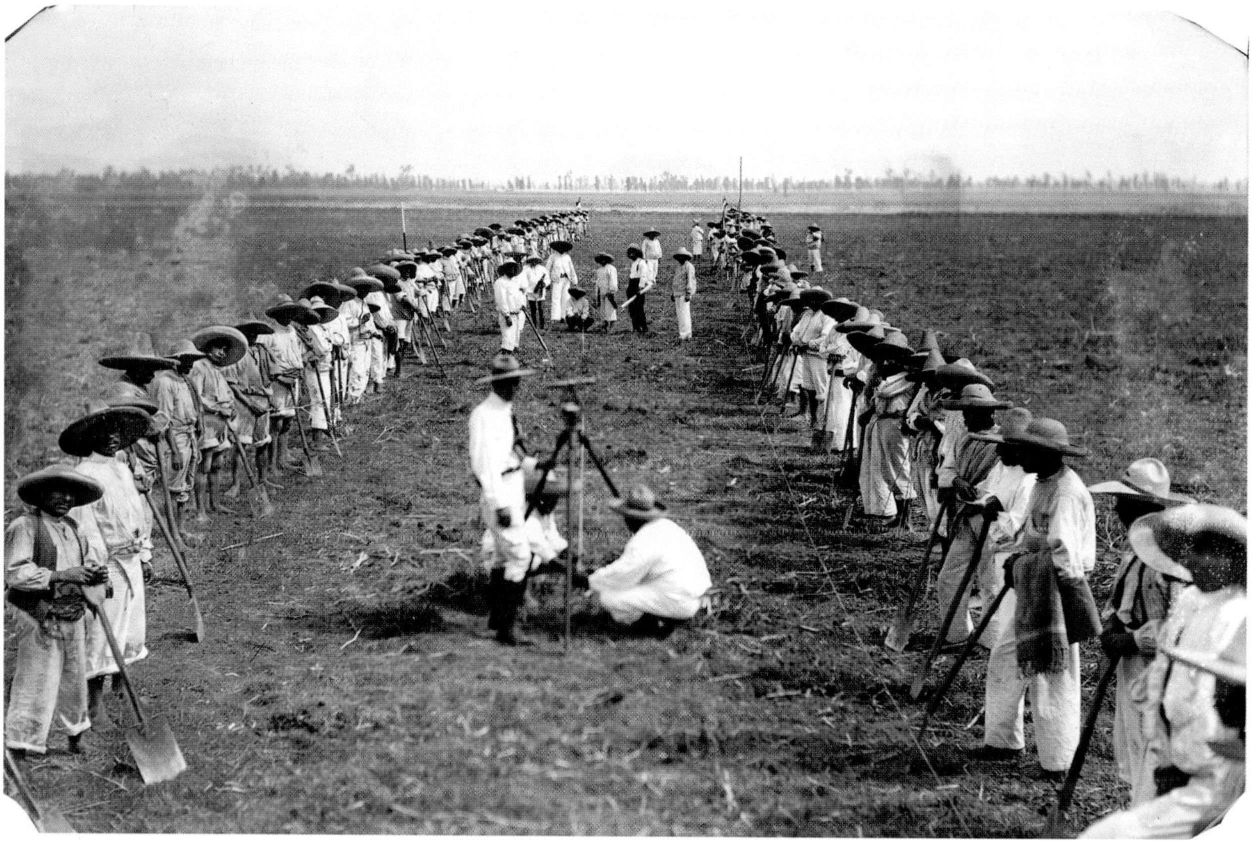

8-35. Campesinos measuring land, ca. 1914. © Inv. #5841, Fondo Casasola, SINAFO-Fototeca Nacional del INAH.

policy; hence, Obregón and, later, Lázaro Cárdenas would take it further, doing away with the older forms of tenancy and exploitation—as well as some of the great properties that had dominated the economy for four centuries.

Opinions about the effects of agrarian reform vary. Economic historian Roberto Vélez Pliego argues that it was an error over the long term: "What it produced was an apparent rise in earnings, and more opportunities over the short run. But, over the medium and long haul, the agrarian reform ended development in the countryside, at least in the central highlands; it was canceled, annulled, and economic growth was transferred to the urban sector, to industry."[91] There are others who see in the campesino rebellion a rejection of modernity; in the felicitous phrase of John Womack, it was made by human beings "who did not want to move and therefore got into a revolution."[92] The option of modernizing, of industrializing agriculture, of uprooting people from their lands and moving them to cities or leaving them no other possibility than going north to the United States, does not shine so brightly in light of the longest-term problem: the ecological crisis that has resulted precisely from the modernizing mentality. Perhaps the backward-looking vision of campesinos who attempted to "interrupt" the contemporary history of Mexico is what we are lacking in facing the most pressing problems of today.

The Icons of the Mexican Revolution

SOME OF THE PHOTOGRAPHS made during the armed struggle have become icons with their reiterated appearances over time and in different places: on political banners both officialist and dissident; in the pages of picture histories, newspapers, illustrated magazines, books, comics, and broadsheets, national as well as international; on the walls of government buildings, banks, and restaurants; on T-shirts and coffee mugs; and in murals painted during the postrevolutionary effervescence, as well as more recently. I find five to be of particular interest: Emiliano Zapata standing stolidly in *charro* raiment, a sash across his chest, with a carbine in one hand and the other on a sword; "Adelita the *soldadera*" peering intensely from the train; Francisco Villa galloping toward the camera; Villa lolling in the presidential chair next to Zapata; and Victoriano Huerta hidden in the shadows together with his general staff. All these icons have been attributed to Agustín Víctor Casasola at one point or another, but the stories of their authorship are much more interesting.

Why these particular images have become icons—and not, for instance, photos of Madero, Obregón, or Carranza—is complex. All but the one of Huerta are largely products of popular sentiment, a consensus among the rank and file (national and international) as to the attraction of the referents themselves as historical actors, and hence as ocular spaces in their imagination that must be filled: the revolutionaries *por excelencia*, Villa and Zapata, and the massive (and unrecognized) participation of women. These functions have largely been carried out through mass media: broadsheets, illustrated magazines, newspapers, books, and television. However, they have also been incorporated in works of public art, such as murals and lithographs.

The incorporation of these images in artistic expressions, and their very attraction to their public, is also a result of their visual power. All of these icons pack an aesthetic punch. Three of them capture a sense of movement characteristic of modern photojournalism: "Adelita" seems to lean into the frame, straining to locate her loved one; "Villa the centaur" gallops toward the viewer, dust kicking up at his mount's hooves; Villa appears to squirm in delight on sitting in the presidential chair. The other two are posed, and might be thought of as images with little interest beyond their referents. Nonetheless, the portrait of Zapata would be a splendid picture, even if it were of a regional chieftain whose name and exploits remained unknown. And, the photo(s) of Huerta "prove" the importance of the aesthetic imperative: the image that has become historical is the "failed" photo with an expressive lighting technique only fully appreciated after the experience of film noir. Within the visual historiography of the Mexican Revolution, these icons are symbols: of popular struggle, of women's participation, and of counter-revolutionary evil.

ZAPATA AS A REVOLUTIONARY *CHARRO*

The picture of Emiliano Zapata in Cuernavaca in May 1911 (Figure E-1) has become an international revolutionary icon equaled only by Korda's famous image of Che Guevara as the "Heroic Guerrilla"; they must be the most reproduced photographs from Latin America.[1] Although authorship of the image was usually claimed by the Casasolas, the caudillo's suspicions of Agustín Víctor probably would have made that very difficult.[2] Later it was argued that Hugo Brehme took the photo.[3] Recent research by Mayra Mendoza Avilés, sub-director of the Fototeca Nacional, seems to have established that it was not Brehme who made the famous portrait, but another foreigner, an F. M. ("Moray" or perhaps "McKay"), in late May of 1911 at the Hotel Moctezuma.[4] The plot thickens, however, upon knowing that another photo, taken at the same time, shows Zapata dressed in the same clothing as in the iconic image, and it is signed by Walter P. Hadsell and F. Wray.[5] As this instance demonstrates, and as I argue in the introduction, a signature is by no means definitive in determining authorship. I believe that the photo was taken by Hugo Brehme, above all for its extraordinary quality. The fact that an outsider (whoever it was) could get that close to the fearsome warrior reinforces the idea of Zapata's concern for constructing his own image; he may have felt that someone from another country would be more neutral than the capital's photojournalists, and that the image would also reach eyes outside of Mexico.[6] Zapata had little trust in the metropolitan press, and rightly so, considering the eventual use it made of this picture.

Before the photo was published in a periodical, the most famous of Mexican lithographers, José Guadalupe Posada, interpreted the image and evidently circulated it as a broadsheet.[7] Posada was an artisan, and his contribution would have to be considered a form of popular culture, although the widespread distribution of broadsheets also made them a mass media of sorts. The popular mythology that envelopes Posada

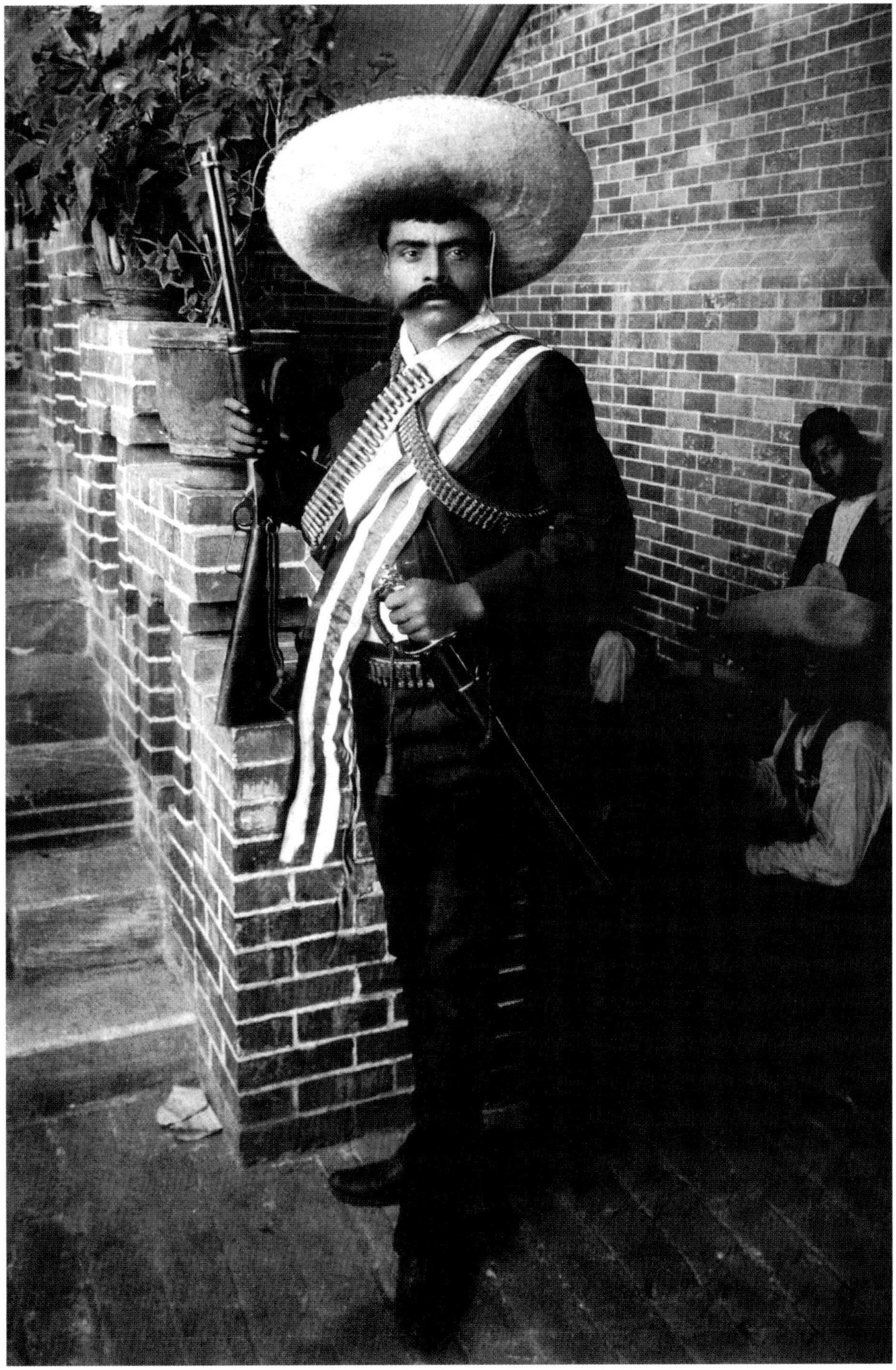

E-1. Emiliano Zapata with rifle, sash, and saber, Cuernavaca, June 1911; Hugo Brehme. © Inv. #63464, Fondo Casasola, SINAFO-Fototeca Nacional del INAH.

and insists that he was a revolutionary artist—in Diego Rivera's words, "a precursor of Flores Magón, Zapata, and Santanón, guerrilla of broadsheets and the heroic opposition newspapers"—was created by postrevolutionary muralists and intellectuals such as Rivera, Dr. Atl, José Clemente Orozco, Jean Charlot, and Frances Toor.[8]

Notwithstanding this broadly accepted belief, recent research indicates that the lithographer was an admirer of Porfirio Díaz and a critic of both the revolutionary movements and their caudillos—in particular, the excesses committed by the Zapatista troops. In fact, Ariel Arnal has questioned whether or not this etching might have been originally intended as a caricature.[9]

It is not surprising that Posada, as an inhabitant of Mexico City, would have been fearful of the Zapatistas. After his death in January 1913, the etching became the centerpiece for broadsheets in which the semantic debility of the image allowed for distinct uses. Around November 1913 it appeared with the poem "El fandango del bautizmo del hijo de Emiliano Zapata" (The party at the baptism of Zapata's son), which is a typical *calavera*, one of the humorous rhymes that appear around All Saints Day and allude to people's foibles, making (usually) good-natured fun of them.[10] This work was composed after June 1913 because it refers to the apprehension of Zapata's mother-in-law, Guadalupe Sánchez, and some of his sisters-in-law, who were photographed by Luis Santamaría in an image published by *La Semana Ilustrada*.[11] Other broadsheets printed during Huerta's regime utilized the lithograph in a much more critical way. One, *The Burial of Zapata*, celebrated the death of the "inhuman" leader.[12] Another, *La jeringa de Zapata* (The plague of Zapata), states that the movement is simply a pretext of thieves to steal whatever they desire. Although Zapata's struggle against the Porfiriato had initially invoked sympathy, some came to view him as a "monster," and thus the broadsheet called for an end to Zapata and the revolution (Figure E-2).[13]

> Zapatismo is the worst;
> Its leaders are bad seeds.
> Their punishment will be
> A bullet for their deeds.

The icon appeared in the press around the same time as these two broadsheets, two years after it had been made, when it was used as a front-page illustration for *El Imparcial*'s attack on Zapata as "Attila of the South." The publication of the photo in the newspaper may have been part of a campaign to discredit Madero, given that Zapata

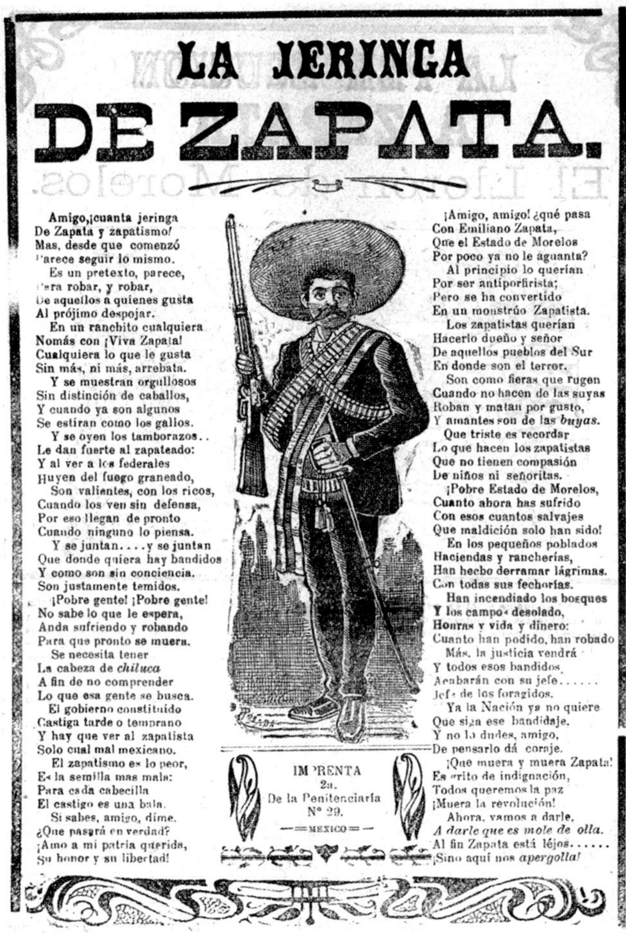

LA JERINGA DE ZAPATA.

Amigo, ¡cuanta jeringa
De Zapata y zapatismo!
Mas, desde que comenzó
Parece seguir lo mismo.
Es un pretexto, parece,
Para robar, y robar,
De aquellos a quienes gusta
Al prójimo despojar.
En un ranchito cualquiera
Nomás con ¡Viva Zapata!
Cualquiera lo que le gusta
Sin más, ni más, arrebata.
Y se muestran orgullosos
Sin distinción de caballos,
Y cuando ya son algunos
Se estiran como los gallos.
Y se oyen los tamborazos..
Le dan fuerte al zapateado:
Y al ver a los federales
Huyen del fuego graneado,
Son valientes, con los ricos,
Cuando los ven sin defensa,
Por eso llegan de pronto
Cuando ninguno lo piensa.
Y se juntan....y se juntan
Que donde quiera hay bandidos
Y como son sin conciencia.
Son justamente temidos.
¡Pobre gente! ¡Pobre gente!
No sabe lo que le espera,
Anda sufriendo y robando
Para que pronto se muera.
Se necesita tener
La cabeza de *chiluca*
A fin de no comprender
Lo que esa gente se busca.
El gobierno constituido
Castiga tarde o temprano
Y hay que ver al zapatista
Solo cual mal mexicano.
El zapatismo es lo peor,
Es la semilla mas mala:
Para cada cabecilla
El castigo es una bala.
Si sabes, amigo, díme.
¿Que pasará en verdad?
¡Amo a mi patria querida,
Su honor y su libertad!

¡Amigo, amigo! ¿qué pasa
Con Emiliano Zapata,
Que el Estado de Morelos
Por poco ya no le aguanta?
Al principio lo querían
Por ser antiporfirista;
Pero se ha convertido
En un monstrúo Zapatista.
Los zapatistas querían
Hacerlo dueño y señor
De aquellos pueblos del Sur
En donde son el terror.
Son como fieras que rugen
Cuando no hacen de las suyas
Roban y matan por gusto,
Y amantes son de las *buyas*.
Que triste es recordar
Lo que hacen los zapatistas
Que no tienen compasión
De niños ni señoritas.
¡Pobre Estado de Morelos,
Cuanto ahora has sufrido
Con esos cuantos salvajes
Que maldición solo han sido!
En los pequeños poblados
Haciendas y rancherías,
Han hecho derramar lágrimas.
Con todas sus fechorías.
Han incendiado los bosques
Y los campos desolado,
Honras y vida y dinero:
Cuanto han podido, han robado
Más, la justicia vendrá
Y todos esos bandidos
Acabarán con su jefe......
Jefe de los foragidos.
Ya la Nación ya no quiere
Que siga ese bandidaje.
Y no lo dudes, amigo,
De pensarlo dá coraje.
¡Que muera y muera Zapata!
Es grito de indignación,
Todos queremos la paz
¡Muera la revolución!
Ahora, vamos a darle,
A darle que es mole de olla.
Al fin Zapata está léjos.....
¡Sino aquí nos *apergolla!*

IMPRENTA
2a.
De la Penitenciaría
N° 29.
—MEXICO—

E-2. Broadsheet "La Jeringa de Zapata" (The plague of Zapata), ca. July 1913; lithograph of Emiliano Zapata by José Guadalupe Posada, private collection.

was wearing emblems linked to that cause, the Maderista general's sash and crossed cartridge belts.[14] The newspaper celebrated the face-to-face battle between Huerta's newly appointed commander, Juvencio Robles, and Zapata, noting that the "Veteran general would utilize the same tactics that [Spanish general Valeriano] Weyler had employed in Cuba in order to exterminate Zapatismo."[15] Weyler had attempted to pacify the Cuban independence movement by "reconcentrating" the rural population and thus taking away support for the guerrillas, a move that caused widespread hunger and radicalized Cubans. Robles was going to "depopulate the state" of Morelos and "resettle" its inhabitants elsewhere.[16] The result, as historian John Womack outlined, was counterproductive: "What Huerta had done in declaring war on the state's rural population was simply to swell the rebels' ranks, to bind together a previously fragmented opposition, and to drive the whole force of the resistance under the command of Zapata."[17]

The research of Arnal has established that the photograph is of intriguing complexity and may represent a startlingly graphic depiction of triumph.[18] Zapata is dressed with the Maderista general's sash and sword that Manuel Asúnsolo had worn as a symbol of his status as the authority in Cuernavaca (Figure E-3).[19] Putting them on was evidently a demonstration of the prerogative Zapata had apparently acquired to determine who would govern the city and Morelos.[20] The icon was probably made on 26 May, when Zapata arrived in Cuernavaca, and the city filled with photographers, foreign and Mexican, to register his assumption of power. "It was the first time that the Southern army and its General Staff could be photographed without fear of falling prisoner to the Zapatistas."[21] Asúnsolo, however, held onto power in Cuernavaca and appointed a planter-friendly banker to be governor of the state, so his surrender of the sash and sword may have been more symbolic than real. Nonetheless, Zapata's wearing of these emblems could represent

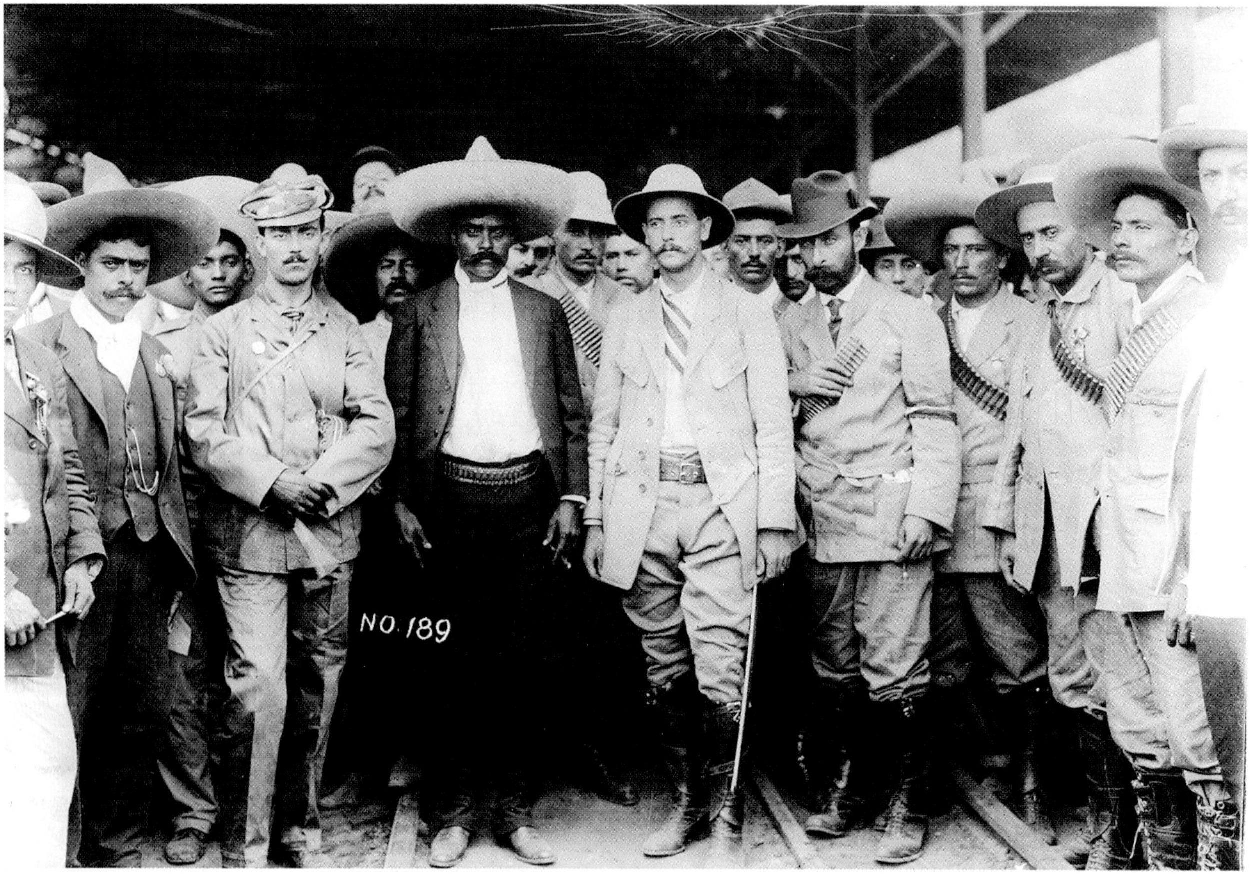

an attempt to legitimate his movement. He and his campesinos were portrayed in the Mexico City press as cruel and ferocious savages, so Zapata may have been attempting to counteract that mindset, presenting himself as a professional soldier, with the rank of general, and thus a man deserving of Madero's political recognition, which was vital at that moment. He may have visually buttressed his Maderismo by assuming the trope of "crossed cartridge belts" (discussed in Chapter 4), borrowing his brother Eufemio's belt to accompany his own (compare this image with Figure 5-18).

The classic image of Zapata has been reproduced many times, usually as an illustration with a one-dimensionally positive connotation. One exception is its incorporation in a painting by Arnold Belkin, where the artist shows the leader as if his body were dissected into geometric forms that are at the same time his skeleton.[22] Another

E-3. Emiliano Zapata and General Manuel Asúnsolo in the Colonia train station to receive Francisco I. Madero, Mexico City, 7 June 1911. © Inv. #5868, Fondo Casasola, SINAFO-Fototeca Nacional del INAH.

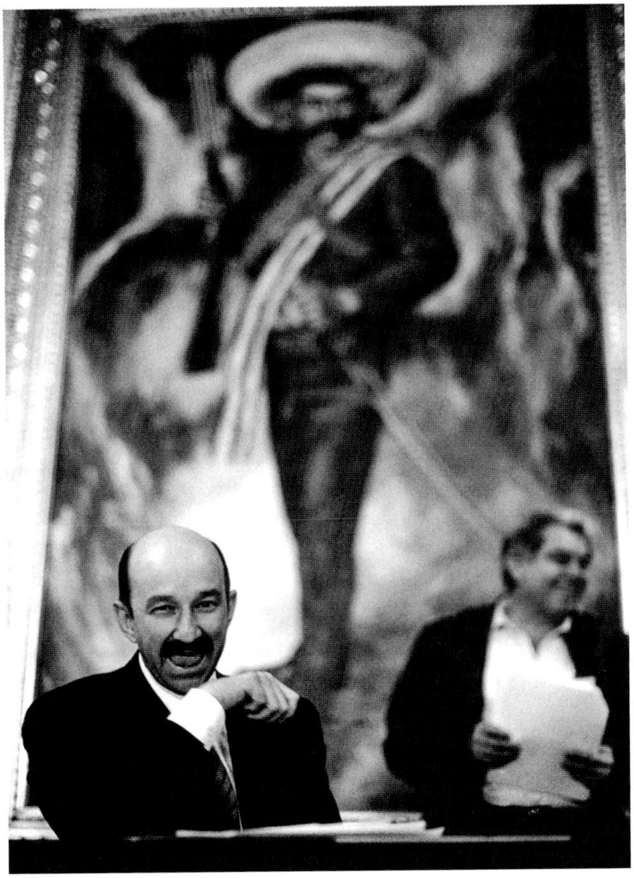

E-4. President Carlos Salinas in a meeting with campesino organizations to reform Article 27 of the Constitution, presidential residence "Los Pinos," Mexico City, 1991. © Elsa Medina, courtesy of Elsa Medina.

is the image constructed by photojournalist Elsa Medina, who integrated it into a photograph in such a way as to offer a dense reading that is also a critique of the party dictatorship, which has been a persistent legacy of the revolution (Figure E-4). Medina has the capacity to recognize simultaneously, in a fraction of a second, both the relevance of an event and the precise organization of the forms through which to express it (or "the decisive moment," to paraphrase Henri Cartier-Bresson).[23] She knows how to capture spontaneous action and, moreover, has the ability to provoke reactions in her subjects. At the same time, President Carlos Salinas de Gortari (1988-1994) was known among photojournalists to be particularly playful with them. The collaboration between Medina and Salinas produced an image in which he makes a grotesque gesture in front of a painting made from Zapata's icon, in the middle of a meeting with Víctor Cervera Pacheco, secretary of Agrarian Reform, at the presidential residence Los Pinos, to essentially do away with Article 27 and any further agrarian reform.

Photography is always a dialectic between the picture and the pictured. As seen from Medina's side of the camera, it is a penetrating critique of how PRI has made use of the revolutionary heritage—incarnated in the gigantic portrait—which has served to legitimate its rule, but which it has not respected. This contradiction was particularly pronounced in the case of Salinas; according to historian Samuel Brunk, his "administration frequently employed the figure of Zapata, both visually and verbally, in pushing its reforms."[24] Although Medina pilloried Salinas, the image is nonetheless an accurate representation of the president's position in relation to the revolution: his neoliberalism broke fundamentally with the formerly reigning ideology of a paternalistic "revolutionary nationalism." Salinas declared an end to the Mexican Revolution, but the publication that employed Medina, *La Jornada*, either did not want to spread that message or thought that the photo was too critical of Salinas, because it was censored.[25]

"ADELITA"

The image of the woman who grips the handrails of a train car, and leans forward to peer intently up the tracks, has been recruited to serve as the personification of the *soldadera* in the Mexican Revolution (Figure E-5). The photograph was taken by Gerónimo Hernández in April 1912 at the Buenavista station, where the woman was standing on the platform of a military train headed north to put down the rebellion of Pascual Orozco, who had risen against President Madero.[26] Its iconic history began with its appearance on the front page of the Maderista newspaper *Nueva Era*, and from that moment the woman was designated a *soldadera* because the cutline proclaimed, "I will defend my Juan."[27] The image disappeared for some thirty years (it was not included in the truncated *Albúm histórico gráfico* of Agustín Víctor Casasola, nor in the book *The Wind That Swept Mexico* by Anita Brenner). It reappeared in the *Historia gráfica de la Revolución*, published by Gustavo Casasola in 1942, where he affirmed, "This *soldadera* has seen all of Mexico, crossing from border to border."[28] In all of its subsequent appearances, the young woman has always been a camp follower, as, for example, on the cover of the book by Elena Poniatowska about those women.[29] For one author she is "The paradigmatic image of the *soldadera*, the Mexican soldier's faithful companion," and her picture has circulated throughout the Americas, Europe, and Asia.[30]

Without identifications that "anchor" photographs to their reality, their aesthetic force generates myths, and they become decontextualized symbols that disfigure our understanding of the past. For example, the series *Historia gráfica de México* provided the following cutline for this image: "Adelita-the-*soldadera*, a photo taken by Agustín V. Casasola en 1910, which would very soon become one of the emblems of the revolution, just like the famous song with almost the same name, 'La Adelita.'"[31] This can only be described as a condensed comedy of errors. We now know that the photo was taken in 1912, but even without that information it should have been clear that the photo was not taken in 1910 because there were few troop movements that year. We also know who the photographer was, and it was not Agustín Víctor. Although the editors of *Historia gráfica de México* did not have that information, they could have assigned authorship to the Casasola Archive. The idea that "it would very soon become one of the emblems of the revolution" is simply not true, as it was not seen for thirty years, until Gustavo Casasola rescued it. Finally, it appears to have been the very editors of *Historia gráfica de México* who named this woman "Adelita," and it was almost certainly derived precisely from the corrido "La Adelita," the best-known of the songs celebrating *soldaderas*.[32]

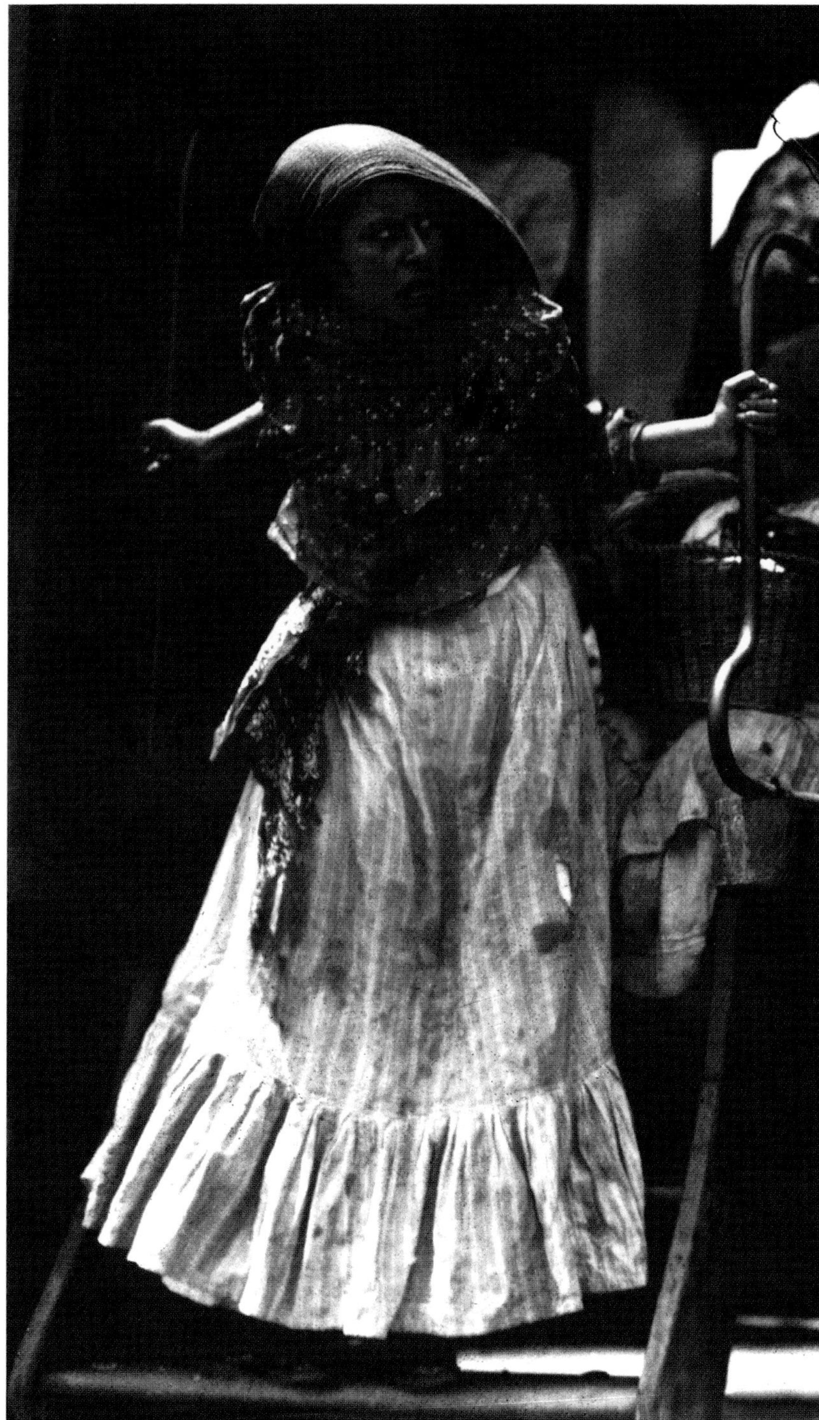

E-5. *Soldadera* (or food seller, or ?) on a train platform in the Buenavista station, Mexico City, April 1912; Gerónimo Hernández. © Inv. #5670 (detail), Fondo Casasola, SINAFO-Fototeca Nacional del INAH.

The series *Historia gráfica de México* followed the usual practice of cropping the negative wherein appears "Adelita," removing the right half of the image (Figure E-6). That part of the glass plate is broken in the original negative, but we can still see a group of women standing on the platform of the train car. When we ask who Adelita was, her location in the train may provide an important clue. *Soldaderas* of the rank and file usually traveled on top of, or beneath, the cars.[33] The women who were inside the cars were probably the privileged followers of federal officers.[34] In an early attempt to demystify the image and contextualize it, I ventured the hypothesis that "it is possible that they were prostitutes."[35] Miguel Ángel Morales was perhaps correct, if not terribly generous, in thinking my speculation was "reckless and erroneous."[36] Nonetheless, one of the most interesting uses that has been made of this image was in the posters that independent sex workers contributed to the celebration of the Grito de Independencia on 15 September 2008 (Figure E-7).

At this point I do not believe that the women in the photograph were prostitutes or *soldaderas*, but Mexico City food venders who attended the soldiers while the train was stopped.[37] Perhaps "Adelita" was eagerly searching for her son or little sister who helped her prepare and sell food. Or . . . maybe she was following her "Juan" along revolutionary paths, like the *soldadera* in Figure E-8, who was in the north, where—because soldiers found themselves at great distances from their homes, and in the absence of quartermaster corps—it was more common to find women who lived from the soldiers' pay (*la soldada*), fed them, cured their wounds, took care of their children, provided social lubrication and entertainment, and sometimes grabbed weapons to defend themselves.[38]

Analyzed as a whole, the image could contribute to our historical knowledge about life during the armed struggle, for it provides "leads" about the living conditions of some women. The cropped version of "Adelita" serves only as another revolutionary myth because the vitality evinced by this woman makes her a repository for, and symbol of, the attributes of the legendary camp followers. A female journalist described the Adelita legend as being the "feminine version of the revolutionary hero," in which women were portrayed as embodying "the attitude of indiscriminately following their men, whether they were right or not"; she asks whether it might not be preferable for women to develop their own criteria, thus "abolishing the 'sublime' concepts of Adelita and the *soldadera*, as well as the never sufficiently praised 'values' that are attributed to them."[39]

Despite efforts to demystify this image—and the myth of the *soldadera* that it incarnates—new versions continue to appear. I would bet that every researcher in

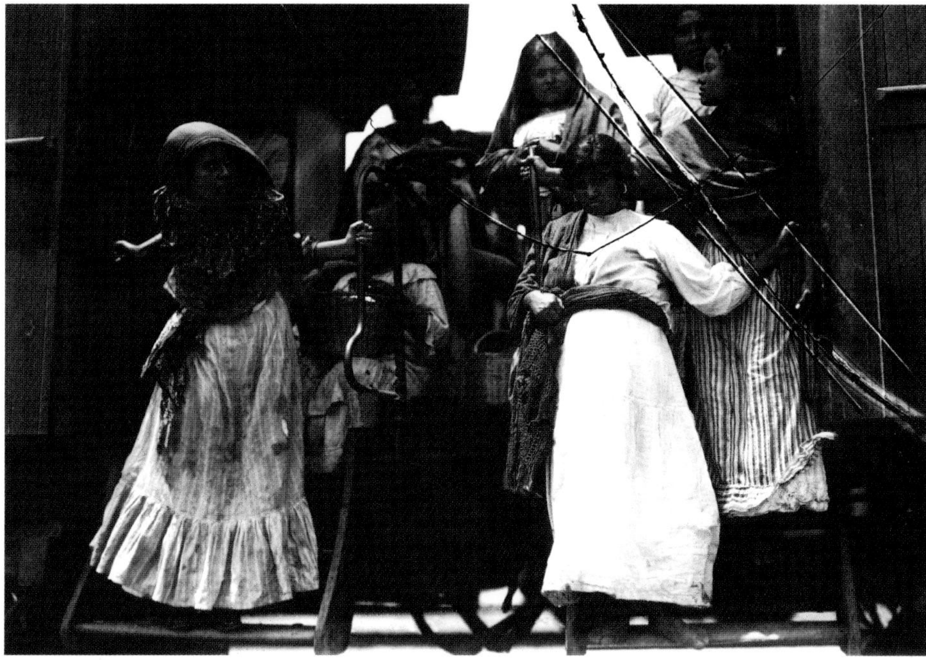

E-6. *Soldaderas* (or food sellers, or ?) on a train platform in the Buenavista station, Mexico City, April 1912; Gerónimo Hernández. © Inv. #5670, Fondo Casasola, SINAFO-Fototeca Nacional del INAH.

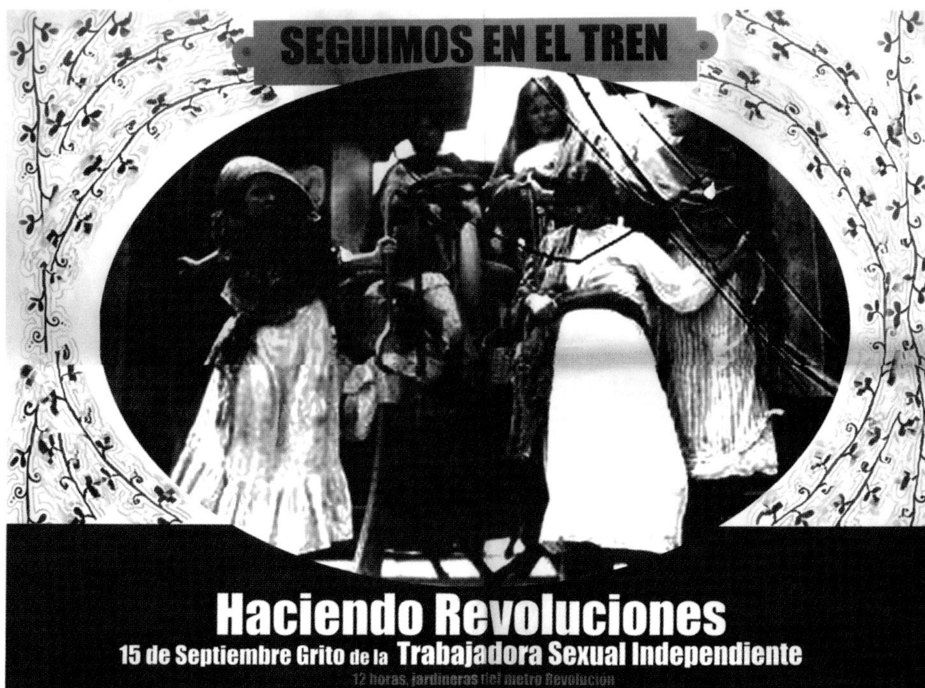

E-7. Poster circulated by independent sex workers, 15 September 2008.

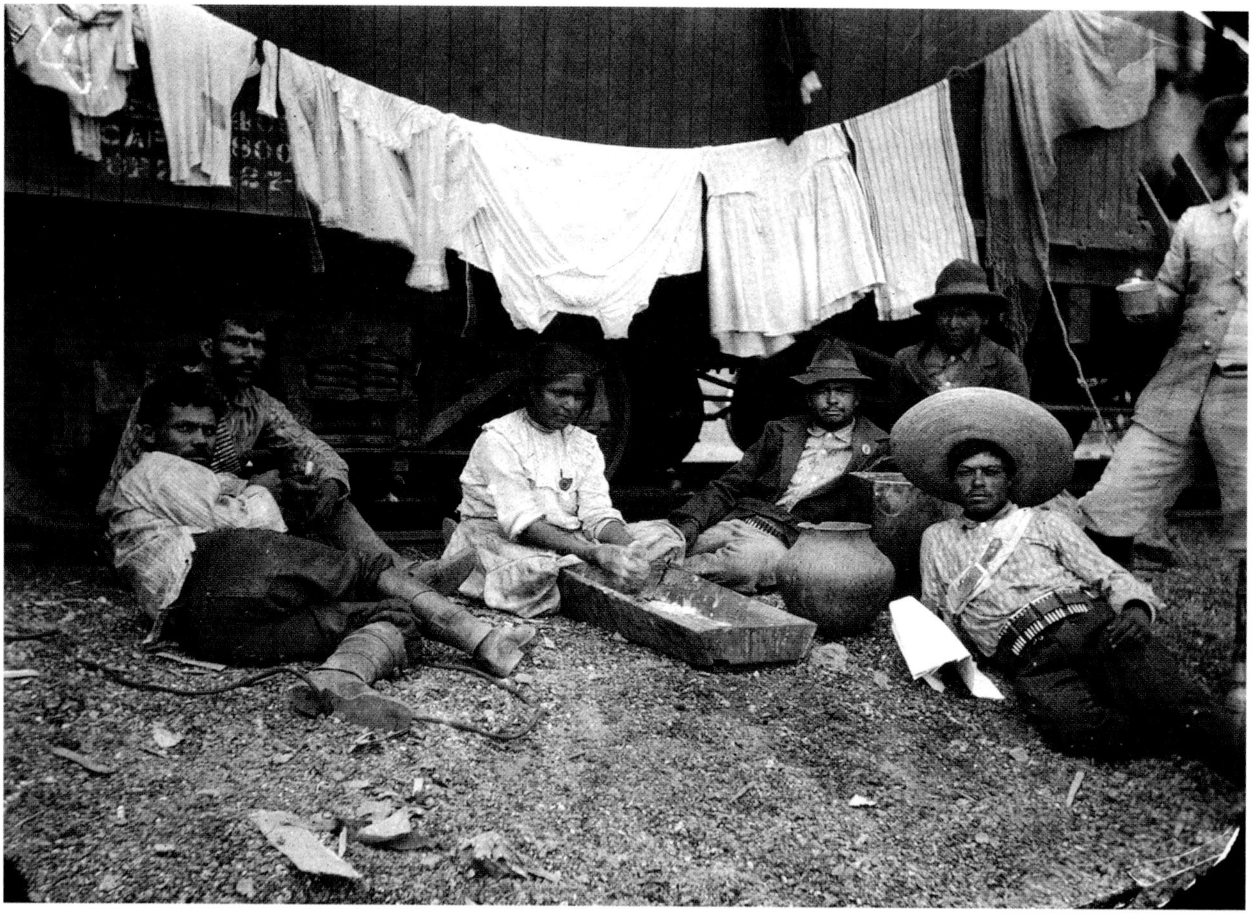

E-8. *Soldadera* with her clients, Lucio Blanco's forces, ca. 1914. © Inv. #6086, Fondo Casasola, SINAFO-Fototeca Nacional del INAH.

Mexican photography has, at one time or another, heard of a little old lady living in a far-off and often inaccessible place who insists that she is "Adelita"; the *viejitas* offer as evidence a copy of the photo on their wall—amplified, blurry, and over-contrasted from being rephotographed by the Bazaar Casasola. A picture history published for the revolution's centennial recently made its contribution to the myth: it asserts to have identified the woman who appears in the photo, an Adelita Velarde, known for her "talent for love and combat."[40] It is, in the end, an image with profound roots in the national consciousness, as can be seen in the photo by José Hernández-Claire, which he titles *La mirada* (The look), but which could be called "Adelita aged" (Figure E-9.)[41]

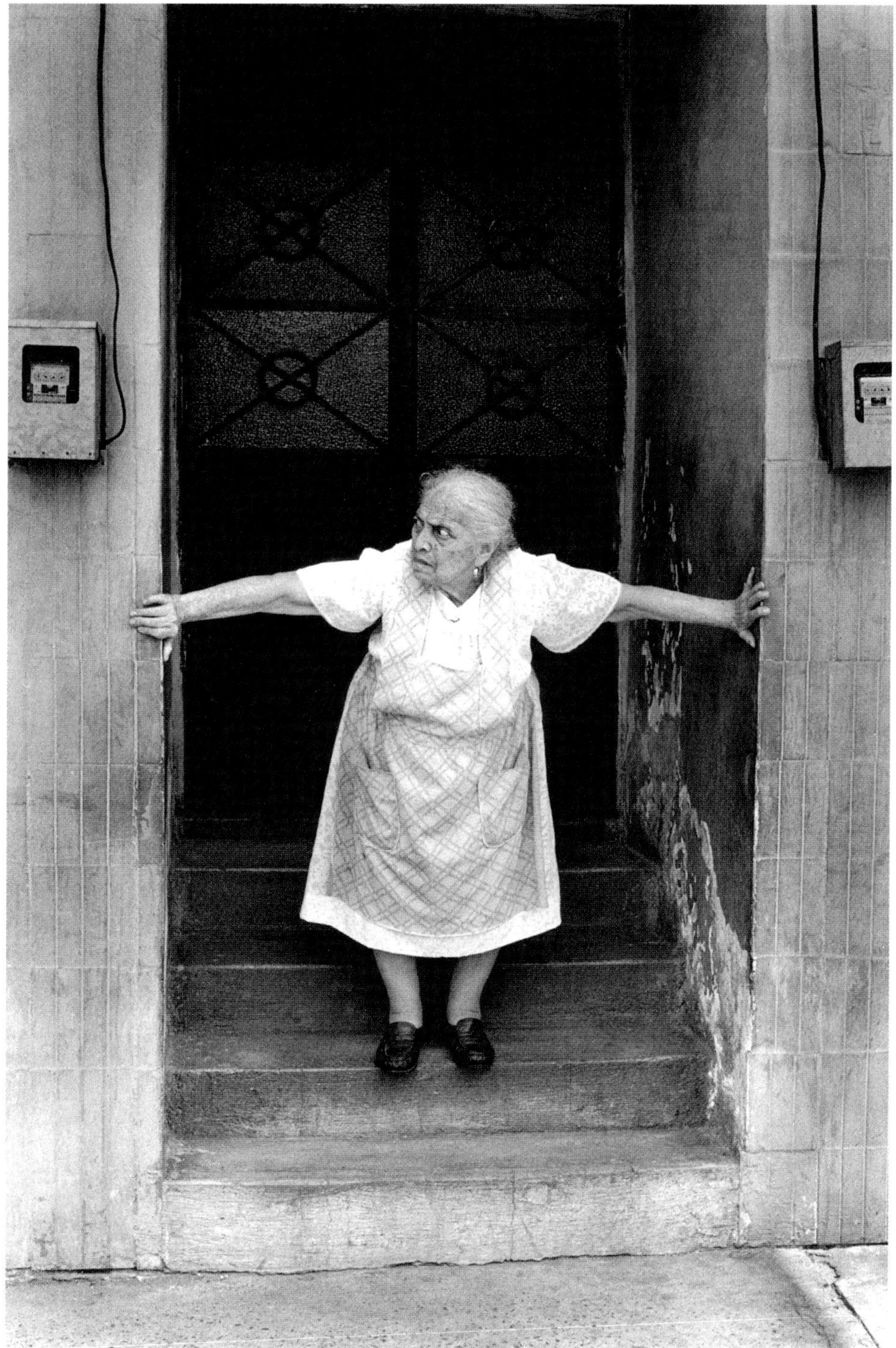

E-9. *La mirada* (The look), 1990. © José Hernández-Claire, courtesy of José Hernández-Claire.

VILLA GALLOPING TOWARD THE CAMERA

Miguel Ángel Berumen states categorically that "All the versions of the Villa myth can be related to the same photograph": that of the centaur who seems to share his mount's wildness (Figure E-10).[42] This icon was born thanks to the contract Villa made with the Mutual Film Corporation in January of 1914, which gave the company exclusive rights to film his battles and executions in exchange for $25,000. In the moment that John Davidson Wheelan took the picture as a publicity still for Mutual while they were filming Villa and his troops prior to the battle of Ojinaga, the caudillo was receiving support from the U.S. government and businessmen, impressed by the discipline he maintained over his forces. Even the reactionary newspapers of William Randolph Hearst backed him during this brief period. He was also the darling of leftists such as John Reed, for whom he was the personification of social revolution. Reed's reports had won Villa the sympathy of President Woodrow Wilson and liberals; moreover, they "gave the revolutionary a legitimacy he had not possessed before."[43] Hence, he was shown in a positive light, and his natural charisma enabled him to project himself to U.S. audiences as a Robin Hood.

The icon first appeared as part of a photo exhibit that accompanied the private premiere on 22 January 1914 of the documentary on Villa made by the Mutual Film Corporation.[44] Shortly after, it was published in the magazine *Leslie's Illustrated Weekly Newspaper*, where it was noted that "Pancho Villa has added a new laurel to his crown by taking cineastes under his protection and making them part of his army."[45] *Collier's* published it two days after *Leslie's,* and in May it appeared in *Reel Life*, where the questions asked by the movie magazine indicated the ambivalence about the caudillo at that point: "Is Villa a bandit or soldier, a Jesse James or a George Washington, a Robin Hood or a Napoleon, a robber and a ruffian or a patriot and a hero?" (Figure E-11.)[46] The answer was provided by the company's cinematographers: "Mutual cameramen, who have spent weeks in the field and who have come to know him well declare that he is a misunderstood and much maligned man."[47]

The ground that Villa had won in public relations was soon undermined by the assassination of William Benton and—as he began to lose battles to the Constitutionalists, who were recognized by the United States as the legitimate government—by Villa's tightening of the screws on U.S. interests. After attacking Columbus, New Mexico, in 1916, his personage was relegated to that of a bandit; rather than posing questions or doubts, the ad that appeared in *The Moving Picture World* for the film *Villa—Dead or Alive* asserted that Woodrow Wilson had made the classic Western call to do away with brigands—dead or alive—and citizens were summoned to fulfill their national duty: "See *your* flag cross the border to punish those who have insulted it" (Figure E-12).[48]

Without doubt, this is the photograph that most circulated during the revolution. *The Illustrated London News* was the publication that followed the U.S. periodicals, and it came out in April 1914 with a page of photos and texts related to "the Benton case." The murdered man had been a British citizen, but the magazine declared that Villa had been absolved of the crime, and "Blackguard as he is, he's a good leader and a brave fighter."[49] The Germans were the next to publish the icon, in the *Berliner Illustrirte Zeitung* in May 1914, and in June of that year it appeared in *Le Miroir* in Paris.

E-10. Pancho Villa, Las Mulas, January 1914; John Davidson Wheelan. © Inv. #287647, Fondo Casasola, SINAFO-Fototeca Nacional del INAH.

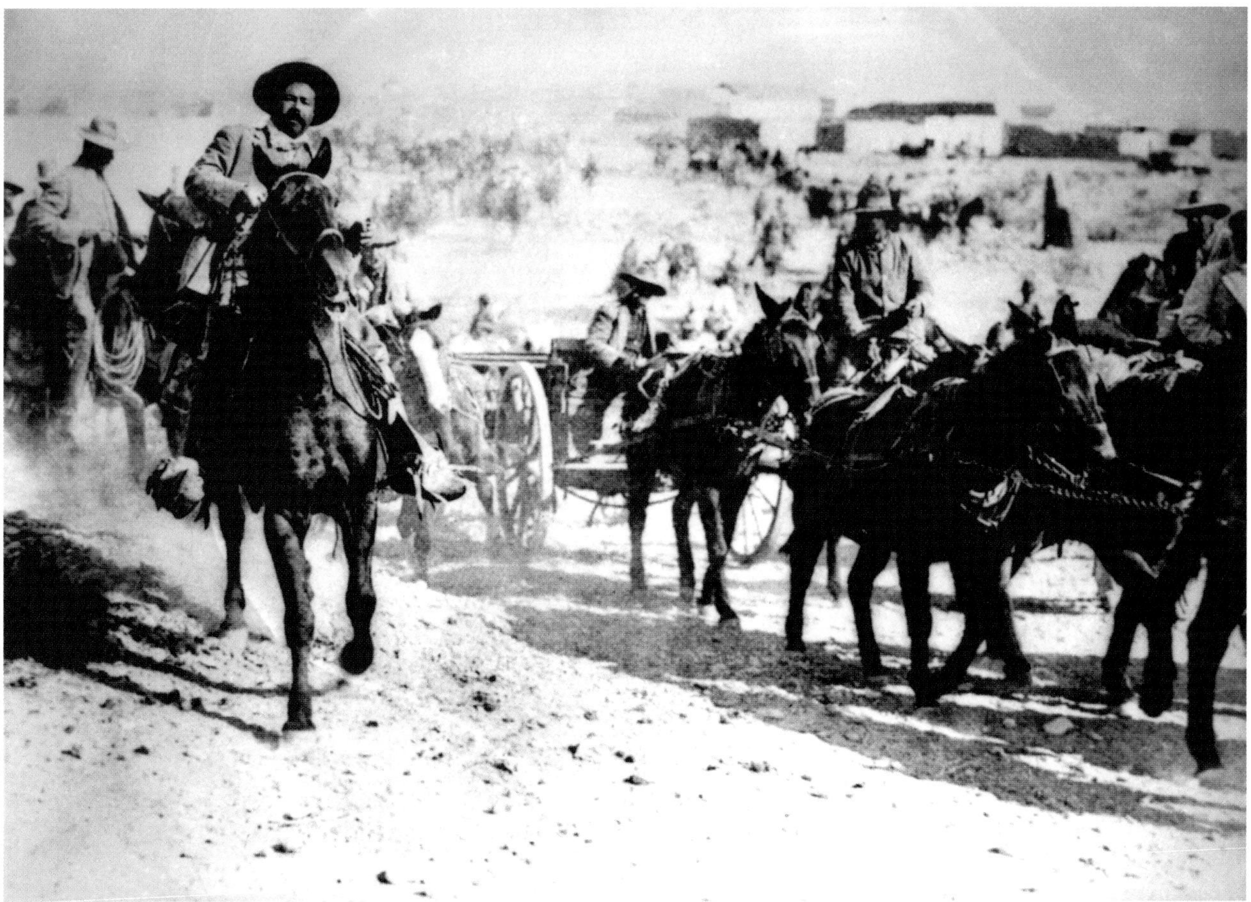

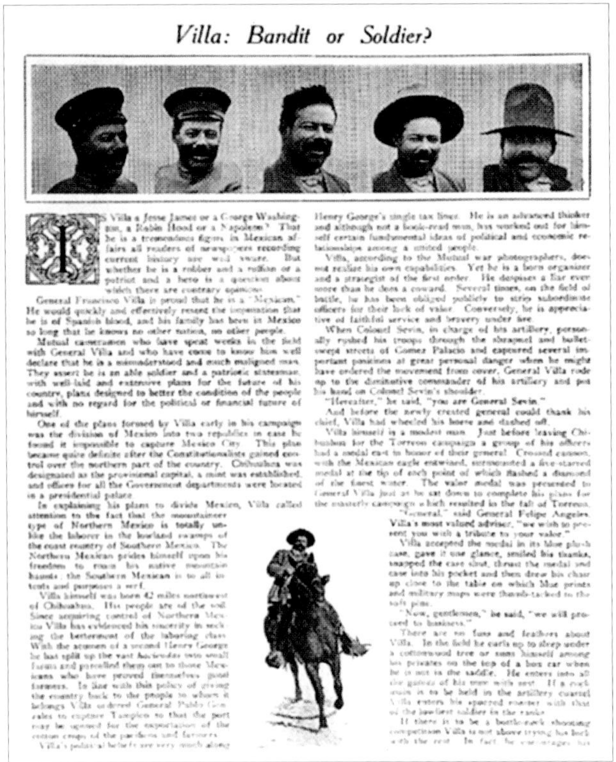

Villa: Bandit or Soldier?

Is Villa a Jesse James or a George Washington, a Robin Hood or a Napoleon? That he is a tremendous figure in Mexican affairs all readers of newspapers recording current history are well aware. But whether he is a robber and a ruffian or a patriot and a hero is a question about which there are contrary opinions.

General Francisco Villa is proud that he is a "Mexican." He would quickly and effectively resent the imputation that he is of Spanish blood, and his family has been in Mexico so long that he knows no other nation, no other people.

Mutual cameramen who have spent weeks in the field with General Villa and who have come to know him well declare that he is a misunderstood and much maligned man. They assert he is an able soldier and a patriotic statesman, with well-laid and extensive plans for the future of his country, plans designed to better the condition of the people and with no regard for the political or financial future of himself.

One of the plans formed by Villa early in his campaign was the division of Mexico into two republics in case he found it impossible to capture Mexico City. This plan became quite definite after the Constitutionalists gained control over the northern part of the country. Chihuahua was designated as the provisional capital, a mint was established, and offices for all the Government departments were located in a presidential palace.

In explaining his plans to divide Mexico, Villa called attention to the fact that the mountaineer type of Northern Mexico is totally unlike the laborer in the lowland swamps of the coast country of Southern Mexico. The Northern Mexican prides himself upon his freedom to roam his native mountain haunts; the Southern Mexican is to all intents and purposes a serf.

Villa himself was born 42 miles northwest of Chihuahua. His people are of the soil. Since acquiring control of Northern Mexico Villa has evidenced his sincerity in seeking the betterment of the laboring class. With the acumen of a second Henry George he has split up the vast *haciendas* into small farms and parcelled them out to those Mexicans who have proved themselves good farmers. In line with this policy of giving the country back to the people to whom it belongs Villa ordered General Pablo Gonzales to capture Tampico so that the port may be opened for the exportation of the cotton crops of the pardners and farmers.

Villa's political beliefs are very much along Henry George's single tax lines. He is an advanced thinker and although not a book-read man, has worked out for himself certain fundamental ideas of political and economic relationships among a united people.

Villa, according to the Mutual war photographers, does not realize his own capabilities. Yet he is a born organizer and a strategist of the first order. He despises a liar even more than he does a coward. Several times, on the field of battle, he has been obliged publicly to strip subordinate officers for their lack of valor. Conversely, he is appreciative of faithful service and bravery under fire.

When Colonel Sevin, in charge of his artillery, personally rushed his troops through the shrapnel and bullet-swept streets of Gomez Palacio and captured several important positions at great personal danger when he might have ordered the movement from cover, General Villa rode up to the diminutive commander of his artillery and put his hand on Colonel Sevin's shoulder.

"Hereafter," he said, "you are General Sevin."

And before the newly created general could thank his chief, Villa had wheeled his horse and dashed off.

Villa himself is a modest man. Just before leaving Chihuahua for the Torreon campaign a group of his officers had a medal cast in honor of their general. Crossed cannon, with the Mexican eagle entwined, surmounted a five-starred medal at the tip of each point of which flashed a diamond of the finest water. The valor medal was presented to General Villa just as he sat down to complete his plans for the masterly campaign which resulted in the fall of Torreon.

"General," said General Felipe Angeles, Villa's most valued adviser, "we wish to present you with a tribute to your valor."

Villa accepted the medal in its blue plush case, gave it one glance, smiled his thanks, snapped the case shut, thrust the medal and case into his pocket and then drew his chair up close to the table on which blue prints and military maps were thumb-tacked to the soft pine.

"Now, gentlemen," he said, "we will proceed to business."

There are no fuss and feathers about Villa. In the field he curls up to sleep under a cottonwood tree or suns himself among his privates on the top of a box car when he is not in the saddle. He enters into all the games of his men with zest. If a cock main is to be held in the artillery cuartel Villa enters his spurred rooster with that of the lowliest soldier in the ranks.

If there is to be a bottle-neck shooting competition Villa is not above trying his luck with the rest. In fact he encourages his

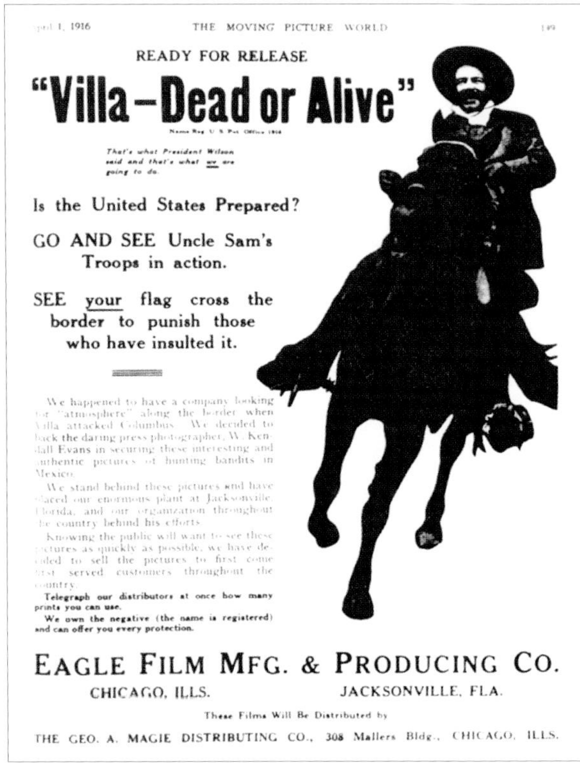

El jefe militar de las fuerzas constitucionalistas

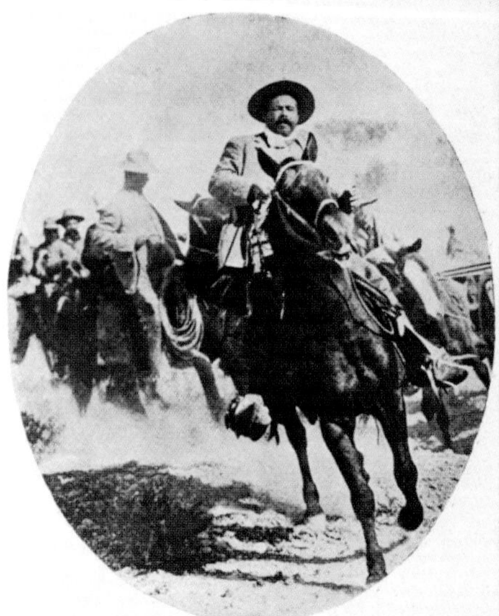

Interesante fotografía de Francisco Villa que por vez primera se publica en México y que representa al jefe revolucionario marchando al frente de sus hombres, al asalto y toma de Torreón.

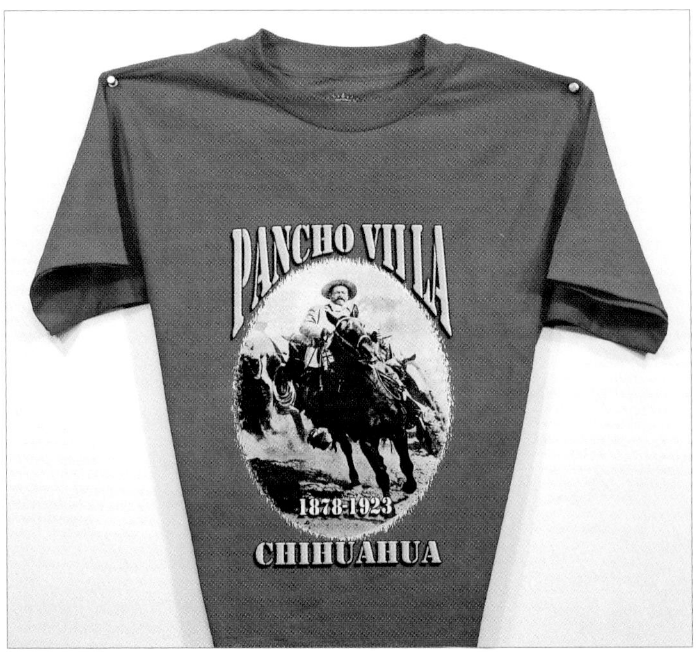

The Spanish periodical *Mundo Gráfico* published it the same month, crediting it to Hugelmann. (*Ilustración Artística* printed it in 1916 and credited to an M. Branger.) It was not published in Mexico until Huerta's fall, when it appeared in *La Semana Ilustrada* on 21 July 1914, and the former *cabecilla* became "The military leader of the Constitutionalist forces" (Figure E-13).[50] Despite the recognition that Villa received during a short period of the armed struggle, he was generally ignored (*ninguneado*) by the capital's press and the government until the 1960s. One example of his exclusion might be the absence of this icon in the first version of *La historia gráfica de la Revolución*, published in 1942.[51] Gustavo Casasola did include it in the large, official exposition, *La historia gráfica de la Revolución*, mounted in 1946, perhaps because that always sharp judge of the aesthetic, Anita Brenner, had placed it in *The Wind That Swept Mexico*.[52] Today you can acquire the image on a T-shirt in the Chihuahua city airport (Figure E-14).

VILLA AND ZAPATA AND THE PRESIDENTIAL CHAIR

Like the image of Villa on horseback, the icon of Villa and Zapata and the presidential chair had both contemporary importance and historical transcendence. Friedrich Katz asserts that "Villa jokingly sat down in the presidential chair for a moment, with Zapata at his side. A photographer recorded the scene, and the picture was soon disseminated worldwide, giving additional proof in the eyes of many observers that Villa had become the real strongman and ruler of Mexico."[53] Writer José de la Colina testified: "Rarely has a photograph obtained such a parallel fixation in history and mythology."[54] Another writer, Paco Ignacio Taibo, relates the icon to presidentialism: "This photo contributed to the growth of the legend around 'The presidential chair.' From that chair arises the referent that will accompany Mexicans during the next 100 years: the idea that the battle is for the chair, the image of the chair as the country's center, as the cupola of the pyramid, as the center of power."[55] However, the icon has the peculiarity of being two different photos made very near in time and space by two photographers who were not those whom one might have expected to have taken them (for example, Samuel Tinoco or Agustín Víctor Casasola).

One image was made by Antonio Garduño, a very experienced photographer who was known as "the master of the masters in photography" and made postcards because "his independence did not permit him to be subject to fossilizing bureaucratisms" (Figure E-15).[56] According to the magazine's cutline, Garduño's image was "a special 'pose' for *La Ilustración Semanal*," where it appeared on 7 December 1914, a day after

E-11. FACING UPPER LEFT "Villa: Bandit or Soldier?"; *Reel Life*, May 1914.

E-12. FACING UPPER RIGHT "Villa—Dead or Alive"; *Moving Picture World*, 1 April 1916.

E-13. FACING LOWER LEFT Villa, "Military chief of the Constitutionalist forces"; *La Semana Ilustrada*, 21 July 1914.

E-14. FACING LOWER RIGHT T-shirt from Chihuahua, 2009; Juan Hernández Rodríguez. Archive of John Mraz.

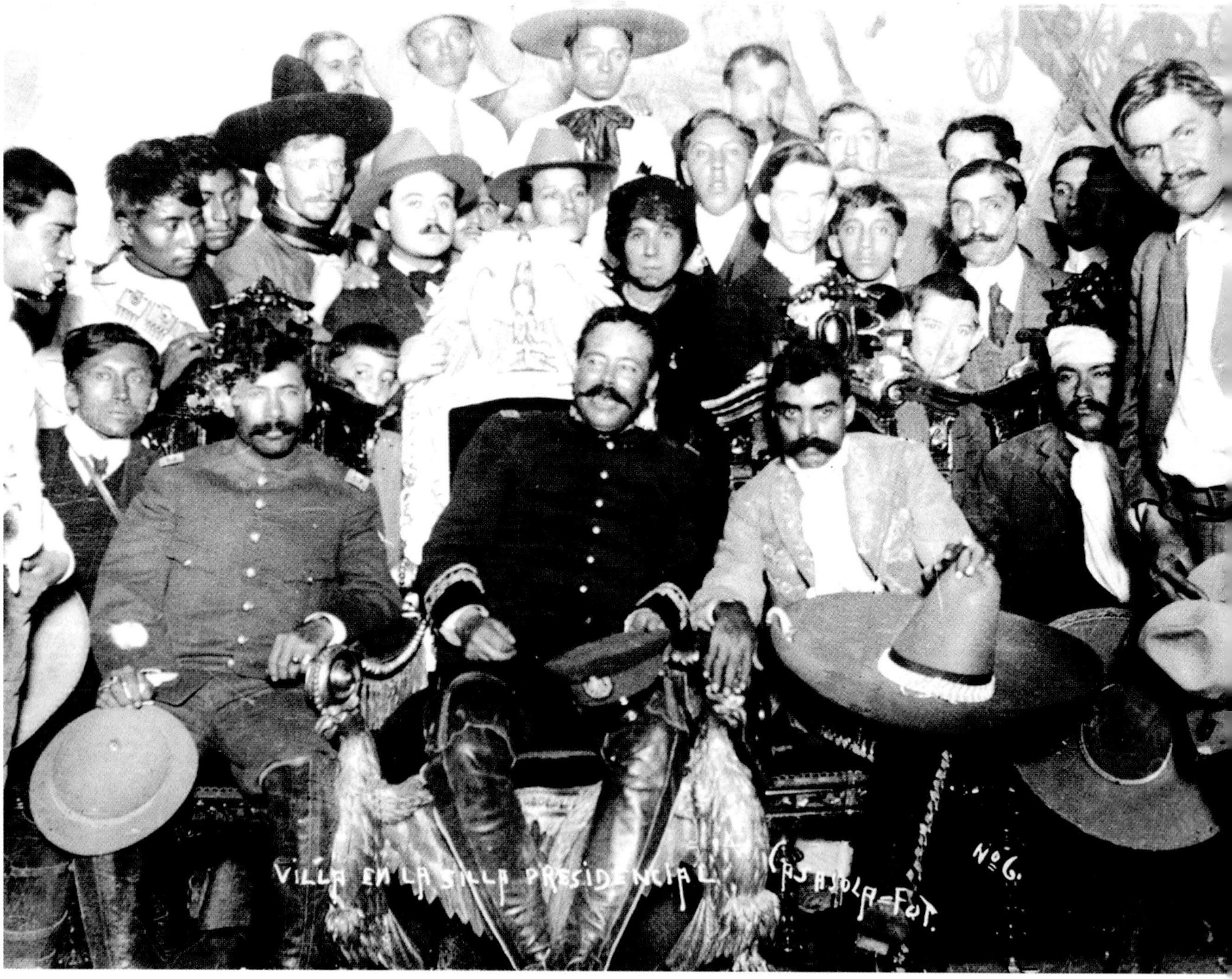

E-15. Pancho Villa and Emiliano Zapata (*seated, second and third from left*) in the National Palace, 6 December 1914; Antonio Garduño. © Inv. #33536, Fondo Casasola, SINAFO-Fototeca Nacional del INAH.

the event.[57] Garduño's treatment of the scene is in the style of studio and art photography that editor Ezequiel Álvarez Tostado promulgated, and to which Garduño was also attracted. The subjects are very conscious of participating in a photograph: all are posing, and most look at the camera. General Tomás Urbina has his eyes open, and Rodolfo Fierro gazes at the photographer. After appearing in the magazine, Garduño's photo was published in the first version of *Historia gráfica de la Revolución* in 1942 and, the following year, in Anita Brenner's book.[58] This version was also incorporated by Arnold Belkin in his mural commissioned by the Museo Nacional de Historia, *La llegada de los generales Zapata y Villa al Palacio Nacional* (The arrival of generals Zapata and Villa at the National Palace) (1979) (Figure E-16). More recently, the neo-Zapatista movement incorporated Garduño's image in a poster advertising *their* Convention of Aguascalientes in Chiapas in 1994: Zapata's visage is replaced by that of Subcomandante Marcos, while the figure of Villa is supplanted by that of Superbarrio Gómez, formerly a professional wrestler and now an urban social activist, who appears in the wrestling outfit he wears in public appearances (Figure E-17).

The other version of this icon belongs more to the genre of photojournalism and was made by the dean of Mexico's graphic reporters, Manuel Ramos (Figure E-18).[59] This photo is a more spontaneous shot, and most of the people are not looking at the camera: Villa and Zapata appear to be talking, Urbina has his eyes closed, and Fierro is observing the caudillos. It was first published in *El Monitor*, 7 December 1914. Even while the armed struggle continued, Álvaro Obregón found this icon of such importance that he included it in his book *Ocho mil kilómetros en campaña* in 1917.[60] Recently, the cartoonists of *La Jornada* added their own, very particular perspective by making fun of this sacrosanct image: "Francisco Villa and Emiliano Zapata gave full compliance to the central demand of their Revolutionary Plan called, 'Land and Liberty to put our seats wherever we want to.' They sat in the presidential chair, called the Casasola brothers to take a photo, and immediately abandoned the place without even bothering to disinfect it."[61]

The Mexico City press in 1914 was more circumspect and made no commentary about the event or the photo beyond identifying the individuals pictured. However, *El Pueblo* in Veracruz (where Carranza's forces held power) did have something to say about Garduño's photo when they published it on page 3, perhaps because of the international notoriety it had acquired. The newspaper felt that to understand Villa, one would have to apply "the paleontology of the amoral," because he was "a barbarian who defends his cavern."[62] The writer seemed to find inspiration in the photograph:

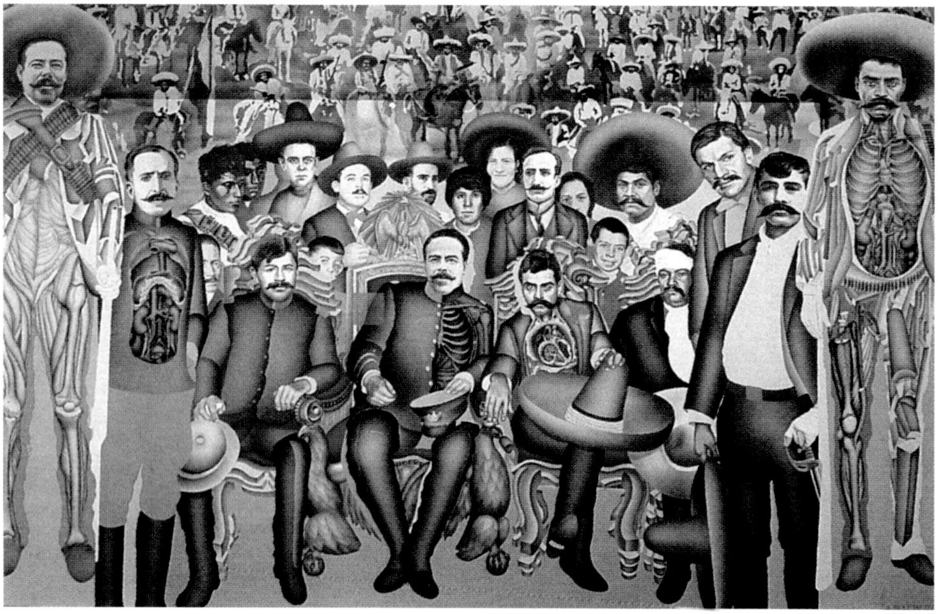

E-16. Arnold Belkin mural *La llegada de los generales Zapata y Villa al Palacio Nacional* (The arrival of generals Zapata and Villa at the National Palace), 1979; Museo Nacional de Historia.

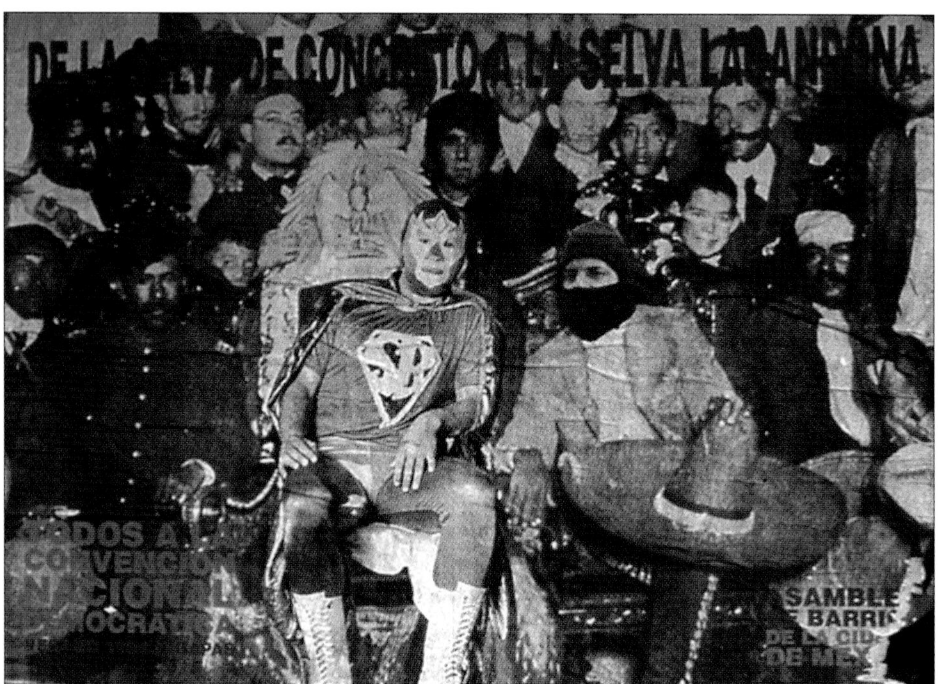

E-17. Poster for the 1994 neo-Zapatista Convention of Aguascalientes (Chiapas), Mexico City, 1994. Courtesy of Samuel Brunk.

The vanity of the primitive dominates Villa in the photo that accompanies these lines. You see a man that, with no premeditation but simply at the impulse of his instinctive passions, always desires to be first among those who are around him. He sits between Zapata and Urbina, in nothing less than the Presidential chair in the palace where the Supreme authority has been exercised by men made eminent by their virtue, talent, and valor, self-denial and even martyrdom. There is no gold, no happiness, no satisfaction on earth that Villa would change for this moment in which he finds himself in a situation that is the perfect antithesis of that offered by the highest expression of virtue in the world: Christ nailed on Calvary, between two criminals. Villa, amoral, the bandit triumphant and smiling, sits between two brigands, amazed at a triumph that unites the three in the same second of arrogance.[63]

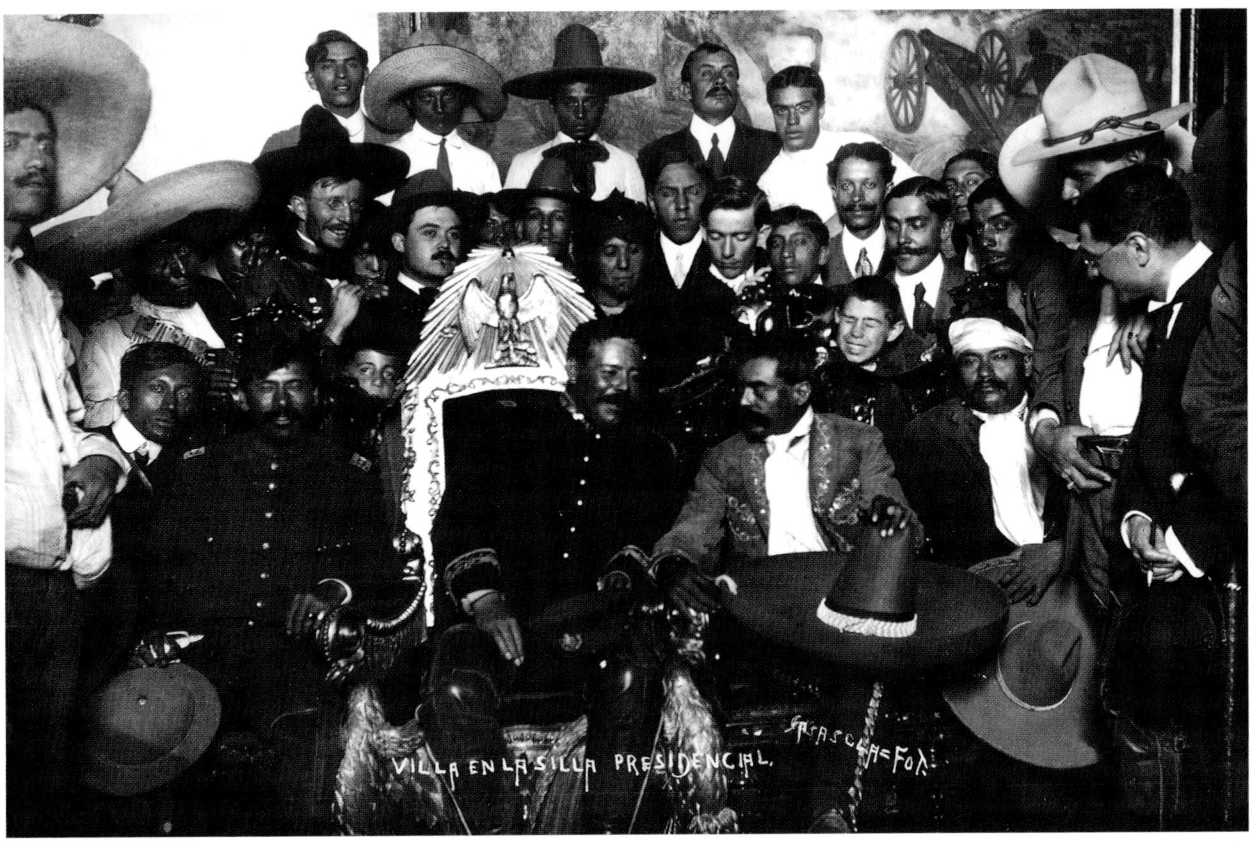

E-18. Pancho Villa and Emiliano Zapata in the National Palace, 6 December 1914; Manuel Ramos. © Inv. #656823, Fondo Casasola, SINAFO-Fototeca Nacional del INAH.

The photos were taken the day that 50,000 Conventionist troops made a triumphal entry into Mexico City and paraded through the Zócalo for six hours. Villa came from Tacuba with the División del Norte, and Zapata from Xochimilco with the Ejército Libertador. Arriving at the National Palace, they went out on the presidential balcony to watch the event and receive ovations from the multitude. Gustavo Casasola said that "Since the parade of numerous contingents was long and tedious, at an opportune moment generals Villa and Zapata went inside, where Villa sat in the presidential chair."[64] Taibo recounts that an old Villista offered a different vision: "Villa said, 'I'm going to be president for a bit,' and sat in the chair."[65] The PRI attempted to incorporate the icon into Agustín Víctor Casasola's myth in their panegyric on the photojournalist by narrating the following scene.

> Another anecdote that they tell about Casasola is when Villa arrived in Mexico City and sat in the presidential chair. Finding the room of the National Palace full of photographers, he directed himself to Agustín Casasola, and asked him, "So, have you been working hard?" Upon being told by Casasola that he had been, in fact, very busy, Villa directed himself to all present, saying, "Be very careful. We don't want a bunch of dead photographers here." In less than a cock's crow, the room in the National Palace was completely empty.[66]

Although the story is part of PRI mythology and Casasola family lore, it is difficult to imagine that Villa would have been moved to address Agustín Víctor, who had been associated with *El Imparcial* and must have represented the more conservative elements of the capital's press corps. It is even more problematic to think of Villa threatening wholesale the assembled journalists, given his consciousness of the power wielded by the media. Also, although I am no fan of psychological readings of photographs, there is no evidence in the images that Villa is somehow upset; instead he seems to be enjoying his moment in the sun, smiling and relaxed, "as if he were the owner of the place, the lord of the castle."[67] Katz commented that this was the acme of the Villista and Zapatista movements:

> That day was perhaps the apex of Villa's career. No one at the time expected that in little more than a year, the enormous armies of the Convention that had marched through Mexico City with a reputation of near-invincibility would be defeated, and that Villa and Zapata would become fugitives in their own states, forced to resort again to guerrilla warfare of a sort that both probably thought, on the day they occupied the capital, they had given up forever.[68]

HUERTA IN THE SHADOWS

The last icon entered late into the photographic pantheon of the revolution. Moreover, while the other icons arose through a (more or less) popular consensus about their importance, this photo-myth had its origin in an officialist attempt to contribute to the visual historiography, when the regime of Miguel de la Madrid (1982–1988) emitted the last gasp of PRI's "revolutionary nationalism." Photographs were an important resource for disseminating the dominant ideology, and a great boon of picture histories occurred, with particular emphasis on the revolution. De la Madrid's government subsidized, among other series, *Así fue la Revolución Mexicana*, *Biografía del poder*, *Historia gráfica de México*, and *Memoria y olvido*.[69] The Casasola Archive had

E-19. Victoriano Huerta and his general staff in the shadows, Mexico City, 3 April 1913; Agustín Víctor Casasola. © Inv. #5764, Fondo Casasola, SINAFO-Fototeca Nacional del INAH.

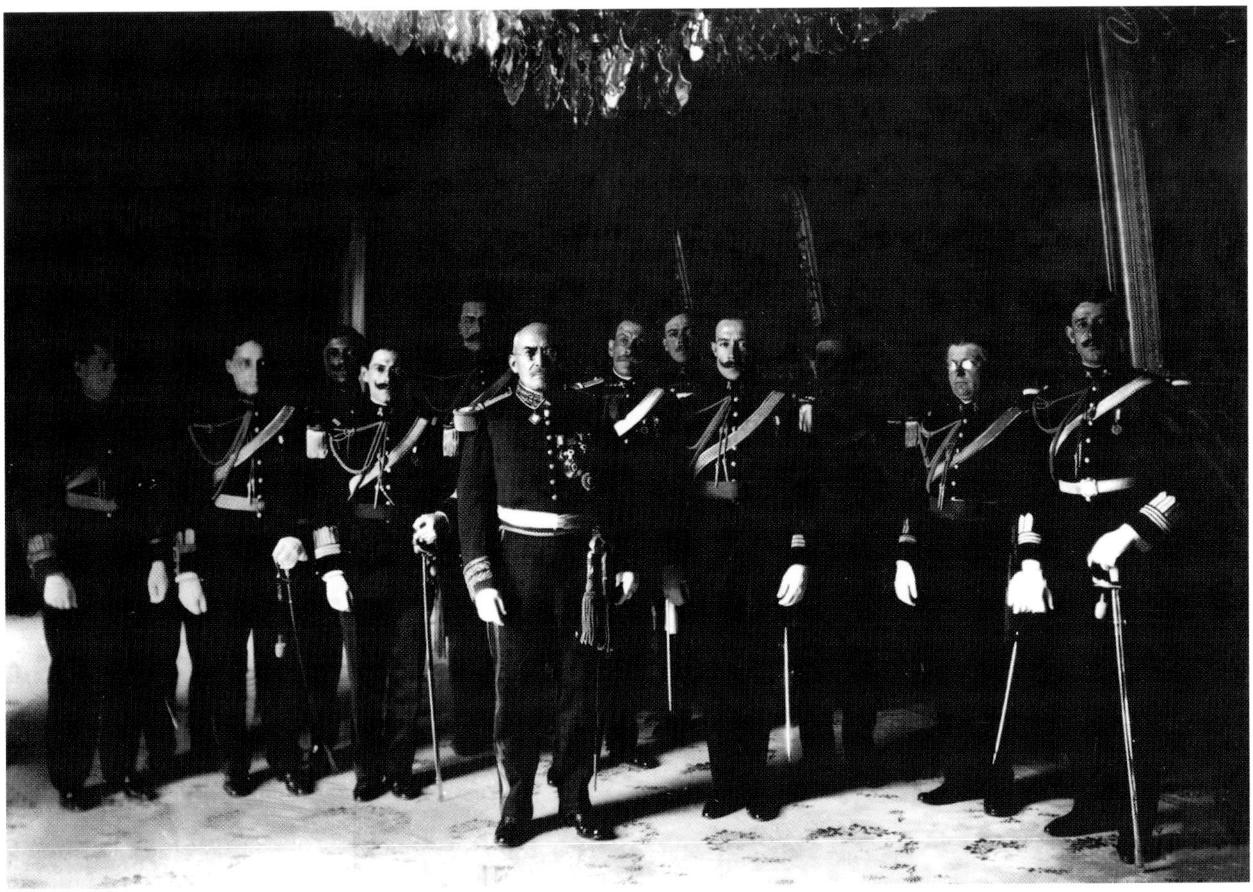

been acquired by the government in 1976, and its photographs were a centerpiece in the illustrated histories and exhibits. According to Eleazar López Zamora, then director of the Fototeca Nacional, this photo of Huerta and his general staff appeared while research was being done for the exhibit *Insurgent Mexico* (1984).[70] Obviously, López Zamora liked the image because he placed it alone on that exposition's poster, thus making it its signature photo. After its discovery and diffusion, it was featured in *historias gráficas* and histories of photography during this era.[71]

The icon offers a fascinating tale of technological failure and revolutionary rescue. The photo was unsuccessful because it lacked light; Huerta and his officers are illuminated only by the luminescence coming in from a lateral source, probably a window.[72] The effect is evocative of the expressive lighting that characterized film noir in the United States during the 1940s and 1950s, from *The Maltese Falcon* (1941, John Huston) to *Touch of Evil* (1958, Orson Welles). This style resulted from experimenting with illumination, altering the "normal" relation between fill lighting and key lighting. Fill lights provide a more general, softer, and less intense illumination that reduces contrast and shadows; it gives the impression of a reality in which the protagonists were attractively and evenly lit, and has no exaggerated areas of darkness. Key lighting creates a chiaroscuro effect, producing high contrasts. This is how noir movies are lit, as cinema researchers Janey Place and Lowell Peterson recount.

> *Noir* lighting is "low-key." The ratio of key to fill light is great, creating areas of high contrast and rich, black shadows. Unlike the even illumination of high-key lighting which seeks to display attractively all areas of the frame, the low-key noir style opposes light and dark, hiding faces, rooms, urban landscapes—and, by extension, motivations and true character—in shadow and darkness which carry connotations of the mysterious and the unknown. Small areas of light seem on the verge of being completely overwhelmed by the darkness that threatens them from all sides. Strange highlights are introduced, often on the faces of the sinister or demented.[73]

Portrayed with this sort of illumination, Huerta embodies the role of "the heavy" in the revolutionary picture, the visual incarnation of the counter-revolution, who "whitens" the reputation of other leaders who were equally corrupt and not much more revolutionary. The "black legend" of Huerta is so ingrained in postrevolutionary culture—and the striking lighting so thoroughly fulfills our expectations of what a "bad guy" looks like—that the photo is often referred to as if it offers a veridical insight into the reality of that history, a perfect embodiment of the notion that "I'll see it when I believe it."[74]

Although the photo is a product of an officialist project, it was also the handiwork of López Zamora, who promoted both research and photographic aesthetics. In this case, an image was discovered that had not been published before because of the difficulty of reproducing from such a dark negative; it could only be utilized with fine printing techniques. Hence, de la Madrid's interest in diffusing "revolutionary culture" and López Zamora's concern to rescue lost images coincided to preserve the photo for history. In fact, the picture's impact depends completely upon its faulty lighting, because the "successful" photo of Huerta and his staff (Figure E-19) is of so little interest that Gustavo Casasola did not include it in the seventy pages dedicated to Huerta's regime in the *Historia gráfica de la Revolución Mexicana*.

E-20. Victoriano Huerta and his general staff, Mexico City, 3 April 1913; Agustín Víctor Casasola. © Inv. #38789, Fondo Casasola, SINAFO-Fototeca Nacional del INAH.

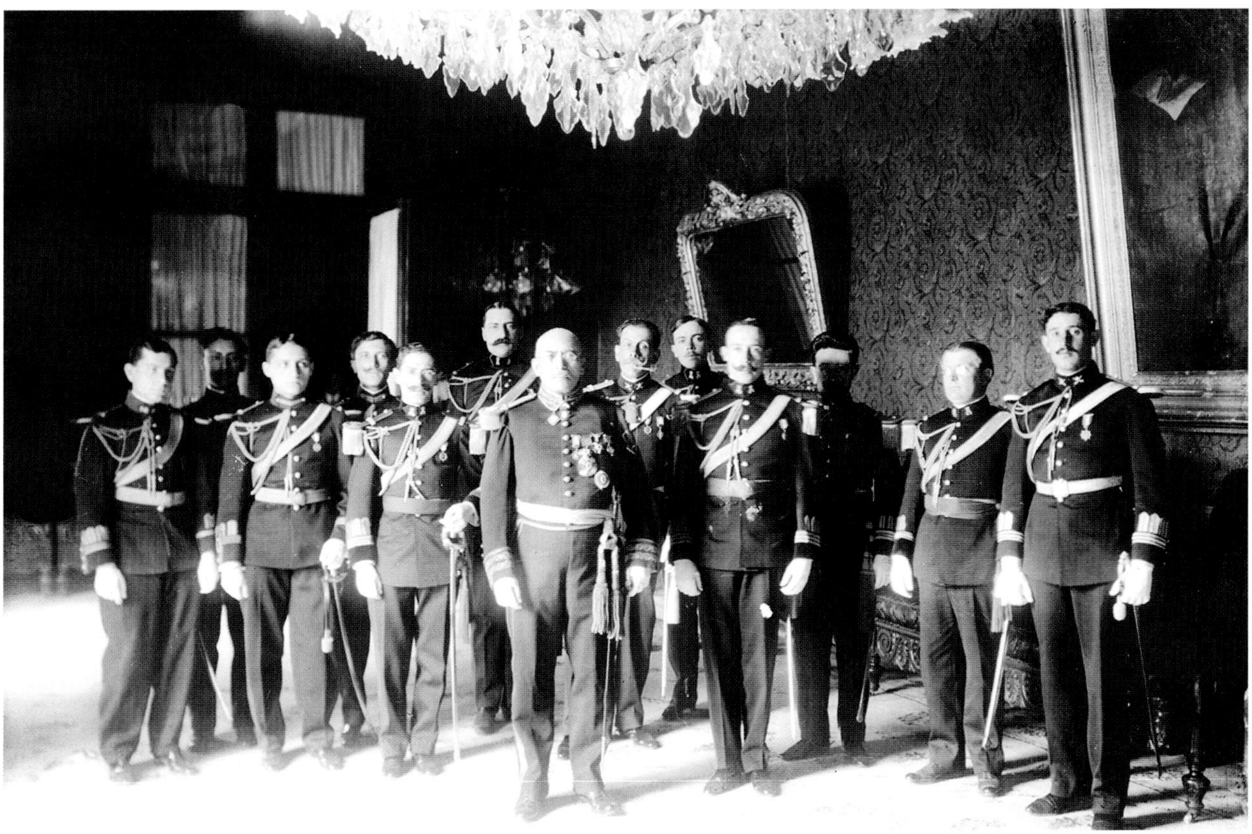

Daniel Escorza is the researcher who has most worked on these images of Huerta. He attributes them to Agustín Víctor Casasola: "The camera placement is that which Agustín Casasola utilized in those years, without tripod, and with the camera held between the breast and the abdomen."[75] The investigator explains the differences between the photographs, and the sequence in which they were taken:

> We can infer that in the first shot, the photographer was slightly nearer the group, and the exposure time was so brief that he decided to make another. For the second, he stepped back a few centimeters, and gave it a longer exposure time. The lamp in the ceiling may also have been turned on to reinforce the lighting. The first shot was a failure, and the photographer knew it immediately, and for that same reason it was poorly developed and fixed.[76]

Photographs float; that is why they travel so easily. Nonetheless, the context always determines the connotation of a photograph, most of the time with words. Hence, the icons have served many masters, and it is revealing to examine the uses made of them today in the postmodern world of the Internet. They often appear in news blogs, above all those with a leftist bent, such as "Romper el cerco informativo" (Break the information fence), "Red Social Club—periodismo humanista," "El silencio que grita" (The silence that shouts), "Iniciativa comunista," and a site whose purpose is to "Stop the train on which we are all going in the direction of self-destruction: The world capitalist system." The Internet permits people to construct their own monuments: in "My Wall of Inspirations," a University of California student included the image of Zapata with carbine and sword—the icon that most appears on Internet sites—together with his favorite sports stars. The reader of another blogspot thanked the creator for having added the icon of Villa galloping: "It is an example that many should follow in defending their rights and helping the needy; don't back down." On the other hand, the polysemia of photographs allows the mercantile world of the Internet to easily incorporate the icons. Zapata as revolutionary *charro* is used to promote karaoke music, the U.S. gun culture, the Costa Alegre Travel Agency, and the rock group La Revolución de Emiliano Zapata, whose biggest hit appears to be "Nasty Sex." Villa in the chair is employed by a rental agency of vacation houses in San Miguel de Allende, and Villa galloping illustrates an ad for cigars. The icons (with the exception of Huerta and his general staff) have not ceased to circulate around the globe.

Notes

INTRODUCTION

1. On the photography of the Mexican Revolution, see the book coordinated by Miguel Ángel Berumen, *México: Fotografía y revolución*; all my notes to this work refer to the original, large edition of 400 pages, not the smaller, re-edition of 240 pages published the same year (which credits Claudio Canales as editor together with Berumen). About the Soviet Revolution, see Baschet, *Russia 1904–1924*. I have found no book dedicated to the photography of the Chinese Revolution. Useful introductions to the photography made by the Vietnamese are *Vietnam, 1954–1975* and *Memorial of a Glorious Time*. There is no book on the photography of the Cuban Revolution, although the Oficina de Asunto Históricos has a good collection of images—of both the guerrillas in the mountains and the urban movement—to judge by the photos published from that archive in Sweig, *Inside the Cuban Revolution*. One of the more important photographers of that urban struggle was Constantino Arias (see Ortiz Monasterio, *Cuba, dos épocas*). I know of no work on the Nicaraguan photographers, but the imagery of two foreigners is worthy of note: Meiselas, *Nicaragua*; and Valtierra, *Nicaragua: Una noche afuera*.
2. The bibliography on Tina Modotti grows daily; among others, see Figarella, *Edward Weston y Tina Modotti en México*. About this period in the Soviet Union, see Tupitsyn, *The Soviet Photograph*; on Rodchenko, see Lavrentiev, *Rodchenko*. For an introduction to what I have called the "epic photojournalism" of the Cuban Revolution, see Mraz, "Cuban Photography," 87–90.
3. See my discussion of this in Mraz, *Looking for Mexico*, 85–91.
4. On the concept of "visual economy," see Poole, *Vision, Race, and Modernity*.
5. The term *technical images* to refer to photography and cinema is Vilém Flusser's; see *Towards a Philosophy of Photography*, 5.
6. Sartre, "For Whom Does One Write?"
7. Martín Luís Guzmán referred to the "fortunes" that photographers could make by portraying Carranza (*El águila y la serpiente*, 338). I explore this question in more detail in my discussion of Constitutionalist photography.
8. González Flores, "Técnica fotográfica y mirada: La fotografía en el país de la metralla," 55.
9. Letter from 1915, cited in Miquel, *Salvador Toscano*, 72. I have decided to focus on photography and to leave cinema aside, even the films produced by photographers who were also cineastes.
10. Gutiérrez Ruvalcaba, "A Fresh Look at the Casasola Archive," 191.

11. García Díaz, *Puerto de Veracruz*, 157.
12. According to historian Paul Vanderwood, "All kinds of pirating went on and could not be controlled. Kodak produced a post card printer in 1910 that was inexpensive and rapid. Many of the postcards were of excellent quality, and could be copied with no problem" (personal communication, January 2009). Photo historian John Turner mentioned several cases of photographers in New Zealand who acquired established studios and erased the names on the glass plates to replace them with their own (personal communication, January 2009).
13. I am grateful to Daniel Escorza for this information (personal communication, 2009). Although the issue of 4 May 1914 does not identify the photographer, one week later *La Ilustración Semanal* specified that the images from Veracruz were "Photos by our correspondent," "Photos: Tinoco," and "Photos: Tinoco and Garduño." It is not clear to whom the magazine refers as its "correspondent," though it could be "the intelligent and active correspondent Torresilla who took this interesting information" and who appears in a photo (*La Ilustración Semanal*, 11 May 1914).
14. See, for example, the response of *Novedades* to *La Semana Ilustrada,* after the latter accused the former of having published photos made originally for *La Semana Ilustrada*: "We have reproduced them with every right, because they are from the very abundant archive of photos taken by Tinoco" (*Novedades*, 12 March 1913). The note informs us that the magazines took the question of rights seriously and, moreover, that Samuel Tinoco had an archive as important as "that of Casasola and Herrerías."
15. *L'Illustration*, 9 May 1914, 397.
16. Brenner, *The Wind that Swept Mexico*, Plate 97.
17. Vanderwood, "The Picture Postcard as Historical Evidence," 214.
18. Brazilians seem to be in the forefront in attempting to define how photographs can be employed rigorously in history; see Kossoy, *Fotografía e historia*; and Mauad, "Fotografía e historia."
19. See Becker, *The Heavenly City of the Eighteenth-Century Philosophers*, 1–33, 72–73. I have offered a critique of one art historian's approach to the photography of the revolution in Chapter 6.
20. The references are to the classic essay of Walter Benjamin, "The Work of Art in the Age of Mechanical Reproduction," reproduced often; to the linguistic theories of Charles Peirce as expounded in "Logic as Semiotic," 102; to the extensive bibliography around the issue of "transparency," as argued by Walton ("Transparent Pictures"), Brook ("On the Alleged Transparency of Photographs"), and Friday ("Transparency and the Photographic Image"), among others; and to Roland Barthes's notion of "That-has-been" (*Camera Lucida*, 80). I have explored this capacity for unintentional documentation in Mraz, "¿Fotohistoria o historia gráfica?", 12.
21. This issue of the thickness or thinness of photographs developed in conversations with Chris Pinney.
22. Lesy, *Wisconsin Death Trip*, "Conclusion," n.p.

23. Levine, *Images of History*, 49. Levine's is an error of "logical types": being shoeless or badly dressed is a condition of some duration; being weary is an immediate state.
24. Lesy anticipates this objection by asserting that Charley Van Schaick, the Wisconsin photographer whom he analyzes, "used plates that permitted half-second exposures" (*Wisconsin Death Trip*, "Introduction," n.p.). He does not, however, examine the conventions for posing in a studio.
25. My discussion of photographic technology during the revolution has a debt to Daniel Escorza; see "Las cámaras fotográficas en los inicios del proceso revolucionario, 1910–1911"; and Escorza Rodríguez and Vera Trejo, "La cámara Graflex."
26. See Guevara Escobar, "Reflex o view."
27. Rosenblum, *A World History of Photography*, 443.
28. I employ the concept of "directed" throughout this work to describe a genre of documentary photography that is characterized by the intervention of the photographer in the scene; see Mraz, "Thinking about Documentary," in *Nacho López*, 169–189, and "What's documentary about photography?".
29. See the covers reproduced in Gautreau, "Questionnement d'un symbole," 96–97.
30. Gautreau, "La Revolución Mexicana a los ojos del mundo," 262.
31. Several comments about the "primitivism" of the photography were made at different lectures in the United States. Perhaps the expectation was for a more photojournalistic imagery, and not the studio format that dominated so much of the early photography of the revolution.
32. Carmichael, *First World War Photographers*, 27; see the photo on p. 50, which was manipulated in printing to remove the breech cover on a rifle because that would have made it clear that it was taken at a training ground.
33. Moeller, *Shooting War*, 126.
34. Carmichael, *First World War Photographers*, vii.
35. Carmichael, *First World War Photographers*, 1–2.
36. Moeller, *Shooting War*, 109–110.
37. Moeller, *Shooting War*, 125. Moeller is discussing US photographers, while Carmichael analyzes the British. My own limited research in British, French, Italian, and German photography of World War I generally confirms Moeller's appreciation.
38. Carmichael, *First World War Photographers*, 71.
39. On the contest of *Le Miroir*, see Beurier, *Images et violence, 1914–1918*; and *Soldati fotografi*. Carmichael also notes that "The press even mounted competitions to attract submissions from men serving on the Western Front" (*First World War Photographers*, 30), but she does not identify the publications.
40. Carmichael, *First World War Photographers*, 44.
41. Baschet, *Russia 1904–1924*.
42. Baschet, *Russia 1904–1924*, 140–141, 144.
43. Baschet, *Russia 1904–1924*, 143.
44. Baschet, *Russia 1904–1924*, 10–18; Riis, *How the Other Half Lives*; Turner, *Barbarous Mexico*.

45. Baschet, *Russia 1904–1924*; see especially 242–243.
46. Baschet, *Russia 1904–1924*, 104–107.
47. I am critical of his picturesque photography in Mraz, *Looking for Mexico*, 77–82.
48. Brehme, "Hugo Brehme: Una vida entre la tradición y la modernidad," 13.
49. The bibliography on Brehme is growing, but scholarly studies are lacking. See Brehme's photographs in *México: Una nación persistente*, *México pintoresco*, *Pueblos y paisajes de México*, and *Hugo Brehme: Fotograf-fotógrafo*.
50. See a selection of photos in Cabrera Luna, *Hugo Brehme y la Revolución Mexicana*.
51. The references to Brehme's importance in constructing a visual nationalism are numerous. See Rodríguez, "La construcción de un imaginario," 39; Lerner, "La exportación de lo mexicano," 30; and Mendoza Áviles, "La colección Hugo Brehme," 43; as well as Garduño Pulido, "Mexico's Enduring Images," 15.
52. Vanderwood and Samponaro, *Border Fury*, 18, 130, 131.
53. Leyda, *Films Beget Films*, 113.
54. Leighton, "The Photographic History of the Mexican Revolution," in Brenner, *The Wind that Swept Mexico*, 288.
55. Debroise, *Mexican Suite*, 174.
56. See the extensive photographic collections in Hanoi (Museum of Vietnam Revolution) and Ho Chi Minh City (War Remnants Museum), as well as *Memorial of a Glorious Time* and *Vietnam, 1954-1975*.
57. I am grateful to Daniel Escorza for information about the lack of photos picturing demonstrations in favor of Díaz.
58. Acosta, "Miguel Ángel Berumen," 47.
59. Berumen was surprised not to find negatives of Villa in the archive of the Cachú brothers, given their relation to the Villista cause, but speculated, "It would not have been strange to get rid of them in that moment, just like any other document that would tie them to him and put both them and their families at risk" (*México: Fotografía y revolución*, 283).

CHAPTER 1

1. Gutiérrez Ruvalcaba, "A Fresh Look at the Casasola Archive," 194.
2. Debroise, *Mexican Suite*, 184. Gutiérrez Ruvalcaba questions the idea that Porfirian photography is dominated by conventional poses ("A Fresh Look at the Casasola Archive," 191), as does Escorza Rodríguez ("Los inicios de Agustín V. Casasola," 27, and "El itinerario fotoperiodístico de Agustín Víctor Casasola," 21).
3. I discuss Modotti's oft-reproduced photomontage *Los de arriba y los de abajo*, of a poor man seated beneath an advertisement from a fashionable men's store, in Mraz, *Looking for Mexico*, 83–84.
4. The amount of the subsidy seems correct, and other papers received much less (García, *El periódico "El Imparcial,"* 59). Both Reyes Espíndola and Limantour wrote openly about the

subsidy after the Porfiriato. Although its importance is debated, I think it is clear that it was pivotal in allowing him to establish his preeminence.

5. Alan Knight comments on "the end of ideology" during the Porfiriato in *The Mexican Revolution*, vol. 1, 15.
6. The subtitle disappeared two years later (García, *El periódico "El Imparcial,"* 31).
7. "Se cumplió en Chalco la pena de muerte impuesta a los reos Arcadio Jiménez y sus camaradas," *El País*, 30 April 1909, 1. Whether the crime and punishment had social origins is difficult to determine. The trial lasted almost two years, and neither it nor the execution were covered in the main opposition paper, *El Diario del Hogar*. Nonetheless, one can well imagine that in Mexico of 1909 the conflict must have had a history, as well as a sequel.
8. "Se forma el cuadro," *El Imparcial*, 30 April 1909, 1.
9. De la Torre Rendón, "Las imágenes fotográficas de la sociedad mexicana," 354. Jane Carmichael found the same difference in Great Britain between the newspapers and magazines: "Photography in newspapers was usually identified with the cheap end of the market. . . . In contrast, the weekly magazines appealed to a better-off audience" (*First World War Photographers*, 6).
10. Del Castillo Troncoso, "El surgimiento del reportaje policiaco en México," 186.
11. Lara Ruiz and Lara Ruiz, "Los 'Caranclanes,'" 124.
12. Piccato, *City of Suspects*, 21.
13. Piccato, *City of Suspects*, 31.
14. Piccato, *City of Suspects*, 31.
15. Lear, *Workers, Neighbors, and Citizens*, 42.
16. This list is compiled from the description provided by Francisco Mejía in Saborit, *"El Mundo Ilustrado" de Rafael Reyes Espíndola*, 245–273.
17. On Kahlo, see Mraz, *Looking for Mexico*, 38–42.
18. Escorza Rodríguez, "El itinerario," 19.
19. Dolores Casasola Zapata remembered, "My father never let go of his camera . . . getting the photo was his true passion" (Malvido, "Archivo Casasola," 36).
20. Casasola was evidently providing images to two illustrated magazines, *El Tiempo Ilustrado* and *El Mundo Ilustrado*, during the transition to becoming a full-time photojournalist (Moreno Irázabal, "Figuras del periodismo mexicano," 6). Escorza asserts that he was working for *El Tiempo* and the *Seminario Literario Ilustrado* in this period ("El itinerario," 26). Agustín Víctor's son Gustavo attributes the bonus to Agustín Víctor's contstruction of a platform that he attached to a telephone pole in order to take photos of an execution in 1907 from which photojournalists had been barred (*Historia gráfica de la Revolución Mexicana*, 2321–2323); this story is repeated by Altúzar ("Agustín Víctor Casasola," 28), as well as in Arroyo and Casanova, "The Casasolas: An Everyday Epic," 205. However, the photographer is identified as José Soriano in the article ("Fusilamiento de los asesinos del Gral. Barillas," *El Imparcial*, 10 September 1907, 1). The true story of the bonus can be found in Moreno Irázabal, "Figuras del periodismo mexicano," 6, and the receipt, dated 31 October 1910, can be seen in *Historia*

gráfica de la Revolución Mexicana, 2323. It is at least curious that Gustavo was so eager to link this recognition to *nota roja* rather than sports.

21. Debroise, *Mexican Suite*, 184. Altúzar asserts that Casasola went to the port on assignment for *El Imparcial* ("Agustín Víctor Casasola," 29).
22. For example, Alejandro Castellanos, currently director of the Centro de la Imagen, wrote, "Without doubt, the most important photographer at the beginning of the century in Mexico was Agustín Víctor Casasola" ("Del México postal a la revolución iconográfica," 17), an affirmation he repeated two years later in "Notas sobre fotografía y sociedad mexicanas," 13. Escorza is developing an investigation of the activities of this photojournalist that promises to deepen our knowledge of him and this period (see Escorza, "El itinerario").
23. "Artistas fotógrafos mexicanos," *El Tiempo Ilustrado*, 1 January 1906, 21–22. The following photographers were found to be worthy of mention: Señor Moreno, Manuel Torres, Ramón Peón del Valle, Antíoco Cruces, Frank Clarke, Emilio Lange, and Emilio Rivoire.
24. Teresa Ramos Sánchez, cited by Maldonado Valera, "Manuel Ramos en la prensa ilustrada," 44.
25. Maldonado Valera, "Manuel Ramos en la prensa ilustrada," 222; Saborit comments that Ramos was "the magazine's photographer" (*"El Mundo Ilustrado" de Rafael Reyes Espíndola*, 190).
26. Teresa Ramos Sánchez, cited by Maldonado Valera, "Manuel Ramos en la prensa ilustrada," 44.
27. *Arte y Letras*, 31 October 1909; cited by Maldonado Valera, "Manuel Ramos en la prensa ilustrada," 117.
28. Alvarado, *La reconstrucción de México*, 32. About the image of Díaz as a military figure, see Gautreau, "Militar o político."
29. González Navarro, *Sociedad y cultura en el porfiriato*, 28.
30. Maldonado Valera, "Manuel Ramos en la prensa ilustrada," 147.
31. Teresa Ramos Sánchez, cited by Maldonado Valera, "Manuel Ramos en la prensa ilustrada," 154.
32. Gutiérrez Rubalcava, "A Fresh Look at the Casasola Archive," 191.
33. About Waite, see Montellano, *C. B. Waite, fotógrafo*; about Scott, see Malagón Girón, "La fotografía de Winfield Scott." See my analysis of Waite and Scott in Mraz, *Looking for Mexico*, 33–36.
34. See these photos in Montellano, *C. B. Waite, fotógrafo*, 41–44.
35. Vargas Sánchez, "La ciudad de México de 1900 a 1920," 175.
36. See Rodríguez Hernández, "Niños desnudos en el porfiriato"; and Montellano, *C. B. Waite, fotógrafo*, 81.
37. See Edwards, "Pretty Babies," 39.
38. Malagón Girón, "La fotografía de Winfield Scott," 279–285.
39. "Las hazañas de un fotógrafo," *El Imparcial*, 5 June 1901, 2.
40. "Las hazañas de un fotógrafo," 2.
41. "El asunto del fotógrafo Waite," *El Imparcial*, 8 June 1901, 2.

42. See the list in Eduardo Ancira, "Fotógrafos de la luz aprisionada," 347.
43. García, *Crónica oficial de las fiestas del primer centenario de la independencia de México*, 150; pp. 148–165 show some thirty-three buildings and houses strung extensively with lights. See also Morales, "Luces y sombras del Centenario I."
44. These two photos by Brehme are part of a previously unknown collection, the "Hoffman," which was acquired by the INAH in the course of activities for the 2010 centennial.
45. See the photo of the troops separating the masses from the rich, who have the best spots to see the historical parade, in "La fiesta interrumpida," *Proceso Bi-Centenario* (6 September 2009): 28–29.
46. Lara Ruiz and Lara Ruiz, "Los 'Caranclanes,'" 123.
47. On Horne, see Vanderwood and Samponaro, *Border Fury*.
48. Anderson, *Outcasts in Their Own Land*, 177.

CHAPTER 2

1. The nickname of González Garza is mentioned in Berumen, *1911*, 192. It would appear that this way of posing was what Roque considered appropriate to the situation; see the photo of him and his brother, Federico, where the latter returns the photographer's (Arriaga's) look while Roque gazes off at history (del Castillo Troncoso, *Isidro Fabela*, 84).
2. Sontag, *On Photography*, 38.
3. E. Herrerías took photos in a more documentary vein; for example, the cavalry of Lucio Blanco (INAH 373894) and Maderistas "Blowing up a bridge" (INAH 373892).
4. See *La Semana Ilustrada*, 24 November 1911, which documents the strike, "uncommon in Mexico City," and the protests in Huatusco.
5. I am grateful to Abraham Guerrero for his research in photo archives of Monterrey and Coahuila that revealed this aspect of González, and for our conversations on this theme.
6. Guzmán, *El águila y la serpiente*, 337.
7. Guzmán, *El águila y la serpiente*, 89–90.
8. Reed, *Insurgent Mexico*, 13–15.

CHAPTER 3

1. Gutiérrez Ruvalcaba, "Los Casasola durante la posrevolución," 37.
2. On "the Revolutionary Family," see Benjamin, *La Revolución*.
3. Rosenblum, *A World History of Photography*, 184.
4. Trachtenberg, *Reading American Photographs*, 33.
5. Debroise, *Mexican Suite*, 185; Arroyo and Casanova, "The Casasolas," 207.
6. *Novedades*, 22 January 1913. For another example of a photojournalist who reprographed images, see the copy that Antonio Garduño made (and signed) of one of the photos of the famous meeting of Madero in the Casa de Adobe (INAH 33506) (published in Rosas, "El primer jefe," 40–41); Berumen published the same photo signed by "FK" (*1911*, 86).

7. Gautreau, "*La Ilustración Semanal* y el Archivo Casasola," 115.
8. [Agustín Casasola], *Albúm histórico gráfico*. Ignacio Gutiérrez states that he "affirmed in the prologue of the *Albúm* that he was the photographer of the Mexican Revolution" (Gutiérrez Ruvalcaba, "Los Casasola durante la posrevolución," 37). None of the copies of the album that I have seen substantiate this; moreover, it is difficult to believe that he would have written something like that just a few years after the armed struggle had ended, because the photojournalists whose images were published would have objected.
9. Moreno Irázabal, "Figuras del periodismo mexicano," 6. Of course, by the time of the Querétaro congress the fighting was largely over, and the Constitutionalists had won.
10. "Murió ayer Agustín Víctor Casasola, el decano de los fotógrafos de México," *La Prensa*, 31 March 1938, 21.
11. *Agustín Víctor Casasola*, 12.
12. Cited in *Agustín Víctor Casasola*, 11.
13. Casasola, *Historia gráfica de la Revolución Mexicana*, 2323.
14. "Don Agustín Casasola Velasco," *Siempre!*, 31 July 1974, 67.
15. *Agustín Víctor Casasola*, 11.
16. Gutiérrez Ruvalcaba, "A Fresh Look at the Casasola Archive," 193–194.
17. Arroyo and Casanova, "The Casasolas," 205.
18. Malvido, "Relata la familia Casasola el devenir de su archivo de fotos," 24.
19. See Gutiérrez Ruvalcaba, "A Fresh Look at the Casasola Archive," 193; Gautreau, "El Archivo Casasola y la representación de la Revolución Mexicana" and "Questionnement d'un symbole."
20. See Gould and Greffe, *Photojournalist*, 100–115. More recently, Miguel Ángel Berumen has analyzed the photography of this combat (see *1911*).
21. "Casasola," 100; "The Casasola Archive is that . . . which is most filtrated in national identity" (Ochoa Sandy, "Historia de un archivo," 11).
22. A publishing history of the Casasolas would be a formidable task. *Historia gráfica de la Revolución* was evidently first published in 1942 and covered the period 1900-1940. In the credits Gustavo Casasola attributes the collecting of materials and the photography to Agustín Víctor, noting that he (Gustavo) directed and finished it; a version of this work was republished in the 1950s. In the 1960s the series became the *Historia gráfica de la Revolución Mexicana*, with a five-volume collection published by Editorial Trillas that extended the period covered to 1960. In 1973 Trillas expanded this to a ten-volume set, which it republished in 1992; this series takes the revolution up to 1970. *Seis siglos de historia gráfica de México* seems to have first appeared in 1962 and has always been published by Gustavo Casasola. The second set was published in 1967-69; the third series appeared in 1971; the fourth version was published in 1978; the latest version appeared in 1989 and was published by the Editorial Gustavo Casasola in conjunction with the Consejo Nacional para la Cultura y las Artes. See Mraz, "Representing the Mexican Revolution," "Picturing Mexico´s Past," and *Looking for Mexico*.
23. See the *proemio* in volume 1, *Albúm histórico gráfico*.

24. Casasola, “Palabras del autor,” *Historia gráfica de la Revolución Mexicana*, vi.
25. Pacheco, “Gustavo Casasola,” 123; Casasola, *Historia gráfica de la Revolución Mexicana*, 2324.
26. See Casasola, *Agustín Víctor Casasola: El hombre que retrató una época*, a book subsidized at least in part by the car manufacturer Chrysler de México.
27. See the essays by Mario Luis Altúzar and Mario Orozco Rivera, in which these statements can be found on pp. 19, 36, and 78 of Casasola, *Agustín Víctor Casasola*. Altúzar wrote the book’s key essay and was undoubtedly little more than Gustavo’s mouthpiece because he states (p. 37) that his prior contact with the Casasola Archive came when he first saw its images in John Womack’s *Zapata and the Mexican Revolution*.
28. Casasola’s speech was published in *La Semana Ilustrada*, 3 November 1911, where it is accompanied by a photo of Casasola standing next to the president. It is reproduced in Casasola, *Agustín Víctor Casasola*, 61; and Ancira, “Fotógrafos de la luz aprisionada,” 347.
29. See the photo published in *La Semanal Ilustrada*, 20 October 1911; and Casasola, *Agustín Víctor Casasola*, 62.
30. Monroy Nasr, “Ezequiel Carrasco”; I am grateful to Rebeca for sharing this unpublished manuscript with me. On *costumbrismo*, see Mraz, *Looking for Mexico*, 28–29.
31. Moreno Irázabal, “Figuras del periodismo mexicano,” 15.
32. I discuss the interview in El Jilguero in Chapter 5.
33. See the photo of Agustín Víctor with the banner in the center of the protest in Casasola, *Agustín Víctor Casasola*, 63.

CHAPTER 4

1. Rivero, *Hacia la verdad*, 22. Of course, it would have been difficult for Madero not to conceive of photojournalists from the official press as “enemies.”
2. See the cases described by Berumen, *1911*, 50.
3. Berumen, *1911*, 85.
4. Abitia Garcés, “Memorias de un fotógrafo constitucionalista,” 1. All the quotations in this and the following paragraph come from this text.
5. Berumen, *1911*, 41.
6. Berumen asserts that only 10 percent of the photos they found to analyze the battle for Ciudad Juárez were taken by Mexicans (*1911*, 22).
7. Berumen, *1911*, 58. Rivero (*Hacia la verdad*, 82) affirms that Fernando Ramírez de Aguilar, war correspondent for *El Imparcial*, was present at the Casas Grandes battle on 6 March 1911. Ramírez does not appear to have been a photographer.
8. On Ignacio Herrerías, see Berumen, *México: Fotografía y revolución*, 382. See Herrerías with his camera in Berumen, *1911*, 25, though it is difficult to know which photos he took because he was given images as well (see Aguirre Benavides, *Madero el inmaculado*, 228). El Archivo General de la Nación (AGN) has twenty-four photos that Herrerías made during 1911 of leaders in Ciudad Juárez. See two of his photos in Casasola, *Historia gráfica de la Revolución Mexicana*, 250, 293.

9. Berumen, *1911*, 25.
10. See these Strauss photos in Berumen, *1911*, 161, 215.
11. Berumen, *1911*, 157.
12. Berumen, *1911*, 30.
13. This photo can be found in Casasola, *Historia gráfica de la Revolución Mexicana*, 696, although it is identified as being of a Constitutionalist in combat against Huerta's army. Another photo in the Casasola volume (p. 549) that seems to come from the same series—of three revolutionaries seated on some rocks (INAH 33510)—is identified as being of Carrancistas in Espinazo, Coahuila, in 1913.
14. The newspaper is cited in Delgadillo, "Legionarios de la luz," Chapter 2, p. 1.
15. Berumen, *México: Fotografía y revolución*, 293.
16. Cited in Gould and Greffe, *Photojournalist*, 74.
17. Berumen, *México: Fotografía y revolución*, 38.
18. Berumen, *1911*, 26. All the citations in this paragraph come from this book.
19. One could argue that the change of clothing was a normal result of having risen in rank, and not a reaction to the cameras. It is worth pointing out that Emiliano Zapata always dressed differently than his followers: he as a *charro*, they as campesinos.
20. See the refugees on the border in Vanderwood and Samponaro, *Border Fury*, 85, 139–143; and in Berumen, *México: Fotografía y revolución*, 171–173.
21. Berumen, *1911*, 59.
22. See the essays published by Arturo Guevara Escobar on the website http://fotografosdelarevolucion.blogspot.com; and Berumen, *México: Fotografía y revolución*, 383.
23. Ocañas and Toscano are cited in Miquel, *Salvador Toscano*, 49, 56.
24. About Guevara Escobar, see http://fotografosdelarevolucion.blogspot.com; and Berumen, *México: Fotografía y revolución*, 314–319, 382.
25. See Guevara Escobar, "El exilio" and "La fotografía de Emiliano Zapata," 23.
26. Miller and Miller, *Picture Postcards in the United States*, 22.
27. Griffiths, "La postal mexicana," 11.
28. See another photo of this scene, INAH 373856. In this period Wells Fargo offered messenger service and transportation in Mexico, but not banking; see "History of Wells Fargo Bank" on the website "Wikipedia: The Free Encyclopedia" (wikipedia.org).
29. Delgadillo, "Legionarios de la luz," Chapter 3, p. 9.
30. INAH 373836, INAH 373854. Arturo Guevara sent me another from this series, "No. 150," on which appears the identification of "Lieutenant Engineer Y. Reyes Retana."
31. This information was provided personally by Arturo Guevara Escobar, 20 November 2010; I appreciate his generosity.
32. Personal communication, 20 November 2010.
33. See Guevara Escobar, "Reflex o view."
34. See another photo in the AGN of Perry taken a few minutes before (because it bears the number 147).

35. Archivo González Garza, Universidad Panamericana. The Herlinda in Figure 4–16 is Herlinda González, according to the writing on the back by her father, Francisco González. This Herlinda was recognized as a veteran of the first phase of the revolution and given the decoration of "Revolutionary Merit" by the secretary of national defense; see *Edición gráfica conmemorativa al Centenario de la Revolución Mexicana*, 58.
36. Douglas C. Nance, "Contador, asaltabancos, mercenario, héroe revolucionario: ¿De cualquier modo, quién es ese hombre en la postal?", presentation in the congress "Los usos documentales de la fotografía en la investigación social," Instituto Mora, 2002.
37. However, see another copy of this photo with different writing in *Edición gráfica conmemorativa al Centenario de la Revolución Mexicana*, 58.
38. Cano, *Se llamaba Elena Arizmendi*, 98–99.
39. Cano, *Se llamaba Elena Arizmendi*, 25. Cano argues that Arizmendi should be seen as part of the generation of modern women, such as Frida Kahlo, Antonieta Rivas Mercado, and Carmen Mondragón (Nahui Ollin), 27.
40. See the lithograph reproduced in Cano, *Se llamaba Elena Arizmendi*, 131.
41. According to Daniel Escorza, all the images of the H. J. Gutiérrez agency in the Fototeca Nacional are postcards (personal communication, 27 October 2009).
42. Curiosly, all the photos of the celebration of the triumph have writing by hand on them rather than the stamp that is common on the photos of the H. J. Gutiérrez agency (Berumen, *1911*, 210).
43. See the photos INAH 373862 and INAH 373849. The different writing on the photos makes it difficult to know which of the photographers associated with the Gutiérrez agency made the images.
44. See the photos in *Así fue la Revolución Mexicana*, vol. 2, 202, 203, 199. The photos of the PND are INAH 373924, INAH 373928, INAH 373930; they can be seen in Casasola, *Historia gráfica de la Revolución Mexicana*, 110, 111, where they have been cropped to eliminate the signature of H. J. Gutiérrez.
45. In another version of this scene (INAH 373867) the young man in the center lunges toward the camera.
46. The photo is in the Archivo González Garza, Universidad Panamericana.
47. The photos that refer to the "popular candidate" are INAH 373922, INAH 373933, and INAH 373925. The photo of Cuernavaca is in the Archivo González Garza, Universidad Panamericana.
48. See Hernández in INAH 373879 and INAH 373830; the photo from Jalisco is INAH 373871.
49. It would appear that Mauricio Yáñez later moved to Monterrey, according to signatures on images reproduced in Treviño, *160 años de fotografía en México* (629, 630). The photos by Yáñez published in Pavelka, *Monterrey en 400 fotografías*, are signed differently (35, 40). Nonetheless, photographic researcher José Antonio Rodríguez stated that Yáñez signed in one way in his first period but changed his signature in the 1930s (personal communication, 30 October 2009). See the information about Yáñez in Rodríguez's essay "Testimonios de la

fotografía en Monterrey." Berumen distinguishes between the studio of "Yáñez y Guillén" in Mazatlán, Sinaloa, and that of Mauricio Yáñez, who arrived in Monterrey in 1917 and associated himself with Jesús Sandoval (*México: Fotografía y revolución*, 386). Nonetheless, Rodríguez says he knows of no other Yáñez, and, moreover, this photographer "traveled much in Mexico—he was in Zacatecas, Guadalajara, Chiapas, etc.—making portraits and postcards" (personal communication).

50. See the photos of Antuna and Meléndez (or Tirado, since the photo identifies Meléndez, but the cutline says the leader is Tirado) in Casasola, *Historia gráfica de la Revolución Mexicana*, 489 and 273.
51. See the cutline of this photo in *La Semana Ilustrada*, 28 April 1911. The published photo does not bear Yáñez's signature.
52. *Crónica ilustrada Revolución Mexicana*, 19.
53. Casasola, *Historia gráfica de la Revolución Mexicana*, 490, 489; INAH 36869, INAH 36804.
54. Casasola, *Historia gráfica de la Revolución Mexicana*, 784; *La Ilustración Semanal*, 17 February 1914. Yáñez covered the US presence in the port of Mazatlán (*La Ilustración Semanal*, 6 July 1914).
55. Berumen, *México: Fotografía y revolución*, 383; personal communication, 27 October 2009. Among the surviving photos of Harris, see Madero on horseback, Chihuahua, February 1911 (INAH 34358) and "Revolucionarios en Santiago" (INAH 373890). This last photo was published in Treviño, *160 años de fotografía en México*, where it is asserted that Harris was active in Mexico City during 1912 (311, 672).
56. Berumen, *México: Fotografía y revolución*, 381.
57. The AGN has seven photos of Arriaga taken at the border. See *Así fue la Revolución Mexicana*, vol. 2, 257; Treviño, *160 años de fotografía en México*, 98. Delgadillo says that Jesús Arriaga made the photos of Maderismo ("Legionarios de la luz," Chapter 2, p. 6); Berumen says it was José Arriaga (*México: Fotografía y revolución*, 381).
58. The AGN has four photos by Andrade. See the photo in Treviño, *160 años de fotografía en México*, 90.
59. INAH 186665.
60. "F. K. MEXICO" could be an agency that, like the Casasola and Gutiérrez agencies, employed different photographers and acquired photos; see the photos of the centenary in *Proceso Bi-Centenario*, no. 3, June 2009, 6, 10, as well as an image from the border and one of a woman revolutionary *coronela* (3, 17); Berumen, *1911*, 86.
61. Berumen signaled the affiliation of Carmona in *México: Fotografía y revolución*, 386. See the photos in Casasola, *Historia gráfica de la Revolución Mexicana*, 403; one by Villalobos of the reception was published in *El Mundo Ilustrado*, 15 October 1911.
62. *La Semana Ilustrada*, 14 April 1911. See them published in Berumen, *1911*, 112; and Casasola, *Historia gráfica de la Revolución Mexicana*, 245.
63. Berumen, *México: Fotografía y revolución*, 384.
64. The photo can be found in INAH-Chihuahua, no. 2026; Berumen mentions the case in *1911*, 50.

65. INAH, 32479; Casasola, *Historia gráfica de la Revolución Mexicana*, 453.
66. Casasola, *Historia gráfica de la Revolución Mexicana*, 261.
67. *La Semana Ilustrada*, 14 April 1911 (my emphasis); *La Semana Ilustrada*, 5 May 1911.
68. *La Semana Ilustrada*, 31 March 1911.
69. *La Semana Ilustrada*, 26 May 1911; the photos of Tinoco and Herrerías appeared in this issue of the magazine.
70. *La Semana Ilustrada*, 26 May 1911. In 1911 Gonzalo Rivero brought out *Hacia la verdad*, a book about the aftermath of the battle for Ciudad Juárez, which was illustrated with Tinoco's photos.
71. *La Semana Ilustrada*, 19 May 1911. Although the magazine asserted that their correspondent had taken the photos, Tinoco did not arrive until after the battle for Ciudad Juárez.
72. Guzmán, *El águila y la serpiente*, 337.
73. *La Semana Ilustrada*, 9 June 1911.
74. *El Mundo Ilustrado*, 3 September 1911.
75. *El Mundo Ilustrado*, 23 July 1911; 22 October 1911.
76. Larrain, "Historia de la fotografía de prensa," 63. When Hernández retired from photojournalism, he gave his archive to Agustín Víctor, and it became part of the Archivo Casasola, in which this photo can be found (Berumen, *México: Fotografía y revolución*, 383).
77. See Madero with the photojournalists in *La Semana Ilustrada*, 22 December 1911; and in Casasola, *Historia gráfica de la Revolución Mexicana*, 431.
78. Magaña, *Emiliano Zapata y el agrarismo en México*, 209. A photo of Madero made by "Rousset y Magaña" can be seen in Treviño, *160 años de fotografía en México*, 534; it is found in the AGN, which has a group of photos by this collective. Benito may not have been a photographer; he declared himself to be a businessman when he crossed the border into the United States, while his brothers said they were photographers (Christine Rousset, personal communication, based on the register of their border crossing, January 2011). I am grateful to Christine for providing me with photos and information.
79. La France, *The Mexican Revolution in Puebla, 1908-1913*, 9. See "Corrido antirreeleccionista," evidently written by Samuel Margarito Lozano, in Avitia Hernández, *Corridos históricos mexicanos*, 265–268.
80. They evidently owned a furniture factory and ranches in the state of Puebla (Javier Pérez Siller, personal communication, December 2010).
81. "Compañeros de Serdán se hallan en México," *Diario del Hogar*, 22 June 1911, front page.
82. "Aprehensiones y cateos en busca de 500 armas de la conspiración fallida," *El País*, 17 November 1910, front page.
83. See Aldo Roberto Rivero Pastor, "Familia Rousset: Proceres de la Revolución Mexicana," unpublished manuscript.
84. "Compañeros de Serdán se hallan en México," *Diario del Hogar*, 22 June 1911, front page.
85. Sánchez Escobar, "Episodios de la revolución en el sur, VII."
86. *Edición gráfica conmemorativa al centenario de la Revolución Mexicana*, 42.

87. La France, *Mexican Revolution in Puebla*, 114.
88. Sánchez Escobar, "Episodios de la Revolución en el sur, VII."
89. Magaña, *Emiliano Zapata y el agrarismo en México*, 211.
90. Archive of Christine Rousset.
91. "Prominent Men of Puebla Sent into the Army," *Mexican Herald*, 10 May 1914, front page.
92. See the photo of the imprisoned Puebla men, with the description of their fate, in the archive of Christine Rousset; *Edición gráfica conmemorativa al centenario de la Revolución Mexicana*, 12, 25, 41.
93. Knight, *Mexican Revolution*, vol. 1, 376. See the photos of the federal army in Juchitán during 1912, taken by a photographer named Mumm; Colección José F. Gómez, Museo de Arte Contemporáneo de Oaxaca.
94. See Benjamin, "Revolución interrumpida." I am grateful to Tom Benjamin for his generous aid in clarifying the Chiapas situation.
95. This narrative is based on Moscoso Pastrana, *Jacinto Pérez*, 37–38.
96. The photo with the giant is INAH 34260. The two photos are published in Casasola, *Historia gráfica de la Revolución Mexicana*, 260.
97. See the reconstruction, as well as a veridical image of Chamulas after their ears had been cut off, in Moscoso Pastrana, *Jacinto Pérez*, 32. Cutting off the Chamulas' ears caused "hilarity" among some of their captors, who thought of it as a "schoolgirl prank" (84).
98. They do not appear in the Moscoso Pastrana book, so they might well have been separated from the other Chiapas images, entering into the Casasola Archive as exotic curiosities.
99. I am here distinguishing between "Indianist" photography, which is that made of Indians by non-Indians, and "Indian" photography, which is that they would take of themselves. On photographing Indians, see Faris, *Navajo and Photography*.
100. Lutz and Collins, *Reading "National Geographic,"* 92.
101. Bhabha, "The Other Question," 70.
102. See the categories of representation in Faris, *Navajo and Photography*, 42. On Rueda's attempts to disarm the groups, see Benjamin, "Revolución interrumpida," 85.
103. On this "partitioning," see Hight and Sampson, "Introduction," 10.
104. Jesús Vargas, personal communication, 22 January 2010.
105. Berumen, *México: Fotografía y revolución*, 384.
106. Treviño, *160 años de fotografía en México*, 678.
107. The photo of the protest is INAH 36799; see it in Casasola, *Historia gráfica de la Revolución Mexicana*, 451. See other photos by Medrano Chávez of the burial in 1913 of Abraham González, INAH 67948 and INAH 68211; and in Treviño, *160 años de fotografía en México*, 413. In 1919 he took a photo of the funeral of Felipe Ángeles in Chihuahua (Archivo González Garza, Universidad Panamericana). This photographer is not to be confused with José Antonio Bustamante Martínez, about whom Acevedo and Morales published a book, *El Gran Lente*.
108. INAH 36800.
109. Escorza Rodríguez and Vera Trejo, "La cámara Graflex," 262.

110. See Whelan, *Robert Capa*, 211.
111. Stomberg, "August Sander," 1383. I thank journalist Blanca González for her observation.
112. I am grateful to Daniel Escorza for the information about the publication of this image in *El Imparcial*, 27 June 1912, and for our conversation. Casasola identified these soldiers as "The warring forces of the División del Norte," *Historia gráfica de la Revolución Mexicana*, 1016. Nonetheless, Villa was a teetotaler and did not tolerate his troops drinking alcohol. Hence, when the cutline of the lithograph in the newspaper refers to "the revolutionaries," it is talking about Orozquistas, and one can imagine that portraying them as drunks was one way to criticize that movement. I thank Jaime Vélez for his careful reading of this image.
113. Some thirty-six photos of this period identified as being from La Rochester are in the AGN; some can be seen in *Así fue la Revolución Mexicana*, vol. 3, 370–372, 377.
114. I am paraphrasing Roland Barthes, *Camera Lucida*, 80.
115. General Guillermo Rubio Navarrete, undated letter, cited by Katz, *Life and Times of Pancho Villa*, 165.
116. Pancho Villa, in conversation with Manuel Bauche Alcalde, undated; cited by Katz, *The Life and Times of Pancho Villa*, 166.
117. Knight, *Mexican Revolution*, vol. 1, 390.
118. Diary, 5 February 1913; Tablada, *Obras-IV, Diario (1900–1944)*, 78.

CHAPTER 5

1. The film was made with material filmed by Salvador Toscano, edited by his daughter Carmen Toscano, and premiered in 1950.
2. Pérez Montfort, "Zapata y Villa en la ciudad de México, 1914–1915: Un tema popular con variaciones y fuga," in *Cotidianidades, imaginarios y contextos*, 235. Various authors have made similar observations. Marion Gautreau: "It makes clear another difference between the two leaders: the smiling and confident attitude of Francisco Villa, who seems comfortable in the presidential chair, and the austere face of Emiliano Zapata" ("La Revolución Mexicana a los ojos del mundo," 228); Ávila Espinosa: "We see a smiling, festive, uninhibited Villa sitting in the presidential chair. At his side, the oblique, uncomfortable, hostile, and untrusting gaze of Zapata" ("Villa y Zapata en la Ciudad de México," 45–46).
3. See Mraz, "De la fotografía histórica," 10; "Mexican History in Photographs," 300–301; and "¿Fotohistoria o historia gráfica?", 21. On re-seeing *Memorias de un mexicano* in 2010, I was struck by Zapata's evident mistrust of the camera; moreover, either because of his nervousness or his customs, he cleans himself with his hand and eats with the knife. Zapata was uncomfortable with the Mexico City media, as well he should have been considering their treatment of him and his movement; however, that does not signify that he did not wish to employ modern media in his service.
4. Jiménez and Villela, *Los Salmerón*, 31, 42. I was not without distinguished company in thinking that Zapatismo turned its back on modern media. In June 2009, one of the visual researchers

I most respect, Ángel Miquel, sustained that it was the only movement that did not show a marked interest in promoting itself with images (Segundo Congreso Regional de Fototecas, INAH-Morelos, 2009). In December 2009, historical novelist Paco Ignacio Taíbo II asserted in his presentation at the Feria Internacional del Libro in Guadalajara that "The southern leaders were not conscious of the modern media." It is worth pointing out that this impression is based on the fact that not only are there fewer surviving photos of the Zapatistas than of other movements, but they have also been studied less than the photos of other armies.

5. Jablonska and Leal, *La Revolución Mexicana en el cine nacional, 1911-1917*, 27.
6. Pérez Montfort, "Imágenes del zapatismo entre 1911 y 1913," 163. I am grateful to Ricardo for our conversations on this theme and his generosity in loaning me materials.
7. Gautreau, "La Revolución Mexicana a los ojos del mundo," 224.
8. Arnal, *Atila de tinta y plata*, 52.
9. Application 6502, Instituto Nacional del Derecho de Autor, August 1913; cited in Berumen, *México: Fotografía y revolución*, 282.
10. "Intentonas de los Zapatistas para llegar a la capital," *Novedades*, 5 August 1914. The photos are credited to Antonio Garduño.
11. Pérez Montfort, "Imágenes del zapatismo entre 1911 y 1913," 205.
12. Brunk, *The Posthumous Career of Emiliano Zapata*, 35.
13. Arnal, *Atila de tinta y plata*, 105.
14. Gautreau, "La Revolución Mexicana a los ojos del mundo," 193.
15. Arnal, *Atila de tinta y plata*, 65.
16. Arnal, *Atila de tinta y plata*, 119–123.
17. Arnal, *Atila de tinta y plata*, 122–123.
18. "La bestia humana en Ayotzingo," *Novedades*, 22 January 1913.
19. Gautreau, "La Revolución Mexicana a los ojos del mundo," 193, 189.
20. For an analysis of a photojournalist who made images that went against the grain of the magazines in which he published—and how the periodicals utilized his photos sometimes in ways contradictory to the intended—see Mraz, *Nacho López*.
21. Moreno Irázabal, "Figuras del periodismo mexicano," 15.
22. See the photos published in Casasola, *Historia gráfica de la Revolución Mexicana*, 492–494, and the following images: INAH 5930, INAH 5933, INAH 5935, INAH 5936, INAH 5937.
23. INAH 5853.
24. Moreno Irázabal, "Figuras del periodismo mexicano," 15.
25. Moreno Irázabal, "Figuras del periodismo mexicano," 15.
26. *Artes y Letras*, 18 August 1912.
27. Moreno Irázabal, "Figuras del periodismo mexicano," 15.
28. Magaña, *Emiliano Zapata y el agrarismo en México*, 208.
29. *La Semana Ilustrada*, 7 October 1913.
30. *La Ilustración Semanal*, 3 August 1914.
31. Arnal, *Atila de tinta y plata*, 95.

32. Arnal, *Atila de tinta y plata*, 95.
33. Pérez Montfort, "Imágenes del zapatismo entre 1911 y 1913," 190.
34. Camacho de la Rosa, *Raíz y razón de Totolapan*, 57.
35. *El Imparcial*, 20 August 1912, front page. I should make it clear that the photo included here (INAH 643135) is not that published in the newspaper (INAH 643006); nonetheless, it is obvious that the two photos were made at the same time. The two photos are published in Casasola, *Historia gráfica de la Revolución Mexicana*, 254, where they are presented as if they represent the Zapatista uprising against Díaz in 1911.
36. It is noteworthy that the text mentions two photos, and there are two that survive in the Fondo Casasola of the Fototeca Nacional.
37. Arnal, *Atila de tinta y plata*, 149.
38. Daniel Escorza says that the negative of photo INAH 643006 is a glass plate. Hence, it was not made by a Kodak Brownie, and most probably was made by a professional photographer, whether of photojournalism or postcards, with his view camera; I am grateful to Daniel for this information.
39. Pérez Montfort, "Imágenes del zapatismo entre 1911 y 1913," 187. In the republication of this essay, Pérez Montfort put below this image the following cutline: "Photos evidenced the difference between poorly armed Zapatista campesinos and well-supplied troops" (*Cotidianidades, imaginarios y contextos*, 169).
40. See my remarks on this in the introduction.
41. This phrase has significance in the context of the most famous photo of Robert Capa, which has acquired different titles, among them *Militiaman in His Moment of Death, Spain, 1936*. The journalist O. D. Gallagher was one of the first to question the veracity of the photo, recounting that Capa had said to him, "If you want to get good action photos, they musn't be in true focus. If your hand trembles a little, then you get a fine action shot" (cited in Knightly, *The First Casualty*, 212). Capa titled his autobiography *Slightly Out of Focus* as a way of ridiculing the notion that he needed "tricks" to make combat photos (see Whelan, *Robert Capa*, 97).
42. Casasola, *Historia gráfica de la Revolución Mexicana*, 400.
43. Gutiérrez Ruvalcaba, "A Fresh Look at the Casasola Archive," 193.
44. The identifications on the photo are written on the back of the copy in the Fondo Dr. Andrés Angulo, INAH-Tlaxcala.
45. My analysis of Amando Salmerón is based on Jiménez and Villela, *Los Salmerón*, as well as the photos that appear therein.
46. Jiménez and Villela, *Los Salmerón*, 32–33; see the photo of her on p. 36.
47. Villela, "Imágenes de la Revolución en Guerrero," 171.
48. Text written by Amando Salmerón; cited by Jiménez and Villela, *Los Salmerón*, 37.
49. Without knowing the archive, it is not clear how much Salmerón photographed anti-Zapatista forces; one example is an image of federal officers (Jiménez and Villela, *Los Salmerón*, 53).
50. This photo also provides a sense of the masses involved, something rarely seen in the photography of this period (Jiménez and Villela, *Los Salmerón*, 52).

51. Villela, "Imágenes de la Revolución en Guerrero," 179.
52. Jiménez and Villela, *Los Salmerón*, 53.
53. Chevalier, "Un factor decisivo de la revolución agraria de México," 177.
54. Arnal, *Atila de tinta y plata*, 76. The photos that Arnal analyzes are in Jiménez and Villela, *Los Salmerón*, 44–45.
55. The letter is reproduced in Villela, "La fotografía de la Revolución Mexicana," 84–85.
56. See the brief note in Berumen, *México: Fotografía y revolución*, 385. Some twenty or thirty photos by Sánchez are preserved in the Instituto de Investigaciones sobre la Universidad y la Educación-UNAM. Reproductions were published in Michel, "Cruz Sánchez y su estudio ambulante."
57. Archivo Gildardo y Octavio Magaña, Archivo Histórico de la UNAM, cited in Cubero Piña, "Catálogo fotográfico Fondo Magaña Cerda," 359.
58. Sánchez Escobar, "Episodios de la revolución en el sur: XIV."
59. Sánchez Escobar, "Episodios de la revolución en el sur: XIV."
60. Berumen, *México: Fotografía y revolución*, 385.
61. Sánchez Escobar, "Episodios de la revolución en el sur: XIV."
62. See the hanged neighbor in Magaña, *Emiliano Zapata y el agrarismo en México*, 81; Sánchez Escobar, "Episodios de la revolución en el sur: XIV."
63. Angulo participated in Domingo Arenas's forces, reaching the rank of lieutenant colonel. Conserving the images of this archive has been one of this project's accomplishments; I thank historian Nazario Sánchez for his collaboration. On some of Hernández's photos the following information appears: "Fotografía Hernández, 4th Street Juan A. de la Fuente, Núm. 3" and, at times, "Concepción 3, Puebla." Jorge Carretero, a historian of Puebla photography, told me that during the 1920s there was a photographer by the name of Juan Hernández E. who was a member of the Club Fotográfico de Puebla; it is not clear whether this is the same Hernández that made the photos of Arenas (personal communication, 4 January 2010). I am grateful to Carretero for this information.
64. See Ramírez Rancaño, *La revolución en los volcanes*, 103.
65. Fondo Dr. Andrés Angulo, INAH-Tlaxcala.
66. Villela, *Sara Castrejón*, 21; "La fotografía de la Revolución Mexicana," 81–82; "Imágenes de la Revolución en Guerrero," 168. Villela is probably right, although we need more research on other figures, such as sisters Adriana and Dolores Ehlers, cineastes from Veracruz linked to Constitutionalism, who worked in both photography and film; I discuss them in Chapter 8. Villela cites a newspaper article by William C. Stewart from the *Los Angeles Times* of 3 October 1968 that claims the first woman to photograph a war was Esther Eva Strauss (discussed in Chapter 4); however, Castrejón documented Maderista troops taking Teloloapan fourteen days before Strauss crossed the border to record the battle of Ciudad Juárez.
67. Villela, *Sara Castrejón*, 31–32.
68. Some issues of the magazine from the end of 1914 and the beginning of 1915 refer to a "Sara," but it is not clear who the photographer is (Villela, *Sara Castrejón*, 35–36).

69. For an introduction to Natalia Baquedano, who evidently did not document the revolution, see Bartra, "Women and Portraiture in Mexico," 221–223.
70. Villela, *Sara Castrejón*, 46–47.
71. Villela, *Sara Castrejón*, 49.
72. Villela, *Sara Castrejón*, 50.
73. Carmichael notes of World War I imagery that "one of the frequent criticisms of official photography [was] that it did not sufficiently convey the colossal scale of operations" (*First World War Photographers*, 70).
74. As with all the photographers of the revolution, we are dealing with "survivors"; the archive was sacked upon her death (Villela, *Sara Castrejón*, 20).
75. Villela, *Sara Castrejón*, 108.
76. Villela, "Imágenes de la Revolución en Guerrero," 181; *Sara Castrejón*, 106.
77. For an introduction, see Cano, "Las mujeres como sujetos de la Revolución Mexicana," 275–286. See Lau and Ramos, *Mujeres y revolución, 1900–1917*, for a preliminary study, a selection of photographs, and an anthology of texts.
78. The name of the woman is written on the copy that appeared on the cover of the magazine *Proceso Bi-Centenario*, no. 3 (2009). There is another photo of this woman, taken at another time, and seated in front of an improvised backdrop, INAH 186387.
79. See Amelia/Amelio Robles dressed as a man, INAH 63944. On this fascinating case, see Cano, "Unconcealable Realities of Desire."
80. Cano, "*Soldaderas* and *Coronelas*," 1358.
81. Arnal, *Atila de tinta y plata*, 132.
82. The photo was published in *La Semana Ilustrada*, 15 June 1913 (see Casasola, *Historia gráfica de la Revolución Mexicana*, 656). Santamaría joined the Carrancista movement (Larrain, "Historia de la fotografía de prensa," 63).
83. See the group that poses for several shots in Hoffman-Brehme-INAH; one of these photos has been reproduced often, although it is usually identified as having been made in the Hacienda de San Ángel during 1914. Berumen would appear to be right in asserting that it was taken in Amecameca during 1911 (*México: Fotografía y revolución*, 106–107).
84. See the photo mentioned in [Brehme], *México: Una nación persistente*, 41, which is usually dated as having been taken in 1913.
85. Brehme, "Hugo Brehme," 15.
86. INAH 5130; Casasola, *Historia gráfica de la Revolución Mexicana*, 306. See another photo of Zapatistas taken from above in *Fotografía latinoamericana*, 142.

CHAPTER 6

1. See the list provided by Arturo Guevara Escobar, "La Decena Trágica, los fotógrafos."
2. Friedrich Katz commented on the "phony war" in *The Secret War in Mexico*, 97.
3. Miret had a studio called La Nobleza where he sold a series of forty-eight postcards on La Decena Trágica; Berumen, *México: Fotografía y revolución*, 384.

4. Berumen, *México: Fotografía y revolución*, 384; Morales, "Eduardo Melhado."
5. See the photo signed by Osuna in Krauze, *Madero vivo*, 71.
6. The photo signed by Osuna can be seen in Krauze, *Madero vivo*, 42; that signed by Miret is INAH 451497, and the one without a signature is INAH 451462.
7. The first, signed by Osuna, is in *La Ciudadela de fuego*, 98, and, signed by Miret, INAH 451488. The second photo, signed by Osuna, is in Krauze, *Madero vivo*, 48, and, signed by Miret, INAH 451489.
8. The copy signed by Osuna is in Krauze, *Madero vivo*, 73; Miret's is INAH 451505.
9. Monroy Nasr, "El tripié y la cámara como galardón," 48. It appears that Monroy's analysis was based on the seventy or eighty photos signed by Osuna that are found in the AGN. The photo historian has just completed an analysis of the photojournalist Ezequiel Carrasco, who worked for *Revista de Revistas* during La Decena Trágica; this work, when published, will shed new insights on the photography of this event, among them her contention that the authorship of Osuna's photography is unclear ("Ezequiel Carrasco").
10. Berumen, *México: Fotografía y revolución*, 384.
11. See the photomontage for the album in *La Ciudadela de fuego*, 53; the copy of Osuna is on p. 100.
12. See the discussion of this photo in Arturo Guevara Escobar, "La Decena Trágica, la competencia," with a copy signed by the Gutiérrez agency. The signature of Gutiérrez has been blacked out in this copy of the photo.
13. Guevara Escobar, "La Decena Trágica, los fotógrafos."
14. The clipping appears in Montellano, *C. B. Waite, fotógrafo*, 65. It is not clear from which periodical it was clipped. See the images that Waite made during La Decena Trágica in the Fototeca Nacional and the AGN.
15. See INAH 466631.
16. Osuna or a photojournalist posed some soldiers and civilians in the same spot and with the same machine gun, but the window is open so that the barrel of the gun can be extended; see Krauze, *Madero vivo*, 55, for the photo signed by Osuna, and INAH 37290 for the unsigned photo.
17. Brehme, "Hugo Brehme," 15–17.
18. See photo 073 in Hoffman-Brehme-INAH.
19. Brehme, "Hugo Brehme," 17.
20. Aguilar, *La Decena Trágica*, 129–130. See the description of the experience of reporter Manuel de la Torre, wounded in the battle in front of the National Palace in de Corpas, "Los chicos de la prensa," 10.
21. Casasola, *Agustín Víctor Casasola*, 12.
22. Casasola, *Agustín Víctor Casasola*, 33.
23. Diary, 13 February 1913, Tablada, *Obras-IV, Diario*, 86.
24. *Novedades*, 24 February 1913. In the course of the revolution, Tinoco collaborated as well in *La Semana Ilustrada* and *La Ilustración Semanal*; Gautreau, "La Revolución Mexicana a los ojos del mundo," 192.

25. The photo of Madero on his way to the Zócalo that is signed by Osuna (INAH 451484) was published in *Novedades* on 20 February 1913. In the same issue of the magazine is another photo of a group in the Zócalo looking at some bodies; the copy signed by Osuna is in *La Ciudadela de fuego*, 61. I consider that the credit given in a publication is a better indication of authorship than signed postcards (see the introduction).
26. Ortiz Monasterio, *Jefes, héroes y caudillos*, 33; the following photographers are mentioned in the essay by Flora Lara Klahr, "Agustín Víctor Casasola: Fotógrafo, coleccionista y editor"; "Manuel Ramos, H. J. Gutiérrez, Ezequiel Tostado, A. Melhado [*sic*], S. Osuna and Schlatman" (105–106).
27. That signed by Miret is INAH 451490; it was published in *Novedades* on 20 February 1913.
28. This photo is credited to A. V. Mendoza in *La Ciudadela de fuego*, 89, 146; Monroy asserts, "Alex B. Mendoza and Manuel T. Pérez are the photographers who captured with their cameras the scenes of the incineration of cadavers in Balbuena" ("El tripié y la cámara como galardón," 49). Nonetheless, this photo was published with credit to Tinoco (*Novedades*, 5 March 1913).
29. *Novedades*, 24 February 1913.
30. Maldonado Valera, "Manuel Ramos en la prensa ilustrada," 194–195.
31. After La Decena Trágica, Hernández "abandoned photography" and joined the Constitutionalist army, in which he reached the rank of major (Larrain, "Historia de la fotografía de prensa," 63). When he retired from photojournalism, he gave his archive to Agustín Víctor, and it forms part of the Fondo Casasola (Berumen, *México: Fotografía y revolución*, 383).
32. A group of "Photographs made and collected by Tostado" of "The disastrous effects of the machine-gunning" were published in *La Semana Ilustrada* on 4 March 1913. Photos of La Decena Trágica published in *La Ilustración Semanal* to commemorate the first anniversary are credited to "Melhado, Tostado, and Lupercio," but those that are not Melhado's were made by Tinoco (*La Ilustración Semanal*, 10 February 1914). Lupercio collaborated in *El Heraldo Ilustrado* and *La Ilustración Semanal* during the revolution, but it is not clear if he took photos during the La Decena Trágica (Gautreau, "La Revolución Mexicana a los ojos del mundo," 198). Garduño worked for *El Diario*, *Revista de Revistas*, *Novedades*, and *La Ilustración Semanal* (Larrain, "Historia de la fotografía de prensa," 63). See Garduño's photos of La Decena Trágica in Krauze, *Madero vivo*, 43, 57, 62, 72, 111.
33. See *El Mundo Ilustrado*, 16 February 1913, cover; this photo is in *La Ciudadela de fuego*, 91. The photo of "the winning generals" is published in Krauze, *Francisco I. Madero*, 103. The two photos are preserved in the AGN, which seems to be the best archive of Melhado's work.
34. Morales, "Eduardo Melhado."
35. See the advertisements in *Revista de Revistas* during June and July of 1916.
36. Casanova and Konzevik, *Luces sobre México*, 163. Another Melhado photo that appears to have been posed after the fact is that of Felicistas in Belem jail (*La Ciudadela de fuego*, 77). I suspect that the staged scenes occurred on 18 February and not afterward.
37. *El Mundo Ilustrado*, 16 February 1913.

38. *La Semana Ilustrada*, 28 February 1913.
39. *Novedades*, 24 February 1913.
40. *Novedades*, 20 February 1913.
41. In fact, the White Cross (Cruz Blanca) was created shortly after La Decena Trágica by a revolutionary woman, Leonor Villegas de Magnón; see Villegas de Magnón, *La rebelde*.
42. Krauze, *Madero vivo*, 43.
43. Knight, *The Mexican Revolution*, vol. 1, 457.
44. Meyer, *Huerta*, 98.
45. See the photo of "Juchiteco Indians in Mexico," a battalion that evidently was accompanied by Juchiteca women in fancy dress (*Novedades*, 23 April 1913).
46. Ramírez Plancarte, *La ciudad de México durante la revolución constitucionalista*, 45–46.
47. *La Ilustración Semanal*, 3 March 1914.
48. *La Ilustración Semanal*, 3 March 1914. The photo in the magazine shows a figure behind the women, as if he were instructing them, either in reality or as an act for the camera; the copy in Casasola, *Historia gráfica de la Revolución Mexicana*, 1298, crops the man at the midpoint of his chest. The man was where the blur is in the upper left-hand corner of the photo published here.
49. Casasola, *Historia gráfica de la Revolución Mexicana*, 1298.
50. González, *San José de Gracia*, 133–134.
51. Méndez Alonso, "Recordando un poquito de mi vida," 206.
52. Berumen, *México: Fotografía y revolución*, 283. Berumen asserts that the hanged could have been "federals or revolutionaries"; nonetheless, who would have prohibited taking them down if not the federal authorities? Hence, I believe that the hanged that stayed hung and had to be photographed were Maderistas.
53. Treviño said this in the videotape *Made on Rails: A History of the Mexican Railroad Workers*, directed by John Mraz, with the collaboration of Gloria Tirado, Puebla, Universidad Autónoma de Puebla, 1987; distributed by the Cinema Guild.
54. See fifteen photos of farewells in Casasola, *Historia gráfica de la Revolución Mexicana*, 721–723.
55. Folgarait, *Seeing Mexico Photographed*, 19–26.
56. Folgarait, *Seeing Mexico Photographed*, 22–25.
57. I am indebted to Arturo Guevara Escobar for his perceptive remarks on this photo (personal communication, February 2011).
58. Salas, *Soldaderas in the Mexican Military*, 43.
59. Morales, "La celebre fotografía de Jerónimo Hernández," 72. Morales makes reference to the following articles of mine: "¿Qué tiene de nuevo la historia gráfica?"; "Historia y mito del Archivo Casasola," *La Jornada Semanal*, 31 December 2000, 6–7; and "El Archivo Casasola: Historia de un mito."
60. Knight, *The Mexican Revolution*, vol. 1, 475.
61. *La Ilustración Semanal*, 16 December 1913. I am grateful to Daniel Escorza for information about the publication of another image of these women taken at the same time.

62. See the photo of the students and their captors in Casasola, *Historia gráfica de la Revolución Mexicana*, 575.
63. Lara Ruiz and Lara Ruiz, "Los 'Carranclanes,'" 131–132.
64. Taracena, *La verdadera Revolución Mexicana*, 62.
65. In fact, Tostado is listed as the "Artistic Director" in the masthead, but it is the highest position, and the only other person who therein appears is the manager, Miguel Langarica.
66. Garner, *Disappearing Witness*, xiv.
67. Garner, *Disappearing Witness*, xvi.
68. Rebeca Monroy ("Ezequiel Carrasco") has a different view of Melhado, arguing that his is a nineteenth-century photography of the pose, and that other photojournalists—she identifies Samuel Tinoco, Manuel Ramos, Antonio Garduño, Gerónimo Hernández, Víctor León, and the Casasola brothers—were more aesthetically modern.
69. De Corpas, "Los chicos de la prensa," 29.
70. Evidently, the magazine was founded by Ernesto Chavero, formerly director of *La Semana Ilustrada*, and a pioneer of the illustrated press during the Porfiriato. Nonetheless, his name never appears in the masthead, where Tostado figures most prominently. Marion Gautreau has carried out an analysis of the magazine that focuses on the role of Agustín Víctor Casasola during the revolution ("*La Ilustración Semanal* y el Archivo Casasola").
71. Lucio de Corpas, "Los chicos de la prensa," 29.
72. Debroise, *Mexican Suite*, 187; Berumen, *México: Fotografía y revolución*, 381.
73. On the development of this type of photography, see von Dewitz, *Kiosk: A History of Photojournalism*; and Hardt, "Pictures for the Masses" and "Sites of Reality."
74. "Le 'petit verre' du President Huerta," *L'Illustration*, 20 June 1914, 548–549. This photo was published in *Novedades* on 22 July 1914, a week after Huerta's fall. Gautreau states that "From the month of August of 1914, the French, German, and British magazines abandoned completely any theme not related to the First World War" ("La Revolución Mexicana a los ojos del mundo," 191).
75. See Vanderwood and Samponaro, *Border Fury*.
76. Even a historian as conservative as John S. D. Eisenhower asserted, "In the United States, the bulk of the public reaction reflected dismay and a desire for peace" (*Intervention! The United States and the Mexican Revolution*, 128).
77. See the photo ggbain 16376, Library of Congress Prints and Photographic Division, http://hdl.loc.gov/loc.pnp/pp.print.
78. Vanderwood, "The Picture Postcard as Historical Evidence," 205.
79. Quirk, *An Affair of Honor*, 123.
80. See the Hare photos published in the British magazine *Sphere* in Gautreau, "La Revolución Mexicana a los ojos del mundo," 218–223.
81. *La Ilustración Semanal*, 18 May 1914.
82. *La Ilustración Semanal*, 25 May 1914 and 8 June 1914.
83. *La Ilustración Semanal*, 20 July 1914. The part of the Geneva Convention relating to the treatment of prisoners was not signed until 1929.

84. It is not clear where Melhado's photos were published, but postcards signed by him can be found in Martínez, *La intervención norteamericana*; they are in the AGN. Miguel Ángel Morales affirms that "It is a mystery whether these photos were made by him, or correspondents, or Mexico City photojournalists who had gone to cover the military occupation" ("Eduardo Melhado"). Although there is one or another photo of the invasion that bears the seal "A.V. CASASOLA" (not the usual identification found on his imagery), it does not appear that he went to the port in this period (INAH 287426). Among those who clearly did not go are Abraham Lupercio, Ezequiel Álvarez Tostado, and Antonio Garduño.
85. Although these photos are signed by Ponciano Flores Pérez, the fact that I found Figure 6-31 credited to Tinoco in *La Ilustración Semanal* (11 May 1914) makes me think that Tinoco took it. I should point out that the previous argument I developed in comparing the photos of Flores Pérez and Melhado was mistaken; see Mraz, "Representing the Mexican Revolution," 27–30. This house must have been a favorite place for staging resistance photos, as a third exists in which riflemen shoot toward the enemy (the bodies on the ground are both distinct from those in Figures 6-31 and 6-32, and in different positions) (*Proceso*, Edición Especial, no. 31, November 2010, 77).
86. They were published in *La Ilustración Semanal*, 4 May 1914 and 11 May 1914.
87. *Novedades*, 22 July 1914.
88. *La Semana Ilustrada*, 2 June 1914. Francisco Rivera Ávila, a Veracruzano who lived during the occupation as a child, had a different take; he said that "The *gringo* soldiers, faced with the scarcity of food, had to open the stores with axes in order to distribute the goods among the population; they gave my mother beans, sugar, cooking oil, fruits, and vegetables" (cited in Ricardo Pérez Montfort, "La invasión a Veracruz en 1914: Aproximaciones a la vida cotidiana de un puerto ocupado," in *Cotidianidades, imaginarios y contextos*, 209–210).
89. *La Ilustración Semanal*, 4 May 1914, 11 May 1914, 18 May 1914; *La Ilustración Semanal*, 4 May 1914; *Novedades*, 20 May 1914; *La Semana Ilustrada*, 2 June 1914.
90. *Novedades*, 6 May 1914.
91. *La Semana Ilustrada*, 28 April 1914.
92. Cited by Pérez Montfort, *Cotidianidades, imaginarios y contextos*, 197.
93. *La Semana Ilustrada*, 28 April 1914.
94. *Novedades*, 10 June 1914.
95. *La Ilustración Semanal*, 21 September 1914.
96. There are nineteen photos attributed to Miret in *La Semana Ilustrada*, 2 June 1914. Two of them show cadavers in the street, but they are images that are known to have circulated before as postcards and were probably taken by U.S. photographers.
97. Pérez Montfort, *Cotidianidades, imaginarios y contextos*, 211. See the photo of Flores Pérez, 212. Images of this photographer can be found in the AGN, and a number are published in Martínez, *La intervención norteamericana*.
98. Berumen, *México: Fotografía y revolución*, 296. The fact that Hadsell signed photos of events at which he was probably not present makes me doubt his authorship in general; see the

photo of Emiliano Zapata in front of his troops on entering Cuernavaca (Casasola, *Historia gráfica de la Revolución Mexicana*, 306, also signed by a "Wray"). Daniel Escorza commented on Hadsell, "I am inclined to think that Hadsell attributed photos to himself that he didn't take, but that is speculation" (personal communication, 9 February 2009).

99. *La Ilustración Semanal*, 11 May 1914; the copy signed by Flores Pérez is in the Archivo General de la Nación.
100. See the versions in which you can see two men in Mraz, *Looking for Mexico*, 71 (signed by Flores Pérez); the unsigned version is in Casasola, *Historia gráfica de la Revolución Mexicana*, 770; and Palomares, *La invasión yanqui en 1914*, 46, where the man who barely appears in the photo published here is identified as "federal sergeant Emilio Contreras," and it is asserted that the photo was taken on 21 April. The most complete version of this photo, in which three men can be seen talking, was published in *The Illustrated London News*, 16 May 1914 (Gautreau, "La Revolución Mexicana a los ojos del mundo," 222). The photos that are published in Palomares, *The Illustrated London News*, and *La Ilustración Semanal* have no author´s identification written on them.
101. *La Ilustración Semanal*, 11 May 1914. Although signed here by Hadsell, the published image had no signature.
102. See the photos on the ships in Cabrera Luna, *Hugo Brehme y la Revolución Mexicana*, 112–113.
103. Historian Leonardo Pasquel says that "numerous colored soldiers were in the invasion" (Pérez Montfort, *Cotidianidades, imaginarios y contextos*, 217).
104. See the U.S. refugees in Vanderwood, "The Picture Postcard as Historical Evidence," 218.

CHAPTER 7

1. See the photos of Villa with the Graflex camera of photojournalist W. H. Durborough, and of his son Agustín, in Berumen, *Pancho Villa*, 109, 169.
2. I am tempted to think that what is believed to be publishable is sometimes not up to speed with the recording technology. This was certainly the case in the 1940s: when the Hermanos Mayo introduced 35 mm cameras into Mexican periodicals, the photo editors did not believe that the tiny negatives could render publishable images; see Mraz and Vélez Storey, *Uprooted*, 15–16.
3. González Flores, "Técnica fotográfica y mirada," 56.
4. See Escorza Rodríguez and Vera Trejo, "La cámara Graflex," 262.
5. Katz, *The Life and Times of Pancho Villa*, 322.
6. Katz, *The Life and Times of Pancho Villa*, 224–225.
7. See the photo of the Villista telegraphers who made sure that the local telegraphers sent messages confirming that the train was controlled by Federales (Casasola, *Historia gráfica de la Revolución Mexicana*, 699).
8. De los Reyes, *Con Villa en México*, 43.
9. De Orellano, "Pancho Villa," 61; De los Reyes, *Con Villa en México*, 41.

10. Katz, *The Life and Times of Pancho Villa*, 325.
11. De los Reyes, *Con Villa en México*, 12.
12. Katz, *The Life and Times of Pancho Villa*, 326.
13. Rufinelli, "John Reed en la Revolución Mexicana," 46.
14. Letter from John Reed, cited in Reed, *Villa y la Revolución Mexicana*, 113.
15. *La Semana Ilustrada*, 19 May 1911; INAH 33694.
16. *La Ilustración Semanal*, 28 October 1913.
17. See the reproductions in Berumen, *México: Fotografía y revolución*, 274–277, and my discussion of this iconic image in the last chapter.
18. *La Semana Ilustrada*, 28 July 1914; INAH 66217.
19. Margarita de Orellano affirms that Villa could not use the uniform designed by the Mutual "on other occasions" ("Pancho Villa," 61); de los Reyes translates an article that appeared in the *New York Times*: "The uniform Villa wears is property of the Mutual Film Corporation. Villa only puts it on when he appears in martial scenes for that company" (189).
20. Berumen, *Pancho Villa*, 51.
21. This subject does not appear to wear the same uniform as the corps of Dorados in a photo of some eighty of them (INAH 65467), but that could be because he was a leader. In another photo he is dressed in a leather jacket with fringe (which can here be seen hanging on the wall behind him) (Casasola, *Historia gráfica de la Revolución Mexicana*, 947); according to Francisco Ramírez Plancarte, "The Villista leaders and officers dressed in a suede jacket that had big fringes of the same leather on the back, the shoulders, and the length of the arms that gave them the ferocious aspect of Comanches" (*La ciudad de México durante la revolución constitucionalista*, 275). The fact that there are two photos of the same man posing makes me think that he may have commissioned them as souvenirs.
22. This photo is reprographed from a clipping out of an illustrated magazine that gives credit to Hugelman (Archivo Roque González Garza de la Universidad Panamericana; see http://biblio.upmx.mx/asp/gl). Berumen says that Hugelman worked for Spanish publications and had photographed the Veracruz invasion (*México: Fotografía y revolución*, 387). The fact that the famous image of Villa on horseback was also (wrongly) credited to Hugelman by a Spanish magazine puts his authorship in doubt generally; see the last chapter. Another photo of the Villista movement that could be of combat was taken during the fall of Ciudad Juárez in November 1913 (INAH 38079).
23. See Montoya's biography in Treviño, *160 años de fotografía en México*, 679.
24. Rodríguez, "The Early Years."
25. Del Moral González, *Las imágenes perdidas de Eustasio Montoya*, 20.
26. See the photo of Montoya, dressed in his Cruz Blanca uniform, in Treviño, *160 años de fotografía en México*, 435. About Pablo González and the Cruz Blanca, see Villegas de Magnón, *La rebelde*, 198.
27. Villegas de Magnón, *The Rebel*, 120.
28. Miranda, "Cronometría de un cine mexicano mudo que nunca fue mudo." There are Montoya photos of General Maclovio Herrera and his general staff in April 1915; Herrera was a

Villista who refused to break with Carranza (Casasola, *Historia gráfica de la Revolución Mexicana*, 1013; Florescano, *Así fue la Revolución Mexicana*, vol. 8, 1614).

29. Letter written in 1938 by Eustasio Montoya; cited in del Moral González, *Las imágenes perdidas de Eustasio Montoya*, 7.
30. See this photo and the text written by Vander Linden in Casanova and Debroise, *Sobre la superficie bruñida de un espejo*, 32–34. I discuss this case in Mraz, *Looking for Mexico*, 17–18.
31. I thank Daniel Escorza for our conversations about photographic technology during the revolution, and his comments on this photo. I am also in debt to photo historians Jorge Carretero and John Turner for their observations about the technology in this photo. See an image of a Kodak Poco in González Flores, "Técnica fotográfica y mirada," 54.
32. Berumen, *México: Fotografía y revolución*, 283, 381.
33. I am basing my analysis on the photos in two archives: the collection "Cachú-Ramírez Juan" of the Departamento de Información y Documentación de la Cultura Audiovisual, Benemérita Universidad Autónoma de Puebla; and the Fondo Cachú, Dirección de Artes Visuales de la Fundación Televisa. I am grateful for the access I was given to both archives, and for the assistance of Fernando Osorio in this regard.
34. See the photos of García in Canales, *Romualdo García*. Canales affirms that García did not photograph the revolution: "The reluctance of García to capture the great events of his time is indicative of his class position, as well as the fact that he was never interested in photography as a medium to document his historic moment; photography for him was an art rather than something to do with the political and the social" (42).
35. Readers may find it interesting that this photo was censured by the INAH museographers from the national exhibit I curated on the centenary of the Mexican Revolution. The polemic generated in the press can be found in the newspapers *La Jornada*, *Excelsior*, *Reforma*, and *Milenio*, on 18 and 19 November 2010. The two photos of Pérez Castro are identified in the Departamento de Información y Documentación de la Cultura Audiovisual, Benemérita Universidad Autónoma de Puebla.
36. The reference here is to Barthes's concept, which he described as "this element which rises from the scene, shoots out of it like an arrow, and pierces me" (*Camera Lucida*, 26).
37. Departamento de Información y Documentación de la Cultura Audiovisual, Benemérita Universidad Autónoma de Puebla. Interestingly, there are no photos of Villa himself in this archive; perhaps they got rid of them when the Villistas lost the war.
38. See the photo of Juan Cachú as a Villista in Berumen, *México: Fotografía y revolución*, 308.
39. Text written over the photograph in the collection "Cachú-Ramírez Juan," Departamento de Información y Documentación de la Cultura Audiovisual, Benemérita Universidad Autónoma de Puebla.
40. Berumen, *México: Fotografía y revolución*, 283.
41. The images in the Fondo Cachú de la Dirección de Artes Visuales de la Fundación Televisa are much more Constitutionalist than those seen in the BUAP collection.
42. See the "Datos biográficos de Juan Cachú Ramírez por María Teresa Cachú Sampers," Dirección de Artes Visuales de la Fundación Televisa.

43. *Novedades*, 2 July 1913.
44. *Novedades*, 9 July 1913.
45. Del Moral González, "El acervo fotográfico de Josaphat Martínez," 41–42.
46. See the copy signed by Martínez in del Moral González, who asserts that this photo "like others of Villa, [has] circulated without due credit" ("El acervo fotográfico de Josaphat Martínez," 42).
47. This photo is in Casasola, *Historia gráfica de la Revolución Mexicana*, 911; INAH 6136 and 655625.
48. Gilly, *La revolución interrumpida*, 140–141.
49. Ramírez Plancarte, *La ciudad de México durante la revolución constitucionalista*, 242.
50. Ramírez Plancarte, *La ciudad de México durante la revolución constitucionalista*, 242–243.
51. Pérez Montfort, "Zapata y Villa en la ciudad de México, 1914–1915: Un tema popular con variaciones y fuga," in *Cotidianidades, imaginarios y contextos*, 235.
52. Womack, *Zapata and the Mexican Revolution*, 219.
53. Vargas Sánchez, "La ciudad de México de 1900 a 1920," 168.
54. Ramírez Plancarte, *La ciudad de México durante la revolución constitucionalista*, 247.
55. "La crisis del papel," *Revista de Revistas*, 11 June 1916, 5; this article is a translation from French and deals with the world paper crisis. See the list of illustrated magazines with their dates of birth and death in Gautreau, "La Revolución Mexicana a los ojos del mundo," 199.
56. *La Ilustración Semanal*, December 1914.
57. Maldonado Valera, "Manuel Ramos en la prensa ilustrada capitalina," 225.
58. See the photo of the mounted Zapatistas in *La Revolución Mexicana*, 32; Ramírez Plancarte describes the dust devils during the parade (*La ciudad de México durante la revolución constitucionalista*, 248). This photo is in the Manuel Ramos Archive, 0017-N; I am grateful to Daniel Escorza for this information.
59. It appears that Gutiérrez made several portraits during the session; see the famous one in Casasola, *Historia gráfica de la Revolución Mexicana*, 957, for whom it was, in 1960, "a little-known photograph"; the copy reprographed by Casasola is INAH 639745.
60. See Guevara Escobar, "La fotografía de Emiliano Zapata," 23, where Guevara Escobar reconstucts the story that his grandmother Consuelo told about what happened in the studio.
61. Ulloa, *La revolución escindida*, 79.
62. Vargas Sánchez, "La ciudad de México de 1900 a 1920," 180.
63. Ulloa, *La revolución escindida*, 83.
64. Casasola, *Historia gráfica de la Revolución Mexicana*, 941.
65. Casasola, *Historia gráfica de la Revolución Mexicana*, 1008.
66. I mistakenly described this photo as "Zapatistas looking for food" in Mraz, "¿Fotohistoria o historia gráfica?," 27; however, I believe that Gustavo Casasola's identification of the place as the Basilica of Guadalupe is the correct one (Casasola, *Hechos y hombres de México*, 68).

CHAPTER 8

1. Gautreau, "Les photographies de la Révolution Mexicaine," 333.
2. See Berumen's comments about the "overvaluation of some authors" (*Pancho Villa*, 20, 29); Acosta, "Miguel Ángel Berumen," 46.
3. Guzmán, *El águila y la serpiente*, 337–338.
4. *Diccionario histórico y biográfico de la Revolución Mexicana*, 246. See also Rivera, "Jesús Hermenegildo Abitia," 56. I also fell into this trap in Mraz, *Looking for Mexico*, 61.
5. Abitia Garcés, "Memorias de un fotógrafo constitucionalista," 1.
6. Abitia Garcés, "Memorias," 1.
7. Sánchez García, "Apuntes para la historia de nuestro cine: Jesús H. Abitia," 23 December 1945, 6.
8. Sánchez García, "Apuntes para la historia de nuestro cine: Jesús H. Abitia," 23 December 1945, 6.
9. Sánchez García, "Apuntes para la historia de nuestro cine: Jesús H. Abitia," 23 December 1945, 6.
10. Sánchez García, "Apuntes para la historia de nuestro cine: Jesús H. Abitia," 30 December 1945, 6.
11. Sánchez García, "Apuntes para la historia de nuestro cine: Jesús H. Abitia," 30 December 1945, 6.
12. Negrete Álvarez, *Valleto Hermanos*, 38, 159.
13. Sánchez García, "Apuntes para la historia de nuestro cine: Jesús H. Abitia," 30 December 1945, 6.
14. Abitia, "Memorias de un fotógrafo constitucionalista," 1.
15. Abitia, "Memorias," 1.
16. Abitia, "Memorias," 1. All the quotations in this and the following paragraph are taken from this autobiography.
17. Miquel, "El registro de Jesús H. Abitia de las campañas constitucionalistas," 13.
18. Abitia, "Memorias de un fotógrafo constitucionalista," 1.
19. Sánchez García, "Apuntes para la historia de nuestro cine: Jesús H. Abitia," 30 December 1945, 6.
20. "Tendremos en México fabricación de películas cinematográficas con asuntos característicos de nuestro pueblo," *El Pueblo*, 22 August 1916, 3.
21. Miquel found a list by Abitia that noted that the film *La campaña constitucionalista* had a length of 36,800 feet, and he calculated that it would have lasted eight hours ("El registro de Jesús H. Abitia de las campañas constitucionalistas," 21). Abitia mentioned that he had filmed "a million feet of cinema from Sonora to Yucatán," but it is not clear if he was referring to his total production or the last project he made for Carranza ("Memorias de un fotógrafo constitucionalista," 6). Evidently two films were made with the title of *Epopeyas de la Revolución*, one edited by Fernando Marcos at an undetermined date, and the other by Gustavo Carrero in 1961; see Miquel, *Salvador Toscano*, 17–21.

22. Abitia, "Memorias de un fotógrafo constitucionalista," 6.
23. Abitia, "Memorias," 6. The word *propaganda* did not scare Abitia, and he used it on numerous occasions. His prodigious production can be found in various archives, including the Archivo General de la Nación, the Fototeca Archivo Fernando Torreblanco, the Fondo Carranza of CONDUMEX, and the Fundación Carmen Toscano.
24. Miquel, "El registro de Jesús H. Abitia de las campañas constitucionalistas," 11.
25. Miquel, "El registro de Jesús H. Abitia," 11.
26. Miquel, "El registro de Jesús H. Abitia," 12.
27. Miquel, "El registro de Jesús H. Abitia," 19.
28. On the Constitutionalist modes of promoting their movement in the United States, see Vélez Storey, "Prensa, propaganda y diplomacia de la Revolución Mexicana"; and Smith, "Gringo Propagandist."
29. Vélez Storey, "Prensa, propaganda y diplomacia," 125–126.
30. See the cover in Vélez Storey, "Prensa, propaganda y diplomacia," 129.
31. Vélez Storey, "Prensa, propaganda y diplomacia," 142.
32. *Novedades*, 30 April 1913.
33. *Novedades*, 29 July 1914.
34. *Novedades*, 5 August 1914 and 19 August 1914.
35. *Novedades*, 19 August 1914.
36. *La Semana Ilustrada*, 30 September 1913.
37. *La Semana Ilustrada*, 28 July 1914 and 4 August 1914.
38. *La Ilustración Semanal*, 27 January 1914 and 6 April 1914. Berumen asserts that Ocampo y Amezcua was active in Morelos and Mexico City between 1910 and 1916 (*México: Fotografía y revolución*, 388).
39. *La Ilustración Semanal*, 25 November 1913 and 1 June 1914.
40. *La Ilustración Semanal*, 24 August 1914.
41. Hernández was a major and Santamaría a lieutenant-colonel (Berumen, *México: fotografía y revolución*, 383, 385).
42. Moreno Irázabal, "Figuras del periodismo mexicano," 6.
43. See Melhado's photo of Carranza on the cover of *La Semana Ilustrada*, 1 September 1914. Melhado registered two series of photos on Carranza with the secretary of public instruction (Morales, "Eduardo Melhado"; "Carranza íntimo," *Revista de Revistas*, 16 September 1917).
44. Berumen, *México: Fotografía y revolución*, 384. See INAH 39461, 41335, 64214; see also the photos in the Centro de las Artes, Fototeca CONARTE, Monterrey, AGENL 5748, 5839, 5620, 5520. I am grateful to Abraham Guerrero for his research in CONARTE.
45. INAH 39461; Gustavo Casasola, *Historia gráfica de la Revolución Mexicana*, 1055; CONARTE AGENL 5480, 5620, 5621, 5839.
46. Casasola, *Historia gráfica de la Revolución Mexicana*, 1215; CONARTE AGENL 5663, 5607.
47. CONARTE AGENL 5691. In fact, it is a tomb that Zapata had built for his men; see a photo in Casasola, *Hechos y hombres de México*, 96.

48. The most reproduced photo of the corpse (INAH 63450) also exists without Mora's signature (INAH 63452), but Casasola did not shoot it because it is a reprograph; see also INAH 63471. The funeral is INAH 4709.
49. Biographical note by Dolores Ehlers, cited in Martínez de Velasco Vélez, *Directoras de cine*, 32.
50. Martínez de Velasco Vélez, *Directoras de cine*, 31–32.
51. Ehlers, cited in Martínez de Velasco Vélez, *Directoras de cine*, 33.
52. Ehlers, cited in Martínez de Velasco Vélez, *Directoras de cine*, 33; see also Sánchez García, "Apuntes para la historia de nuestro cine: Las hermanas Ehlers," 7.
53. Sánchez García, "Apuntes para la historia de nuestro cine: Las hermanas Ehlers," 7.
54. See del Castillo Troncoso, *Isidro Fabela*.
55. Del Castillo Troncoso, *Isidro Fabela*, 157, 158, 162, 163, 169, 171, 173, 180, 181.
56. Del Castillo Troncoso, *Isidro Fabela*, 30.
57. Del Castillo Troncoso, *Isidro Fabela*, 119, 123.
58. See Berumen, *México: Fotografía y revolución*, 385; INAH 287605, 641439, 39150, 32606, and 39166.
59. See the photo of Carranza and General Francisco Murguía in Casasola, *Historia gráfica de la Revolución Mexicana*, 1415.
60. See Berumen, *México: Fotografía y revolución*, 385; INAH 32937; CONARTE AGENL 5337, 6079, 5334.
61. See Berumen, *México: Fotografía y revolución*, 387; CONARTE AGENL 6031, 6033, 6039, 5379, 5319.
62. Berumen, *México: Fotografía y revolución*, 382. See fourteen photos by García in Pavelka, *Monterrey en 400 fotografías*, 168–171.
63. See the photos of García in the Carpeta Venustiano Carranza, Colección Gráfica y de Sonido del Instituto Nacional de los Estudios Históricos de las Revoluciones Mexicanas, and in the Museo del Obispado, Monterrey. I am grateful to Abraham Guerrero for his research in the Museo del Obispado.
64. INAH 37804; CONARTE AGENL 5361.
65. See the photos of Villistas in Cabrera Luna, *Hugo Brehme y la Revolución Mexicana*, 132–133.
66. The complete photo was published in *La Ilustración Semanal*, 27 July 1914.
67. Knight, *The Mexican Revolution*, vol. 2, 418.
68. Ramírez Plancarte, *La ciudad de México durante la revolución constitucionalista*, 348.
69. Lear, *Workers, Neighbors, and Citizens*, 310.
70. Ramírez Plancarte, *La ciudad de México durante la revolución constitucionalista*, 351–352.
71. Vargas Sánchez, "La ciudad de México de 1900 a 1920," 170.
72. Lara Ruiz and Lara Ruiz, "Los 'Caranclanes,'" 134.
73. Cuenya Mateos, "Reflexiones en torno a la pandemia de influenza de 1918," 151.
74. Knight, *The Mexican Revolution*, vol. 2, 421–422.
75. Márquez Morfín and Molinar del Villar, "El otoño de 1918," 138.

76. Cited in Ramírez Racaño, "La epidemia de influenza española en México," 69.
77. See Piccato, *City of Suspects*, 140.
78. See four photos of this event in Casasola, *Historia gráfica de la Revolución Mexicana*, 993. Lear identifies this photo (Fig. 21) with the cutline "Consumer riots even extended to the posh commercial stores in the heart of the city center," but I doubt that is the case.
79. Guzmán, *El águila y la serpiente*, 143–145.
80. See the photos of Indians in the north in Miquel, *Acercamientos al cine silente mexicano*, between pp. 88–89, and Obregón, *Ocho mil kilometros en campaña*, between pp. 48–49; Jiménez and Villela, *Los Salmerón*, 52.
81. Guzmán, *El águila y la serpiente*, 67.
82. Casasola, *Historia gráfica de la Revolución Mexicana*, 1213.
83. To reconstruct this event, I am employing various sources which at times contradict themselves: the newspaper reports in *El Pueblo* (Veracruz), 10 and 11 June 1915, and the letters of Lobo Guerrero published therein, as well as Urquizo, *Recuerdo que*, 156–158.
84. *El Pueblo*, 11 June 1915.
85. Urquizo, *Recuerdo que*, 157.
86. Urquizo, *Recuerdo que*, 158.
87. Knight, *The Mexican Revolution*, vol. 2, 203.
88. Cumberland, *Mexican Revolution*, 1972, 347.
89. I have analyzed this case in Mraz, "'En calidad de esclavas'"; the citations come from de Beraza's reports.
90. See Title VI, Article 123, reprinted in Florescano, *Así fue la Revolución Mexicana*, vol. 6, 1206–1208.
91. Interview in "On the Case of Rosalie Evans," a digital production directed by John Mraz, Instituto de Ciencias Sociales y Humanidades, Universidad Autónoma de Puebla, 2004.
92. Womack, *Zapata and the Mexican Revolution*, xi.

EPILOGUE

1. Known as "Korda," Alejandro Díaz Gutiérrez was one of the greatest photographers of revolutionary Cuba. Although Zapata's icon has not produced many reflections, one by Subcomandante Marcos, leader of the 1994 Chiapas neo-Zapatista rebellion, is of interest. A personage invented by Marcos, Old Antonio, visits the guerrilla; the old man brings Marcos the Zapata icon and tells him, "I have asked many questions of this photo. That is how I got here. Take it, so that you learn to ask, and to walk" ("Relatos del Viejo Antonio," http://www.extremaduralternativa.net/chiapas/texto1.html).
2. Agustín Víctor claimed authorship, at least implicitly, as early as 1921, when he published the image in the *Albúm histórico gráfico* as if it were his.
3. See Ruiz, "Brehme, autor del Zapata de Casasola."
4. Mendoza Avilés, "El Zapata de Brehme," 83–84.

5. Casasola, *Hechos y hombres de México*, 19. Hadsell worked in Veracruz, but it appears that Wray may have established himself in Morelos. This photo is a useful comparison because Zapata projects a much less dignified and powerful presence, although he is dressed the same way.
6. Dennis Brehme believes that foreigners had an important advantage because the revolutionaries considered them neutral ("Hugo Brehme," 27).
7. See the *hoja suelta* of the etching with the name "ZAPATA" above it in *José Guadalupe Posada*, 395. It was issued by A. Vanegas Arroyo, and the date of its making is said to be "1910–1912" (496). It is difficult to know how Posada saw the photo, but it may well have circulated as a postcard.
8. The quote from Rivera was in a special issue of *Mexican Folkways* dedicated to Posada's etchings, *Monografía de 406 grabados de José Guadalupe Posada*, cited in Barajas Durán, *Posada: Mito y mitote*, 27, a critical analysis that runs counter to the popular myth. Toor was the editor of *Mexican Folkways*. See also Frank, *Posada's Broadsheets*.
9. Barajas Durán, *Posada: Mito y mitote*, 389; see Arnal, "El río que cambia."
10. See the broadsheet in *Posada y la prensa ilustrada*, 223. I am grateful to Ricardo Pérez Montfort for information about *calaveras*. Barajas Durán argues that this broadsheet represents Zapata as a drunk and celebrates the apprehension of his family by Huertista troops (*Posada: Mito y mitote*, 385, 389). Nonetheless, I fear that Barajas Durán overstates his case and, moreover, fails to recognize that these broadsheets were produced after Posada's death. It would have been impossible for Posada to have collaborated in "pro-Huertista" publications because they did not exist until after his death.
11. I refer to this photograph in Chapter 5, on Zapatista imagery.
12. See Tyler, *Posada's Mexico*, 254.
13. I first saw this broadsheet in Zavala, *Mexico Beyond Its Revolution*, 75.
14. Arnal, "El río que cambia."
15. *El Imparcial*, 18 April 1913, front page.
16. Womack, *Zapata and the Mexican Revolution*, 165–167.
17. Womack, *Zapata and the Mexican Revolution*, 166.
18. See Arnal, *Atila de tinta y plata*, 80–91; and "Construyendo símbolos," 65–70.
19. The relationship, in time and space, between Figures E–1 and E–3 is not clear. Gustavo Casasola identified the second as "General Manuel Asúnsolo turning Cuernavaca over to General Emiliano Zapata" (*Historia gráfica de la Revolución Mexicana*, 307), and this is the description employed in the Fototeca Nacional. That would place this photo in Cuernavaca around 26 May 1911, when Zapata's authority was recognized. Nonetheless, Guevara Escobar establishes that Figure E–3 was taken on 7 June 1911, and in the station of the Ferrocarril Colonia, Mexico City, when Zapata and Asúnsolo went there to welcome Madero upon his triumphant arrival ("Reflex o view"). Zapata retained recognition for about a month, until 20 June (or a few days thereafter). Hence, although the sash and the sable are the same, the photos were probably not taken the same day nor in the same place, and the exact chronology is difficult to determine. As John Womack remarked, "While the symbolism of detail

is often wonderfully revealing, I think it's also often random and contingent, in those days in particular, nothing 'uniform' in any sense" (personal communication, January 2011).

20. On the incident, see Womack, *Zapata and the Mexican Revolution*, 81–96. I am grateful to John Womack for helping me understand this situation.
21. Arnal, *Atila de tinta y plata*, 84.
22. See this work, *Serie Zapata II* (1978), in Arnal, *Atila de tinta y plata*, 49.
23. Cartier-Bresson, *The Mind's Eye*, 42.
24. Brunk, *The Posthumous Career of Emiliano Zapata*, 2.
25. Interview with Elsa Medina, 28 January 1996. I formerly saw only the critique of Salinas; see Mraz, "The New Photojournalism of Mexico, 1976–1998," 341–343.
26. See Morales, "La celebre fotografía de Jerónimo Hernández." Because the photograph had been published in the first and all successive *historias gráficas* of the Casasolas, authorship had been assigned by default to Agustín Víctor.
27. *Nueva Era*, 8 April 1912, front page.
28. Casasola, *Historia gráfica de la Revolución*, 664.
29. Poniatowska, *Las soldaderas*, cover.
30. Rodríguez Lapuente, *Breve historia gráfica*, 74.
31. This was the caption used in the original fascicle, Héctor Aguilar Camín and Lorenzo Meyer, *Siglo XX*, 7, published in 1987, 100–101. In the series published the next year, the cutline was changed to read, "In the lens of Agustín V. Casasola, women were incorporated in the revolutionary disorder" (Aguilar Camín, *Historia gráfica de México*, vol. 7, 100–101).
32. No reference is made to the name "Adelita" in any other *historia gráfica*, though this photo is invariably reproduced; however, journalists had employed this name previously in referring to *soldaderas*, and coverage of Morales's discovery makes it clear that it has stuck to this image. See Jiménez, "Identifican al verdadero autor de la fotografía de la Adelita"; and Haw, "Prueba que 'Adelita' no es de Casasola."
33. Salas, *Soldaderas in the Mexican Military*, 43.
34. See the photo of a better-dressed woman serving alcohol to federal officers in a train car (Ortiz Monasterio, *Jefes, héroes y caudillos*, 47).
35. Mraz, "El Archivo Casasola," 213; and "Historia y mito del Archivo Casasola," *La Jornada Semanal*, 31 December 2000, 7.
36. Morales, "La celebre fotografía de Jerónimo Hernández," 72.
37. This observation was made by Alfonso Morales.
38. See Cano, "*Soldaderas* and *Coronelas*," 1358.
39. Alegría, "Pero, ¿existió La Adelita?". The illustration for this article is Mauricio Yáñez's photo of General Iturbe and his "Feminine General Staff" (Figure 4-20).
40. *La Revolución Mexicana*, vol. 1, 15, 37. The cropped photo is published twice with the woman's name; however, this series is not reliable.
41. Hernández-Claire commented to me, "Obviously, I didn't make the photo of the old lady thinking about the one from the revolution, but there are images that stay in your head without you being conscious of them" (personal communication, 2000).

42. Berumen, *Pancho Villa*, 55.
43. Katz, *The Life and Times of Pancho Villa*, 321.
44. Berumen, *Pancho Villa*, 56.
45. *Leslie's Illustrated Weekly Newspaper*, 5 February 1914.
46. *Reel Life*, May 1914.
47. *Reel Life*, May 1914.
48. *The Moving Picture World*, April 1916. Interestingly, this photo is probably the only one that is printed correctly, with Villa holding the reins in his left hand, as any experienced rider (above all, a cavalryman) would do.
49. I am constructing the history of its publication in the European magazines based on the reproductions in Berumen, *México: Fotografía y revolución*, 274–277.
50. *La Semana Ilustrada*, 21 July 1914; the magazine erroneously identified the photo as being of the "assault on and taking of Torreón."
51. On the *ninguneo* of Villa, and his popular acceptance, see O'Malley, *The Myth of the Revolution*, 95, 97, 111, 112.
52. See photos of the exhibit in Del Castillo Troncoso, *Isidro Fabela*, 101; Brenner, *The Wind That Swept Mexico*, no. 86.
53. Katz, *The Life and Times of Pancho Villa*, 437. Unfortunately, Katz does not document the international circulation of the icon, which would have given us some leads to follow.
54. De la Colina, "Breve lectura de la fotografía *Villa en la silla presidencial*," 12.
55. Taibo, *Pancho Villa*, 454. Taibo includes some interesting reflections on the question of whether it really was the presidential chair that Villa sat in, as Carranza is said to have taken it with him to Veracruz.
56. Larrain, "Historia de la fotografía de prensa," 63.
57. *La Ilustración Semanal*, 7 December 1914.
58. Casasola, *Historia gráfica de la Revolución*, 875; Brenner, *The Wind That Swept Mexico*, no. 108.
59. See the photo signed by Ramos in Berumen, *México: Fotografía y revolución*, 364.
60. Obregón, *Ocho mil kilómetros en campaña*, 353.
61. Ahumada et al., *El tartaranieto del Ahuizote*, 79.
62. José Ortíz, "Villa jugando a la presidencia," *El Pueblo*, 14 March 1915, 3.
63. Ortíz, "Villa jugando a la presidencia."
64. Casasola, *Historia gráfica de la Revolución Mexicana*, 941.
65. Taibo, *Pancho Villa*, 452.
66. *Agustín Víctor Casasola*, 13. This anecdote appears on the pamphlet of the opening of the Museo de la Fotografía in Pachuca, Hidalgo, in November 1976. Gustavo Casasola recounted it, and it was confirmed by his son, Gustavo Casasola Salamanca (Daniel Escorza, personal communication, 2009).
67. De la Colina, "Breve lectura de la fotografía," 12.
68. Katz, *The Life and Times of Pancho Villa*, 437.
69. Florescano, *Así fue la Revolución Mexicana*; Krauze, *Biografía del poder*; Aguilar Camín, *Historia gráfica de México*; Martínez Assad, *Memoria y olvido*.

70. Conversation with Eleazar López Zamora, June 2000.

71. This photo appeared in all the *historias gráficas* and was also published in the following works: *Tierra y Libertad!*, 38–39; *El poder de la imágen y la imágen del poder*, 36; Ortiz Monasterio, *Jefes, héroes y caudillos*, 39; and Rodríguez Lapuente, *Breve historia gráfica*, 59.

72. Exactly what happened with the light is unclear. Some researchers, such as Juan Carlos Valdéz, believe that the magnesium flash failed; others, such as Daniel Escorza, think that the ceiling light was not turned on.

73. Place and Peterson, "Some Visual Motifs of Film Noir," 327–330.

74. I have heard congress presentations in Mexico that turn completely around how this photo "proves" Huerta's evil nature.

75. Escorza Rodríguez, "Imágen y apariencia de Victoriano Huerta después de La Decena Trágica."

76. Escorza Rodríguez, "Imágen y apariencia."

Bibliography

Abitia Garcés, Jesús H. "Memorias de un fotógrafo constitucionalista." *El Universal* (revista de la semana), 22 de febrero de 1959, 1, 6.

Acevedo, Marta, and Alfonso Morales. *El Gran Lente: José Antonio Bustamante Martínez*. Mexico City: Secretaría de Educación Pública, 1992.

Acosta, Anasella. "Miguel Ángel Berumen: Villa sabía que el poder militar no lo es todo." *Cuartoscuro*, no. 98 (2009): 46–47.

Aguilar, José Ángel. *La Decena Trágica*, vol. 1. Mexico City: Instituto Nacional de Estudios sobre la Historia de la Revolución Mexicana, 1981.

Aguilar Camín, Héctor, et al. *Historia gráfica de México*. 10 vols. Mexico City: Editorial Patria-INAH, 1988.

Aguirre Benavides, Adrián. *Madero el inmaculado: Historia de la Revolución de 1910*. Mexico City: Editorial Diana, 1962.

Agustín Víctor Casasola. Mexico City: Partido Revolucionario Institucional, 1988.

Ahumada, Manuel López, et al. *El tartaranieto del Ahuizote*. Mexico City: La Jornada, 1991.

Alegría, Juana Armanda. "Pero, ¿existió La Adelita? Reconsideraciones del mito." *Siempre!*, 26 February 1975, 34.

Altúzar, Mario Luis. "Agustín Víctor Casasola: Cazador de instantes históricos." In Casasola, *Agustín Víctor Casasola: El hombre que retrató una época*, 5–48. Mexico City: Editorial Gustavo Casasola, 1988.

Alvarado, Salvador. *La reconstrucción de México: Un mensaje a los pueblos de América*. Mexico City: Instituto Nacional de Estudios Históricos de la Revolución Mexicana, [1919] 1985.

Ancira, Eduardo. "Fotógrafos de la luz aprisionada: Asociación de fotógrafos de la prensa metropolitana de la ciudad de México, octubre-diciembre de 1911." In *Imágenes e investigación social*, edited by Fernando Aguayo and Lourdes Roca, 334–353. Mexico City: Instituto Mora, 2005.

Anderson, Rodney D. *Outcasts in Their Own Land: Mexican Industrial Workers, 1906–1911*. DeKalb: Northern Illinois University Press, 1976.

Arnal, Ariel. *Atila de tinta y plata: Fotografía del zapatismo en la prensa de la ciudad de México entre 1910 y 1915*. Mexico City: INAH, 2010.

———. "Construyendo símbolos—fotografía política en México: 1865–1911." In "Cultura visual en América Latina." Special Issue, *Estudios Interdisciplinarios de América Latina y el Caribe* 9, no. 1 (1998): 55–73.

———. "El río que cambia: La fotografía de Zapata y la historiografía visual contemporánea." Unpublished manuscript, 2011.

Arroyo, Sergio Raúl, and Rosa Casanova. "The Casasolas: An Everyday Epic." In *Mexico: The Revolution and Beyond: Photographs by Agustín Víctor Casasola, 1900–1940*, edited by Pablo Ortiz Monasterio, 203–210. New York: Aperture, 2003.

Ávila Espinosa, Felipe Arturo. "Villa y Zapata en la ciudad de México." *Relatos e Historias en México*, no. 3 (2009): 42–50.

Avitia Hernández, Antonio. *Corridos históricos mexicanos: Voy a cantarles la historia (1819–1910)*. Mexico City: Porrúa, 1997.

Barajas Durán, Rafael (El Fisgón). *Posada: Mito y mitote: La caricatura política de José Guadalupe Posada y Manuel Alfonso Manilla*. Mexico City: Fondo de Cultura Económica, 2009.

Barthes, Roland. *Camera Lucida: Reflections on Photography*, translated by Richard Howard. New York: Hill and Wang, 1981.

Bartra, Eli. "Women and Portraiture in Mexico." In "Mexican Photography." Special Issue, *History of Photography* 20, no. 3 (1996): 220–225.

Baschet, Eric. *Russia, 1904–1924: The Revolutionary Years: A History in Documentary Photographs*. Zug, Switzerland: Swan, 1989.

Becker, Carl. *The Heavenly City of the Eighteenth-Century Philosophers*. New Haven: Yale University Press, 1932.

Belliter, Erika, ed. *Fotografía latinoamericana, desde 1860 hasta nuestros días*. Barcelona: Ediciones El Viso, 1982.

Benjamin, Thomas. *La Revolución: Mexico's Great Revolution as Memory, Myth, and History*. Austin: University of Texas Press, 2000.

———. "Revolución interrumpida: Chiapas y el interinato presidencial, 1911." *Historia Mexicana* 30, no. 1 (1980): 79–98.

Berumen, Miguel Ángel. *1911: La batalla de Ciudad Juárez*, vol. II: *Las imágenes*. Ciudad Juárez: Cuadro por Cuadro, 2003.

———. *Pancho Villa: La construcción del mito*. Mexico City and Ciudad Juárez: Oceano and Cuadro por Cuadro, 2005.

———, coord. *México: Fotografía y revolución*. Mexico City: Fundación Televisa y Lunwerg, 2009.

Beurier, Joelle. *Images et violence, 1914–1918: Quand "Le Miroir" recontant la Grand Guerre*. Paris: Nouveau Monde, 2007.

Bhabha, Homi K. "The Other Question: Stereotype, Discrimination and the Discourse of Colonialism." In Homi K. Bhabha, *The Location of Culture*, 66–84. London: Routledge, 1994.

Brehme, Dennis. "Hugo Brehme: Una vida entre la tradición y la modernidad." In *Hugo Brehme: Fotograf-fotógrafo*, 13–27. Berlin: Verlag Willmuth Arenhövel, 2004.

[Brehme, Hugo]. *México: Una nación persistente: Hugo Brehme, fotografías*. Mexico City: CONACULTA and INBA, 1995.

———. *México pintoresco*. Mexico City: Porrúa-INAH, [1923] 1990.

———. *Pueblos y paisajes de México*. Mexico City: Porrúa-INAH, 1992.

Brenner, Anita. *The Wind That Swept Mexico: The History of the Mexican Revolution 1910–1942*. New York: Harper and Brothers, 1943.

Brook, Donald. "On the Alleged Transparency of Photographs." *British Journal of Aesthetics* 26, no. 3 (1986): 277–282.

Brunk, Samuel. *The Posthumous Career of Emiliano Zapata: Myth, Memory, and Mexico's Twentieth Century*. Austin: University of Texas Press, 2008.

Cabrera Luna, Claudia, Mayra Mendoza Avilés, Friedhelm Schmidt-Welle, and Arnold Spitta, eds. *Hugo Brehme y la Revolución Mexicana / Und die Mexikanische Revolution*. Mexico City and Germany: DAAD, INAH, and SINAFO, 2009.

Camacho de la Rosa, Gerardo. *Raíz y razón de Totolapan: El drama de la guerra zapatista*. Mexico City: Secretaría de Desarrollo Social, Gobierno del Distrito Federal and Ceácatl, 2007.

Canales, Claudia. *Romualdo García: Un fotógrafo, una ciudad, una época*. Guanajuato: Gobierno de Estado de Guanajuato-INAH, 1980.

Cano, Gabriela. *Se llamaba Elena Arizmendi*. Mexico City: Tusquets, 2010.

———. "Las mujeres como sujetos de la Revolución Mexicana: Una mirada historiográfica." In *El siglo de la Revolución Mexicana*, vol. I, edited by Jaime Bailón, Carlos Martínez Assad, and Pablo Serrano Álvarez, 275–286. Mexico City: Instituto Nacional de Estudios Históricos de la Revolución Mexicana, 2000.

———. "*Soldaderas* and *Coronelas*." In *Encyclopedia of Mexico: History, Society and Culture*, edited by Michael S. Werner, 1357–1360. Chicago: Fitzroy Dearborn Publishers, 1997.

———. "Unconcealable Realities of Desire: Amelio Robles's (Transgender) Masculinity in the Mexican Revolution." In *Sex in Revolution: Gender, Politics, and Power in Modern Mexico*, edited by Jocelyn Olcott, Mary Kay Vaughan, and Gabriela Cano, 35–56. Durham: Duke University Press, 2006.

Carmichael, Jane. *First World War Photographers*. London: Routledge, 1989.

Cartier-Bresson, Henri. *The Mind's Eye: Writings on Photography and Photographers*. New York: Aperture, 1999.

Casanova, Rosa, and Olivier Debroise. *Sobre la superficie bruñida de un espejo: Fotógrafos del siglo XIX*. Mexico City: Fondo de Cultura Económica, 1989.

Casanova, Rosa, and Adriana Konzevik. *Luces sobre México: Catálogo selectivo de la Fototeca Nacional del* INAH. Mexico City: CONACULTA and INAH, 2006

"Casasola." *Siempre!* (3 July 1974): 100.

[Casasola, Agustín Víctor]. *Albúm histórico gráfico: Contiene los principales sucesos acaecidos durante las épocas de Díaz, de la Barra, Madero, Huerta y Obregón*. Mexico City: Agustín V. Casasola e Hijos, 1921.

Casasola, Gustavo. *Hechos y hombres de México: Gral.: Emiliano Zapata*. Mexico City: Editorial Gustavo Casasola, 1994.

———. *Historia gráfica de la Revolución, 1900–1940*. Mexico City: Editorial Gustavo Casasola, 1942.

———. *Historia gráfica de la Revolución Mexicana*. 4 vols. Mexico City: Trillas, 1960.

———, ed. *Agustín Víctor Casasola: El hombre que retrató una época*. Mexico City: Editorial Gustavo Casasola, 1988.

Castellanos, Alejandro. "Del México postal a la revolución iconográfica (1900–1920)." *Foto Zoom*, no. 101 (1984): 14–19.

———. "Notas sobre fotografía y sociedad mexicanas." *Foto Zoom*, no. 131 (1986): 12–15.

Chevalier, Francois. "Un factor decisivo de la revolución agraria de México: El levantamiento de Zapata (1911-1919)." *Cuadernos Americanos* 63, no. 6 (1960): 165-187.

La Ciudadela de fuego: A ochenta años de La Decena Trágica. Coordinated by Rafael Vargas. Mexico City: CONACULTA, Archivo General de la Nación, INAH, and the Instituto Nacional de Estudios Históricos de la Revolución Mexicana, 1993.

Crónica ilustrada Revolución Mexicana, no. 5. Mexico City: Publex, 1966–67.

Cubero Piña, Gustavo Adolfo. "Catálogo fotográfico Fondo Magaña Cerda." *Licenciatura* thesis, History, UNAM, 1990.

Cuenya Mateos, Miguel Ángel. "Reflexiones en torno a la pandemia de influenza de 1918: El caso de la ciudad de Puebla." *Desacatos*, no. 32 (2010): 145–158.

Cumberland, Charles C. *Mexican Revolution: The Constitutionalist Years*. Austin: University of Texas Press, 1972.

de Corpas, Lucio. "Los chicos de la prensa: El mundo de nuestros reporteros." *Revista de Revistas* (4 May 1913): 10, 29.

de la Colina, José. "Breve lectura de la fotografía *Villa en la silla presidencial*." *Alquimia*, no. 9 (2000): 12–13.

de la Torre Rendón, Judith. "Las imágenes fotográficas de la sociedad mexicana en la prensa gráfica del porfiriato." *Historia mexicana* 48, no. 2 (1998): 343–373.

de los Reyes, Aurelio. *Con Villa en México: Testimonios de camarógrafos norteamericanos en la Revolución, 1911–1916*. Mexico City: UNAM, 1985.

de Orellano, Margarita. "Pancho Villa: Primer actor del cine de la Revolución." In *Cine mexicano*, edited by Jorge Alberto Lozoya, 61–62. Mexico City: IMCINE-Lunwerg, 1992.

Debroise, Olivier. *Mexican Suite: A History of Photography in Mexico*. Translated by Stella de Sá Rego. Austin: University of Texas Press, 2001.

del Castillo Troncoso, Alberto. *Isidro Fabela: Una mirada en torno a la Revolución Mexicana*. Mexico: Gobierno del Estado de México, 2010.

———. "El surgimiento del reportaje policiaco en México: Los inicios de un nuevo lenguaje gráfico (1888–1910)." *Cuicuilco* 5, no. 13 (1998): 163–194.

del Moral González, Fernando. "El acervo fotográfico de Josaphat Martínez en Monclova, Coahuila." *Alquimia*, no. 10 (2000): 41–42.

———. *Las imágenes perdidas de Eustasio Montoya: El rescate de un camarógrafo*. Mexico City: Arqueología Cinematográfica, A.C.-AGN, 1994.

Delgadillo, Willivaldo. "Legionarios de la luz: Fotógrafos, revolucionarios y filibusteros durante la toma de Juárez de 1911." http://docentes.uacj.mx/willi/.htm.

Diccionario histórico y biográfico de la Revolución Mexicana, vol. 1. Mexico City: Instituto Nacional de Estudios Históricos de la Revolución Mexicana, 1991.

Edición gráfica conmemorativa al centenario de la Revolución Mexicana. Mexico City: Secretaría de la Defensa Nacional (SEDENA), 2010.

Edwards, Susan H. "Pretty Babies: Art, Erotica or Kiddie Porn?" *History of Photography* 18, no. 1 (1994): 38–46.

Eisenhower, John S. D. *Intervention! The United States and the Mexican Revolution, 1913–1917.* New York: Norton, 1993.

Escorza Rodríguez, Daniel. "Las cámaras fotográficas en los inicios del proceso revolucionario, 1910–1911." Unpublished manuscript from the Segundo Encuentro Regional de Fototecas, 2009.

———. "Las fotografías de Casasola publicadas en diarios capitalinos durante 1913." *Alquimia*, no. 25 (2005): 35–40.

———. "Imagen y apariencia de Victoriano Huerta después de La Decena Trágica." Unpublished manuscript from the IX Encuentro Nacional de Fototecas, 2008.

———. "Los inicios de Agustín V. Casasola como reporter-fotógrafo." *Alquimia*, no. 27 (2005): 24–35.

———. "El itinerario fotoperiodístico de Agustín Víctor Casasola, 1910–1910." *História* 26, no. 2 (Sao Paulo, 2007): 19–42.

Escorza Rodríguez, Daniel, and Heladio Vera Trejo. "Las cámara Graflex en la campaña federal maderista contra Pascual Orozco, 1912." *20/10: Memoria de las Revoluciones*, no. 10 (2010): 254–265.

Faris, James C. *Navajo and Photography: A Critical History of the Representation of an American People.* Albuquerque: University of New Mexico Press, 1996.

Figarella, Mariana. *Edward Weston y Tina Modotti en México: Su inserción dentro de las estrategias estéticas del arte posrevolucionario.* Mexico City: UNAM, 2002.

Florescano, Enrique, ed. *Así fue la Revolución Mexicana.* 8 vols. Mexico City: Senado de la República-Secretaría de Educación Pública, 1985–86.

Flusser, Vilém. *Towards a Philosophy of Photography.* Göttingen: European Photography, 1984.

Folgarait, Leonard. *Seeing Mexico Photographed: The Work of Horne, Casasola, Modotti, and Álvarez Bravo.* New Haven: Yale University Press, 2008.

Frank, Patrick. *Posada´s Broadsheets: Mexican Popular Imagery, 1890–1910.* Albuquerque: University of New Mexico Press, 1998.

Friday, Jonathon. "Transparency and the Photographic Image." *British Journal of Aesthetics* 36, no. 1 (1996): 30–42.

García, Clara Guadalupe. *El periódico "El Imparcial": Primer diario moderno de México (1896–1914).* Mexico City: Centro de Estudios Históricos del Porfiriato, 2003.

García, Genaro, ed. *Crónica oficial de las fiestas del primer centenario de la independencia de México.* Mexico City: Centro de Estudios de Historia de México Condumex, 1991; facsimile of the 1911 publication by the Museo Nacional.

García Díaz, Bernardo. *Puerto de Veracruz*, vol. 8: *Veracruz: Imágenes de su historia.* Veracruz: Archivo General del Estado de Veracruz, 1992.

Garduño Pulido, Blanca. "Mexico's Enduring Images." In *México: Una nación persistente: Hugo Brehme, fotografías*, 13–16. Mexico City: CONACULTA and INBA, 1995.

Garner, Gretchen. *Disappearing Witness: Change in Twentieth-Century American Photography.* Baltimore: Johns Hopkins University Press, 2003.

Garner, Paul. *Porfirio Díaz.* Harlow, Great Britain: Pearson, 2001.

Gautreau, Marion. "El Archivo Casasola y la representación de la Revolución Mexicana." Unpublished manuscript, 2006.

———. "*La Ilustración Semanal* y el Archivo Casasola," *Cuicuilco* 14, no. 41 (2007): 113–142.

———. "Militar o político: La imagen del presidente durante la Revolución." *Historias*, no. 68 (2007): 71–80.

———. "Les photographies de la Révolution Mexicaine dans la presse illustrée de Mexico (1910–1940): De la chronique á l'iconisation." Doctoral thesis, Université Paris IV-Sorbonne, 2007.

———. "Questionnement d'un symbole: Agustín Víctor Casasola, photographe de la Revolution Mexicaine." Master's thesis, Université Paris IV-Sorbonne, 2002.

———. "La Revolución Mexicana a los ojos del mundo: Diferentes perspectivas en la prensa ilustrada." In *México: Fotografía y revolución*, coordinated by Miguel Ángel Berumen, 187–280. Mexico City: Fundación Televisa y Lunwerg, 2009.

Gilly, Adolfo. *La revolución interrumpida*. Mexico City: Ediciones El Caballito, 1971.

González, Luis. *San José de Gracia: Mexican Village in Transition*. Translated by John Upton. Austin: University of Texas Press, 1972.

González Flores, Laura. *Otra revolución: Fotografías de la ciudad de México, 1910–1918: Colección Ricardo Espinosa*. Mexico City: UNAM, 2010.

———. "Técnica fotográfica y mirada: La fotografía en el país de la metralla." In *México: Fotografía y revolución*, coordinated by Miguel Ángel Berumen, 53–61. Mexico City: Fundación Televisa y Lunwerg, 2009.

González Navarro, Moisés. *Sociedad y cultura en el porfiriato*. Mexico City: CONACULTA, 1994.

Gould, Lewis, and Richard Greffe. *Photojournalist: The Career of Jimmy Hare*. Austin: University of Texas Press, 1977.

Griffiths, Gloria Fraser. "La postal mexicana." In "La tarjeta postal." Special Issue, *Artes de México*, no. 48 (1999): 8–15.

Guevara Escobar, Arturo. "La Decena Trágica, la competencia." http://fotografosdelarevolucion.blogspot.com/2009/01/la-decena-trgica-los-fotografos.html.

———. "La Decena Trágica, los fotógrafos." http://fotografosdelarevolucion.blogspot.com/2009/01/la-decena-trgica-los-fotografos.html.

———. "El exilio." http://fotografosdelarevolucion.blogspot.com.

———. "La fotografía de Emiliano Zapata." *Relatos e historias en México*, no. 9 (2009): 22–23.

———. "Reflex o View." http://fotografosdelarevolucion.blogspot.com/2009/03/reflex-o-view.html.

Gutiérrez Ruvalcaba, Ignacio. "A Fresh Look at the Casasola Archive." In "Mexican Photography." Special Issue, *History of Photography* 20, no. 3 (1996): 191–195.

———. "Los Casasola durante la posrevolución." *Alquimia*, no. 1 (1997): 37–40.

Guzmán, Martín Luís. *El águila y la serpiente*. Mexico City: Colección Málaga, [1928] 1978.

Hardt, Hanno. "Pictures for the Masses: Photography and the Rise of Popular Magazines in Weimar Germany." *Journal of Communication Inquiry* 13, no. 1 (1989): 7–29.

———. "Sites of Reality: Constructing Press Photography in Weimar Germany, 1928–33." *Communication Review* 1, no. 3 (1996): 373–401.

Haw, Dora Luz. "Prueba que 'Adelita' no es de Casasola." *Reforma*, 16 February 2007, section "Cultura," 6.

Hight, Eleanor M., and Gary D. Sampson. Introduction to *Colonialist Photography: Imag(in)ing Race and Place*, edited by Eleanor M. Hight and Gary D. Sampson, 1–19. London: Routledge, 2002.

Jablonska, Aleksandra, and Juan Felipe Leal. *La Revolución Mexicana en el cine nacional, 1911–1917*. Mexico City: Universidad Pedagógica Nacional, 1997.

Jiménez, Arturo. "Identifican al verdadero autor de la fotografía de la Adelita." *La Jornada*, 16 February 2007, 4a.

Jiménez, Blanca, and Samuel Villela. *Los Salmerón: Un siglo de fotografía en Guerrero*. Mexico City: INAH, 1998.

José Guadalupe Posada: Ilustrador de la vida mexicana. Mexico City: Fondo Editorial de la Plástica Mexicana, 1992.

Katz, Friedrich. *The Life and Times of Pancho Villa*. Palo Alto: Stanford University Press, 1998.

———. *The Secret War in Mexico: Europe, the United States, and the Mexican Revolution*. Chicago: University of Chicago Press, 1981.

Knight, Alan. *The Mexican Revolution*, vol. 1: *Porfirians, Liberals and Peasants*. Lincoln: University of Nebraska Press, 1990.

———. *The Mexican Revolution*, vol. 2: *Counter-Revolution and Reconstruction*. Lincoln: University of Nebraska Press, 1990.

Knightly, Phillip. *The First Casualty: From the Crimea to Vietnam: The War Correspondent as Hero, Propagandist, and Myth Maker*. New York: Harcourt Brace Jovanovich, 1975.

Kossoy, Boris. *Fotografía e historia*. Translated by Paula Sibilia. Buenos Aires: Biblioteca de la Mirada, 2001.

Krauze, Enrique. *Biografía del poder*. 8 vols. Mexico City: Fondo de Cultura Económica, 1987.

———. *Francisco I. Madero, místico de la libertad*. Mexico City: Fondo de Cultura Económica, 1987.

———. *Madero vivo*. Mexico City: Clío, 1993.

La France, David. *The Mexican Revolution in Puebla, 1908–1913: The Maderista Movement and the Failure of Liberal Reform*. Wilmington, DE: Scholarly Resources, 1989.

Lara Klahr, Flora. "Agustín Víctor Casasola: Fotógrafo, coleccionista y editor." In *Jefes, héroes y caudillos: Archivo Casasola*, 99–109. Mexico City: Fondo de Cultura Económica, 1986.

Lara Ruiz, Miguel, and Spencer Lara Ruiz. "Los 'Caranclanes.'" In *Mi pueblo durante la revolución*, vol. 1, 113–149. Mexico City: INAH, 1985.

Larrain, Marcos G. "Historia de la fotografía de prensa." *Mañana*, 19 September 1953, 57–70.

Lau, Ana, and Carmen Ramos. *Mujeres y revolución, 1900–1917*. Mexico City: Instituto Nacional de Estudios Históricos de la Revolución Mexicana, CONACULTA, and INAH, 1993.

Lavrentiev, Alexander. *Rodchenko: Photography, 1924–1954*. Edison, NJ: Knickerbocker Press, 1995.

Leighton, George. "The Photographic History of the Mexican Revolution." In Brenner, *The Wind That Swept Mexico: The History of the Mexican Revolution 1910–1942*. New York: Harper and Brothers, 1943.

Lear, John. *Workers, Neighbors, and Citizens: The Revolution in Mexico City*. Lincoln: University of Nebraska Press, 2001.

Lerner, Jesse. "La exportación de lo mexicano: Hugo Brehme en casa y en el extranjero." In "Hugo Brehme: Los prototipos mexicanistas." Special Issue, *Alquimia*, no. 16 (2002–2003): 30–38.

Lesy, Michael. *Wisconsin Death Trip*. New York: Pantheon, 1973.

Levine, Robert. *Images of History: Nineteenth and Early Twentieth Century Latin American Photographs as Documents*. Durham: Duke University Press, 1989.

Leyda, Jay. *Films Beget Films: A Study of the Compilation Film*. New York: Hill and Wang, 1964.

Lutz, Catherine A., and Jane L. Collins. *Reading "National Geographic."* Chicago: University of Chicago Press, 1993.

Magaña, Gildardo. *Emiliano Zapata y el agrarismo en México*. Mexico City: Instituto Nacional de Estudios Históricos de la Revolución Mexicana, 1985.

Malagón Girón, Beatriz. "La fotografía de Winfield Scott: Entre la producción comercial y la calidad estética de la fotografía." Doctoral thesis, UNAM, 2003.

Maldonado Valera, Acacia Ligia. "Manuel Ramos en la prensa ilustrada capitalina de principios de siglo, 1897–1913." *Licenciatura* thesis, History, UNAM, 2005.

Malvido, Adriana. "Archivo Casasola: 100 años de historia fotográfica en México." *La Jornada*, 19 November 1991.

———. "Relata la familia Casasola el devenir de su archivo de fotos." *La Jornada*, 21 November 1991, 24.

Márquez Morfín, Lourdes, and América Molinar del Villar. "El otoño de 1918: Las repercusiones de la pandemia de gripe en la ciudad de México." *Desacatos*, no. 32 (2010): 121–144.

Martínez, Andrea. *La intervención norteamericana: Veracruz, 1914*. Mexico City: Martín Casillas Editores, 1982.

Martínez Assad, Carlos, ed. *Memoria y olvido: Imágenes de México*. 20 vols. Mexico City: Martín Casillas-SEP, 1982–1983.

Martínez de Velasco Vélez, Patricia. *Directoras de cine: Proyección de una mundo obscuro*. Mexico City: IMCINE-CONEICC, 1991.

Mauad, Ana Maria. "Fotografía e historia." In *Imágenes e investigación social*, edited by Fernando Aguayo and Lourdes Roca, 464–473. Mexico City: Instituto Mora, 2005.

Meiselas, Susan. *Nicaragua*. New York: Pantheon, 1981.

Memorial of a Glorious Time: Photographic Material on the Vietnam War. Vietnam: Nhà Xuat Ban Tong Hop Thanh Pho Ho Chi Minh, 2003.

Méndez Alonso, Ignacio. "Recordando un poquito de mi vida." In *Mi pueblo durante la revolución*, I:189–213. Mexico City: INAH, 1985.

Mendoza Áviles, Mayra. "La colección Hugo Brehme." In "Hugo Brehme: Los prototipos mexicanistas." Special Issue, *Alquimia*, no. 16 (2002–2003): 41–43.

———. "El Zapata de Brehme: Análisis de un caso." *Alquimia*, no. 36 (2009): 83–84.

Meyer, Michael. *Huerta: A Political Portrait*. Lincoln: University of Nebraska Press, 1972.

Michel, Paulina. "Cruz Sánchez y su estudio ambulante." *20/10: Memoria de las revoluciones*, no. 6 (2010): 138–149.

Miller, George, and Dorothy Miller. *Picture Postcards in the United States, 1893–1918*. New York: Clarkson N. Potter, 1976.

Miquel, Ángel. *Acercamientos al cine silente mexicano*. Cuernavaca: Universidad Autónoma del Estado de Morelos, 2005.

———. "El registro de Jesús H. Abitia de las campañas constitucionalistas." In Ángel Miquel, Zuzana Pick, and Eduardo de la Vega, *Fotografía, cine y literatura de la Revolución Mexicana*, 7–30. Cuernavaca: Universidad Autónoma del Estado de Morelos, 2004.

———. *Salvador Toscano*. Mexico: Universidad de Guadalajara, Universidad Veracruzana, Gobierno del Estado de Puebla, UNAM, 1997.

Miranda, Raúl. "Cronometría de un cine mexicano mudo que nunca fue mudo." 25 March 2009. http://www.correcamara.com.mx/index.php?mod=historia_detalle&id=823.

Moeller, Susan D. *Shooting War: Photography and the American Experience of Combat*. New York: Basic Books, 1989.

Monroy Nasr, Rebeca. "Ezequiel Carrasco: Entre los nitratos de plata y las balas de bronce." Unpublished manuscript.

———. "El tripié y la cámara como galardón." In *La Ciudadela de fuego: A ochenta años de La Decena Trágica*, 47–52. Mexico City: CONACULTA, Archivo General de la Nación, INAH, Instituto Nacional de Estudios Históricos de la Revolución Mexicana, 1993.

Montellano, Francisco. *C. B. Waite, fotógrafo: Una mirada diversa sobre el México de principios del siglo XX*. Mexico City: Grijalbo, 1994.

Morales, Alfonso. "Luces y sombras del Centenario I." *Luna Córnea*, no. 12 (1997): 67–71.

Morales, Miguel Ángel. "La celebre fotografía de Jerónimo Hernández." *Alquimia*, no. 27 (2006): 68–75.

———. "Eduardo Melhado." Fotografía en México, http://miguelangelmorales-fotografos.blogspot.com/2009/03/eduardo-malhado.html.

Moreno Irázabal, Luis G. "Figuras del periodismo mexicano: Don Agustín Víctor Casasola." *El Demócrata*, 11 April 1926, magazine section: 6, 15.

Moscoso Pastrana, Prudencio. *Jacinto Pérez, "Pajarito": Último líder chamula*. Chiapas: Gobierno del Estado de Chiapas, 1972.

Mraz, John. "El Archivo Casasola: Historia de un mito." In *El siglo de la Revolución Mexicana*, edited by Jaime Bailón Corres, Carlos Martínez Assad, and Pablo Serrano Álvarez, 207–214. Mexico City: Instituto Nacional de Estudios Históricos de la Revolución Mexicana, 2000.

———. "Cuban Photography: Context and Meaning." *History of Photography* 18, no. 1 (1994): 87–90.

———. "De la fotografía histórica: Particularidad y nostalgia." *Nexos*, no. 91 (1985): 9–12.

———. "'En calidad de esclavas': Obreras en los molinos de nixtamal, México, diciembre, 1919." *Historia obrera*, no. 24 (1982): 2–14.

———. "¿Fotohistoria o historia gráfica? El pasado mexicano en fotografía." *Cuicuilco* 14, no. 41 (2007): 11–41.

———. *Looking for Mexico: Modern Visual Culture and National Identity*. Durham: Duke University Press, 2009.

———. "Mexican History in Photographs." In *The Mexico Reader: History, Culture, Politics*, edited by Gilbert Joseph and Timothy Henderson, 295–331. Durham: Duke University Press, 2002.

———. *Nacho López, Mexican Photographer*. Minneapolis: University of Minnesota Press, 2003.

———. "The New Photojournalism of Mexico, 1976–1998." *History of Photography* 22, no. 4 (1998): 312–365.

———. "Picturing Mexico's Past: Photography and *Historia Gráfica*." In "Memory and Nation in Contemporary Mexico." Special Issue, *South Central Review* 21, no. 3 (2004): 24–45.

———. "¿Qué tiene de nuevo la historia gráfica?," *Elementos: Ciencia y Cultura*, no. 61 (2006): 49–57, http://www.elementos.buap.mx/num61/htm/49.htm.

———. "Representing the Mexican Revolution: Bending Photographs to the Will of *Historia Gráfica*." In *Photography and Writing in Latin America: Double Exposures*, edited by Marcy E. Schwarts and Mary Beth Tierney-Tello, 21–39. Albuquerque: University of New Mexico Press, 2006.

———. "What's documentary about photography? From directed to digital photojournalism." *Revista Zonezero*, www.zonezero.com, 2002.

Mraz, John, and Jaime Vélez Storey. *Uprooted: Braceros in the Hermanos Mayo Lens*. Houston: Arte Público Press and University of Houston, 1996.

Negrete Álvarez, Claudia. *Valleto Hermanos: Fotógrafos mexicanos de entresiglo*. Mexico City: UNAM, 2006.

Obregón, Álvaro. *Ocho mil kilometros en campaña*. Paris and Mexico City: Libería de la Vda. de Ch. Bouret, 1917.

Ochoa Sandy, Gerardo. "Historia de un archivo." *Luna Córnea*, no. 13 (1997): 10–15.

Ortiz, José. "Villa jugando a la presidencia." *El Pueblo*, 14 March 1915, 3.

Ortiz Monasterio, Pablo, ed. *Cuba, dos épocas: Raúl Corrales, Constantino Arias*. Mexico City: Fondo de Cultura Económica, 1987.

———. *Jefes, héroes y caudillos: Archivo Casasola*. Mexico City: Fondo de Cultura Económica, 1986.

———. *Mexico: The Revolution and Beyond: Photographs by Agustín Víctor Casasola, 1900–1940*. New York: Aperture, 2003.

O'Malley, Ilene. *The Myth of the Revolution: Hero Cults and the Institutionalization of the Mexican State, 1920–1940*. New York: Greenwood Press, 1986.

Pacheco, Cristina. "Gustavo Casasola: Todos nuestro ayeres." In *La luz de México: Entrevistas con pintores y fotógrafos*, edited by Cristina Pacheco, 116–125. Mexico City: Fondo de Cultura Económica, 1988.

Palomares, Justino. *La invasión yanqui en 1914*. Mexico City: n.p., 1940.

Pavelka, Jeffrey James, ed. *Monterrey en 400 fotografías*. Monterrey: Museo de Arte Contemporáneo de Monterrey, 1996.

Peirce, Charles. "Logic as Semiotic: The Theory of Signs." In *The Philosophy of Peirce: Selected Writings*, edited by Justus Buckler, 98–119. London: Routledge and Kegan Paul, 1940.

Pérez Montfort, Ricardo. *Cotidianidades, imaginarios y contextos: Ensayos de historia y cultura en México, 1850–1950*. Mexico City: CIESAS, 2008.

———. "Imágenes del zapatismo entre 1911 y 1913." In *Estudios sobre el zapatismo*, edited by Laura Espejel, 163–208. Mexico City: INAH, 2000.

Piccato, Pablo. *City of Suspects: Crime in Mexico City, 1900–1931*. Durham: Duke University Press, 2001.

Place, J. A., and L. S. Peterson. "Some Visual Motifs of Film Noir." In *Movies and Methods*, edited by Bill Nichols, 325–338. Berkeley: University of California Press, 1976.

El poder de la imagen y la imagen del poder: Fotografías de prensa del porfiriato a la época actual. Coordinated by Marco Antonio Hernández. Chapingo: Universidad Autónoma Chapingo, 1985.

Poniatowska, Elena. *Las soldaderas.* Mexico City: Era, CONACULTA, and INAH, 1999.

Poole, Deborah. *Vision, Race, and Modernity: A Visual Economy of the Andean Image World.* Princeton, NJ: Princeton University Press, 1997.

Posada y la prensa ilustrada: Signos de modernización y resistencias. Mexico City: Instituto Nacional de Bellas Artes, 1996.

Quirk, Robert E. *An Affair of Honor: Woodrow Wilson and the Occupation of Veracruz.* New York: Norton, 1967.

Ramírez Plancarte, Francisco. *La ciudad de México durante la revolución constitucionalista.* Mexico City: Ediciones Botas, 1941.

Ramírez Rancaño, Mario. "La epidemia de influenza española en México: 1918." *20/10: Memoria de las revoluciones en México*, no. 4 (2009): 68–93.

———. *La revolución en los volcanes: Domingo y Cirilo Arenas.* Mexico City: UNAM, 1995.

Reed, John. *Insurgent Mexico.* Danvers: General Books, 2009.

———. *Villa y la Revolución Mexicana.* Mexico City: Nueva Imagen, 1983.

La Revolución Mexicana: 100 años de historia: 2 vols. Mexico City: Editorial Cordillera, 2009.

Riis, Jacob. *How the Other Half Lives.* New York: Dover, 1971.

Rivera, Emiliano. "Jesús Hermenegildo Abitia: 'El Fotógrafo Constitucionalista.'" *Fotozoom*, no. 37 (1978): 56–63.

Rivero, Gonzalo G. *Hacia la verdad: Episodios de la revolución.* Mexico City: Compañía Editora Nacional, 1911.

Rivero Pastor, Aldo Roberto. "Familia Rousset: Proceres de la revolución mexicana." Unpublished manuscript.

Rodríguez, José Antonio. "La construcción de un imaginario." In *Hugo Brehme: Fotograf-Fotógrafo*, 28–43. Berlin: Verlag Willmuth Arenhövel, 2004.

———. "Testimonios de la fotografía en Monterrey." In *Monterrey en 400 fotografías*, 77–104. Monterrey: Museo de Arte Contemporáneo de Monterrey, 1996.

Rodríguez, Roberto. "The Early Years: The Portrayal of Minorities in Hollywood Film Industry." 16 June 2007. http://diverseeducation.com/article/7443/1.php.

Rodríguez Hernández, Georgina. "Niños desnudos en el porfiriato." *Luna Córnea*, no. 9 (1996): 44–49.

Rodríguez Lapuente, Manuel. *Breve historia gráfica de la Revolución Mexicana.* Mexico City: G. Gili, 1987.

Rosas, Alejandro. "El primer jefe." *Relatos e historias en México*, no. 9 (2009): 38–45.

Rosenblum, Naomi. *A World History of Photography.* New York: Abbeville Press, 1989.

Rufinelli, Jorge. "John Reed en la Revolución Mexicana." In John Reed, *Villa y la Revolución Mexicana*, 11–106. Mexico City: Nueva Imagen, 1983.

Ruiz, Blanca. "Brehme, autor del Zapata de Casasola." *Reforma*, 4 October 1995, 12.

Saborit, Antonio. *"El Mundo Ilustrado" de Rafael Reyes Espíndola*. Mexico City: Centro de Estudios de Historia de México Condumex, 2003.

Salas, Elizabeth. *Soldaderas in the Mexican Military: Myth and History*. Austin: University of Texas Press, 1990.

Sánchez Escobar, Rafael. "Episodios de la Revolución en el sur, VII: En defensa de la vida del caudillo." *Revista de Revistas*, 6 November 1932, n.p.

———. "Episodios de la revolución en el sur, XIV: Antecedentes sobre la toma de Yautepec." *Revista de Revistas*, 25 December 1932, n.p.

Sánchez García, José María. "Apuntes para la historia de nuestro cine: Las hermanas Ehlers," *Novedades*, 25 February 1945, sec. 3, p. 7.

———. "Apuntes para la historia de nuestro cine: Jesús H. Abitia." Suplemento dominical, *Novedades*, 23 December 1945, 6.

———. "Apuntes para la historia de nuestro cine: Jesús H. Abitia." Suplemento dominical, *Novedades*, 30 December 1945, 6.

———. "Apuntes para la historia de nuestro cine: Primeros fotógrafos." *Novedades*, 11 February 1945, sec. 3, p. 8.

Sartre, Jean-Paul. "For Whom Does One Write?" In *Literature and Existentialism*, translated by Bernard Frechtman, 67–160. New York: Citadel Press, 1949.

Smith, Michael M. "Gringo Propagandist: George F. Weeks and the Mexican Revolution." *Journalism History* 29, no. 1 (2003): 2–11.

Soldati fotografi: Fotografie della Grande Guerra sulle pagine de "Le Miroir." Roverto: Museo Storico Italiano della Guerra, 2005.

Sontag, Susan. *On Photography*. New York: Dell, 1973.

Stomberg, John. "August Sander." In *Encyclopedia of Twentieth-Century Photography*, edited by Lynne Warren, 1383–1386. New York: Routledge, 2006.

Sweig, Julia. *Inside the Cuban Revolution: Fidel Castro and the Urban Underground*. Cambridge, MA: Harvard University Press, 2002.

Tablada, José Juan. *Obras-IV, Diario (1900–1944)*, ed. Guillermo Sheridan. Mexico City: UNAM, 1992.

Taibo, Paco Ignacio, II. *Pancho Villa, una biografía narrativa*. Mexico City: Planeta, 2006.

Taracena, Alfonso. *La verdadera Revolución Mexicana: Segunda etapa (1913–1914)*. Mexico City: Editorial Jus, 1960.

Tierra y Libertad! Photographs of Mexico 1900–1935 from the Casasola Archive. Oxford: Museum of Modern Art, 1985.

Trachtenberg, Alan. *Reading American Photographs: Images as History: Mathew Brady to Walker Evans*. New York: Hill and Wang, 1989.

Treviño, Estela, ed. *160 años de fotografía en México*. Mexico City: Conculta-Oceano-Televisa, 2004.

Tupitsyn, Margaret. *The Soviet Photograph, 1924–1937*. New Haven: Yale University Press, 1996.

Turner, John Kenneth. *Barbarous Mexico*. Chicago: Charles Company Cooperative, 1911.

Tyler, Ron. *Posada's Mexico*. Washington, DC: Library of Congress, 1979.

Ulloa, Berta. *La revolución escindida*. Vol. 4 of *Historia de la Revolución Mexicana*. Mexico City: El Colegio de México, 1982.

Urquizo, Francisco. *Recuerdo que: Visiones aisladas de la Revolución Mexicana*. Mexico City: Secretaría de la Defensa Nacional, 1993.

Valtierra, Pedro. *Nicaragua: Una noche afuera*. Mexico City: Cuartoscuro, 1991.

Vanderwood, Paul. "The Picture Postcard as Historical Evidence: Veracruz, 1914." *The Americas* 45, no. 2 (1988): 201–225.

Vanderwood, Paul, and Frank N. Samponaro. *Border Fury: A Picture Postcard Record of Mexico's Revolution and US War Preparedness, 1910–1917*. Albuquerque: University of New Mexico Press, 1988.

Vargas Sánchez, Eduardo. "La ciudad de México de 1900 a 1920." In *Mi pueblo durante la revolución*, vol. 1, 151–190. Mexico City: INAH, 1985.

Vélez Storey, Jaime. "Prensa, propaganda y diplomacia de la Revolución Mexicana: *The Mexican Review* (1916–1917)." In *El orden cultural de la Revolución Mexicana: Sujetos, representaciones, discursos y universos conceptuales*, edited by Leonardo Martínez Carrizales, 111–143. Mexico City: Universidad Autónoma Metropolitana-Azcapotzalco, 2010.

Vietnam, 1954–1975. Tokyo: Tokyo Metropolitan Museum of Photography, 2006.

Villegas de Magnón, Leonor. *The Rebel*. Edited by Clara Lomas. Houston: Arte Público Press, 1994.

———. *La rebelde: Leonor Villegas de Magnón*. Edited by Clara Lomas. Mexico City and Houston: CONACULTA, INAH, and Arte Público Press, 2004.

Villela, Samuel. "La fotografía de la Revolución Mexicana." *20/10: Memoria de las Revoluciones en México*, no. 5 (2009): 80–88.

———. "La fotografía de la Revolución Mexicana." www.terra.com.

———. "Imágenes de la Revolución en Guerrero." In *Obra de un pueblo*, 168–183. Chilpancingo: Gobierno del Estado de Guerrero, 2004.

———. *Sara Castrejón: Fotógrafa de la Revolución*. Mexico City: INAH, 2010.

von Dewitz, Bodo, ed. *Kiosk: A History of Photojournalism*. Göttingen: Steidl, 2001.

Walton, Kendall L. "Transparent Pictures: On the Nature of Photographic Realism." *Critical Inquiry* 11, no. 2 (1984): 246–277.

Whelan, Richard. *Robert Capa: A Biography*. New York: Alfred Knopf, 1985.

Womack, John. *Zapata and the Mexican Revolution*. New York: Alfred Knopf, 1968.

Zavala, Adriana, et al. *Mexico Beyond Its Revolution / México más allá de su revolución*. Medford, MA: Tufts University Art Galleries, 2010.

Index

Abitia, Jesús Hermenegildo, 3, 40, 173, 203, 204; as Constitutionalist photographer, 2, 194–198; photographs by, *197*, *199*; saves Madero's life, 53–55
agencies, photo, 3, 45–46
Alemán Pérez, Dr., *89*
Alexander, Jim, 55
Almagro (Mexico City photojournalist), 200
Alvarado, General Salvador, 27, 42–43
Álvarez Bravo, Manuel, 2, 14, 154
Álvarez Tostado, Ezequiel, 24, 34, 48, 50, 123, 133, 251; as editor of *La Ilustración Semanal*, 11, 153–155, 184, 201; photograph by, *154*; photograph of, 51
amateur photographers, 13, 56, 155, 157
Andrade, Manuel L., 74,
Ángeles, Felipe, 198
Apreza, Eucaria, 109
Arenas, Domingo, 2, 114, *115*
Arizmendi, Elena, 68
Arnal, Ariel, 94, 95, 102, 104, 111, 118, 236, 237
Arriaga, José, 74
artistic photography, 50, 154–155, 251
Aultman, Otis, 55, 57
authorship and credit, 7, 16, 46

Banderas, Juan (El Agachado), *74*
bandits and banditry, 142, 179, 184, 207, 236, 246, 247; photograph of, *179*
Baquedano, Natalia, 116
Bartra, Eli, 116
Becker, Carl, 9,
Belkin, Arnold, 238, 251; mural by, *252*
Berumen, Miguel Ángel, 16, 57, 70, 75, 112, 126, 162, 202; on Cachú brothers, 143, 180; on Maderismo, 53, 55, 64, 74, 118; on Villismo, 59, 170, 180, 193, 246
Blanquet, Aureliano, 133, 152
Bonilla, Ignacio, 57, 73; photograph of, *74*
Botte, M. Louis, 155; photograph by, *156*
Branger, M., 249
Brehme, Hugo, 3, 14, 46, 154, 204–207; during the Tragic Ten Days, 123, 128–129; during Veracruz invasion, 163–166; photographing Zapatistas, 118–121, 234–235; photographs by, *35*, *120*, *129*, *130*, *164*, *165*, *166*, *205*, *206*, *207*, *235*
Brenner, Anita, 7, 15, 240, 249, 251
Brown Bros. Agency, 7
Brunk, Samuel, 95, 239

Cachú, Juan and Antonio, 2, 3, 118, 143–144; photographs by, *145*, *179*, *180*, *181*; as Villista photographers, 177–181
cameras, 154–155, 167, 195; Kodak, 55, 155, 177; Kodak Brownie, 11, 157, 167, 227; Graflex, 11, 83, 167; photographs of, *124*, *178*; reflex (single lens reflex), 11, 68, 167; view, 11, 68, 167, 177
Cananea, 37–38, 195; photograph of, *37*
Cano, Gabriela, 68
Capa, Robert, 85
Carmichael, Jane, 12
Carmona, V., 75
Carranza, Venustiano, and Carrancistas, 4, 16, 46, 48, 133, 162, 181, 183, 201, 202, 214,

229, 233, 251; and consciousness of modern media, 42, 175, 193–194, 196, 198–199; photograph of, *218*
Carrasco, Ezequiel, 123
Cartier-Bresson, Henri, 154, 239
Casa del Obrero, 79, 180–181; photographs of, *79*, *180*
Casanova, Rosa, 134
Casasola, Agustín Víctor, 5, 9, 144, 147, 234, 240, 249, 251, 258; and Constitutionalism, 48, 202; and El Jilguero interview, 99, 100, 102; myths about, 2, 4, 45–52, 105, 194, 233, 254; photographs by, *21*, *255*, *257*; during Porfiriato, 16, 25, 27, 34; during the Tragic Ten Days, 123, 130, 132
Casasola, Gustavo: participation of, in the revolution, 48, 187, 223, 254; and picture histories, 4, 9, 46–47, 49, 50, 143, 182, 240, 249, 257
Casasola, Miguel, 46, 251; participation of, in the revolution, 48, 105, 123, 130, 132; photograph by, *18*; during Porfiriato, 17, 34
Casasola Archive, 4, 17, 28, 46, 240, 255
Castrejón, Sara, 2, 93, 114–118; photograph by, *117*
Centennial of Independence, 14, 34–35, 108; photographs of, *35*
Cepeda, Rafael, 57, 74; photograph of, *59*
Cervantes, Captain Librado, 141; photograph of, *140*
Chamula Indians, 80–82; photograph of, *81*
child pornography, 32–34; possible photograph of, *32*
children, 9, 19, 23, 32; photographs of, *19*, *20*, *23*, *29*, *31*, *32*, *33*, *36*, *47*, *63*, *70*, *98*, *126*, *129*, *131*, *136*, *137*, *140*, *141*, *183*, *186*, *210*, *212*, *215*, *218*; in the revolution, 9, 98, 137, 141, 167, 216
cinema, 93, 167, 168, 194, 203–204, 234, 246, 256; and photographer-cineaste "hybrids," 40, 82, 173, 175, 194, 196
Ciudadela, 126, 127, 128, 133
Ciudad Juárez, 14, 53, 55–60, 64–71, 74, 76, 168
Constitutionalist movement and Constitucionalistas, 14, 15, 108, 109, 114, 118, 147, 166, 181, 193–231, 246; and consciousness of modern media, 16, 55, 193, 196, 198–199; and Constitutional Congress, Querétaro, 20, 48; photographers of, 2, 46, 48, 155, 175, 177, 180, 201–204; photographs of, *181*, *197*, *199*, *201*, *202*, *205*, *206*, *207*, *208*, *209*, *212*, *213*, *214*, *218*, *219*, *220*, *221*, *222*, *225*, *226*
Conventionists, 14, 93, 95, 182–191, 202, 207, 254; photographs of, *183*, *186*, *187*, *188*, *189*, *190*, *250*, *252*, *253*
Convention of Aguascalientes, 48, 182
Corral, Leonides, 42; photograph of, *42*
Corrales, Raúl, 1
Cruz Blanca Nacional (National White Cross), 3, 68, 137, 167, 175

De Bereza, Juan, 227–229; photograph by, *228*
Debroise, Olivier, 15, 17, 27, 155
De la Fuente, General David, photograph of, *83*
Del Castillo, Alberto, 204
Delgadillo, Willivaldo, 66
Del Moral, Fernando, 173, 182
De los Reyes, Aurelio, 168
Díaz, Félix, 123, 125, 133, 152, 153; and Felicistas, 125, 126, 128, 132, 133, 134; photographs of, *127*, *134*, *136*
Díaz, Porfirio, 19, 48, 53, 65, 72, 80, 108, 121, 151, 196; photographs of, *20*, *26*. *See also* Porfiriato
directed photojournalism, 57, 127, 128, 158, 163, 176, 177
diseases, 131, 132, 214

Ehlers, Adriana and Dolores, 203
Escobar Castellanos, Aurelio, 65–69, 71, 127, 153, 185; photographs by, *66*, *67*, *69*, *71*

Escorza, Daniel, 7, 258
Espejo, Josefa, 119; photograph of, *120*
Evans, Walker, 134

Feldman, Fred, 55, 56
Figueroa, Jesús, 42, 57; photograph of, *43*
Flores Pérez, Ponciano, 5, 7, 162–163; photographs signed by, *6*, *158*
Folgarait, Leonard, 144–148
foreign photographers, 3, 55–58, 120, 157, 234
Fototeca Nacional, 4, 16, 105, 133, 256

García, J. Z., 74
García, Refugio Z., 204
García, Romualdo, 177
García Díaz, Bernardo, 5
García Joya, Mario (Mayito), 1
Gardner, Gretchen, 154
Garduño, Antonio, 46, 48, 109, 123, 133, 200, 201, 249–251; photographs by, *136*, *202*, *250*
Garza Flores, Don Tomás, 61; photograph of, *62*
Gautreau, Marion, 11, 94, 95, 97, 193
Gidal, Tim, 155
Gilly, Adolfo, 182
Gómez, José (Che), 80; photograph of, *80*
González, Herlinda, 68; photograph of, *70*
González, Pablo, 16, 42, 112, 175, 193, 200, 202, 203
González Flores, Laura, 3, 167
González Garza, Roque, 39, 42, 68, 175, 176; photograph of, *39*
González Navarro, Manuel, 28
González y González, Luis, 142
Goodman, Clara, 56, 118
Guerrero, J., 159, 200; photograph by, *142*
Guevara Escobar, Arturo, 64, 67, 127
Gutiérrez, Eulalio, 93, 185
Gutiérrez Escobar, Heliodoro Juan, 34, 56, 109, 185; and Maderismo, 2, 3, 64, 65, 68, 70–73; photographs by the agency of, *66*, *67*, *69*, *71*, *72*, *127*; in the Tragic Ten Days, 123, 126
Gutiérrez Ruvalcaba, Ignacio, 4, 28, 45, 48, 105
Guzmán, Martín Luis, 42, 76, 193, 218, 223

Hadsell, Walter P., 5, 7, 162, 163, 165, 166, 234; photographs signed by, *6*, *160*, *163*
Hare, Jimmy, 48, 55, 57, 157, 163; photograph by, *58*
Harris, Carlos, and "La Rochester" Agency, 56, 74, 86; photograph by, *88*
Hernández (Puebla photographer), 2, 93, 114; photograph by, *115*
Hernández, Gerónimo, 24, 34, 46, 94, 100, 123, 202; and Maderismo, 2, 3, 77, 133, 240; photographs by, *241*, *243*; photograph of, *124*
Hernández-Claire, José, 244; photograph by, *245*
Herrera (Puebla photographer), 114
Herrerías, E., 40, 56; photographs by, *40*, *42*
Herrerías, Ignacio, 50, 55, 56, 59, 75, 100; photograph by, *60*
Hine, Lewis, 28
histories of art, 9, 144–148
histories of photography, 7, 9, 256
Horne, Walter, 38, 55
Huerta, Victoriano, 55, 65, 79, 86, 94, 109, 123, 179, 200, 233, 234, 237; photographs of, *88*, *156*, *255*, *257*. *See also* Huertismo
Huertismo, 120, 123–166, 196, 198, 201; photographers of, 2, 46, 48, 73, 117, 123–134, 155, 177; photographs of, *127*, *132*, *134*, *136*, *137*, *138*, *139*, *140*, *141*, *142*, *146*, *149*, *153*, *154*
Hugelman, 170, 249; photograph by, *174*
hunger, 185, 208

icons, 9, 52, 168, 169, 233–258
illustrated magazines (Mexican), 4, 5, 7, 9, 12, 39, 40, 73, 99, 121, 155, 159, 163, 182, 184, 233; conservative but chameleon-like character of, 3, 76, 95, 124, 134, 169, 200; Porfirian, 28, 34, 55, 75, 76
—*Arte y Letras*, 27, 100

—*La Ilustración Semanal*, 7, 95, 115, 133, 143, 157, 162, 163, 169, 184, 200, 201, 204, 249; artistic-symbolic photography of, 11, 104, 153, *154*, 155; photographs published in, *5*, *96*, *101*, *201*, *209*, *250*
—*L'Illustration*, 7, 155; photograph published in, *156*
—*The Mexican Review*, 198
—*El Mundo Ilustrado*, 19, 22, 24, 27, 76, 104, 133, 134
—*Novedades*, 46, 94, 97, 131, 132, 134, 160, 161, 162, 181, 182, 200; photographs published in, *47*, *98*
—*Revista de Revistas*, 133, 202
—*La Semana Ilustrada*, 53, 55, 56, 73, 75, 76, 101, 134, 160, 161, 163, 169, 200, 236, 249; photographs published in, *201*, *248*
—*El Universal Ilustrada*, 74
—*Zig-Zag*, 204
illustrated magazines (non-Mexican):
—*Berliner Illustrirte Zeitung*, 247
—*Collier's*, 55, 57, 157, 246
—*Ilustración Artística*, 249
—*The Illustrated London News*, 247
—*Leslie's Illustrated Weekly Newspaper*, 246
—*Le Miroir*, 13, 247
—*The Moving Picture World*, 246; photograph published in, *248*
—*Mundo Gráfico*, 249
—*Reel Life*, 246; photograph published in, *248*
Indians and Indianist photography, 81–82, 198, 213, 214, 220; photographs of, *81*, *213*, *221*
Iturbe, General Ramón F., 73; photograph of, *74*

El Jilguero interview, 99–100
Jiménez, Blanca, 93, 111
Juchitán, 80, 138, 139

Kahlo, Guillermo, 25; photograph by, *25*
Katz, Friedrich, 86, 168, 169, 249, 254
Kiefer, Harvey, 55
Knight, Alan, 208, 224
Korda (Alejandro Díaz Gutiérrez), 1, 234
Krauze, Enrique, 137
Kurt, Juan (J. C. Curd), 177

Lear, John, 24, 209, 211
Leighton, George, 15
León, Víctor, 46
León de la Barra, Francisco, 50, 78, 80
Lesy, Michael, 10
leva (gang pressing), 137–141, 151, 216; photographs of, *137*, *138*
Levine, Robert, 10
Limantour, José, 17; photograph of, *18*
López (Guaymas photographer), 200
Lupercio, Abraham, 24, 46, 48, 95, 102, 109, 123, 133, 151, 160, 162, 207; photographs by, *96*, *101*, *152*, *208*, *209*; photograph of, 101
Lupercio, José María, 24, 46

Maderista movement, 2, 14, 40, 53–91, 116, 128, 151, 175, 237; photographers of, 64–75, 78–79, 133, 153, 155, 196, 203; photographs of, *54*, *56*, *58*, *59*, *60*, *61*, *62*, *63*, *64*, *66*, *67*, *69*, *70*, *71*, *72*, *74*, *76*
Madero, Francisco I., 48, 50, 99, 109, 121, 123, 127, 134, 196, 200, 233, 236, 238, 240; and consciousness of modern media, 53, 55; photographs of, *51*, *54*, *77*, *124*. *See also* Maderista movement
Magaña, Gildardo, 78, 100
Magonista movement, 195, 236
Márquez, Luis, 154
Martínez, Josephat, 182
Medina, Elsa, 239; photograph by, *239*
Medrano Chávez, Ignacio ("El Gran Lente"), 2, 3, 40, 82–83, 173, 204; photographs by, *83*, *84*
Melhado, Eduardo, 2, 34, 46, 123, 133, 154, 159, 163, 202; photograph by, *134*

Mendoza, José and Pedro, 203–204
Mendoza Avilés, Mayra, 234
mentalities, 10, 187–188
Mexico City, 14, 71–72, 74, 78, 79, 114, 151, 160, 195, 196, 204, 229; Conventionists in, 93, 182–191; photojournalists of, 4, 48, 98, 102, 161, 202, 203, 208; during the Porfiriato, 17, 24, 28, 34, 35; the Tragic Ten Days in, 123–140
Meyer, Michael, 137
Michoacán, 140, 141, 143, 179
Miquel, Ángel, 198
Miret, Félix, 123, 124, 132, 160, 162; photographs by, *125*, *136*
modern media, Mexican revolutionaries' consciousness of, 13, 53, 59, 109, 168, 193, 203, 234
Modotti, Tina, 1, 14, 17, 154
Moeller, Susan, 12
Mondragón, Manuel, 123, 133
Monroy, Nestor, 152; photograph of, *153*
Monroy Nasr, Rebeca, 50, 125
Montoya, Eustasio, 40, 68, 173–178, 204; photographs by, *70*, *176*, *178*
Mora, José, 42, 202–203
Morales, Miguel Ángel, 148, 242
Mutual Film Corporation, 4, 59, 168, 169, 246

Negrete, Claudia, 195
newspapers, 34, 39, 40, 73, 100, 154, 184, 233
—*Amigo del Hogar*, 133
—*El Heraldo de México*, 204
—*El Imparcial*, 16, 19, *20*, 21, 22, 25, 27, 34, 45, 48, 50, 86, 91, 102, 103, 104, 162, 236, 254
—*El Liberal*, 204
—*El Monitor*, 251
—*Nueva Era*, 133, 134
—*El País*, 64, 134
—*El Porvenir*, 204
—*El Pueblo*, 204, 224, 251
—*Regeneración*, 195
—*El Tiempo*, 55, 108
—*La Tribuna*, 134
—*Vida Nueva*, 170
nota roja (police news), 21, 86, 95, 154, 202

Obregón, Álvaro, 16, 48, 55, 181, 193, 196, 198, 198, 200, 230, 233, 251; photograph of, *199*
Ocampa y Amezcua, Ignacio, 200
Ocañas, Antonio, 65
Orozco, Pascual, 39, 46, 67, 68, 70, 86, 179; photographs of, *39*, *71*, *88*
Orozquista rebellion, 2, 74, 82–86, 240; photographer of, 82–83; photographs of, *83*, *84*, *85*, *86*, *87*, *88*
Osuna, Sabino, 123, 124, 125, 126, 132

Partido Revolucionario Institucional (PRI), 15, 45, 46, 47, 254, 255
Pérez Montfort, Ricardo, 93, 95, 162, 184
Perry, Herlinda, 68; photograph of, *69*
photography: "candid," 155; combat, 57, 102, 104, 109, 170; paparrazi, 155; polysemia, ambiguity, and semantic debility of, 7, 9, 27, 38, 49, 95, 102, 105, 185, 236, 258; spontaneous, 57, 155, 167, 170, 207
photohistories, 7, 9, 62–64, 105–108, 135–137, 185, 207–223
photojournalism and photojournalists, 3, 4, 7, 12, 13, 50, 251; cameras used by, 11, 83, 167; and Constitutionalism, 204, 208, 216; and Huertismo, 147, 154, 155, 159, 162; and Maderismo, 57, 65, 68, 70, 83, 85; modern, 83, 85, 233; photographs of, *99*, *101*; during the Porfiriato, 17, 27; in the Tragic Ten Days, 123, 131, 133; Zapatismo, 98, 104, 120
Piccato, Pablo, 24
Pichardo (Toluca photographer), 161
pictorialism, 11, 50, 154
picture histories (*historias gráficas*), 7, 15, 46, 48, 49, 50, 52, 104, 143, 182, 233, 240, 249, 251, 255, 256, 257

Pino Suárez, José María, 91, 134
Porfiriato, 17–38, 62, 66, 134, 141, 223, 236; media of, 3, 16, 19–22, 24, 40, 91; photographers of, 2, 14, 24–38, 195; photographs of, *18*, *20*, *21*, *23*, *25*, *29*, *30*, *31*, *32*, *33*, *35*, *36*, *37*, *58*, *63*
Posada, José Guadalupe, 70, 234–236, *237*
postcards, 3, 7, 11, 40, 116, 121, 198, 249; of Maderismo, 57, 64, 65, 68, 70; during the Porfiriato, 34, 38; of the Tragic Ten Days, 123, 125, 127; of the Veracruz invasion, 162, 163, 166
psychological readings of photographs, 10, 93, 191
Puebla, 77, 114, 144, 161, 179, 204

railroads, 144, 148–151, 185
Ramírez Pimental, Luís, 75
Ramírez Plancarte, Francisco, 138–139, 184, 208, 213
Ramos, Manuel, 2, 11, 24, 27–28, 34, 46, 86, 123, 132, 133, 184, 185, 251; photographs by, *26*, *88*, *253*
rape, 142–143, 179
realism, 12, 61, 102, 104, 109, 153–155
Reed, John, 44, 167, 169, 246
refugees, 64, 135, 166
Reyes, Bernardo, 123
Reyes Espíndola, Rafael, 19, 24, 25, 27
Reyes Retana, Ismael, 66–67; photograph of, *67*
Reyguad, P., Jr., 201
Riis, Jacob, 14, 28
Rivera (Mexico City photojournalist), 100, 102
Robles (Zacatecas photographer), 181–182; photograph by, *182*
Robles, Amelia/Amelio, 118
Robles, Carmen, 118; photograph of, *119*
Rodchenko, Alexander, 1
Rodia de la Peña, Clara, photograph of, *41*
Rodríguez (Constitutionalist photographer), 204
Rodríguez, Antonio, 46
Rojas, R., 161, 201
Rosenblum, Naomi, 11
Rousset brothers (Antonio, Guillermo, and Benito), 78–79
Rubio Navarrete, Guillermo, 79, 89
Rueda, Policarpo, 80–82; photograph of, *81*
Rufinelli, Jorge, 169
Ruíz Sandoval, A., photograph by, *87*
Rurales, photographs of, *21*, *137*

Salas, Elizabeth, 18
Salas, Osvaldo, 1
Salazar Cázares, José Cruz, 204
Salgado, Amparo, 116; photograph of, *117*
Salinas, León, 103–104; photograph by, *103*
Salmerón, Amando, 2, 3, 93, 108–112; photograph by, *110*
Salomon, Erich, 155
Sánchez, Cruz, 2, 93, 112–114; photograph by, *115*
Sánchez, Refugio, photograph of, *115*
Sander, August, 85
Santamaría, Luis, 46, 120, 202, 236
Scott, Homer, 55, 57
Scott, Winfield, 28, 30, 34; photographs by, *29*, *30*, *31*, *32*, *33*
Serdán, Aquiles, 78, 109
She, L. O., 204
Sontag, Susan, 39
Soriano, José, 100
Sosa, Fernando, 204
Soviet Revolution, photography of, 13, 14, 15
Strand, Paul, 2, 134
Strauss, Esther Eva, 56, 118
studio photography, 3, 4, 11, 12, 39, 153, 251; and Constitutionalism, 195, 203, 204; and Maderismo, 57, 61, 65, 68, 70, 78, 82; during the Porfiriato, 17; and the Tragic Ten Days, 126, 133; and Villismo, 177, 180, 185; and Zapatismo, 115, 116

Tablada, Juan José, 91, 130–131
Taro, Gerda, 85
testimonies, 7, 9, 32, 42, 131, 143, 185, 208, 214, 218–219, 224
Tinoco, Samuel, 7, 34, 46, 48, 55, 75, 98, 102, 123, 131, 132, 133, 157, 159, 162, 163, 200, 249; photographs by, *47*, *98*, *132*, *158*, *163*
Torresilla (photographer of Veracruz invasion), 157
Toscano, Salvador, 4, 65, 68
Tragic Ten Days, the (La Decena Trágica), 2, 14, 48, 121, 123–137, 154, 196
Turner, John Kenneth, 14

Ulloa, Berta, 187
United States, 53, 64, 73, 76, 121, 129, 151, 182, 203, 231; invasions of Mexico by, 4, 38, 79, 121, 123, 156–166, 177, 226; and the media, 55, 57, 65, 75, 118, 128, 168, 169, 170, 173, 194, 198, 199, 246; and photographs of armed Americans in Mexico, *5*, *6*, *37*, *227*
Urbina, Tomás, 44, 251, 253; photographs of, *250*, *252*

Valleto brothers, 195
Vanderwood, Paul, 156, 166
Vasconcelos, José, 68
Vélez Storey, Jaime, 199
Veracruz, 14, 48, 203, 204, 251
Veracruz, invasion of, 4, 14, 47, 121, 133, 148, 156–166, 202; photographs of, *5*, *6*, *158*, *159*, *160*, *161*, *163*, *164*, *165*, *166*
Vietnamese revolution, photography of, 15
Villa, Francisco ("Pancho"), 2, 16, 48, 57, 68, 86, 193, 199, 200, 226, 233, 246–254, 258; and consciousness of modern media, 167–169; and Mutual Film Corporation, 4, 168–170; photographs of, *60*, *89*, *247–248*, *250*. *See also* Villismo
Villalobos, 75
Villegas de Magnón, Leonor, 175
Villela, Samuel, 93, 109, 111, 114, 116, 118
Villismo, 147, 155, 166, 167–191, 207; photographers of, 2, 143; photographs of, *170*, *171*, *172*, *173*, *174*, *175*, *176*, *178*, *182*
Virgin of Guadalupe, 64, 161, 162, 188

Waite, C. B., 28, 30, 34, 123, 127, 128; photographs by, *29*, *31*
Weeks, George F., 198
Weston, Edward, 2, 14, 154
Whelan, John Davidson, 168, 246; photograph by, *247–248*
Womack, John, 184, 230, 237
women in the revolution, 68, 109, 118, 142–143, 175, 185, 203, 207, 208, 211, 227, 233, 234, 240–245; photographs of, *41*, *69*, *70*, *117*, *119*, *120*, *142*, *149*, *152*, *186*, *188*, *205*, *208*, *210*, *212*, *215*, *228*, *241*, *243*; as *soldaderas*, 148, 188, 207, 240–245
women photographers, 56, 114–118, 203
World War I, photography of, 11, 12, 13, 15, 104, 121, 155
Wray, F., 234

Yáñez, Mauricio, 73–74; photographs by, *74*

Zacatecas, 170, 181
Zapata, Emilio, 16, 48, 50, 65, 199, 203, 226, 233–239, 249–254, 258; and consciousness of modern media, 93; photographs of, *110*, *120*, 162, *235*, *238*, *250*, *253*. *See also* Zapatismo
Zapatismo, 10, 64, 93–121, 134, 147, 155, 166, 183–191, 202, 207, 208, 220; photographers of, 2, 78, 108–118; photographs of, *43*, *47*, *96*, *97*, *98*, *101*, *107*, *108*, *113*, *115*, *117*, *119*, *120*, *183*, *186*, *187*, *189*, *190*
Zazueta, A., photograph by, *54*